The
GREAT
DECEPTION

A Dissection of Religion

Robert E. O'Neill Jr.

Print ISBN: 978-1-54391-238-8
eBook ISBN: 978-1-54391-239-5

CONTENTS

PREFACE

Before sitting down to write this, I experienced grave trepidation. Primarily, because I still felt a trifle fearful of the possible consequences, both spiritual and physical. After all, I would be assaulting "the Lord" by committing my most secret thoughts to composition. My early religious indoctrination forced me to weigh the possibility that God might strike out at me. Jesus personally uttered this warning, *"If anyone should cause one of these little ones {children} to turn away from his faith in me, it would be better for that man to have a large millstone tied around his neck and be drowned in the deep sea."* [Mt. 18:6; Mk. 9:42 & Lu. 17:1-2] My mind asked — how far could I go before He would react?

Also, if I continued with my exposé I would be flaunting the religious predispositions (prejudices) of my Catholic, Jewish, and Protestant friends. Could I ever convince them that my belief *–in no belief–* was correct, and that their beliefs were only instilled biases implanted during their childhood? Every moderately intelligent person should be able to pierce the façade of truth that religion presents, or to identify the blatant impossibilities it excuses as divine mysteries.

When we revert to this type of emotional palliative and forsake intelligent appraisal, we are really reverting to our childhood days. The world of make-believe and the real world interweave so compactly that soon we are unable to distinguish the one from the other. However, in this case, knowing what was/is happening and preventing it from continuing to happen *–regrettably–* are two separate realities.

All this troubled me during the weeks, the months, and the years that I struggled to reach my goal of presenting my total views on religion in writing. It bothered me that so much of what I knew and understood about religion was nothing but human invention. Articles of Faith were being printed, read, talked about, or shown on television and –*most bothersome*– they were being <u>believed</u>! I could readily visualize myself as a modern David of Truth facing the Goliath of religious falsity, but without the aid of the Lord.

Rather, I should have pictured myself as the child in the fantasy story of the Emperor's New Clothes. Everyone pretended they could see the splendid clothes fake weavers claimed to have spun for the King lest those onlookers be accused of being "not pure of heart." But when a guileless child failed to see the nonexistent clothing, the people all realized that the foolish King was parading in the nude while the deceitful weavers made off with his gold.

Religious myths, such as "God made me" really provoke my ire. If a personal God exists, and if everything that religion teaches is true — this proposal would still be false. Only for this argument's sake, grant that God did create Adam and Eve. Still, the answer to "Who made me?" is "My parents." Why lie or exaggerate a point? Does God need our magnification to attain greatness? Is He, in reality, something less than He is proclaimed to be? These questions demand answers if religionists persist in attributing every occurrence to the Creator.

If every action in this world is caused by God, then I am free to do whatever I please. I am acting with God's consent. Or more candidly, God is directing me; I am <u>never</u> accountable personally. Of course, God isn't responsible for my every action. How could He be? Some of my actions, or all of my actions, must be my own. Do you agree? I am certain you do.

Newspapers and periodic magazines have featured sections on religion. Have you ever read a syndicated column promoting atheism? No, you have not —and it is improbable that you will any time in the anticipated future! Demanding equal time to promote atheism is impossible for there would be little time for anything else.

Now, a few words of necessary illumination about the writing of this book before I bid you: *"provocative & stimulating reading!"* All references to the Supreme Being, God(s), and Jesus are capitalized as they would be in a book written by a believer. Because it matters not at all to me, and because a minor item such as this could cause distraction to believers troubled with doubts —I capitalized out of respect for their sensibilities, not out of reverence for a non-existent personage (concept).

To make certain points, or to expose certain incongruities, at several places I framed my writing much as a believer might. My reasons for doing such were solely academic. I felt those passages read better that way. Several different biblical translations have been quoted/referenced, throughout this work.

At this juncture, authors invariably list their acknowledgements and dispense written kudos to those who have aided them in the preparation of their manuscript. My namesake son has earned the first kudo from me. My further kudos are reserved for those of you who will read my manuscript. To each of you, my heart-felt thanks. There is no point to writing if no one ever reads your work.

By incontrovertible admission, all errors in this work are mine alone. All I can add to that statement is that none of them were intentional, nor were they recognized by me as such.

If anyone feels impelled to write to me about this work, I will gladly read their correspondence. Just to know that my written thoughts have pro-voked a response from someone else is both gratifying and pleasing. *(Even if you disagree with me!)* My lifelong passion has been to read. You can be assured, I, personally, will read all correspondence.

So I sincerely invite you to read —to question, and in hope —to enjoy my book. If you share my beliefs, then talk about this book to your friends. If not, then write your own. In all probability, I will buy it —if only to dispute your tenets! And after completing my work, if you still aren't convinced of the non-viability and the unavailability of any cosmic deity, then I ask that your "God" comfort you. You are obviously troubled by profound doubts, and I haven't helped you. I will deeply regret that eventuality.

R. E. O'Neill Jr.
Philadelphia, PA
1983 – 2017

CHAPTER 1

The Greatest Deception Ever

WHO AM I?

Who am I? Where did I come from? Why am I here? Because I deemed to ask these questions, an enigmatic further question arises: What fate (if any) will befall me after I die? To the current reader: Who are you? Where did you come from? Why are you here? Lastly, what fate awaits you after your death? I have asked myself these questions uncounted times, and throughout written history numberless others have asked similar, if not identical, questions.

The answers recorded are as multifaceted as are the persons who have asked them. Many came to believe that they had divined the ultimate solution to those eternal posers and with passionate zeal sought to convince others of the cosmic correctness of their vain and intrinsically spurious pontifications. Yet, inevitably, there always arose another person who wasn't convinced or converted by those conjured answers that renewed the quest till ultimately either he came to believe he had been endowed with his own infusion of personal or celestial enlightenment, or he expired while still questing. "She" is appropriate in all the previous.

The first question isn't difficult for one seeking a direct answer. You know who you are, just as I know who I am, and I am not referring to a name! No one else knows totally who I am unerringly. I do! You, alone, know who you are. "Where did I come from?" This can be answered simply and factually "From my mother's ovum and my father's sperm." "Why am I here?" is best answered as "To live a biologically limited mortal life that is (in hope) self-fulfilling and relevant to human society."

The above answers aren't merely true, they are demonstrably true. Well, if they are so obviously true, why do so many people keep looking for alternate answers? The reply to this query is embodied in the fourth question. The fourth question led to the genesis of this book. "What fate will befall me after I die?" Seemingly, no one is willing to accept the undeniable resolution to that question. To wit: "I am going to be cremated or buried, and all too soon be forgotten." This is an answer that almost no one appears to want to confront or acknowledge. Finding an alternate answer to our destiny query is humanity's perennial preoccupation, and it also forms the cornerstone of the frame of mind that is called religiosity.

We all know that our human body won't last evermore, especially after we pass our prime years and we are startled to note subtle changes in our most noticeable organ, our skin. The message becomes more unavoidable with each passing year. No mortal has ever cheated the grave yet, and it appears eternally unlikely that anyone ever will. Despite this incontrovertible reality, civilized man has universally striven to extend his existence endlessly, and for most of that time he has been duped by a pervasive mental accomplice known as supernaturalism.

Supernaturalism (aka 'religion') provides an enticing elixir that most humans find too irresistible to forgo. If you believe in this tenet and that dogma; if you have performed the required rites under the appropriate circumstances, then your soul (theoretically, the spiritual animating essence of you) will never experience final death. It will be rewarded with endless life in a magnificent spiritual locale named 'Heaven.' What a comparatively meager price to pay for such eternal munificence. Conversely, if you disbelieve the essential truths of a religion and you refuse to perform the required rites and rituals, then your soul will be punished by endless confinement with incessant torture in a horridly unpleasant spiritual locale called 'Hell.'

Hell is a bargain also, albeit, a negative bargain. One ritualistic miscue can purchase eternal regret. In Heaven you will experience great joy, while in Hell you will experience immense suffering. *'Choose one!* Incidentally, most Christian denominations even offer a form of instant jackpot payout of either Heaven or Hell. If, the instant before you die you are able to perform one very simple mental task, namely, to feel remorse, then you win! You go straight to Heaven. If however, you commit an equally facile mental blunder such as experiencing a moment's doubt, then you lose! You go straight to Hell.

The whole concept of Heaven, and conversely of Hell, is so muddled that we should examine both with a critical, unbiased perspective if we are to derive any valid conclusion as to their existence. Let me state here categorically: "If there is no Heaven, then dying becomes exactly that: ceasing to live — finis!" First, our body will undergo decay, and then it will revert to some basic form of inert chemical matter. If you already think this to be the finality for humans on Earth, then read no further. If you are an average human being with the genetic traits attendant to that classification of being, then you will have to continue reading to evaluate for yourself the arguments I have presented that contest or counter the existence of Heaven.

HEAVEN DEFINED

What is Heaven? Heaven, I am told, is a place where I will experience unremitting bliss with God. It is a place where I will exist not in body, but in spirit form entirely without the cares, the wants, and the needs of my earthly existence. It is a place where I will exist forever in rapture. It will be (and is?) a thoroughly Utopian place to be eternally domiciled. This seems irresistibly enticing until you take a closer look. Can any place offer such contentment and can any locale be that perfect?

My earthly existence is totally dominated by my bodily needs. Here on Earth I am most pleasured when my bodily needs are being attended. Many of the conditions that please mankind are physically stimulating. Humans invariably seek pleasurable stimulation. Religious indoctrination causes them to undergo sensations of guilt after they have experienced that pleasurable stimulation. Pleasant self-gratification, to religious formulators, is deemed shameful, sinful, or even sacrilegious. We all engage in various forms of self-gratification, yet, we often scandalize others when they pamper themselves to the same end.

In reality, Heaven doesn't offer happiness. What Heaven basically promises is a lack of unhappiness, i.e., an absence of envy, guilt or shame. To my mind, none of us will be content in Heaven. Heaven, and the life it allegedly encompasses, is so alien to everything I have come to know and enjoy in my physical life that I can hardly be expected to yearn for the day I may arrive there. Ask a blind man to describe a cloud and he will fare better than asking me to describe Heaven. A blind man has access to sighted persons who can provide him with a visual description of a cloud. I've never had acquaintance with an eyewitness to Heaven.

What makes life so enjoyable to me, and seemingly to others, is the pleasant stimulation of the body's senses. To be appreciated an item must be smelled, tasted, heard, seen, or felt. Even a state of mind must be contemplated to be enjoyed. To reply that Heaven is a wholly dissimilar level of awareness doesn't end my confusion. If Heaven is so absolutely foreign to my human existence, then why should I aspire to go there? True, someone could tell me that I would relish living in Heaven; that would prove nothing! I have been told I would like scotch whiskey once I acquired a taste for it. I have tried it, and tried it, and still, I hate it!

The absence of feelings isn't the same experience as is happiness. Happiness is the titillating sensation of receiving pleasurable physical stimuli; the longer the duration, the greater the sensation (of pleasure!). Why would God give me a body that needs and seeks bodily pleasures if He wants me to forgo those pleasures and deny those needs?

Should a loving parent buy a guileless child a fascinating toy, and then forbid the child to play with this toy? What reward would be forthcoming to the child who obeyed this senseless order? 'To cut off the child's arms and legs? 'To blind the child? 'To disconnect all his other senses, so that he no longer desired to play with toys, or to do anything else whatsoever?

Heaven would weary a normal, human being. This is what religion is portraying to me. If I deny myself the pleasures of my body, God will blunt all my senses, God will decompose my body, and God will reanimate me as a brainless spiritual zombie. This is questionable recompense, and it is unworthy of an Entity who could create a Universe. Ancient superstitious fantasies have evolved into today's glorified theological mysteries.

My observance of life informs me that although our human needs are similar, our human enjoyments are vastly dissimilar. A Heaven that promises a complete lack of want seems to me to be entirely lacking itself. How can I be happy without wants that are being satisfied? Put aside bodily requirements for a moment. Consider the mental state, which is the closest human concept we have that could approximate a spiritual state of being.

My personal greatest pleasure is reading and learning about subjects in which I am interested. Tell me that Heaven is full of books for me to read. Tell me that I can spend eternity reading. Or better yet, tell me that I will have an angel read to me unceasingly. Let that angel never tire of reading aloud and explaining those books to me. This would be my Heaven. Unfortunately, this Heaven would hardly appeal to some people I know. There are people who detest having to read. Many persons would reckon my visualization of Heaven as their apprehension of a torment in Hell.

WHO FIRST FORMULATED HEAVEN?

Who were the formulators of Heaven? No one will ever know now. However, we can surmise that they were of the same reference sort as the formulators of the 'Supreme Being' postulation. They were persons who rationalized a concept that abounds in irrationality.

The early developers of the notion of Heaven must soon have realized that a Heaven that catered to every person's whims would be a multifaceted Heaven indeed. Some events that others appear to relish positively bore me. I couldn't bear being present while they basked in their pleasures. My Heaven would be replete with books that interest me along with an angel to read them aloud and elucidate the books for me. My Heaven would also have to be without distractions that lessened my bliss. Regrettably, not even Heaven could be endowed with the wherewithal to satisfy everyone. For me, a perfect Heaven wouldn't merely contain endless personal delights. Simultaneously, it would have to be free of all annoyances or distractions as well.

This restriction must have posed a seemingly insurmountable obstacle to the early theologians. Ultimately, they determined that the only unanimously acceptable 'Paradise' was one where persons existed wholly without wants, thereby eliminating the impossible task of satisfying the innumerable and conflicting gratification appetites of the entirety of mankind. Besides, everyone knew you didn't take your body with you into Heaven, and you could hardly expect your spirit to hold a book, or any other material object either.

Today's technology has exposed another barrier to belief in the existence of Heaven. Namely: "Where is it?" With our modern telescopes we can see billions of light-years into the Universe which, in all such instances, is also into the past. Early man imagined his Heaven as located in the sky just beyond the clouds, little realizing the vast expanse of the cosmos.

I am aware that presently our theologians refer to Heaven as a spiritual universe. They could hardly do otherwise. It is provable that Heaven doesn't exist in the physical universe. This doesn't solve my problem; it compounds it. How can I be happy in spirit form when my entire existence, every event that I have ever experienced, has occurred in the physical world? I am hopelessly unqualified to make an intelligent, rational, studied decision regarding a spiritually renewed life in that esoteric locale termed "Heaven."

A spiritual existence is beyond my comprehension. I am unable to relate intelligibly to that type of existence. I would become, quite factually, a different being as a spirit. In reality, I could no longer speak of "I" as a person. If I exist at all, I exist in my mind. If I don't have a physical mind, then without qualification I no longer exist. Offer me that Heaven and you offer me a phantasm. Any meaningful continuation of living must improve on life as I know it, not promise a totally indefinable, unfathomable, unimaginable and literally lifeless existence. Tell me that I will return to life as a honey bee in the Garden of Eden. That, I can relate to more cogently.

Why does Heaven exist? Does it have to? The answer is that it doesn't. Heaven is a thoroughly human concept. The similarity between the words Heaven and haven is suspicious. I think they both describe the same place: a place of safety, hence, of happiness and contentment. Mortals surely need such a place. The Immortal Creator irrefutably doesn't. Rationally, to position God in any limited space does just that; it limits Him! God doesn't need a haven; God doesn't need a shelter. God doesn't need, nor could He ever need, anything!

Pure spirits, that are impervious to all natural phenomena such as rain or snow, heat or cold, gravity or acceleration, likewise should have no need for Heaven. Then why does it exist in the minds of so many? It exists because all religious creations are only comprehensible in human terms. The need for a Heaven isn't a spiritual requirement. It is a physical one.

Humans need a place to rest that is protected from predators as do all other cognitive life forms. Instinctively, we are drawn to a location that offers security from danger, or refuge from storm. We call this the instinct to survive. I think it is better described as seeking to lower our anxiety level. Whenever we or other discerning creatures discover ourselves in a situation where we sense we are insecure, or we are vulnerable to harm, we have our anxiety modality activated. Then, as the perceived peril is heightened, so too is our anxiety reaction. This anxiety stimulus is neither a pleasurable nor a desirable sensation. We tend to skirt anxiety stimulants chiefly by avoiding them. However, we can't avoid sleep; therefore, our need for a safe haven is our third most vital requirement. It ranks directly after breathing and eating.

Belief in a spiritual life hereafter dictates that we will not have to agonize over the first two concerns. In Heaven there should be no problem breathing because air pollution is unheard of there. 'As for eating? Spirits would seem to need no food whatsoever, so that human frailty is eliminated. However, the third: "security," isn't so readily dismissed.

Religion teaches (and our innermost fears tend to confirm) that there are evil spirits in abundance in addition to benevolent spirits. How can I be assured that an evil spirit won't attempt to harm my spirit? One has to assume that evil spirits perform evil deeds, even in the spirit world. Therefore, God will have to provide me with a secure shelter protected from those malevolent spirits. Again, religion teaches that He has. My reasoning informs me that He needn't bother. If I am a pure spirit, and if pure spirits are indestructible and impervious to all external actions, I would have no use for a secure haven, or in religious terminology, a heaven.

If this line of deduction is valid, then Heaven is redundant, and Hell is an anomaly. Unlike pure spirits, impure spirits discernibly are not impervious to pain. (Hell-fire burns!) They can be confined and restricted to a designated place (Hell). They share only immortality with pure spirits. Damned souls will suffer everlastingly!

A pivotal doctrinal query must be raised here. How can an eternity of suffering be justly imposed for a moment's sin, or even for the comparably short period of one lifetime of sin, contrasted against an endless eternity? I am aware that some sects deny the existence of Hell professing resurrection for the saved only; those not "saved" expire for all time. The question of the severity and the eternal permanence of the punishment are identical. This is one of the many muddled notions concerning Heaven and Hell. You could ponder the above incongruity (injustice) for a lifetime and no logical explanation, nor just solution, would ever be discerned.

Heaven and Hell are a human invention seeking to compensate the 'good,' and to punish the 'wicked,' in the afterlife. Why in the afterlife? Obviously, because so many of the wicked were being rewarded in this lifetime, and so many of the deserving were being deprived. If you believed in a personal God, and you had made any effort to observe mankind's earthly happenstance, postponed justice rendered in Heaven was the ultimate feasible scenario. Here, as ever, I find we have a theological conception expressed, and thence validated, within human parameters.

If Heaven makes little sense to you, then Hell will be just as senseless. In Hell, we are told, we will suffer mightily for our sins. Our bodily sense of experiencing pain will be all too alert and functional. Just how this pain and suffering is possible absent a human body has never been explained to me. Today, the entire concept of Heaven and Hell (or they could be identified as, 'your reward or your punishment') is vastly different from the original notion. Primitives looked for their reward immediately after performing a specific rite, or shortly after petitioning the Divinity. Contrariwise, they feared imminent retribution if they offended their tribal Deity.

There was (and remains) a refreshing simplicity to their childlike directness. No obscure, murky, cryptic, dubious theological hocus-pocus about the ways of the Lord being too inscrutable for us lowly creatures to comprehend. If you pleased Him, then invariably you earned His beneficence. If you displeased Him, then just as assuredly, you courted His fury. "...*for great is the wrath of the Lord....*" [2 Chr. 34:21]

WHENCE CAME HEAVEN?

Heaven never existed until after man had acquired a civilization. How can I, or anyone, know this? Rather easily, if we only trouble to examine and analyze the many clues left behind by the confidence men who sold mankind the fictitious notion of a Heaven. Begin by listing the things you know about Heaven, and then examine each item rationally, but critically as well.

We are told that the streets of Heaven are paved with gold. Why gold? Obviously, because gold is highly valued on Earth. In the earliest civilizations human kings greatly admired and greatly desired gold. The more gold a king possessed, the more esteem he received from his peers, and the more envy he evinced from his kingly rivals. Gold is highly malleable, tarnish free, and can be polished to a brilliant sheen. Kingdoms and Empires were evaluated by the amount of gold they could flaunt. If God's kingdom was indeed greater than mankind's kingdoms, He, too, must brandish a lavish quantity of gold. God did; He lined the streets of Heaven with it. No earthly king could match that. Continually bear in mind, that Heaven was understood by all its early adherents to be a faithful replica of the principal cities of the ancient world, different not in design and function, but always in splendor and magnificence.

The gates of Heaven, we know, are made of pearl. [Cf. Rev. 21:21] Pearls are highly lustrous, and likewise, greatly prized. Of all the precious stones, pearls were assigned the highest value by early civilized man. If they had possessed our knowledge of metal finishing, the gates of Heaven might have been constructed of stainless steel or, at least, have been chrome plated. By the way, why does Heaven need gates? The answer is apparent, but only if you pause to reflect on the underlying purpose of the formulators of Heaven. They felt that God was in direct competition with the kings on Earth. Their King (God) and His kingdom (Heaven), likewise, must be greater, more resplendent, and infinitely more glorious than the kingdoms of Earth. God was the greatest king of all. His kingdom must attest to His greatness. God's kingdom even resembled the earthly kingdoms. That because God's proponents wanted to be able to contrast His kingdom in high favor against the world's kingdoms.

If the earthly kingdoms had a gate permitting or barring entrance to the capitol city, then God's city had one also … a finer one! If the human king paved his streets with stones (paved streets were a rare sight, consequently impressive to the average man), then God outstripped man by paving His entire city with blocks of gold. The king commanded, and was protected by, a large army. God was adored and surrounded by a host of angels. What are angels? Angels are God's super soldiers. [Cf. Ps.

103:19-20 & Mt. 26:53] Why, in heaven's name (endure the allusion), would the Almighty, Invincible Creator of the Universe need a bevy of angels? This proposition dumbfounds me, but it seems everything an earthly king possessed, God must surpass.

What purpose do the gates of Heaven serve? 'To keep the inhabitants in? That is fatuous. 'To keep someone out? That is unnecessary. The wicked have been condemned to Hell, and, presumably, they are securely confined therein. It is ludicrous to visualize damned souls skulking about the Universe trying to burgle or storm their way into Heaven. If the virtuous are all ensconced in Heaven, and the vile are all locked in Hell, whose spirit can be flitting about unencumbered attempting a break-in of Heaven? Nonetheless, and despite the inanity, God's capitol city has a gate … a most resplendent one.

WHERE IS HEAVEN LOCATED?

The visualization of God's Throne located in the sky is a remnant from the days when mankind thought the World to be flat. To those scientifically naive people it was evident that God observed the Earth at a height sufficient to scan the entire flat surface in a single glance. Personal experience indicated to everyone that whenever they stood on an elevation they increased considerably the area they could effectively view. When approaching a low-lying village from a nearby hill, the entire community could be seen in one viewing. Common sense would further deduce that an unsurpassed vantage point would have been directly over the village. Not only was Heaven the best observation post, it was the only one that might account for the hidden knowledge that their God, by implication and accusation, seemed to possess.

If God was accountable for all the misfortune that befell ancient mankind, then, obviously He was watching when humans did something forbidden. Whenever calamity struck, it surely came from the hand of God and only in reprisal for some transgression on mankind's part. How did God know of our concealed transgressions? Evidently, He could observe actions of ours that could effectively be hidden from most others.

"We are sinners all." [Rom. 3:23] Evangelizers prey on this ubiquitous imperfection. All religions have taboos. These taboos were formulated by religiously predisposed persons who were attempting to explain the misadventures that assailed their lives. If all things that happen to you derive from God, and if something deleterious happened, then you might search your memory to determine what it was that you did that moved God to visit that misfortune upon you.

Inevitably, a list of prohibitions was compiled that might precipitate God's retribution. Conversely, another list of behavioral acts that didn't provoke God could be created by noting those times when God's vengeance was expected, or even warranted, but didn't materialize. Anytime we did something that could have caused God's anger to be vented on us, and that punishment did not eventuate, we must somehow have assuaged His anger. Again you would search your memory to determine what you did to obviate His anticipated reprimand. The most prevalent reason deduced must have been that you were truly contrite after the misdeed.

Quite naturally, all of us are remorseful when we anticipate imminent retribution for an act of ours. Or we may simply regret the results of our wrongful deed. The opprobrium of a loved one, or someone respected, sometimes causes us to rethink the appropriateness of our past actions with the result that we rue the event after the fact. Whichever!

More often than not, the above framework will be all that you will find when searching back through your memory. Occasionally, a 'mystical' action will be attributed to forestalling or moderating God's reprisal. When this apparent though incidental act is credited, a new religious ritual is founded. If a second event of similar circumstances occurs with the identical result (no retribution from God), then the efficacy of the exculpating ritual will be validated and the ritual will be replicated for many years afterward.

Concomitantly, in a completely reversed situation where God's vengeance struck, and where the effectuating action was profane, you would see a taboo born. Rituals and taboos are both magical; either one can impel God to react in a predictable, albeit opposite, manner.

Imagine how burnt offerings were initiated as a means of ingratiating oneself to, or propitiating, the Sky Deity. There is nothing sensible in burning up an animal carcass, or firing up cereal grain. Yet, we know this is precisely what the early Hebrews did to conciliate Yahweh. Their unsophisticated minds reasoned that God resided in the heavens (just above the crystal semi-globe that over-arched the flat earth). Smoke from their holocausts rose in the air and seemed to reach the heavens; therefore, although they couldn't reach God directly, they could touch His nostrils through the rising fumes of their burnt offerings. At their level of knowledge of the physical world, this was more than logical; it was obvious as well, provided only that our abode (the Earth) is truly a flat surface and that Yahweh truly resides overhead in the heavens.

But the Earth is a globe (virtually). For that reason, when I point down toward the abode of the Devil, I am pointing in the same direction that an Australian would point to for his Heaven. Contemplate this: he is looking for salvation in the same direction I was taught to expect damnation. Someone's perception is wrong. The situation is reversed for an Australian pointing out the direction of Hell. He points in the same direction I pray to when I am talking with God. The only way this directional discrepancy can be reconciled is for Hell to be located in the center of the planet. Heaven, the home of God, His angels, and all the 'saved' souls of humanity, therefore must completely encompass our globe. There is a modicum of circumstantial evidence that would support the existence of Hell in the center of the Earth, for it is arguably extremely hot there. Certainly, it is impossible for anyone to get there in their mortal body, only a true spirit could achieve that physical impossibility. But, under no logical circumstance, can Heaven exist in every direction above our planet.

The Bible would have us think that a supplicant at the North Pole looking directly overhead would be facing the same Heaven that his fellow man at the South Pole was facing when he raised his eyes to the southern skies. Here we are looking in completely opposite directions and expecting to behold the same Heaven. Several imperative questions are forced by the supposition that Heaven exists in all outward directions. Measured from the surface of the planet, at what altitude does the boundary of Heaven begin? Are its frontiers one mile, two miles, a million miles, or a light year away? Does Heaven begin where the Universe ends? No one knows where that is, but it is at least ten billion light-years distant. We now can peer that far (and farther) with our present telescopes. Quasars, thought to be the most distant objects ever viewed, are calculated to be at least ten billion light-years (13.7 BLY?) removed from our Solar System. That distance is so inconceivable that it might just as well be infinity.

An unanticipated difficulty interposes itself at distances the magnitude of a light year ... the fourth dimension "Time." Traversing such vast stretches of space can't be accomplished in a reasonable time interval. In distance, a light-year is approximately six trillion miles. This means that a photon of light moving at one hundred eighty-six thousand miles per second travels that far in an Earth year (365 days). Even at that tremendous speed, travel to the rim of the Universe would take more than ten billion years and, very likely, much longer. If Heaven was sited beyond the Universe, our death-liberated spirit could spend eternity just getting there.

One of the aspects of space is time. Time can be measured in distance and, conversely, distance can be measured by time. A 'second' is now defined as the time it takes an electron to travel from one measurable point to another. Instant teleportation, i.e., moving from one spot to a distant spot instantaneously, is ridiculous. Any essence that has a boundary, including spirit essence, must expend time to reach any point beyond its boundary. If any essence can instantly move from one spot to another, then that essence must be as large as the distance involved. In other words, it hasn't moved at all, it merely concomitantly spans both locales.

The modern rationalization that Heaven exists on a spiritual plane apart from our physical world, yet sharing the same space, is just as ridiculous. Mary, the mother of Jesus, was assumed into Heaven bodily, that is, 'in the flesh.' Where in Heaven is her body now, and why can't we see it with our telescopes? I won't press the argument here. I am certain that you recognize my present intent.

How uncomplicated Heaven was while the world was flat. God's home was above, and the Devil's fiery pit was below. When the ancients died, the faithful ascended to Heaven, and the wicked descended into Hell. I wonder, what became of those unfortunate souls who fell off the edge? Did they fall into the sinister grasp of Satan? Or did an Angel of the Lord swoop down from Heaven and rescue the deserving?

Religion is the invention of a child-like imagination, and should be discarded when we mature to adulthood and can reason more deeply. Somewhere in the Bible it reads, *"Verily I say to you, whosoever shall not receive the kingdom of God as a little child, shall not enter it."* [Mk. 10:15 & Lu. 18:17]

That is a clever epigram, but it doesn't affirm Heaven's reality, it challenges it! A child accepts the reality of Santa Claus as readily as he or she accepts the teaching of a spiritual Heaven. Not because Santa Claus is a fact, but because lying adults perpetuate the myth in each generation. I think the time has arrived for all of us to stop lying to one another about God and Heaven.

MOTIVATION — A REASON FOR LIVING

In addition to bodily needs, we humans also have emotional needs. One poignant need, possibly the most basic of the emotional needs, is motivation. The three most effective motivations influencing our behavior are: (In order of their potency to goad us to action) Advantage to ourselves; Acceptance by our peers; and Advantage to our community. The last item could be rephrased as altruistic communal behavior. Reversing the priority of this list may be the noblest action we could perform, but not necessarily the wisest action we could perform. Universal altruism must eventuate in eternal impasse. If altruism ever became universal, then "Heaven" might be attainable. Not in a strange, far-off locale peopled by ghostly specters, but here on Earth; enjoyed by corporeal beings. We wouldn't have to constrain or deny our wants in that place. We could pamper them to their fullest. My ideal of a realistic Heaven is thoroughly physical, not spiritual.

By nature, humans always require a motive factor to explain every eventuality in the Universe, however grand, however trivial the eventuality. Humans even reexamine their own motivations. Alas, in this endeavor they err most frequently and most glaringly, invariably ascribing lofty, noble motives to crass, selfish actions. Motivationally, almost every action we perform, or neglect to perform, is intended to benefit ourselves primarily. That we seek a secondary rationale for our actions, which we can profess to justify those actions, is equally true. This is done more to assuage our own conscience than to dupe another person. But, by this process, the person most deluded is one's self. The ordinary person would deny the intrinsic precision of this observation. Most psychologists, et al., know through both training and experience that humans do exactly this. They justify their self-indulgent actions with self-aggrandizing rationalizations that present a verbal façade of respectability for those actions. Humans are quite adept at convincing their conscience of the most devious of falsehoods.

Why do we rationalize our behavior? Is it to gain admittance to a Heaven that we, in our deepest introspection, perceive we might not be entitled to enter? Conditionally, Yes. We crave acceptance. Humans, and most other primates, are gregarious, tending to gather into homogeneous groups. This instinct to form into familial bands was beneficial to our species, and thence became genetically inbred. Hermits, and their ilk, are exceptions; they are aberrant of the human family. Family or group living isn't a panacea that guarantees a happy or successful life. Group living demands group harmony. No group could long survive that constantly, or ceaselessly, bickered and disputed among its members. Does group living thereby require that no member of a group seriously disrupt the collective stability of the group through selfish actions? Quizzically, No!

LEADERS

Most groups have one individual who is the most selfish of all; one who insists that his needs, his wants, and his desires are met first. Disputing with this individual always leads to dire consequences for the disputer. The other group members are ever aware of this individual and inevitably acquiesce to his insistence. This individual has an exclusive title. We call him "The Leader." Whenever humans gather regularly, one person always ascends to the leadership role.

Groups can have any number of followers, but let there be more than one contender for leadership and a conflict is bound to ensue. The conflict will be resolved in only one of two ways: the defeated contender will attract followers to a newly formed splinter group, or he will be ejected from the group. Keep this in mind when later we consider why we are confronted (and confounded) by so many fragment denominations of all of the world's religious faiths.

Formalized religion was early man's determined effort to control that which formerly was beyond his control. Sometimes it rained, and that rain was beneficial. Sometimes it rained (and rained!), and that rain wasn't beneficial. Why did it rain when it wasn't needed as often as it rained when it was needed? Man was baffled. He recognized his impotence at influencing the forces of nature, and you would think that he, thereafter, would simply have accepted his futility and conducted his life accordingly. 'Not so!

Man refused to accept that anything was completely and immutably beyond his control. Someone had to be controlling the rain. If man couldn't control the rain directly, then perchance, somehow he could influence "He" who did control the rain. Anyone who could manipulate the Rain-Maker would wield much authority in his society. All of man's feeble efforts to regulate his life and his destiny might be rewarded if such secondary (indirect) control were possible. Although all men recognized this 'truth,' only egotistical, domineering leaders had the arrogance to avow that they alone might manipulate the Rain-Maker.

It is tempting to speculate that the origin of the 'God' concept had, as its ultimate goal, the control and influence of other human beings. Potential leaders needed some way to wrest the leadership role from the incumbent. If the contender wasn't physically stronger, then he, necessarily, had to be more potent in another area of human need … the need to exercise some control over the forces of nature (read: "Acts of God"). The first Shaman (pl.) were undoubtedly shrewder than those gullible people whom they deceived with their quasi-religious chicanery.

Leaders, as in all other subjective classifications of humans, come in varied and diverse temperament. The one standard factor they evince is an ungoverned impulse to dominate others. This is a character trait inborn in many mammals, particularly primates. It isn't illogical to ascribe that same trait to humans, although some would deem the ascription to be derogatory.

The importance of the above in the formation and the profusion of religious sects cannot be overstated. All sects (likewise cults, et al.) can be traced back to one persistent, forceful, charismatic leader. His biography would undoubtedly indicate that the religious propositions he espoused existed initially and that he merely championed those propositions. Quite the reverse is the fact. He formulated his beliefs first, then, subsequently, he sought an arena to expound those beliefs with the expectation of gathering a faithful, subservient retinue.

Try to imagine a leadership candidate who had nothing new to offer; no novel or imperative reason why you should accept him as your leader; one who promised simply to continue leading exactly as had the incumbent leader. Ridiculous, isn't it? Every politician knows that in any elective contest one has to have an issue. Either that or one must create the semblance of a vital issue. Some pertinent grounds (or grounds considered pertinent to the beholder) must exist to rouse the inertial crowd to action. The intended action being: a switch in allegiance from one leader personality to another.

This is often accomplished after the leadership role of a long established group has passed to a person who maintains his role by default. By default I mean: Older sects tend to attract and hold, few potential leaders, but many submissive supporters. After a time, all that remains as prospective leader replacements are docile, fully indoctrinated devotees. Of necessity, eventually one of those will have the leadership role thrust upon him. He, administering by default only, is no match for a new, vigorous, overly-ambitious, unrelenting usurper. The result is hardly surprising.

The orthodox leader either surrenders to the aspiring leader, or he faces certain schism. The blossoming charismatic personality will siphon off a number of adherents regardless of (and in spite of) the validity of his proposed novel beliefs. A casual evaluator would describe the events as a clash of conflicting ideologies, and reckon the thesis with the largest backing as the 'true' doctrine. An in-depth appraisal would discover merely a clash of personalities, each vying to control the entire congregation. All such conflicts are occasioned by vanity, not by imperative doctrine; never by revelation from any Deity.

The Old Testament chronicles the most noteworthy details in the lives of the ancient Israelite "leaders." By name, Noah, Abraham, Moses, Joshua, the Judges, Samson, Samuel, King Saul, David and Solomon to identify those most prominent that come readily to my mind.

AUTHOR'S CAVEAT

At this point in my composition, I ask your indulgence. Shortly, I will be scrutinizing the teachings, and the stated, emended, inferred and extrapolated beliefs of a man who many people believe to be the literal 'Divine Son of God.' He is considered to be coequal with God while remaining an intermediary between the Almighty and mankind. Frankly, no description of mine would be adequate to define the connection between the uncreated Creator and His purported Son, Jesus; nor their affinity to the Third Person of the Trinity, the Holy Ghost. Today, it is fashionable to refer to this Third Entity as the Holy Spirit for 'ghosts' have come to be recognized as spurious creations of the superstitious mind. But, to me, the two appellations are unequivocally identical.

If an objective scrutiny of the personality of Jesus offends you, then I suggest you either put this book down, or skim through those sections. I feel it is necessary to expose some of the many inconsistencies surrounding Jesus Himself, for without such scrutiny, this writing would be deemed negligent and demonstrably incomplete. If the human being Jesus was/is also an indivisible partner in the universal Divinity, then nothing I write could diminish Him in the slightest. If He was not, then this book has value.

I believe that Jesus was a remarkable individual. He was a unique leader. But He wasn't a God, or the offspring of a God, or even a demigod. He was a thoroughly human man. His life, and the philosophies it generated, satisfies an insistent primal urge in man; the urge to be wanted; the urge to be loved; the urge be thought to have personal worth!

From the moment of our first consciousness, we need affection. We spend the remainder of our lives seeking affection, from ourselves to a major degree, and from others to a lesser degree. Religion (particularly the Christian religion) pacifies this impulse to be loved, to be held in esteem, and to possess an inherent worth. All human behavior can be explained by this hypothesis. I won't enlarge on my human behavior theories further because that would be a distraction from the overall intent of this composition.

So, after that forewarning I bid my reader to proceed. I aver here that at no place have I purposely slandered nor ridiculed Jesus, His mother, or His fathers (Yahweh – Joseph). Nowhere was my purpose to denigrate anyone, although undeniably there have been holy men, proselytizers, clerics, and all manner of religionists in the past who were not worthy of the homage that was bestowed upon them.

If, by exposing the irrationality (and even the deceit) of many religious teachings, I unavoidably may tarnish the reputation of someone. If that be so, then it will only be due to the exigencies of writing a book such as this is intended to be. I offer no apology. I seek only after universal truth. This book is a testament to that which I have found through my research. I may have erred. But nowhere have I knowingly deceived!

CHAPTER 2

Introducing God

GODS AND DEMONS

Most of what persons of this age would call 'superstitious behavior' had their origins in primitive religious beliefs. The earliest cults had nothing whatever to do with morality. They revolved around magical symbols, behavioral cajolery, ritual delusion, and mystical communication, all directed at influencing the actions (or reactions) of incomprehensible Supernatural Forces. Ancient Gods weren't ethical beings. They were powerful, turbulent, unconstrained demons.

In earliest Hebrew, the word "Elohim" was the plural form of the word "El" or "Eloi." [Cf. Mk. 15:34] meaning: strong, mighty, i.e., an almighty supernatural being. (Current word demon is similar in meaning, but not identical). This is the word used in Genesis 1:1, "*In the beginning 'Elohim'* {the mighty g<u>ods</u>} *created the heavens and the earth.*" That word later came to be used exclusively referring to the singular Hebrew God, Yahweh. However in Genesis, several times God Himself speaks in a manner confirming that there are other gods. Two examples: *"And God said, Let <u>us</u> make man in <u>our</u> image, after <u>our</u> likeness."* [Gen. 1.26] Speaking of Adam: *"And God said, 'Lo, the man has become as one of* <u>us</u>' ...."* [Gen.3:22] {Author's underlines} These evidential examples indicate to me that the original author of the beginning of Genesis truly believed in multiple deities, and his writings reflect this belief. Conclusion: "Elohim" in the original Genesis texts is, and was intended to be understood as, a plural proper noun. To wit: "In the beginning the gods {"Elohim"} created the heavens and the earth." {Author's translation}

Demonology, in religious supposition, has never been as fully, or as extensively, developed as has theology. Once having been formulated, it persists. That which demon attributes lack in specifics, they compensate for in generalities. Consider the many guises, powers, limitations, and confusions surrounding belief in the Devil.

What functions do demons fulfill in the scheme of religion? Obviously, they create a counter balance, an opposite. They complete the logical deliberations of religious theorists. Just as hot must have cold, and near must have far, so, too, must good have evil. They complement each other and are as indivisible as are the two ends of a straight bar. Would it be fair or equitable for an Almighty God to contend with a puny adversary? No. In comic book adventures, does Superman do battle with mere mortals? Of course not! Super Heroes require Super Villains.

God's super villain is Lucifer, Prince of the Fallen Angels. Note that Lucifer is only a prince, whereas God is a king. Yet, virtually everything that God can do, Lucifer can mimic. For that reason, Lucifer is also known as a master deceiver. How, you may ask, can one unerringly distinguish God's benevolent acts from the Devil's deceitful acts? This is exceedingly difficult for often they are similar, if not precisely the same act.

I am more than slightly amused at the solution offered by one "enlightened" religious leader known through his long-running television program. He, sagely suspicious of all actions, even his own thoughts, will boldly proclaim that if what he perceives is not from God, he wants no part of it. Then he will invoke the quasi-magical name of 'Jesus' that invariably vanquishes the Devil. How he reconciles this with the well-documented cases of thoroughly evil acts being performed in the name of 'Jesus' eludes me. Nonetheless, he retains unshakable faith that Jesus guides him personally and unfailingly through the trials of the Powers of Darkness, i.e., the Devil.

In practicality, the prevalent method of determining if an action was initiated by God, or was concocted by the Devil to fool humanity, is to look back at the result of an event to determine if the action has ended in a beneficial or an odious outcome. Then the faithful, with pious certitude, can ascribe the witnessed intervention to either God or Satan. Is this reasoning true discernment, or is it merely biased religious dialectic?

GOD, THE INSCRUTABLE DEITY

Original man invented the Gods to account for the ostensibly unfathomable acts of nature and the capriciousness of life. To him, Nature must have appeared utterly unpredictable and wholly incomprehensible. Surely there had to be some order to this apparent disorder. The least complicated way that natural events could be understood logically was to conceive and assign a different deity to every separate, unexplained occurrence. To early man this made sense. Constrained by their limited comprehension, it would to you also. A multiplicity of gods isn't wholly illogical. Although a single arbitrary, yet mutable, deity is less complex to visualize.

Presently we picture the Creator as kind, benevolent, and loving. If an event occurs that is indecipherable, or worse if it is detrimental, we are informed that it isn't God's deleterious act that is enigmatic; it is only our comprehension of that event that is puzzling. Somehow, every act of God will ultimately devolve to our personal favor. When you strip away the verbal veneer, this belief makes as much nonsense as anything the ancients believed.

Lacking an extensive knowledge of cause and effect, the original Homo sapiens were perplexed by the original question "Why?" Why did this happen? Why didn't that happen? There is one inarguable distinction between mankind and all other creatures: It is man's ability and propensity to wonder "why." Man never seems to tire asking why; furthermore, he invariably provides an explanatory answer, although seldom with unerring accuracy.

Once the preternatural, i.e., Supreme Being(s) concept, was promulgated, it was certain to be tested. Man continued to ask why. Why did the God of good deeds become the God of evil deeds? No amount of rationalization could square with the observed facts. Someone had to invent Anti-Gods, and so they did! Our Anti-God is the Devil (aka Satan). If something welcome happened, obviously, the good God was to be credited. If something unpleasant happened, then just as obviously, the evil personage (Anti-God) was to blame.

A parallel observation turned man's thought processes in an alternate direction. He noticed that if he was performing a specific act before an event took place, the event proved beneficial. Conversely, other actions seemed always to precede a malevolent eventuality. This perception wasn't, and isn't, restricted to religious speculation. This superstitious propensity presented an obstacle to would-be proselytizers. If mankind was able to seek God in his own individual manner, there would be no leaders, no privileged caste of priests, and no organized religious conformity. This couldn't be tolerated. Frankly, this would only conclude in an intellectual and doctrinal "Tower of Babel." [Cf. Gen. 11:1-9]

In the earliest human societies, the need for extensively defined religious behavior was minimal. A study of existing primitive groups shows a dearth of formalized rituals on the scale we in the West currently practice. That isn't to opine that religiosity didn't exist in those communities. Quite the contrary! Religiosity is ubiquitous in all human societies. Believers point to this observation as proof for the existence of a Supreme Being. They conveniently neglect to note the utter dissimilarity of those beliefs that, if indicative, merely posits that man is susceptible to believing virtually anything in the realm of the preternatural or the supernatural.

Everyone knew that certain actions evoked predictable reactions from other persons. The more intimate you were with that person, the more predictable their reactions would be. Perhaps the Gods were no different. Becoming intimate with the Gods, however, posed no minor difficulty. Further, the Gods proved discouragingly less predictable than humans. One moment a given action would produce the expected result. Later, the same action would fail to produce any reaction at all; or worse, it would effect an adverse reaction. This was very perplexing. To complicate the matter even further, it was noted that certain individuals were successful, more often, at producing desired results than other individuals, or at least alleging such! Thus was born the priesthood.

Actually many persons sought religious guidance, or simply found it more prudent to support insistent leaders, or more advantageous to acquiesce to persuasive personalities than to develop a theology for themselves. The cognitive religious authorities grasped this opportunity to set about codifying their own beliefs and formalizing their own ceremonies. This seemed the best way of checking the spread of the ever-expanding miscellany of religious practices and beliefs.

Next, the leaders had to secure the acceptance and to enforce the observance of their individual creeds. One method was to assert that their doctrines were divinely inspired, accordingly, in full accord with God's will. Yet how was God's will to become known to man? The answer: God had to speak to man, and that He did! If the words were the words of man that was one thing, but if they were the revealed truths of God, that was quite another. Stable civilization necessitates unquestioned authority, and it also requires strict obedience to its dictates. So, too, does stable religion. The inspired words of God were the invention of civilized man. He needed divine authority to outlaw religious self-determination that led unfailingly to 'false' beliefs and practices, or even more worrisome, to schism!

Every successful religious leader has asserted to have been in communication with a Deity as the foundation for his authority. More often, the Deity sought out the leader to accomplish some vital, doctrinal mission. Usually this required the formation of a new 'inspired' sect. True, each leader propounded his individual creed. In that respect, each was unique. Their common bond was the belief (or assertion) that the Supreme Being had singled them out from the chaff of humanity. They were the chosen, 'the Elect of God.' The wisdom of the Ultimate Intelligence of the Universe spouted from their mouths. An affront to their person was tantamount to an affront to God Himself. Expanded, that belief led inexorably to the religious disciplinary excesses that have been impressed onto the backs of gullible followers and powerless adversaries by pompous, vindictive, jingoistic religious authorities since the advent of communal living.

One belief that appears constant and unchanging (principally in Christian theology) is the paternal depiction of the senior member of the Trinity, God the Father. He is always understood as just that: a father! He has all the desirable attributes of a human father, but few if any of their human failings. He loves you exclusively, just as your real father does. True, you do have brothers and sisters (fellow adherents to your creed), but illogically, you continue to believe that notwithstanding this reality, God's every action will ultimately devolve to benefit you personally. You believe this even though God's professed actions, seemingly at times, are quizzical or even injurious to you.

A real human father could never be so perfect. Your experiences informs you that your real father is fallible. This is disheartening, but true! Not being capable of soothing your innermost pains is his greatest failing. God the Father can ease even these very deep-seated aches, you are told. It is postulated that God the Father has <u>no</u> shortcomings. All you must do to obtain His ministrations is believe in Him, and obey His earthly representatives. If your emotional pain is relieved soon after espousing a novel belief then, "Praise the Lord; God loves you!" If your distress isn't alleviated, then evidently, your faith isn't strong enough, or maybe you haven't performed the effectuating ritual properly. God never fails those who truly trust in Him!

This type of self-fulfilling principle has gulled so many persons that it is almost laughable … almost! A person can only suffer mental anguish if he allows it, or even encourages it. He will continue to feel this anguish until he decides, consciously or subliminally, to forgo it. Any diversion that helps him to cease dwelling on the cause of his anguish will perceptively, but not factually, be credited for the relief he experiences. Placebos accomplish the identical effect through the same principle. Religionists are quick to credit God with any 'cure' you experience while being indoctrinated into their respective belief system.

Contrarily, if you don't obtain relief, this isn't your divine Father's failing. God is only responsible for beneficial results, the Devil should be blamed for all else. If one is going to formulate a spiritual Father, perforce, one must delineate Him as perfect. Mankind has done just this. What else would a perfect father provide you with but a perfect home? God has done this also, but we don't call that place "home." We call it Heaven.

All the actions of the Deity are explained as His way of attending us; an idealized form of self-indulgence! Early religionists concentrated on obtaining earthly benefits from the Deity. All rituals had the sole goal of profiting the practitioner. Yet, God failed early man as often as He accommodated him, as He discernibly does to this day! This frustrated early man and created doubts in his mind. However, once again, human ingenuity provided reconciliation.

The Earth was postulated as an arena for moral testing. First, God subjected us to many and varied trials while on Earth. Then if we subsequently demonstrated our worthiness, we would be rewarded with an eternity in Heaven. But if we failed our trial, without recourse we would be justly punished in Hell. Although God is credited as all-knowing in everything, discernibly, He is uncertain which of us mortals is inherently worthy of Heaven. He must continually test each of us with adversity before He decides our deservedness for eternal happiness. The obvious fact that some are burdened with more adversity than others, in no way diminishes the perfect justice God hypothetically dispenses. This inequality of adversity, as with all other facets of life, is more sensibly explained as randomness of natural events than as impositions concocted via the undecipherable will of an 'allegedly just' Divinity. Yet the 'Godhood' myth endures!

GOD — COMMUNING WITH HIM

In primitive groups, where everyone knew everyone else, direct communication with the Deity would have been ridiculed. Trances or dreams were another matter altogether. Anyone could have them under unusual, extraordinary, or contrived circumstances. Opiates and hallucinogens were employed worldwide to induce trances. Trances seem to be the usual means of communicating with the Supreme Being where this entity is indistinctly defined, i.e., when the Supreme Being is other than a recognizable human being. If the Deity is a mystical, paranormal, supra-natural Entity, then normal means of communication would be inappropriate, if not impossible. A supra-natural message via our supra-natural inner consciousness would seem to satisfy a human proclivity to 'normalize' an abnormal situation; that being, communicating with the Spectral Deity who resides somewhere high in the earth's atmosphere.

If a society envisioned the Supreme in human terms, then, of course, direct intercourse with the Deity was not only possible, it was highly probable. We need read only Genesis for confirmation of this assertion. [Cf. Gen. 3:8-10 ff] On the other hand, in a society where the form and substance of the Supreme was ill-defined (as was the exact status of the Risen Jesus the day Saul traveled that fateful road to Damascus), the most acceptable means of communication should have been the trance. The day that Saul had his vision of Jesus, he (Paul) was uncertain of the exact nature of the crucified man the Apostles preached to be the Jewish Messiah.

This seems to have been the usual case in most primitive cults. That communication with the Deity was (and continues to be) necessary, was (and is) self-evident. Human existence is incredibly complex. Situations that ostensibly required divine guidance multiplied with the increasing complexity of human cultural advancement. Legalistic, moralistic, and ritualistic questions arose that the earliest proselytizers hadn't foreseen. Clarification, edification, or inspiration was clearly considered presently necessary.

Not all religionists were brazen enough to allege direct communication with the Deity. The number of persons in any age who were brash or presumptuous enough to allege to know the Divine Will unerringly was exceedingly small. A truly devout person never makes such a blatantly bogus allegation. Only a consummate egotist can presume that God speaks to them exclusively, and upon subpoena at that. A curious paradox arose from this consideration.

Devout, yet skeptical, believers required proof. If God spoke to humans, why couldn't they hear Him? In every contact incident, weren't they as worthy as the prophets? Didn't they strive as mightily as they could to perform the rites, accept the tenets and obey the religious strictures, with as much devotion (possibly more) than the already highly honored seers? What plausible reason could God have for not communicating directly with them? Surely, no one could be more receptive, nor be keener to follow those directives. Reasonably, if God spoke to anyone it should have been to those who believed so faithfully. But, alas, that was not the observed case. How that perplexity was resolved is a further tribute to human creativity. (Otherwise to human deviousness!)

Clearly, those questing devout souls required tangible proof of God's intentions. They would have to be shown something tangible that would guarantee their continued submission to that belief system. What the ancient priesthood needed was a magician's apparatus. An apparatus that looked normal and innocuous to the uninitiated, but for God's intimates, it possessed a power beyond its appearance. Lacking the technical skill to build such equipment didn't hinder the persistently devious. If they couldn't build a device, then they must find one in nature. Therefore, they submitted the use of a mystical contrivance whereby God's Will would not only become known, but could be shown as well. Medicine sticks, tea leaves, calves livers, dice, et al., all served this nefarious purpose. The number of mystical appliances recognized as prophetic and utilized in a revelatory manner was as countless as was the number of persons gullible enough to believe in them. Superstition and religiosity are twin manifestations of the identical human idiosyncrasy.

An alternate method of communicating with the Deity indirectly, as via a visual occurrence, was to interpret cryptic appearances in the sky. Many natural events (storms, et al.) originated from the heavens. Heaven is the abode of the Almighty Spirit; therefore, it was the Deity who caused those manifestations, obviously! Why did God cause these portentous meteorological events? Was it to send us mortals a message? Were these events the Deity's arcane method of displaying the Divine Will? Similarly, a solar eclipse or a spectacular comet was alleged to be a worrying omen of the Divine Will. Yet, because of the multiplicity of ways God supposedly chose to exhibit His Will, only His adepts could explain them fully and convincingly. Fortunately for the more humble of humanity, there always chanced to be an adept nearby who professed the ability to decipher God's coded messages unerringly as discerned through His emanations from or in the unreachable skies.

Occasionally, the sign would be so visible and so obvious that everyone knew its meaning. A flash flood in a low lying valley after a prolonged rain that perished an entire village was an unmistakable sign that God was displeased with the behavior of all of the village inhabitants. People with today's sense of justice would be appalled by such a massive, all-encompassing penalty meted out to the very guilty, the slightly guilty, and the innocent; all in equal measure. There is no possible way for every person in a community to be so far beyond redemption as to deserve to be drowned or buried alive. It didn't make sense in the past, and it doesn't make sense today. Is the bursting of an earthen dam during a violent storm a vengeful act of God, or is it the incompetent workmanship of man?

Almost no one now thinks that a natural disaster, such as a hurricane, an earthquake, or an erupting volcano, is anything other than what it clearly appears to be. Namely, a random occurrence that is comprehensible, although maybe not immediately explicable because of our imperfect knowledge of the workings of nature. Some biblical proponents would have us believe that natural disasters are explained by the pseudo-intellectual axiom "The ways of the Lord are mysterious." That absurdity may appease the slow of wit, but should offend anyone with 'God given' intelligence.

Is God the Ultimate Wisdom of the Universe, or is He merely the grand mystery drama writer whose sole aim is to confound and confuse His creatures with inexplicable eventualities? What is your reply to that query?

GOD HEARS OUR PRAYERS?

('Some thoughts on the efficacy of prayer: more directly: "Are prayers answered?"')

That there can be no Divine intervention in the affairs of man can be deduced with a small expenditure of effort, and a reasonable application of logic. Roughly half of the requests a supplicant might make would require that something not only would have to be given him, but necessarily, that thing would have to be taken away from someone else. The other half, that being good health, could be given one petitioner, yet denied many others. How is the granting and denying determined? 'By devoutness? That can be disproved! 'By worthiness? This is easily challenged! Whatever your criterion, you could or would be shown obvious exceptions.

"God moves in mysterious ways," is a time-worn adage, and the fact that it has endured a lengthy time proves one thing at least, 'No reasonable, comprehensible, rational or intelligent explanation can be given for the seemingly random happenings of life other than randomness itself.' If you reflect honestly on the events of your life and how they transpired, then search objectively for the reason why, the answer invariably is blind, aimless, haphazard "chance."

So much of what happens to us in life is clearly the result of a vast, complex interplay of the actions of many persons interweaving with the actions of many other persons. Sorting out all the relevant factors contributing to the end discernible is nigh on impossible, especially if one calibrated the relative impact of those factors. If God was to influence even minor events in our lives, He would have to control the actions and the thoughts of many others in ever so many sundry ways. And, if God were altering our thoughts and our actions, could we then be held accountable for them? Hardly! How about evil, harmful episodes in our lives? Does

God trigger them? You would have to answer "Yes," if we can believe the countless tales of surprising benefits that eventuated from initially adverse situations. "Praise the Lord!"

Was it God who was directing the plotting of the "Son of Sam" murderer? Who orchestrated the victims' movements so that they would be exactly where they had to be in order to be killed? Jack the Ripper was responsible for many a prayer directed to the heavenly Father. Was "Jack" thence unwittingly acting robotically via God's inscrutable guidance? Blasphemy, you charge? 'Not really, just the logical extension of an initial fictitious premise.

Surely, there are few preachers who haven't used the emotional (and frankly erroneous) argument for the discernibly universal belief in a Supreme Entity: 'There are no atheists in a foxhole.' Wherever the intelligent exist there have been atheists, and there always will be! Grant that, in a war zone, atheists are a minority. That doesn't prove God's reality. It exposes mankind's perfidy.

Religionists have a one-dimensional perspective of the happenings in life. If an event seemed to them to be propitious, then surely God designed it. If an event was seen as harmful, then surely the Devil initiated it. However, if something beneficial later eventuated out of the formerly credited disastrous event, then the cry is reverted to: 'The Lord Moves in inscrutable ways, His wonders to perform.' Aren't they aware of their unabashedly biased inconsistency?

Consider the hard-working, God-fearing farmer who prayed for rain the day before the Flood. Did anyone from Sodom recognize the perversity of his neighbors and fret that Yahweh might one day discipline that town? Surely there was one unsuspecting Japanese soul who petitioned God to provide clear skies over Hiroshima (an indispensable A-bomb dropping criterion) the day the Atom bomb was exploded. If wars turn mankind to prayer and help launch religious revival, then perhaps, we should celebrate wars as boons to humanity. In war, we enhance both our probability of earning Heaven, and the odds that we will arrive there shortly!

Sober reflection by any thoughtful person will convince her/him of the accuracy of my previous pronouncement that there just isn't any Divine intervention. An omniscient Creator, granting His creatures' unrestricted free will, by that enactment would exclude Himself from their every affair. If we have free will, and beyond question we do, then neither our actions, nor the actions of those who affect our lives, are controlled in any fashion whatsoever by God.

Clearly, the rewards and the adversities of life are neither evenly nor fairly dispensed. 'Not on an individual basis. 'Not on an area basis. 'Not even by Nation or Continent. Which theory best fits the observable evidence: That God, in His wisdom has parceled out what each man's physical and material portion will be? Or that fickle fate, spinning the wheel of fortune, coupled with the ability and persistence of the individual, has determined the present distribution of health and wealth, or poverty and want? In virtually every discernible case, the most appropriate response must be unconditional, unpredictable, and impersonal 'happenstance.'

The most materially blest of the world's nations are predominantly Christian. Does this indicate that Jesus Christ has favored those nations to the exclusion of all other nations? If your response is 'yes,' then answer me: "Why do the Muslims now control the most valuable commodity on Earth"? By name: petroleum. Evidently, Allah dispenses favors also. So I ask, "What of China with her almost uncountable masses?" After an all-out nuclear war the greater part of the survivors (assuming there were survivors) would offer their gratitude to Confucius. If sheer numbers determined whether prayers were answered, then God's grace should have been bestowed chiefly in the Far East. Oriental people far outnumber the remainder of humanity.

If you look earnestly you will see that not only can most events on Earth, if not all events, be more convincingly explained by mere coincidence. The obverse is equally compelling. Too many events on Earth are wholly incomprehensible when we ascribe them to the enigmatic machinations of an intelligent, loving Creator. The continual warfare and strife that mankind has engaged in since the dawn of human proliferation testifies strongly as an argument validating evolution, i.e., "survival of the fittest." This verifiable axiom is in unmitigated disagreement with the proposition that God manipulates any sphere or facet of human behavior whatsoever.

Would an all-powerful and entirely-just Deity permit man to commit those atrocities that we know, throughout history, have been inflicted on humanity? All too many outrageous incidents have occurred under the aegis of religiously motivated authorities. The biblical God, Yahweh, would have punished mankind down to the fourth generation for the worship of an idol. [Cf. Ex. 20:5 for an example] What retribution fits the unpardonable crimes that have been committed in the glorification of a Divinity? (Zeus, Odin, Quetzalcoatl, Jesus, Allah, et al.)

Can you picture today's world if Hitler had been aborted in his mother's womb? Did humanity have to suffer through World War II? Why? To prove we are deserving of Heaven? How many sinless children lost their lives as a direct result of that war? If they hadn't yet reached the age of reason and responsibility, they couldn't have sinned grievously enough to warrant death. Most victim children of that time hadn't matured enough to know how to sin.

Does anyone really believe that our life on Earth is only a proving ground for us to demonstrate to God our worthiness to exist eternally with Him in Heaven? This rationale for our existence is so flawed that I am mildly surprised that it is the sole reason advanced by religionists. But then I realize that without it religionists have no argument at all, and are thence confronted with the chagrining prospect of conceding an impersonal creative impetus, and the ultimate of all horrors by their reckoning, evolution! Without reconsideration, that discovery/theory is everlastingly anathema to every religion. "No Creator" predicates "No God."

The flaws in the proposition of an earthly moral proving ground permeate the entire spectrum of that postulate. However, to me, the death blow is struck by the undeniable observation that some people never get a chance to demonstrate their deservedness. I am referring to those who die before reaching the age (or mental maturity) of accountability. Should someone opine that children and mentally deficient adults automatically go directly to Heaven, then I question: "Why isn't everyone granted this reward?" Yes, reward! Unending bliss in Heaven is the supreme gift. Nothing God could grant you in recompense would approximate that eternal gratuity.

Next I would ask: "What have they done (unborn children, infants and other non-accountable persons) to warrant such preferential treatment"? The answer must be: "Nothing" … absolutely nothing! In sympathy, someone might offer that Heaven is "just compensation" to them for the loss of an adult life, but this can hardly be deemed just. This theorem posits earthly life as a benefit, not as a trial. The essential prerequisite of any fair test is that everyone must be given the same test or at least a comparable test.

At once, you can see that false theories breed false conclusions. If all mankind is adjudged sinful through Adam, then all mankind should be tested equally or with reasonable equality at a minimum. What is the observed case? The observable truth is that fortune favors the few, and misfortune attends the rest. Injustice is rampant. Or is it? No! Judicious observation leads me to conclude cogently that humanity isn't victimized by the gods; we are merely collectively disparaged, disdained or ignored by the gods. {Actually, by nature}

GOD THE ENIGMATIC

Is the celestial Father aware of all the misfortunes that strike our lives, or is the father analogy only operational when benefits accrue to us? Is it possible that a benevolent, benign, gentle, sympathetic, merciful, considerate and concerned Supreme Being, capable of averting, deflecting, preventing, circumventing, substituting or stopping any event whatsoever from transpiring ... could He tolerate that which we are all aware has been tolerated on Earth? Directly asked: "Do we humans have total and unconditional free will to act in any manner whatsoever without the slightest interference from anyone, including God? Or, are we restricted to only those approved actions that are acceptable to the Universal Creator?"

The skeptic's reply is obvious. Still I will concede that this is a bothersome question for someone who is still intimidated by the doctrinaire tenets of his religious upbringing. One day all of us must confront that doctrinal dilemma if we are to grow to full intellectual maturity. We can evade it temporarily as a child strives to evade a troublesome situation, or we can attempt to reconcile the reality of life against the rationale of religiosity as every adult should.

Read the newspapers daily and then ask yourself objectively: Is there a knowing, caring Deity monitoring the happenings on Earth with the power to alter every event? To answer that it isn't our prerogative to question the actions of God, is intellectual myopia. All other bio-forms experience life in intellectual ignorance. Are we also intended to suffer through our life in mental servitude? Several passages in the Bible seem to suggest just that. As an example: in Corinthians it reads, *"The wisdom of this world is foolishness with God."* [1 Cor. 3:19] Does it then follow: 'The foolishness of this world is wisdom with God'? It must!

Here is what the ancient writer of that scriptural passage was really conveying: 'Facts be damned. Whatever I promulgate is to be treated as universal truth.' This is precisely what I perceive as the self-elevating rationalization of immature persons. Every proof, every confirmation, every recalled wisdom of an adult can be invalidated with an inane, superficial remark. About all the above biblical quote has to recommend it is the fact that it is so utterly ridiculous that it fits squarely into the realm of demagoguery. Any statement that devoid of logic and believability must be accepted without reservation because no one would make such an outrageous assertion unless it was unquestionably and unalterably 'a truth.' [Cf. 1 Cor. 3:18]

If there is one overriding attribute that a Creator of this Universe must possess, it is intelligence. If that Creator is a personal God to mankind, we should be able to come to know Him by recognizing the intelligent artifacts He has created. A great sculptor leaves behind great sculptures. A great architect leaves great architecture, and so on. Is God the real author of the collected writings we call the Bible? Is it He who speaks of the four corners of the Earth? The author of that comment didn't know that our world is a sphere. Only a flat or cubed Earth can have four corners. [Cf. Isa. 11:12 & Rev. 7:1]

And notwithstanding the biblical references to "pillars of the earth," or "the ends of the earth," and other references that are Irreconcilable with a spherical Earth. [Cf. 1 Sa. 2:8 & Job 37:3 respectively] Did God inspire the idea that the stars can fall to the Earth? Matthew and Mark thought stars could fall. [Cf. Mt. 24:29 & Mk. 13:25] Can the stars fall to the Earth? No! Even more fantastic is the prediction in Revelations that one-third of the stars will fall to Earth. [Cf. Rev. 12:4 & 8:12] There are six thousand magnitude 6 stars visible from the earth. Every single one of those is many times more massive than is the Earth.

Our Earth couldn't survive the near collision of a single star, much less by two thousand stars. The person(s) who wrote these verses thought of the stars as tiny balls of light attached to a crystal globe overarching the flat

Earth. The depth of their astronomical ignorance is startling today. Didn't the Divine Inspirer know of the enormous mass of even the smallest of stars? Neither was that Inspirer cognizant of the uncountable number of stars in our galaxy alone. It is small wonder that religious protagonists were so adamant against intelligent scrutiny of their precepts, and remain so into this day! Thoughtful examination of their fabulous and misguided pious allegations could have exposed these protagonists for exactly what they were: Charlatans, dupers, deluders, sham prophets, liars, and vainglorious manipulators.

Even more confirming of the biblical falsities posing as predictions is the continuation of the cited verses from Matthew identified immediately above. To wit: *"Likewise, when you see all these things, you may be certain that he is near, even at the doors. Truly I say to you, 'This generation will not come to an end till all these things are complete. Heaven and earth will come to an end, but my words will not come to an end.'"* [Mt. 24:33-35 & Mk. 13:30] While it is true that these words of prophecy live on even to this day (Matthew's cited verses), the "generation" that Matthew was writing to did 'come to an end' more than 2000 years ago, therefore this Evangelist's prophecy has proved entirely false. So far, not a single star has fallen to the Earth, nor has the Earth come to an end, plus Matthew's contemporaries are all dead. Matthew's gospel words have survived; only his horrific disaster prediction has failed.

If there is sin in this world {I aver there is}, the greatest sin is incurred by suppressing our intellect. Religionists preach that God has given humanity many gifts, beginning with the gift of life. Including the planet we live on and a plethora of other putative gifts. The greatest gift, absent a doubt, is the gift of intelligence. If we suppress this gift, I feel that we have forfeited any claim we have to the rest of God's purported gifts.

The story of the fall from favor of Adam in the Garden of Eden is blatantly anti-intellectual. The entirety of mankind along with Adam was punished for thousands of years because Adam ate fruit from the Tree of Knowledge. Here are God's words: *"Indeed, the man has become like one of us* {sic} *knowing good and evil. And now perhaps he will put forth his hand and take from the Tree of Life and eat and live forever!"* [Gen. 3:22] Evidently, the fruit that conferred knowledge wasn't one hundred percent enlightening, for if Adam had been a bit wiser, he could have hastily eaten from the Tree of Life and never suffered death at all. Why was there a "Tree of Life" in the Garden?

The entire Garden of Eden story is riddled with fable-like inconsistencies. If you regard this Bible-opening anecdote as a divinely inspired means of informing future generations of how God created the Universe, or as facts beyond review that are to be believed explicitly and without reserve, then surely God must have intended us to be dimwits or juveniles our entire lives. The Creation story is utterly ridiculous. However, if you read it knowing that it is exactly what it appears to be: that is, a folk legend that was designed to offer a fanciful explanation (to the unsophisticated ancient listener) for the creation of mankind, the pain of childbirth, the necessity for manual labor, the origin of shame at nakedness, and several other human idiosyncrasies, then the story does lose its believability entirely. But it gains immeasurably therewith in charm and entertainment.

I can picture knowing adults winking to one another as they related the creation story to their children. The story has a very direct and poignant message for the young: 'Do as you are told or you will surely regret that you have not.' An intelligent Deity, who knew the future, without doubt and with no additional effort could have inspired a tale that didn't contradict the now-known facts quite so flagrantly; quite so absolutely!

The culmination of the Flood story can be used to illustrate this contention convincingly. Rainbows are formed by the diffraction of light passing through certain mediums that spread it into its constituent colors. In the biblical instance, the medium is rain. Rainbows can be produced on sunny days by anyone with a garden hose set for fine spray if the hose is held up between your eyes and the Sun. Plainly, rainbows are a natural occurrence, not a divine spectacle. Are all rainbows a sign from Yahweh that He will never again flood the Earth? If so, then what is proved on days when the rain stops suddenly and no rainbow is formed? That perchance He will flood the entire Earth again?

Isaac Asimov, writing in his book, <u>Light, Magnetism, and Electricity</u> (page 50, par. 3), informs us thus: "One such phenomenon known to men of all ages, is the rainbow, the arc of varicolored light that sometimes appears in the sky, when the Sun emerges after a rain shower. The rainbow was startling enough to attract a host of mythological explanations. A common one was that it was a bridge connecting Heaven and Earth."

Science can demonstrate that light from distant stars, passed through a prism, will split into a tiny rainbow called a spectrum. Anywhere in the

Universe, where the effectuating conditions are present, rainbows will form. They aren't confined to Earth, or to the aftermath of rain showers. Does the Bible urge us to think that rainbows didn't exist before the Flood? Yes, it does. This is untrue, and an Omniscient Inspirer would have known that it wasn't factual.

Incidentally, this characteristic of light has proven to be an invaluable tool in determining the likely composition of the Milky Way Galaxy and the Universe beyond. Accordingly, we can "Thank God" that rainbows aren't exclusive to the Earth after a rainstorm. Intelligent, thinking, questioning men have used rainbows (in the form of galactic spectra) to unravel a few of the mysteries of the Cosmos.

GOD'S EMOTIONS VS. GOD'S ACTIONS

Can God be known other than via divine revelation? The implication being this: All cultures, however primitive, have a bent toward the development of notions of religiosity. Religiosity, for purposes of discussion here and throughout, is defined in its broadest sense: "The belief in a paranormal intelligent force superior to man's power and intellect." The single criterion of that intelligent force is that it must be constantly cognizant of man. This is a curious concept, but an indispensable one. God must attend to mankind without distraction. Man is thereby elevated to a position of preeminence throughout Creation. Religion is not man's attempt to glorify God, but is mankind's egocentric method of glorifying man himself.

Why does God perform miracles, inspire revelations, confer grace, forgive transgressions, dispense favors, and exude love? Clearly, it is because He desires mankind's reciprocation. God needs man to honor Him. That conclusion is inescapable. Analyze the interrelationship between a mother and her infant. The mother receives as much satisfaction and pleasure from the infant as the infant receives from her. They both seek gratification of an inherited impulse, and both find that gratification in their mutual relations.

God doesn't exist, so it is impossible to know His emotions; therefore, man feebly ascribed to his God, the familiar emotions he instinctively recognized as an infant in his relationship with his mother (or substitute care giver). It is gratifying to visualize a God who responds to man's petitions in a predictable manner. The visualization is easy to maintain as long as we don't stray from the emotional responses of the Deity onto His physical responses.

God's emotions are stable, constant, but most comforting, they are predictable. When your behavior is praiseworthy, don't you just know that God is pleased with you? Certainly you do! God's emotions never vary. What God thinks, we all know. What He does, is an altogether other matter. God's actions are totally chaotic. In fact, you could state paradoxically that God's actions are predictably unpredictable. This paradox has never been explained by revelation, for revelation doesn't exist either. The true resolution lies in our thinking processes.

The reason God's emotions never vary is because they can't be tested or verified, they can only be surmised. God's emotions exist only in our imagination, and nothing in creation can refute our imagination. If you opine that God is saddened by your sins, then of course, He truly is saddened. There is no proof, no evidence, nothing tangible I could produce to prove otherwise. Your belief that you know the mind of God rests solely on faith. God only exists in faith, not in fact.

But tell me that God acts in any discernible manner whatsoever, and that I will take issue with. God doesn't act. This can be proven. Can God move mountains? "Yes," you reply. Then let us ask the entire Christian world, Muslim world, and Jewish world to pray that the Golan Heights of Syria (Israel) be leveled. Not only would this be an irrefutable proof of God's existence, but it would remove one of the obstacles to peace in the land where His beloved Son was born; it is the land called "Holy" in the Bible (ostensibly authored by God the Third personally).

Has God raised the dead? "Yes," you repeat. Why shouldn't we ask God to resurrect Hitler so that we could put him on trial for the holocaust? Or should we all intercede with Him to resurrect Moses, or Saint Paul? There are today many religious fantasizers who assert that God is still performing the resurrection miracles of the Bible. Why not resurrect someone unquestionably worthy or deserving of resurrection? What a catalyst this would be toward mass religious conversions.

Does God provide for those who heed His words? The Bible conveys that He does. In Mark, we are told that Jesus fed five thousand with five loaves and two fish, and then gathered up the fragments that filled twelve baskets. [Cf. Mk. 6:35-44] Matthew lowers the audience to four thousand men and begins with seven loaves and a few fish. [Cf. Mt. 15:32-38] Despite having started with more food and feeding fewer men (*"beside women & children"* [v. 38]), the leftovers only filled seven baskets. [Also Cf. Mt. 14:15-21; Mk. 8:19-20; Lu. 9:12-17; & Jn. 6:5-13; Compare 2 Kings 4:42-44]

Nonetheless, the four (including Luke & John) agree that Jesus, not wanting to send the people away hungry, performed His multiplication miracle and the attentive gathering was fed. In the stories, the throng was fed merely as an expedient. All presumably had homes and finances, and surely could have purchased their own food. In today's world there are many who aren't nearly as fortunate. Why couldn't we round up twelve or more pious Christian ministers and then send them to an area of extreme famine with a planeload of Bibles and a few baskets of bread and fish? God could then multiply the victuals and the Bibles, so that all would be fed and, undoubtedly, converted to Christianity shortly thereafter.

You and I both know that nothing even remotely resembling the above scenario will ever eventuate. All the physical evidences maintained to prove the existence of God have been attributed after-the-fact. Restated, after an incident has occurred, someone then recognizes that incident as a miracle that proves the existence of God.

The common denominator of all denominations is faith … that, and nothing more! The faithful must have faith, not in God; but in the human instinct that impels them to believe in a God. The continual exploitation and subsequent gross distortion of this instinct is a boon to zealous pros-elytizers. They ask that you have faith in God, but what they truly are anticipating is fealty to their chosen creed. I believe in the instinct, but I also think that our application of this instinct is a substitution for a sur-vival impulse associated with our relationship toward our initial care-giver (mother). The instinct is as ancient as the evolution of offspring born with a dependency period. Without this instinct, there can be no humanity. If humanity dies, imagination dies with it. Then, once imagination dies, God also dies!

GOD THE MALE GUARDIAN?

I have heard that demographics in Christian countries show that many more women than men regularly attend religious services. Why should this be so? My surmise to explain this otherwise irrational imbalance rests on my observance of the dependence of women on men for protection. The Christian religion offers masculine protection, i.e., God the Father and Jesus. Females are more inclined to be comforted subliminally by the thought of an All-Powerful, Loving, Accessible Male Protector than are men, who depend instinctively on their own physical strength for protection.

Despite the rabid insistence of obdurate feminists, the Supreme Being is still universally envisioned as a male entity. Unanswerable inquiries inevitably arise if we subject this concept to a deeper scrutiny. To begin, if God is a male, who (and where) is His female counterpart? Doesn't He need one? Then why is He male? Postulating a female God doesn't resolve that problem; it raises an identical one. Does She have a masculine consort? If She doesn't, then why is She female? Additional questions could be asked relating to menstruation and lactation, but they are unnecessary. A female Deity is even more incongruous than is a male Deity. Contemplating a neuter God is somewhat more rational, but it has the inherent disadvantage of being more than slightly inconceivable, and it conjures up visions of eunuchs and the like. This is hardly inspiring. Also, it destroys the anthropomorphic aspect of Western religion that is one of the enduring allurements that Christianity possesses.

Churches, to the dismay of their hierarchy, have degenerated into a stand-by service that must be ready to attend only when a distinct need arises. Weddings, funerals, and baptisms comprise a large portion of a Christian cleric's duties. For a sizable portion of congregants, attendance at weekly services is tolerated as a bothersome inconvenience, rather than as a spiritual rejuvenation, or as a joyful experience. This harms the Church most in the collection basket; therefore, more and more we see religions functioning in the entertainment and business world to raise the funds needed to perpetuate their denominations.

I am referring to the increasing incidence of church carnivals, lotteries, sale of overpriced merchandise, and kindred money garnering schemes not excluding the stock market and primary business enterprises, such as, health resorts, health maintenance organizations, homes for the elderly, life insurance, and other sources of profit-making formerly provided exclusively by the 'free enterprise' system. This lays a solid foundation for reconsidering the tax free, tax reduced, privileged status of officially recognized religions. Another bothersome observation regarding today's religions is the preponderance of old folks at services. Seniors constitute the greatest share of all contributors to television Evangelists. It is difficult to avoid the obvious conclusion that the elderly are simply hedging their bet. Having lived their lives and sinned their sins, they now seek to obtain a boarding pass for their eventual flight to Heaven made possible through their generous late-in-life collection basket donations. Unquestionably, there is much to gain and little to lose by this stratagem.

The elderly realize that each day their demise beckons more insistently. They can't ignore its call indefinitely. If, as I maintain, that is finis, there is nothing they can do to prevent it, and no exculpatory religious enactment will be effectual in fending off that fate. However, if there is a personal God, and if He has provided a Heaven for the earthly dead, they unwaveringly wish to resume their existence in that place.

Evaluate both options yourself. Shun all religious services and be certain of a plot in the cemetery. Or join the congregation, and perchance be empowered to pry the gates of Heaven open just enough for a questionable soul to slip in. Considered solely on that basis, even I might opt for religion. It can't hurt, particularly if I am too old to do much sinning even under the optimum of opportunity.

The doctrinal fact that Heaven promises none of the mortal pleasures is no deterrent at all. Most of us mentally embrace the viewpoint "Try anything once." Any style of life, however insipid, is preferable to eternal death. Withal, it annoys me to think that some gross sinner, who has enjoyed so many of the illicit pleasures of this life for so many of his/her adult years, as the end approaches, can buy their way into Heaven with a timely tithe or a belated repentance. To counter that God knows the heart of all, won't suffice. A hypothetical example will clarify my analysis. Present a million dollars to most individuals, and they would undoubtedly spend the money in the most outrageous methods imaginable. After the gift money was spent, many, if not all, would feel true remorse … honest regret! I wouldn't question the depth of their eventual penitence. God could search their soul and find nothing but contrition. Shouldn't we consider the opposite of this example, and shouldn't God also?

Consider the individuals who weren't the recipients of that fortune? Those persons who were beset instead with poverty their entire lives. They may, as their demise nears, feel resentment toward the God who never favored them in this life. Orthodox Christian doctrine teaches us that the favored former will be welcomed into Heaven. Whereas, the neglected latter will be shunted off to Hell. In the Sermon on the Mount, Jesus indicated He recognized that mankind's worthy attributes vary from one individual to another. Different degrees of worthiness compel different levels of reward. The meek were to receive one reward and the pure of heart another. [Cf. Mt. 5:3, 8] Well, the same should hold true for the domineering, and the vile of heart. 'Not so! In the either/or concept of Heaven and Hell, either you are saved, or you are damned.

Yet, if we throw out the instant lottery aspect of religion and substitute a balance scale, good deeds versus bad deeds, then I envision a Heaven where loneliness would be the prevalent emotion. It would be the domain that Heaven occupies that could pass readily through the eye of a needle. Conversely, Hell would have a waiting line an eternity long before one could attain entry. One other perverse outcome of the above substitution comes to mind. On balance, if your life has been predominantly immoral or amoral at age fifty, then odds are you will never be able to counter-balance your iniquities with subsequent moral rectitude. Accordingly, your waning years could better be spent committing as much iniquity as you are capable of at that point in your life.

Thinking mankind should challenge the whole problematic precept of deservedness through pious actions. If a personal God were all-knowing and all-seeing, couldn't He judge each of us according to our known and observed human merits? Why are we rated on ritualistic performance more heavily than we are on mental attitudes? A decent human being, who keeps the spirit and intent of the commandments (ignoring the first few, iconic/idolatrous ones), starting with "Honor thy father and thy mother." He need never bend his knee, nor bow his head to entitle himself to the highest spiritual reward attainable by mankind. 'Whatever that reward may be! Notwithstanding, I am persuaded that if man doesn't receive a reward in this life, its proposed bestowal in a non-existent afterlife will avail him naught.

GOD PROTECTS US

A number of years ago, an acquaintance known from my youth was shot through the left side of his abdomen. He was a policeman, and he was wounded while on duty. Fortunately, the bullet didn't strike any vital organs, and several hours after the incident he was well enough to be interviewed from his hospital bed by a local television reporter. The video tape was shown on the evening news that very night. As expected, the officer was gratified to be alive. He piously gave thanks to God for this "miracle."

I couldn't have been more astonished. How, in this century of human enlightenment, can God be given interventionist credit for this tragic occurrence? Intelligent reasoning reveals that the gunman's aim, together with the officer's instinctive avoidance movements, were the prime causal factors determining the point of entry of the bullet.

It is flattering to the human ego to delude ourselves into believing that a Divine Being cares enough about us to keep us from harm. The facts in this incident contradict this delusion. The police officer couldn't accept that sheer chance had kept him from death or serious harm. There had to be a more significant reason than mere coincidence; his religious convictions supplied that most cogent reason. God spared him because God loves him. If true, that would be wonderful. But is it true? I doubt it!

Try to visualize this event from a universal perspective. High up in Heaven sits God on his magnificent throne smiling down on our minion of the law: Just as the bullet is fired, God's power zips out and deflects the projectile away from life-supporting internal organs into less lethal intestinal matter. Devout persons offer this as an example of God's love. And, frankly, we all are awed by the presumption of God's love. Yet, what emotion should we postulate to explain why God permitted the officer to be shot at, and wounded, in the first instance? Was this an example of God's perverseness? Was it a specimen of His sadism? Was God venting a little callousness by allowing the officer to be injured without being killed?

The time for God's merciful action was before the policeman was wounded, if indeed, God acted at all. If every occurrence on Earth is either directed or sanctioned by the Supreme Being; how can this event be defended logically? Why didn't the Lord deflect the bullet so that it missed the officer altogether? Everyone with a sufficiency of intelligence should realize that the reasons (there were other contributing factors) why the officer was shot, yet didn't die, had their explanation in human actions coupled with ordinary happenstance, not celestial intervention.

Ignorant of, or ignoring, the *bona fide* facts of life, the officer persisted in his contention that his life was spared because God loved him. His line of reasoning, if fully examined, would conclude that God cared enough to preserve his life, but not enough to prevent him from being injured. Perhaps God only likes us. After all, when we are born (and mostly for long thereafter) we haven't done anything to earn His love. By the same reasoning we can deduce that all police officers who are killed on duty are less loved, or maybe even disliked, by God. More than this, we can infer that any officer, who is fired at and missed, is truly one of God's favorites. Ultimately, we must concede that any officer, who serves until full retirement without once being shot, should be canonized; he must be a saint. God's affection toward that divinely protected person was unreserved.

In this same incident, the culprit was wounded superficially by another officer. What was God's role in that eventuality? What would have been God's motivation for deflecting the path of the bullet that superficially injured the criminal? Does God play a role in every shooting? … Half of all shootings? …Ten percent? …One in a million? When deliberated sensibly, the best resolve is: None whatsoever! If I raise a gun and discharge it at someone, I alone am accountable for whatever consequences are the result of that action. This is true for harmful actions, this is true for beneficial actions, and it is true for indifferent actions.

Religionists, with their selective interpretation of natural and human events, would have us determine that the Supreme Being initiates some events, intervenes in other events, and is oblivious to the remaining events. This proposition must be accepted solely on faith, which places it squarely in the same category as are superstitions, fairy tales, astrology, paranormal manifestations, and all other unverifiable claims. They never concede that He is powerless in every event. When all things are considered, that should be the foremost possibility. To my mind, it definitely is the most probable.

Religionists submit that prayers are effectual, while in the same instance they admit that God acts in His own cryptic ways. He rejects our prayers at times and imposes His own inexplicable (yet, hopefully beneficial) ministrations. In the light of this, I must conclude that prayers are a waste of time, for God always favors us with whatever He deems is best for us in every case. To think otherwise is to propose that God will grant us favors that are not in our best interests, and that are other than that which He would have provided us, had we not prayed to Him for a divergent intervention. Restated: God's love for us causes Him to send us that which ultimately benefits us most, unless we pray to Him for a lesser favor. In which case, He may acquiesce to our prayers, thereby substituting that which helps us less, for that which would have helped us best. Nonsensical, isn't it?

Intellectually, God is either the supervisor of all mortal events, or He is responsible for none. The 'efficacy of prayer' proposition implies that He passively just observes in most human occurrences, but can be moved to action by prayer in selected other instances. All three postulations: responsible for all; responsible for none; responsible for some; must cause us to reconsider the personality of the entity we are told to render reverence and exaltation toward. Whichever of the options you embrace will demand a redefinition of all the laudable attributes of the Lord. Divine love, Divine justice, Divine mercy, even Divine Wisdom must be scrapped and Divine Whimsy must be postulated.

If God unfailingly (and without invitation) acts in our lives, then Jesus lived in vain. His teachings are invalid. His philosophies are ineffectual. He taught that God conditionally loved us all, but He preached that God would reward (here and in Heaven) those alone who believed in the Fatherhood of God (the condition). His ideology revolved around a doctrine that only personal worthiness could win God's ultimate mercy for one's self. Two thousand years hence that postulation remains unproven, unlikely, and to be blunt, untrue!

GOD — THE FATHER OF ALL?

Christians profess that God is their father. Indeed, He is the father of all. Together, let us explore this avowal. If God is our Father mustn't it follow that He will do all in His power to protect His children? This certainly seems logical, and the New Testament continually echoes this theme. Can we test this proposition, or must this also be consigned to the arena of doubtless and unconfirmed trust?

The first refutation of this baseless thesis is that God created disease as well. Our real father would do all within his province to protect us from disease. Not so, our Father God! Secondly, our father would protect us from those who would do evil to us. God permits criminals to rob us, to wound us, even to kill us. How does this square with the postulation of God as our father? It doesn't, and the "free will" interjection is the weakest apologetic ever proffered. This ground has been covered already. By actual observation, the supposition that God interferes in the everyday workings of humanity and of nature should be renounced as continually disproved by reality each and every day of our mortal lives.

So let us instead contemplate the spiritual world. If God is our Father, why does He suffer Satan to tempt us to eternal damnation? A father, knowing his child was under the influence of an evil person, would act to intervene. The least he would do would be to arm his offspring against the machinations of that person who sought to harm his child. Religionists assert that God does aid us in our trials with Satan. But, in truth, our weapons are patently inadequate and unavailing. The unequivocal proof of this is the admission that all of us, without exception, are continual sinners. Metaphorically, God has armed us with a pea-shooter against a foe firing a bazooka. We are certain to lose every sustained encounter. Worse, even than this, is the postulation that God also created our adversary, and if He had the inclination, God could vanquish our antagonist with a mere thought. This reputed fact should give religionists their most instructive cause for retrospection. Why does God permit the Devil to direct so many of us into eternal damnation? God could prevent this eventuality so easily. Yet, He doesn't!

Furthermore, if God has foreknowledge of everyone's eventual final destination, why does He insist that we experience a pain filled and burdensome human life beforehand? Religionists weave inspiring stories about "saints" who endured unrelenting hardships in life, yet maintained their faith and ultimately attained a divine reward. The contemplation of that eventuality is soul-uplifting, but why not reflect on those who suffer misery and deprivation all their life, and in a final act of defiance, curse the Deity who afflicted them so mercilessly? Compassionately, God should have canceled that person's life and delivered him directly to Hell.

There is no theological impediment herewith. But, there is no theological gain either.

The real fact-of-the-matter is that no Personal Creator exists. No Devil exists. Heaven and Hell are mythical creations, and all religiosity is a mental sham. Religionists are perpetrating a hoax on humanity with their otherworldly mystifications. We can put an end to their deception. This will be achieved only after we have purged all superstitions from our minds and our hearts. Most especially our hearts: because religiosity is almost exclusively a fabrication of our emotions. Our piety is engaged only in a futile effort to recoup the imperfectly recalled happiness and imagined security of our infancy and early childhood.

Our biological father never was as invincible as we initially imagined, and there is no 'Sky Father.' Now is the time for all of us who have reached our adulthood to accept our maturity, to assume our responsibilities, and to plan for the future of the entirety of the human family, including those who are still immersed in childhood fancy, or who have become stricken with elderly senility. The fully adult must commence their roles as stewards and guardians of the only safe haven (Heaven) we will ever inhabit. By name: Planet Earth!

GOD IS OMNISCIENT?

God is all-knowing. He knows all things. Is this a fact? No, it is not a fact; it is a religious postulate that obtains its support from speculative extrapolation. In our pious reveries we imagine a God possessing the ultimate of all superlatives. God is All-Good; God is All-Powerful; God is All-Entirety! The theory is flawless, but only as long as no one tests this premise intellectually. The moment one does, God's imputed faculties begin to evaporate.

A self-contradicting poser: Can God create another God who is more intelligent than Himself? This question shows how preposterous some theories can be. Even an imaginary super being does, and must perforce, have some limitation. Re-think the proposition that God knows everything. Does God know what my next action will be? Does He know what my next thought will be? I don't know what my next thought or action will be because I haven't decided this yet.

In our speculations, we grant God abilities that are quite impossible because they are contradictions. God can't create a greater God than Himself because we declare that God is already the greatest entity possible. Well, the same consideration makes it quite impossible for God to know the future. If all human actions are granted total freedom from His control. If humans have the totally ungoverned prerogative to act in any manner that they, themselves, choose; further, if those choices are made at the caprice of the individual, then no one, not even God, can know how this individual will react until that individual has finalized his own course of action. Unconditional prescience is absolutely a contradiction, even for a Deity!

In case I have just failed to convince you, let me restate this assertion. Not until a decision is made can anyone, including that person himself, know what his final decision will be. God can't know the unknowable. My future acts are unknowable, even to me. Knowledge of the future is impossible unless the future is foreordained. Knowledge of the future is a contradiction if free will is a fact.

Can God fashion a circle that isn't round? Most people would agree that this is a contradiction; ergo, it is an impossibility. Yet, if I ask if God can create a viable bio-form that doesn't require nutrition, religionists would be quick to aver: "Yes, God can create a bio-form that doesn't require nutrition." Yet a bio-form not requiring nutrition is just as absurd as is a cubed orb, only in a less obvious manner. There are laws of physics (i.e., nature) that are inviolable. If you want to postulate a Being who is the author of those laws of nature, I can't prevent you. I can expose the fallacy of your belief that this Being can controvert the observed "laws of nature" whenever and wherever it suits His pleasure.

One of the more potent arguments assailing evolution is that cats only reproduce cats, never giving birth to dogs. The Bible reads: 'Each animal shall reproduce its own kind.' [Gen. 1:24] (Paraphrased) Yet, the Bible also reports that Aaron threw down his staff and it turned into a serpent. The Egyptian priests, magically, were able to duplicate Aaron's trick. [Cf. Ex. 7:8-12] How? How did Aaron cause a wooden staff to transform into a snake? By the power of God, you declare. Fine! Who enabled the Pagan priests to perform the same wonder? By the power of Satan, you declare. Fine again!

Once more, I have religionists out on a limb. Now I will proceed to hew off the limb. If God can change a stick into a snake, why can't He change a cat into a dog? The same question could be posed about the Devil. Therefore, the facetious rebuttal to the objection that cats only produce cats is that "The Devil caused evolutionary species diversity."

Forget Aaron and the priests now. They have served their purpose. My real point was to show that any proposition can be rationalized once you concede an initial fabulosity. If you grant that there is a personal Deity, or a Master Demon, then all religious suppositions become more than viable; they approach the imperative. Contrariwise, if you begin a story with the words "Let's pretend," one would be assured that the story will contain elements that are not only unbelievable, but are patently bogus as well.

I am aware that none of my above arguments is conclusive. In the realm of the imagination, no argument can be inarguable. I do have one remaining refutation of God's omniscience. I have God's own words in the Bible. They were spoken by God to Abraham, face-to-face.

"Then the Lord said to Abraham, 'There are terrible accusations against Sodom and Gomorrah, and their sin is very great. I must go down to find out whether or not the accusations that I have heard are true.

"Then the LORD said, 'The outcry against Sodom and Gomorrah is so great and their sin so grievous that I will go down and see if what they have done is as bad as the outcry that has reached me. If not, I will know.'" [Gen. 18:20-21]

So God had heard! He didn't know beforehand! God, Himself, told us through His inspired words in the Holy Scriptures, that He doesn't know everything. If you persist that God is All-Knowing, then you must argue with the Holy Spirit. It was He who informed us that God wasn't fully omniscient. There are several instances where the Bible informs us that God is not omniscient.

When God instructed Moses to return to Egypt to escort the Hebrews to the "Promised Land" He instructed Moses to perform two "miracles" to frighten the Egyptians into releasing the Hebrews from bondage. The first was the well-known walking staff changed into a snake. [Cf. Ex. 7:9] The second 'miracle,' much less known, was for Moses to place his hand in his tunic and pull it out covered with leprosy-like scaling. Then when Moses repeated those actions his hand came out perfectly healthy. [Cf. Ex. 4:6-7]

Upon empowering Moses with these miracles, "The Lord said, 'If they will not believe you or be convinced by the first miracle, then this one will convince them.'" [Ex. 4:8] Take note that God used the word "IF." Plainly, God didn't have foreknowledge of which "miracle" would achieve the goal of convincing Pharaoh to release the Hebrews from Egypt, i.e., the staff to snake, or the leprosy stricken hand back to healthy hand. (Neither "miracle" worked!) Shouldn't an "omniscient" God have known beforehand which of those 'tricks' would succeed with the Egyptians? The factual answer is: 'YES!' The Bible's answer is 'NO!'

GOD CAN — BUT WOULD HE?

The New Testament scrutinized intelligently, *sans piety*, is no more believable than is the Old Testament. It, too, appears to be copious embroidery attached to a ragged piece of cloth.

Our Universe is more complex than the average person knows (or cares). Consider the basic units that make up all matter in the Universe: The proton, the neutron, and the electron. Then consider that not only aren't those three the basic units, they are only a few of the burgeoning number of 'elementary' particles that do comprise matter. Now theorists are convinced that much smaller units, called quarks, are contained within the so-called elementary particles rendering them as more complex than basic matter. (Disregarding "strings" and "superstring" vibration theories)

The form and the properties of combined elements is another wonder. The 'gas' hydrogen and the 'gas' oxygen joined together, form the 'liquid' water (H_2O). Every school child knows this, but most adults never seem to grasp the profound incongruity of this knowledge and its intrinsic implication. This Universe is as intricate as the human mind can conceive. In truth, it may well exceed the ability of solitary man ever to comprehend.

It would be safe to state here that no single man (or woman) will ever possess the wisdom of the Universe within his own skull. We may never attain the capability to even store, and to retrieve coherently, the accumulated wisdom of mankind into any separate memory system, regardless of the number of computer data storage chips we link together. I am not denigrating man's ability to devise computer memory systems, but I am paying due homage to the vastness and intricacy of the Universe and all that is contained therein.

How is all this related to a discussion of the Godhead of Jesus? In this manner: If Jesus was (is) God incarnate, then He must possess the totality of knowledge that abounds in the limitless Cosmos. Can He repress that knowledge? Was He a selective amnesiac while He lived on Earth. Did He cease being God while He walked among us? Can God will Himself down to mankind's level of ignorance for thirty-three years?

The answer is that God can do everything. To Him, nothing is impossible. That is fine, as a generalization, but it isn't an answer, it is an excuse for not having an answer. If God can perform any act whatsoever, can He then exchange personalities with Satan? Of course, He can. Can God transform a viper into the Holy Spirit? Of course, He can. But the practical question remains: "Has He ever performed anything approximating such absurdities?" No, He has not. And, in all likelihood, He never will. Therefore, all hypotheses of what God has done or will do aren't confirmed by conceding that all is possible with God. Rather, the validity of all such conjectured actions of God must pass the inquiry of whether or not He is likely to have performed that action, or is likely to perform such anytime in the future.

GOD EXISTS ALONE IN ALL THE COSMOS

Reason this along with me. How long did God exist entirely by Himself? 'A million years? 'A billion years? 'An eternity? How long was He alone before He decided to create the Angels? At what point in time did He first experience the need for companionship? Not that He was completely alone. Jesus and the Holy Spirit were with Him. But, then, you can't count them, for they don't count. That is, together with Him, the three only add up to one. We are concerned here with time. How much time passed before God created? This question is meaningless to an infinite being. Time only exists for finite entities. To a universal deity, all time is instantaneous. For a timeless being that had no beginning and shall have no end, all events past and future, would exist in His present. All time would be simultaneous.

Is God aware of the passage of time? When we conceptualize Him, we accept the inference that He is cognizant of elapsed time. Logically reasoned, God can't be limited either 'in or by' time. Yet, in order to intervene in human affairs, God must possess awareness of time. As Einstein pointed out at the turn of the century, time is a dimension just as is length, width, and depth. Time is the fourth dimension. If we can measure God in time, then we have proved He isn't infinite.

To the average person, this line of deduction borders on the incoherent. 'It needn't! Ponder this: "Will we be conscious of the march of time as we are idling away the hours in Paradise?" The bliss of Heaven is scheduled to last for all eternity. How will we measure the progression of time? Will we enjoy it minute by minute? I am sure there are no wristwatches in the afterlife. Is a steadfast angel assigned the task of charting the movements of some celestial spirit-sun in order to measure the passage of time? Without a cognizance of the duration of our stay in Heaven the reward of 'eternity' becomes a profound absurdity. Being in a comatose state is the nearest anyone will ever approach to approximating endlessness.

This point is perhaps better appreciated if we consider a parallel situation. Suppose you were instructed to measure the length of a highway in the sky? Looking down the highway in either direction discloses nothing but an endless expanse of roadway. You suspect that the highway is indeed endless no matter which direction you would proceed. How may your measurement be calibrated? 'In inches? 'In yards or meters? 'In kilometers or miles? 'In astronomical units or light years? Of course, it is pointless to wonder, and fruitless to try. More cogently, it is senseless to even consider.

An eternity of Heaven is just as senseless in that there would be no way to appreciate it. Timelessness is an eternal impossibility. When we conceptualize timelessness, the most we can do is contemplate the indefinite, not the infinite. Infinity, like equality, belongs in the realm of mathematics where it serves a valid function. Invoking mathematics, answer this question: "What is the greatest (largest) number there is"? Obviously, using our numbering system, whatever the number, it would have to begin and end with a nine, and contain nothing but nines. The ultimate number would be the numerical equivalent of God. Now take this number, the final number, and add one to it. Now what number do you have? Wait! It can't be done, you aver? True enough, for if we factually have discovered the ultimate number then there can be no higher number. Nothing can be added to the ultimate number. Neither can we add anything to God the ultimate being. Not by prayer, sacrifice, ritual, or praise.

Can we subtract from God? Yes, we can. When we think that any human action diminishes His number, then we truly have lessened Him. In effect, we have accomplished what Lucifer attempted, yet failed to do. We have dethroned God.

CHAPTER 3
Sampling Religiosity

A TESTIMONY TO YAHWEH

The Bible is not primarily a moral guide. This may surprise some, but not those who have troubled to read it studiously. A thorough reading of the Old Testament, up to the advent of the Judges, will reveal that it is principally the biography of a few personages whose only common bond was belief that one God, among the many that existed, was leading them personally, guiding their destinies, and providing them with an abundance of the material rewards of this life. The Old Testament deals only tangentially with the concept of Heaven.

Because the early adherents honored the Semite God Yahweh, their fortune was assured despite glaring and repeated ritual & liturgical lapses in their behavior. It wasn't until the ascendancy of Moses to a position of leadership that the Bible treats the Hebrews as a distinct group of people. Before that we have individuals, seemingly at odds with the world, yet favored materialistically by their personal Deity. In those pre-mosaic times the behavior of the leaders (they are commonly called Patriarchs) hardly improved. Nonetheless, Yahweh continued to prosper His adherents: but not ceaselessly, as we can gather from Psalm Forty-Four. (Forty-Three in some translations)

In the first stanza, the Psalm extols the past partiality of Yahweh toward His people. Verses four to eight read: *"You are my king and my God; you give victory to your people, and by your power we defeat our enemies. ... In God we make our boast all day long, and we will praise your name forever."* [Ps. 44:4-8 excerpted. Some versions Psalm 43]

Those words begin the verses, but read now the end of this Psalm. The tone and the level of homage completely reverse. Yahweh is no longer praised, He is questioned. His actions (in the present of the writer) are inexplicable. If He is the Lord who dispensed favors so unfailingly to the ancestors of the writer, how is it that the contemporary Hebrews found themselves in such lamentable straits? If the legendary history of the 'special' people purportedly chosen by Yahweh was factual, why was the present generation of the Psalmist afflicted so? Obviously, the author of this Psalm was mired in the same quandary we find ourselves in today. If every occurrence in the world transpires only with the consent of the Director of the Universe (God), then His actions are irredeemably paradoxical. Most of the taxing events of human life can better be reconciled by assuming that the Deity naps frequently and thereby is often unaware of a substantial portion of the occurrences on this planet.

Carefully read the pertinent continuation of this Psalm; not with anticipatory reverence, but with intelligent objectivity. Then ask yourself earnestly: "Are these the inspired words of God, or are they the bewildered, pleading, soul-wrenching thoughts of a perplexed human being attempting to reestablish favorable rapport with a Deity, once munificent, now oblivious?"

Psalm 44 (43), verse 9 to conclusion.

9) But now you have rejected us and let us be defeated;

you no longer march out with our armies.

10) You made us run from our enemies,

and they took for themselves what was ours.

11) You allowed us to be slaughtered like sheep;

you scattered us in foreign countries.

12) You sold your own people for a small price

as though they had little value.

13) Our neighbors see what you did to us,

> and they mock us and laugh at us.

14) You made us a joke among nations;

> they shake their heads at us in scorn.

15) I am always in disgrace;

> I am covered with shame

16) from hearing the sneers and insults

> of my enemies and those who hate me.

17) All this has happened to us,

> even though we have not forgotten you

> or broken the covenant you made with us.

18) We have not been disloyal to you;

> we have not disobeyed your commands.

19) Yet you left us helpless among wild animals:

> you abandoned us in deepest darkness.

20) If we had stopped worshiping our God

> and prayed to a foreign god,

21) you would surely have discovered it,

> because you know our secret thoughts.

22) But it is on your account

> that we are being killed all the time,

> that we are treated like sheep to be slaughtered.

23) Wake up, Lord! Why are you asleep?

> Rouse yourself! Don't reject us forever!

24) Why are you hiding from us?

> Don't forget our suffering and trouble!

25) We fall crushed to the ground;

we lie defeated in the dust.

26) Come to our aid!

Because of your constant love – save us!

Source: Good News Bible – - – Catholic Study Edition

This, from the self-same author (?) who gave us Psalm 23 (22), *"The Lord is my shepherd."* Why isn't Psalm 44 (43) as widely known, or as oft repeated? Pro-Biblists and religionists are very judicious when promulgating the words of God. Only that which furthers their aims or seemingly confirms their dogmas is ever presented. To counter that I am doing just the opposite is an apparent observation that doesn't correspond to the actuality.

I am not presenting a book and asserting divine authorship. I am taking the evidence proffered by the proponents of the Bible and debunking their divine inspiration assertions with their own evidence. If my challenge is short of perfection; or if it is deemed deficient in half of its conclusions; or if some regard it as utterly without merit, then this itself proves something very damaging to pro-Biblists. Namely, that the proposition of the Devil is false. If such an entity exists, surely he would have aided me in this effort. He, being a near equal of God, would undoubtedly have inspired me with a more potent repudiation of religiosity, and of the belief in a benevolent heavenly being.

Trust me, when I affirm that I had no assistance whatsoever from any spiritual source, whether angelic, demonic, satanic or divine. Every page, every sentence, and even individual words came haltingly. There were nights when I spent hours rewriting a single sentence, or rephrasing a single idea, striving to verbalize my thoughts as I conceived them into words that would convey my precise meaning to a future reader. More often than not, I failed. My thoughts were firm, but my words were flabby. I can no more pass my writings off as the words of Satan than the Bible's authors can pass their writings (Scripture) off as the words of God. Clearly, both have had uninspired, flawed, exclusively human, origins.

MIRACLES ARE PROOF OF GOD'S EXISTENCE?

The most damning *corpus delicti* (body of evidence) against the divine origin of the Old Testament is derived from its own writings. The O. T. provides an entertaining look into the past of that portion of this planet known as the Levant (Middle East). If we consider it in its proper perspective, only then can we truly enjoy its very human stories. Start by renouncing the stifling and repressive dogma that these are the inspired words of a Divine Deity because this precept raises impossible queries that can only be answered with: 'You must have faith.'

No one alive today can verify or refute the Bible beyond repudiation. If you are a believer, you believe simply because you so choose. The overwhelming preponderance of evidence, i.e., tangible, verifiable, observable, (and most telling) demonstrable evidence, posits against the existence of a personal Deity, hence against any Divine Inspirer.

Miracles, or those events we are prone to identify as miracles, prove nothing. First, none can be predicted. Second, the same results we call miracles often occur in situations where the Deity hasn't been importuned and isn't even acknowledged. Third, most are concerned with sickness, and frankly, we just don't know enough about the curative capabilities of our body to differentiate between natural healing and putative divine healing. Fourth, why aren't severed limbs ever restored, or a lost eye regenerated? At His arrest, Jesus reattached a man's severed ear. [Cf. Lu. 22:50-51] Have His powers diminished since His ascent into Heaven? Finally, all recent miracles are recorded to have been accomplished through natural agencies such as: spontaneous remission. Show me an incontrovertible miracle and I will become a believer also.

If God desired a miracle that would convince the world of His existence, I can think of several that would leave no uncertainty. Why not a personal appearance? God could announce a time and a place for His appearance with the major Television Networks providing world-wide coverage via satellite. He could materialize instantaneously, indicate His true or favored religion, allow His wounds to be inspected (in the event He announces for Christianity), then be lifted into Heaven on a glorious cloud. Whatever the shortcomings of this proposal, the advantages thereto greatly outweigh the latent disadvantages.

Let us return to an evaluation of the Bible. If the 'God Directs All' attributions in the Bible are fact, then nothing that is apparent to our senses is real. Water isn't really wet; up is down; the Sun truly does revolve around the Earth; and the richest man in the world should be elected Pope, God has demonstrated His affection for that man above all others.

Frankly, no proposition stands entirely alone. If we affirm that one plus one equals two, then two minus one must invariably equal one. Also, one minus one must equal the absence of one (we call that zero). Progressing, one plus one, plus one again, must equal one more than two (aka three), and so on. This is where religious beliefs fail so blatantly and so utterly. Their tenets, being false to begin with, can't survive logical extension. Most tenets won't abide close scrutiny in the first instance. This is where science shines brightest in comparison with religion. Water boils at 212 degrees Fahrenheit (compensating for difference in atmospheric pressure, et al.), regardless of who puts the kettle on the stove.

USE YOUR BRAIN

The outwardly innocuous doctrine that "God made me" is replete with broad-range consequences. If God made me, He obviously intended me (i. e., humanity) to be different from the rest of His creatures for He made me (us) different. How am I different? I am different because I can think, because I can perceive, and because I can reason. More importantly, I am different because I can communicate my thoughts. I can pool my acquired knowledge and my past experiences with another human being and thereby enhance the probability of accomplishing whatever tasks I attempt. My superior brain allows me to do these things. By using my versatile human brain I am able to do infinitely more than any other life form known to me. God's 'gift' to me (and to all of mankind) is a superior brain. Yet, as this book evidences: my brain tells me that there is no God; not in the generally accepted present-day sense.

I look at today's religions and I see beliefs and rituals that clearly refer back to a period when man was just emerging from primitive, backward beginnings. There is absolutely no point to the advancement in knowledge of the physical world if the Christian Bible is the embodiment of God's infallible instructions. To live a Christian life requires very little knowledge, and is repressive of our investigative impulses. Why should humanity search after any data whatsoever when 'God in His Holy Writ' has provided all the knowledge necessary? {Christian 'truism'} 'Provides what? 'Starvation? A farmer who trades his plow for a Bible necessarily must learn to eat paper, or gather a gullible following so that he can pass the collection plate, or he thereafter will starve.

The Bible's proponents astonish me. How can they believe such unfounded, improbable, sanctimonious drivel? I am not unalterably antagonistic toward religion. I sincerely wish I could believe in the Christian 'mystery' episodes. My 'God given intellect' won't allow this. My brain tells me that if I am to accomplish anything in this life, I must use my brain, not confuse it! And, it is only in this life that I will be able to accomplish anything. The lone way I will ever enjoy a semblance of eternal life is if I am able to leave something behind that others coming after me deem worthy of retaining. I can live on only in the memory of those who live after me. Once I have been forgotten, only then have I truly suffered eternal death.

Mankind's track record for recalling its ancestry is disheartening. A person is many times more likely to be remembered for having done something deleterious than for having done something beneficial. What was the name of Lot's wife? She must have been a righteous woman for God initially spared her from the fate of the wicked Sodomites. Observably, He didn't care enough about her to reveal her name to future generations. [Cf. Gen. 19:26] He did inspire the name of Noah's disrespectful son … the one who walked into Noah's tent when his father lay naked in a drunken stupor. His name was Ham. [Cf. Gen. 9:22] He became the ultimate ancestor of the future Canaanites via his son, Canaan.

Matthew and Mark both tell of a woman who had 'great faith.' She was a Samaritan who had come to ask Jesus to heal her daughter of possession by a demon. Jesus was reluctant to assist a Samaritan. His words, *"It isn't right to take the children's food* (the Children of Moses) *and toss it to the dogs."* (Dogs = Samaritans, among other non-Hebrews) But the woman would not be dissuaded. She replied, *"Even the dogs eat the scraps that fall from their Master's table."* (Master = the Hebrews) Jesus was impressed with her self-effacing riposte; He cured her daughter. [Cf. Mt. 15:26-27 & Mk. 7:27-28] What was this woman's name? No one knows! Now if I asked you to name a harlot, prostitute, or loose woman from the Bible, could you do so?

I'm certain you could. There are enough of them prominently identified in the Bible and thereby individually glorified.

WHY DID GOD CREATE MANKIND?

The keystone philosophical argument for the existence of mankind is the emotionally aggrandizing notion that God created us out of love. He loves us in the same manner that a parent loves his/her children. This notion is exceedingly facile to visualize and relate to; will this rationalization retain its apparent accuracy if it is subjected to even a cursory analysis?

Avail me while I do just that. Begin by asking yourself: "What is parental love?" Parental love is a survival instinct that many (but not all) life forms have evolved that aids in the perpetuation of their species. Parental love is an effective survival trait, and those species that don't possess it usually compensate for this lack by being prodigious parents. That is, they produce offspring in such numbers that invariably a few individuals some-how manage to survive the hazards and rigors of sub-adult life. Ultimately, the surviving adults live long enough to become prodigious parents them-selves, thereby propagating their respective species. If God created human beings because He loved them exclusively, why did He create the gamut of non-human life forms? Why are all life forms predatory on other life forms, including mankind as both predator and as prey? Pointedly, why did God create carnivores and other predators?

WHAT IS OUR PURPOSE FOR BEING?

What is our purpose? Why are we here? The obvious and most plausible answer is the response that scientists give us today. We are the evolutionary progression of an original life form that began on this planet billions of years ago. You might then ask cunningly "Who is the Creator that caused this original life form?" I would be forced to confess that I don't know. My lack of knowledge, however, in no way proves your 'uncreated' Creator postulation. If God exists, He exists despite my ignorance, not because of it.

The answer to the enigmatic question of why we are here can only proceed from our intellects, not from an ancient book. A book written by persons who never dreamed of man's present technological accomplishments; persons who were awed by sights and sounds they couldn't readily comprehend; persons who believed the most preposterous events imaginable. They wrote a book, and we hold it to be inspired by God. A book that is nothing more than a miscellany of disparate stories that culminate in the life and death of a male person who was able to perform spectacular miracles for others (reputedly), but was unable to save himself from being crucified due to the rabid insistence of the self-professed 'chosen people' of His Father.

That man was Jesus, whose very existence is mainly attested by a person (Paul) who admittedly never saw Him alive. Paul communed with Jesus through a hallucinatory trance. I stated earlier that trances were common when the nature of the Deity was indistinctly understood. This was the case here. Saul (Paul) was confused regarding the nature of Jesus. His followers professed He had risen from the dead, which unquestionably proved that He was more than a mortal man. Yet, hadn't He been killed by ordinary men? Couldn't He have saved Himself? Surely His Father could have saved Him from death. Or disdaining this, God could have wreaked terrible vengeance on those who perpetrated this lethal sacrilege. The God of Noah, Abraham, and Moses most assuredly would have.

To Saul (Paul), this paradox must have been perplexing. Hopefully the Messiah, Jesus, would return soon to establish His worldly kingdom. Perhaps then, Paul could ask Him to clarify His exact nature. That Jesus would return soon Paul had scant doubt. The common belief of the initial adherents was that many of those alive in the first century of their current era would live to see the glorious and triumphal reappearance of the Messiah. [Cf. 1 Thes. 4:14, el al.] Those faithful who died before the Second Coming would be raised up bodily to share in the majesty of the messianic age when His second advent dawned. Rome, the Babylon of the messianic age, would be smitten by the God of Abraham and Isaac through His 'anointed one,' Jesus. The Hebrews would be restored to their former glory and would avenge their national degradation with righteous vengeance. Charity for the repentant, but great woe to the unrepentant! The Golden Age of Judaism would reign evermore. {Author's surmise}

How did we learn such astounding 'truths'? We learned them from the New Testament. The New Testament was written by the Evangelists, Paul, and a few Apostles, but was dictated by the Holy Spirit (of God). If God the Father, or Jesus, or the Holy Ghost inspired the New Testament, why is it so inadequate? Why is it so obscure? Why is it so incomplete? Why is it so inaccurate? Matthew 2:1 has Jesus being born during the reign of Herod the Great, King of Judea. King Herod died in the year 4 BC. This indicates that the posited year of the birth of Jesus is wrong by at least four years. In Luke 2:2, we are told that Quirinius (Cyrinus) was Governor of Syria when Jesus was born. Quirinius became Governor in AD 6, ten years after the death of King Herod. These incontrovertible errors can't be attributed to faulty translations.

Another thought regarding translations: Why were the original texts allowed to disappear? Why go through the bother of inspiring infallible books if only to permit those books to be lost. The oldest N.T. texts extant are dated more than two hundred years after the death of Jesus (ignoring fragments). We are asked to believe that God assiduously oversaw the composition of the Bible, then after completion, He promptly lost interest in His own words. Later, He further compounds His negligence by tolerating scribes who miscopied, added to, and omitted His divine words. It took a thousand years before any verse tampering was realized. Were these errors uncovered through divine inspiration? They were not! They were found through diligent study and research by men who rightly suspected that the formal Christian Church (the Roman Catholic Church), along with its entrenched hierarchy, held no singular commission (from the Holy Spirit) to translate the earliest New Testament Scriptures.

If all the above be true, I still haven't answered the question: "Why am I (or any of us) here"? I could answer that question with another. "Why does there have to be a why?" If truly we are the serendipitous creation of the haphazard interplay of natural elements (primarily carbon), then we not only don't need a reason why; we frankly do not have a preordained reason "why."

If that offends your dignity, I apologize. That doesn't render my answer invalid. However, maybe there is a rectifying reason we can advance. If there is, then the most logical one I can think of is to come to know God, and to appreciate His universal accomplishments without resort to egocentric holy men (or women), a priestly hierarchy, or any other such pretensions!

This is not an endorsement of the Bible. If, as pro-Biblists declare, God gave us enlightenment through the Bible, then He did a very poor job of it. Witness the many irreversible human catastrophes that have attended the various interpretations of the Bible. Of its very nature, all religiosity is biased, bigoted, hypercritical and intolerant. Those who believe they act in God's stead are as doctrinaire and as intractable as is possible. Frankly, they are a continual menace to believers in an alternate religion, to all doubters, and to all non-believers.

EVERLASTING LIFE

What purpose do we serve if we live forever in heaven? Most people don't accomplish anything worthwhile in a human lifetime. What benefit derives to anyone, save the individual, who lives on and on everlastingly? 'None that I can conceive. The sterile, vapid, zombie-like existence that Heaven promises wouldn't seem to offer much opportunity to fulfill any latent human potentialities either.

Intelligently pondered, a resurrected human being only makes sense if that person is thence able to accomplish some worthwhile deed/feat impossible in human life. What can life in Heaven really be about? Could it be likened to a continual and never ceasing orgasm? I disdain invoking a more base aspect of human existence into this exposition, but frankly, this is the most intense and pleasure generating sensation I have ever experienced physically. There are many happenings that give mental titillation and enjoyment, but they lack the climactic explosiveness of sexual culmination. Sexual gratification is a biological imperative that can't be wished away, dismissed, rendered irrelevant, or sermonized out of existence.

I wonder! How can the pleasures of Heaven endure into infinity? There isn't anything I can imagine that I would not tire of, if I were exposed to it for a never-ending span of time. Unless my spirit awareness is vastly different from my earthly consciousness, I would eventually weary of Heaven's allurements.

Now answer this earnest question: "Why resurrect my physical body?" Is it to enable me to enjoy a spiritual reward in the afterlife? A physical body can't react with non-physical entities. If we believe in the existence of Heaven at all, we must contend with the reality that a physical entity can never interact with a non-physical entity. At least, this we know is true from personal, physical observation. A physical entity can't perceive a spiritual entity through its own abilities; therefore, the reverse should be equally true. My experience on earth indicates this is so.

The more one contemplates everlasting life, the more ominous the potentialities of that state of being become. To develop this thought, imagine now that you (the reader) have died and, having led a good Christian life, you are rewarded with immortality. Then further imagine that after a time period of quintillion years, you weary of Heaven. Is there any means of escape? Is suicide possible in heaven? Can one break out of Heaven and seek adventure elsewhere? To answer these queries with a declaration that no one will ever become bored with Heaven because Paradise bestows eternal happiness just won't persuade me. In this life (so far) there hasn't been anything that I have experienced that I haven't grown disenchanted with once I have mollycoddled myself overly much. So I appeal to whoever controls such eventualities, "Please don't confine me in Heaven for all eternity. Yes, issue me a universal entry ticket to Paradise, but also allow me to spend a great deal of time spiritually exploring this vast universe that has been revealed to me by our diligent, able, and wholly mortal intellectuals."

Zipping effortlessly throughout the entire universe exploring every nook and cranny therein; that would be the greatest Paradise for me. More poignantly, that enterprise positively would necessitate an 'eternity' to conclude.

THE TRAGEDY OF GUYANA

While this book first was being composed a major tragedy was broadcast to the world. In Guyana, South America, a fanatical cult leader, Reverend Jim Jones, induced hundreds of his followers to drink poison in a mass suicide rampage. Those who were rational enough to balk were shot dead by militant henchmen. More than nine hundred persons lost their lives because of the paranoia of their leader. Is this nothing more than an isolated incident? I wish that it was. It is not! Hardly a week passes without reading of deaths, injury, cruelty, or injustice heaped onto trusting believers by religious zealots. The day this sentence was first conceived, the News concerned civil strife in Iran where radical Muslims were acting violently against fellow Muslims who spurned religious taboos. The report stated that women in Iran were uncovering their heads and wearing western dresses. How heinous! How blasphemous! How unforgivable! They all must be punished severely.

Unfortunately, a very low level of intelligence will suffice to live a "pious Christian life", or in the above instance, a "pious Muslim life." Personal freedom, political democracy, and scientific inquiry are not only superfluous, but should be outlawed. They can only eventuate in religious heresy. What, then, should sensible people do religiously?

Well, if God is out there (or up there?), we can find Him through our intellect. We can come to know Him through His works, i.e., the workings of nature. When we have learned all there is to learn about the physical universe; when the words 'mystery of nature' are removed from human vocabularies, then and not before, will we be able to truthfully declare "I know God!" For me, indeed, for the multitude of searchers who lived before, and the numberless seekers who will come after, that phrase: "I know God" (Nature!) will open the gates of Heaven; gates that have been closed and barred since the dawn of sentient human kind. On that day, we will all be resurrected. Not in a physical, nor even in a spiritual way, but in the mind of humanity. Remember me and I will live evermore. Forget me and it won't matter that I have ever lived.

If it appears to you that in the previous paragraph I am, in essence, merely formulating another cult, there is some justification for that. On the surface, it does appear that I am. I have no such purpose. What that paragraph is intended to convey are my thoughts concerning the unknown. I make no claims to a divine enlightenment, no claims of visions or trances, no hint of a personal mission in life, divinely inspired or otherwise. I state my case thus: "If a personal God exists; if a Creator of all things dwells in the Universe; if a Supreme Being does know and care what my thoughts, words, and deeds are, then I should be able to come to know Him through the unique gift that He endowed me with, that being: my intelligence."

Whenever I exercise my 'God given intelligence,' it convinces me that there is no God. No God in the image of man; No God dispensing favors or withholding needed assistance; No God initiating every occurrence, monitoring every thought, and recording every utterance. No God in the sense He is commonly understood in the Christian faith. (Or any other faith for that matter) A faith that teaches, and therefore believes, that God has talked face to face with man; has appeared in trances; spoken in dreams; sent messages via ostensible divine agents, or via natural events; finger sculpted commandments into stone tablets (that Moses smashed to pieces shortly afterward); took the form of a dove; was born of a virgin; walked the Earth as a child and man; performed unbelievable miracles; was crucified; resurrected; appeared to those who knew Him intimately, yet was unrecognized; and finally: ascended back into Heaven on a cloud. 'So much for a smorgasbord of Christian beliefs!

My intelligence rejects all of the above hyper-physical fictions. Two that trouble me most often are: The commandments and the cloud business. If God appeared to me and carved stone tablets with His finger before my very eyes, I would have revered and cherished those tablets, protecting them with my life if the need arose. Yet Moses shattered them in anger. No eventuality could have induced me into doing what Moses did.

Secondly, I am troubled by His ascension into Heaven on a cloud. [Cf. Acts 1:9] Why a cloud? Does Jesus need a physical conveyance to travel? That story reeks of human invention. Most clouds appear substantial, but now we know they aren't, and we similarly know that clouds could never support the weight of an adult body. They can scarcely suspend specks of dust and water vapor. We know this, and surely God must know this. Only the ancient writer was that ignorant. The author, likewise, didn't know the upper limit clouds can reach. Did Jesus, the Son of God, end His ascension at the altitude of the clouds? Or did He transfer to a passing comet? Forgive the injection of sarcasm, I am sincere. In the story of the Flying Carpet (1001 Arabian Nights), which possessed the magic: the traveler or the carpet? The same would be valid for Jesus and the cloud. Jesus should not have needed a cloud to transport Him to Heaven.

Catholic doctrine troubles me even further. Would God hide His existence under the appearance of a thin wafer of unleavened bread? Why? Why do we need to ingest the body and blood of Jesus? (The Son of God, yet still, one with God) If the Divine Being is a spirit, why do we need a worldly substance ingested into our body to receive God's essence? Why can't we simply receive the spirit of God into our own spirit? Why should the earthly substance that converts (transubstantiates) into Christ's body and blood be from the plant world, rather than from the animal world? Could not God have had us eat red meat, and then have that transubstantiate into Christ's body? Yes, He could have. Changing wine into His blood is indeed more logically consistent than is converting bread into His flesh.

Today, the evolved dogma seems to be that the wafer is both the entire body and the fullness of blood of Jesus thus effectively skirting the tacky question of separating Christ's blood from His body, also the indelicate matter of which portion of His anatomy was being consumed. If your answer to the Eucharist (host) question is that God doesn't have to be logical, then my reply to you is: Don't try to sell your belief in God with the very logical argument for the existence of a Creator, viz., "Who created the Universe." Wily Evangelizers throughout this country are forever appealing to our simplistic sense of logic to advance the belief in their version of an Eternal Creator.

Listening to an effective preacher, it all seems to make sense. What he tells you generally does make sense. It is that which he doesn't explain that should be deeply scrutinized. The entire Judeo-Christian fable is ludicrous when viewed with open eyes and a clear mind. For example: Eve was created from Adam's rib? She was tempted by a talking serpent? Both she and Adam were expelled from Eden because they ate fruit from the Tree of Knowledge? What tree bears fruit that imparts knowledge? What knowledge did they lack? They lacked "The knowledge of good and evil." In a word, they were ignorant. God loved them when they were dumb, but as soon as they gained knowledge, He drove them out of the Garden. The story indicates that it is wiser to be uninformed. You then will be bountifully provided for by God. This parallels the generally comforting notion that only the poor can readily attain Heaven. [Cf. Mt. 19:24; Mk. 10:25 & Lu. 18:25] Heaven is the one place where the majority (i.e., the intellectually dull and materialistically deprived) holds worthwhile advantage over the minority (i.e., the talented and the ambitious).

Eden, we can deduce, was not Heaven because Adam had two wants. First, he was lonely. We could guess that he had seen the animals paired, male and female, and correctly reasoned that he, too, should have a mate. Second, he desired knowledge. In both cases he proved he was truly human. He needed a woman, just as all healthy, normal men do. And, after satisfying his bodily needs, he sought to satisfy the necessities of his human mind. Granted, the story is just that, a story! It does, however, illustrate the point that everything we humans do must be expressed in human terms, particularly storytelling.

One of the factors assailing the accuracy of the Bible is the time progression in the Old Testament. Adding (with liberality) all the antecedents of Jesus back to Adam, you arrive at a proximate date for the earth's creation at 5000 (five thousand) BC. Every student of Anthropology, Geology, Oceanography, and several other learning disciplines, will know that this figure is utterly ridiculous. Double it, triple it, quadruple it, and you would be nowhere near the scientifically provable date. The actual time span since the creation of the earth is almost one million times the biblical reckoning. The generally accepted figure is 4.5 billion years since the formation of our planet. The proofs of the approximate age of the Earth are so numerous that I wouldn't begin to list them all here, but against all that evidence the religious person has only one refutation, i.e., the Bible: a book that discourses on the "*four corners of the earth.*" [Rev. 7:1] The Bible also discourses on "*the ends of the earth.*" [Prov. 17:24 & Acts 13:47] A globular planetary body (which is what the Earth is) has no corners; has no ends!

And still, all too many of you believe that God inspired every word in the Bible? Meanwhile, the scholars who translated the Bible from the ancient languages of its origins are uncertain about many of their translations. A fact easily verified by anyone who bothers to read the preface to any of the numerous English translations of the Bible. Or examine the identical footnote that is found at the bottom of virtually every fourth Bible page, to wit: "Hebrew unclear." Religionists have much more confidence in the words of the translator than the translators themselves had in their translations. That fact, and it is a fact, exposes religionists for the unmitigated sanctimonious human dogmatists that they truly are.

INTELLIGENCE SHOULD RULE

Intelligent leaders have never been prolific religious proselytizers and likely never can be. To be intelligent is to question. Each intelligent leader must ultimately travel his personal path. If he is forthright with his followers, he will unavoidably encourage dissent. Sycophantic followers would sap his cognitive drive. For an intelligent leader this poses an impossible-to-solve dilemma. If he admonishes his disciples to accept nothing; to question everything; to form their own views, then assuredly he will lose followers. This should remain true until that distant day when all things are known; when all questions are answered; when the last 'why' has been resolved. On that day, God's authentic chosen people, the questing intelligentsia, will march triumphantly into Heaven. Not as many might suppose, to sit at the right hand of God; but to share His Throne with Him. For on that day man will genuinely *"… have become like one of us."* [Gen. 3:22] Man, thereby, will have merged with the elementary intelligence of the physical Universe.

The age of intelligent leadership appears to be long overdue. Why place so much emphasis on intelligence? Am I, too, guilty of overblown human vanity? No, that is one of the least active factors motivating me. I recognize human inquisitiveness as the strongest urge impelling me to seek satisfactory answers to the questions posed at the start of this extensive retrospective. The question "Why am I here?" continually intrudes itself into my mind. If I don't have a divinely prescribed purpose on Earth does that doom me to a pointless, profitless, pitiful human existence?

My answer is an unequivocal "No." I can give my life a purpose … a meaningful objective. That espoused objective is to add something beneficial to mankind. It needn't be spectacular or earth rattling; and it surely doesn't have to be the uncovering of a profound or obscure truth that will forever alter the future of humanity. It can be comparatively minor and relatively inconsequential. The essential element is that it must add to the reserve of knowledge that mankind heretofore has accumulated. Knowledge is the true Nirvana.

Presume my goal as an attempt to assist in building a beach. If during my life I add one grain of sand, then I have contributed to the creation of that beach. However, if I add nothing, or worse still, if I take some sand away, or cause some sand to be lost, then I will deem that I have lived in vain. Such is the extent of my personal vanity.

Religionists, by my evaluation, have curtailed the accomplishments of mankind. A narrow survey of the good that has been performed in the name of religion would seem to contradict me. But a panoramic view that measured and weighed the 'good' in totality against the 'bad' in totality would weigh heavily on the side of the bad. Religion has restricted the intellectual growth of humanity. Just as an overly protective parent will stifle the emotional growth of a child; so has religion repressed the realization of mankind's intellectual potential.

RELIGIONISTS SPREAD IGNORANCE

Fundamentalists insist that every word in the Bible is God-inspired; hence, it is indisputable fact. Their porcine insistence irks me. The Flood fable is amusing, not enlightening. If Noah, in his naked drunkenness [Cf. Gen. 9:21], was the worthiest of extant mankind, then it is small wonder that Yahweh destroyed the remainder of humanity. I am also profoundly inquisitive as to what unreported sins the little children were guilty of prior to the Flood. Whatever! We do know that their offenses were so heinous that Yahweh condemned even the entirety of the world's infants and children to death along with every adult except Noah and his family. [Cf. Gen., Chap. 7, particularly v. 22]

I resent the affront to my intelligence that is imputed to me by haughty religionists who intrude their cultic tenets into my life. I am distressed by the audacity of modern evangelizers who piously exhibit mock sympathy for those of us who have not conceded or recognized their "enlightenment." To them I submit: "Perhaps they have stared too long at their own self-perceived illumination." Possibly they have been affected by ego-provoked pseudo-sunstroke. Their brain has been addled or worse yet, it has failed to develop post-puberty so that they are unable to differentiate between fact and fable. They choose to embrace a fable and disregard the facts, just as most sub-adults do (children and their mental peers). There is more conceit-pampering gusto believing that a white knight will rescue you from all harm, or that the ugly frog that you are can be transformed into a handsome prince, if only someone will kiss you. Not only are the infantile-minded certain that a pot of gold rests at the base of the rainbow, but everyone can travel there, gather some gold, and the pot is never empty. The lure of these fables is patently irresistible … to the immature mind!

Everyone loves a story with a happy ending. Why not end life on a happy note? 'Specifically, in Heaven. Who wants to die anyway? We all desire to live on everlastingly. Methuselah lived nine hundred and sixty-nine years. [Cf. Gen. 5:25-27] Why not me? Imagine living all those years! He died the year of the Flood, presumably in the Flood, or he might still be alive. Imagine also the number of children he may have fathered, and also the magnitude of the 'generation gap' he thus would have had to cope with.

While we are considering the length of Methuselah's life, let us examine the biblical record for the life span of mankind in those days immediately after the expulsion from Eden. The lifetimes of the antediluvian personalities is a bothersome enigma for both those who are 'pro' and those who are 'anti' the Bible. A casual look at the age at which the early men fathered their children, rules out the possibility that a lunar calendar was used to calculate the yearly passage of time. There are approximately thirteen lunar cycles in one year. If Mahaleel fathered Jared at the bible-recorded age of sixty-five years based on lunar cycles, he would have been five years old by our present reckoning. [Cf. Gen. 5:15] That is impossible. However, a lunar cycle calculation of the longevity of Methuselah becomes a more reasonable seventy-four and one-half years old at the time of his death. $\{969 \div 13 = 74.5\}$

All of the forbearers of Noah had fathered children before the biblical age of two hundred. Calculated in lunar periods, two hundred Moon years equates to our sixteen years of age. Sixteen, I feel, is a minimum age for reaching the maturity necessary to begin fathering a family. Yet, most of the earliest fathers, computed in Moon cycles, would have been half that age, approximately eight years of age. This would seem to rule out a lunar calendar. However, if one divides the recorded age of all the long-lived antediluvian biblical characters by ten, then almost every instance of longevity becomes somewhat reasonable by today's averages. Whatever the actual solution, the resolution won't be discerned from the Bible. Further enlightenment by archaeologists and scholars, aided perhaps by the uncovering of ancient manuscripts, much in the manner of the Dead Sea Scrolls, is questing mankind's best to only hope of resolving the enigma of the recorded protracted lives of the antediluvian personalities.

What does reality have to offer in rebuttal of lifetimes in the hundreds of years? First and foremost, that you will die, that your life span on

Earth is limited, and that inevitable misfortune must assuredly befall you at some time during that life span. And, if good fortune does smile on you at another period during your life, you will probably be resented by your peers, and every effort will be attempted to deprive you of your good fortune. The natural order of life's happenings is for the many to have little, and for the few to have much. You, by all inevitability, will be one of the many. To get to be one of the few, in addition to intelligence, you will need a combination of luck, dogged perseverance, or an enhanced endowment of avarice.

Contrary to liberal doctrine, some of us are inferior to others. Some people manifestly have more talent in one endeavor than the majority. Most of the truly successful people are markedly smarter than the majority. Brain power is what has given man his preeminence on this Earth. Only brain power will keep him there. The sorriest effect of religious domination is the propensity it has to inhibit intelligent inquiry. The crude Neanderthals could easily become exemplary Christians, but they could never become adequate scientists, or modest physicians.

The most naïve and the most primitive of peoples are the ripest for conversion to formalized religious sects, a fact not lost on the early evangelizers nor forgotten by their successor missionaries. Providing food is a universal method of influencing human behavior (and most animal behavior also). When we scrutinize Christian proselytizers, we find that they all engage in charitable works. This is commendable, but might it not also be a tactic to ingratiate themselves to a needful community. Charity doesn't do anything to hinder their efforts at obtaining conversions to their respective creeds. This has been proven amply.

Have you noticed the increasing incidence of finding a small bowl of wrapped hard candies on the counter of retail stores? Why is it there with a tiny sign reading "Have one"? Is it because the merchant wishes to lose money by giving away an item that he paid for? No, it is the knowledge that once we accept a gift from someone, we are intuitively impelled to return the courtesy. In this example: To buy some merchandise. This is human nature, and merchants are fully aware of this fact. Televangelists employ a related technique. They ask you to send money in with your prayer requests. It seems probable to the petitioner (but it shouldn't) that the more money sent, the greater is the chance that the prayer will be favorably answered. The greater your gift, the more likely it is that your gift will be reciprocated by the Divinity. 'Perceptively, this is so!

Are all those who proselytize merely insincere money grubbers? Probably not! Are all who proselytize sincere advocates for your betterment? Same response: *Probably not!* On the other hand, are any that proselytize facilitating God's favor toward you? 'Absolutely none! If God exists as we perceive Him in our Western culture, then He is all-knowing, and all-caring, and all-provident. You don't need anyone else to pray to God for you. God hears everyone. God loves everyone equally. No one has any more influence with God than you do yourself.

Good works won't atone for previous evil deeds. Is a bedridden quadriplegic less able to attain Heaven than a wealthy man who spreads largesse throughout the community? 'Of course not! Charity does aid in recruitment to the Sect dispensing it, but no kind act will avail you if, basically, your heart is abounding in evil. (The foregoing is theological reasoning)

The above is why I question the underlying motives of ministers of any sect who dispense charity endlessly, while concomitantly ignoring blatant disbelief. To me they are banking on the human propensity to reciprocate when a kindness is received. I deem it more appropriate to nourish only those who adopt your beliefs. Missionaries have found themselves more successful dispensing food and crediting God as the true benefactor. No one bothers to inform these naïve primitives of the many persons toiling in far off fields and working diligently at arduous tasks who in fact supplied the provident missionaries with the victual means of converting them.

To be sure, the good missionaries did have food to give, but they should have been truthful with the natives. It wasn't God who conferred the agricultural provisions for distribution. It was another human being who produced more than he consumed that provided the foodstuffs the improvident natives accepted so readily. It was industrious human labor, applied intelligently to demanding toil, that produced surpluses that could be transferred to less industrious, less prudent human beings.

Many persons have commented on the harshness of primitive life. What they fail to likewise observe is that primitive people work only hard enough to survive the day. "The more primitive – The less provident!" Most animals lack the foresight to plan ahead. Regrettably, many humans match them in this lack. I don't write this to demean or to ridicule anyone. What purpose do we accomplish if we don rose-colored glasses and remark how rosy the world is? The promise of Heaven appeals strongly to artless people, but providing nutritional or material benefits is the real converting factor. 'Rice Christians' is a term applied derisively, plus descriptively, to this type of convert.

To be honest, I don't fault the natives. They are reacting in their own best interests. What I do not condone and that which irritates me most, are the supposedly intelligent people who consciously choose to believe in a personal God without being enticed by victual bribery. It isn't that I don't comprehend. I do! Still, it disturbs me that so many people opt to believe, in the vain hope of prolonging their life in an afterlife, rather than accept the less appealing prospect of a limited mortal existence that one day will end in irretrievable death for all time.

To me, they seem to be wagering: "If there isn't a life hereafter, then it doesn't matter what I believe. Yet, if there is, then it behooves me to do whatever is necessary to partake of that life hereafter." On balance, what do they stand to lose, as opposed to that which they stand to gain? {Pascal's Wager} This type of shallow, hedonistic reasoning vexes me. The petty logic it embodies generates a steadfast resolve against all religiosity by judicious evaluators.

This line of reasoning permits, and even encourages, the intolerance that permeated the 'Middle Ages.' I am convinced that many persons living in those days knew that the world wasn't supported by four pillars. [Cf. 1 Sam. 2:8 & Job 9:6] And that the Bible contained many other fallacies. [Re: "foundations" Cf. Ps. 81.5] However, as long as no interpretation of the Bible threatened or chastened them personally, they chose not to speak out. I am aware of the extraordinary and pervasive authority the Church of those days wielded. But they wielded it with the passive assent, if not the active consent, of the customarily influential Middle Class.

Those who would argue that religion is generally benign and beneficial to humanity are doubtlessly not students of history. We in the West exist during an age when Christian religions no longer exercise temporal power and must rely on moral persuasion to obtain their ends. Whenever and wherever Christianity has held the whip hand, they have not flinched from using that whip. If all the murdered and brutalized persons since the founding of community-based religions (all religions, not just Christianity) were gathered on one side of a huge teetering board, and all those happy with and helped by state-approved religions were gathered on the other side, that board would tilt heavily downward on the end opposite to the "pious" believing side.

If only that religious zeal … the fervor … this tireless energy, could be directed into endeavors which truly benefited humanity, then a 'heaven' could be constructed by man. Why doesn't humanity set this as its ultimate goal? Religionists have misdirected our objectives. They desire increasing numbers of adherents to their creed. However, that isn't an end; it is a carousel. We eat to live, so that we may live to eat. It isn't the quantity of life that matters, it is the quality. Feed the hungry masses, so that they can reproduce the even hungrier mega-multitudinous masses? Charitable Christians have long been feeding those children who have matured health-ily into the anti-Christian religious armies that are threatening the very existence of Christianity. The greatest peril any religionist will ever face is not the enmity of atheists; it is the fanatical religious fervor of religionists of a competing faith. Deeply held beliefs are the fostering of unalterable intolerance toward those whose beliefs are different.

HUMAN BEHAVIORAL TENDENCIES

An infant receives affection and is contented. A toddler learns to give some affection to receive much more in return. School age children quickly learn that all adults don't readily give affection or accept it. In actuality, a few adults rebuff any demonstration of affection by the child. Very early in life we all learn that when we aren't either giving or receiving affection, we must distract our attention from the need to be loved (and protected) by those around us.

Puppy love and young love develop at a period in our lives when we are able to return as much love as we receive. We are able to meet another individual half way, but alas no farther. Later, we become parents and we are confronted with an individual (infant) who gives nothing, yet expects everything. If we have matured emotionally, we are perfectly capable of coping with this inevitable, natural reversal of role.

In life, not everyone reaches this last stage of development. Some never outgrow their juvenile emotions. Criminals, thieves, and other troublesome individuals simply haven't matured beyond a given point in their childhood. They give little, and expect much. Then, if their wishes aren't fulfilled, or their needs aren't forthcoming, they strike out against persons, institutions, or even against society as a whole.

For the average person, religion is a substitution for young love. We bestow love on God. He bestows love on us. We meet God half way. We must be able to conceive that God returns our love, or we won't be able to sustain our proffered love for Him. The only justification a preacher can proffer for the benefits (blessings) God allegedly grants you, is His love for you. Absent love, no benefit God confers on us makes sense. We, by returning His love, ensure future payback from Him (expectantly). How comforting and how enticing religion is as long as we believe this is true. The philosophy is flawless. However, the facts don't vindicate this hypothesis. The facts refute them.

In religion, we supply the entire amount of love mentally, our share and God's share. However, we direct all that love back upon ourselves. That is why all religious leaders are so self-centered. They all have super egos, and they demand much more esteem in return than they have given. They are vindictive toward non-believers (in themselves) and benevolent toward their adherents. They vent their most vitriolic imprecations against their detractors because pampered vanity leads inexorably to vain pride. That pride creates dogmatism. Dogmatism quickly morphs into domination. We can readily discern these personality links by observing the personality transition that occurs with persons who have "found God" in their lives. In the beginning they are humble. Then, as their pride matures, they become a bit haughty and self-righteous. From haughty, they become religiously definitive and dogmatic. In the final stages they wax dictatorial and begin proselytizing others. This is the real reward they seek by adopting religion, that being to assemble an admiring coterie. This self-sanctifying process always begins with pandered vanity.

"Vanity of Vanities" laments the Preacher. *"Vanity of vanities; all is vanity."* [Ecc. 1:2,] Every action that we perform has the underlying ultimate goal of shoring up our own egos. In our vanity we have conjured up a deity to reinforce our vanity. 'But to what ultimate end? If the God concept is real,

everything else is illusory. If God is fact, we are all a fiction of His incomprehensible imagination.

RELIGION IS ANTI-INTELLECTUAL

The world, as yet, has never been ruled by the intelligent. The one serious flaw in intelligent reasoning is the notion that because a fact is true and verifiable, everyone will accept that fact. Every demagogue, and for that matter, any accomplished religious proselytizer, can attest that quite the opposite is the actual case. The bigger the lie and the more preposterous is the alleged fact, the greater the number of believers one can attract. It is almost as if the moderately intelligent thought to themselves: 'He couldn't possibly expect me to accept such utter nonsense unless it was true.' This application of inverted rationale is all too prevalent.

Political and religious leaders have thriven on this mortal propensity since the founding of communal living. Even God, seemingly, is infected with this contra-logical reasoning. In Genesis, Abram (Abraham), whose wife was barren, impregnated his wife's maid … with his wife's concurrence. God is so pleased with this dalliance that He inexplicably now enables the wife, Sarai (who is ninety years old) to bear the child, Isaac. Couldn't God have rendered Sarai pregnable before Abram committed adultery? Sarai (renamed Sarah by God) was complicit in Abram's infidelity, yet, she was rewarded also. [Cf. Gen. Chap's 16 & 17] Maybe this event, after Divine introspection, imbued Yahweh with the motivation for one of the Ten Commandments dictated later to Moses? *"Thou shall not commit adultery."* [Ex. 20:14 & Deut. 5:18]

A brief aside: Sarah's pregnancy shouldn't be counted a single miracle since not only her conceiving would have been unparalleled, carrying to term and bearing a living infant required nine months' duration for the completed miracle. That a ninety-year-old woman could survive a full-term gestation period and deliver a normal, healthy child is, by far, a greater miracle than simply producing a viable ovum.

Returning to my example: Even the impregnated maid, Hagar, is honored in this enigmatic tale. She is told by an angel speaking for the Lord, *"I will give you so many descendants that they will be too numerous to count."*

[Gen. 16:10] The author of that pronouncement never anticipated the modern science of demographics, nor was he privy to the future occurrence of a method of numbering people known as a Census. Perhaps this is why Yahweh was so angry with King David for ordering a census of the Hebrews nine hundred years later, for doing so invalidated His sacred words to Hagar. [Cf. 2 Sam., Chapter 24 & 1 Chr., Chapter 21] Then again, Yahweh utilized a later Census to fulfill a prophecy that the Divine Savior Jesus would be born in Bethlehem the birthplace of David. [Cf. Mt. 2:6 & Lu. 2:1-4]

Of course Abram, now called Abraham, didn't receive this largesse entirely without reciprocation. He had to render an acknowledgment continually and ceaselessly to God. All his male heirs, male members of his household, and even his male slaves, had to be circumcised. Why God desired this particular form of genital mutilation is never divulged, and to this day it eludes sensible deduction. The implicit fact that God doesn't condemn slavery is glossed over by evangelizers, and is dismissed as commonplace by biblical apologists. In this story, Yahweh speaks directly to Abraham and could have informed him personally that slavery was abhorrent to the Creator of all mankind. God didn't, and this should raise crucial moral inquiries for the Bible's defenders. It is apparent here, as in so many other verses in the Bible, that slavery is condoned by the imputed Creator. The evidence gleaned from the above cited tale will only support the conclusion that religion is man's invention, not God's inspired enlightenment.

All that can be discerned here is that a newly-conceived religion condones whatever are the prevailing moral and ethical standards. The emerging sect reinforces the fixed taboos and sanctifies the current beliefs. However, once the decreed new doctrines have set through the hallowing passage of time, the now-established Sect becomes wholly obstinate to change, hence the future need for, and emergence of, new or schismatic groups. More often, splinter groups don't redo the moral perspectives of the older group. They frequently redefine the precepts, and create an original propriety to exhibit their differences. What begins as informal practice, in later generations becomes obligatory ritual, oftentimes with fanatical insistence.

A case instance: The ringing of the Church bell to summon the faithful to services is an obsolete remnant from a past era. Before the widespread ownership of timepieces, the practice was necessary. A clock mounted in the church steeple served the same purpose in a later age. The church clock, a continual expense, seems on its way to extinction. Oddly, this isn't the case with the church bell. Today, in our insulated homes, with televisions, radios, and stereos blaring, the clanging of church bells is both unnecessary and unheard; and increasingly unheeded. Yet, the practice survives, and in all probability shall continue long into the future.

If you posit any belief on a bogus premise, eventually that belief will be challenged by someone who questions its believability. Then, if your premise is examined very closely, that same someone is bound to find a discrepancy in the belief. Now the formulator (or a defender) of the bogus belief has only two alternatives. One: Abandon his false belief. (Hardly anyone chooses this option) Or Two: Alter the false belief, or expand it to account for the uncovered discrepancy. (This option is infinitely more appealing)

The belief in a Supreme Being has undergone just such a compelled metamorphosis, many times over. Each time an inconsistency intruded, a clever apologist would restate or redefine the concept to surmount the variance. Yet each attempt to further explain God, only further mystified Him. In Genesis, presumably in human form, God met face-to-face with Adam and Eve. [Cf. Gen. 3:8-19] Today, this divine appearance in Eden is proffered (conjectured) as allegorical.

Our present theology and that of the ancient Hebrews are worlds apart. Tenets of the belief in a personal God most likely have followed generally the path of the now disproved dictum of the Earth being the 'center of the Universe.' When the motions of the Planets were plotted with a small degree of accuracy, the 'Geocentric' theory promptly came under assault. To avoid abandoning this self-aggrandizing 'truth,' apologists postulated epicycles along the orbital paths of the Planets. As more and greater deviations in the orbits of the Planets were observed, more and more epicycles were added to account for these deviations. Finally, with much reluctance and a great deal of restating of past doctrine, the Christian Churches agreed with the astronomers and surrendered to the Sun its rightful place at the center of our Solar System with the planets encircling in elliptical orbits. Perfectly circular orbits proved to be perfectly incorrect!

Why the Geocentric theory was so imperative to the Church baffles me. Nonetheless, Galileo was forced by Pope Paul V to retract his "heretical" proposition that the Sun occupies the center of our Planetary System. Galileo was summoned before the Inquisition at Rome in AD 1633, and was admonished to recant his belief that the Earth moves around the Sun. His theories violated an interpreted 'biblical truth' supposedly inspired by the Universal Divinity. 'The Earth is the center of the Universe!' Galileo spent the remainder of his life under suspicion, and under house arrest.

To my mind, the actions of the then Pope and the members of the Inquisition board annulled the dogma of Divine intervention. Historically, whenever God's punitive judgment wasn't immediate, the ministers of religion were quick to apply their own version of 'divine' retribution. Why wait for God to act when you have the power and the inclination to mete out punishment yourself? Acting in God's stead is always warranted for those few pious appointees who are closest to Him (as measured by their personal yardstick).

GALILEO WAS NOT ALONE

Strive to view the official acts of the medieval Church from an atheist's perspective. How many persons are aware of the vigor with which the empowered Church harassed and pursued scientific inquirers in an unholy attempt to stifle what was condemned as satanic curiosity? The fate of Galileo is amply attested in historical records. Ask yourself now though, how many budding or potential inquisitors were directly or indirectly dissuaded from a scientific career because they apprehended the physical peril of so doing? What contributions to scientific advancement (not exempting the comfort and well-being of mankind) were discouraged, delayed, even permanently lost through the repressive acts of the tyrannical Church? We can never know what might have been!

Can we excuse the misguided zealotry of the Church hierarchy of past ages? No, because other actions the reigning pontiffs took cannot be excused. I am referring here to those actions that the Popes "loosed" on earth. Actions, such as granting absolution to tyrants, and even to murderers; dissolving imprudent royal marriages; even the improvident marriages of their illegitimate children so as to consolidate the Church's oppressive power over the common people. An excess of religious zealotry is reprehensible enough of itself. What utterly repulses me are the excesses of diplomatic skullduggery, political maneuvering, or however else one may describe the Papal double-dealings of those days when the Church wielded uncontested power to do so.

What part in those tainted machinations can we ascribe to the Holy Spirit? Where did His influence begin, and where did it end? Does this point need to be elaborated? It is impossible to assign a dominant ameliorating role to any "good" Spirit entity, even 'God the Third Party.' About the only means of exculpating the Holy Spirit is to relegate the scandalous faults of past Popes to God's granting of 'free will.' Yet, 'free will' does not absolve the Holy Ghost of complicity in the prevalent transgressions of the Popes. Coincidentally, it strips Him of the imperative, if not the power, to halt wrong-doing by His surrogates on earth. Without the defense (alibi) of 'free will,' the Holy Spirit would be rightly indictable for malfeasance, misfeasance and predominantly nonfeasance in the conduct of His spiritual leadership of the Christian Church. Everyone concedes that there have been many "bad" Popes. Once having made that admission, we must now reconcile the inherent corollaries to that concession.

Did the Holy Spirit inspire the selection of the wrong men to be elected Pope? Were the 'right' men elevated, but then induced to perform wrongful actions by the Devil? Surely, not by the Holy Spirit! Or did the Holy Spirit merely monitor and permit mortal Cardinals (and other prelates) to exercise their 'free will' to select whomever they fancied to become their Pope without divine guidance? Is divine guidance intrusive or suggestive; imposed or proffered; demanded or presented? These alternatives, repugnant though they be to a religionist, must be frankly determined if the Holy Spirit is indeed active in the affairs of any Christian Church.

None of the six alternatives queried above are viable. Either the Holy Spirit acts dictatorially in all ecclesiastic deeds, or He acts compellingly in some ecclesiastic deeds and not in others, or He has ignored all Christian ecclesiastic deeds enacted during the reign of the Popes succeeding Peter up until the present day. Any of the foregoing options makes Him grievously liable to justifiable criticism by lay Christians. He is thereby rendered guilty of either an error of commission, or an error of omission. The Holy Spirit's only salvation is to find an apologist who is exactingly selective when that proponent ascribes divine intervention in highly selective examples of past Papal issuance.

And just so that I do not convey that only the Roman Catholic Church was guilty of religious devilment, my research has informed me that virtually every religious leader once having obtained dictatorial powers, has become a frightful dictator over his followers, and often (always?) a physical threat to his intolerable apostate/heathen/infidel competitors!

THE SYNOD HORRENDA

In March of the year AD 896, the then Pope, Stephen VII, convened what has come to be known as the "Synod Horrenda." The purpose of this ghastly Synod ostensibly was to prosecute a previous Pope for a violation of Canon law. Former Pope Formosus (r. 891-896 AD) was charged with accepting the Bishopric of Rome while he was still Bishop of another diocese. The charge itself was merely a ploy to exact vengeance against the Roman faction that had supported the elevation of Formosus. And, we can presume, later had opposed Pope Stephen's election.

Such was the petty bickering and spiteful revenge of late ninth century Roman religious politics. The Papacy, always a religious plum, wasn't yet the power base it would become later; the irreparable schism of the Eastern Orthodox Church had yet to occur; the Protestant Reformation was centuries away. If you were a Christian in those times, then you belonged to the only Christian Church that lawfully existed, the Roman Catholic Church.

Everything about this trial was so unimportant that it would have escaped the pages of history, save for one unbelievably shocking fact. Pope Formosus had been dead for eight months! His body literally was dragged from its tomb, dressed in the sacerdotal vestments, and propped in the Papal throne for the trial. The deceased Pope was even assigned legal counsel, but the record shows that this counselor wisely remained as silent as did poor Pope Formosus.

During the trial, Pope Stephen mockingly urged the decaying Formosus to reply to the charges. Eugenius, recording the event for posterity comments: "Would not all that appalling crowd have fled, screaming with terror? Who, then, would have judged Formosus?"

Predictably, the Synod, (which included a certain Cardinal Sergius), condemned the cadaver, and you would think that would have ended it. 'Not for the despicable Pope Stephen. Afterward, the condemned Pope was stripped of the sacred vestments, and the three fingers of benediction on his right hand were hacked off. The corpse was dragged through the palace and hurled to a yelling mob that dragged it through the streets, and eventually threw it into the Tiber River. Compassionate fishermen later recovered the corpse, and gave it a decent burial.

Up to this point, God had not intervened. Although, you would have to admit that there was ample provocation. But wait! The incident isn't quite finished. It seems that shortly after this gruesome exhibition, an earthquake struck and overthrew the ancient Lateran basilica. And, by early autumn of the same year, Pope Stephen (r. 896-897 AD) was seized and strangled. It would appear that with this revelation I have outwitted myself, for if the previous doesn't outline a *prima facie* case of Divine Retribution … what does it describe?

Earlier, discussing miracles, I advised that we shouldn't merely look at the preliminary results to discern and declare a supernatural intervention. We should examine the final results of the alleged intervention. Some benefit, or some notable improvement, must follow the conjectured intervention. The aftermath of this speculated intervention was anything but an improvement for the Roman Christians, or for the Catholic Church.

I will summarize the events following Pope Stephen's strangulation. His party, still active, elected the previously mentioned Cardinal Sergius as Pope while an opposing faction concurrently elected Pope Romanus (r. Aug-Nov 897 AD) to the Papacy. The world now had two Popes!

A papal battle ensued. Sergius and his followers were driven out of Rome. Over the next twelve months, four Popes ascended the throne, and four Popes died. Seven Popes and an Anti-Pope appeared in a little more than six years. Finally, early in the start of the millennium century, Cardinal Sergius reappeared after seven years of exile. And, with the aid of the swords of a friendly feudal lord, he was able to scramble back into the Chair of Peter.

Cardinal Baronius (first of the great Papal historians), writing six centuries later, observed that such a monster (Pope Sergius III, r. 904-911 AD) had been unleashed against the Church to show the supernatural strength of its foundations. No other structure could have survived such an ignominious onslaught from within. Pope Sergius' conduct was gross even measured by his venal contemporaries. He died in AD 911, but not before consigning a living legacy to the Church! He fathered a boy named John by the recently pubescent, Marozia, daughter of the Senatrix of Rome, Theodora.

Marozia, scion of the powerful House of Theophylact and former mistress of a Pope, later became a power in her own right. By the spring of AD 932, Marozia had succeeded in:

1. Imprisoning & causing the murder of her mother's former lover, the pitiable Pope John X.

2. Marrying twice —her second husband was blinded and imprisoned by his half-brother.

3. Getting married for a third time to the same half-brother of her second husband.

4. The marriage ceremony was solemnized by no less than the twenty-year-old reigning Pontiff, Pope John XI who (you will find this difficult to believe!) was the child born of the illicit union of Marozia and Pope Sergius, the Cardinal who survived the earthquake and eventually succeeded to the Papacy.

John XI, the bastard child of Pope Sergius, had himself been ordained Pope of all Christendom twenty years after his illegitimate birth. Perhaps it was fitting that he should be the one to bless the third marriage of his mother, who was marrying her second husband's murderer (his half-brother). Lovely Marozia! The Blessed Virgin she wasn't! Yet her blood coursed through the veins of more Popes than any woman who has ever lived before or since! In all, five Popes trace their ancestry back to Marozia, and many more procured their election directly through 'House of Theophylact' influence.

If the earthquake and the death of Pope Stephen can be attributed to Divine intervention, then God became a conspirator before the fact (through Sergius, and through him, Marozia) to adultery, murder, incest, concubinage, banditry, papicide, and a host of other crimes and mortal sins. He is also guilty of improvidently withholding Divine intervention against the iniquitous House of Theophylact, and against the dissolute Popes of the period. If ever there was an age that pleaded for heavenly intervention, and above and beyond that, divine retribution … this age was it! Yet no divine reckoning was ever exacted against all those (oh, so deserving) ancient malefactors. Throughout all religiosity, the term "Divine Justice" mostly has been a malapropism for the more accurately applicable term "Devoid of Justice."

CHAPTER 4
Morality

RELIGIOSITY IS MORALITY?

To a Christian the concepts of religion and morality are interchangeable. They both encompass one and the same concept. The one can never be separated from the other. This is an apparent fact, but not an actual fact. It only appears so from a modern Christian's vantage point. The Merriam-Webster Dictionary's first entry under religion is: "The service or worship of God or the supernatural." None of the subsequent entries mentions morality, nor should they. Morality is a tenet of the Judeo-Christian religion, one of its doctrines. It may be the single belief that distinguished it from the extant creeds of the ancient Middle East. However, Post-Exodus Judaism didn't insist upon universal morality, but it did insist upon the morality of each Hebrew toward every other Hebrew along with unconditional & exclusive fealty to the god Yahweh.

It is taxing for anyone steeped in a Christian heritage to discuss the aspect of morality without reflexively linking it to his religion. There is no compelling reason for this, and it is doubtless a matter of evolved history rather than any intrinsic coupling that links the two. The original Ten Commandments, as anyone can verify, only applied within the Hebrew community. To covet thy neighbor's wife only offended Yahweh if your neighbor was an Israelite. Read your Bible to learn what the Hebrews did to the peoples God helped them to defeat. Few were spared from a cruel death, and they were either women for base reasons, or children to be raised as servants (slaves) to Yahweh's chosen people. The ancient Hebrews had no doctrinal restrictions prohibiting lying to, cheating, coveting, enslaving, or even murdering their Canaanite neighbors. In Exodus, Chapter 3, God personally instructs Moses to lie to the Pharaoh. *"… to the king of Egypt, and thou shalt say to him: The Lord God of the Hebrews hath called us: we will go three days' journey into the wilderness, to sacrifice unto the Lord our God."* [Ex. 3:18] This was a blatant, deliberate falsehood. Moses was scheming to lead an Israelite Exodus out of Egypt! Was this the actual reason Pharaoh eventually permitted the Israelites to exit Egypt? [Cf. Ex. 10:24]

Jesus, a rebel against Sadducee & Pharisaic ritualistic exactitude, created new rules. This despite His disclaimer: *"Do not think that I have come to destroy the Law or the Prophets. I have not come to destroy but to fulfill."* [Mt. 5:17] Jesus laid a heavy moral burden on the religious hypocrites of His day. He expanded, logically, the commandment against killing and stated that you violated the stricture by merely feeling anger toward your brother. [Cf. Mt. 5:22] No mention was made by Jesus of non-Hebrews. Further, He advised that a sinner should remove the occasion of his sin, e. g., *"If your right eye sins, pluck it out; … your right hand, cut it off and cast it from thee."* [Mt. 5:29-30 & Mk. 9:46]

The sentiments of the 'Sermon on the Mount' are esthetically ennobling, but as a practical guide they are wholly impractical, patently irrational, and realistically unworkable. [Cf. Mt. 5:3-11 & Lu. 6:20-25] Religionists extol them pridefully, while at the same instant effectively side-stepping them, and even completely ignoring them. In any event, Jesus never intended that His words that day should be taken literally. He was attacking the hypocrisy of the religious authorities of His day. They weren't devout of spirit. The outward signs of religiosity were meaningless to Jesus. He correctly saw them as mere holdovers from, or substitutes for, past pagan practices. Jesus taught that the Father God judged individuals by the hidden sentiments that they held in their hearts, not by their ostentatious posturing or the verbal sentiments that they expressed in the presence of other Hebrews in the Synagogues.

Paraphrased, this is what I believe Jesus taught: 'You can deceive your acquaintances, you can deceive your family, you may even deceive yourself at times, but you can never deceive God the Father.' {Author's extrapolation}

MORALITY ISN'T RELIGIOSITY

Moral codes and moral attitudes aren't exclusively the province of the Church. Reasonable, rational determination would impart to anyone the need in civilized societies for civilized (meaning polite) behavior. No one needed to be crucified to acquaint me with the wrong in injuring a person who wasn't harming me or my society. I act kindly and courteously toward others because I sincerely believe this is the proper way to act, not because I hope to gain a heavenly benefit from an all-seeing invisible Deity. Religion is a pathetic less-than-best reason for decent human behavior. If a kind act isn't intrinsically worthy of being performed, then receiving a reward (immortality in Heaven) for performing such doesn't enhance its actual worth.

But the matter of good deeds isn't the point of greatest contention between religionists and non-religionists. The main point of contention is reached when religionists are able to control our actions, and to a lesser degree, to influence our thoughts. The attempt at total control begins with the proposition: 'God made you, therefore, everything you do must be directed toward the honor and glory of God.' (< – a ubiquitous Christian precept)

Taken objectively and analyzed, the second proposition doesn't necessarily insist upon the first. If God did make me, then assuredly He is much greater than me. Why God would want or need me to convey to Him how glorious He is … puzzles me. That concept is all too suspiciously human. Worldly kings are notoriously disposed toward seeking adulation, and in encouraging flattery from their fawning subjects. But God the Almighty Being (?): can He, too, be charmed with compliments and beguiled with blarney? The belief that the Supreme Being is in constant need of human adoration becomes ludicrous when expressed in anything but sanctimonious idiom. Parents know the elation they experience when their small child hugs them and tells them they are the greatest parent ever. The undeniable fact that the child is a demonstrably unqualified 'expert' affirming this proposition in no way diminishes the delight of the parent upon hearing that compliment. If God is the Father of all, then (to a religionist) He also would be elated to be similarly complimented by His created children, who are just as unqualified at evaluating the quality of His Godhood.

Repeatedly, we see an overlay of human sentiments and traits onto a personal Deity. In some ways we are compelled, and in other ways we are obstructed mentally, grasping so esoteric a conception as a Supreme Existence. Mankind hasn't yet grown to the collective intellectual maturity where we are able to infallibly comprehend a Universal Creator. We have, nonetheless, begun our intellectual development, and should now cease believing in a "Santa Claus" Deity bestowing wondrous gifts on persistently undeserving children. A popular Yuletide song admonishes us not to wait till the night before Christmas "to be good." Christian dogma informs us otherwise. At the stroke of midnight we can repent our mischievous ways and still receive a stocking full of goodies in Heaven. How magnanimous; how grossly unjust, but how sublimely magnanimous!

This is the paramount reason why I so stubbornly deny the existence of a personal God. In every instance, in every example, in every characteristic that God exhibits (as attributed by religionists), He shows Himself to be not so much superhuman as simply and patently human, yet concomitantly having super powers ascribed to Him. He possesses every worthwhile human trait, along with some that are considered less desirable. He exhibits love & jealousy, altruism & envy, forgiveness & vengeance, and even openness & deviousness. Patently, if one can define an admirable trait, God possesses that trait beyond refutation via our perception. Whatever negative reactive trait one can detect in human beings, (again, in our perception) God possesses that trait beyond repudiation also. Delineating the Godhood is the embodiment of supernatural anthropomorphism. {Anthropospiritism?}

I cannot conceive the Creator of the vast Universe and all that is encompassed within it as being so persistently and so continually egocentric, thus so utterly human. The explanation for His humanity is evident. He is the creation of humans. How else could they describe, animate, and propagandize His existence? His creators were human and only functioned within human parameters. Religionists might advance this point as only proving man's humanity. But I reply that it contends decisively against divine revelation, and unintentionally against the reality of any celestial entity whatsoever.

The historic fact that a coherent theology only developed over a long period of time, rather than at a revelatory occurrence, and that it was expounded copiously by many diverse individuals, substantially verifies the theory of religious doctrine by gradual human accretion, as opposed to dogma through intermittent divine disclosure. That some very talented and intelligent persons have striven to accurately delineate a Supreme Being and His appropriate worship is evident. That they have fallen significantly short of their desired goal is equally evident to me.

THE NATURE OF MORALITY

Morality defines that which is admirable, from that which is evil. There is almost no middle ground, for even the most innocuous action (e.g., a fleeting thought) tends to lead toward either sanctity or sinfulness. To aver that all mankind has a sense of morality is to state an absolute fact. To declare that there is an unconditional, uniform, universal morality infused by God and applicable to all mankind is to state a demonstrable falsehood.

By observation, morality is nothing but manifest survival instincts tempered by our life's experiences. Unlike man, a turtle has no discernible morality because its survival instincts have evolved along different paths than our own primate line. From the moment a turtle is born, until it inevitably dies, it is solely dependent upon itself for both sustenance and safety. Natal survival in all mammalian species, and in most advanced forms of life, is dependent upon maternal instincts of protection and the care tendered to their young. Many other bio-kingdoms, however, survive quite adequately without maternal /paternal care. Both options are viable in nature, ergo, both exist.

In the primate line, not only is maternal care the rule, it is an indispensable necessity. Humanity evolved from primate lineage; thus, all humans begin life needing maternal care. Females provide maternal affection and nutritional sustenance. Our first human stimulations arise within our own body as a fetus, and our requirements are met through the agency of our mother's reproductive system. After birth, when our needs aren't filled automatically, we cry to get the attention of the person who supplies those needs, that being our mother (in most cases). Upon reaching maturity, human females are endued with the predisposition and the physical means to provide for the survival needs of their infants.

It would seem to be only natural for us to love our mother. And, indeed, eventually this is so, but not immediately. At first, we merely need our mother, and we feel no more love for her than we would (as an adult) feel affection toward a water fountain when we are thirsty. All too soon we learn that there is a noticeable difference between the inanimate objects around us and our mother. The difference being: 'Our mother is progressively less manageable and less predictable than the other objects in our infant lives.'

As our awareness of events outside our body increases, we begin to learn also that all of our pains aren't swiftly relieved by the mother who handles us so gently. Once, when we reached out and squeezed the nose of our mother with our sharp little fingernails, she scolded shrilly and smacked the hand that committed the unintentional transgression. Although too young to understand the nature of our indecorum, we nonetheless learned not to repeat the offense that generated such an unforgettably intimidating response. We had just experienced our first lesson in morality: 'Don't pinch Mommy's nose, that's bad!'

All morality springs from our experiences as an infant and child, and is learned through our interactions with others. The central core of mankind's morality pervades every human society. But only because the central core of human culture is similar throughout the world. The range of the finer points of morality is the result of differences in our early experiences. If our morality was infused by God, no behavioral differences would exist, nor would we have the need to learn the Ten Commandments.

A cannibal would recoil at the suggestion of killing and eating a favorite relative, yet wouldn't experience the slightest misgiving at devouring an enemy or an unknown stranger. Civilized man is horrified by the mere thought of cannibalism. But don't confuse learned conditioning with inspired morality.

Both moralists and religionists insist that there is a common denominator of morality for all humanity. So there is; but not for the reason that God has implanted that moral imperative! More fundamentally, it is because that instinct is inbred in our species and derives not from our impulse toward religiosity, rather from our instinct to avoid unpleasant recriminations, plus being taught societal etiquette from our early associates.

The human species does share a certain commonality of genetic inheritance as well as equivalent infantile experiences; therefore a core similarity in ethics is to be expected throughout the world. This shared ethical core is much too scant to evidence religionists' declaration of infused fundamental ethics. To the contrary, it jibes well with the assumption of learned morality through the experiences of life. Apparent animal participation in laudable ethical behavioral instincts, to me, is the clincher that positively debunks divinely-infused morality.

Crediting God with implanting a moral propensity in animals doesn't alter this conclusion. Plus it has an added disadvantage in that it raises the question of why God would implant the seeds of morality in animals, for they also exhibit much of the basic morality of mankind. Most of the higher land animals possess the rudiments of familial morality in their everyday behavior. Not consciously, of course, they are merely responding to genetically imprinted tendencies. Early naturalists, observing this apparent ethical behavior were quick to identify almost all laudable animal mannerisms to conscious moral judgment, as if animals had inherited implanted rules of moral behavior. They haven't. Now all serious investigators realize this instinctual behavior is neither moral nor ethical. In actuality, it isn't even consistent. Individual animals act with as much unpredictability as individual humans. Animals learn social etiquette in the same manner that humans do, assuming they are able to learn societal "etiquette" by any means.

I will always remember the anthropomorphic "truism" that carnivores only attack prey when they are hungry. Systematic inquiry has disproved this crass attempt to ennoble carnivores (and thereby to blacken mankind's reputation by implied comparison). The truth is: Most carnivores are opportunistic, never spurning a tasty meal if that meal inadvertently blunders within easy reach of the predator. Notice also, that most carnivores are lazy. When they aren't hungry, they mostly just lounge about doing nigh on nothing. This has the effect, without the intention, of obviating the attempt to capture prey when the carnivore isn't hungry. The non-sentient actions of animals mock the imputation of inherent morality in humans. Our natural instincts impel us to satisfy our personal needs at the expense of all others. We learn to act morally the same way we learn not to touch fire ... by painful experience! In humans that pain can be either physical or emotional.

Anyone who has ever owned a kitten can scotch the notion that carnivores only attack when they are driven by hunger. What carnivore is better fed than our own pet cat? Yet, our felines will attack any small moving object that comes to its attention, even a ball of yarn. This isn't cruel behavior, it is instinctive behavior. Evolutionary development has programmed your cat to pounce on small moving objects.

When kittens in a litter frolic with one another, we imagine they merely are playing. This is typical anthropomorphism. What they are doing is practicing their inherited 'capture' techniques. Inadvertently, but indelibly, they soon learn not to attack another kitten. Not for reasons of morality, but simply for the very expedient reason that other kittens counterattack very effectively. This is why and how they learn not to attack their own kind. Morality has nothing to do with it.

Place a pair of human babies together in a playpen, then stand back and observe. You will soon learn how moral behavior is implanted in our species. Eventually one of the infants will strike the other. The younger the infants, the more likely the blow will be unintentional. But the reverse is the impetus toward morality. The older the infants, the more likely it will be that the hurt is inflicted consciously. The nearby mothers will swiftly react. The attacked youngster will be soothed. The aggressor youngster will be scolded. Both, however, will have learned a lesson applicable to their future lives, i.e., one of the prime morality rules of communal coexistence.

The morality we exhibit isn't morality infused by God. It is the ethical standards of the adults who cared for us during our childhood. Don't, however, expect a child's behavior pattern to be a carbon copy of that of his parents. In all likelihood, the parents will have slightly differing moral values themselves. In some instances, one parent will have profoundly different ethical standards from his/her mate. Additionally, all of our moral principles aren't imbued in us by our parents. Nor are they always learned directly or formally. Adult relatives and adult neighbors have their input also, as do older and younger siblings.

Lastly, the role of heredity cannot be dismissed offhandedly. Traits like aggressiveness and passivity, kindness and cruelty, even weakness and strength, are largely inherited. How much, and what degree of effect our genes have, is arguable. But anyone who denies that inheritance is less than fifty percent causal is one-hundred percent wrong. Those who propose that inheritance has no role in behavior aren't suited for participation in this analysis of morality.

To pursue this matter with fairness would require more space than I am willing to allot in this work. So, reluctantly, I will break off here. If I have convinced you that moral behavior in humans is mostly learned, not wholly inherited or divinely infused, then I have made my point. The most arduous chore we have as parents isn't teaching our children how to survive, but is, 'How to become socialized.' It is this task that requires fifteen or more years.

HOW MORALITY EVOLVED

Behavior that thwarted maternal protection in our species would be suicidal. If baby monkeys instinctively attacked their mothers, or instinctively performed any other action that drove the mother off before the baby monkey's dependency period passed, how could the baby monkeys survive? The unequivocal answer is: they couldn't! Only behavior that reinforces the mother/infant relationship is viable in the primate species. So, if we observe harmonious relations in a band of monkeys, we needn't infer morality. We are only witnessing practical evolution as it providentially functions.

Human beings need stable family relationships for the very same reason … to survive! Could a farmer thrive if every time he harvested his crops a band of marauding outlaws swept in and stripped him of the fruits of his labor? No. He would soon stop planting, and all would starve. How long could a community tolerate a persistent murderer? Undoubtedly, no further than the point where he murdered everyone but himself. In actuality, only until he murdered someone the group, or an individual from the group, felt deep affection for.

Communal living must forbid both murder and theft. Man also needs woman, and family continuity is best served by monogamous relationships. We are less insistent in this instance however, and discreet deviations are generally tolerated, although seldom (never?) encouraged within a community. Community coherence must also discourage promiscuity.

Now if the foregoing maxims are beginning to read familiarly, then they should because they form the nucleus of the Commandments of God. Omitted are the first few commandments, which are nothing but superstitious taboos appended by Moses to solidify (and legitimize) his own authority. There just wasn't any possibility of consolidating his leadership without the endorsement of an extant Semite Deity. Yahweh was only one of many gods the Hebrews deemed existent and potent. Moses taught the Israelites not that Yahweh was the only extant divinity, but, more pragmatically, that Yahweh was the lone God who promised to favor only them. By inference and by precept, other gods favored other peoples.

The average Israelite could see, via his own observations, how the gods of Egypt aided the Egyptians. Keep in mind how the people three thousand plus years ago perceived gods and Nature. If a baby was born blind, they believed this was a manifestation of God's anger with the parents, not that the child suffered from some genetic imperfection. Quite literally, everything that happened in a person's life was the direct result of intrusion from the spirit world.

Believing people believed in all manner of spirits. We all know that spirits can inhabit human bodies, or herds of animals. We read of just such events in the Gospels. Even Jesus believed in possessive demons. The people of King Saul's time believed the Lord (Yahweh) might send an evil spirit into a person's body. The Bible testifies to this purported actuality. [Cf. 1 Sam. 18:10; 19:9] *"The Lord's spirit left Saul, and an evil spirit sent by the Lord tormented him. His servants said to him, 'We know that an evil spirit sent by God is tormenting you.'"* [1 Sam. 16:14-15]

Moses certainly comprehended this and incorporated this human idiosyncrasy into his own agenda. He desired to be the leader of his people, but he needed authorization from God. It was no accident that Moses led the Israelites to Mount Sinai. This Mount, which enclosed an active volcano, was greatly intimidating to the superstitious. Moses required some menacing natural marvel that he could attribute to a Hebrew Deity that would physically terrify his followers. A fiery volcanic mountain filled this requirement more than adequately.

This postulation is entirely consistent with what we read of the Exodus in the Bible. Recall that the author related how the Lord guided the Israelites in the form of a column of smoke by day, and a column of fire by night. [Cf. Ex. 13:21] Obviously, Moses led them directly toward an active volcano. Upon reaching the mount, Moses informed the tribes that he would ascend the noisily quaking mountain to confer with God. The people trembled with fearful apprehension at the intensity of the rumblings caused by the thermal activity of the volcano. The now panic-stricken Israelites implored Moses, *"If you speak to us, we will listen; but we are afraid that if God speaks to us, we will die."* [Ex. 20:19]

Forty days later, when Moses returned from his supposed parley with Yahweh, the people had lost all fear of the mountain. At least half of them had lapsed into idolatry, including Aaron, the religiously waffling brother of Moses. [Cf. Exodus, Chap. 32] After ordering the slaying of three thousand idolaters (Aaron not being among them), Moses returned to the mountain to obtain replacement tablets from Yahweh, for he had smashed the first set upon viewing the Golden Calf Aaron had fashioned, and the riotous behavior of the Israelites while rendering homage to that idol.

After his second visit, Moses is recorded to have been forced to wear a veil over his face to shield onlookers from its brilliance. [Cf. Ex. 34:29-35] Inferentially, meeting God face to face (and living to tell of it), causes one's face to glow with radiance. My guess (if this report is historical) is that the face of Moses may have been seared through volcanic activity, or perhaps, when approaching too near a "burning bush," or even sleeping too close-by his own campfire.

The most valuable legacy of Moses, however, wasn't his religiosity; it was his code of morality. Moses correctly theorized that the only method of keeping this disruptive assemblage of Semites united was to enact a series of ordinances that everyone was commanded to abide by. Writing laws to govern people wasn't novel. All rulers have recognized this imperative. What Moses did was to invoke Yahweh as the authority behind those laws. This not only was innovative; it also was eminently successful. Because the directives were mandated by the Deity, any infractions of the law weren't offenses against the secular authorities (Moses) alone; they were sins against their benefactor God to whom the Israelites owed unconditional fealty.

The miracles during the Exodus were calculated to show Yahweh's concern for the welfare of the Israelites. Reduced to its essence, the tale of the Exodus is a story of reward or reproof. When the people were faithful to the God Yahweh, He favored them. When they were wicked, He punished them. I am convinced Moses reminded his followers often of how Yahweh held back the waters of the Sea of Reeds for His chosen people, but crashed the waters down on the (Egyptian) enemies of the Israelites. There are many speculations as to what really happened at the outset of that fateful Exodus, but do they matter? Every eventuality that befell that meandering troop became mystified into a supernatural occurrence. Always, the trigger for every event was the behavior of the people; or so they were informed!

If the people minded the commandments, Yahweh blest them. If not, beware! For Yahweh was a wrathful and vengeful God. Fearing the Lord could be more advantageous than loving Him. But above all else, Moses demanded honesty, morality, and civility from every Israelite toward every other Israelite. Codified ethical behavior was the adhesive that held an otherwise disparate assemblage together.

Today's moralists look at the final six ethical commandments and marvel at how comprehensive they are. They then proceed to declare that only God could have inspired such an all-embracing, yet concise, list. They conveniently neglect to expound on the veritable volumes Moses produced in fully defining the Mosaic Laws (chiefly Deuteronomy and Leviticus, but parts of Exodus and Numbers as well). Also completely overlooked by both the Hebrews and their fellow Christian Bible worshipers is an ordinance delineated in Deuteronomy. *"No one of illegitimate birth shall enter the assembly of the Lord, none of his descendants, even to the tenth generation, shall enter the assembly of the Lord."* [Deut. 23:2] Ponder that ordinance!

Also overlooked are the rules Moses instituted to pardon the sins of his followers. All minor infractions could be expiated through an offering to the priesthood. Lest anyone question the validity of the last sentence, let him read the following quote from Numbers: *"A murderer must be put to death. He cannot escape the penalty by the payment of money."* [Num. 35:31] By obvious inference, all other infractions could gain exoneration by an exchange of coin.

The priesthood, you will recall, was reserved to Moses' own tribal family, the Levites. These rules may or may not have enriched Moses' clan, but the rules positively did nothing to impoverish the Levites either. All monetary penalties for sin were payable to the Priests. Clearly, Moses wasn't averse to nepotism, and in honesty and in fairness this must be assessed against him.

ANOTHER LOOK AT MORALITY

Is Fornication a Sin? Is Murder a Sin?

Is it really a sin for unmarried men and women to fornicate? Does this offend God? Is it a sin for animals to copulate? How about insects? The answers: 'No,' for insects. 'No,' for animals. 'Yes,' for men and women. Why? Why does God hate to see human beings performing an act that He, Himself, made so enticing, so pleasurable … almost imperative?

Evolutionists have an answer that no religionist will accept. Notwithstanding, the answer of the evolutionists is irrefutably the actuality. "God had nothing to do with implanting human lust." We inherited our carnality from our pre-human predecessors, and they inherited their carnality from their pre-primate antecedents, and so on back into the opaque eons of evolutionary beginnings. Carnality isn't a sin, it is a biological indispensability. We all know the result of sexual activity between male and female … the creation of another male or female offspring of that species. Have you ever wondered why coitus is so enjoyable? Why is the desire to consort with the opposite gender so commanding? These two questions insist upon a resolute reply.

Religion doesn't have those two answers, at least, not satisfactory answers. In religious apology we are told that our lusts are nothing but the seductions of the Devil. Yet, if so, then Satan must be tempting the birds and the bees also, for they appear to be every bit as randy as is mankind. By observation, they are much less constrained than are human beings. Frankly, though, it is difficult to picture Satan engaged in such trivial matters as the lechery of salamanders, or the licentiousness of any other of the passionate species. No, the facts don't fit the religious explanation. Religionists insist that our lusts arise from the inducements of the Evil

One. Yet, our passions are no different than those of the lower animals and most insects. Whatever the impetus is toward copulation, that impetus is common to all sexually differentiated bio-forms and it demonstrably isn't dependent upon diabolical intrigue.

Evolutionists have a far simpler explanation, and it is this: Sexual attraction between dimorphic members within a species is an evolved impulse that is indispensable for the perpetuation of that species. Animals can't reason. They don't copulate with the intention of producing offspring, but merely to satisfy an inherited natural urge. This has proved to be a successful biological trait. Remember this; we are only able to view the successes of the evolutionary process. The evolutionary failures primarily don't live long enough to produce living heirs. This has the irreversible effect of terminating disadvantageous evolutionary divergences before that randomly evolved trait is added to that species' gene pool.

The evidence of evolution indicates that mankind's sexual proclivities are hereditary remnants from our pre-human animal ancestors. We humans know what to do to create babies, and we recognize the compelling desideratum to continue our species. Recognizing this, the lust imperative in mankind is evidenced to be superfluous, it is redundant, and more, it is the cause of much of our grief as well. It is conceded that we humans need children to perpetuate our species, but we don't need the passion that precedes the copulation act that produces children. If the pleasure generating aspects of sexual activity somehow were excised from all mankind today, would we face certain extinction as a species thereafter? Definitely not!

To illuminate my point consider this: A farmer experiences no sensual pleasure while planting crops. He doesn't even reap his reward until many months later. Does either of these facts dissuade the farmer from his labors? No. Neither would the absence of orgiastic recompense deter humanity from producing offspring. Some other explanation for human sexuality must exist. We could well do without the lust inducement, as God should know. But, still we have it. Why? Whose explanation best fits the facts; Religionists or Evolutionists?

Patently, from an evidentiary standpoint, the evolutionists have the only cogent solution. All that religionists offer is the presumptive question: "If God didn't model us the way we are, then who did?" The question forces its own answer. A respondent is compelled to answer that 'someone' rather than 'something' or 'some principle' is responsible for our lechery. Religionists persist in personalizing the creative impetus against all the evidence available to the contrary. Evolution isn't a competing religion that must be embraced or rejected on faith. It is the best (only?) logical resolution to the enigma of the diversification of life forms on Earth. Evolution is provable fact. Creationism is vain deduction.

Did you ever wonder why human babies are born without the ability to walk, or even to crawl? Why do babies have to learn to talk? If God had so desired, couldn't He have enabled us to walk at birth as can many other mammalian newborns? Why didn't He? Why do humans require such a long period of childhood and adolescence? (Paleontologists have a theory called neoteny that concerns maturation time lapses, but that is a tangential subject) What purpose of God is served by delaying our maturity for 18 to 25 years? One quarter to one third of our lives are spent in growing up. No religious objectives necessitate such a protracted maturation.

Evolutionists theorize that the increase in human intelligence caused a decrease in inherited animal instincts. Once intelligence guided our actions to a greater degree, then our instincts would control our actions to a lesser degree. The more we were able to learn, the less dependence we would have on inherent behavioral impulses. Surely the domestication of animals came as a direct result of the diminished reliance of domestic mammals on instinctual responses to stimuli, and the magnified reliance on learned responses to stimuli provided by humans. Humans are no different in this respect, only more evolved.

Ironically, there are evolutionists afflicted with a superstitious bent of mind also. They preach a doctrine of Divine design in the natural processes of evolution. Sadly, the evidence won't support this conclusion either. The progression of evolution seems to be completely random. Yes, it is opportunistic! But is it purposeful? No! Man, himself, might just be the result of biological serendipity, rather than either fated inevitability or divine design.

Our binocular vision evolved in our proto-simian antecedents as a necessity in order to accurately gauge leaping distances from branch to branch traveling through forests. Our opposable thumb and grasping fingers evolved in response to a tree dwelling life (or maybe the reverse).

Whichever! We could never have evolved directly from quadruped mammal to bipedal man without the intermediate phase of arboreal primate.

Yet, after acquiring these specialized adaptations for a life above the forest floor, our genetic predecessors came down out of the trees and learned to walk upright on open terrain. Most other arboreal species, having left their optimum habitat, would have been ill-prepared to compete with the already established ground dwelling species. But our predecessors enjoyed an advantage over their new competitors. The prehensile hands of primates could grasp objects that they then utilized as tools or as weapons, whichever the situation required.

The food supply at ground level wasn't necessarily more abundant, but it was more varied. That is how and why man became omnivorous. There was one drawback to life on the open savannas. It was the presence of predators, particularly members of the feline and canine families. This was a serious impediment in the quest for successful adaptation to a life away from trees. There is, however, one indispensable requirement for predators, and it is this: 'Predators must be more cunning than their prey is resourceful.'

At first, these homeless primates must have paid a frightful and devastating price for invading the treeless habitat. But evolution turned this new disaster into a disguised boon for our ancestors. Not all species have been so fortunate (or blest), excepting the Whales, otters, and penguins, among other representations that could be exampled.

Evolution has been described as "survival of the fittest." The phrase is a hopelessly imprecise generalization of the reason for one individual's survival, and for another's demise. Species survive because individuals develop a nullifying response to a potentially lethal environmental pressure. On Earth, the appropriate response to environmental pressures can be either physical or intellectual. Most of the existing mammalian species have employed both responses at various times throughout their evolutionary history in order to survive. Mammals have evolved mentally to a greater extent than all other animal families. Predators, as stated previously, are invariably more intelligent than are their stalked quarry.

Now, concerning our primate ancestors, the pressure was on. No physical response could overcome the absolute advantage the carnivores had over these primate immigrants. The carnivores were physically superior to the primates, and they were highly endowed in intellect as well. If the primates were to survive in this new and hostile environment, they would have to evolve an appropriate strategy to combat the onslaught of the carnivores. That they did evolve a winning strategy, we are all living proof. What was that stratagem? Today, we can only surmise, but one thing we can say with certitude is that the response wasn't physical in the case of man's direct antecedents. (It may have been for the immediate ancestor of the gorilla?)

My guess is that the carnivores weeded out the least intelligent of the primate species. Those clever enough to seek shelter on cliff faces, or any other inaccessible nook, survived. They were able to climb high up into trees. The ability to throw objects accurately may have aided. Learning to use or make fire may have contributed. But most likely, how our ancestors survived was through their nimble wits. Then, by reducing the number of low intellect individuals contributing to the racial gene pool, the carnivores unwittingly, yet assuredly, increased the percentage of high intellect individuals adding to the collective human gene pool. An aside: Nature abhors the weak, the unlucky, and the incompetent. There is a brutal, perturbing, even repugnant lesson to be learned thereby. But do today's leading societies have the firm fortitude, the unwavering courage, and the unyielding determination to cease thwarting nature's predisposition to eliminate the evolutionary inferior for the betterment of the entirety? Therefore: Should we encourage Euthanasia? No. But should we cease facilitating low intellect individuals from breeding indiscriminately? As abhorrent as this biologically imperative answer may be, the intellectually imposed reply is 'Yes!'

The tendency of the mammalian order to produce intelligent offspring continued in the case of our primate predecessors. The primates couldn't outrun nor outfight their adversaries, so they, therefore, had to out-think them to survive. Intelligent, provident mankind is the victorious result of the epic struggle between the carnivores and the first land-roving primates.

OF THE NEED FOR LAW AND MORALITY

Part of the human impulse toward religiosity is engendered by the perceived and evident need for order and predictability in our lives. The very fact that we can conceive of a tomorrow makes it imperative that we do something today to ensure that the next day is either a better day or, at minimum, is no worse than is this day. This behavior pattern is learned; it isn't inherited. Children have little concern for the future. Adult people plan for the future only if they have matured sufficiently. Not all twenty-one-year-old humans, however, are adult. Some persons never reach full maturity and need perpetual caring from a dependable adult (or a surrogate parent such as the government). Persons who spend a lifetime seeking and receiving governmental charity aren't adult … excluding the despicably indolent Welfare scammers.

Earlier, it was stated that anti-social behavior was an act of immaturity, and so it is. It doesn't take a super intellect to realize that if all of us were criminals, none of us could survive. It is only possible for some of us to be criminals, because most of us are not. Mental maturity is the key to the success of the human species, and for that matter, all the higher species.

But I must curtail the mundane ramifications of this dissertation and concentrate only on the philosophical. What I am referring to is the religious aspect of this human propensity that attempts to control, or failing that, alternately to predict the future. In many ways religiosity is juvenile. Yet, it finds adherents among the fully mature population as well. Seemingly this is contradictory and inexplicable.

The dichotomous nature of the aggregate of religiously oriented persons becomes intelligible only if we concede a dichotomy. For instance: the farmer's need to predict adequate sunshine and rainfall is surely reasonable. But the practice of burning a holocaust to the gods to ensure those needs is superstitious immaturity. Looking back at some of the early rituals of religionists indicates to an unshackled intellect, that those first deifiers of nature, precursors of the Israelites, were inspired by ignorance, not by a spiritual divinity.

If this is fact, does it then follow inexorably that everything the Pre-Judaic theorizers believed in was false? No. The premise for a belief can be in error without the belief itself invariably being fully erroneous. In a like manner, a premise can be correct, yet a conclusion drawn from that premise may be incorrect. This does not insinuate that correct premises mostly result in counterfeit conclusions. If the premise itself is correct, much more often than not, a reasonable conclusion derived from that premise will likewise be correct. This is why we must continually strive for the facts and forgo superstitious illogicality (sanctioned mysteries, et al.).

In the case of the Judeo-Christian religion, morality is mandated by the Commandments of Moses, and is reinforced by the teachings of Jesus. Both men, Moses and Jesus, received their authority from God. (One considerably more direct than the other?) Yet, if I deny their authority by denying the existence of God, do I likewise deny the need for morality? No. Morality, decent behavior, respect for the reasonable rights of others, all these have genuine legitimacy. Their legitimacy is mandated by their value and necessity to communal mankind. Actions that disrupt the cooperative enterprises of civilization are violations against the community weal, and for this reason apart, they must evermore be legally and morally prohibited.

The prohibition alone, however, won't ensure against the perpetration of a proscribed act. A law's chief utilitarian benefit to civilization is that it permits the administration of a punishment against an offender. This may sound vindictive, and it is in one aspect, but it is also viable and therein resides its utility. The imposition of a penalty for violations of the law serves two purposes. First, assuming the sentence is severe enough, soon enough, and is justly applied, the punishment is a deterrent to future infractions. Secondly, it is a vicarious reward for those who obey the laws of a community. Liberals assiduously overlook the second aspect, while paternalistically denigrating the first aspect. Liberals mindlessly, yet effectively, would have us invert these two principles. They would exonerate the guilty by inventing a mitigating (hopefully unassailable) excuse for their offense, and they would indict the innocent by faulting society for some presumptive causal action, or negligent causal 'lack of action' that accusatorially occasioned the criminal act.

Liberals espouse the irrational. Here, I will provide an example that is almost trite by comparison to other examples I might have provided. Concomitantly, there is an additional message in this triteness that, if discerned, amplifies my point. In Philadelphia, as in all other cities, we have vandals who travel around scrawling all manner of pointless yet defacing graffiti over every high-visibility surface they can reach. (The extent of their "reach" is phenomenal)

One such miscreant was so pernicious that his juvenile sprayed "autograph" became infamous throughout the city. Worse still, his "tag" (personal logo) became much copied by other malefactors. Finally, his real identity became known to the authorities. Relieved, the decent citizens all presumed this criminally motivated defacer was soon to reap his long-delayed punishment. This was not to be, for an all-too-liberal press rushed to defend (excuse) him. To the press and other liberals, he wasn't a destructive dispenser of graffiti; he was a frustrated artist. That is, a budding, albeit untutored, future Rembrandt.

While a vocal (yet influential) minority began glorifying this hoodlum criminal, a few of the normally silent majority spoke out. Several sensible people in our community asked that this individual be compelled to remove the disgraceful scrawl he created on our transit system (and elsewhere) as recompense for his crime, and as a deterrent to others with his inclinations. Gratifyingly, this would also have provided relief and respite to all those who suffered distress, day after day, while being forced to view the wanton defilement of their community.

But the liberals had their way, and the spray-can wielder was ceremoniously conveyed to Art School. Several years later a small notice appeared on the inside pages of our newspapers informing us that this Media-created 'hero' had dropped out of art school. Who knows who bore the cost of the Art School? (We all do know.) I can tell you who paid to clean up his mess. It was the very community that was so offended by his nauseating defilement. How much additional anguish was felt by parents of decent children with real artistic talents who were unable financially to send their children to Art School can only be conjectured?

What does the Bible inform in matters such as the foregoing? To be honest, the Bible is so diverse and contradictory that one can find virtual validation for whatever actions one takes. Culling a few pertinent passages will justify the previous statement, yet, it won't truly resolve the aforementioned question.

Jesus asserted that the Temple merchants defamed the House of the Lord, and He drove them out with a whip of cords. [Cf. Mt. 21:12-13; Mk. 11:15-17; Lu. 19:45-46 & Jn. 2:13-16] If the greedy merchants had been brothers of Jesus would He have turned His other cheek? [Cf. Mt. 5:39 & Lu. 6:29] Jesus taught us to love our enemies. Why didn't He love the greed-motivated merchants? Jesus also advised us to love our neighbors as we love ourselves. [Cf. Lu. 10:27] Fine! Who are our neighbors? Modern theologians declare that we are all neighbors, still, this isn't what Jesus taught the Apostles. In the parable of the Good Samaritan, both the Temple Minister and the Levite (priestly caste) passed by the injured man. They weren't neighborly to the needful man. Only the ill-thought-of Samaritan stopped and aided the hapless robbery victim. [Cf. Lu. 10:29-37] Today's preachers repeat this story, and then solemnly declare that all men are brothers, or at least neighbors. I choose to differ. What the parable teaches is that those who help us are our neighbors; those who do not help us, are not our neighbors!

Lest someone wishes to dispute this point, let him read Luke. *"Anyone who is not for me is against me ...."* [Lu. 11:23] The proposition that everyone is a neighbor to everyone else is neither promulgated nor verified in the Bible. The proposition is a modern accommodation to aid in obtaining Church membership by Christian missionary sects.

But these aren't the biblical passages a liberal would quote to justify his liberality. Rather, he would repeat the parable of the Lost Son. [Cf. Lu. 15:11-32] As most will know, the gist of the story is that the father held a great feast to celebrate the return of his wastrel son. Overlooked in the parable is the justifiable resentment of the steadfast son. Read from Verse Twenty-Eight forward. The faithful son was so angry he refused to go into the house. He berated the father for never having given even a small feast in honor of his worthy, steadfast son. The eldest son evaluated correctly, and indiscernibly, so did the younger son. The younger son, when he confessed to his father, *"I have sinned against God and against you, I am no longer fit to be called your son; treat me as one of your hired workers,"* was incontrovertibly precise in his assessment. [Lu. 15:21] This is precisely what he deserved.

The foremost culprit of this parable was the foolish old man. The logical continuation of this parable would be for the younger son to demand that the father's estate be divided in half once again so that he might resume his life of dissolute squandering. In the end, the worthless son never repented until after he had spent all his initial inheritance. Why should we expect him now to abandon his hedonism? What is even more insidious about this parable is the thought that the prodigal son may repeat his selfish ways seven times over. If a brother can transgress seven times and be forgiven biblically, a son should have the right to at least as many violations.

If you read the parable closely, you will see that the younger son wasn't so much repentant as he was resourceful. He reasoned, shrewdly, that a hired worker on the father's estate lived better than he was living after having dissipated his inheritance. The younger son, true to form, was once more seeking what was most beneficial to him. The world is over-brimming with persons who continually and unfailingly 'promote their own best interests.' Who needs them? The trustworthy, the devoted, the reliable, these are the people we need to celebrate. It is they who have created the utmost in our civilizations, not the hedonists.

It has often been remarked that "there is no justice in this world." On a subjective matter such as this, there are no absolutes. Still, there is enough truth in this axiom to render it appropriate in aptly applied instances. The world doesn't have to be devoid of all justice, especially not today's world. We have the knowledge and the resources to mete out justice in a more even-handed fashion than ever before in history. Yet, do we? No. For it seems we lack the will to do so. We have allowed cheerleader liberals to foist their pseudo-ethics (contra justice) upon all of us.

It must be conceded here that many religionists today resist the liberal perversions of our 'English Law.' Nevertheless, when the liberals inject Christian pragmatism into secular affairs, religionists are forced to support them. Christian moralists are cowed into grudging acquiescence when liberals invoke the commandment against killing to oppose the rightful sentence of execution for the crime of murder. The contrary is how I interpret Judeo-Christian jurisprudence. God decreed that every sin requires a punishment. In the Old Testament He punished errant mortals often, and He punished them harshly, even to their death.

What is God's punishment for each person who dies in mortal sin? The punishment is eternal damnation. Murder is a mortal sin; so are many acts of a lesser gravity. Still, the punishment is the same. Yahweh was never a bleeding-heart liberal. Today, the Christian formulary, "judge not and you shall not be judged," [Mt. 7:1 & Lu. 6:37] is twisted so perversely as to allow the most heinous of crimes to be 'tolerated,' thereby exonerated. Yet, every day these same liberals "judge" the conduct of non-liberals. They judge the innocent to determine if the innocent have violated the "rights" of the guilty. In this pursuit, they are ever vigilant and most diligent. They, themselves, are villains!

Our Courts today are being subverted because of the arduous path the prosecution must traverse in order to obtain a conviction. Liberals congratulate themselves daily for ensuring that no "innocent" man ever goes to prison. In actuality, going to prison isn't always the worse fate that can befall an innocent man. We release hundreds and thousands of guilty persons by bending over backward to avoid sending one innocent person to jail. This makes sense to a liberal. No one can convince them that those guilty persons, so inappropriately spared from prison, go on to inflict countless crimes against truly innocent persons that include murder, rape, assault, robbery, and a proliferation of other offenses.

Doesn't anyone recall cartoonist Al Capp's newspaper comic substrip hero "Fearless Fosdick"? The premise of one story line was that a can of poisoned beans was accidentally released to the public. Fosdick went around shooting holes into the heads of everyone he found eating beans … to protect them from being poisoned! We accomplish the same end when we fail to incarcerate fittingly arrested criminals. The released guilty thereafter prey on innocent people who would have been protected if we hadn't been so foolish (squeamish) to give the captured criminals further opportunity to victimize society.

The puerile presumption of innocence until proven guilty is illogical and, strictly speaking, impossible. If we presume someone innocent, then why investigate them? Why bring charges against them? Why conduct a trial at all? The act of convening a trial presumes guilt. What is really necessary in our criminal system is for the jury, alone, to withhold their final judgment until all the evidence is presented to them, and the defense has had an ample opportunity to refute the evidence. (Notice I didn't write "to confuse" the evidence) Too many of our younger citizens think that unless an unambiguous video tape of the crime is presented, they must acquit the defendant because there may be some slight chance that the accused is not guilty.

Allow me to return to a point made several paragraphs ago regarding the reversal of guilt and innocence. Not too many years ago, a merchant continually had his warehouse burglarized. In frustration, the merchant set a shotgun trap for his habitual predator. The persistent burglar repeated his crime once too often and was shot in the legs for his persistence. Arrogantly, the thief sued the outraged merchant and won! The court found that the thief had been trapped by the merchant, and the judge ruled that no human being, regardless how low or how despicable, should ever be entrapped. Theologically, 'we are all God's children.' The innate dignity of man transcends his debased behavior. This is fundamental Christian ethos. Nevertheless, it thwarts justice, and mocks the sensibilities of the decent segment of any civilized community.

Opponents of the death penalty invoke the Mosaic commandment against murder as Divine approbation of their position. This, notwithstanding the verifiable fact that Moses never proscribed lawful executions; He ordered them! [Cf. Ex. 32:27] God, personally, was set to execute Moses at the start of the mission to escort the Israelites out of Egypt because Moses had not yet circumcised his sons. [Cf. Ex. 4:24-26] Absolute justice is the attribute that will be the salvation of mankind, not universal love. Justice is a function of the intellect, unlike love, which is governed by our emotions. Here, innumerable examples could be provided to make the point, but none shall be provided. Instead, I ask you to imagine your own examples. Contemplate the major problems facing mankind today, and then ask yourself if they wouldn't be solved permanently if "just" solutions could be found for those problems. Yet, take care, for liberals have so polluted the meaning of justice that most confuse paternalistic benignity with unmitigated justice.

Justice, to be effective, must be wholly impartial, and must not be diluted with the squeamish aversion to the imposition of punishment called mercy (modern terminology: 'compassion'). For instance: All murderers, without exception, would face a death sentence. Criminal negligence resulting in death would automatically face life in prison, and so on. The mitigating circumstances would apply after the sentenced person had served time "with absolute good behavior" by reducing the sentence. Each day served with strict adherence to prison rules could reduce a convict's sentence by one day. Defiance toward penal authorities, or even uncooperative behavior, would result in additional incarceration time being added to the miscreant's sentence. At a certain point, unrepentant or unmanageable criminals could have their sentence upped to the death penalty irrespective of the original sentence. Trust me! That stipulation absolutely would prove to be rehabilitative!

Over the past thirty years our prisons have become cesspools of anti-social behavior without attendant punishment. There is more brazen criminality in prison than anywhere else in this nation. Under true justice, incorrigible inmates would "earn" their way into an execution chamber. Rehabilitation comes from within the person. There is no way anyone, no matter how well-intentioned, can infuse another with the will to behave sociably. If the threat of execution, or even of life in prison, doesn't alter behavior, then cable television, gym privileges and conjugal visits won't either.

We should treat prisoners humanely, provided they act as a decent human being must act by obeying rules, expressing remorse for their crimes, and doing nothing to hamper the efficient administration of the prison. Unearned benefits only create the expectation (demand?) of more and superior unearned benefits. Establishing rehabilitation programs in prison is futile if we force every criminal to attend them. Rehabilitation isn't a cloak that can be wrapped around a person against his true wishes. Frankly, believing that society can rehabilitate anyone is exactly as deluded as believing one can influence the weather through prayerful petition.

If a number of people assembled and continually performed a rain ritual; one day their efforts would attain success. This is the same apparent "success" result we observe with rehabilitation programs. Understand this: 'Whenever we improve the overall conditions of confinement in prison, we reward every criminal, not just the repentant.' A benefit given without merit destroys the initiative of those who would undertake to earn their benefits.

Religionists offer the same easy salvation as liberals. 'Sin all you might, for when you accept Jesus as your personal Savior ... you are forgiven!' {The foregoing axiom does not exist anywhere in the New Testament.} Can you see the interconnection between religious propositions and liberal premises? The Church proposes that people sin because the Devil tempts them. Liberals propose that criminals commit crimes because society has wronged them. Both religionists and liberals preach the supremacy of mercy over punishment. But all either faction produces is present day injustice and future criminality.

CHAPTER 5

To Live Again

BEING REBORN

Reincarnation is a very ancient religious belief that predates Christianity's belief in bodily resurrection. Yet Reincarnation and Resurrection are two aspects of the same belief, denial of inescapable and irreversible death. Reincarnation, as understood and interpreted by Asiatic mystics, was considered an undesirable yet unavoidable occurrence in human existence. Life was exceedingly harsh: accordingly, the greatest joy (i.e., relief from misery) would be obtained by ceasing to continue to be reborn into a life of poverty, grief, and strife. At first glance, suicide might seem a rectifying antidote, but not so. You would inevitably be reincarnated and your tribulations would again commence. The only lasting salvation attainable was to terminate your reincarnations, and thereby attain the blissful death state of Nirvana.

To Buddha, each reincarnation would prove just as pain-filled and wretched as the last. This agony was caused by man's unrealized desires. Buddha correctly fathomed that misery is produced by imposed negation of pleasure realization. If you earnestly desire something, and that thing is forever denied you, you will perpetually be tormented by self-actuated anguish. His solution, only partially successful at best, was to suppress all desires. If a person has no desires whatsoever, obviously he will never suffer any degree of distress through deprivation.

His logic is flawless. Regrettably, we are all human and our desires are as intrinsic to us as is our consciousness. All living matter has desires, whether perceived or not, matters not. The more complex the life form is, the more desires it acquires. In mankind, we find the apex of sensate desires. In actuality, the only means of purging all personal pleasure goals is to die. Our present Christian concept of a 'heaven' was formulated after the life of Buddha, and discernibly was somewhat influenced by his negative conjectures about life/rebirth.

Reincarnation is undergoing a mild revival in the Western World today, but in a somewhat altered form. It appears to be devolving into a human mental ploy to avert the clutches of Hell. Just when the Devil thinks he has gained another miscreant soul, that person is reincarnated and given another chance to re-direct his final destination. Yet, even reincarnation couldn't avoid being rationalized by those embracing a quasi-logical, metaphysical mysticism. In essence, reincarnation defies and denies pragmatic logic.

Reincarnation, were it factual, appears to be utterly arbitrary, though possibly opportunistic on first consideration. A living person dies and his soul is liberated from its imprisoning torso only to immediately begin seeking a new torso to become incarcerated into. Just how one particular human embryo is chosen, over the millions available, seems the result of happenstance. Does a liberated soul animate the very next newly conceived zygote it encounters? Do male souls seek only male impregnations in their next incarnation? Does God assign, or do the souls select? Is randomness operable? A boundless number of intriguing and pertinent queries could be posed in an effort to expand on the concept of reincarnation.

Reversing a popular and recurring theme: "Why do so many former Egyptian kings and queens choose to reincarnate as a comparative nobody?" Now, after centuries of mystery, the resolution to that poser has been revealed. In a book by Allen Spraggett titled, Ross Peterson: The New Edgar Cayce, reincarnation itself is visualized as mankind's Heaven or Hell.

Unfortunately (yet somehow predictably), most of the cases cited relate to Hell. Goodness in one earthly life is rewarded with health and fair fortune in the next reincarnated earthly life. More preponderantly, villainy, wickedness, or meanness in a previous existence is punished (atoned for?) by misfortune and sickness in your next existence. Let us explore this concept by reading from Mr. Spraggett's book. Quoting excerpts from Chapter Six:

"The law of karma is the law of the harvest. Whatsoever a man soweth, that shall he also reap. What the soul committed in a previous life determines its circumstances in this life. This is the answer of reincarnation to the vexing question of human life inequality of life experiences. Why is one man born a prince, the other a pauper? Why is one born physically perfect and the other damned into the world with gross deformities? 'It is the law at work,' writes Peterson. 'Each entity reaps exactly what it has sown. The law is perfect. There are no mistakes, no excesses, and no imbalances. It is just.'"

Later Peterson states, "I can accept the idea that everything I have experienced in my life, or have not experienced, for good or for ill, is the result of my own deeds or thoughts in a previous lifetime." An illustrative reading rendered by Peterson:

"A man suffering from diabetic blindness was told that in a previous life he had exulted in putting out the eyes of others. So in this life, like a boomerang, his eyes had been put out. How do people react when they are told in a Peterson reading that their present plight is the result of their own misdeeds or troublesome attitudes in a former life? Peterson reveals: 'Ninety-nine times out of a hundred —the person relates to the reading instantly and feels comfortable with it. He or she feels that if this is something they deserve, then they can live with it.'"

If Peterson's law of karma reads familiarly, it should! Substitute 'will of God' for the words 'law of karma' and re-read the paragraph. Buddha was correct in his evaluation of reincarnation (if factual). For the mass of the people on this planet, being reborn will only result in your having the opportunity to endure another agonizing life. Is this God's will?

A personal God is only believable if he aids mankind. An evil, injurious, malignant Deity would be man's adversary, not his benefactor. (A being to be fought; not to be worshiped) The enigma of life's hardships has plagued religious scholars ever since the contrivance of the personal God concept was inaugurated. A perfectly good Deity can't perform even slightly evil acts. Yet evil exists; yea, it proliferates! Does mankind therefore discard the personal God premise? No, he expands his theology to include the Devil to account for the presence of Evil.

The Devil is the perpetrator of all evil. But still poignant posers remain unresolved, so the theology expands again and again to cover more and more discrepancies in the theory. The simplest and most logical resolution is that there is no personal God. All events can then be seen for exactly what they are, the coincidental interactions of mankind and nature. Nature has power; but man has intellect. Religion maintains the ability to harness nature's power through the intercession of God. But only science can empirically demonstrate the ability to at least predict some of nature's more violent outbursts. In case you haven't already noticed, your local weather person is generally able to fairly accurately predict the weather pattern five days in advance. In the days of Noah and his contemporaries, that ability would have been declared "God-Like."

Mystery breeds superstition. Superstition breeds Deities. Deities breed controversy. Thus, is reincarnation one of God's gifts? Or is it one of His Trials?

REINCARNATION ATTESTED

The Bible and sacred traditions have already acquainted us with the physical appearance of spiritual Heaven. However, in our generation we are thrice blest. For today, in addition to the Bible and sacred traditions, we have expert eyewitness testimony from persons who miraculously ascended to Heaven and returned. Blessedly, they are magnanimously amenable to share with us less fortunate the wonderment of their privileged audience with Almighty God and His resurrected Son. I am referring to those who have been diagnosed clinically dead; flitted off to Heaven; met the Deity, and returned to Earth revived and unscathed.

Specifically why God performs such miracles is the greatest mystery of all. If His purpose is to report the existence of Heaven, He had already done that adequately. Nor could it be to correct any misinformation concerning Heaven we may have become heir to, for the disclosures of the returnees confirms that Heaven exists precisely as Revelations describes it. [Cf. Rev., Chap. 21]

Then are these additional resurrections God's means of flaunting His unparalleled powers? 'Not likely! Resurrecting Himself was, by far, much more compelling. Perhaps it wasn't God's decreed time for that person to enter Heaven. If so, why did He permit the person to clinically die in the first instance? Maybe it is to honor those He bestows the resurrection miracle upon. This being the case, the way of the Lord truly is mysterious for although some of the honorees (those so honored) are saintly, others are admittedly habitual and barely repentant sinners. The resurrection honor, it appears, is conferred (or withheld) indiscriminately. Focusing hindsight on those supposedly raised up through the intervention of the Deity leaves one steeped in ignorance as to how God makes His selections. There is no satisfactory resolution to this manifest mystery.

Accept for a minute that there is no personal God intervening in the affairs of humanity. Suppose, instead, that all such wonders (reincarnations, et al.) are empirically established as natural occurrences. Apparent resurrections then would take place arbitrarily, regardless of the moral or religious convictions of the resurrected. Saints and sinners would have an equal prospect of being revived naturally or spontaneously from apparent death. This fits more snugly with the currently reported instances of human revivification, and solves the enigma of the selection process. The world would witness resurrections randomly, absent divine favoritism.

The most conceivable outcome from the belief that God restores life only to a select few is an increase in the number of believers for the sect proclaiming such restoration. The vain prospect of possible resurrection has won many hopeful converts to the several groups professing that enticing capability. If this was God's intention, then think how much more effective His proselytizing efforts could be if He simply enabled the adherents to His authorized sect to live vigorously and in moderate health until age one hundred. I would join any congregation that provided such readily discernible and verifiable authentication.

Restated: If God's prime reason for resurrecting anyone was to foster converts to a given sect, then the uncertainty, the unpredictability, the ambiguity of His present-day choices disputes against conversion to the claimant sect. If indeed, arbitrary resurrections could ever argue for specific conversion. Once we strip away the convenient shroud of obscurity over the selection process, we are left with a fumbling, inept attempt to harvest followers hardly worthy of a Super Intelligent Being. More likely, what we are witnessing is the tireless endeavors of hyper-ambitious evangelizers to grasp any occurrence that is thought to be beneficial or desirable in life. They then will attribute that occurrence to the 'Hand of God,' for the sole purpose of enlarging their personal (Christian) convert tally.

During the past several years increasing attention has been focused on the unsettling resuscitation of persons declared clinically dead. Several books on the subject have already reached the Best Seller lists and, without doubt, many similar books will be written in a greedy attempt to capitalize on the reading public's credulity regarding this subject. What are the facts in this matter? Do they support the contentions of the authors? Are dead people being returned to life? Before you can make your own determination, you first must be apprised of the difference between clinical death and biological death. {Below, read this non-expert author's description.}

Clinical death (essentially) is the absence of detectible life signs such as breathing, beating of the heart, or brain wave activity. Biological death is the actual deterioration of cell matter in the body. Without exception, all of today's apparent resurrections are of the clinical variety, and none have been of the biological variety. In the former instance, a doctor, or possibly someone with lesser training, examines a seriously ill patient, is unable to detect one or more of the obvious life signs, and therefore declares the person clinically dead. Fortunate for the resurrected however, none of his/her vital organs had begun to decay, for that truly would be irreversible.

These miraculous resurrections, in tandem with healing miracles, can only be accomplished if or when the body remains whole and intact. If the purpose of miracles is to prove God's omnipotence, why doesn't He show us a truly astonishing miracle? Reviving a week-old decaying corpse, or by making whole an amputee, would stifle all dissenters … under a proviso that there was given foreknowledge of the intended miracle. But don't look for such wonders anytime soon. Rephrasing: "God works only in cryptic ways, never openly and unmistakably."

RESURRECTION OF THE BODY

It is ironic that the first recorded belief in a life after death came not from persons who were deprived in this life, but by those who had all the delights of life at their command. I am referring to the Egyptian Pharaohs. That they understood their Heaven to be exactly like our Earth is indisputable. We are all aware of the lengths they went to preserve their earthly body. It is unsettled in my mind whether they believed that resurrection was accessible to all, or was it restricted to the upper classes? What is certain is that only those who could afford the costly process of mummification accessed the method required to be reborn. One wonders, whether the Egyptian belief in resurrection of the body was gained through divine revelation, or was it the result of flawed human deduction? In either case, we do know that none of the mummified Pharaohs, all of whom are still dead, has yet returned to reclaim his throne.

We also know that their heaven was quite literally a return to earth-style living. The Egyptians not only recognized that they would have bodily needs; they studiously labored to ensure that those future needs would be sufficiently provided beforehand. Their post-death happiness would derive not from a lack of want, but from unending gratification of their every want and whim. They sought a heaven with all the desirable trappings and accessories of their former life on Earth. The Egyptian Paradise was called the "Field of Reeds." They believed this was a place where giant wheat plants grew, where no one was ever hungry, and where everyone was happy all the time. In the Field of Reeds everyone would live everlastingly in a renewed life after their mortal death, provided their spirit could survive the perils and pitfalls of the journey from the place of their death, through the underworld, to the "Field of Reeds."

The average man could never aspire to attain such bliss. Or could he? The sons of Abraham (Jacob's descendants), living in Egypt, wondered? Their God, Yahweh, had made them a people of promise. Having read their history one would have reason to question precisely what was that promise. It seems Yahweh was going to establish a worldly kingdom exactly like the material kingdoms they knew, and with the Israelite tribes presumably as the overlords of His earthly kingdom. But many years had passed, and still the promise remained unfulfilled. [Cf. Gen. 15:18] What reward would Yahweh provide for the faithful who died before the attainment of His promise to Abraham? Obviously, to the ancient doctrine formulators, the departed faithful would be raised up from death and be restored in their former bodies to enjoy the fruits of that Promised Land that "flowed with milk and honey." [Ex. 3:8]

There were two critical obstacles to the Hebrews' vision of the glory to come while they were in Egypt. They had neither the finances, nor the political power to have their bodies mummified and stored in a tomb, even less so in a pyramid! They also lacked the resources (and possibly the desire) to build a temple to their God that could compete with the transcendent majesty and stately magnificence of the Egyptian edifices. You might ask here if the Hebrews formulated their belief in a resurrected life after associating with the Egyptians or vice versa. It appears highly unlikely that the ruling Egyptians would even have known of the supernatural beliefs of the common Hebrews.

The argument isn't resolvable either way. What is known with certitude is that the Egyptians invented a form of writing and were the first to write of an earthly return to life after death. The most logical and most plausible deduction is for the Hebrews to have adopted the notion of a renewed life-after-death from the envied Egyptians. Clearly, the Patriarchs sought their 'reward' (i.e., benefits from the gods) here on earth, and they never expected a home in 'heaven' to commence in a divinely resuscitated future existence. Even today, Moses seems completely ignorant of the eternal reward of a life hereafter in 'Heaven' for the Israelite faithful. Moses promised the faithful Hebrews a 'heaven of earth' located in God's 'Promised Land of Canaan.'

It is quite obvious that the Hebrews in Egypt espoused some of the bizarre beliefs of the Egyptians. Quizzically, the Hebrew alphabet (after it evolved) more closely resembled the cuneiform characters of the Middle East instead of the pictograph lettering of the Egyptian hieroglyphs. Notwithstanding this, my supposition is that the Hebrews 'borrowed' the belief in bodily resurrection from ancient Egyptian mythology.

A FINAL LOOK AT RESURRECTIONS

If we can believe the books on resuscitation after death, many who have died clinically (that is, to the extent of man's knowledge and ability to judge such) have been returned to life through the resurrecting prerogatives of Jesus Christ. True, most cases can be classified as an instance wherein a lone doctor declared a person dead because of an absence of detectable life signs. The intelligent skeptic can always recourse to the disclaimer that the physician was mistaken, and that the dead person wasn't truly dead; hence, his resurrection was untrue ... merely an advocate's biased inference. This is undoubtedly the answer in all such cases.

The current interpretation of bodily resurrection is slightly wide of the creedal mark. Resurrection of the body, to the early Church Fathers, referred to the complete restoration of a decayed, corrupt, disembodied skeleton. Today's proponents apply the miracle to whole, intact, uncorrupted human bodies. For discussion purposes we are going to disregard the latter notion and dwell on the former older concept of a final resurrection.

The acceptance of a spiritual Heaven and the belief in a bodily resurrection are contradictory. If Heaven is a spiritual dimension, what would we do with a human body there? Besides, physical resurrection isn't the unmixed blessing that unthinking Christians accept it to be. Consider these questions: Will an infant be resurrected in its infant body, unable to walk, or to talk, or to care for itself? Will cripples remain crippled for all eternity? Consider also, the mentally defective, the emotionally flawed, or those persons otherwise denatured.

Does a person who died of the infirmities of old age return to his aged body? Will our entire body be reassembled? Suppose a cannibal had eaten your hand (after you cast it from you for sinning). Your hand will have been digested by the cannibal and become part of his body. Think! Will racial differences still exist? Will Samson be just as strong, and will Tom Thumb be just as tiny? Will beauty of face and form, or lack thereof, persist? Or will we all be resurrected as clones of Adonis or Venus? Will gender differentiation survive death? How will we be clothed in Heaven? Will we wear clothing in Heaven? Adam and Eve were naked and unashamed while in the Garden of Eden. When we are resurrected bodily in Heaven will that body be clothed or not? Someone give me enlightenment for these queries.

I could expand and expound on the dogma of bodily resurrection *ad nauseam*, but that proposition could still be dashed with a sincere yet insistent "Why?" Why bodily resurrection? The ancient Hebrews would have answered unhesitatingly: 'Because Yahweh's anointed one was coming to establish His earthly kingdom.' We know precisely what they understood this to entail: a palace, a throne, fine clothing, riches, splendor, unqualified contentment, servants (slaves) waiting banquet tables, et al. *In toto*:

unending pleasure for the elite; the favored; the Chosen! Need I reveal exactly who they were expected to be?

What of the remainder of humanity? The unspoken but understood fate of those would be just as it was in the days of old: death to the men; concubinage for the women; and servitude for the children. In contrast, Christians may know of bodily resurrection, but few can tell what objective God has in mind to necessitate reanimating our bodies. If God is going to raise us up in the flesh, then some purpose is to be realized that can't be realized for a spirit. If you are going to inform me that this is another of God's mysteries; please don't! I would sooner suppose physical reanimation was a requirement for me so that I could shovel coal in Hell, and for you so that you can play the harp in Heaven. That, figuratively, would be superficially rational.

A few last questions concerning a bodily resurrection before I move on. A man who wore a beard for half his life, yet was clean shaven the other half, would he be resurrected with or without a beard? Would an amputee have his limb restored? "Of course," you opine. Then what of those who have had sex change operations? Which sex will they be resurrected as? Just how far will God go to restore the complete me? Will all my fingernail clippings, my trimmed hair, and the skin I have sloughed off every day of my life … will all of that be restored to me? Ponder the case of conjoined twins who were never able to be separated; will they be resurrected separate or still conjoined? The whole concept becomes bogged down in imbecilic possibilities when you delve completely through this juvenile, ignorant, superstitious precept of bodily resurrection.

Halt! I can almost hear you shouting at me that I don't understand. You cry out: 'God will resurrect us in a perfect human body.' That isn't what Mark records. His words were: *"It is better for thee to enter into the kingdom of God with one eye."* [Mk. 9:46] Earlier in the same chapter he expresses the same sentiment about a hand or a foot. [Cf. Mk. 9:42, 44] Are these the expressions of Jesus as recorded by Mark, or are they not? Matthew records them as the words of Jesus. [Cf. Mt. 18:8-9] Remember, also, that the resurrected body of Jesus still bore His scars from the crucifixion. [Cf. Jn. 20:27] Yet, today's religious fantasy formulators would raise our reanimated corpse in unblemished perfection.

That sounds fine, but still I ask: "What will that perfect body look like?" If this is a mystery, then I am stymied. God is so full of mysteries that it is a wonder we know anything at all about Him. If it isn't a mystery, then I can assume my resurrected body will either be the same as it was when I died, or it will be different. The question is reasonable. If God does shed some illumination on the afterlife, then someone reading this may answer my queries, provided they satisfy me (via proof, not via piety) that they speak for God.

If we all are revived essentially as we were in this life … then we all will be different. We all will be true individuals with differences that can, and always have, led to comparisons favorable and unfavorable. Consequently, the racial differences will remain, and I find it improbable to envision an entirely harmonious diversified co-existence for all of mankind. If any variance whatever is retained; then that variance will ultimately result in ethnic strife, barring only a personality alteration for the entirety of humanity. Tampering with individual personalities, regardless of motive, would seem to be just as amoral in Heaven, as it is deemed here on Earth.

Considering the opposite case presents problems as well. If we are all cloned to some perfect human stereotype, whose stereotype will it be? Will God clone us to be giants? Giants supposedly roamed the Earth in the days of Genesis. If we all looked alike would we be numbered to tell us apart? Would there be any need to tell us apart? Cloning is irrational.

From any perspective we view it, resurrection, whether spiritual or physical, poses insuperable impediments. It is much easier now for me to empathize with the early Christian theologians when they resorted to divine mysteries to cover their own lack of understanding of the interrelationship of multifaceted, incongruous beliefs (actually, religious imaginings).

The Bible reveals there will be a resurrection, so unquestionably there will be. The only dilemma not adequately resolved yet is: "Will our resurrection be spiritual, or will it be physical?" Here, once again, we have two disparate tenets that were conceived at different times, to serve different purposes, by different peoples, bizarrely lumped together. Metaphorically: A blind seeing-eye dog! It doesn't have to make sense; it is an incontestable article of faith.

Shortly, we will consider why the disappointed Christians invented a spiritual Heaven. First we will consider why the parochial early Hebrews could so readily conceive of an earthly kingdom. The early Hebrew world consisted of Egypt, the eastern Mediterranean Lands, and the Tigris-Euphrates valley communities. Both Babylon and Thebes served as a model for the Hebrew's conception of what Yahweh's earthly future capital should look like. Only this time, it would be the Hebrews who would be the masters. During the period of the messianic theorem's formulation, the strongest state, therefore the ruling state, was always the one that could unite or conquer the greatest number of city states. The grand plan of messianism was to consolidate all of Yahweh's chosen (Israelite/Hebrew) so that they could dominate their neighbors to a greater extent than even had David, their greatest king.

After the anticipated Messiah had established His new material kingdom with Jerusalem as its capital, the already deceased faithful would be raised up to enjoy this physical realm. If you can see a close parallel between their beliefs and that of the Pharaohs, I can too. One or the other had to have borrowed from an earlier theorist's rebirth speculations.

A spiritual kingdom was postulated by the confused Christians to account for the failed appearance of a physical messianic kingdom. The idea was fostered to placate the disillusionment of the second generation converts who, by then, were shaken with doubts about the Second Coming. The original teaching preached that many of those alive to hear the original disciples preach would not experience death before the return of the Savior. [Cf. Mk. 8:39; Mk. 13:30 & 1 Thes. 4:14-16] After a hundred years, many would naturally become apprehensive. Surely, after one hundred and fifty years the apprehension turned to bafflement and anyone could predict a spate of rampant skepticism, even disbelief, before very much longer.

There must have occurred a period of retrospection when the dwindling number of believers gathered and expressed their doubts communally. It was during this period, I believe, that the impetus to copy down the oral traditions and to collate those written manuscripts reached its culmination. Doubtless, this is how the New Testament originated.

Pro-Biblists marvel at the similarity of some of the New Testament stories. I marvel at the dissimilarity. If God inspired every word, there shouldn't be any disparity whatsoever. None of the original New Testament writings exist, and maybe for a cogent reason. If Jesus was returning within a lifetime, what need was there for committing to writing all the things that He did or said? 'None! When it was realized rather late that the first Christians were all dead, converts hastily began to gather whatever data they could find pertaining to the life of Jesus. The four Gospels are the result of their collection and collation endeavors.

However, the four Gospels simply don't read as though they are first-hand reports. None of the mundane, everyday actions of people are ever mentioned. Every act, every word, every setting, has meaning and import. The disciples only speak when they can provide Jesus with a lead-in to a sage parable, or a stirring rejoinder.

The wedding feast at Cana is a typical example of what I am alluding to when I write that the mundane is missing. The only incident of note, hence recorded, is the miraculous transformation of water into wine. [Cf. Jn. 2:1-11] Didn't Jesus have even a moment of fun there? Didn't Jesus toast the couple with wine? Did He dance with the bride? Typically, weren't there any bawdy remarks made, as at most weddings? Did Jesus laugh? Did Jesus ever laugh? Is there a single, intentional incidence of humor reported anywhere in the Bible? There are none that I can find. The Christian Bible ranks right up there with the dourest book ever written. The "Good Book" is utterly and altogether humorless.

ISAIAH ON RESURRECTION

[Isaiah 26:19-21] *"Thy dead men shall live; together with my dead body shall they arise. Awake and sing, ye that dwell in dust: for thy dew is as the dew of herbs, and the earth shall cast out the dead. Come, my people, enter thou into thy chambers, and shut thy doors about thee: hide thyself as it were for a little moment, until the indignation be overpast. For behold, the Lord cometh out of his place to punish the inhabitants of the earth for their iniquity: the earth also shall disclose her blood, and shall no more cover her slain."* {King James Version}

[Isaiah 26:19-21] *"Those of our people who have died will live again! Their bodies will come back to life. All those sleeping in their graves will wake up and sing for joy. As the sparkling dew refreshes the earth, so the Lord will revive those who have long been dead. Go into your houses, my people, and shut the door behind you. Hide yourselves for a little while until God's anger is over. The Lord is coming from his heavenly dwelling place to punish the people of the earth for their sins. The murders that were secretly committed on the earth will be revealed, and the ground will no longer hide those who have been killed."* {Good News Bible – Catholic Study Edition}

Isaiah lived approximately 2,700 years ago. He said that 'his people' need only hide from the Lord's anger for a "little while" longer. Just how long is "a little while"? Then, "our people ... will live again." You don't suppose that Isaiah meant that only Hebrews would be resurrected? Who were "the people of the earth" who would be punished "for their sins"?

No one can answer the above questions. Do not accept any person who asserts that he or she can answer those queries informatively and flawlessly. The original author of those verses personally was ignorant of the answers to his own queries. How, then, can anyone else provide an accurate resolution to those evermore unanswerable posers?

THE SPIRITUAL WORLD — IS IT REAL?

Can anything that happens in the spirit world be thought of as real? What is real? Are fairies real? Are gnomes real? Are ogres real? Are the more than one hundred other mythical beings listed in a book titled "The Impossible People" written by Georgess McHargue, real? 'No,' you answer. Only that which supports the Christian beliefs and imaginings is real, even though these can never be proved either. If you imagine that a thing exists, then it must exist.

All superstition is make-believe, and it can be ridiculed safely unless it is religious superstition. Religious superstition is to be believed on faith. Faith can verify the impossible. No supernatural 'fact' has ever been substantiated. If you disagree with the last statement, I have an even more crucial question that I will ask. "If any single supernatural event can be verified, why can't they all be verified?" Expanded: If God chooses to allow one supernatural event to be checked, it can only be to convince a skeptic. Believers don't ask for verification. They must and do accept everything the Deity's advocates profess on groundless trust or on boundless faith.

Surely, God knows that proof of a supernatural event only needs to be shown to non-believers. Well, here is a news flash: "Today there are a greater number of doubters, even a greater percentage number of doubters, than have ever existed on Earth prior to the advent of Christianity." We ask, we beseech, and we even implore the Creator of the Cosmos to give us some proof … to give us some sign. I am aware that the Bible reads *"no sign will be given this generation,"* but that was many generations ago. [Mk. 8:12] [Cf. Mt, 12:39; 16:4 & Lu. 11:29] The Bible doesn't state that no sign will ever be given again. Are we ever to have a sign? No generation in history ever needed a sign, a proof, a confirming action from the Almighty more than this generation does. Why is the proof of God's existence being withheld from this generation?

St. Thomas the Apostle was granted his wish to see, to touch, and to place his fingers into the wounds of the resurrected Jesus. Why not me? Being an Apostle, he was already more abundantly graced than me. If a person who traveled with, and lived with, who was an eyewitness to all the wonders, who saw the miracles, who heard the assertion that Jesus was the incarnate Son of God; if he had doubts, how can I be castigated for my disbelief? Does God love me less? 'Provably so, for I have never been blest via any of God's marvels. I am willing to believe, but I need some sliver of evidence that I can personally verify. Don't offer me another's testimony, for that leads back to my previous (prevalent) question: "Does God love me less?"

The New Testament cautions us to beware of bogus teachers and anti-Christs. To me, all religion is sham testimony. Reading the Epistles I am perplexed by a suspiciously recurrent admonishment. In each instance, the faithful are warned to guard themselves against false teachings. Somehow this seemed odd to me. How could it happen so soon after the Ascension that heresy and unorthodoxy waxed competitively? We can only blame the Devil, but that presupposes that Satan held power even over the Apostles. They were infused with the Holy Spirit, and preached under His inspiration, yet their message was subverted (rather easily we can surmise) by faux teachers inspired by Satan. [Cf. 2 Pet. 2:1-3; 1 Jn. 2:18; 1 Jn. 4:1-6;

2 Jn. 1:7 & Tit. 1:10-11] If that was true in the time of the Apostles, what chance do we have today to discern the genuine message of the Apostles versus that of loquacious heretics? None! Peculiarly, since one of Paul's Epistles cautions us to be wary of "false Apostles." [Cf. 2 Cor. 11:13-15]

The Lord is reported to have said: *"Blessed are they who haven't seen, yet have believed."* [Jn. 20:29] Down through the Christian era there has been no lack of persons who have believed that which they couldn't see. Their numbers defy counting. But what has been the result of their unsubstantiated beliefs? The result has been an unmanageable explosion of Christian denominations; many legitimizing themselves with the above quote. If that quote were declared apocryphal and expunged from the Bible, religious charlatans would have a more complicated time with their deceptions. Jesus, in His omniscience, knew that this factionalism would occur. He either condones a plethora of Christian sects, or He is powerless to prevent their formations. Which one of those "either" — "or" options explains the present reality?

Faith without foundation, and belief in the unbelievable, are the very reasons we are encumbered by so many denominations. Christianity is splintered many times over precisely because so many feckless individuals believed utter nonsense, or had unquestioning faith in foolish pronouncements. The first tenet of religious indoctrination is "Shun the sensible." Why is this so when the only biological trait we have developed more extensively than the animals is intelligence? My reflections advise that if a proposition disturbs your sense of logic, it may be wrong. If it assaults your credence, then chances are it is wrong. If it outrages your intelligence, then surely, it is a damnable lie. You should denounce it outright.

My attitude toward religion has progressed along just such scenarios. In my earliest recollections of religion, I have always been unsettled by pious pontifications of religiosity. Too many of its basic propositions bordered on the incredible. Yet, early indoctrination caused me to fear the consequences of disbelieving the teachings of my faith. I was bursting with unresolved questions, but I knew intuitively that merely asking those questions would guarantee me serious difficulties with my religious overseers. God loved us, but only so long as we unfailingly obeyed the teachings of His surrogates … the priests and the nuns. In honesty, early on the priests affected my life only tangentially. But the nuns were another matter altogether.

The Nuns not only hawked every move we school children made, but more, (Acting in God's stead?) they were quick to intervene when they detected anything less than total obedience. Not only that, but more portentously, they intimated rather unambiguously that if they couldn't enforce their will on us, a priest would be summoned, and some horribly unimaginable fate would befall us. I was reasonably brave with the Nuns, but frankly, I never initiated a confrontation with a priest until my High School days.

This writing isn't an autobiography, so I will resist the temptation to make it become that. The behavior and the attitude of the Nuns who taught me proved to be no holier, no more intelligent, no more uplifting than that of the other adults in my life. Secretly, I hated two of the Nuns who taught me, yet concurrently, the person I loved most aside from my family, was also a Nun. Her worthiness of my love, however, didn't emanate from her religiosity; rather, it came from her warmth, her affection for us children, and her unflagging commitment to teaching us both academically and morally. {Sister Madeline Louise, S.S.J.} The two Nuns I despised had few of her admirable traits. Most of the Nuns I knew personally were admirable, as were the priests.

My observations confirmed the unfathomable fact that all too many adults who frequented church weren't "nice" people. Alternately: that just as numerous non-churchgoers were decent, loving individuals. If God was watching (at that time I had no doubt that He was), and if He blessed those who attended Mass, then how could my conclusions be correct? Quite the opposite should have been the actuality. Resignedly, I conceded that it wasn't. My heart wished to believe, but my mind remained ever skeptical.

Then, inspirationally, the resolution came to me: God was biding His time. Soon, when it was propitious for God, all untoward matters would be righted. The thought was comforting, and I am inclined to reflect that we have all entertained similar delusory rationalizations. Daily, I observe more injustice than justice. Now I am convinced that the concept of justice is just as illusory as is the concept of Heaven.

From my own observations, I have noted that persons known to attend revivals, rallies, rebirths, and the like, are habitual attendees at every religious pageant. They flit from crusade to crusade and give testimony equally to all. One day they profess one belief and the next day they profess another. In this manner evangelizers have one of their many ego cravings requited. Everyone involved departs from the spiritual spectacle with a feeling of having accomplished something uplifting. This increases their self-esteem and temporarily quiets that subliminal hyperphysical (religious) compulsion that resides within all of us.

Well, not everyone is relieved thus. It saddens me to witness this: but some persons accept literally every pious pronouncement of the preacher. They come away from religious rallies with a feeling that they are exactly what the preacher declares that they are, that is, 'miserable sinners unworthy of the pristine love that God bestows on them.' It is true that their numbers are few, but their plight is nonetheless lamentable. You see, these few don't have that arrogant egotism that would convince them they are a worthy recruit for God to bring into His fold. They leave these religious festivals bewildered. Why would an all-knowing Deity love them? Surely He knows their doubts; He knows their secret thoughts; He knows that when the next opportunity to sin presents itself, they probably will succumb. Why would God ever forgive those who can't forgive themselves? The truly sincere 'godly' are a troubled lot indeed. It is they whom I foremost wish to relieve of their recurring torment.

But what of the prideful preponderance who leave the revival with swollen chests, secure in the knowledge that they are saved? Everyone else may be perched on a ledge teetering to this side or to that side. But the religiously confident know that their feet are firmly set on the stairway to Paradise. Whenever they choose, they can ascend into Heaven and commune with their near peer. i.e., God Himself. They see themselves resting snugly on the breast of Jesus. Of course, Jesus has His arms protectively around His admired companion. Others might profess Jesus and be accepted, but these individuals consider themselves "close family." God has no choice but to adore them. They aren't required to live by a rigid set of rules; they just live as it pleases their fancy, dispensing their favors to those who recognize and honor their elevated human status as intimates of God Himself.

But, Beware! They will vilify anyone brash enough to question their exalted stature. They rush out into the world of religious instruction and make bold pronouncements that they arrogantly ascribe to the Mind of God. They are unbending in their views concerning the morality or amorality of every human action. Their thoughts accurately reflect the thoughts of the Creator. They are inerrant in their affirmations.

Thank goodness these people have been removed from positions of authority in Western cultures and can no longer enforce their will on anyone. The Inquisition would seem a feeble attempt compared with the excesses today's technology could provide to them. The potential danger these people represent stems from their unmitigated belief that they are pontificating with God's authorization; thence, there can be no appeal of their 'divinely instructed' decisions (via the New Testament). This may be tolerable for a short while if there factually was a personal Deity; and if He did openly and invariably intervene in all practical or theological affairs. There isn't; and He doesn't!

CHAPTER 6
Two Israelites

MOSES, THE DELIVERER

A solitary man is seldom able to appreciably alter the evolution of history. Nonetheless, whenever history has been drastically altered, the cause invariably has been one irrepressible individual. Moses, the founder of Judaism, was just such a man. He not only altered the history of the Jewish people, but indirectly, the broad history of humanity. (Perhaps, in perpetuity?)

Moses lived during the Israelite sojourn in Egypt. Although raised as an Egyptian nobleman (aristocrat), Moses never forsook his humble Hebrew ancestry. [Cf. Ex. 2:1-10] In early adulthood Moses formulated a plan to unite all those who acknowledged Abraham as their ultimate forefather. The tribal divisions were already firmly set, a fact that militated against Moses' plan. If he was to be accepted as the Hebrew leader, he would need a method of uniting the tribes under his stewardship. He chose the twin impetus of ethnicity and religion. He then provided a final clincher by offering them a homeland of their own where they alone would rule; namely, the lands promised to Abraham that flowed with milk and honey. In order to ensure their submission to his generalship he revived the ancient cult of Yahweh, the ascribed personal God of their common ancestor, Abraham. [Cf. Gen. Chaps. 12 through 25]

Of course, Moses' plan wasn't without obstacles. For one, Moses realized that Yahweh couldn't compete successfully with the ensconced divinities of Egypt. In Egypt, proof of Yahweh's impotence was everywhere. In those days, the power of a Deity was determined in the present. If a person, or a group of persons, held power and position in their society, this proved their god's affection for them. If anything, the reverse was doubly true. Moses correctly saw that the Hebrews would never ascend to dominant positions as long as they remained in Egypt. The decision to move his people to the 'Promised Land' was thereby self-imposed on Moses.

There is strong inferential evidence that the peoples Moses sought to lead had forgotten Yahweh as completely as He discernibly had forgotten them. The protracted existence of the twelve tribal divisions, rather than a sense of 'one people,' is indicative of the disparity (if not the disunity) of those Moses asked to follow him. The actions of that diverse gathering during the Exodus and later (after settlement in the "Promised Land"), demonstrates just how disparate each tribe was. Moses needed a strong bond to bind these divided Semites together. He had witnessed the binding power of religion in Egypt and chose this as his method of uniting the Hebrew tribes. The ancient God of the Patriarchs would guide "His" Semites to the land Yahweh had promised to Abraham and his descendants. [Cf. Ex. 13:21-22ff]

The theoretical considerations resolved, only theological determinations remained. If the people were to worship Yahweh, that God must prove Himself more potent, less vulnerable, indeed, wholly invincible in the looming battle with the Egyptian gods. Yet, how do gods fight with one another? 'Certainly not with spear, sword, or bow & arrow. Being creatures of man's imagination, gods are diminished whenever they are depicted in physical terms. Factually, Moses fancied Yahweh as a super Human Being, rather than as a Superhuman Being. The dilemma arose because the Egyptians pictured their gods with separate spheres of responsibility, consequently one god could fail his responsibilities without pulling down the rest of the Egyptian pantheon. Moses resolved the dilemma shrewdly. He took his single Deity and endowed Him with more powers than the combined Egyptian pantheon possessed. As was universal in those days, his chosen Deity owed exclusive allegiance to the twelve Hebrew tribes, not to humanity as a whole, and certainly not to the Egyptians.

Incidentally, Moses' postulation of one supreme God, instead of a plethora of minor gods, wasn't a completely original concept. For a transient period, the Egyptian Pharaoh, Amenhotep IV (r. 1375-1358 BC), attempted to guide the Egyptians in the worship of the greatest god, Aten, the "Sun God," represented by a golden solar disk. Amenhotep changed his ruling name to Akhenaten and moved his capitol out of Thebes. He encountered fanatically passionate resistance however, from the priests of the more ancient cult of the gods of his domain: Amun, Ra (Re), Osiris, Isis, et al. Akhenaten's attempt to impose his generally monotheistic views on his subjects was terminated shortly after his death. Polytheism was officially restored during the reign of Akhenaten's son and successor, Tutankhamun. (Originally Tutankhaten)

Akhenaten's Empire extended over much of the Middle East, including all of what later became the Hebrew's Promised Land, Knowing this, we can surmise that both the Hebrews living inside Egypt and those within its Empire would have been cognizant of Pharaoh's 'One Chief God' postulation. Moses, adopted by Pharaoh's daughter, educated and reared in the royal palace, surely knew of this interlude that had occurred less than a hundred years previous.

Moses mulled over his deity creation; there was something missing. He had no visible means of portraying his new God. If Yahweh was more powerful than a crocodile, faster than an eagle, stronger than a lion, brighter than the 'Sun God,' and wiser than mankind, then how should He be depicted? No earthly form would suffice, and most of the exotic combinations already had been fashioned by the enterprising Egyptians. Again, Moses resolved the issue through the only method possible. His God would have no perceptible physiognomy; Yahweh was un-viewable. Meaning, if a human being were to see Yahweh's visage, that human would die instantly; therefore Yahweh ceaselessly hid His countenance from mankind. This relieved Moses of the impossible task of competing with the Egyptian image makers. They were far superior in that endeavor, and Moses sagely recognized this.

But Moses couldn't completely escape from a human conception of the Deity. His God talked directly with Moses. Yahweh personally scribed the Ten Commandments; therefore He must have had a hand. He indeed had a face, because Moses had looked upon it. But beware! Only Moses could view the face of God (after singular dispensation). Yahweh was so majestically splendiferous in person that any human who beheld Him expired frightfully at the merest glance. So, although the God of Moses (Yahweh) was invisible to the masses, He did have some definable physical features. In Genesis we read that God created man in His own image, leading to the assumption that although God was a spirit, that spirit had form, and the form corresponded visually to the physical form of mankind. [Cf. Gen. 1:26-27 & 5:1]

MOSES MIMICS HAMMURABI

As did all religious leaders before him, Moses was cognizant that belief alone isn't enough to ensure the beneficence of the Deity, nor for a practical matter, occasion the subservience of the adherents to His embryonic religion. Actions often do speak louder than words. Just as human behavior could influence the way a worldly king would react toward his subjects: so too, the heavenly king could be influenced by mankind's worship behavior, Moses reasoned.

Because of the disunity of his hoped-for following, Moses needed a set of rules governing their behavior, and controlling their comportment within and between the disparate tribes. The last four books of the Pentateuch (Exodus, Leviticus, Numbers, & Deuteronomy) are partially a record of these rules. What few persons realize is that the regulations of Moses only applied within the Hebrew community. Those peoples outside of Yahweh's Covenant were excluded from the protections of Moses' ordinances. If one Hebrew murdered another Hebrew, that was a serious crime under Mosaic Law. However, if a Hebrew murdered a non-Hebrew, he putatively was acting with inferred consent/absolution from Yahweh via Moses, hence he was blameless.

Moses was exacting with most of his statutes, imposing precise penances or punishments for specific violations. Most of these are culturally outmoded today. But six general principles survive intact: The six (of a total of ten, beginning with "Honor Thy Father and Thy Mother") that Yahweh is alleged to have etched into stone with His finger. We will discuss them next, just after a few words about the personality of the Supreme God of Moses. Although Yahweh suffered none of the human frailties, He seemed to possess all the human emotions: love-hate; charity-envy; forgiveness-vengeance; but above all, He possessed a super vanity. An offense to Yahweh's pride was perilous indeed.

The First Commandment clearly shows us which human misdeed was paramount in the eyes of the Supreme Being. (Or was it in the mind of Moses?) Murder, fornication, theft, lying and coveting; these were all subordinate to the First Commandment. Never should Yahweh's supremacy be challenged. Somewhat shortened the first precept reads thus: *"I, the Lord, am your God … you shall not have other gods but Me."* {Rephrased: *'You shall not elevate other gods over Me.'*} Later, it adds: *"I, the Lord your God, am a jealous God inflicting punishment for their father's wickedness on the children of those who hate Me, down to the third and fourth generation."* [Ex. 20:1-5] Isn't it curious that the most grievous sin you could commit against an earthly king also was to consider another king superior to him? How very human the God Yahweh seems when viewed through the eyes of the ancient Hebrews. His wrath could be expected on the good, the bad, even the unborn of later generations when His ego was injured.

Analyzing the wording of the first commandment I am struck by a curious, yet unavoidable, inference. Yahweh's words (discounting that the words are not exclusively from Moses) seem to indicate that there is more than one God. Yahweh appears to be advising the Hebrews that He, and He alone, is their God. This coincides aptly with the earliest Hebrew teaching that although there were many gods extant, only the God Yahweh chose this particular Semite branch (Abraham's descendants) as His very own favorites. Yahweh would be protective and provident toward the Hebrews, if they, in return, would revere and serve only Him.

If we look closely, Yahweh tacitly admits that other deities exist. His stricture states that the Hebrews shall not place any of these other gods before Him, i.e., subordinate His position of preeminence. Genesis uses the plural form of the word 'God' when describing the creation. "In the beginning Elohim (literally, 'the Gods') created the heavens and the earth." Only in Deuteronomy and Isaiah have I found the declaration that "The Lord" is the only God. *"I am the Lord, there is none else; there is no god beside me."* [Deut. 4:35, 39; 32:39 & Isa. 45:5-6; 44:8; 46:9]

In Genesis, Chapter 1, all words rendered as "God," grammatically should be rendered as "Gods." ('Elohim' is the plural of 'Eloi') After Adam ate from the Tree of Knowledge, God remarked, *"Indeed, the man has become as one of* us.*"* [Gen. 3:22] Again we find the plural form. There are several other instances of "God" (Eloi) speaking to fellow gods. An example: God speaks after observing the Tower of Babel, *"Let* us *go down and mix up their language."* [Gen. 11:7] {Author's underline added twice in this paragraph}

In Chapter 2, one notes a significant change. The Deity is now referred to as the "Lord God." [Gen. 2:4, et al.] The pertinence of this appellation is that the God referred to by this title is 'Lord' over all other gods. The ancient author perceptively believed in the supremacy of one God over the other 'gods.' This "Lord God" walked in the Garden of Eden. He bestowed protection to Cain against the other peoples of the world (inferentially created by someone other than Himself). *"If anyone kills Cain, Cain shall be avenged sevenfold. So the Lord put a mark on Cain."* [Gen. 4:15] What are we to make of this wording? Cain and Abel were the "first born" of Adam and Eve. Most pro-Biblists would insist that the translators have made a mistake, but this can be disproved. The best translations available read essentially as presented above.

Also, you must remember that the Bible is infallible. God inspired the Bible. Accordingly, if God indicates that more than one Deity exists, then irrefutably they do. So if you choose to disregard these verses in the Bible, then you open a door for everyone else to exit through also. They can choose the verses of the Bible that they wish to reinterpret, or even to disregard.

Today, the First Commandment is obsolete. Christianity suffers not from competition with other gods, but from a growing lack of belief in any deity. God may not be dead already, but He is mortally wounded with terminal disbelief. His case requires intensive care if He is to survive this malady. Revivalists, crusaders, and their pious brethren have accurately diagnosed His illness. They are feverishly trying their best to apply a resuscitating cure.

Another Twentieth Century phenomenon that portends no gain for Christianity is the growing popularity of Eastern, self-realization, self-glorification, godless religions. (If such can accurately be classified as religions?) By their doctrines, all men are a rebirth of the Creative Force of the Universe. This invisible Force (God) dwells within every one of us;

therefore, we are all linear descendants of the universal Godhead. How grand! I never knew I had such a resplendent heritage.

THE GRANDFATHER OF MOSES

Exodus informs us that Moses was the son of Amram, the son of Kohath (aka Caath). Kohath, Merari and Gershon were the sons of Levi, the founder of the tribe of Levites. [Cf. Ex. 6:16] This is a biblical fact. But this fact (?) clashes with other biblical 'facts.' Below are the conflicting facts. *"On the first day of the second month of the second year after the people of Israel left Egypt, the Lord spoke to Moses ...'You and Aaron are to take a census of the people of Israel by clans and families. List the names of all the men twenty years old or older who are fit for military service.'"* [Num. 1:1-3] {Why would God need a census?}

The tribe of Levites had three divisions corresponding to the three sons of Levi. The census records that the sub-clan of Gershon had 7,500 males, the sub-clan of Kohath had 8,600 males, and the sub-clan of Merari had 6,200 males. [Cf. Num. 3:21-34] Imagine that: Kohath with all those descendants, not counting the females. Concede that Kohath did live for 133 years. [Cf. Ex. 6:18] Concede that Kohath's eldest son, Amram lived for 137 years. [Cf. Ex. 6:20] Still, the Bible records that Kohath had only four sons and that his son Amram had only two sons (Moses & Aaron). Where did all the remaining 8,594 male descendants of the sub-clan of Kohath come from?

You can work on the mathematics and discover for yourself the absurdity of these biblical "truths." What I discover here is just more proof that the Bible contains obvious falsehoods. If Kohath was the son of Levi, then Moses wasn't his grandson. If Moses was his grandson, then Kohath was many generations removed from Levi. The final conclusion one must draw from this example is that the Bible is intrinsically flawed; this is proof that it wasn't dictated by an omniscient (all-knowing) Deity. Factually, the Bible is completely man-made. The evidence is incontrovertible. The evidence is conclusive. This invalidating evidence derives from the Bible itself.

THE EXODUS

Yahweh's 'justice' is so twisted and unpredictable that it can't properly be termed justice. The word whimsy better fits the following two incidents (and much else also), i.e., if we are to maintain the exclusive 'Actions of God' proposition. An intelligent appraisal of the Old Testament should conclude that if the events recorded therein reasonably did occur, then the miraculous was misapplied, and the mysterious was misconstrued as miraculous.

How can the attribution of the miraculous be misapplied? It would be impossible to satisfactorily explain every miracle without firsthand information of all the circumstances accompanying that miracle. All we have to scrutinize these past wonders are accounts written by persons who wanted to believe in the miracles. Believers can never be considered impartial observers, and they can rarely be relied upon to supply patently consistent or even overtly conflicting evidence. Yet, surprisingly enough, some of the bible marvels can be explained with only the information available in the biblical texts viewed in the light of today's knowledge.

Here are two such: During the early days of the Exodus, the Hebrews grumbled that they had no meat to eat, and that author tells us that Yahweh sent quail for them to eat. [Cf. Num. 11:31 & Ex. 16:13] Yet, I have read elsewhere that formerly there was a twice yearly migration of quail, once south and once north to return, over the Sinai regions. On the southbound trip, the quail are so exhausted that they fly only a few feet above the ground and even wearily tumble down where they can easily be captured. On the return flight, the quail rest in the Sinai for the arduous flight back across the Mediterranean. To us, fowl migrations are a natural event. To the Egyptian-born Hebrews that migratory flight was God sent, hence, a provident miracle.

In the notes on page one hundred of the Confraternity Edition of the Catholic Family Edition of the Holy Bible, even the 'manna from heaven' is explained naturally. Confer with the note for Exodus, Chapter 16, verse 4. It concludes, "Perhaps it was similar to a natural substance that is still found in small quantities on the Sinai Peninsula." Elsewhere, I have read that certain insects pierce the skin of a plant that causes a sweet liquid discharge that dries into small flakes. Was this the Divine "manna"? Probably so!

The crumbling of the walls of Jericho is similarly explicable when a person is forearmed with today's knowledge of seismic physics. Joshua had forty thousand armed troops that he marched daily around the besieged city of Jericho. It is a well-established fact that soldiers tramping in cadence can create disastrous vibrations. Add to that the constant blowing of rams' horns by the priests, and you can imagine the din. Then surpass that on the final day when the entire assemblage, numbering many thousands, perhaps up to six hundred thousand (Cf. Ex. 12:37), marching defiantly around the beleaguered fortress city seven consecutive times. Then culminate that earth-vibrating march with a thunderous shout in unison by every available soul and it is small wonder that the then six-hundred-year-old walls of Jericho fell. Only God's intervention could have prevented the walls from toppling. Unfortunate for that city, God (Yahweh) was supporting and aiding the Israelite attackers, not the inhabitants of Jericho, who were likewise His created creatures.

PARTING THE RED SEA

The Hebrew Exodus from Egypt and the miraculous parting of the Red Sea are considerably diminished when we study the internal evidence provided. The Hebrews lived in Goshen, in the Nile delta area of northern Egypt. It is highly unlikely that they ever came near the Red Sea when exiting Egypt and entering the Sinai desert at the start of the Exodus. Where they did cross (arguably) was the "Sea of Reeds," a section of the Bitter Lakes, one of many areas in the wilderness that is subject to periodic flooding or extreme drought. These factors shed further illumination on God's 'parting of the waters' miracle reputed today to be the Red Sea. [Cf. Ex. Chap. 14]

Re-constructed, the reality appears to be: The Hebrews left Egypt with Pharaoh's permission for three days to worship and propitiate Yahweh. The six hundred thousand (?) men on foot, "not counting children along with livestock and very numerous flocks and herds," departed from Rameses toward Socchoth and thence the distance to the Sea of Reeds

(Yam Suph) area. [Cf. Ex. 13:18] At the moment of their arrival, this tract was being swept by a strong desert dry east wind blowing throughout the night that turned the Sea of Reeds into dry land. The Hebrews crossed safely. In the interim, the Egyptians, some distance behind (3 days behind — Cf. Ex. 3:18; 5:3; 8:27), had camped for the night. *"Just before dawn the Lord looked down from the pillar of fire and cloud at the Egyptian army and threw them into a panic. He made the wheels of their chariots get stuck."* [Cf. Ex. 14:20-25]

What was this fiery cloud? Obviously, it was a severe thunderstorm. What clogged the chariot wheels? The answer: Mud, formed by the sudden torrential rains. Why did they panic? Outnumbered more than 500 to 1 and being unable to maneuver their chariots in a drowning rain is reason enough for judicious men to panic. The miracle can thus be explained, but a serious discrepancy remains. Historians are troubled over the lack of confirming evidence of the Exodus in Egyptian records. The Egyptians were prolific, almost persnickety, record keepers. If, as the Bible states, *"six hundred finest* (chariots) *commanded by their officers"* had indeed perished in the Sea of Reeds, why wasn't there a record of this military debacle? [Cf. Ex. 14:7] By compensated comparison, such an event would rank with the most devastating defeats in history. Yet, the Egyptian chroniclers remained inexplicably silent.

The ancient miracles aren't looked upon as proof of the reality of God by religious apologists of today. All too often, they are logical embarrassments. Every modern sect professes God-given ability to perform miracles. To accept parts of the Bible as a moral guide can be profitable. However, we must exercise prudence when making our selections. There are events described in the Bible that are unfit for children, or youths, and even episodes that adults may/will find morally offensive. Some of those are discussed in Chapter 7 of this book. Frankly, I was hesitant to include them lest someone charge that I invented them. Also, the revulsion engendered by these episodes could easily be transferred to this composition through associative proximity. (Blame the messenger for the message!)

Historically, the Bible has caused at least as much harm as it has bestowed benefits. The scope and gravity of the harm perpetrated by over-zealous, dogmatic, and intransigent proponents of the Bible could only be known in its totality by an Omniscient Being. And, if He knew, He should have done something to rectify or ameliorate the cause; 'that cause being a perverse, obdurate (mis)interpretation of the Bible.

The fact that nothing inspired by the Holy Spirit has been added to the Bible for two thousand years proves one of two things. First, the Bible is complete and needs no additions. (This is demonstrably untrue) Second, God the Third is still speaking to His prophets, but no one will listen. (This is specious)

THE GOLDEN CALF

Are there any biblical examples of Yahweh's bewildering application of uneven punishment for sin? Yes, there are many. This short example illustrates one of His most egregious. *"Elisha left Jericho to go to Bethel, and on the way some boys came out of a town and made fun of him. 'Get out of here, baldy!' they shouted. Elisha turned around, glared at them, and cursed them in the name of the Lord. Then two she-bears came out of the woods and tore forty-two of the boys to pieces. Elisha went on to Mount Carmel and later returned to Samaria."* [2 Ki. 2:23-25] Just punishment for the 'crime' of calling a man "Baldy" could never, in any society, or in any age, warrant being torn to pieces by ferocious bears. Yet, in God's own words (the Bible) we are informed that Yahweh caused this to happen to forty-two disrespectful boys!"

Additionally, the tale of the golden ox calf depicts this same divine injustice propensity unequivocally. Keep in mind, the prime offender in that brazen idolatry was Aaron. Read now of Aaron, who was to be appointed the future and first High Priest of Yahweh.

"When the people became aware of Moses' delay in coming down from the mountain, they gathered around Aaron and said to him, 'Come, make us a god who will be our leader; as for the man Moses who brought us out of the land of Egypt, we do not know what has happened to him.' Aaron replied, 'Have your wives and sons and daughters take off the golden earrings they are wearing, and bring them to me.' So all the people took off their earrings and brought them to Aaron, who accepted their offerings and working this gold with a graving tool, fashioned a calf.

"Then they cried out, 'This is your God, O Israel, who brought you out of the land of Egypt.' On seeing this, Aaron built an altar before the calf and proclaimed, 'Tomorrow is the feast of the Lord.' Early the next day the people offered holocausts and sat down to eat and drink, and rose up to revel." [Ex. 32:1-6]

Who is the most culpable person in this idolatry? Aaron, in full command in the absence of Moses, should have borne full responsibility for the actions of the people he directed. Aaron conceived the idea of a golden idol. Aaron, himself, sculpted the form of a calf. Aaron, personally, built an altar to this idol of a god. It was Aaron who proclaimed the morrow as a feast day to the golden calf. The whereabouts of (sister) Miriam is unrecorded in this incident.

Moses returning found the Israelites reveling riotously and worshipping that golden calf. Moses flung the Commandment tablets to the ground shattering them and ordered the Levites to slay every one of three thousand idolaters. [Cf. Ex. 32:26-28]

Acting through Moses and his Levite brethren, God caused the death of three thousand idolatrous Israelites. But, did Moses slay his brother for his part in violating the First and Second Commandments? Were Aaron's sons among the idolaters? Aaron not only escaped the fate of the three thousand lesser idolaters; astonishingly, he is shortly afterward rewarded by Yahweh through his appointment to the newly created post of High Priest. Only the High Priest could enter the inner recesses of the Ark of the Covenant tent. In addition, the Levites, who were supported by tithes from the other eleven tribes, were required to pay Aaron and his progeny a tenth of all that they received: a hefty stipend in any age! [Cf. Num. 18:25-30]

Was Aaron so rewarded because he found favor with Yahweh, or because he was brother to the leader, Moses? The commandments also state that the offspring of violators, down to the third or fourth generation, will likewise be punished for the wickedness of their fathers. [Cf. Ex. 34:7; Num. 14:18 & Deut. 5:9] The offspring of Aaron also went unpunished; they instead were rewarded undeservedly as the title of High Priest was made hereditary. Aaron's descendants were decreed by Moses to be the successors in perpetuity to the High Priesthood (ostensibly via relayed command from God Himself). [Cf. Ex. 28:41-43]

Nepotism, in most matters, isn't the reprehensible act that some would condemn it as. Effective leaders need persons assisting them whose fealty they can rely upon totally. Who would be more loyal than a brother or a sister? Moses, by promoting Aaron to the post of obvious succession, appears to have made a prudent selection. We will place that generalization under scrutiny as soon as we dispose of another matter.

Moses could have spared and then promoted Aaron on his own authority. He was the unchallenged leader of the Israelites, but instead he chose to lie and deceive. He made the elevation of Aaron the choice of God, Himself. Yahweh is placed in the ignominious position of having to bestow honors upon the man who had just recently flagrantly dishonored Him.

Leviticus details the elaborate ceremony that preceded Aaron's ordination:

"The Lord said to Moses, 'Take Aaron and his sons, together with the vestments, the anointing oil, the bullock for a sin offering, the two rams, and the basket of unleavened food. Then assemble the whole community at the entrance of the Meeting Tent.' Moses told them what the Lord had ordered to be done. Bringing forward Aaron and his sons, he first washed them with water. Then he put the tunic on Aaron, girded him with the sash, clothed him with the robe, placed the ephod on him, and girded him with the embroidered belt of the ephod, fastening it around him. He then set the breastpiece on him, with the Urim and Thummim in it, and put the miter on his head, attaching the gold plate, the sacred diadem, over the front of the miter, at his forehead, as the Lord had commanded him to do.

"Taking the anointing oil, Moses anointed and consecrated the Dwelling, with all that was in it. Then he sprinkled some of this oil seven times on the altar, and anointed the altar, with all its appurtenances (accessories), *and the laver, with its base thus consecrating them. He also poured some of the anointing oil on Aaron's head, thus consecrating him. Moses likewise brought forward Aaron's sons, clothed them with tunics, girded them with sashes, and put turbans on them, as the Lord had commanded him to do."* [Lev. 8:1-13]

Numbers adds: *"But only Aaron and his descendants shall you appoint to have charge of the priestly functions. Any layman who comes near shall be put to death."* [Num. 3:10] Is Aaron grateful to Moses for neglecting to punish him for his idolatry? Indeed, for rewarding him by creating the position of High Priest? If so, his gratitude is expressed in a perverse manner. Aaron and Miriam, their sister, envious of Moses, ask aloud, *"Is it through Moses alone that the Lord speaks? Does He not speak through us also?"* [Num. 12:2]

These last two short sentences bellow an evident fact. The fact is that Aaron and Miriam, the closest persons to Moses, aren't unduly impressed by the miracles of Moses, nor are they awed with his personal visitations from God. They, privy to the true facts, declare that they, too, can hear the voice of Yahweh; they venture that their words carry the same authority as do the words of Moses. They obviously knew something that others didn't, to wit: Moses only maintained to be inspired by God, and they rightly (by their own evaluation) also could maintain divine guidance. They knew the actual circumstances of God's speaking with Moses, yet they rated Moses no holier and no closer to the Supreme Being than were they.

So angry was Yahweh at this turn of events that He afflicted Miriam with snow white leprosy that lasted seven day. [Cf. Num. 12:10] What happened to Aaron? Nothing! It seems as though, in the eyes of the Lord, Aaron can do no wrong. Twice Aaron sinned wickedly against Yahweh, and twice Yahweh ignored his iniquity, while simultaneously lashing out against lesser offenders. This is debatable behavior by a purportedly "just" Deity. But, nothing in the Universe remains everlastingly static, and shortly before Aaron dies, the Lord becomes displeased with him and pronounces a punitive sentence against him. What was the unforgivable transgression that finally roused Yahweh's ire against the at-times obstreperous Aaron? True to His past form, Yahweh punishes Aaron for something that Moses did. Moses had doubted that the Lord would again forgive the grumbling, rebellious, duplicitous Israelites.

The people were suffering from drought, so God told Moses *"speak to the rock"* and the rock would then pour forth water for all to drink. [Num. 20:8] Moses disobeyed and struck the rock instead. But Moses had to strike the rock a second time before the miraculous water flowed; he 'doubted' when he struck the first blow. [Cf. Num. 20:10-12; Cp. Ex. 17:5-6] If that sin seems less grievous than those of which Aaron personally was guilty. It is! But who are we to question the judgments of God. For their joint punishment, God decrees that neither Moses nor Aaron would be permitted to enter into the Promised Land. [Cf. Num. 20:12] If we discount the miraculous ('not unreasonable!) and read this story from the vantage point of a devout author who desired to explain the forty-year diversion of the Israelites during the Exodus trek as the actions of a justifiably angered Deity, then the punishment of Moses and Aaron becomes a bit more warranted, and somewhat less mystifying. All of the Egypt – escaping Israelites are denied entry into the Promised Land. [Num. 14:29-30]

Suppose, for example, that you are the ancient editor of the Exodus events. You aren't an eyewitness, but you do have access to first-hand accounts from a reliable witness. If your source tells you that Moses and Aaron died before entering the Promised Land, then you or he must supply rationalization why they were so denied, always presuming that every occurrence is dictated by God, ergo in conformance with His Will.

Imagine, also, that Miriam contracted leprosy during their travels. You ask your witness why the sister of Moses would be afflicted so by God. His reply: "Obviously, because she did something to anger the Lord." The source searches his memory and recalls that she, at one time, vied with Moses for the leadership of the assemblage. This must be it, he can think of no other reason. The fact that nothing happened to Aaron during the Exodus precludes you or him from reporting a vengeful act of God against Aaron. Grant this exception to the previous sentence: Moses may have personally murdered Aaron at the presumptive behest of God. [Read Num. 33:38] Apply this same backward-reasoned rationale to every biblical episode, and you will view those distant events through altered eyes.

One last anomaly connected with Moses and then we will leave him in peace for the remainder of this chapter. Moses, Aaron, and Miriam were born of the union of Amram and his wife, Jochabed. Jochabed was a blood relative of Amram, she was his father's (half?) sister, i.e., she was Amram's Aunt. Subsequently, she became Amram's wife. [Cf. Ex. 6:20] Moses, himself, later condemns such close blood marriages as incestuous. *"If a man has intercourse with his aunt, both of them must suffer the consequences for incest."* The Old Testament brands Moses as a child born of incest. Where does one find this proof? In the book of Leviticus written by Moses himself! [Cf. Lev. 18:12-14 & 20:19] A question: Did Moses himself write the Book of Leviticus?

KING DAVID

Christianity had a long period of prenatal development. It was born of a mixed marriage, that is, a Hebrew father and a Greco-Roman mother. As with all other progeny, Christianity inherited traits from both parents and, quite naturally, you would expect that each genetic manifestation could be traced to one parent or the other. A point by point comparison of all inherited 'traits' is beyond the scope of this endeavor. I will, however, expound on a few.

The notion of soul or essence was inherited from the Greeks. The Jews were immanently practical, they didn't believe in soul and spirit to the exclusion of body. They, likewise, didn't believe in esoteric punishment for wickedness, or immaterial reward for righteousness. To them Divine reactions were real, direct, and never withheld during one's lifetime.

The Greeks craftily animated their gods, literally, in the image of man. That simple reversal had profound consequences. Their gods behaved in the manner of the most depraved of human beings. They were full of lust, treachery, and infidelity, all interwoven with a vein of model heroism, and even with seeming altruism at times.

If nothing else, the Greek gods, on the whole, were much more lovable and laudable than was the vengeful Yahweh. The Greek Deities were closer to the ideal of the universality of the Gods than was the tribal God of Israel. Yahweh was the private benefactor of the Hebrew nation alone. His sole purpose for existing seemed to be to vend His powers to the conquests of the Israelites in exchange for their acknowledgment of Him as the Lord Paramount of the Middle Eastern Deities.

Ever since Paul founded the heterogeneous religion called Christianity, his successors have been forced into Herculean scriptural gymnastics in order to fit the Judaic parochial views into the catholic (universal), ideological framework of the new "Christian" religion. The greatest hurdle, yet one that has been successfully leaped, was the switch in Yahweh's allegiance from the orthodox ethnic Jews of the Promised Land, to the heterodox multi-ethnic Gentiles of the Roman world. This was no minor achievement. By the time of Paul, Yahweh was credited with a long history of devotion to the Jewish Nation exclusively (albeit with notable lapses). Even the personality of the Supreme Being had to be altered.

The benign, philanthropic depiction of God the Father was profoundly counter to the stern, rancorous, vengeful portrayal of Yahweh. Worse yet, Yahweh seemed to have a penchant for misdirected justice and uneven punitive sentences.

Review these examples: When King David took Bathsheba in adultery (or was it rape?), and then contrived for her husband to be killed in battle, these acts displeased the Lord so grievously that He caused the illegitimate child born of that illicit liaison to die as a punishment to David. [Cf. 2 Sam. 12:14-15] A more fitting penalty might have been to render David impotent or to curse Bathsheba with infertility; but that would have altered a future event. You see Jesus, through His foster father Joseph, was a descendant of David and Bathsheba's son Solomon [son Nathan, according to Luke 3:31], thus fulfilling later prophecy that the Messiah would be born of David's seed. [Cf. Mt. 1:6] We will pass over the gross impropriety of punishing an infant for the sins of the parents. What I attempted to illustrate here was the direct act of retribution God executed against what He decreed was wrongdoing. In Hebrew theology, when you incurred Yahweh's enmity, zap, you were stricken forthwith via His retribution.

It isn't that Yahweh perpetually was unforgiving. He forgave, but only after some atoning, expiatory penalty was levied against someone. Frequently, the main spate of vengeance befell persons only tangentially connected with the infraction, while the chief culprit was either wholly unpunished, or else received only the equivalent of a mild reprimand.

Another Davidic episode is enlightening, but not as the biblical author intended. Upon ascending the throne after King Saul, David ordered a census of the people to be taken. [Cf. 2 Sam., Chap. 24 & 1 Chr. Chap. 21] Inexplicably, this kindled the ire of the Lord against David. No reason is ever given why Yahweh became so angry at David for ordering a census. Of all the sins that David committed in his lifetime, this would seem to be among the least felonious. Discount the previous, on this occasion Yahweh decided to punish David directly. So what penalty did God inflict on David? Unbelievably, God invited David to choose his own punishment.

Speaking to the prophet Gad, the Lord thus informed: *"Go and tell David that I am giving him three choices. I will do whichever he chooses."* [1 Chr. 21:10 & 2 Sam 24:12] David truly was favored among men; he could even choose the form of chastisement that he desired the Lord to exact against him.

The three options were: 1. Seven years of famine in the land. 2. Three months of fleeing from his adversaries. 3. Three days of pestilence. [Cf. 2 Sam 24:13 & 1 Chr. 21:12] Here David displays his wisdom; he chooses the pestilence. However, the pestilence doesn't afflict David directly. It rages against his subjects. This is comparable to punishing a wayward minister by flogging his congregation. What a heroic leader David was to choose this form of expiation from God's punishment. The first two choices would have afflicted David more directly. From a personal standpoint, David chose exceedingly well.

David's response to the prophet merits a direct quote. *"I am in a desperate situation! But I don't want to be punished by men. Let the Lord himself be the one to punish us, for he is merciful."* How does the Lord respond? *"So the Lord sent an epidemic on Israel, which lasted from that morning until the time that he had chosen. From one end of the country to the other seventy thousand Israelite men died."* [2 Sam. 24:14-15 & 1 Chr. 21:13-14]

Regarding: "Seventy thousand men"? Either we have a faulty translation here, or God caused a tremendous number of widowed Hebrew women to be left to the unreliable mercy of charity. What inspirational message can we glean from this 'inspired' story? Should we vehemently oppose any census we are involved in, or should we resign ourselves to unwarranted misery and a cruel death anytime some witless leader of ours rankles the Lord?

And lest someone absolve Yahweh of direct involvement in this slaughter of innocent people, read on: *"When the Lord's angel was about to destroy Jerusalem, the Lord changed his mind about punishing the people and said to the angel who was killing them, 'Stop! That's enough!' The angel was by the threshing place of Araunah, a Jebusite."* [1 Chr. 21:15 & 2 Sam. 24:16]

God is as culpable here as any Commander who ever sent troops to make war against civilian non-combatants. The people of that city (then named Jebus, later Jerusalem) were predominantly non-Hebrew, and surely had no involvement with the census ordered by David. Even King David recognized the injustice of Yahweh's vengeance. His words: *"I am the guilty one. I am the one who did wrong. What have these poor people done? You should punish me and my family."* [2 Sam. 24:17] The wording in Chronicles varies somewhat, but still conveys the identical recrimination against Yahweh's misdirected reprisal. [Cf. 1 Chr. 21:17]

To my mind, the only noteworthy attribute David possessed was his attainment of the pinnacle of power in the glory days of the Hebrew ascendancy. His personal deportment was scandalous. He may well be the sorriest example anyone could cite of a venal leader whose corrupt conduct has been piously recorded in the Bible for future posterity to revere and glorify.

Is there anyone who would extol the life of David as the type of behavior that was generally pleasing to God? To be singled out as the premiere precursor of the 'anointed one' of the Lord was an unparalleled mark of distinction. Was David so chosen because of his intrinsic worthiness? Hardly! In this life (by human evaluations), nothing succeeds like success itself. To the ancient chroniclers, the very fact that David ascended to the throne of Israel was undeniable proof that Yahweh favored him above all others.

If today you would begin to view every notable world occurrence as a direct act of God, those actions would be no less darksome, enigmatical, and unintelligible than are the events in the Old Testament. If you enlarge your perspective to include the individual lives of the world's leaders, again attaching to each personal event the machinations of a Supreme Being, the result can only be an incomprehensible undulation between 'beneficial' and 'harmful'; with many other events halting at the 'indifferent' determination. The lack of any credible design or logical scheme to the historic incidents attendant would mismatch perfectly with the befuddling Old Testament narratives.

Contrarily, try picturing all events in the absence of a personal, puppet-master Deity and the mystery of God's indecipherable intentions dissolves completely. Happenstance is an antonym to design. Mostly, our human tribulations have their genesis in human conduct. A God who continually smote us with adversity would have to be an insatiable sadist. What pleasure can He derive from our suffering or our anguish? Religionists arrive at the doctrine of heaven-sent trials that prove our steadfastness of belief through a process of sheer elimination, not divine enlightenment. If there is a personal God (and the devout ardently labor to believe that there is), then no other solution is practicable or reasonable.

The religionists adamantly refuse to believe the most obvious of all solutions, i.e., there is no personal God, no Divine guidance, and no celestial intervention. That the world exists exactly as we see it is an unpalatable, unacceptable, abhorrent alternative to them. A religionist reasons (vaingloriously) that somewhere in the vast cosmos there must exist a rational super being that more than just knowing everything about these pious persons, this super being holds unflagging love for them as well. This is a grand belief. It just happens to be wholly, eternally, and provably false!

JESUS — DESCENDANT OF DAVID

Much ado is made of the descent of Jesus through King David. What was so religiously celebrated about King David? When I read the first book of Samuel, the only behaviorally distinguished person I can locate is Jonathan. Jonathan was the first-born of King Saul; therefore, he was also the rightful heir to Saul's throne. David, in actuality, was a usurper. Not only that, but he was, at one time, a traitor to his people as well; he fought on the side of the Philistine King, Achish, against the Israelites. Read the biblical proof below:

"Some time later the Philistines gathered their troops to fight Israel, and Achish said to David, `Of course you understand that you and your men are to fight on my side.'* *"'Of course,' David answered. `I am your servant, and you will see for yourself what I can do.'" [1 Sam. 28:1-2] Morally and socially, David was a disgrace to early Judaism. Book 1 Samuel states that David raided and killed non – Israelites, but lied to King Achish telling him that his (David's) raids were against Israelites. I believe that the Old Testament lies here, just as David purportedly lied to King Achish.

While hiding from King Saul, David attacked the Jews of Judea and murdered everyone so that his treasonous behavior wouldn't become known to the entire Israelite (Hebrew) nation.

During that time David and his men would attack the people of Geshur, Girzi, and Amalek; He would raid their land; Killing all the men and women, and confiscating the sheep, cattle, donkeys, camels, and even clothing. Then he would come back to {Philistine king} Achish, who would ask him, 'Where did you go on a raid this time?' and David would tell him

{Achish} that he had gone to the southern part of Judah. David would kill everyone, men and women, so that no one could go back and report what he and his men had really done. This is what David did the entire time he lived in Philistia." [1Sam. 27:8-11] (Edited .... Quote)

Why was it necessary (or desirable) for Jesus to be born of the peasants Joseph and Mary, yet, be of the lineage of King David? If Saul was the first legitimate King of the 'Chosen People,' why wasn't he an ancestor of the Messiah? Why wasn't Jesus descended from Jonathan, the admirable son of King Saul?

But was Saul a legitimate King? Was the monarchy itself really sanctioned by Yahweh? The solitary evidence in the Bible indicates that the monarchy wasn't the inspiration of God at all; it was the agitation of the people. Here is what the Bible records regarding the establishment of the Kingdom of Israel: *"And they said to him, {Samuel} `Behold, thou art old, and thy sons walk not in thy ways: make us a king, to judge us, as all nations have.' And the word was displeasing in the eyes of Samuel that they should say: `Give us a king...'*

"And the Lord said unto Samuel: ... 'They have rejected me, that I should not reign over them.'" [1 Sam. 8:5-7] Later, Samuel reproaches the Israelites. *"And when ye saw that Nahash the king of the children of Ammon came against you, ye said unto me, 'Nay; but a king shall reign over us': when the Lord your God was your king."* [1 Sam. 12:12]

The inspiration for a physical Ruler over the Hebrews didn't come from God. Neither was it suggested by His prophet, Samuel. Noting that all other nations had a monarch, the Hebrew people decided that they no longer wanted the invisible sky God (Yahweh) as their sovereign. They wanted a mortal king. What does this incident portray about God's Omniscience? Which is the more likely: That God is all-knowing? Or that mankind is ever gullible; mankind is fickle; mankind is duplicitous?

CHAPTER 7
Ten Disreputable Tales

NOT-FOR-SUNDAY-SCHOOL READINGS

Reading and pondering the events of the past two thousand years, I marvel that academic western civilization survived. That improbable survival is truly a living testimonial to reasoning mankind's tenacity. Small pockets of enlightenment, no doubt buffeted incessantly by religious bigotry and doctrinal intransigence, clung precariously to an intellectual existence that for centuries had to be hidden from the notice of narrow-minded religionists. Religionists who confidently decreed that their 'God inspired' Bible contained all the knowledge that mankind would ever need. Further, that knowledge was unerring and complete! The stake and a flaming bonfire awaited anyone foolish enough to voice even a moderate doubt concerning biblical interpretations that inadvertently found its way to the ears of a vindictive cleric.

I wonder if religionists from the pre-printing press era ever read a Bible. Did they own a Bible? Before printing, few persons could afford a hand-scripted copy ... if such had been available. They weren't! How comprehensibly did the Christian Community as a body know the Bible before the invention of the printing press? For the first fifteen hundred years of the current era all that the average Christian knew about the Bible were the selected gospel readings chosen by the Bishop to be read at Mass on Sundays and Holy Days.

If odds were now calculated, those odds would favor the proposition that early Christians didn't read the Bible, and knew very little of its full contents. The betting line for today would still weigh heavily against those religious devotees who haven't read the Bible extensively.

Permit me to read your mind here. You are thinking to yourself "I'll take that bet." My reply is "I accept." Here are the conditions of the wager: I will list ten short sections from the Bible, each relating incidents in the lives of prominent, recognizable biblical personalities. You will have to consult your own Bible to read the entirety of all ten episodes. I won't supply the complete story to you for reasons that I will justify later. However, I do risk a charge of editorial coloring or deceptive emphasis by excerpting the text (isogesis), but my wager remains open. Can we agree?

You will read the stories; you will ascertain the facts; and you will make the decision as to who won this bet. If you have never heard of the event before yet deem it pertinent enough that it should have been widely disseminated, then I am awarded one point. If the opposite occurs, namely, if you knew beforehand of the event and feel that it is generally known to Bible quoting adherents (proselytizers), then you garner one point. Ten total points could permit a 5 to 5 tie. But confidently, I predict that this wager will be decided heavily in favor of one side or the other. The bet is joined! Have your Bible handy as you read the contents of this chapter.

RECOMMENDED BIBLICAL READINGS (NOT)

1. Ruth, The Entire Book (Four Chapters)

This is the tale of a brazen seductress who, incidentally, was an ancestress to Jesus. Ruth was a young Moabite widow living with her Hebrew mother-in-law, Naomi. She wasn't of God's chosen people, so it shouldn't be expected that she would entrust her fate to Yahweh. Rather, she took matters into her own hands. She seduced Boaz, and her mother-in-law instructed her how.

'Bathe yourself, perfume your body, dress in your best attire, wait until he has eaten and drunk to contentment, then lie at his feet in the dark of the night when no one can see you,' was the advice her mother-in-law,

Naomi, gave to Ruth. Naomi knew that randy male human nature would write the finale to that contrived scenario. Whether or not Ruth and Boaz had sexual relations their first night is immaterial. Ruth kindled a passion in Boaz's heart for her feminine form and he, as with any unmarried and (by inference) older male, was impelled to action through sexual arousal, not via Divine direction. [Cf. Ruth 3:1-18]

If Naomi believed that God was protecting Ruth from the Moabites, why did she advise her to stay away from fields other than those of Boaz, warning Ruth that she might be violated somewhere else? [Cf. Ruth 2:22] Surely Yahweh would protect her from sexual assault wherever she gleaned in the grain fields. Naomi's actions speak louder than her words. Was she aiding the Lord in His designs, or did she design her own aid? Despite all circumstance, Ruth and Boaz were destined to become ancestors of King David, thereafter of Jesus also.

In the event that the reader is unfamiliar with this story, here is a brief synopsis: Naomi's son, husband to Ruth, died leaving both women without support. Naomi, related by family to Boaz, determined that he should be the financial support both women required. Ruth went to "glean" in the fields of Boaz, but at first Boaz took only compassionate notice of Ruth. This is when Naomi concocted her stratagem. But Naomi had to act fast, the wheat and barley harvests were at an end, and Boaz hadn't made the expected advances yet. Naomi induced Boaz to lust after Ruth in the manner of a conniving, determined schemer.

Imagine yourself back then. Would you permit your daughter, or encourage your daughter-in-law, to go in the middle of the night to lie at the feet of a prospective husband? If the thought occurs that perhaps this tawdry behavior was acceptable in those days, that notion is dashed by Boaz. He orders (his servants?), *"Let it not be known that this woman came to the threshing floor."* [Ruth 3:14] No! Seduction and casual sexual relations (fornication) were scandalous even in Old Testament times.

This tale well could have inspired the adage that 'God helps those best who first help themselves.' Naomi was well cared for the remainder of her days thanks to her own connivance, and thanks also to her daughter-in-law Ruth's feminine appeal. One question remains. What part did God play in this conspiracy of seduction and fornication? If none, then why is it included in the sacred writings?

2. 1 Samuel, Chapter 18, Verses 20-30

This grisly little tale could never be shown on public television, and I am certain that it has never been selected for recital at Christian services. It is ironic that we are asked to believe every word of this story, yet, we dare not cite it to decent people for fear of scandalizing them.

The story concerns an incident between King Saul and the young David. Earlier the Bible informed us that in all Israel there is no one "goodlier" (more handsome) than was Saul. [1 Sam. 9:2] God Himself told the prophet Samuel to anoint Saul as the first ruler over His chosen people, the Israelites. [Cf. 1 Sam. 9:17] Later, the spirit of the Lord departed from Saul and an evil spirit from the Lord troubled him. [Cf. 1 Sam. 16:14 & 18:10] King Saul seized the opportunity David afforded him (to wit: asking permission to marry Saul's daughter) to vent his envy and hatred by exacting a weird and gruesome bride's fee from David.

'One hundred foreskins of the Philistine soldiers,' was Saul's price for his daughter. [Cf. 1 Sam. 18:25-27] As reported, the Lord looked with favor upon David and helped him to slay not one hundred, but two hundred Philistines so that David could meet Saul's nuptial demands. After his victory, David (or his troops?) performed the macabre task of posthumous 'circumcision' under Yahweh's approving eye. Returning in triumph, David proudly counted out his nuptial fare before the king and was rewarded via his marriage to Michal, daughter of Saul.

Manifestly, the mutilation of dead bodies didn't violate any of the Hebrew Divinity's sacred commandments, nor did it offend Him; for if it had offended God, He would have punished David forthwith. Instead, we next read of God protecting David from the treachery of King Saul who attempted to kill him shortly afterward. [Cf. 1 Sam. 20:1ff]

Another fact that attests to God's partiality toward David was His magnanimity in assisting him in the slaying of twice the required number of Philistines. It seems the Sixth Commandment, *"Thou Shall Not Kill,"* is waived or suspended when one of God's favorites is seeking a wife, even if she is only one of many others to follow. [Cf. Ex. 20:13, et al.] Moreover, Michal may not have been David's first wife, and she positively wasn't his last! [Cf. 2 Sam. 3:2]

3. Esther, Chapter 1, Verses 9-12; Chapter 2, Verses 1-17

The king, Ahasuerus, who fulfills the leading role in this story, is speculated today to be the historic Persian Monarch, Xerxes, (r. 485-465 BC). When his beautiful wife, Vashti, refused to disrobe and be leered at by the drunken assemblage in his court (an act that God should have admired and rewarded), the king removed her from the throne, and thence, from the pages of the Bible also.

The explanation why the king was so "wroth" with his wife is because he reasoned that if he failed to punish Vashti harshly, all the other wives in his domains might thereafter attempt to flout the orders of their husbands in replication of the Queen's defiance of the commands of king Ahasuerus. A wife disputing with her husband was intolerable in those days!

In order to replace the deposed queen, Ahasuerus initiated a beauty & talent contest. Mordecai, a captive Jew, blest by the Lord with a wily mind and a stunning adopted daughter, Esther, entered her in the contest. (Esther was the daughter of Mordecai's uncle.) After twelve months of preparation with oils and myrrh, perfumes and sweet spices, Esther was ready for her big night. She got to sleep with the king, who (influenced by God?) was so enamored of her charms and talents, that he selected her to be the new queen.

The Bible leaves us to wonder if Esther ever exhibited her female allurements before the king and his besotted royal court, but regrettably, we are never so informed. We do know that she wasn't replaced, and we can only surmise that in all her future actions she pleased her husband unfailingly. One question persistently troubles me reading this sacred account. Is a woman who prostitutes her body to one man for a great price, less of a harlot than the woman who sexually favors many men for smaller fees?

Not only is Esther rewarded for her 'God given talents,' but her adoptive father and likewise her Hebrew people, also derived benefit from her shameless sexual promiscuity. Her cousin (Mordecai, who had adopted her) earned his reward by advising her not to reveal her Jewish nationality. He advised her to act out a lie. Of course, Yahweh is pleased as this aids His people and lightens the yoke of their oppression. Oddly, God Himself is charged with responsibility for burdening them with their oppressors (the Babylonian Captivity) as earned punishment for their past sins. This proposition highlights the irrational and contradictory logic of ascribing all events to the premeditated actions of an inscrutable, interventionist Deity.

There is mightily inverted, convoluted, and twisted rationale being applied here and truthfully, throughout theologically biased biblical mythology. Still, this is the only means of reconciling the concept of a personal God with the bizarre, though biblically 'factual' (?), events of history. To me, the Old Testament reads as an extremely partial, quasi-historical account of the traditional lore of an unspectacular ethnic group. Through early persistence and later luck, this group ultimately managed to have those tribal remembrances glorified into the very words of a universal Divinity. However, when their history is compared against that of their contemporaries, the Hebrew people are seen to be neither favored nor disfavored materialistically more so than their neighbors. A religionist might read the mystical into the chronicle of the Israelite-Hebrew-Jewish peoples, but never would a historian!

4. Genesis, Chapter 12, Verses 10-20 & Chapter 26, Verses 6-8

Here we have two similar tales. In truth, they are literally <u>too</u> similar. The most probable explanation is that we have one legend, which is told twice, each time in a slightly altered form. (Factually, if Genesis, Chapter 20, verses 1 thru 18 is included, the tale is repeated thrice.)

Abram (Abraham) lied to the Egyptians about his wife, Sarai (Sarah), telling them that she was his sister. The Pharaoh, covetous of her charm and beauty but ignorant of her marital status, took her as a wife. Abram permitted the deception to continue because, through her favors, Pharaoh favored him with "flocks, herds, he-asses, men servants, maid servants, she-asses and camels."

Yahweh is angered because the compliant, if not enthusiastic (?), Sarai is violated through the intrigue of her avaricious husband. God lashed out, not against the two guilty parties (Abraham and his wife, Sarah), but against the duped Pharaoh and his entirely innocent subjects. Great plagues struck the Egyptians. The Lord's unfailing, but misdirected, injustice (wrath) is recounted in His own words in the first book of the Bible, Genesis.

[Gen. 26:6-8]

<u>In The Second Banner Story, The Nearly Identical Event Unfolds</u>. Isaac, the son of Abraham (a truly faithful reproduction) proves the genetically accurate maxim "Like father, like son." He, fearing that the Philistines

would kill him to steal his beautiful wife Rebecca, introduced her as his sister. The Lord was overjoyed with this lie, and blest Isaac with a hundredfold harvest that year. Isaac's riches, afterward, increased until he was very wealthy.

The moral of this segment: 'Yahweh rewards His people who deceive and defraud their associates, while prostituting their women for their own profit.'

The hoax was uncovered when the Philistine king observed Isaac 'fondling' Rebecca. He correctly fathomed that she truthfully was Isaac's wife. But why? I am not quite sure! It is historical fact (and presumably known during this period) that the Egyptian royalty intermarried brother to sister; therefore, I am surprised that the king didn't suspect sibling incest of the two, rather than deceit. Maybe he was the beneficiary of another of God's edifying infusions?

What inspiring message are we to derive from these two tales? Abraham permitted his wife to commit adultery, and thereby, was greatly rewarded by Yahweh. Then his son, Isaac, lied to the Philistines about his wife, and he, too, was greatly rewarded. There is an unavoidable conclusion to be drawn from these tales regarding biblical honesty and marital fidelity. But, frankly, the civilized world would be better served if everyone dismissed that conclusion.

Re: **Genesis 20:1-18**

In this obvious repeat of the earlier tale Abraham and Sarah again deceive the local king by declaring that they are brother and sister. The king, Abimelech of Gerar, was enamored of the feminine charms of Sarah and had her brought before him, presumably to admire or perhaps to leer. But this time God interferes before Sarah can demonstrate her talents. *"You are going to die, because you have taken this woman; she is already married,"* said God to Abimelech in a dream. The king responded to God, *"... Abraham himself said that she was his sister, and she said the same thing ... I have done no wrong."* God's final reply: *"... give the woman back to her husband. He is a prophet, and he will pray for you, so that you will not die...."* {The word "prophet" here is rendered from the Hebrew word, *"Nabi."*}

The next morning Abimelech confronted Abraham. *"Why did you do it?"* Abraham responded: *"... I thought that {you} would kill me to get my wife.*

She in actual fact is my sister. She is the daughter of my father, but not of my mother, and I married her." {Author's aside – >} *"God's curse on anyone who has intercourse with his sister or half sister."* [Deut. 27:22 & Lev. 20:17]

Abimelech, fearful of Yahweh's vengeance (?), rewards Abraham's deliberate lie by giving him sheep, cattle, and slaves. He also gave Abraham and Sarah a thousand pieces of silver. But his magnanimity doesn't completely requite Yahweh's anger at him. The final verses of this chapter of Genesis record that, as punishment for allowing Abraham and Sarah to deceive him, that *"the Lord made it impossible for any woman in Abimelech's palace to have children." "So Abraham prayed for Abimelech, and God healed him."* Thereafter, Abimelech's wife and his slave girls could again have children. Evidently, Abimelech already had a palace full of young pubescent girls and pre-menopausal women before the deceitful Abraham came on the scene.

In closing this segment I will enlighten the reader a bit more. At the time of this incident, Sarah was more than sixty-five years old! In this case there must have been some act of divine manipulation or interference; why else would the king have 'lusted after' a sexagenarian?

<u>5. Genesis, Chapter 29, Verses 16-35 –</u>
<u>Genesis, Chap. 30 Verses 1-24</u>

This is the saga of the founding of the twelve tribes of Israel. There is little comment that I can add to it; the story defies explication.

Jacob fathers twelve male children: Four by his first wife, then two by the maid of his second wife, then two by his first wife's maid, then two more, again, by his first wife, giving her a total of six male children and giving him a total of ten male children. The first wife falters at this point and bears a girl child. Meanwhile, the second wife, barren until now, finally conceives the child Joseph, followed some time later by the twelfth and last boy, Benjamin.

Now if the above is confusing to you, it is to everyone else also. That God would choose such a serpentine course to achieve the historically inconsequential division of His chosen people cries out for some sensible clarification. None is provided! The real baffler is "Why?" Why did God inspire Jacob to act out this boudoir version of the game of musical chairs?

The second wife, Rachel, it would appear, is merely a vessel of the Lord when she offers her sister (Jacob's first wife, Leah) the exchange of some mandrakes for the privilege of again sleeping with Jacob. Leah, an apparent shrewd bargainer, accepts the barter of the few herbs of Mandrake in return for Jacob's manly services. He proves to be quite a bargain, for his services span a period over which Leah conceives three separate times.

Rachel, it seems, has fared poorly from the trade. But wait! God hears her anguished prayer and now blesses her by ending her barrenness. Or perhaps it was the mandrakes? Mandrakes were assumed by the contemporary peoples to be an aid to conception, and that sheds light on the entire matter. Rachel may have prayed to God for personal fertility, but she also ate the herbs. In today's parlance, this is called 'fading both ends of a bet.'

Rachel longed for a child, and she was willing to try anything, even sharing her husband or experimenting with exotic herbs to have one. None of the actions of the people in this story are shocking from a human standpoint, but neither are they inspirational. It is only when we inject the Supreme Being as the mastermind of the affair that the story becomes sordid. When you invoke the Christian Deity, you inject morality. Then, as a consequence, the story must be viewed from an entirely different perspective.

Jacob is indicted as a lecherous satyr, begetting children indiscriminately so that the twelve tribes of Israel could be founded. Did the relatively short-lived existence of their division have any importance or relevance to that age or, for that matter, to any age? Reading the remote history of the Hebrews, I find few cogent reasons for more than one tribe, and none at all for twelve tribes! Religionists force me to conclude that the Supreme Being's actions are as mysterious and as unfathomable as the sequence of numbers drawn in a lottery. Most likely, for the same reason: They are both determined by pure chance that can be rationalized only through the faux contrivance of inventive hindsight.

So, why were the Israelites divided into twelve tribes? Solution: 'Because it happened!'

6. Genesis, Chapter 34, Verses 1-31

This section concerns the rape of Dina, the lone (recorded) female child born to Jacob via Leah. The perpetrator of the violation afterward fell in love with the girl, and subsequently offered to marry her as restitution. The offer was spurned. Her brothers, the heroes of the story, exacted a vengeance that must have pleased Yahweh. I wonder: Did God inspire their method of reprisal? Read on and you will learn why I ask.

The revenge tactic conceived by the brothers rivals the stratagem of the ancient Greeks with their "Trojan Horse" in its spuriousness. We can all agree that rape is a heinous crime that should be appropriately punished. But there are strong mitigating circumstances here that must be weighed against any possible retribution. Sechem, the attacker, repented and asked permission to marry the girl. His father, Hemor the king of the Hivites, came to Jacob and agreed to meet whatever terms the family would set if they would consent to a wedding between his son and the ravished Dina.

All in all, the father of the young rapist acted in a forthright and conciliatory manner. Yet, how did God's chosen tribal founders respond? They replied with deceit and deception. They pretended to agree to the marriage only if all the male inhabitants of the Hivite kingdom would undergo circumcision. Hemor, the king, ordered all his male subjects to comply. As soon as these painful surgeries were completed but not yet healed, Jacob's sons and their hirelings struck. Were they intent on punishing only Sechem, the guilty party? No, they "advanced boldly against the city and slew all the males." They then proceeded to loot the city of all its wealth. They stole all the flocks, herds, and asses. The women and children were carried off and we needn't engage our imagination very deeply to deduce their inevitable fate.

Perhaps, when we consider Yahweh's lopsided judgments against the Hebrews, we can temper our repugnance toward this Hebrew instance of "justice." This story is not without its dogmatic anomalies. If all the male inhabitants accepted the initiating circumcision rite of God's covenant with Abraham, didn't that make them His chosen people also? Of course, it did! They all became converted Jews! But, alas, that wasn't good enough for Yahweh. Their leader's son offended Him, so He permitted (possibly aided) the sons of Jacob to slay every Hivite male despite their willingly enduring Yahweh's (Israelite) mutilating initiation ritual.

To modern theologians, I direct a question. Did these slain innocents go to Heaven or to Hell? Aren't they martyrs of the Israelite religion?

Allow a small digression. The Christian Church speaks often, and with pride, of the martyrs among their early converts. They depict the persecuting Caesars as Satan-inspired monsters, and show revulsion at the methods Nero and his successors used in an attempt to eradicate Christianity. Several centuries later we find the now powerful Church employing methods equally atrocious to exterminate paganism or heresy, but now we are advised that God approves these acts of violence against His own creatures because the punishments were decreed by His surrogates here on earth, by name, the newly empowered Christian hierarchy.

7. Judges, Chaps. 19-21, & Genesis, Chap. 19 Verses 1-11

The unnamed hero of this first epic fits perfectly the mold of the other 'valiant' Old Testament Hebrews whom God chose as His own. As with other sections of the Bible, this story parallels the second cited story so strikingly that, again, I can only presume that a single legend has come down to us in two separate forms. Either this or I must conclude that God orchestrated two very similar events to exhibit double emphasis on the moral intended. Later, read more regarding that moral at the end of these duplicated tales. First: The story related in Judges.

Traveling back toward his home with his unfaithful wife (concubine), a Hebrew man spurned staying overnight in Jerusalem because, at that time, it was a non-Israelite city known as Jebus. Lacking inspiration from the Lord (or was his destiny foreordained?), he unwisely elected to continue on to Gibeah, a city in the Hebrew controlled territory of the Tribe of Benjamin.

So, how did God's chosen people, the race to which the man and his woman also belonged, welcome the traveler in Gibeah? The townsmen surrounded the house of the man he was staying with and they shouted, "Bring out your guest, that we may abuse him." (Homosexually) Yes, their intentions were repugnant, but the response of the host landlord was even more reprehensible. He volunteered his virgin daughter to the lecherous mob. Then the craven husband decided to divert the rabble's lust from his person by thrusting his wife out the door. The foul herd of moral swine ravished the hapless and helpless woman all through the night. But then, in the morning, a bizarre event unfolded as recorded in the Bible.

Her 'gallant' husband emerged safely from the house and spoke to his wife who had crawled back to the bolted door earlier. He received no reply because she was dead. He returned home, carved her corpse into twelve pieces and sent them, respectively, to each of the twelve tribes.

The aftermath of the debauchery is so illogical that I am tempted to believe every word, for no one would dare to lie so outrageously. The horrified and enraged eleven tribes wreaked murderous vengeance against the tribe of Benjamin, but not before forty thousand of the avengers themselves were killed. However, the Benjaminites lost twenty-six thousand men and all their women and children. So thoroughly were the Benjaminites eradicated that only six hundred spouseless men survived the onslaught. Then, incredibly, the avengers concocted a perverse strategy to avert the impending irreversible demise of the entire tribe of Benjamin.

The town of Jabesh had sent no soldiers to assault the Benjaminites; therefore, the Israelites sent an army to destroy the entire population of that city, excepting only four hundred young virgins to be given to the spouseless six hundred Benjaminite male survivors. Noting that they were two hundred virgins short, the Hebrew leaders now instructed the two hundred spouseless men to go to Shiloh and kidnap an equal amount of that town's virgins. Despite all else, and no matter how iniquitous the Benjaminites were, they remained a crucial part of the Lord's beloved people! The most irksome aspect of this atrocious episode is that God was advising the Israelite avengers during each barbarous attack that they committed. [Cf. Judges 20:18, 23 & 28]

Genesis Chap. 19, Verses 1-11

The story of Sodom and Gomorrah is similar in many respects, but it differs in one conspicuous feature. The Sodomites (who, incidentally, never satisfied their lusts) weren't God's chosen race; they only acted as if they were! Yahweh punished their wickedness by expunging both cities so completely that their ruins haven't been located (arguably) to this day, despite diligent searching by numerous archaeological teams.

This story features the pusillanimous Lot, Abraham's nephew. Two angels had come to warn Lot to leave the doomed city of Sodom with his family. When the angels were about to retire for the night, the Sodomites surrounded Lot's home and demanded that he surrender the two angels for the townsmen to abuse. (Homosexually) Lot offered to substitute his two virgin daughters. (Shortly after this event, Lot personally deflowered his virgin girls in a cave.)

Moses clearly forbade Lot's offer. *"You shall not degrade your daughter by making a prostitute of her; else the land will become corrupt and full of lewdness."* [Lev. 19:29]

We all know the conclusion of this tale: God blinded all of the avowed pederasts before they could perform their aberrant dereliction. I am still pondering the moral; the purpose; the divinely inspired message that we future readers of His Holy Writ were supposed to derive from the two degenerate incidents reported here. To me, these abhorrent, abominable tales raise question after question, but resolve nothing. A few select queries will illustrate my point.

Did Lot think that the Lord's angels would be powerless to resist the foul intentions of the mob at Sodom? Does the Lord count homosexual rape more grievous than heterosexual rape? Was it necessary to incite the death of seventy-five thousand souls (or more!) to assuage God's anger? What attributes did God find most attractive in those whose lives He spared, to the exclusion of those whose death He later orchestrated when He rained down "fire and brimstone" on Sodom and Gomorrah? Beyond all else I ask: "Who does God hold liable for the deaths of those innocent people whose only sin was that they resided in locales (Sodom and Gomorrah) that became the object of Yahweh's murderous wrath?"

8. Genesis, Chapter 19, Verses 30-38

Lot, who was spared by God from the fate of all other inhabitants of Sodom and Gomorrah, presumably because he was more virtuous, led his two mature daughters up into the hills and lived with them in a cave. Yahweh had recently turned Lot's wife into a pillar of salt on the plains of Moab because she didn't control her curiosity. After being ordered not to do so, Lot's wife looked back on the destruction God rained down on the two iniquitous cities. Her fatal punishment left Lot with no female companionship to share the lonely nights, and to relieve his masculine impulses. It would seem that the next move would have been Lot's. 'But not so! As we read in the Bible, here is what transpired next:

Lot's eldest daughter conceived a plan, and thereby conceived a child as well. Her words, "Our father is old and there is no man in the land to marry us as is the custom everywhere. Let us give our father wine to drink, then lie with him that we may have offspring by our father."

Lot drank the wine. Then the inspired author informs us, 'He miraculously was successful in impregnating his daughter. Yet, because of his drunkenness, he never knew it.' (Interpreted) The next night the same scene is enacted by the younger daughter with the exact same results. On two successive nights this old man performed two amazing physical feats at the very time that he was so intoxicated that he wasn't cognizant of his accomplishment!

Forgive my bluntness, but that story is a damnable lie. First and foremost, as a man, I can state without anticipation of contradiction, that if he was able to consummate the act of copulation, then he was sensible and conscious enough to know who his partners were. Did he imagine they were female angels from Heaven sent down to entertain him? Only he and his daughters lived in the cave. Is the Bible implying that this is one of God's interventionist schemes? Are Lot's daughters merely facilitating one of God's master plans? The elder daughter bore a son called Moab who became the ancestor of the people known as the Moabites. The younger daughter also bore a son, and named him Ben-ammi. He became the ancestor of the Ammonites.

This founding of tribal clans would seem to be the type of work a Deity might engage. However, as the story is presented, I am unable to discern whether its author considered the stratagems of the daughters as immoral or as inspired. The narrative doesn't offer a clue as to why the incestuous cave incidents are included in the Bible. If we accept that the story contains a nucleus of truth, then I have to chuckle when I read it. The Hebrew are casting ignominious derision on their Semite kin. They, the Hebrew, are legitimate heirs of Abraham. But the Ammonites and the Moabites are the illegitimate descendants of Abraham's lascivious nephew, Lot, and his two incestuous daughters.

Another peculiar point is just why Lot left the town of Zoar (aka Segor). An angel of the Lord told Lot that he would be safe there; the same angel who had predicted the destruction of Sodom. Yet Lot ignored the assurances of a supernatural being that had just accurately foretold a frightful event. This is puzzling. The Bible records that Lot was "afraid." What he feared, it neglects to mention! Lot just may have been fearful of his Israelite neighbors. Had they learned of his sexual escapades with his daughters, all three would have been stoned to death by the religious authorities of that day.

If I appear to be an authenticator of the Bible's stories at this point, be assured that this appearance is illusory, and it is temporary. Of course, some portion of what is written in the Bible is factual. That isn't because God inspired it, but because it is almost impossible to write, or even to think for that matter, without writing or pondering about something that has occurred. The most outlandish fiction you could conjure up has some foundation in fact or in reality. You couldn't imagine something if first you hadn't encountered a real event whose similar (or related) image wasn't imprinted into your memory.

Departing from a philosophical delineation and returning to the story we have been evaluating: If Lot left the apparent safety of Zoar, it was because he wasn't privy to any divine or spiritual revelation. In his mind the events that took place in the two destroyed cities might just as likely be repeated in Zoar. Reading the biblical verses (lines), then extrapolating between the verses (lines), is most enlightening here. Make a conscious effort to eradicate all imputed meddling by any Deity, then read my reconstruction of this story. Here is how it might have occurred:

Lot was absent from his home traveling with his wife and two daughters toward the city of Zoar. A violent earthquake (or other natural calamity) struck in the vicinity of Sodom and Gomorrah and destroyed both cities. Lot's wife was killed while the family was scurrying to shelter. When the tumult subsided, Lot and his daughters emerged from their hastily found refuge to discover the older woman missing. The only apparent remains on those plains of Moab were the (still existing) salt formations. Just prior, Lot may have admonished his wife to hurry along and not look back as he excitedly sought safety. After the discovery of her disappearance he presumed that she had been punished by God for her disobedience. True to their times, Lot and his contemporaries ascribed to God all the actions of nature. Accordingly, it was elementary to conjecture that God had punished the wife by turning her into one of those variously shaped salt formations. But God had spared Lot and his daughters for some divine purpose.

Back to written biblical scenario: Apprehensive about returning to Zoar, Lot decided the safest place to survive any future disasters would be in the mountains. Consequently, he moved the remainder of his family to a cave. The finale of the story reads almost exactly as the Bible portrays it, *sans* divine causation. The only eyewitnesses to the events that transpired in the cave were Lot and his daughters. (If you are a believer: 'God' observed) If either Lot or his daughters revealed the details, then each of us is free to attach whatever credence we feel the story warrants. But if we suppose that these particulars are from God's inspiration, then we must accept every item as irrefutable fact. This doesn't present too great an obstacle to belief in the story. But if I begin to wonder why the all-knowing Christian Deity chose to divulge the sexual peccadilloes of Lot's family for the entire world to read then I propose that there should be some moral significance gleaned from this tale. Regrettably, but predictably, no such significance can be divined or discerned.

Lot is the man whom the Lord chose to save from the destruction He rained down on all the men, all the women, and all the children of Sodom and Gomorrah. Lot may have been the most worthy denizen of those two reputedly depraved communities, but he definitely was not a moral icon within our current morality. Did God spare Lot just so he could incestuously father the two tribes that later would fight with, and kill, His chosen people? This is all that sparing Lot accomplished. If this is so, then why the subterfuge of having Lot become intoxicated before he impregnated his daughters? This tale is morally mystifying in that it is thoroughly decadent.

Why didn't the two angels who foretold the "fire and brimstone" disaster advise Lot that God desired him to have sexual relations with his daughters for by so doing he would be furthering the designs of the Lord? You and I both can answer that question. The events that enfolded in that cave were a shameful disgrace in any age. An ethical God, who continually intervened in the affairs of mankind, would have severely punished the guilty parties. Lot, a mature adult, should have been dealt with harshly. The two (obviously pubescent) daughters should have been severely disciplined by the God who had just destroyed the entire populations of Sodom and Gomorrah, presumptively for being more debauched than Lot and his daughters.

Didn't Lot question his daughters when their incestuous stratagem became obvious? Did Lot suppose that what he evidenced was miraculous conceptions by two virgin mothers? Unfortunately (or is it fortunate?), we never read again of Lot and his degenerate daughters. If this was a fairy tale, we might expect to read that Lot and his offspring 'lived happily ever after.' But this is the 'God inspired' book called the Bible, and as is so often the case, we can only speculate as to what became of the divinely delivered trio. The most rankling aspect of this anecdote is that later Lot was declared "a righteous man" by the Apostle Peter. [Cf. 2 Pet. 2:7]

9. Genesis, Chapter 38, Verses 1-30

Our word onanism comes directly from this biblical adventure. Judah, the progenitor of the Hebrew tribe that bore his name, reneged on a promise to his daughter-in-law. Her name was Tamar and her husband's name was Er (aka Her). Because of some unspecified wickedness, the Lord killed Er. The Bible never informs us why Er was divinely executed; but, as was the custom in those days, Judah instructed his second son, Onan, to perform a spouse's duties with the widow so that the family name would be perpetuated through a child by Tamar.

Onan agreed to have relations with Tamar, but refused to impregnate her. He withdrew at the last moment and "wasted his seed on the ground." Not surprisingly, this is the literal meaning of onanism. Yahweh was furious with Onan over this, and slew him also. In our day, we are told that God will damn us to hellfire for impregnating our widowed sister-in-law, but in those days the exact reverse was a mandatory obligation. Judah still had one remaining son who hadn't been assassinated by God, alas, he was too young! Consequently, Tamar was told to wait until the youthful lad had matured, so that one day in the future she might conceive a child of the family of Judah via the youngest son.

The years passed and the son, Selah, grew to manhood. However, to make the story more interesting, if for no other reason, Judah failed to redeem his promise to Tamar that she would be made pregnant with seed of his seed. But the patient and persistent Tamar would not be denied. Through trickery and deceit she arranged to become pregnant by Judah himself, thereby forging another link in the genealogical chain that culminated in the birth of Jesus. Yes, that is astonishingly correct! With the Bible's own words we are informed that another of the forebears of Jesus was conceived through a union that was legally, morally, and biblically condemned as incestuous.

By present standards, sexual relations between father and daughter-in-law aren't chargeable as incest. But, when Yahweh instructed Moses on the rules governing sexual taboos, such an act was irrefutably deemed incestuous. *"If a man lies with his daughter-in-law, both of them shall be put to death."* [Lev. 20:12] But Judah and Tamar weren't put to death; God permitted them to create a life. Their illegitimate son, Pharez, became a direct ancestor of Joseph, the foster father of Jesus. You are probably asking here what Judah and Tamar did to merit this singular distinction. Judah, amid his other 'accomplishments,' solicited a prostitute for her services. Tamar pretended (?) to be a prostitute and sold her body to Judah hoping to become pregnant by him. It happened! Those two may not have been personally worthy, but their behavior matched closely (in presumption, admirably!) with the bulk of those God similarly blest. As evidenced in the Bible, Yahweh invariably rewarded immoral sexual indiscretion.

10. 2 Samuel, Chap. 3, Ver. 1-5 + Chap. 5, Ver. 13-16 + Chap. 11, Ver. 2-5: 1 Kings, Chap, 1, Ver. 1-4 & 1 Chronicles, Chap, 3, Ver. 1-9

This last section briefs us on the amours of David with a few words added about Solomon. Although not as obscene or as gross as some of the preceding examples, it nonetheless belongs in this section because it highlights the utter unworthiness of David to be either the divinely selected King of God's chosen people, or the most illustrious ancestor of the Son of God, Jesus.

The following list of David's wives and male children is compiled from two separate biblical sources, so, as is often the case, God inspired two different 'infallible' lists. One source is the second book of Samuel, and the other is the first book of Chronicles. It is highly probable that David had other male children, and it is absolutely certain that, other than Dina, he fathered many female children not recorded in the Bible.

The male list: Amnon of Ahinoam from Jezreel; Chileab of Abigail from Carmel; Absolam of Maacah from Geshur; Adonijah of Haggith; Shepatiah of Abital; Ithream of Egiah, all from Hebron. Plus: Shobab; Nathan; Solomon; and Shimea of Bathsheba. [2 Sam. 5:13 & 1 Chron.

14.3] *"And David took more concubines and wives."* [2 Sam. 5:13] The male list continued: Shammua; Ibhar; Elishua; Nepheg; Japhia; Elishama; Eliada; Eliphelet; and Nogah, all born of an unknown "woman." (women?) Only God knows if one mother is instrumental here, or several, but He opted not to inform us!

All that can be learned from this section of the Bible is that David was a womanizer of the first magnitude, surpassed only by his successor, a son born to him adulterously through Bathsheba. Solomon is, on this charge, inarguably his father's son. In 1 Kings, Chapter 11, Verse 3, it relates that Solomon had seven hundred wives as Queens, and three hundred concubines. Wow!

Alas David, in his last years, is only a shadow of his former self. His servants, troubled because David was always cold, tried their best to warm him. They procured a beautiful young Shunammitess virgin named Abisag, to lay with the aged monarch and to ease his affliction, but to no avail. The Bible is explicit about David's infirmity, it states: *"She slept with the king; and served him, but the king did not know her."* [1Ki. 1:3-4] David's ultimate impotence is exposed by God for all the Scripture reading future generations to contemplate. But I ask humbly, yet quizzically, "To what sanctified purpose?"

END OF TEN REPREHENSIBLE BIBLE STORIES

That completes the ten (or so) selected stories from the Bible that have been glossed over, conveniently forgotten, or most probably, simply hidden from decent, respectable believers. Why aren't these events published and discussed with the same zeal and ardor, as indisputably, are some of the other Old Testament biblical anecdotes? I know, and now you must know also. They are a disgrace to the moral convictions of the religion they fostered. Abraham, Isaac, Jacob, Tamar, Rahab, Ruth, David, Bathsheba, Solomon (Nathan?), et al., could never qualify on merit as ancestors of the Savior of all of Human Kind.

I am cognizant of the incontrovertible fact that no human could ever meritoriously qualify as a worthy or deserving antecedent of God Incarnate. But, if the Bible is factual, then the Lord must have searched diligently for the least worthy and the least deserving to accomplish His designs. He was eminently successful in His quest, for a less likely clique of humans destined for divine honors would be nearly impossible to gather through random selection.

My rationale for the two preceding paragraphs follows. If Adam and his descendants are justly punished for the sin of eating a piece of fruit that was forbidden them; if that magnitude and duration of punishment fits Adam's transgression along with all of his descendants for several millennia, then the above identified antecedents warranted, yea even richly merited far more dire, far more disastrous, and far more agonizing retribution. Justice should be meted out in some proportion to the gravity of the offense that provoked the imposition of that justice.

A person who accidentally strikes and kills a pedestrian with his automobile isn't nearly as accountable as is a terrorist who plants a bomb in a crowded establishment and deliberately kills scores of innocent people. The latter intentional murders are unquestionably deserving of a greater punishment than is the former accidental death.

In real life other factors can rightly be taken into consideration. Considering the evidence in the Bible, and evaluating only the circumstances accessible, my sense of justice convinces me that Abraham and Sarah weren't deserving of a divinely decreed son. Each of those named near the beginning of this segment were respectively unworthy of their ennobling and enshrining elevation as ancestors to Jesus that they received from God.

Tragically, not only is this God, Yahweh, overly generous and forgiving toward some culpable individuals; contrarily, He is excessively harsh and punitive toward other less culpable individuals. These observations can't be harmonized with the modern conception of a supremely 'Just' Heavenly Creator. In my judgment, those two purported divine beings, Yahweh and God the Father, are not the same divinity. At best, they could only have been very distantly related, not consubstantial.

As to the wager between you (my current reader) and the author: Who won?

SHAME ON SOMEONE!

There is information I feel the earnest reader would desire to learn, if only because this would add to his/her comprehensiveness in a scrutiny of the Bible. All of the following quotes come from the King James Translation of the Bible.

<u>WARNING</u>: The wording of the selected quotes from the King James translation of the Bible may be offensive to some readers. If the present reader is one of these, please feel free to skip over these excerpts. The information that I include here is supportive of my accusations demystifying the Bible, but these quoted texts aren't crucial or imperative to my arguments!

So either skip now to Chapter 8, or read on. Below are the selected quotes:

"But Rabshakeh said unto them, hath my master sent me to thy master, and to thee, to speak these words? Hath he not sent me to the men which sit on the wall, that they must eat their own dung, and drink their own piss with you?" [2 Kings 18:27 & Isaiah 36:12]

"So and more also do God unto the enemies of David, if I leave of all that pertain to him by the morning light any that pisseth against the wall." [1 Samuel 25:22]

"For in very deed, as the Lord God of Israel liveth, which hath kept me back from hurting thee, except thou hast hasted and come to meet me, surely there had not been left unto Nabal by the morning light any that pisseth against the wall." [1 Samuel 25:34]

"Therefore, behold, I will bring evil upon the house of Jeroboam, and will cut off from Jeroboam him that pisseth against the wall, and him that is shut up and left in Israel, and will take away the remnant of Jeroboam, as a man taketh away dung, till it be all gone." [1 Kings 14:10]

"And it came to pass, where he began to reign, as soon as he sat on his throne, that he slew all the house of Baasha: he left him not one that pisseth against a wall, neither of his kinfolks, nor of his friends." [1 Kings 16:11]

"Behold, I will bring evil upon thee, and will take away thy posterity, and will cut off from Ahab him that pisseth against the wall, and him that is shut up and left in Israel." [1 Kings 21:21 & 2 Kings 9:8]

One could blame the translator(s) for the vulgarities contained in the above biblical quotes. If that be so, then I ask "Who inspired the thoughts that the author expressed?" The idiomatic expression, 'he that pisseth against the wall' unmistakably refers to males alone. Why didn't the Holy Spirit imbue the author with the words "man" or "men" to exclude women from the predicted revenge against men alone rather than permitting the author to delineate the intended victims of God's vengeance via a coarse elimination characteristic uniquely applicable to men.

I invite the reader to form his or her own conclusions about the above verses. Modern translations have removed the offensive words from their renditions. Ninety-Five percent of all modern translations will print "men" where the oldest extant texts read, "him that pisseth against the wall." Joseph Smith's "Inspired Version" (Bible of the Mormon Church) retained the original biblical wording.

Wherein resides the true 'inspiration' of the authentic words of God? Who will ever be able to say?

CHAPTER 8
Old Testament Anecdotes

GOD'S POWERS & THE EXODUS

The Old Testament chronicles God's concern for the Israelites. Arriving at the Promised Land to find it occupied by peoples who had no inclination to relinquish their ownership of the area. Joshua, while attacking the combined armies of the five Amorite cities, prayed to God for the Sun to stand still in the sky. God heard Joshua's petition and this was the result: *"The sun stood still and the moon did not move until the nation had conquered its enemies. This is written in The Book of Jashar. The sun stood still in the middle of the sky and did not go down for a whole day. Never before, and never since, has there been a day like it, when the Lord obeyed a human being. The Lord fought on Israel's side!"* [Jos. 10:13-14]

Did this unprecedented wonder happen? No, it didn't. [Cp. 2 Kings 20:9-11 & Isaiah 38:8] As a first rebuttal, the Sun doesn't revolve around the Earth; the Earth rotates on its axis, which creates the apparent motion of the Sun moving across the sky. The only way Joshua could have known this truth of the actual celestial motions within our Solar System was for God to inspire him with that knowledge. It is obvious today that God didn't infuse Joshua with the knowledge of the Sun's central position in our Solar System, or of the fact that the earth would have to stop its spinning for the Sun to appear to halt in its apparent (though deceptive) daily transit across the Earth's sky.

Secondly, such a celestial event wouldn't be just a local singularity; it would have been worldwide. Every nation's day would have seemed to halt in place for twenty-four hours. No record of such a momentous, startling, and portentous event can be found in historical records. Ramses II ruled Egypt, but the Egyptians failed to notice that the Sun never moved for a day. Shalmaneser ruled in Assyria, yet the written accounts of the period make no mention of the Sun standing still. The Mycenaean civilization was flourishing, as was the Hittite, still neither record this spectacle. The Chinese civilization was a thousand years old, but they must have slept through the twenty-four hours of darkness that remained over their domains, for their historical records fail to confirm this unforgettable (utterly terrifying to most) event. The actual catalyst for this unbelievable scriptural invention was many times less wondrous and eminently more practical.

This story was fabricated solely as an attempt to intimidate the superstitious inhabitants of the land of Canaan. (Discernibly!) The Canaanites believed the tales of Yahweh's powers and His inscrutable use of those powers. The paragraph preceding the stationary Sun paragraph tells us that God rained down great stones (hail?) from the sky killing more of the Canaanites than their Israelite foes did. [Cf. Jos. 10:11] That fiction would have duly frightened the gullible ancient citizenry of Canaan. But today we should see the halted Sun for what it was designed to be: a fantasy horror story glorifying the terroristic God of the Israelites. His unpredictable antics always managed to make the Hebrew tribes a victor in their wars of conquest. The psychological advantage the Israelites enjoyed when their foes believed their gory stories combined with their numerical superiority, and together, guaranteed them victory almost every time. The Bible informs us this: *"The Lord made the Amorites panic at the sight of Israel's army."* [Jos. 10:10]

Don't read 'gospel truth' into these tales. Instead, discover the wisdom of these authors when they acclaimed (thereby immortalized) their tribal God, Yahweh. The ancient foes of the Hebrews couldn't help but be intimidated when they were told of the wonders Yahweh performed to aid His chosen people. If He could cause all the calamities that befell the Egyptians, and if He could part the waters of the Red Sea, and if He would rend asunder the Earth and cause it to swallow up men alive, then what chance did the Canaanites have against the Israelites? [Cp. Deut.

11:6] If their enemies could be induced to believe in Yahweh's superhuman power, and His dogged devotion to the Israelites, then the battle was half won before the first arrows flew. This is the only explanation that satisfies all inquiries raised by the 'constrained' Sun tale.

From the time Moses returned to Egypt until the successful assault on Jericho, how many wonders and signs did Yahweh perform before the very eyes of the Hebrew tribes? Begin with the ten afflictions: Water turned to blood; the invasion of the frogs; the attack of the gnats; the swarms of flies; the pestilence that afflicted the livestock; the festering boils that affected all Egyptians, including their magicians; the rain of hail; the plague of locusts; the three days of intense darkness during which only the Israelites had light; and finally 'the clincher,' the death of all the firstborn males of Egypt both of man and of beast. [Cf. Ex. 4:18 thru 12:36]

After witnessing any one of these marvels I would have been a reformed skeptic for the remainder of my days. But were the Israelites? Not then, and not after many other miraculous wonders were performed in full view of the entire assemblage. God himself appeared as a column of smoke in daylight and as a column of fire by night to guide the Israelites out of Egypt and toward the Promised Land. [Cf. Ex. 13:21] He parted the Red Sea and allowed them to walk unharmed between the walls of water, but the pursuing Egyptians were all drowned when the walls of water collapsed after Moses stretched out his arms. [Cf. Ex. 14:26-29]

Once they arrived in the desert, Yahweh instructed Moses how to purify the waters of Marah. [Cf. Ex. 15:23-25] When they complained of the lack of meat, He sent them quail to eat. Next the Lord sent them manna from Heaven to eat. [Cf. Ex. 16:13-15] When they were thirsty once more, he poured water forth from the rocks. [Cf. Ex. 17:6] Arriving at Mount Sinai, God appeared as a point of fire atop the mount. As He spoke to Moses, the people heard the peal of thunder and very loud blasts of a trumpet. [Cf. Ex. 20:18; Ex. 19:19; variant, Deut. 5:23-24]

Maybe the Israelites didn't love Yahweh, but after all of these manifestations, they should have mortally feared Him. The Bible informs us they did just that. At the foot of Mount Sinai they entreat Moses, *"You speak to us and we will listen; but let not God speak to us, or we shall die."* [Ex. 20:19; alt. Deut. 5:25] Moses' reply explained God's motive for this frightful display.

"Do not be afraid for God has come to you only to test you and put His fear upon you, lest you should sin." [Ex. 20:20]

And the wonders didn't end there. Whenever Moses returned from speaking with God, his face became so radiant he had to shield the glow with a veil. [Cf. Ex. 34:29-35] But all of God's signs weren't beneficial to the community as Nadab and Abihu discovered. They were sons of Aaron, thereby, priests of the Ark of the Covenant. The report in Leviticus explains that they offered "strange" (unauthorized or profane?) fire to the Lord, who became so incensed He caused the fire to consume them, a foreboding manifestation to anyone who took Yahweh's strictures too lightly. [Cf. Lev. 10:1-2]

{Excuse my straying from the main theme of this section momentarily so that I may make another point that is as appropriately made here as anywhere. It concerns the imposition of punishment for lawbreakers.}

In a few isolated instances God imposed His own punishment on violators of His rules, as in the previously cited story of Nadab and Abihu. Yet, all too often, He (allegedly) instructed mankind to apply His penalties for Him. Why? Why doesn't He always strike out against sinners Himself? If adultery is such an abomination to Him, why doesn't He stone the adulterers personally, from Heaven, as He did when He rained down stones on the Amorites at Beth-Horon? [Cf. Jos. 10:11] If certain infractions were so "profane" that they warranted the death penalty, why didn't God execute the sentence Himself, in every instance and without human assistance? [e.g., Gen. 38:7] Everyone knows the stock answer to these two questions, but so few are willing to concede the obvious true answer. If mankind didn't enact God's punishments for Him, almost invariably, the guilty went unpunished. Oftentimes the malefactor ostensibly was rewarded, either through his transgression or despite his transgression.

If men truly believed in God, and unreservedly believed in divine intervention, then mankind would leave all discipline or retribution to that infallible prosecutor and that incorruptible judge, the Supreme Being. God shouldn't ever need a surrogate to act in His stead. If accepted Christian theology is valid, all God needs to do is to cease thinking of a person and that person will cease to exist.

Reflecting back, one can hazard why God didn't execute all adulterers Himself. If He had done so with David and Bathsheba, He would have altered His own Son's destiny, for those two were ancestors of Jesus. There were many other offenses that the progenitors of Jesus were guilty of, including murder (David devised the stratagem that directly led to Uriah's death). [Cf. 2 Sam. 11:15] However, none of Christ's ancestors committed the ultimate of all human sins, offering "profane" fire to the Lord, as did Nadab and Abihu!

That written, I return to the early days of the Exodus of the Israelites. In May, the second month of the Exodus, the people began grumbling against God and Moses because they had no meat to eat. (Who can reveal what became of their numerous herds and flocks?) [Cf. Ex. 12:38] God, in His benevolence, sent quail into their midst. [Cf. Ex. 16:13] Yet, in revenge, He concurrently struck them with a *"very great plague."* [Num. 11:33]

Yahweh's next disciplinary act was to punish Miriam with seven-day leprosy for contending with Moses for leadership of the Community. [Cf. Num. 12:10] Aaron was a party to the same conspiracy as was Miriam, yet he remained unpunished, which must have puzzled at least some of that assemblage.

Soon thereafter, the multitude reached the borders of the Promised Land. Moses sent out twelve spies to reconnoiter the area, but they returned with disheartening news. The inhabitants of the land were all giants (Anakim, aka Rephaim, Zuzim and Emim, i.e., very tall peoples) who lived in well-fortified cities. They were most unlikely to accommodate the Israelites in their desire to annihilate them. [Cf. Num. 13:33-34]

You should surmise after all that had occurred to this point, the people would not only have requested Yahweh's assistance; they should have expected it. You would surmise so, but you would be wrong. The despondent tribes were more disposed to retreat than to attack. Moses, Aaron, Joshua, and Caleb tried to dissuade the Israelites from their intention to return to Egypt. To understate the actuality, the people's response to the urging of their leaders was singularly unappreciative. 'The entire community threatened to stone all four rather than face the Anakim in battle.' [Cf. Num. 14:10]

Even God is perplexed by their lack of faith. His words, *"How long will this people spurn me? How long will they refuse to believe in me, despite all the signs I have performed among them?"* [Num. 14:11] If God can ask these questions, then my repeating those questions can't be too unreasonable. Ruefully, I must inform you that the Bible contains no answer for this apparent disparity of perceived perception. But next, I will attempt to supply a reasoned explanation for that perceptual difference.

None of the asserted miracles was a miracle at all. Whatever were the real facts, most of the people must have viewed the events in Egypt and during the Exodus as the random manifestations of nature, not the purposeful actions of a patronizing Deity. Briefly, I will comment on most of the signs the Israelites witnessed during this period, injecting my speculations periodically so that you may ponder these events from my perspective.

Of the ten plagues, five lend themselves readily to a natural explanation: The frogs, the gnats, the flies, and the locust are a recurring problem in many parts of the world. Severe hailstorms occur with just enough repetitiveness to enable anyone to associate their occurrence with some momentous human event. The water turning to blood isn't easy to explain, but the Bible relates that *"the Egyptian magicians did the same by their magic arts,"* and that causes me to suspect trickery. [Ex. 7:22] I am almost embarrassed to offer an obvious solution to the red water plague. At flood time, the Nile carries large quantities of red silt down into the lower regions of Egypt. Isn't it possible Moses merely stirred up the red mud with his staff?

The pestilence, which only affected the Egyptian livestock, could well have been caused by the Israelites themselves. This possibility must have occurred to Pharaoh. The festering boils most probably were nothing more than blistered skin caused by a caustic element which Moses mixed with the soot he threw into the air. [Cf. Ex. 9:8-11]

The intense darkness for three days would appear to surpass the bounds of a natural phenomenon; yet, the text itself sheds illumination. *"Men could not see one another, nor could they move from where they were."* [Ex. 10:23] If so, how was Pharaoh able to summon Moses to bring him to the royal residence to bargain with him? Perhaps it wasn't quite as dark as the above text indicates. Ever since the Sahara desert evolved, Egypt has been beset with sandstorms that are fierce enough to blot out the Sun, even for days at a time. At this point, Pharaoh relented. He informed Moses that the Hebrew people could leave, but their livestock had to remain. Moses rejected this condition. [Cf. Ex. 10:24-27]

The last plague, the death of the male firstborn of Egypt, is almost totally unbelievable. From either party's perspective, the tale reeks of literary invention. Assume the position of the Egyptians first: You awake in the middle of the night to find your firstborn male child dead. Do you suspect that an invisible spiritual entity (Angel or God) killed your offspring, or do you suspect a human intruder? If anything could have frozen my mind into an obstinate mode; that would have done it. I would have sought immediate revenge on the first Hebrew I could lay my hands on. [Cf. Ex. Chapter 12]

The Hebrew perspective likewise would have generated suspicions and retaliation. The Israelites were instructed to smear blood on their door posts so that the avenging angel of their God would bypass (pass over, hence 'Passover') that house, thereby sparing their firstborn male. Why would God's angel need a blood sign on a door post? Didn't God know who His chosen people were? He did, but human assassins might not; therefore, the actual need for a visible identifying sign. Also, why would God wait until midnight to strike? Did He need the cover of darkness to aid Him in His mission to murder so many of His own creatures? I offer that the real reason was because He was experiencing shame at what He had decreed, and accordingly, ordered the murderous deeds be carried out under the anonymity of midnight darkness.

We will never become privy to whatever induced Pharaoh to permit the Israelites to leave Egypt. But the internal evidence refutes, rather than supports, divine intervention. The evidence indicates that the Israelites weren't overly imbued with confidence in Yahweh's partiality toward them. The obvious conclusion as to why they weren't convinced was because they didn't witness any inarguable proofs of that partiality. The Exodus was a toilsome hardship that was endured with only the greatest reluctance. The meandering path that it took toward the Promised Land informs me there was no sentient heavenly being directing that staggering trek for forty years (if it did endure 40 years?). Clearly, several of the attributed miracles of the Exodus were nothing more than natural occurrences. Once these occurrences had been defined as miraculous, they provided the inspiration for the imputation of Yahweh's intercession in all events during the journey, both events that aided and events that hindered the trekkers.

Shortly after the Israelites arrived at the Promised Land, many of the Canaanites began hearing (and believing?) of the prodigious wonders Yahweh could and would perform for His adherents. How did this tribal information come to be known by other than the Israelites? Understandably, the Hebrews were astute enough to broadcast, to as wide an audience as possible, the frightful power of their personal Lord of all Gods, Yahweh.

Equally obvious is the assumption that had the Israelites been certain of Yahweh's unremitting intervention, it just may have been unwise to forearm their enemies with this intelligence. Wide distribution of numerous examples of the awesome manifestations of their personal Deity could only have aided the Israelites psychologically. But, as you can well imagine, such psychological advantage would have greatly abetted their military efforts. The rationale behind this premise can be framed thus: If Yahweh unfailingly provided His chosen people with military victories, what advantage was gained by alerting their foes beforehand?

The glorious stories of Yahweh's interventions in the affairs of the Israelites were retold with such convincing repetition that eventually the succeeding generations of Israelites came to believe them personally. Boastful stories designed to dupe and intimidate their adversaries, eventually became scriptural 'truths' to the Hebrew tribes themselves.

The last postulation isn't a grand revelation. This is simply how all anecdotal "folk myths" eventuate into "revered facts." Most legends are charming as long as they are recognized as legends. The Greek mythologies attest compellingly to this. Throughout the world, wherever people travel, they bring their ethnic myths with them. It is delightful to hear those enticing stories about ogres and giants and a myriad of other wondrous creatures, cavorting through charmed forests or enchanted lands wielding magic lanterns and other mythical artifacts. This is great fun, provided no one takes these tribal myths seriously. Yet, this is precisely where the Hebrews went astray; they ultimately succumbed to their own glorified Deity folklore. Because of this, untold miseries have been inflicted upon countless persons, all under the guise of honoring the greatest folk myth of all: The Supreme Being, God!

A HORRIFIC TEST OF OBEDIENCE

Heavenly Beings, to the ancients, weren't the least bit explicable. The manifestations of Nature (which they believed were God's method of demonstrating His majestic faculties) were patently unpredictable, logically irrational, and seemingly deliberately obstructionist. Therefore, the God who controlled nature didn't need man's love, but undeniably, He did need to be appeased! Abraham had this understanding of his God (Yahweh), so when he was commanded by Yahweh to kill his son, Isaac, and to fire the son's remains in a holocaust offering, Abraham never questioned this barbaric directive. Yahweh was not to be trifled with! He was a vengeful God and Abraham 'knew' that Yahweh had destroyed the entire world several generations earlier. If the slaughter of his young (and only legitimate!) son could win Yahweh's favor, it seemed a small price to Abraham.

Apologists of the Bible deflect the real implication of this story and attempt to portray it as a glowing example of obedience to God's will. It was, in actuality, the acting out of ritualistic human sacrifice meant to gain Abraham some material benefit. Abraham should have realized that it would have been deceitful for Yahweh to miraculously send him a son if He was going to negate that beneficence ten years later. [Cf. Gen. 22:1-13] Ordering the killing and incineration of a youth is the command of a despot, not a test of obedience by an alleged clairvoyant (all-knowing) Deity. [Cf. Ezekiel 16:36 –*Yahweh condemns Jerusalem for child sacrifices*]

The murder and fiery immolation of children wasn't unknown in the time of Abraham. Afterward, we find the Hebrews excoriating their neighbors for such sadistically abhorrent religious practices. This particular child-sacrificing rite was associated with the Cult of Molech and it is conceivable, even probable, that Abraham was dallying in a ghastly ritual of this pagan religion, rather than following Yahweh's dictates. [Cf. Lev. 18:21 & Lev. 20:2-5] In this biblical story Yahweh relents and spares the boy's life. But, to my mind, the moral and doctrinal damage had already been done. The immorality of such a repugnant test of obedience is self-evident. God's omniscience is likewise compromised. If He knew that Abraham would obey the Divine command without question, what was the point of testing him with a directive that was so ethically and so socially revolting? Immolating children was/is barbarous!

The two principal conclusions I draw from this story are: 1. Yahweh wasn't a kind, loving, noble Deity tending His devotees with paternalistic care. 2. Yahweh couldn't foretell the future; He didn't know if Abraham would or would not obey His order. Ponder the opposite; if this was a 'sacred' test from God, to what 'evil' tests might Satan subject us? It is soul-shuddering even to contemplate that potentiality.

THE BRONZE SNAKE

In Numbers, Twenty-One, the Israelites again grumble against Yahweh and His sparse munificence during their desert sojourn. I presume they are complaining against the miraculous manna from heaven when they decry, *"We are disgusted with this wretched food."* [Num. 21:5] For once Yahweh's vengeance was directed at the guilty parties, for He sent seraph (burning) serpents to harry the Israelites. Many died of snakebite, and wisely, the remainder appealed to Moses to seek deliverance for them. Moses prayed to the Lord for relief, and God answered the plea. He instructed Moses to fashion a bronze serpent and to mount it on a pole. Moses complied and, thereafter, anyone bitten by a serpent, that subsequently was able to approach the pole and behold the replica of the serpent, had his life spared. [Cf. Num. 21:6-9]

Beholding an iconic image seems to be a very circumspect require-ment to cure your chosen people; moreover, it also could invite belief in the potency of idols. Was it the bronze serpent that cured, or was it God? God is everywhere, so you would surmise His healing powers are likewise everywhere. Conversely, if the healing power resided in the emanations coursing out from the bronze form, you would presume that you would have to be exposed to those emanations to be cured. Stated plainly, it is the bronze serpent icon itself that cures!

One last alternative might suggest itself to an inveterate skeptic. Namely, that only those persons naturally resistant to the venom's toxicity would be able to travel to the locale of the magical icon after having been bitten. They also would be the most likely to survive the venom's effects, with or without gazing at a bronze likeness of a snake! The suggestive power of the incidence of the first survivors would also influence those later bitten by snakes allaying their despair, instilling hope, and perhaps even promoting the release of internal combative and curative antibodies.

More enlightening is the information provided at verse six of the tale when the ancient author admitted that not all those bitten by the serpents died even before Moses manufactured his bronze idol. *"And they bit the people and many of the people died."* (Many died, but not all!) [Num. 21:6]

The Bible's defenders today must be greatly perplexed to read how years later, the serpent's image, crafted by Moses at God's direction, was

188

finally consigned to its proper niche in history. King Hezekiah (r. 726-698 BC) unceremoniously destroyed the bronze serpent of Moses because the people of his day were burning incense to it. Hezekiah called it Nehushtan. (Hebrew: 'little copper thing') [Cf. 2 Ki. 18:4] God's potent talisman was ultimately exorcised!

THE TALKING ASS

The Old Testament of the Bible is replete with evidence of the ignorance and superstitious gullibility of its authors. The story of Balaam and the talking ass is representative. Balaam was neither an Israelite, nor an adherent to the Laws of Moses. The story alleges that he was an oracle that the gods spoke with and through. Yes, that is correct; Yahweh 'the Lord God of Israel' also attended to the summons of Balaam. What is more, if Balaam cursed you, then Yahweh (or some other god?) enforced that curse upon you. [Cf. Num. Chaps. 22, 23 & 24]

Balak, the king of Moab, after hearing of the Israelite defeat and annihilation of the Amorites and their king, dispatched messengers to Balaam. The messengers besought him to pronounce a curse on the Israelites in order that they might be defeated in battle. Balaam, an Amauite, informed the messengers that he must confer with the God of Israel first. Being an oracle, Balaam (presumably) could conjure at will all extant deities of the Canaanite lands, calling forth even Yahweh.

The Lord of Gods (Yahweh) dutifully responded to Balaam's summons and asked him who his visitors were. Why would Yahweh have to pose this question? Didn't He know? Or was this just His method of initiating a conversation. Balaam explained their mission to the Hebrew Deity who instructed Balaam: *"Do not curse this people for they are blessed."* [Num. 22:12] Did God also think that Balaam's curses had potency? Balaam followed the Lord's instruction and turned the petitioners away. They returned to Balak with their mission unfulfilled.

Still, Balak, the king of the Moabites, would not be rebuffed. He sent more distinguished emissaries who again entreated Balaam to pronounce a curse on the Israelites. The emissaries relayed Balak's offer to reward Balaam handsomely if he but complied with their entreaty. Balaam again beckoned the Lord God (Yahweh) whose words then were, *"You may go with them; yet only on the condition that you do exactly as I tell you."* [Num. 22:20]

The next morning Balaam arose, saddled his ass, and set off with the princes of Moab who were sent by Balak. Incredibly, the whimsicality of Yahweh surfaced again. Inexplicably, His anger flared up against Balaam for doing precisely what He had instructed him to do just the previous night. God stationed an invisible angel with an invisible drawn sword on the road to Moab. Balaam couldn't see the angelic assassin, but fortunate for the seer, his ass could. Three times the animal refused to pass the unseen angel with the sword standing in the roadway. Each time Balaam heatedly lashed the unfortunate beast for his seeming obstinacy.

After the third beating, the Lord endued the animal with the ability to speak. It asked Balaam, *"What have I done to you that you should beat me these three times?"* Neither surprised nor shocked at having an animal question him, Balaam answered, *"You have acted so willfully against me that if I but had a sword at hand, I would kill you here and now."* The ass responded to Balaam, *"Am I not your own beast, and have you not always ridden upon me until now? Have I been in the habit of treating you this way before? 'No,' replied Balaam."* [Num. 22:28-30] Just then God permitted Balaam to see the angel with the sword blocking the roadway. Then the angel imparted the frightful news that had the ass attempted to pass that spot on the roadway Balaam would have been slain. [Cf. Num. 22:31-33]

Incidentally, the idiomatic expression 'Lord God,' which the Israelites used for Yahweh, is enlightening to us all if we but reflect on its meaning. Lord God means master god or chief god, implying that its user acknowledged that there existed subordinate or lesser gods! *"The Lord God of gods."* [Jos. 22:22] {*"For those who have ears, let them hear!"*} [Mt. 11:15, et al.]

The 'Talking Ass' tale is contradictory in some aspects and mystifying in another. If God told Balaam to go to Moab, then why did He dispatch the angel to kill him? If God really wanted to kill Balaam, then why didn't He simply cause him to die? Why did the ass receive the power to talk? Inarguably, what the ass said was neither profound nor notable. Clearly, the whole conversation was trivial. The story is pointless; I am mystified why God inspired the author of Numbers (whomever that might have been) to include it in his O. T. narrative.

At this juncture, 'Numbers' informs of how the Israelites slaughtered those who were occupying the Promised Land, or who were so unfortunate as to live on the approaches to those lands. None of the participants in the 'Talking Ass' tale are Israelites, so the only way the story could be known to its biblical author is through inspiration. The author definitely wasn't a personal witness, nor was he a confidant of Balaam when Yahweh spoke with him. Soberly considered, the tale is either holy inspiration or wholly invention. No plausible third alternative is possible.

So what became of Balaam, the man who at will could page the various gods of the ancient Promised Lands? With nothing more deferential than a terse sentence in the Bible, he is dispatched by the Israelite Army. "... [A]*nd Balaam, the son of Beor, they put to death with the sword.*" [Jos. 13:22 & Num. 31:8]

THE SPIES OF JERICHO

An incident related to the future conquest of Jericho should be a shameful memory for the moral and ethical Heavenly Father whom Jesus Christ urged us to venerate. Yet, for Yahweh, the fearsome, jingoistic God of the Israelites, this incident ruefully is typical. This tale amply evinces Yahweh's cruel concept of mercy and His distorted application of justice.

[Joshua, Chap. 2, Verse 1ff.] Joshua sent two spies into Jericho to reconnoiter for the coming siege and intended annihilation of its inhabitants. The spies proceeded into the city and eventually entered the house of a harlot (madam?) named Rahab. The king of the city received a report of the spies and sent men to Rahab's house. Alert, or alerted, she secreted the Israelites and diverted the king's men onto a fool's search mission outside the city. The grateful spies then swore an oath not to harm Rahab or her family during the coming invasion because she had shielded them. Of all the people in that doomed city, Yahweh chose a harlot to spare. She, a traitor to the city that gave her protection, and likewise provided the patrons for her profession, was the person upon whom the God of Israel (Yahweh) elected to bestow His dispensation. Who could have been less deserving than Rahab? [Cf. Jos. Chaps 2 & 6]

It is said that virtue is its own reward, but it would appear that with Yahweh, treachery, deceit, and promiscuity merits extraordinary distinction. Can anyone countenance the biblical fact that God chose a harlot (Rahab), a seducer (Ruth), and 'in essence' an adulterer (Bathsheba) as precursors of His only begotten Son? [Cf. Ruth Chaps. 2 thru 4] [Cf. 2 Sam. Chap. 11] These are only three of the tainted women in the lineage of Jesus. Judah, the founder of the tribe which bears his name, fathered Perez and Zerah in an incestuous liaison with his daughter-in-law, Tamar. [Cf. Gen. Chap. 38]

You've already read of Abraham and Isaac, both of whom prostituted their wives. Without doubt most of us have antecedents of whom we are less than proud. However, we had no choice in selecting our antecedents. God did!

Rahab, the harlot, was honored through Yahweh when He made her an ancestor to Jesus. Rahab was a wife to Salmon, and the mother of their son, Boaz. Boaz was the father of Obed. Obed was the father of Jesse. Jesse was father to King David. [Cf. Mt. 1:5-6] Wasn't there a single righteous woman in all of Jericho who was more worthy? By my determination, Rahab must have been among the least worthy of all the women in that doomed city.

THE MISPLACED ALTAR

Even certain Israelites noted the twisted sense of retribution Yahweh directed against His chosen people. For some unexplained reason the eastern tribes of Reuben, Gad, and the half tribe of Manasseh built an altar on the east bank of the Jordan River. [Cf. Jos. 22:10] In the minds of the other Israelites this was certain to bring Yahweh's vengeance down upon the entirety of the twelve tribes. But let the author enlighten you in the Lord's own words as they appear in the Deity-inspired Bible. This quote begins with a spokesman for the remaining tribes admonishing his injudicious brethren.

"What act of treachery is this you have committed against the God of Israel? You have seceded from the Lord and rebelled against Him by building an altar of your own. You are rebelling against the Lord today and by tomorrow He will be angry with

the whole community of Israel. When Achan violated the ban, did not {God's} wrath fall upon the entire community? Though he was but a single man, he did not perish alone for his guilt." [Jos. 22:16-20] (Excerpted for brevity)

Achan had stolen treasure from the conquest of Jericho that should have been turned over to the priests. For this crime, Achan, his family, his servants, his men, even his animals were all put to death by Joshua via the dictates of Yahweh. [Cf. Jos. 7:18-26]

This ancient protestor evidently knew the story of the Exodus well and he feared that Yahweh would strike out violently and indiscriminately against the entirety of Israel. The faithful were as liable to lethal retaliation from Yahweh as were the actual malefactors. Was it true that God, moved by anger at his misguided adherents, would direct great injury to afflict his faithful adherents as well, simply to vent His spleen? No! In actuality, God neither helped nor harmed the Israelites —*ever!* Mostly, Yahweh's vengeance was enacted by holy (?) men claiming to act in God's stead, presumptively at God's personal behest.

At other times natural events are attributed to Divine intervention occasioned by His anger. The notion of Divine intervention is preposterous. But a person who attributed every significant occurrence affecting his life to the willful actions of an unfathomable Divinity would necessarily be apprehensive about the unpredictable reactions of a presumptively provoked Deity who was believed (known?) to be capricious as well.

Unintentionally, the person who originally composed those verses concerning Achan informs us much about the superstitions of his day. Yet, looking around me today, I see abundant indications that this same credulous mentality flourishes into this age. Not that we still indict the Lord for every natural disaster. However, as a violent hurricane bears down upon a coastal community we learn that numerous persons (self-styled 'holy' men foremost among them) prayed to the Lord to spare the populace from great property damage or personal injury.

Today, the belief is that God doesn't initiate the natural disaster, but if we beseech Him fervently enough, He will moderate the suffering attendant to that natural disaster. We have refined our superstitions; but we haven't renounced them. How often do we assign credit to God when someone with a serious illness experiences a seeming remission of their debilitating medical condition? 'More often than not, I suspect! Why don't we question the Supreme Being at the outset as to the reason He permitted us to be so stricken? What of those who die after prayer?

Oh yes, I have almost forgotten, we are all sinners; therefore we are all deserving of punishment. But if so, I ask why the greatest sinners among us aren't stricken with the greatest punishment? The response: This is another of God's endless mysteries. Don't ask again!

GOD ACCEPTS A HUMAN SACRIFICE!

A reprehensible example of the superstitious mindset of the people of the Old Testament period occurs in Judges, Chapter 11, verses 30 to 40. Jephthah, a Judge of Israel for six years, made a vow to the Lord that he would offer up, in fiery sacrifice, the first person that came out of Jephthah's door when he returned home. This vow was offered in exchange for God's deliverance in war of the Ammonites to Jephthah's army. Well, God dutifully delivered up the Ammonites, but to Jephthah's stunned regret, the first person to greet him upon his return home was his only child, a daughter. Yahweh, knowing the future, must have known who would first greet Jephthah, yet He failed to make objection to Jephthah's vow. Thence, Jephthah, as he had vowed, soon afterward conflagrated his daughter in a ghastly holocaust as recompense to the Deity who had accepted his vow of a human sacrifice and provided him a military victory. [Cf. Judg. 11:39] [Cf. Num. 30:1-3]

There are many actions which that perverse Deity, Yahweh, could have taken to circumvent Jephthah's appalling oath. But in this case, He took none. Why Jephthah would even tender the offer of a human sacrifice is illuminating if one but reflects on it. In a commentary note at the end of the Roman Catholic Book of Judges, the Christian editor wisely disassociates God and the ancient author from Jephthah's act by observing, "The inspired author merely records the fact; he does not approve of the action."

To the contrary, I opine that Yahweh's lack of recorded disapproval proves just the opposite. In numerous other incidents, when Yahweh was displeased with the actions of His petitioners, He made His displeasure known immediately or shortly thereafter. No such disavowal is evident in this account, and none should be imputed or inferred. The fact that Yahweh delivered up the Ammonites after the vow was made would have been evidence enough of His approval in other cases of vows tendered; subsequently accepted and recompensed; why not this one? The answer is: Simply because a Twentieth Century apologist knows that by today's ethical standards, Jephthah's act was ritualistic murder, and it was a gross violation of decent, sensible, (Christian?) behavior!

How did Yahweh deal with the man who murdered his own daughter? Chapter Twelve informs us. He helped Jephthah defeat and murder forty-two thousand Ammonites (who also were 'Children of Abraham' through Lot and his debauched daughter!). [Cf. Gen. 19:38] Then, *"After having judged Israel for six years, Jephthah the Gileadite died and was buried in his city in Gilead."* [Judg. 12:7] Now for all time, Jephthah will be revered and respected as an honored and righteous "Judge of Israel."

SODOM REVISITED

Just how wicked were the towns of Sodom and Gomorrah? Aren't there places on Earth today where the people are just as depraved? It is difficult for me to imagine just how wicked those ancient debauchees were, to have so incurred God's remorseless reprimand.

In November of 1980, a devastating earthquake struck southern Italy killing several thousands of people. Three hundred of the dead were killed in the collapse of a church. What message should I extract from this tragic event? If the church had been unscathed by the quake while nearby edifices had been destroyed, I know what interpretation religionists would have given this eventuality. This clearly would have been a miracle from God! A point is being labored here, I realize. Yet, how does one combat the willful ignorance that attributes supernatural significance to arbitrary natural events, as most religionists are always eager to do?

The people from the village where the calamity struck were even more perplexed over the tragedy than I am. You see, the town, Benevento, has a deceased patron saint that reputedly protects it from harm. Saint Januarius (AD c.305) is his name. Every March and October a reliquary containing congealed blood from the Saint is examined to determine the state of his blood. If the blood remains congealed, the town is feared to be in peril. However, if the blood liquefies, the town is considered to be safe from disaster for another six months.

At both expositions in 1980, the blood liquefied. So why was the town struck? Why was the church destroyed? Why were three hundred people crushed to death by the collapsing roof of the 'House of God?' Why did God's anger flare up so viciously against people who were engaged in acts of worship toward Him? You know my answer. What is your response?

I asked this question of a devout (converted) Catholic whom I knew. His reply will appear vague and evasive when you read it. But to him, his response was complete and self-evident. His reply: "God didn't directly kill anyone; earthquakes are natural events. Besides, we all have to die some-day. The dead, because they were engaged in activities honoring God, probably went straight to Heaven." Can you see the flaws in his logic? Is there any logic in what he said? All I can see is biased rationale. To this man, everything that happens proves the existence of God. If it rains, this is proof of a Supreme Being. If it doesn't rain, that also is proof of a Supreme Being. This is classic apologetic disguising unconstrained reli-gious bias.

Had this man been born three thousand years ago in Egypt, he would have been just as supportive of Osiris and Isis. This is what is wrong with faith. Faith finds immutable proofs for the most outrageous beliefs imaginable in faith alone. Faith is an opaque partition that shields the real-ities of life from a religionist. Faith is the eternal foe of truth. Religious proponents ask their followers to have faith because they don't have any facts for them. Faith masquerades as a noble virtue when, in actuality, it is a pernicious vice!

QUESTIONS ABOUT THE TWELVE TRIBES

Can you name the twelve tribes of the Israelites? Perhaps you can, but most people cannot. My response to the most previous question will be given before this segment ends.

First, recall the story of Jacob (later renamed "Israel") in the Old Testament. Remember he labored seven years for his Uncle Laban in order to obtain Rachel as a wife. Laban double-crossed Jacob, however, and Leah, the eldest daughter, was given as the payment for the seven years' labor. Jacob, refusing to be dissuaded, agreed to another seven years' indenture in order to possess the more desirable daughter, Rachel.

So, after fourteen years, Jacob had two wives, and those wives each had a personal maid. The maids' names were Zilpah (Leah) and Bilhah (Rachel). The how and why of the remainder of the story of Jacob are irrelevant to the purpose of this segment. The result is all that will concern us.

Jacob fathered six male children by Leah; two by Rachel; two by Zilpah, and two by Bilhah. [Cf. Gen. 29:16-35 & 30:1-24] A quick calculation will reveal a count of twelve male children, but don't conclude too hastily that these twelve are the founders of the twelve tribal territories. Ten of them are, but two aren't. Levi became the father of the priestly caste that didn't inherit any territory in the Promised Land three hundred or more years later. [Cf. Jos. 13:14 & Deut. 10:9]

The reader can also consult a historical map of the Promised Land after the invasion of the Israelites and note that there isn't a territory named Joseph. Joseph was the most illustrious of the sons of Jacob, and it was he who was responsible for the migration of the other sons of Jacob into Egypt prior to the Exodus. [Cf. Gen. 37:26-28, 42:1-3 & 46:3-4]

This leaves us with only ten territories named after Jacob's sons. Who were the other two territories named after? The solution: son Joseph had two sons, and just before Jacob (now "Israel") died, he adopted his two grandsons (per Joseph) as his heirs. [Cf. Gen. Chap. 48 & 49:1-28] This, thereby, made them eligible to become heads of clans, just as their ten uncles became ancestors to the Tribes of Israel. Their names were Manasseh and Ephraim.

So here follows the names of the twelve sons of Jacob, and listed beside those are the names of the twelve land divisions by tribe:

Mother	Son	Territory	Territory
Leah	Reuben	Reuben	Reuben
—	Simeon	Simeon	Simeon
—	Levi	—	Levi
—	Judah	Judah	Judah
—	Issachar	Issachar	Issachar
—	Zebulun	Zebulun	Zebulun
Bilhah	Dan	Dan	—
—	Naphtali	Naphtali	Naphtali
Rachel	Joseph	Ephraim	Joseph
—	—	Manasseh	Manasseh
—	Benjamin	Benjamin	Benjamin
Zilpah	Gad	Gad	Gad
—	Asher	Asher	Asher
—	[Gen. 35:22-26]	[Jos. Chap's 13-21]	[Rev. 7:4-8]

You are probably wondering why there has been included a third list of names of the descendants of Jacob. The resolution of your wonderment is also the impetus for this segment.

Look back at the lists. John's list from Revelations is different from either the names of the sons, or the names of the tribal territories. John (In Revelations) omits Dan, who was a son of Jacob, and he also omits Ephraim, who was a son of Joseph thereby, an heir to Jacob. Why does John the Evangelist (Revelations) give us a different list than the Old Testament authors?

I don't know, and I am reasonably certain no one else does either. But I have a suspicion, which if correct, completely dashes the dogma of divine inspiration. John gave his list from memory, inadvertently skipping Dan and mistakenly listing Joseph, instead of Joseph's son, Ephraim. What other explanation is there? If the Holy Spirit directed John's hand as he wrote, then God made the mistake.

I can appreciate that my supposition is total speculation. That is, the supposition isn't based on substantiated fact. Yet, neither does any verifiable evidence support the supposition that the Holy Spirit guided John. The only fact I can discern here, is the fact that no factual information is contained in Revelations. All of its prophecies have failed, while most of the ancillary verses are either too fantastic for belief, or they are biological impossibilities! *"And there was seen another sign in heaven: and behold, a great red dragon, having seven heads and ten horns, and upon his heads seven diadems."* [Rev. 12:3] *"And the beast which I saw was like unto a leopard, and his feet were as of a bear, and his mouth as the mouth of a lion: and the dragon gave him his power, and his throne, and great authority."* [Rev. 13:2]

Sadly, Revelations is self-exposed as nothing more than a bewildering exposition of fantastic trumpery encompassing ludicrous imagery.

SATAN TORMENTS JOB

"There was a man named Job, living in the land of Uz, who worshiped God and was faithful to him." [Job 1:1] Job had seven sons and three daughters. He was exceedingly wealthy, owning thousands of sheep, camels, cattle and donkeys in addition to very many servants (slaves). However, in Heaven there came a day when all the otherworldly creatures (Angels) would appear before "The Lord" (God). Among those present was Satan (the former Archangel Lucifer?). God spoke to Satan and told him of Job: *"There is no one on earth as faithful and good as he is. He worships me and is careful not to do anything evil."* [Job 1:8] To this Satan replied, *"Would Job worship you if he got nothing out of it? ... But now suppose you take everything he has —he will curse you to your face"* [Job 1:9-11]

God's reply, *"'All right,' the Lord said to Satan, 'everything he has is in your power, but you must not hurt Job himself.' So Satan left."* [Job 1:12] Satan causes Job to lose all of his sheep, camels, cattle and donkeys along with all his wealth. His seven sons and his three daughters are killed when a "violent wind" caused their house to crash down upon them. On another day, God permits Satan to physically harm Job, but not to kill him. Satan causes a painful ulcer to afflict Job from his head down to his toes. Still, Job tenders obeisance to God.

The point of this segment isn't so much what happened to Job, but is the biblical fact that God 'invited' Satan to cause the dreadful and torturous afflictions of Job. Note also that God and Satan appear to be cordial social acquaintances, rather than irreconcilable opponents!

POTPOURRI DEBUNKING DIVINE INSPIRATION

Source: <u>Religion Outlines for Colleges – Course II</u>, by John M. Cooper, D.D., second edition, revised

Below I have excerpted passages from Dr. Cooper's book. Following his excerpts I have added my comments challenging his apologetic, sometimes reinforced with biblical quotes supporting (I believe!) my opinions.

"The sacred writers, when mentioning such things in passing ..." {Ibid. page 39}

Rabbits chew the cud? [Cf. Lev. 11:6 & Deut. 14:7]

A viper's tongue can kill? [Cf. Job 20:16]

Rabbit' chewing a cud wasn't a 'passing remark,' it was an integral part of the dietary rules given by God to Moses. The Holy Spirit, if He inspired any other portion of the Bible, inspired those words as well.

P. B. Rabbits <u>do not</u> "chew the cud!"

{Ibid. page 41} "Most of the Bible is as clear as plate glass. But here and there ... correct interpretation demands very reverent care and cautious exact scholarship..."

Why? Why is the Bible crystal clear in some areas, and extremely opaque in others? God, in His perfection, could easily have rendered the entirety 'as clear as plate glass.' It is clear to me why the Bible isn't perfectly clear. The Bible isn't perfect because none of its authors, spiritual (?) or human, was perfect!

One concise example: In 1 Samuel, a quaint tale of the introduction of David to King Saul is related. [Cf. 1 Sam. 16:21-23] In the next chapter we read of an entirely different initial meeting between

David and Saul. [Cf. 1 Sam. 17:55-58] Who is confused here, God or the mortal author(s)?

"Pope Leo XIII had this to say concerning the inspiration of the Bible: 'The Holy Ghost Himself, by His divine power, stirred up and impelled the Biblical writers to write and so assisted them in writing that they conceived in their minds rightly, and committed to writing faithfully, and rendered in exact language and with infallible truth, all that God commanded and nothing else.' (Council Vatican)"

If the Pope and that Vatican Council were being inspired by an 'omniscient' Deity, then why do we find wholly inaccurate texts such as the following? *"After this I saw four angels standing at the four corners of the earth, holding the four winds of the earth, that no wind should blow on the earth, or on the sea, or upon any tree."* [Rev. 7:1]

Pope Leo XIII (r. 1878 – 1903) declared that The Holy Spirit inspired Revelations (actually the entire Bible) in "exact language" and with "infallible truth." So I ask my reader: Exactly where are the "four corners of the earth"? [Cf. Rev. 7:1; 20:7] A globe, which is what our planet Earth is, has no corners whatsoever!

BIBLICAL REFERENCES TO
NON-CANONICAL BOOKS

Book Referenced	Book of Bible	Chapter & Verse
Wars of Yahweh (Jehovah)	Numbers	21, 14
Song of the Well*	Numbers	21, 17
Book of Jasher	Joshua	10, 13
Song of Deborah*	Judges	5, 1
Fable of Jotham*	Judges	9, 7
Book of Nathan	1 Chronicles	29, 29
Book of Gad	1 Chronicles	29, 29
Book of Iddo	2 Chronicles	9, 29
Book of Shemaiah	2 Chronicles	12, 15
Book of Jehu	2 Chronicles	20, 34

Source: The Laughing Jesus, page 67

Why would the Holy Ghost reference books that could never be read by future adherents of the Bible? The fact that these referenced books are no longer extant indicates that the author wasn't cognizant that those books wouldn't be preserved for future generations. Candidly, whoever composed those references didn't know the future! This positively eliminates God from any part in the authorship of the cited Biblical books or passages.

UNPRESERVED BOOKS
MENTIONED IN 2 CHRONICLES:

"The Vision of Isaiah the Prophet, the Son of Amoz" [2 Chr. 32:32]

"The Kings of Judah and Israel" [2 Chr. 32:32]

Why did the Holy Spirit (of God) inspire the author of '2 Chronicles' to mention these two books if He (the Holy Spirit) knew they would never be available for future generations to consult?

CHAPTER 9
New Testament Times

THE ACCURACY OF THE NEW TESTAMENT

What follows was excerpted from <u>Creeds, Councils, and Controversies</u>. (Saint) Jerome wrote a response letter to Pope Damasus in the year AD 383. {Ibid. page 167} The letter speaks on the request from the Pope for Jerome to undertake to revise, correct, and reconcile the many divergent versions of the New Testament extant in that day.

The gist of Jerome's reply is this: "You urge me to make a new work out of an old one ... the scriptures now scattered throughout the whole world ... differ from one another {you ask me} to decide which of them agree with the true reading of the Greek original ... readings at variance with the early copies cannot be right ... if we are to pin our faith to the Latin texts ... {I must discover which texts} for there are almost as many forms of texts as there are copies ... why not go back to the original Greek and correct the mistakes introduced by inaccurate translators and the blundering alterations of confident, but ignorant critics, and further all that has been inserted or changed by copyists more asleep than awake? ... {Matthew's Hebrew original} as we have it in our language {Latin} ... is marked by discrepancies ...."

Then, discernibly having completed his task of revising the New Testament, in a subsequent letter Jerome declares: "... they {the three Gospels} have been revised by the comparison of the Greek manuscripts

... But to avoid any great divergences from the Latin ... I have used my pen with some restraint, and while I have corrected only such passages as seemed to convey a different meaning, I have allowed the rest to remain as they are."

(End of excerpts. Braces { } enclose my insertions, not found in the book being quoted.)

Jerome was chiefly responsible for the translation of the Bible known as the Vulgate. What can we derive from this knowledge? Many things! First, that there exists no document from the hand of the original author; only imperfect copies of earlier copies are available to us. Remember also, that the nascent Church was severely persecuted, and that there were few locales in the ancient Roman world where the Church held secular power as a religious entity before the emergence of Constantine (AD 306) (r. AD 324-337). The consequences of this lack were many. Scarce few scholars or intellectuals were found in the congregations until the Emperor officially legitimized Christianity in the third decade of the Fourth Century. Before then, the unrecognized Church consisted of autonomous congregations loosely affiliated with one another by a common belief in the special, though vaguely understood, status of Jesus, who was long overdue to return to establish God's kingdom on Earth. There existed no orthodoxy of beliefs, and no single written document expounding *in toto* those beliefs in the manner of a modern catechism.

After Constantine's decree (AD 324-25), the Church promptly formed into ruling units paralleling the structure of the secular hierarchy, and it exercised the same governing authority over its constituent parts. Heresy, evident from the days of the Apostles, remained rampant. The initial acts of the now empowered leaders of the Church were an attempt to homogenize the divergent doctrines of the scattered congregations. The request of Pope Damasus to Jerome was consistent with that attempt. This occurred around the year AD 386.

If anyone still retains reservations about accepting the Bible, especially the New Testament, as the unadulterated 'Word of God,' let him consult any annotated Bible and read the frequent disclaimer, "not found in the best Greek Manuscripts." Let him further reflect on the fact that the earliest surviving document of the New Testament dates from the middle of the second century of the current era and is only a tiny fragment.

The first copies of the Gospels were written on fragile parchment (papyrus rolls?) and were handled frequently; thereafter, the necessity for frequent reproductions. The impulse to add a word here, or to drop a phrase there to validate a local tradition, must have been irresistible for the copyists. That many scribes succumbed to the impulse is undeniable. All that remains to be discovered is just what has been deleted from, or amended into, the originals; whose texts have been lost to us forever. This discovery may no longer be possible.

What Christianity could sorely use today is a contemporary inspiration from God concerning His mortal Son's life on Earth. But then, how could we authenticate such a fabulous and improbable eventuality? For example: Can one unerringly critique Mormon founder, Joseph Smith's, 'Inspired' translation compiled in mid nineteenth century? No! Nor can I or anyone else prove that Humpty-Dumpty was just an invented character in a child's nursery rhyme. I don't believe that Humpty-Dumpty was real. But I can't prove that he was imaginary either. Suppose he was a space-traveling, exotic egg-like being from another galaxy? Can you prove contrariwise? 'Positively not!

THE VIRGIN BIRTH PROPHECY

"Therefore the Lord himself shall give you a sign. Behold a virgin shall conceive and bear a son and his name shall be called Immanuel."
[Isa. 7:14]

The word 'virgin' here is translated from the Hebrew word "almah" that, strictly speaking, means 'young woman of marriageable age.' The Hebrews had another word "bethulah" to express 'virgin.' It might be argued persuasively, that in biblical times a young woman was expected to be a virgin as well. The argument has much weight, but if we postulate divine inspiration of the author, the weight shifts to the counter argument. God, knowing the future, should have been more explicit. If He intended the verse to be translated as 'virgin' and not as 'young woman,' then He should have inspired the author to use the appropriate Hebrew word.

The following is tangential to the purpose of this segment, but it is applicable notwithstanding; hence, it shall be included at this position.

The quote from Isaiah, *"Behold, a virgin shall conceive and bear a son..."* is not a messianic prophecy. Read his seventh chapter yourself. This "virgin" portent was a sign to King Ahaz of Judah that he would prevail against King Rezin of Syria and King Pekah of Israel who had formed an alliance against Judah. Incidentally, King Ahaz did not prevail against his enemies despite the authenticating sign from God that he would prevail. [Cf. 2 Chr. 28:5-8] Matthew inserted his "virgin" verse out of context! [Cf. Mt. 1:23]

THE NATIVITY

According to John the Evangelist, Jesus, just prior to dying, entrusted the care of His mother to the *"disciple He loved."* [Jn. 19:26] We are taught that John himself was the disciple indicated by this phrase. If so, then a curious fact intrudes itself into the Nativity story. The curious fact is that the Nativity isn't recorded in John's Gospel. John's Gospel is replete with miracles, yet, one of the greatest of miracles (the Virgin birth) isn't mentioned. If John the Evangelist didn't know of that history-altering event, and if his was the last Gospel committed to writing, then how and by whom did the two Nativity stories (Matthew & Luke) originate?

John's isn't the only Gospel that doesn't contain the (supernatural) genesis of Jesus. Mark's Gospel omits it also. The fact that so momentous an event was missing from Mark's account of the life of Jesus is injurious to that story's veracity. There is no way that Mark would have left that incident out had he known of Mary's miraculous conception of Jesus through the agency of the Holy Spirit. It can only be assumed that Mark wasn't aware of the 'Virgin birth.' Mark was a nephew of Barnabas, and traveled at one time with Paul as well. Later, he is reputed to have associated with Peter. His Gospel is said to reflect the teachings of that chief Apostle. It is inconceivable that Mark (and, by logical extension, Peter) wouldn't have known of Christ's unique nativity through Peter. It is equally inconceivable that knowing ... Mark would have omitted this incredible revelation. Evidently, 'Mark' never knew of 'Luke' either.

There is no evidence that Mark's Gospel is incomplete in its beginning as we now have it. Therefore, the fact that Mark doesn't record a Nativity is more than just a thoughtless omission; it is deduced evidence against a paranormal birth for Jesus. Beside which, we profess that God inspired him; accordingly, even if Mark was ignorant of the circumstances of the birth of Jesus, the Holy Spirit could have imbued him with this knowledge. He didn't, and we skeptics are left speculating why. The first (and best!) solution that presents itself to my mind is that the Nativity myth is a later fabrication (after AD 70) appended only to the Matthew and Luke manuscripts, and in fact, is not fact! This is the most logical explanation, and it jibes well with the suspicion that the Bible isn't infallible, isn't consistent, and manifestly, wasn't divinely dictated. But then, I am a confessed, herewith confirmed, disbeliever!

This unit began by noting that the Nativity story was missing from John's Gospel. Axiomatically, if Mark's omission was injurious to the veracity of the Nativity, for John to have omitted it must be deemed fatal. If indeed John did receive Mary into his home as an adopted mother as his Gospel states, then he should have been the Evangelist who informed us of Gabriel's visit to Mary; her visit to her cousin Elizabeth; the census; the birth in Bethlehem; the shepherds; the Wise men; the slaughter of the innocents; the flight into Egypt; the teaching in the Temple by the twelve-year-old Jesus; and all the other pre-public ministry details that only Matthew and Luke report. Accounts of the childhood of Jesus would be expected to come from John, more so than from anyone else. Yet, this isn't the verifiable case.

One could reasonably accept that John wouldn't necessarily record every incident in the life of Jesus. Yet, John omits the entire childhood of Jesus. Apparently, John doesn't even know what two of the Synoptic chroniclers have written about the infanthood of Jesus. Or perhaps he did, and this is why his followers wrote in the next-to-the-last verse in John's Gospel: *"And we know that what he said was true."* [Jn. 21:24] Is this a judicious yet cryptic insinuation that other Jesus stories extant at that time were less than true?

And, as for the very last verses, *"Now, there are many other things that Jesus did. If they were all written down one by one, I suppose that the whole world could not hold the books that would be written. Amen."* [Jn. 21:25] If this isn't a brazen addition by some pious scribe, then there never has been a single instance of inserted text anywhere in the Bible. In fact, the very last word, "Amen" is no longer contained in most modern translations of the text under scrutiny. But the King James Version currently appends that word! (As do several other translations)

John, himself, informs us that Jesus commended Mary into his care. As a consequence, John should be the richest font of information about Christ's life before the advent of His public ministry. Instead, He is the poorest source. He records nothing whatsoever of Jesus before the commencement of His proselytizing career. John doesn't even tell us what became of Mary. He doesn't furnish the slightest detail of her death, or of her traditional (legendary) "Assumption into Heaven." Why? John's Gospel dwells so heavily on the more spectacular miracles of Jesus that he must be held at least partially accountable for an early heresy that denied the human nature of Jesus while Jesus lived among mankind. (Docetism)

One more curiosity in John's Gospel should be pondered. Mary, the mother of Jesus, is referred to several times, but never by name! Confer John 2:1-5 & 6:42 & 19:25. In the last cited reference John writes: *"Standing close to Jesus' cross were his mother, his mother's sister, Mary the wife of Clopas, and Mary Magdalene."* [Jn. 19:25] John never informs us of the name of the mother of Jesus. Didn't he know her name?

Now read the final Johanine mention of the mother of Jesus: *"Jesus saw his mother and the disciple he loved standing there; so he said to his mother, 'Woman, here is your son.' Then he said to the disciple, 'Here is your mother.' And from that time the disciple took her to live in his home."* [Jn. 19:27] Now can you see why I am so astonished when John doesn't know anything about the early life of Jesus? It is inconceivable to me that John wouldn't have told us of the miraculous birth of Jesus, had he known of it. What if he didn't know of the immaculate conception of Jesus? That question answers itself!

The opening of John's Gospel could be construed as verifying the virgin birth stories of either Matthew or Luke. (Not both, for those two are in substantial conflict with one another) *"And the Word was made flesh and dwelt among us, (… the only begotten of the Father.)"* [Jn. 1:14] Yet, a moment's reflection would convince an objective person that he was merely alluding to the (professed) fact that God (the Word) became man, which is quite another proposition. The Nativity narratives, as presented, prove that God didn't need a human male to work His reproductive miracle. Why, then, did He need a human female? Couldn't the Angel Gabriel, holding the baby Jesus, have appeared to

Mary and Joseph and then inform them specifically who that baby was? Alternatively, couldn't Jesus merely have appeared on Earth as an adult and thenceforth commence His ministry?

If Mary didn't tell John the Evangelist of her singular distinction among women, how did the story come to be known? Could it be that the story of the birth of Jesus is just that: a fanciful canard appended to the basic story of His ministry? Deities impregnating human women aren't anomalous in historic literature. An Egyptian legend from the Westcar papyrus [The Riddle of the Pyramids] relates an incident from the time of the Pharaoh Khufu, more than two thousand years before Jesus was born. The gist of that text is reproduced below.

Dedi, a magician of Meidum, predicted that the descendants of Khufu would rule over Egypt for three more generations but, then, the next three kings would be triplets begotten by Re himself (a Sun God), and borne by the wife of his high priest. This is one example, there are many more!

Theologians have been diligent on these logical suppositions for centuries. Their conclusions, condensed to their essence, are that Jesus became man to prove that He could live a human life. They stress how very human Jesus was. The pain of the scourging and the crown of thorns, the humiliation and degradation of the crucifixion, after the 'Agony in the Garden' where He foresaw what was soon to happen to Him, all combine to elicit our sympathy; our pity; and our regret. But only if Jesus experienced the trauma exactly as would an actual human person! God can't feel pain, or if He can (our sins pain Him!), then He can punish forthwith those who cause His discomfiture.

God didn't punish the Roman Centurion and his cohorts who crucified Jesus. Eventually, He did punish the Jews of Jerusalem (because of the High Priest Caiaphas?), but not until thirty-some years later. {Ref., The destruction of Jerusalem in AD 66-70.} The humanity/divinity of Jesus is an unjustifiable extrapolation. Either Jesus was a human being (period); or He was a deity posing as a human being. He could not have been both! 'God to man — man back to God' is an impossible contradiction.

THE NATIVITY ACCORDING TO
MATTHEW AND LUKE

Having discussed the absence of the Nativity story in John and Mark, let us now consider the ramifications of that event as it appears in Matthew and Luke. In addition to his Gospel, Luke is also credited with writing the Acts of the Apostles. Luke was a Gentile by birth, and a companion of Paul. He never saw Jesus, nor is there any direct evidence that he knew or had ever met Mary, the mother of Jesus. 'Acts' does mention that Luke accompanied Paul on his last recorded visit to Jerusalem in AD 61. If, as tradition indicates, Mary didn't die until AD 66, then it is possible that Mary and Luke did meet. However, it is extraordinarily incredible that Luke never recorded such a meeting if it had occurred!

Then how did Luke learn of her virgin status; her visit from the Angel Gabriel; the wondrous birth of John the Baptist to Zechariah and Elizabeth; Mary's visit to her cousin; Mary's song of praise; Zechariah's prophecy; the shepherds and the choir of angels at the birth of Jesus; the Circumcision; and the Presentation in the Temple? [Cf. Lu. Chap. 1 thru Chap. 2, vv. 1-38]

If Luke knew all this (and no one else records any of the above), how did he fail to know of the visit of the Magi and their guiding star; of the flight into Egypt to escape the jealous fury of King Herod; and of the slaughter of the innocents? [Cf. Mt. Chap. 1 thru Chap. 2, vv. 1-18] This is comparable to a historian writing the history of World War II and neglecting to mention the attack on Pearl Harbor; Hitler's invasion of the Soviet Union; the Holocaust; or the dropping of the two Atomic bombs. The reliability of this historian's account of the entire conflict would have to be seriously questioned.

Logically, Luke should have been the least likely source of any intimate knowledge of the early life of Jesus. Instead, he is the sole source of much of the written witness to Jesus Christ's human origin. Even an admittedly gullible person should have critical reservations about accepting Luke's testimony as 'gospel truth.'

Matthew, under close scrutiny, fares similarly. He would have us believe that the mothers and fathers of Bethlehem and its neighborhood, permitted their sons, two years old and younger, to be killed without recorded resistance or revenge. So heinous a crime could hardly escape the notice of contemporary historians. The reverberations from that revolting act would have been heard throughout the land. Surely, the people of nearby Jerusalem would have known about it … if it were factual! No citation to/of such a dastardly commission can be found outside Matthew's Gospel. The other Evangelists, who should have been anxious to supply any evidence of Christ's singularity, also fail to record this appalling episode. Even Luke, who provides so much detail concerning Christ's birth, doesn't confirm this emotional catastrophe. There is only one cogent explanation for this omission by Mark, that being: because it never happened!

Flavius Josephus (AD 37 – c.101), a historian contemporary with the first Christians, knew of Jesus, yet didn't know of His virgin conception. Nor does Josephus record a slaughter of children by Herod. Josephus is very expansive about the Jews during the period of Christ's life. Josephus informs us that the Jews rebelled against Pilate because Pilate brought images of Caesar Tiberius into Jerusalem (AD c.26). Josephus is thoroughly conversant with the period of Jewish history that encompassed the lifetime of Jesus. He reports numerous accounts of events that transpired during Herod's reign. Many of the events were particularly reprehensible. Yet, there isn't a word about the slaughter of infants, the arrival of pagan priests heralding the birth of the Jewish Messiah, or the appearance of a portentous star in the heavens over Judea. Josephus gives mute witness against the virgin birth scenario by neglecting to mention it at all.

The internal and external evidences all point toward the complete fabrication of 'the slaughter of the innocents.' Herod the Great was king of Judea, but he ruled at the discretion of the Romans, and factually, his throne rested on a patently insecure foundation. All during his monarchy, his enemies continuously plotted to dethrone him. Josephus chronicles many (all?) of Herod's tribulations.

An example: Complaints were made to the Roman Procurator against Herod when he had Hezekiah slain. The Jewish laws of those times forbade the execution of even an exceedingly wicked man without the approbation of the Jewish Sanhedrin. A provision of the Law of Moses provided that convicted criminals, particularly where death sentences were applicable, could appeal their sentence to the Supreme Council of seventy-one at Jerusalem. By slaying Hezekiah, Herod had acted on his own without the prior approval of the Sanhedrin.

All this notwithstanding, the most devastating question is this: "Who carried out Herod's order to murder infant children?" Surely not the Romans! Yet, can you believe that the Romans permitted Herod to have an army of soldiers so loyal to him that they would commit infanticide? An army that loyal might turn on the Romans themselves. No! Herod ruled because the Romans trusted his fidelity to them, and because of his ability to pacify the turbulent Hebrews. The new-born son of a common Jewish carpenter was no threat to either Rome or to Herod!

Would Herod have so jeopardized his already tenuous position by murdering twenty, perhaps forty, infant boys on the basis of some improbable astrological prognostication delivered by strangers from a foreign land? This stretches my believability beyond its limits. But we are further asked to believe that such atrocities could have been kept from the ears of his enemies so completely that Josephus, who elucidates the period of Herod's kingship in no fewer than one hundred and fifty thousand words {my estimate}, yet fails to provide one word in confirmation of Matthew's deplorable 'slaughter of infants' accusation against Herod?

Josephus does attest one miraculous event. (Doubtless he simply recounts an unusual aerial marvel.) He reports the story that the "sun turned away his light from us" at the murder of a certain great man. [Ant. Judg., Book XIV, 12, 3] To the dismay of Christian research historians, however, he is referring to a celestial manifestation that transpired at the death of Julius Caesar in 44 BC, not the death of Jesus the Christ in AD 33. Such an intimidating occurrence is charged with explicit and implicit portent; surely, this is why three Gospel authors (minus John) appropriated a parallel solar myth (three hours of extreme darkness) to the death of Jesus on the cross. If God made manifest so ominous a heavenly sign at the death of Julius Caesar, how frightening an atmospheric omen would God display at the death of His only begotten Son?

NATIVITY DISAGREEMENTS BETWEEN
MATTHEW AND LUKE

The Nativity stories are absent from the Gospels of Mark and John; moreover Matthew's account differs from Luke's on many salient points. These differences have been explored earlier, so here they will be contrasted only.

Luke writes of the miraculous pregnancy of Elizabeth; Matthew does not. Luke informs us of the visit of the angel Gabriel to Mary; Matthew does not. Luke informs us that Mary visited Elizabeth; Matthew does not. Luke doesn't mention Joseph's dream where an angel explains Mary's divine impregnation; Matthew does. Luke writes that Mary and Joseph lived in Nazareth. Matthew merely writes that Jesus was born in the town of Bethlehem. Luke informs there was a Census that required all Jewish citizens to register in their ancestral town. Why the Roman Emperor, Augustus, would insist on this provision, which may have been important to a Jewish Ruler, but would hardly have mattered to a non-Jewish Roman ruler, leaves me nonplussed! Matthew knows nothing of a census, or that Joseph and Mary travelled from Nazareth.

Incidentally, the Jewish historian, Josephus, doesn't record such a momentous upheaval of an entire Jewish population. The repercussions of this senseless "ancestral home" requirement are beyond imagining. The founding of these ancestral towns took place one thousand years earlier. Just to gain an inkling of the vastness and the societal impact of this idiotic decree, grant that tomorrow our President ordered all of this country's citizens to return to the town that their ancestors occupied in the year 1776, so that they could be recorded in a Census. If you think through all the ramifications of that speculation you will necessarily conclude that not only is this stipulation highly unlikely, but that it is absolutely unachievable!

Caesar Augustus did decree a Census in the year 7 BC, which required three years to complete. But there is no evidence that such a meaningless (to him) genealogical requirement was included. That such a stipulation was enforced, and did occur, should be revered by believers as the greatest miracle recorded in the Bible. Without argument, it would have been the most prodigious!

Matthew reports there was a star in the sky that led the Magi to Bethlehem. How many Magi arrived is never reported, the number three is conjectured because they offered three gifts: gold, frankincense, and myrrh. Luke doesn't mention either the star or the Wise men; he writes of the Shepherds in the fields, and the appearance of a host of Angels singing praises to God. Matthew knows nothing of angels or shepherds. Matthew posits that Jesus was born in a house [Cf. Mt. 2:11], while Luke informs that Mary gave birth and laid Jesus in a "manger" implying that she and Joseph were in a stable because *"there was no room for them in the inn."* [Lu. 2:7] Then Matthew records the Holy Family's flight into Egypt, and Herod's 'slaughter of the innocents.' Luke directly contradicts this event. He reveals that Joseph and Mary took the infant Jesus into Jerusalem and presented Him in the Temple. [Cf. Lu. 2:22]

Luke finally delivers what I consider the *coup de grace* to the insidious fable of the 'slaughter of the innocents.' First he writes of Simeon who *"had been assured by the Holy Spirit that he would not die before he had seen the Lord's promised Messiah."* [Lu. 2:26] Upon viewing the infant Jesus, Simeon recited his canticle giving thanks to God. Then the prophetess Anna not only also recognized Jesus as the Messiah, but perilously, she *"spoke about the child to all who were waiting for God to redeem Jerusalem."* [Lu. 2:36-38] How could Herod Archelaus have failed to learn of this momentous event which occurred in the Temple of Jerusalem, within sight and sound of the High Priest, and with Herod's palace only a short walk distant? Someone's story is amiss; Matthew belies Luke; or Luke belies Matthew. 'Or both are discredited!

Proceeding with the comparison: Luke concludes the Nativity story by reporting that the Holy Family returned to their hometown of Nazareth. Meanwhile Matthew, who has burdened us with the tale of the murder of the infants, records the flight of the Holy Family into Egypt where they *"stayed until Herod died."* [Mt. 2:19] It seems the flight was occasioned to fulfill the prophecy, *"I called my Son out of Egypt."* [Mt. 2:15 citing Hosea 11:1] At the death of King Herod the Great, Joseph was told by an angel to *"go back to the country of Israel,"* {but} *"Joseph was afraid to settle there."* So, after further angelic instructions in a dream *"He came and dwelt in a city called Nazareth"* [Mt. 2:19-23]

Reading Matthew, you would have to conclude that Joseph and Mary were not originally from Nazareth, but lived in Bethlehem before the birth of Jesus. Also, answer why Herod killed children two years old and younger. Was it because Matthew believed, and broadcast to the world, that the Holy Family lived in Bethlehem for almost two years before the flight into Egypt?

Why, you may rightly ask, does Matthew's version differ so substantially from Luke's? 'Primarily because neither was inspired by the Holy Spirit of God! That alone explains the difference. But a secondary explanation is that they proceeded from two different motivations. Luke's Gospel seems to be directed at an established group of Gentile believers. His narrative is reinforcing for an audience already predisposed toward belief, whereas, Matthew is intent upon converting unconvinced Jews. For instance: Why does Matthew have the Holy Family move to Nazareth? So that the prophecy *"He will be called a Nazarene"* would be fulfilled. [Mt. 2:23 per Isa. 11:1?] The term "Nazarene" cannot be found in the Old Testament.

Why does the Holy Spirit impregnate Mary? To fulfill another prophecy, *"The virgin will become pregnant and give birth to a son."* [Mt. 1:23 citing Isa. 7:14] When Herod calls his teachers together and asks where the Messiah will be born, they recite, *"Bethlehem, in the land of Judah."* [Mt. 2:4-6 citing Micah 5:2]

Matthew assumes that Mary and Joseph already lived in Bethlehem, in a house (not a stable!), when Jesus was born. [Cf. Mt. 2:11] In the same vein he has "Wise Men" attest to the Messiahship of Jesus. [Cf. Mt. 2:1-2] A "star" in the heavens points the way to Jesus. [Cf. Mt. 2:9-10] Who can deny such an incontestable assurance from the very sky domain of Almighty God? Why did Herod kill the little children? [Cf. Mt. 2:16] Yes, you guessed correctly: To fulfill yet another ancient prediction! The Prophet Jeremiah had written: *"A sound is heard in Ramah, the sound of bitter crying and weeping. Rachel weeps for her children; she weeps and will not be comforted, because they are all dead."* [Mt. 2:18 quoting Jer. 31:15]

Rachel's connection in this prophecy is somewhat circumspect. It is recorded that she was buried near Bethlehem, but biologically, the inhabitants of Bethlehem weren't her children. You will recall, she was the wife of Israel (nee Jacob) and the mother of Joseph and Benjamin, consequently her descendants are found in the tribal territories of Benjamin, and Joseph (Ephraim and Manasseh). Bethlehem is located in the territory of Judah, the son of Leah and Jacob.

Before Matthew's attribution of this text to the slaughter of the innocents, Jeremiah had interpreted the lament of Rachel as a result of the Babylonian Captivity (597-582 BC?). Several (apparent) matches have transpired. 'Another seeming fulfillment: The lament of Rachel foretold of the destruction of Israel by the Romans after the Jewish Revolt of AD 66-70. Jeremiah's depiction fits more convincingly than any other ascription. (Guesses!)

Again, at the start of His public ministry, Matthew has Jesus move to the town of Capernaum. Once more this is in fulfillment of yet another prophecy, this time from Isaiah. *"Land of Zebulun, land of Naphtali, in the direction of the sea, on the other side of the Jordan, Galilee of the Gentiles! The people who live in darkness will see a great light! On those who live in the dark land of death the light will shine!"* [Mt. 4:13-16 quoting Isa. 9:1-2]

Matthew seems to be writing to/for skeptical Jews throughout. Only in his Gospel do we find the spurious pronouncement from Jesus: *"Do not think that I have come to do away with the Law of Moses and the teaching of the prophets ... As long as heaven and earth last, the least point or the smallest detail of the Law will not be done away with —not until the end of all things."* [Mt. 5:17-18] Was Paul aware of what Matthew wrote here? 'Seemingly not! Beyond denial, Paul later set aside all but a few of the ritualistic regulations of the Old Testament.

Whom should Matthew's audience obey, the teachers of the Law, or Jesus? Matthew informs them, *"I tell you, then, that you will be able to enter the Kingdom of Heaven only if you are more faithful than the Scribes and the Pharisees."* [Mt. 5:20] Academically, the Nativity stories could be subjected to yet closer scrutiny with the same results, but I won't belabor the point here. That point being: The four Gospels occasionally confirm one another; but they frequently and unambiguously contradict each other irreconcilably.

THE NATIVITY VERIFIED?

Many of the details of the Nativity are liable to inquiry. Notwithstanding, there have always been scholarly defenders of the veracity of the entirety of the Gospels. In my research I have encountered several such authors. In one book [Born in Bethlehem], the author concentrated on the Nativity and set out to authenticate as much collateral material as he was able. This segment will dissect his findings.

The author begins with a plausible explanation of the "Census" by deducing that what factually took place was only a tax assessment on propertied persons. His 'theory,' (while reading his book it isn't always apparent that this is all that it is) supposes that Joseph owned property or held some inheritance rights in Bethlehem. Joseph traveled to Bethlehem to register his possessions for taxing purposes.

Author Smit's conjectures throughout are generally tenable, if not somewhat forced. But what must be borne foremost in the mind of an inquisitor is his occasional deviation from, or contradiction of, those scriptural passages that he can't reconcile with his conjectures. His initial detour comes in the first several pages. His understanding of the Census only requires those with taxable assets outside the locale of their permanent residence to have to journey to another location in Roman-occupied Israel. He enumerates all the obstacles to the requirement that every Jew return to his ancestral home territory. He correctly assesses these obstacles as insuperable. Not the least of the difficulties, for the census takers, would have been the universal resistance of the Jewish population to almost any Roman decree.

He must, of necessity, alter the words of Luke. Luke wrote: *"At that time Emperor Augustus sent out an order for all the citizens of the Empire to register themselves for the census … Everyone, then, went to register himself, each to his own town."* [Lu. 2:1-3]

Mr. Smit dismisses the words 'all' and 'everyone' and offers that only a relative minority were involved in this forced migration. Altering the inspired words of God might seem a minor accommodation to him; but I see it as a rejection of the Bible's assertion of unique authorship via divine inspiration. If the Bible in general, and the Gospels in particular, are nothing more than human history books as amenable to revision as any other written account, then Christianity is founded on an unreliable and questionable foundation. If God's Will didn't ceaselessly and unerringly guide the hand of the human authors of the Bible, the legitimacy of Christianity is hopelessly compromised.

Mr. Smit's book has much to recommend it. I invite everyone to read it, believers and non-believers alike. Catholics needn't shun his work for it is endorsed with both a Nihil Obstat ('nothing hinders'), and an Imprimatur ('let it be printed'). Much research went into the writing of Mr. Smit's book, and the exposition of the regulations and traditional ethics of those times is interesting and illuminating from a historical perspective. The damage to the Gospel texts is minimal. This is all the more laudable when it is observed that his two chief sources wrote conflicting and incompatible accounts of the Nativity.

The thorniest path this author must travel is making viable Mary's lifelong virginity. There just aren't any loopholes in the mores and customs of the period to permit this unwarranted extrapolation of the virgin birth myth. The ancient prophecy only required that the woman be virgin until the birth was accomplished. The author's path through this doctrinal dilemma is tortuous, but as expected, he arrives at his destination with the doctrine intact. First, he ages Joseph into his fifties. Then he leaves us with the impression that at his senescent (old) age the masculine fires of concupiscence had died; accordingly, Joseph no longer desired sexual gratification from his sixteen-year-old wife. He then makes the utterly unsubstantiated assertion that Mary openly scorned the singular, customary role of women in those days, namely, marriage attended by motherhood!

In ancient Israel virginity after marriage would have been a disgraceful blot marring the character of Mary, not the meritorious virtue we ascribe to it. Luke confirms my previous statement in the beginning of his Gospel. Discoursing on Zechariah and his wife, Elizabeth (Mary's cousin and mother of John the Baptist), Luke relates Elizabeth's relief and gratification when she learns she is pregnant. *"Now at last the Lord ... has taken away my public disgrace."* [Lu. 1:25] In Genesis, read the words of Rachel, Jacob's second wife. *"So she conceived and bore a son and said, 'God has taken away my reproach.'"* [Gen. 30:23]

Mr. Smit envisions Mary as making a vow of eternal chastity, and depicts Joseph as a compassionate widower who marries her to shield her out-of-wedlock pregnancy from the taunting invective of her peers. His speculations all hinge on two unsupported theses. One: that Matthew and Luke weren't attempting to give a factual and complete biography of the birth of Jesus. Two: that neither Evangelist wrote down all they knew of the Nativity. Yet, the words of God as related through Luke avers that he was writing an *"orderly account ... so that you will know the full truth about everything which you have been taught."* [Lu. 1:4] If Luke averred that he was relaying the full truth, how can Mr. Smit argue that the actual truth was considerably more than Luke provided? Perhaps it was Mr. Smit who was inspired by the Holy Spirit with the totality of the Nativity scenario, not Luke or Matthew!

JOSEPHUS ATTESTS TO JESUS

In the edifying account of the history of the Jewish people, Flavius Josephus, in his Jewish Antiquities (Book XVIII), attests to the historical reality of Jesus. However, the 'witness' of Josephus is not without its critics. Over the centuries since its composition many scholars have contended that the reference by the Jewish historian to "Christians" soon after the death of Jesus is an addendum by a pious (Christian) redactor (long?) after Josephus {fl. c.38-101} had completed his work. Is the text written in the paragraph below, that of Josephus, or is it the bogus witness of another? That dispute won't be resolved in this work. There are secular scholars on both sides of that issue. Here, then, is what Josephus purportedly wrote:

"Now there was about this time, Jesus, a wise man, if it be lawful to call him a man, for he was a doer of wonderful works, a teacher of such men as receive the truth with pleasure. He drew over to him both many of the Jews and many of the Gentiles. He was [the] Christ; and when Pilate, at the suggestion of the principle men amongst us, had condemned him to the cross those that loved him at the first did not forsake him, for he appeared to them alive again the third day as the divine prophets had foretold these and ten thousand other wonderful things concerning him; and the tribe of Christian, so named from him, are not extinct at this day." {< – Josephus? Or a Christian redactor?}

A (somewhat) related item was culled from the Philadelphia Daily News of Thursday, December 22, 1983. "Two Oxford University astrophysicists maintain April 3, AD 33, as the date of the death of Jesus based on lunar eclipses." (I incline to the year AD 30; but I do not insist upon it!)

JOHN'S GOSPEL

John's Gospel is so different from the other three gospels that scholars treat it separately from the so-named Synoptic Gospels. One source of mine vindicates this difference by explaining that John assumed that his readers were already familiar with the Synoptic Gospels. This explanation is devoid of authentication. John doesn't supplement the other Evangelists, he composes his own gospel! His primary concern is to prove to all disbelievers that Jesus is divine; that Jesus literally is God Incarnate. John takes the core story of Christ's life and intersperses his own copious fictions, all to prove that Jesus was a human God.

John's Gospel describes the baptism of Jesus in a circumspect manner. Candidly, relying upon John alone, one could advocate that Jesus never sought the Baptist's services. The text merely states that the Baptist recognized Jesus as the person who would baptize with the Holy Spirit, whereas John himself baptized only with water. The Baptist exclaims, *"Here is the Lamb of God."* [Jn. 1:29] (The lamb, I reason, being a symbol of sacrifice?) Sometime after the conclusion of the Baptism, John states, *"and I tell you that he is the Son of God."* [Jn. 1:34] A devout Jew would have treated this utterance as blasphemy beyond toleration. But here it passes itself off as divine enlightenment; while all the Baptist's followers dutifully nod their heads in complacent agreement. (Inferred)

At the call of Nathaniel in John's Gospel (whom none of the other Evangelists name as an Apostle), Jesus revealed to Nathaniel that he had been under a fig tree when Philip informed him of Jesus. Nathaniel's response to the apparent clairvoyance of Jesus is almost predictable, *"Teacher, you are the Son of God!"* [Jn. 1:49] How could he form so fantastic a conclusion on such flimsy evidence? Couldn't Jesus simply have guessed that Nathaniel was resting under a fig tree when Philip called him to meet Jesus? In Funk & Wagnall's Encyclopedia in Book 9, page 453b, under 'Fig' it states: "This tree is the true sycamore, mentioned several times in the Old Testament, and is a favorite shade tree in the Middle East." Even Jesus is amazed by Nathaniel's declaration; Jesus remarks: *"Do you believe just because I saw you when you were under the fig tree?"* [Jn. 1:50]

John continued to provide proof of the divinity of Jesus. In Chapter Three, Nicodemus, a Pharisee, said to Jesus, *"We know, Rabbi, that you are a teacher sent by God."* During the conversation, Jesus made open claim to Divinity and Sonship. His statements, copied in context: *"No one has ever gone up to heaven except the Son of Man, who came down from heaven."* Plus, *"God loved the world so much that he gave his only Son."* Also, *"God didn't send his Son into the world to be its Judge, but to be its Savior."* [Jn. 3:2, 13, & 16-17, respectively] At the conclusion of Chapter Three, John the Evangelist quotes John the Baptist. *"The Father loves the Son and has put everything in his power."* [Jn. 3:35]

Chapter Four: Jesus stayed two days in the Samaritan city of Sychar preaching to the people. As He prepared to leave, the people profess to the Samaritan woman, *"We believe now, not because of what you said, but because we ourselves have heard him, and we know that He is really the Savior of the world."* [Jn. 4:42] It isn't recorded just what the Samaritans heard from Jesus, and this is regrettable, for many a skeptic might have been converted if later preachers could have reprised this irresistibly convincing and converting sermon by Jesus.

Hardly a verse exists in John where someone doesn't acknowledge Jesus as the actual Son of God, or where Jesus Himself doesn't profess it. The five thousand, whom Jesus fed miraculously, ask Jesus, *"What can we do in order to do what God wants us to do?" Jesus answered, "What God wants you to do is to believe in the one he sent."* [Jn. 6:28-29] That seems to be John's guiding philosophy throughout; to wit: to convince his readers of the divinity of Jesus and His Sonship to Almighty God.

If any Jew had lingering reservations as to the exactitude of Jesus' claim to be God's Son, those misgivings should have been dispelled when Jesus said to the Jewish leaders, *"I tell you the truth … Before Abraham was born, I Am."* [Jn. 8:58] No claim could be stated so unmistakably. Jesus used the very words God uttered on Mount Horeb. When Moses asked God what His name was, Yahweh replied, *"I AM, WHO I AM: and He said, This is what you shall tell the Israelites: 'I AM sent me to you.'"* [Ex. 3:14] {Capitalization added}

No learned Jew could mistake the unequivocal meaning of the words of Jesus. He was laying unambiguous claim to Godhood. Shortly afterward, Jesus further elucidates His claim. *"The Father and I are one."* [Jn. 10:30] The audience understood fully what Jesus had said, and the very next verse shows their reaction. *"Then the Jews once more picked up stones to throw at him."* [Jn. 10:31] John finished his narrative by noting its purpose.

"These have been written that you may believe that Jesus is the Messiah, the Son of God." [Jn. 20:31] Oddly, there is one more chapter to John's Gospel containing three topics and the conclusion to his Gospel. The purpose of this last chapter seems to be to authenticate the primacy of Peter. But, skeptically, it appears more conspicuously to be a calculating redactor's anonymous addendum.

Here a summarized reprise of the final Post-Resurrection Chapter of John's Gospel (actually his human ghostwriter's Gospel as I will 'prove' shortly): Peter and six other Apostles, including the "Apostle whom Jesus loved" [Jn. 21:20] go nighttime fishing without success. In the morning the risen Jesus, appears on the shore unrecognized, and instructs the apostolic group how to catch a net full of fish. Once on shore, and without the Gospel's author elucidating how, the Apostles realize that the previously unrecognized man is the resurrected Jesus. Jesus now proceeds to elevate Peter to the leadership role among the Apostles. [Cf. Jn. 21:15-19] This final chapter addendum is highly suspect!

Next, Peter asks of 'the Apostle Jesus loved' (John?), "Lord, what about this man?" [v. 20] Jesus answered him, 'If I want him to live until I come, what is that to you?'" [v. 21] The Gospel text then explains Jesus did not intend to inform Peter that John would live to see the return of Jesus. [v. 23] How would the original author of these words know that John would never live to witness the Triumphal Return of Jesus? Obviously, because John had already died and Jesus hadn't yet returned at the time this Gospel was composed. The previous is my "proof" that the Evangelist John did not write the Fourth Gospel as it has come down to us.

John's Gospel has been the subject of more speculation than any of the other three have — *with reasoned cause!* During the second century of the current era, many early Church Fathers even questioned its inclusion in the Canon of the New Testament. Much of the speculation revolved around its date of original composition. In some respects John's Gospel gives evidence of a late date for its composition, perhaps as late as the year AD 90.

The chief reason for assigning a later date for its composition than those proposed for the Synoptic Gospels is because John's Gospel is more theologically advanced. John's Gospel begins with the assertion that Jesus is the Son of God Incarnate, and never wavers from that central theme.

The Synoptic Gospels are much less emphatic on this point, and Matthew in particular, seems more intent on proving that Jesus was the expected Messiah, a separate proposition from the Sonship of Jesus! It is reasoned that had the other Evangelists had access to John's Gospel they would have incorporated more of his material into their accounts of the ministry of Jesus than is the observed case; thus, John's Gospel must be of a later date!

The other indicator for supposing that John's Gospel was written late in the first century is his frequent identification of "the Jews" in a negative, adversarial manner. The consensus is that "the Jews" weren't deemed as enemies of Jesus until long after His death, and after the destruction of Jerusalem around the year AD 70. By then, many Gentiles had espoused Christianity and many, if not all, Jewish Christians had been ostracized from the Jewish meeting houses. The antagonisms between Christian and Jew were gradual and hadn't fully crystallized when the Acts of the Apostles was written, or when Paul composed his Epistles. Paul's Epistles can be dated with a degree of exactitude from internal evidences.

The arguments for a late composition of the Fourth Gospel are compelling, but not conclusive. There are several contentions for an early composition predating the Synoptic Gospels. The most compelling, to me, is a sentence from the story of the curative pool of Bethesda. The sentence reads: *"There is in Jerusalem…"* [Jn. 5:2] Note that the writer states that there "is", not that there "was" in Jerusalem. Every Gospel translation that I have read has the word "is." There are a few Gospel exceptions that read "was." This is strong evidence that Jerusalem hadn't been destroyed {AD 66-70} at the time that the author of the Fourth Gospel first wrote of the curative pool incident.

The absence of a Nativity story, although not determinative, is indicative of an early composition. Once that fiction had circulated, anyone writing about Jesus would have had to repeat it, repudiate it, or justify why he did neither. John appears to have been totally ignorant of the Virgin birth story; therefore, the logical deduction is that he wrote his version of the life of Jesus before that fabrication was formulated, or before it had attained general dissemination.

The question of who authored the Fourth Gospel also has been raised. The open vitriol against 'the Jews' would seem to indicate a non-Jew. Yet, the author not only knew of Jewish religious customs and Palestinian topography, he even knew the names and relationships of several biblical personalities that the Synoptic authors didn't. One example: John is the only Evangelist to mention the name of the man whose ear was cut off during the arrest of Jesus. John informs us that his name was Malchus. [Cf. Jn. 18:10] There is no pertinent reason for providing this information outside of the fact that the author knew his name. Rephrased: "If John fabricated the name Malchus, to what purpose was he moved to broadcast such a fabrication?"

Despite all the scrutiny, however, John's Gospel remains an enigma. Some scholars hold to a pre-revolt date of composition. Others insist that a post-revolt date is more likely. Most scholars credit John the Apostle as the author. An adamant minority propose a disciple of John who has become known as John the Elder. The minority offer their proof in the attestation near the end of John's Gospel; and a very odd testament it is!

John's ministry narrative ends abruptly at verse 23 in Chapter 21. The next verse contains a quizzical and unexpected declaration from its unidentified copyist. *"He is the disciple who spoke of these things, the one who also wrote them down; and we know that what he said is true."* [Jn. 21:24] Jesus had just finished speaking to Peter about the 'disciple he loved' and, presumably, the 'beloved' referred to throughout this Gospel is this same disciple. Although this revered disciple is never named, much evidence indicates that he is John. One need not quarrel with that identification. (Although one notable exegete identifies James, the brother of Jesus, as the "beloved Apostle.") But this doesn't reveal who the 'we' is who knows that what 'John' reported is historical fact. The most obvious conclusion to be drawn from the statement is that someone, acting singly or with others, has redacted John's Gospel.

Then he and the others bear witness to the truth of John's recollections. The unnamed copyist speaks for himself in the concluding verse. *"Now there are many other things that Jesus did. If they were all written down one by one, I suppose that the whole world could not hold the books that would be written."* [Jn. 21:25]

Notice here the copyist refers to himself, alone, when he writes, 'I suppose.' John would have known how much of the life of Jesus was missing from his account. But with only fragmented knowledge, the author of the final verse could only surmise how much pertinent information was omitted. This would seem to indicate that our extant version of the Fourth Gospel wasn't personally written by John the Apostle, but was composed by someone associated or acquainted with him.

Ordinarily, I have an aversion to solutions that bestride a controversy, but in this instance I will grant myself a dispensation from that disinclination. I believe our current Gospel according to John contains the reminiscences of a contemporary of Jesus, but his remembrances have been embroidered upon, much edited, and generally glorified. John, himself, in his zeal to acquire adherents to the cult of Jesus, may have been responsible for some of the glorification. But the bulk of the editing and embroidery came from the hand of another. The Synoptic Gospels suffered a similar fate, but not by the hand of John's unidentified redactor.

John's editor, who was probably his successor also, took the basic witness of the Apostle and embellished it to substantiate the beliefs as they had evolved after John's death. By then (perhaps as late as AD 100), Christianity had become almost exclusively Gentile in composition. John, his followers and his Gospel (conjecturally), had lost touch with the mainstream of Christianity, which were Paul's Gentile-dominated Christian communities.

There is one final anomaly that is unique to John's Gospel; that is, John's Gospel contains only one unambiguous parable! [Cf. Jn. 10:1-6] Curiously, John's Gospel does mention parables; *"I have told you these things by means of parables. But the time will come when I will use parables no more…"* [Jn. 16:25] There are miracles aplenty! There are many minor sermons interspersed. There are a few incidentals mentioned that detail the travels of Jesus, and that provide background information. But there is only one parable. If the original author of this Gospel intended to convey a discernible message by his omission of the many parables recounted in the Synoptic Gospels, I have failed to discern his purpose. But I must confess that my curiosity has been piqued by their absence from John's Gospel.

FAITH IN THE NAME "JESUS"

Jesus prayed after the Last Supper, *"O Holy Father! Keep them safe by the power of your name."* [Jn. 17:11]

What is the name of God? The Israelites/Hebrews/Jews knew His name, but refused to utter it, even in prayer! Very ancient folklore superstitions taught that to know someone's secret name was to possess magical power over that person. Moses commanded the Israelites not to use the Lord God's name in vain. From there, the stricture evolved into an edict never to speak His name at all. In the Jewish sacred writings, wherever God's name appeared (presumptively 'Yahweh') the copyist would superimpose the Hebrew letters 'YHWH' (omitting the vowels). The narrator of the scriptures would then be reminded not to voice God's real name, but to substitute the word Adonai, i.e., "Lord." In that manner the reader avoided offending Yahweh.

Nineteenth century scholars, attempting to decipher the ancient Hebrew liturgical texts mistakenly added the vowel components of the word Adonai to the four consonants of the name YHWH and confidently announced that the name of the ancient Semitic Divinity was, 'Jehovah.' Eventually, their mistake was discovered, but not before the name Jehovah had been taken up by several denominations. Today, every serious scholar agrees that Jehovah was not the actual name of the Hebrew Deity.

Part of the problem of discovering what name the Hebrews gave to their Deity arises from the custom of the Semite scribes to omit the vowels from words, printing the consonants only. God's name was written using four consonants now called the Tetragrammaton. The four letters were: *Yodh, He, Waw, and He.* In English the name sounds phonetically as "Yah' way" {Yahweh}. This is as close as we can come to pronouncing the Israelites' name for their Tribal Supreme Deity. This is doubtless the name Jesus was referencing in John's quote. Yet, if you stop to reflect, we have no name for God the Father today. Our Christian God has no name. We use descriptive titles for Him, such as: Heavenly Father, Almighty Creator, and Lord of the Universe, and more. But we have no personal name for Him.

However, we do have a name for His Son whom we profess is God also. We call this other God "Jesus." No one doubts (no one steeped in Christian religiosity *per se*) the power of the name of Jesus. Evil spirits flee at the sound of it. Hopeless cripples can walk again when some pious man intones this name. The Devil himself must retreat when that holy name is invoked against him. Not only does Jesus wield the powers of God; His name of itself is invested with these powers. That such superstitious tripe is believed is a smirch on the collective intellect of mankind. Do you ask why? Well, primarily because the man who was crucified two thousand years ago wasn't named 'Jesus.' This is a fact that can be verified by anyone able to read, even at an elementary level.

To begin: The letter "J" didn't exist in the ancient Semite alphabet, nor does it exist in the Modern Hebrew alphabet. It doesn't and didn't exist in the Greek language. So where did it originate? The letter "J" first appeared in late Roman times and usually represented the consonant sound of the letter "I", which to our ears sounded similar to our present letter "Y", not as the letter "J" does today. The current sound of the letter "J" didn't come into general use until the late seventeenth century of this era. In the first King James translation of the Bible, printed in 1611, the name "Jesus" is appropriately rendered as "Iesus." You will recall that the inscription above the head of Jesus on the cross is always represented by "I.N.R.I." where the first letter indicates His name (Iesus) and the last letter represents the word used when referring to Jews (Iudem).

How did we come to pronounce His name 'Jesus'? Probably, because the early Roman copyists used the "J" symbol created to convey the consonant sound of the letter "I": that is, the "Y" sound. Phonetically, Jesus' name in Aramaic sounded much like Yeshua or Yehoshua. In fact, all the first letter "J" names in the Bible should properly be pronounced as is our present letter "Y."

What effect this information has on religious intransigents can be gleaned after reading of my experience with just such a person. He approached one day and began reciting from the Bible. *"Everyone who calls on the name of the Lord will be saved."* [Rom. 10:13 & Acts 2:21] I asked him what the name of the Lord was. He replied, "Jesus." I countered that the person referred to in that quote was named Yeshua, not Jesus. His response was that he didn't believe me. He then added that his Bible taught that "Jesus" was the name of God's Son. Abruptly, his attitude changed to near defiance, and he stated emphatically that the Bible was the 'Holy Word of God.' He only believed what was written in it; not in any book that was written by man!

He had unshakable faith in the Bible, and this faith insulated him from the deceits of man. But his professed faith caused me to rethink just what faith is, or what it should be! To me, faith is that which is required in the absence of knowledge. Faith is needed where facts are not known, yet a decision must be rendered, or a conclusion formed. Properly, faith should be substituted for knowledge only when there exists the necessity to form an immediate opinion, or when there is a future possibility of obtaining the evidence that will justify your faith.

A prudent person may hold with faith and then hope that the facts, when known, will validate the object of his faith. But when the facts are uncovered, and when each new item of evidence bears witness against the object of faith, then faith is no longer a virtue, it is a character flaw! To be sure, it shows constancy; it shows bullheaded constancy! Before his conversion, Paul had absolute faith in his Pharisaic tutoring. It took a vision from Heaven and an intimidating miracle to convert Paul from Judaism to Christianity. [Cf. Acts 9:3-20]

These men of great faith appear to me more as men of set will. They are canine in their loyalty. We all know how the family dog will protect his master from assault, or protect his home from intruders. But this canine virtue doesn't arise out of intelligence; it is a genetic, instinctive trait. The dog doesn't distinguish between right and wrong, good and bad, even between friend and foe in the strictest sense. Dogs welcome the known, and repel the unknown. Doctrinaire religious champions do exactly the same. They are extremely protective of familiar teachings and beliefs, but implacable enemies of any dogma that isn't offered by their recognized master, be that master a living person or a revered tradition, or even a glorified book!

This isn't an attempt to infer that rock-ribbed religionists only possess the level of intelligence of dogs. But it is an observation that many of those who exhibit unquestioning faith in religious pronouncements aren't exercising their intellects. They close their minds to physical facts, and cling to fantasy worlds; worlds where Angels and Devils flit constantly about strengthening men, or tempting men. 'Worlds where God manipulates mankind in indecipherable, cryptic ways. Imagination is man's greatest attribute in these worlds. Man's intellect, not his imagination, is determined to be 'the great deceiver.'

Your intellect tells you that man is a first cousin to the anthropoid apes (by anatomical & biological comparison). The chief difference between those two is that very intellect. Yet, how does a Christian refute this conclusion? By insisting that man is different primarily because he possesses an immortal soul. What soul? I am willing to wager eternal life against the reality of an immortal soul that exists anywhere outside of man's imagination.

Blind faith in a proposal that is disproved by every observable fact isn't commendable. Further, if that faith leads to actions that reinforce the proposal, and as a consequence contravene those facts, then this faith is not only deplorable, it is abhorrent! An analogy, paralleling the previous statement, would be the case of a tribal witch doctor. For the witch doctor to believe in his personal incantations and spells is deplorable. But if a diseased or injured person is subjected to the ineffective ministrations of a witch doctor, in lieu of a medical doctor, and if mumbo-jumbo is permitted to replace medicine, then whatever defining term we apply to the sham of (quasi)religious machinations of a witch doctor must be denounced, and thereafter be combated!

If mankind insists on exercising his/its imagination, then try imagining this: Imagine that man never utilized his intelligence. The wheel would never have been invented; no tools would exist; no clothing would be worn. Man's only shelter would be caves or forests. Communication would consist of grunts or barks or screeches. Food could only be gathered, not grown. The family unit would consist of a small, interrelated group highly protective of its feeding area. Mankind would be restricted to the tropical regions of the world. In all essentials we would be apes. Our higher intelligence is all that separates us from our near relative, the anthropoid. Lastly, God would be dead! It is our intelligence that isolates mankind from the rest of Earth's bio-forms, not a conjectured illusion called a soul!

Does a soul confer intelligence? No! If it did, then all of the higher animals must be endowed with at least a partial soul for each of them exhibit undeniable signs of intelligence. As a consequence, either animals have souls, or intelligence can exist without soul. This leads inexorably back to the question: "What is soul?" Some persons equate the spiritual soul with possession of a sense of morality. But morality is the resolution of experience, learning and intelligence, not a manifestation of spirituality!

JESUS — MAN OR GOD?

One of the earliest New Testament heresies was occasioned by the confusion surrounding the belief in the true nature of Jesus. Was He God;
or was He merely man? Was He both simultaneously? Did He alternate
between God and man? Was His divinity sublimated while He was on
Earth? Did His human nature suppress His divine nature?

The answer, you might have guessed, is that this is a divine mystery.
No lowly mortal can grasp the solution to so esoteric a poser. This rationale is a convenient dodge for proponents of the Godhood of Jesus. To
perform the miracles we read of, He must have been a God. But to die on
the cross, He must have been a human man. How can anyone reconcile
these diametrically opposite postulations? They can't, thus the obfuscation
intended by ascribing these mutually exclusive beliefs to the unfathomable
realm of divine mystery.

In reality, He is either God, or He was a man, but not both! If Jesus
was God, it would have been impossible for Him to cease being God,
even for an instant. Can Almighty God will Himself into non-existence?
Mystery or no mystery, that absurdity is impossible. God is, or God is not.
There is no mystery intrinsic to that incontrovertible pronouncement.

Read Paul's Epistle, 1 Corinthians 11:3, as interpreted by the
American Bible Society in their <u>Good News for Modern Man</u>. *"But I want
you to understand that Christ is supreme over every man, the husband is supreme over
his wife, and God is supreme over Christ."* <u>The Catholic Family Edition</u> of the
Confraternity of Christian Doctrine text expresses the same idea. *"But I
would have you know that the head of every man is Christ, and the head of every woman
is the man, and the head of Christ is God."* In plain, easy-to-understand words,
'<u>Jesus Christ is above mankind, but is lower than God</u>.' That is what Paul
believed, and he was infinitely more informed about Jesus than everyone
who lived after him. He told us that Jesus wasn't God, but that Jesus was
subject to God.

The above text refutes the doctrine of a Trinity of Gods. By name:
God the Father, God the Son, and God the Holy Ghost. Having thus eliminated the Second Person are we then left with a Duality of Gods? 'Not
likely! God the Holy Ghost is purported to be the 'Spirit' of God, clearly
testifying that God in the first Person has an essence that is more than spirit

essence. Restated: God has both substance and spirit, just as man supposedly is composed of both flesh and spirit. There is such an obvious flaw in this doctrine that if I have to identify for you what the defect is, then you probably will not be able to comprehend it anyway.

When God the Holy Spirit appears as a dove, then He is no longer a spirit. He is substance; the substance of a dove. Somehow, the thought of God appearing as any sort of animal is debasing to Him, and could generate visions of a zoogenic Godhood. Why a dove? Why not a loathsome viper, or a disgusting caterpillar, or a poisonous green mold on an odious mildewed slice of bread? If the Holy Spirit insists on being a member of the avian family, He might appear as a vulture, or a buzzard, or some other repugnant, carrion-eating bird. Why not? Is it because the aforementioned are abhorrent to mankind? Must God appease human preferences when He chooses to appear in the guise of a sub-human member of His creation?

Does God despise certain of the creatures of His own creation? A dove is more endeared by mankind than most other flying creatures, but I would imagine that God would love each variety of His own composition equally, favoring none (excluding mankind) over another. This evidently isn't so! According to the Law, as given to Moses, only perfect, unblemished animals were to be sacrificed to Yahweh. Offering a deformed lamb was an affront to the Almighty even though He, putatively, caused the animal to be born deformed. [Cf. Deut. 15:21, et al.] It appears that the Almighty embraces many of mankind's biases also. The evidence here indicates that God is possessed of the partiality and preferences of mankind, rather than exhibiting an all-encompassing love of every creature of His own conception and formation.

The Godhood of Jesus becomes more incongruous the closer we examine that concept. Pointedly, exactly how did God cause Mary to become pregnant with Jesus? Did God create a divine sperm that subsequently pierced Mary's ovum? If this was the case, then Jesus was (is) only half divine. 'Unacceptable? 'Agreed! Accordingly, the question remains: "How did God cause Mary to become pregnant?" Did God create a divine zygote (an impregnated ovum before the first division) and implant this zygote in Mary's womb to become an embryo, a fetus, and finally the infant Jesus? If this is the case then Jesus is God incarnate, but He isn't a true human being; only an apparent one. A divine zygote would have evolved into a divine baby. 'Still unacceptable? What then? No one can ever know! This is another heavenly (biblical) ambiguity.

The question is nonetheless relevant. When did Jesus cease being {a} God and start being human? I will rephrase the question: When did God the Second Person shed His divinity and become a human being exclusively? Or was He both simultaneously? However I phrase the question, there is no answer. Any distinction I could fashion wouldn't negate the obvious impossibility of the 'One-and-Only' Deity in the Universe from becoming a human being. Folksy evangelizers delight in extolling Christ's human nature; offering His humanity as an example to be emulated. They then proceed to exhort us all to strive to attain some measure of the human perfection that they speciously ascribe to Him. Jesus is ever proclaimed as a perfect human being; this despite much contrary evidence!

You (the reader) are human, so I ask "Have angels ever ministered to you after being tempted by the Devil?" Or have you ever been able to walk on water; or to tell a paralytic to rise up and walk; or have you ever been able to change water into wine; or to multiply loaves and fishes; or to calm a violent storm; or to cure all sorts of maladies, including restoring the dead to life? Have you ever been able to perform any miracles of any variety? You haven't? Neither have I. I wasn't born of a virgin either! Therefore, the humanity of Jesus was vastly different than is my humanity. [Cf. Gospels of Matthew, Mark, Luke & John]

How could Jesus, with all his supernatural faculties, be considered a mere mortal? Effectively, He retained all His Divine prerogatives, including the power to know the future, e.g., He knew exactly how He would die, and when He would be resurrected. That knowledge alone separated Him from the glut of humanity by an everlasting unbridgeable chasm. It is ironic, yet it is inevitable concomitantly, that the evidence religionists' put forth to prove the humanity of Jesus, concomitantly disproves His divinity, and *vice versa*!

Regarding the humanity of Jesus: Was it the same as mine? Was He attracted to females as I am? Homosexuals might ask if He was attracted to other men as they are. (The consummation of such attractions needn't be inferred, nor conceded, for the question to remain germane.) Stated generally, was He wholly human, in every fashion or facet, and did the Devil tempt Him with the same enticements as he does all other humans?

From the religionist who answers "Yes, Jesus was fully human," I request proof of this contra-logical extrapolation.

If Christ's humanity is to have any relevance to mankind, He must have been subject to the same cravings and frailties that other human men are afflicted with; except in His case, He need never have succumbed to those temptations. We can accept this and yet still ask "How was He able to resist the Devil's allurements?" Was it via the same power that permitted Him to hide Himself from the Jews who sought to stone Him in the Temple? [Cf. Jn. 8:59]

Did Jesus ever forget He was God? Did He ever stop remembering that anything whatever He wished for would happen? Wasn't He continually cognizant that anything that men might do to Him could be avoided or reversed, even if they went so far as committing murder on His human body? Can you or I call upon twelve legions of angels to assist us in a moment of peril? [Cf. Mt. 26:53] The humanity of Jesus is exposed as a farce if we can believe in His divinity; conversely, His divinity is incontestably refuted if we believe in His humanity.

These arguments don't specifically indicate that any act is impossible to God. If we postulate an infinitely powerful God, then all actions must be possible to Him. But this concession doesn't admit that God has performed all actions. Answer this if you will: Can God be Himself and the Devil at the same instant? He can if all things are possible to Him. But in actuality, some actions are contradictions of the possible. In this example, God can't be the essence of Goodness at the same instance that He is the essence of Evil. Those two concepts are measures of opposition and cannot be coexistent at the same locale, at the same time. For the same reason, God can't create a seven foot tall midget. That, too, is an impossible contradiction.

Now, to return to the opening question of this segment: Can infinite God become finite man? No! More than any other example I could offer, that is an impossible contradiction. Man knows that he is finite, yet subliminally, he wishes that he was infinite. So how can he attain his ardent wish? He can pretend that he is immortal until the day that he dies. Or he can invent a God who will grant him his impossible dream. Mentally, he can endow that God with all the capabilities that he himself lacks, but which he fervently desires to possess.

If Jesus Christ was God, then He never lived on Earth. If He lived as a human being, then He wasn't God, but only a mortal man. And, if He was a mortal man, then He couldn't perform miracles! The one perpetually impossible act (the ultimate contradiction) is for God to cease being God. God always was! God always is! God always will be! Unless, **factually**, there is no God!

THE TEMPTATION OF JESUS

In Matthew, the Devil tempted Jesus in a desert. Satan took Jesus to a very high mountain and showed Him all the kingdoms of the world and the glory of them. *"Then Satan said to Jesus, 'All this I will give you' he said, 'if you will bow down and worship me.'"* [Mt. 4:9] In Luke the wording is different, *"And he said to him, 'I will give you all their authority and splendor; it has been given to me, and I can give it to anyone I want to. If you worship me, it will all be yours.'"* [Lu. 4:6-7] Contemplating the above story, only two alternatives are possible.

One: The incident is nothing more than an abject fiction (albeit, conceived by a human). If Option One is correct, we can dispense with further consideration. This leaves only Option Two open to dissection. Number Two can't be dismissed lightly, for it implies much more than the author intended.

Two: The event happened much as it is written. We can't decide unerringly because these two versions (Matthew & Luke) are noticeably different. Mark records this event without dialogue. *"And immediately the Spirit* {as a dove} *drove him out into the desert. And he was in the desert forty days and forty nights, and was tempted by Satan."* [Mark 1:12-13] John doesn't mention the temptation, or even the sojourn into the desert.

The first and most obvious inference I gather from this temptation incident is that the world is flat. It must be flat because that is the only shape that would allow a person to stand atop a very high mountain and view all the kingdoms of the world simultaneously, even if we limit the statement to encompass only the kingdoms known to the ancient author. The person being tempted couldn't be a supernatural being (God) for obvious reasons!

Further, if we postulate that the highest mountain on Earth is magically transported to Galilee, a person on the pinnacle of that mountain couldn't see Rome, the pinnacle of the then world's domains. (Also, in the opinion of the Christian writers: the pinnacle of wickedness in the world!) Only a flat Earth will allow such a panoramic view from that vantage point. A manned satellite orbiting one hundred plus miles above the Earth might just be able to see all the kingdoms known to the ancient writer, but, without the most advanced optics from today, Jesus would not have been able to resolve those kingdoms visually with His human eyes.

Certainly, we could grant that the Devil had god-like capabilities ... given to him by God. Who else? Through his sorcery, the Devil (Satan) could have projected geographical vistas for Jesus to view. But then, why did he need a very high mountain? Why should the Devil have moved Jesus from the desert at all? With only the knowledge of Eratosthenes (who in 250 BC knew the world was not flat, and who had estimated the circumference of the round Earth with a high degree of accuracy), Matthew would have recognized the juvenility of this fable. The information that the world was a globe was available to the ancient author, but we can reasonably conclude that he didn't have that knowledge. Alas, God didn't inspire him to seek that knowledge! Matthew could have learned the true shape of the Earth from the library at Alexandria in Egypt, if God had so imbued him.

Satan, of course, should have known that the world wasn't flat and that transporting Jesus to the top of the mountain not only would have been unnecessary, but also would have been altogether ineffective. Skeptics have ample cause to doubt this entire 'temptation' episode. The God of the Universe couldn't be so hobbled of brain as to think any but the dullest human beings would believe the Devil could have acted so feeblemindedly. Also, that Jesus, by His acquiescence and indulgence, would have molly-coddled Satan so obligingly.

DID JESUS CONSIDER HIMSELF A GOD?

New Testament quotes that implicitly prove (or tend to prove) that Jesus wasn't a part of the Godhead: Jesus rebukes the Devil, who has just asked Jesus (God the Son?) to worship him. *"Begone, Satan! For it is written, 'You shall worship the Lord your God and him only shall you serve.'"* [Mt. 4:10 & Lu. 4:8]

Jesus warns that many who invoke His name, and are verbally able to drive out devils and perform miracles, will not enter Heaven because they have not done what the Father of Jesus wanted them to do. [Cf. Mt. 7:22-23] So, invoking the name of Jesus will allow you to drive out demons, but it won't admit you into Heaven! Oddly, casting out demons could also be performed by ordinary men other than the Apostles invoking the name of Jesus. [Cf. Mk. 9:37-39]

Jesus, having ordered the Twelve out to gather the 'lost sheep of Israel' allayed their fears: *"Do not be afraid … Whoever confesses publicly that he belongs to me, I will do the same for him before my Father in heaven."* [Mt. 10:32] *"I tell you, whoever confesses publicly that he belongs to Me, the Son of Man will do the same for him before the angels of God."* [Lu. 12:8] Jesus praises God. *"O Father, Lord of heaven and earth! I thank you because you have shown to the unlearned what you have hidden from the wise and the learned."* [Mt. 11:25 & Lu. 10:21]

If you look carefully you will notice that Jesus invariably advises that all should acquiesce to the Will of God, including Jesus Himself! Nowhere does He instruct you to worship "The Son." Jesus directs us to worship God only! From here to the end of this segment, biblical quotes stating that identical dictum will be presented. Begin:

Jesus is accused of deriving His powers from Beelzebub. But He counters this charge by informing his accusers, *"No, it is God's Spirit who gives me the power to drive out demons … I tell you: men can be forgiven any sin and any evil thing they say; but whoever says evil things against the Holy Spirit will not be forgiven. Anyone who says something against the Son of Man {Jesus} will be forgiven; but whoever says something against the Holy Spirit will not be forgiven —now or ever."* [Mt. 12:31-32; Mk. 3:28-29 & Lu. 12:10] Clearly, Jesus considers Himself less significant than is the Holy Spirit. If three is one when considering the Trinity, how can an insult to any one personality be more defamatory than an insult to the other two? Can a Spirit God be more vulnerable to denigration than is a more-than-spirit God (Yahweh) or a mortal God (Jesus)?

In response to a rich man's calling Him by the title, "Good Master," Jesus says: *"Why callest thou me good? There is none good but one, that is, God."* [Mt. 19:17; Mk. 10:18 & Lu. 18:19] The quote is explicit; God is the only good. No one else, not even Jesus, is "good."

It is God who will allocate a person's place in Heaven, not Jesus! The Apostles James and John ask Jesus to reserve the right and left hand side of His throne for them. Here is the reply Jesus gave: *"I do not have the right to choose who will sit at my right and left. These places belong to those for whom my Father has prepared them."* [Mt. 20:23 & Mk. 10:40] Does this indicate that Jesus shares a common will or mutual authority with God Almighty?

Jesus, editorially, chastises the city of Jerusalem, *"From now on you will never see me again, I tell you, until you say, 'God bless him {Jesus} who comes in the name of the Lord' {God}."* [Mt. 23:39 & Lu. 13:35] It is ludicrous to ask God {Yahweh} to bless God {Jesus}.

Speaking on the Second Coming, Jesus informs us that He doesn't know when it will happen. *"No one knows, however, when that day and hour will come —neither the angels in heaven nor the Son —the Father alone knows."* [Mt. 24:36 & Mk. 13:32]

Jesus, Himself, can't command the angels. At His arrest He rejects aid from a disciple. *"Don't you know that I could call on my Father for help and at once he would send me more than twelve armies of angels?"* [Mt. 26:53]

To me, the following is among the most perplexing statements in the Bible. At the moment of His death Jesus cries aloud, *"Eli, Eli lema sabachthani? That is to say, my God, my God, why hast thou forsaken me?"* [Mt. 27:46 & Mk. 15:34] (While experiencing the distressing tribulations of mortal life, this author has uttered a similar lamentation!)

The following is an anecdote that only appears in Luke. 'The twelve-year-old Jesus spent three days in the Temple amazing the Jewish teachers.' First, remind yourself that Jesus is God the Son; then interpret the last sentence of the Temple incident. It reads: *"And Jesus grew up, both in body and in wisdom, gaining favor with God and men."* [Lu. 2:52] What 'wisdom' did Jesus gain that caused Him to find 'favor' with Himself? Can God grow in wisdom? Did God the Father admire His Son {Jesus} less before He {Jesus} 'gained favor'?

The people of Capernaum desired Jesus to tarry with them, but Jesus cannot. He replied to them, *"I must preach the Good News of the Kingdom of God in other towns also, for that is what God sent me to do."* [Lu. 4:43] In the first place, this looks suspiciously as a post crucifixion insertion. The 'Good News' was the message of the Apostles proclaiming that Jesus was the expected Messiah. But that isn't my point here. The point is that Jesus discernibly didn't consider Himself equal to God or even co-existent with God. Jesus was "sent."

The disciples have just brought food to Jesus, but He declines it and expounds cryptically: *"My food is to obey the will of him who sent me, and to finish his work."* [Jn. 4:34] What was God's "work" that Jesus was to finish? Also, a person can only be sent by someone who has authority over him. In this instance, as in all the others where Jesus states unconditionally that God sent him, He informs us that He is subordinate to God. That violates the current theory of a Trinity of Gods —*all equal* —*all in harmony* —*all with a unity of thought.* God cannot be sent by God if there is only one God. If one God can send another God, then we have two Gods. One is superior to the other, and gives orders to the lesser. God the Son is subject to the jurisdiction of God the Father. This necessitates two distinct Gods with two distinct wills, and with two disparate levels of authority!

Speaking to the Pharisees on the source of His authority, Jesus says: *"I can do nothing on my own; I judge only as God tells me, so my judgment is right, because I am not trying to do what I want, but only what he who sent me wants."* [Jn. 5:30] Would one God have to "tell" another God what to do if both Gods were the same God? Emphatically, "No!" The very question is silly. The affirmation that three distinct Gods add up to one united God is even more ridiculous! Throughout the Gospels Jesus iterates often that He was sent by God, not that He Himself is God! Is it possible that the mortal Jesus didn't know that He was consubstantial with Yahweh?

Most scholars agree that John's Gospel was the last one committed to writing. {AD 90?} In conjecture, John's Gospel was composed after the notion of the divinity of Jesus already had been promulgated and generally accepted. Every page contains some proof that Jesus is, in actual fact, the literal 'Son of God.' Yet, nowhere is a trinity or duality of God(s) mentioned. So what were John's thoughts in this matter? Did he believe in one God encompassing three divine persons? The evidence culled from his Gospel is inconclusive inasmuch as he never unambiguously deals with the subject. His testament is doubly puzzling in that John doesn't mention the paranormal conception of Jesus. As observed previously, John the Beloved, before all others, should have known intimately of a heavenly impregnation of Mary, if it was factual!

If John's was the latest composition, I would assume that the author would have heard of Matthew's and Luke's Nativity narratives. Wouldn't he have commented, either confirming or refuting their version? Engaging my mind on that topic, I can only conclude that John never knew about

Mary's fertilization by the Holy Spirit. This despite the 'gospel truth' declaration that he was the appointed provider/protector of Mary after the crucifixion of Jesus. [Cf. Jn. 19:27]

My own understanding of John's Gospel leads me to believe that the author wasn't a strict monotheist. Obviously, he considered Jesus as a form of demigod, i.e., a man with more capabilities than a mortal, yet with fewer powers than a god. If this analysis is valid, then that author, likewise, was never a devout Jew, thus eliminating the Apostle John from authorship.

Read John, Chapter Six. In this relatively lengthy homily in the synagogue at Capernaum, Jesus stated that He was the bread of life, conferring eternal life on all those who ate His flesh and drank His blood. Not unexpectedly, the people were aghast. The very notion was repugnant to them. Of course, we today know that Jesus was referring to bread and wine transubstantiated into His Body and Blood. [Cf. Jn. 6:48-59]

Several sentences endorse my belief that Jesus didn't exalt Himself to a level coequal to God. They are: *"This food {the bread of life} the Son of Man will give you because God, the Father, has put his mark of approval on him {Jesus}."* [Jn. 6:27] And, *"The living Father sent me, and because of Him I live also."* [Jn. 6:57] Finally, *"For I have come down from heaven to do the will of him who sent me, not my own will."* [Jn. 6:38] Jesus appears to be stating that His will differs from God's will; however, He nonetheless deferred to His Father's outline for mankind, and forsook whatever His own mortal inclinations were.

Read further: *"Whoever is willing to do what God wants will know whether what I teach comes from God or whether I speak on my own authority?"* [Jn. 7:17] If Jesus cannot speak on His own authority, then He isn't homologous with God. Jesus is God's emissary, but He isn't co-equal to Him (nor co-existent with Him). This distinction became blurred very early in the evolution of Christianity.

"If you loved me, you would be glad that I am going to the Father, because he is greater than I." [Jn. 14:28] The disclaimer here is explicit. One can only wonder how those who conferred Godhood on Jesus can reconcile this unequivocal statement with their contradictory teachings. Jesus prayed (audibly?) to God. *"And this is eternal life: for men to know you, the only true God, and to know Jesus Christ, whom you sent."* [Jn. 17:3] Here we read still

another incidence of Jesus detailing His separateness and distinctness from the Godhead.

Shortly after this sentence you can read where Jesus stated that He and the Father are "one," and superficially this may be read as a confirmation of the oneness of Jesus and God. An objective reading, however, leads to an entirely different discernment. Here is the Good News for Modern Man translation of the text: *"Holy Father! Keep them {the Apostles} safe by the power of your name, the name you gave me, so they may be one just as you and I are one."* [Jn. 17:11]

We read this today as meaning that Jesus and God are mystically and mathematically one. Was Jesus asking God to make the Apostles mystically and mathematically one also? No, He was not! What He was petitioning for was that they would remain in harmony with one another just as Jesus felt that He was in harmony with His Father (God). The final portion of John's Gospel is replete with exhortations from Jesus to His Disciples to love one another as He had loved them. Two people that truly love one another will invariably react with a singleness of purpose; it is this type of unity and accord that Jesus petitioned God to grant to His disciples (Apostles).

The words of Jesus here mustn't be taken too literally unless one is willing to embrace polytheism. Examine the following, which is a continuation of the passages under scrutiny: *"I do not pray only for them {the Apostles}, but also for those who believe in me because of their message. I pray that they all may be one. O Father! May they be one in us, just as you are in me and I am in you."* [Jn. 17:20-21]

Was Jesus praying that the Apostles should be given a share of the Godhead just as Jesus shared the Godhead with the Father? A dogmatic fundamentalist would, of necessity, have to reach just this conclusion. Let me repeat the phrase, *"May they be one in us just as you are in me and I am in you."* [ibid.]

(Arguably) Jesus was petitioning that the Apostles would become one with Jesus and God. That would have swelled the Trinity to fourteen (minus Judas) and would have been altogether too many persons for even the all-too-liberal Roman world to accept as one God.

Mary Magdalene was crying at the empty tomb when Jesus appeared to her. At first she didn't recognize Him, but when He spoke her name, she cried out in Aramaic, *"Teacher."* Then Jesus gave her a peculiar caution. *"Do not hold on to me … because I have not yet gone back up to the Father. But go to my brothers and tell them for me, 'I go back up to him who is my Father and your Father, my God and your God.'"* [Jn. 20:17] Yahweh is the "Father" of both Jesus and Mary Magdalene?

Notice how Jesus tells Mary that His relationship with the Father God was the same as her relationship to the Father God. His preceding remark, *"Go to my brothers"* if taken literally, repudiated the dogma of His Mother's eternal virginity. Moreover, if we interpret that phrase figuratively, it reinforces my belief that Jesus Himself never claimed to participate in the Godhead. If the Apostles were His 'brothers,' they shared His heritage, and were as equal to Him as a biological brother would have been. Notice, also, that John's Gospel informs us that the Father was His God also. Restated: Yahweh was the God of Jesus!

The blasphemous doctrine that incorporates Jesus into the Godhead of the Universal Creator diminishes His human stature —*it doesn't enhance it!* Those who would deify Jesus, perform a disservice on Him. His actual greatness flows out from His humanity. That one man could have inspired so many men to strive to live an exemplary life, espousing so many exemplary actions, is glorious tribute to a human being. Notwithstanding this, lamentably few have attained their striving, and fewer still have maintained that striving, and this fact alone precludes His Divinity. Almighty God couldn't have been such an overall failure. If Jesus and God share a communion of powers and knowledge, and if we measure His accomplishments with a divine yardstick, then the "Divine" Jesus must be classified as an arrant underachiever.

Only God the Father knows when "Heaven and Earth" will pass away. Jesus doesn't! [Cf. Mt. 24:36 & Mk. 13:32] How, then, can Jesus be an integral person of the singular "Trinity" and not the middle member of a three person reigning 'Triumvirate?' The foregoing concludes the effort to prove with the very words of Jesus that He truly wasn't a God, and that He never considered Himself to be co-existent and consubstantial with the Father and the Holy Spirit.

If we could find the Gospels in their original autographs I believe they would report that Jesus was exclusively human. I would wager that the original authors believed that Jesus was a remarkable man, not that He was a part-time God and only a one-time human!

THE TRANSFIGURATION

Can anyone inform me what religious message God intended to make when He orchestrated the Transfiguration? Why did the Holy Ghost inspire all three of the Synoptic chroniclers to record this wondrous triviality? The story is nothing but a fabulous inanity. 'Judge for yourself!

Here, interspersed with my comments, is how the story unfolds. Jesus took three disciples (Peter, James, and John) up a high mountain. Once there, Moses and Elijah joined Jesus. How do we know the two personages were Moses and Elijah? Don't inquire; this is yet another inexplicable mystery! [Cf. Mt. 17:1-13; Mk. 9:1-13 & Lu. 9:28-36] [2 Pet. 1:18?]

Later in the story, God the Father's voice was heard speaking out of a shining cloud. This audible revelation would seem to rule out divine inspiration of those present. Why would God have infused into their minds at one minute, and then deem it was necessary to speak aloud into their ears at the next moment? Also, how did Matthew come to know of this magnificent incident? He wasn't there. Why did John, who was there, omit this unforgettable and extraordinary occasion from his Gospel?

God thought this event was so theologically imperative that He inspired three separate Evangelists to report it. Only John, of the three eyewitnesses to the Transfiguration, later wrote a Gospel. Yet, only John, of the four Gospel Evangelists, doesn't record the Transfiguration. This is more than suspicious, but I will permit you draw your own conclusions from this 'gospel truth.'

Returning to the initial question: "How did the three disciples know who the two miraculous visitors were?" No one knows. We do know that no picture or statue was ever made of these two steadfast Israelites. Also, there isn't any description of Moses or Elijah contained in the Old Testament. For all the disciples knew, those two men could have been Isaiah and Jeremiah, Zechariah and Obadiah, Joshua and Nehemiah, or anyone else from the Hebrew past! How did the Apostles know that they weren't witness to the Archangels Gabriel and Raphael in earthly garb? Of one thing we can all be sure, and it is this: Neither of the visitors was Methuselah! At age 969 years, He would have been more wrinkled than a prune, and more bent than a palm leaf. The slightest breeze on the mountain would have blown him over a precipice!

Next question: "Why were Moses and Elijah there?" Obviously, they were there to confer with Jesus. Why? Was Jesus telling them something they didn't know? Or were they informing Him of something He didn't know? From this event onward, Jesus spoke openly of His impending death. Did He learn of His future crucifixion from Moses and Elijah? Was this the secret message they delivered to Jesus in such an auspicious fashion? If so, was His execution foreordained by His Father, thus exonerating all human participants? If not, then what message did Moses and Elijah impart to Jesus?

There are innumerable suppositions we could make as to the content of the conversation between Jesus and the two dead Israelites. But none of them is satisfactory if/after we impute the Godhead to Jesus. I can think of no information Jesus (as God) would need from those two. If, however, three of the Evangelists thought Jesus to be a man chosen by God to be the Messiah, rather than His incarnate Son, then this scene does become a bit sensible. Moses and Elijah were heavenly messengers from God informing the mortal Jesus what was in store for Him when He was manifest as the Messiah. That assumption makes a modicum of sense!

The future first Pope (?) obviously didn't think Jesus was co-extensive with God at this point. Peter, after viewing the majestic event, offered to build three tents to honor the three transfigured persons. He was willing to honor all three as equals. But Luke characterizes this proposition better than I could. He added the parenthetical comment attacking Peter's proposal: "*(He really did not know what he was saying.)*" [Lu. 9:33] I have no way of knowing Luke's motive for inserting this sagacious characterization. But I accept his pronouncement as reported. Peter's proposal definitely was inappropriate to the event, if Jesus was a Deity! Neither Moses nor Elijah has ever been depicted as deities.

Perhaps, we can gain some insight from the statement of Jesus after the human group had descended back down the mountain. Luke reports that the three Apostles were "*heavy with sleep.*" [Lu. 9:32] Jesus said, "*Don't tell anyone about this vision....*" [Mt. 17:9] From the Gospels themselves, we learn that what the three Apostles saw wasn't reality, it was a vision! A vision is something seen only in the mind. It is a mental event created by our imagination. In plain words, it isn't an actual happening. I think this explains all religiosity! Imagination is an astounding faculty; it didn't create the Universe, but it surely gave birth to the spectral personality (God) that humans have credited with the act of creating it.

JESUS WAS MORTAL

Pope Pius XII granted an indulgence of three years for reading the Books of Sacred Scripture fifteen minutes a day, each day for a month. (You must also kiss the Bible; an unsanitary act of abasement, which I consider on a par with symbolic ritual magic. But this isn't germane to our current topic. He stipulated, however, that you read the sacred book piously as a "spiritual reading with the reverence which is due the word of God." {*sic*}

Not me! I want you to scrutinize the Bible skeptically. Then, at the end of each sentence, I want you to ask yourself the question: "Would God Almighty have acted thus? The Old Testament is preposterous when examined thoughtfully; you can skip it! The New Testament is less so, but then, this may be due to the increased sophistication of the writers and their audience, not to any inherent quality intrinsic to the narratives.

It is difficult to discount the assumption that Jesus would have been many times more informative toward His contemporaries if He was {a} God. In retrospect, we can now see that Jesus can't be God because He just wasn't as knowledgeable as He should have been. The novel, <u>A Connecticut Yankee in King Arthur's Court</u>, explores only a miniscule fraction of the enlightened actions Jesus could have performed while He traversed the Holy Lands.

Jesus spoke to the people in parables, which He often had to interpret afterward. He spoke cryptically of the Second Coming that no one to this day can decipher unerringly. He may have accomplished miracles that are still beyond human comprehension and repetition, but He didn't add one jot of practical knowledge to mankind's accumulation. At times, He even appeared to be as misinformed as were His contemporaries. Driving out demons demonstrates this unambiguously. Today, we know that which Christ's contemporaries diagnosed as demonic possession was epilepsy or dementia, i.e., insanity. In Jesus' day, no one was ever afflicted with mental disease; they were all considered infested with malevolent spirits.

Why did Jesus permit the populace to persist in their error? Insanity would have been more facile to comprehend than any portion of the Apocalypse {Revelations}, and would have led to more compassionate behavior toward those ill-treated, afflicted persons. In every case, as God, He was responsible for their mental illness wasn't He? Why didn't He moderate their suffering by explaining to the people what was the actual affliction of the 'possessed'?

But no, He helped perpetuate a false conclusion. He contended with the *"demons."* Jesus even held a dialogue with a concentration of demons that called themselves *"legion."* It seemed this group of demons was bedeviling some poor, wretched soul. The demons discoursed with Jesus, acknowledging Him to be the *"Son of God."* Jesus ordered them to leave the man. They replied by asking permission to enter a nearby herd of swine. Jesus permitted the demons to enter the swine, which promptly stampeded over a cliff, fell into a lake and drowned. [Cf. Mt. 8:28-32; Mk. 5:1-13 & Lu. 8:26-33]

From the plentiful questions that could be asked here, only two will be explored. First: Who compensated the owners of the pigs for their loss? The owners hadn't done anything to justify the death of two thousand swine. Jesus gave the demons His permission to enter the swine, so He is partially accountable at a minimum.

Second: What became of the 'legion' (mob) of demons? Did they enter into a school of fish and cause the fish to act insanely? Somehow that suggestion appears frivolous. But the solution can only be resolved speculatively, for the Scriptures are silent after the swine drowning. Formulate your own resolution to the eventual destination of the "legion" of demons, and then ask yourself this: "Why didn't the demons go there directly? Why did a herd of animals have to perish?" In Matthew, Jesus described a frightening scenario for an unclean spirit {demon} who had vacated a mortal man. It returned with seven others worse than itself to re-infect the man! [Cf. Mt. 12:43-44] *"... and the last condition of that man is worse than the first."* [v. 45]

The demons/swine story alone raises a third question: At the end of the narrative all the people of the territory besought Jesus to leave their area. The local people saw Jesus as a menace, not as a 'wonder worker.' Why? [Cf. Mt. 8:33-34; Mk. 5:17 & Lu. 8:37]

One last point regarding demons can be made here. The Gospels inform us that Jesus had competition in the driving out of demons. In Mark's and Luke's version, the Apostle John informed Jesus that a man was driving out demons utilizing the name of Jesus, although the man didn't belong to Christ's selected band of followers. (Oddly, but tellingly, John's Gospel omits both the swine tale and a subsequent discussion concerning strangers driving out demons.) Jesus isn't angered; He used this incident to assert to John, *"Whoever is not against us is for us."* [Mk. 9:38-40 & Lu. 9:49-50] That generality isn't valid, but it is pithy, and it embodies an earthy folk logic that holds emotional appeal for the less-than-discerning.

Unintentionally, this exorcising episode validates an improbable fact: You don't have to be the Son of God to dispossess demons. You don't even have to be one of the followers of Jesus. Apparently, this reported demon-exorcist was working free-lance and reportedly was performing quite successfully as well!

If Jesus retained His Divine prerogatives while on Earth, didn't He also retain His Divine wisdom? Why didn't He ever perform a wonder that could have been verified by someone not present? I am thinking that He could have told a parable that only today could be substantiated by science. The aim here is this: Jesus performed miracles so that the people would believe that He had all of the potentials of Heaven (intrinsic or granted) at His command. Nonetheless, if we reflect on His miracles, none of them is verifiable today.

To illustrate: John informs us that Jesus healed a man who had been paralyzed for thirty-eight years. Jesus said to him, *"Get up, pick up your mat, and walk."* [Jn. 5:5-9] The man was cured instantly; he picked up his mat and walked. This is impressive. However, just a few verses earlier one reads that the man was lying there by a miraculous pool (public bath) waiting to be healed by the actions of an *"angel of the Lord."* In God's own inspired words, we learn of this incredible pool. It seems a large gathering of the sick and the infirm daily surrounded the pool. Each day they would congregate beside the pool apprehensively awaiting a whimsically motivated angel to stir up the waters. [Cf. Jn. 5:4] Then, with the water stirred, whoever was agile enough to be the first one into the water was cured of whatever malady afflicting him. Can we believe this? We must … it is in the Bible!

What utter fiction! Regrettably, the real significance in this fiction is the inarguable observation that the author of the fable believed an angel was stirring the water, and further, he obviously shared the belief that the first person (and only the first!) into the pool would be cured. Can this witness be relied upon as a credible reporter of the miracles of Jesus? Maybe you are too polite to impugn his veracity. Still, you must seriously question his gullibility. The author of the Fourth Gospel believed in the 'Angel of the Pool of Bethesda.' This indelibly compromises his credibility throughout. Furthermore, it inflicts yet another disabling wound on the proposition of an inspired Scripture (in tandem with its alleged Inspirer!).

If John's Gospel is divided into approximately eighty segments (incidents, scenarios, or changes of topic), then only about twenty of these segments are correspondingly related in one of the other Gospels. Yet, most of even those are worded so dissimilarly as to raise the possibility that John's version of the replicated stories aren't inspired compositions, but simply they are a local adaptation of already circulating verbal anecdotes about Jesus. Below are some enigmatic specimens.

The anointing at Bethany is probably the best example. John writes that Mary, the sister of Lazarus, poured the ointment over the feet of Jesus in the house of Lazarus. [Cf. Jn. 12:3] Matthew writes that the anointing took place in the house of Simon the Leper where an unnamed woman poured the nard on the head of Jesus. [Cf. Mt. 26:7] Two millennia later, we still don't know if the perfume was poured on head or on feet, nor whether it was in the house of Lazarus, or in the house of Simon the Leper.

Previously, I pointed out that John's Gospel was curious for what it didn't discuss (the early life of Mary and her Son, Jesus). Now I am stating that John's Gospel is further suspect for what it does relate. Three-fourths of the incidents in John's Gospel are original, i.e., they don't appear in the Synoptic Gospels. For this reason, although scholars categorize Matthew, Mark, and Luke together (Synoptic Gospels), they treat John separately. (Johannine Gospel)

John informs us of Christ's revivification of Lazarus immediately prior to Passion Week. [Cf. Jn. 11:1-44] How could the other three Evangelists have omitted such an unprecedented and spectacular miracle? "Miraculous cures" may have been common in John's day, but I doubt that "resurrections" ever have been. John's account also contains three Passover holidays, while the Synoptic Gospels tell of only one; consequently, John is the sole source of Jesus' postulated three-year ministry. [q.v., Jn. 2:13; 6:4 & 11:55] John's Gospel also informs us that Peter and several other Apostles returned to their fisherman occupation after the Crucifixion. Chronologically, this report appears to have occurred after the infusion of the Holy Ghost in John's version of Pentecost. In an earlier spectral visitation, Jesus breathed on the Apostles and bid them, *"Receive the Holy Spirit."* [Jn. 20:22] The very next paragraph recounts the incident of the unbelief of 'Doubting' Thomas. Yet, here are five Apostles: Peter, James, John, Thomas and Nathaniel, along with two unnamed disciples (after the Pentecost recorded by John) fishing without success on Lake Tiberius (Sea of Galilee). John's version of the tale of the miraculous catch of fish follows. [Cf. Jn. 21:1-6]

This episode is debatable on two counts. The first question being: "Isn't this John's Post-Resurrection miraculous catch of fish the same event that Luke records occurred at the start of the public ministry of Jesus?" [Cf. Lu. 5:4-11] The second query is: "Why didn't the Apostles recognize Jesus in John's miraculous fish catch tale?" John's Gospel informs us that the Apostles had traveled with Jesus for several years. They had just seen Him in His glorified body shortly before; still, they didn't recognize Him at John's miraculous fish catch? To me, this undeniably is too implausible for belief.

But these two points are secondary. The main thrust is this: Why were the Apostles out fishing after the Holy Spirit had descended upon them? Didn't Pentecost begin the organizing and proselytizing career of the Apostles?

Do this with an expendable New Testament: Open to Matthew, Chapter One and proceed through to John, Chapter 21, verse 25, deleting every miracle, and excising every improbable event. Surprise! What you will be left with is a stirring sermon by a very human person exhorting each of us to live a moral life dedicated to a spiritual Father who spies upon us endlessly. What you won't find is an all-wise and all-benevolent Deity posing as a man. You may discern the pronouncements of a philosopher, but decidedly not the elucidation of a scholar!

THE POWERS OF THE APOSTLES

Luke, Chapter 9, verse 51-54:"*And it came to pass, when the days of his assumption were accomplishing, that he steadfastly set his face to go to Jerusalem. And he sent messengers before his face; and going, they entered into a city of the Samaritans, to prepare for him. And they received him not, because his face was of one going to Jerusalem. And when his disciples James and John had seen this, they said: Lord, wilt thou that we command fire to come down from heaven, and consume them?*" Did the brother Apostles, James and John have the power (with permission from Jesus) to "command fire to come down from heaven"? How many Samaritans did they propose to burn up (murder) because they "received him not"? (Jesus) What other death-delivering powers did James and John possess? What about the other Apostles, what lethal powers were they granted?

Luke alone, who never knew of Jesus until two decades later, is the recorder of this event. John, who was a purported participant, does not report this fear-engendering event. Why is this event broadcast by someone who wasn't present either in time or in location, while someone who is averred to have been present as it happened does not record it? What went amiss with the 'inspiration' of the Holy Ghost?

THE ARREST OF JESUS

The Gospels tell us what happened to John the Baptist who wasn't an Apostle of Jesus. Yet, they don't tell us what became of Mary, His Blessed Mother; or of Paul, His greatest proselytizer; nor of Peter, His chosen successor. (Arguable) Isn't it mildly suspicious that Mark, whose Gospel is said to reflect the teachings of Peter, writes thus at the arrest of Jesus in the Garden of Gethsemane: "But one of the bystanders drew his sword and struck the servant of the high priest and cut off his ear." [Mk. 14:47] The point being made is that Mark (allegedly speaking for Peter) doesn't know who struck the blow. Meanwhile, only in John are we told that, "Simon Peter, having a sword, drew it and struck the servant of the high priest and cut off his right ear." [Jn. 18:10] If Peter tutored Mark, then Mark would have known who drew the sword.

Indeed, all four Evangelists record a story of the arrest of Jesus, but each records it differently. Mark, who speaks for Peter doesn't know who struck the blow, nor does Matthew, who was there, nor does Luke, who writes for Paul who wasn't there. Only John, who was there, reports the swordsman was Peter. Oddly, only one of the Gospels mentions Jesus healing the severed ear. Luke's Gospel so informs us. What is doubly suspicious in Luke's rendition is this: Only Luke, whom we know to have been a physician, reports that Jesus used His power to restore the man's ear. A physician comprehends the trauma of losing an ear. Obviously, none of the other Evangelists did. But, the honest biblical scholar has to wonder if this curative restoration wasn't a pious addendum on Luke's part, rather than a historical fact.

But even Jesus, there in the Garden, commits a *faux pas*. Matthew discloses that Jesus rebuked the sword wielder (whomever he was!) saying, *"Don't you know that I could call on my Father for help and at once He would send more than twelve armies of angels."* [Mt. 26:53] No one else but the swordsman and Matthew must have heard this, for none of the other Evangelists records it, another indication that Peter wasn't the swordsman! Now back to the remark of Jesus. Why, in heaven's name, would Jesus need more than twelve armies of angels? Were they needed 'to protect Him'? Does God need the protection of angels just as a worldly ruler needs the protection of armies of loyal soldiers?

The writer of that sacred scripture thought so, but I would wager that you could think of ten swifter, more effective and more imaginative alternatives than Jesus threatened on that night. What is more, if we remember Jesus' boast that He could call on His Father's assistance and surely receive it, how should we understand His words as He died on the cross? *"Eli, Eli, lema sabachthani?"* ("My God, My God, why did you abandon me?") [Mt. 27:46 & Mk. 15:34]

The apparent understanding of the foregoing verse is that Jesus silently called on His Father, but received no response. The only consistent interpretation is that Jesus, although not expressly calling for rescue, (in actuality) did expect to be rescued. Either explanation condemns the future dogma that Jesus held a central position in a unique Trinity of the Divinity. Additionally, it dashes the doctrine that Jesus shared a common will with God!

A GOOD THIEF?

At this juncture I want to interject that everything I write about Jesus isn't necessarily beyond questioning because my only source of data is the Bible. The underlying scheme of quoting biblical inconsistencies, improbabilities, fallacies, contradictions and their like is to expose their human origins. If there is a personal Deity, and if He did inspire the writings in the Bible, then those texts would be free of error. Likewise, they would be free of contradiction as well. The four Gospels are replete with unresolved contradictions. One uncomplicated specimen should suffice to confirm the foregoing assertion.

The stories of the two thieves crucified with Jesus will provide this example. Matthew reports that both thieves reviled Jesus. [Cf. Mt. 27:44] Mark agrees with Matthew. [Cf. Mk. 15:32] Luke disagrees. He records that one thief hurled insults while the other asked Jesus to remember him when Jesus returned as King. [Cf. Lu. 23:42] John neglects to mention any comments of the two thieves crucified with Jesus, which could (should!) be interpreted as a disclaimer that they spoke to Jesus in any manner. [Cf. Jn. 19:18] John was the only disciple to witness the crucifixion. If he didn't hear the thieves speak to Jesus or hear Jesus respond, how did the three other Evangelists, who weren't there, come to know of this dialogue? Why didn't John, who reportedly was present, know what the thieves said to Jesus?

Dwell on these four different accounts; which one describes the actual event? Barring some unexpected and highly unlikely revelation/discovery, the texts we have today are all the evidence we will ever possess; therefore, we will never resolve the question of how (or if) the two persons crucified with Jesus verbally communicated with Him.

Suppose, for the sake of disputation, that only John gave a report of the two thieves. Then the doctrine of instant salvation would have lost one of its vital supports. But a new devotional could have been promulgated. Religious extrapolators would have extolled the capacity of Jesus to endure excruciating pain and still converse with those watching His execution. The two thieves would have been portrayed as being too agonized to speak. Another miracle would have been attributed to Jesus, just as all others are attributed —*a priori*.

On the other hand, if the only Evangelists recording the event were Matthew and Mark, then the cult of the "Good Thief" could never have gained a devoted following. Don't you suspect a little selective accreditation when the Church advances one version (or is it perversion?) that clashes with three others? This is precisely what we find here. Luke's rendition best fits the designs of a proselytizing organization (and Christianity is ceaselessly proselytizing); thereby we have the promulgation of the "Good Thief" paradigm.

So where does the truth reside? Who can determine when all we have to guide us is the self-contradicting Gospels. We will never know if there was one good thief (Luke), or two bad thieves (Matthew and Mark), or two silent thieves (John). The incontestable 'Word of God' (the Gospels!) is surely highly contestable here.

MULTIPLE RESURRECTIONS ON GOOD FRIDAY

Were the Evangelists plagiarizers as well as deluders? According to Matthew, Jesus wasn't the only one resurrected during that original 'Holy Weekend.' Matthew embellishes the tale of that fateful weekend, and as a consequence, raises my suspicions mightily. To quote: "*... and the earth quaked, and the rocks were rent, and the tombs were opened, and many bodies of the saints who had fallen asleep arose; and coming forth out of the tombs after His resurrection, they came into the holy city, and appeared to many. Now when the Centurion, and those who were with him keeping guard over Jesus, saw the earthquake and the things that were happening, they were very much afraid, and they said, 'Truly, he was the Son of God!'*" [Mt. 27:51-54] Luke contradicts Matthew. He reports the centurion's words: "*... Indeed, this was a righteous man.*" [Cf. Lu. 23:47]

As you can read for yourself: many 'sleeping bodies' (a Hebrew idiom for 'the dead') arose and appeared in Jerusalem. No one else records such a frightful event. Imagine having the streets of your town filled with the reanimated bodies of persons known to have died and been buried. Such an event would have caused utter pandemonium. The populace would have been thrown into a panic-stricken turmoil, fleeing frantically to avoid the embraces of the (presumably) exuberant resurrectees. What of those resurrected? What became of them? Weren't they inquisitive to know how they came to be alive again? After learning, wouldn't they have been more than willing to give witness to the wonderment of Jesus? Wouldn't all the Evangelists have sought them out as unimpeachable proof of the Godhood of Jesus? Wouldn't the other Evangelists have at least mentioned this unprecedented miracle in their narratives if it was factual?

But of course, these additional resurrections weren't true. Thankfully so! The deleterious consequences of such an occurrence cannot be disregarded as inconsequential, or as too trivial to dwell upon. The legal, emotional, and disruptive result of mass resurrections defy contemplation, and couldn't be kept secret, even if a valid reason for doing so existed!

The Gospels have been rewritten and edited so frequently in the first two centuries of the current era (C.E.) that you would expect all of the obvious signs of appended material would have been excised. But, in the instance of the Gospels, that wasn't so. Reread the quoted texts, or more convincingly, examine them in your own Bible. What the writer seems to be stating is that the "saints" were resurrected at the moment of Christ's death, but they didn't appear before the people until after Christ had risen. Excerpted: 'the Temple curtain was torn —*the earth shook* —*the graves broke open* —*and the dead arose.*' The author is speaking in the present, i.e., Friday. [v. 52] Continuing: 'after Jesus was resurrected, the resurrectees went into the Holy City.' [v. 53] Now the author is speaking of Sunday, or later! Concluding: 'The Centurion and the soldiers saw the earthquake.' Now we are back on Good Friday. [Cf. Mt. 27:54]

The indications here are that either we have confused recollections by the original author, or we have hasty addenda by an inexperienced copyist. A judicious questioner, after reading of Matthew's multiple resurrections, must arrive at the same conclusion; to wit: those verses are untrue and weren't written by the Apostle Matthew; neither did the Holy Spirit inspire them.

This unknown redactor was a liar. ('A pious liar perhaps, but a hereby proven liar!) In order to magnify Christ's greatness, our scribe multiplied the number of the resurrected. His rationale was probably not far removed from today's religious theorists. They see God's hand behind every beneficial occurrence. I am convinced that they would fabricate a fictional story or expound any rumored event that would bolster the belief in a personal God, and all that attends it. Their goals are pure, so this excuses their deceitful method of furthering those goals. Divining not-so-subtle proofs of God's reality from overstated and embroidered events isn't just the distracted vocation of a few misguided advocates; it is the fervent preoccupation of a sizeable portion of our religious communities.

Another query arises with the identification of Jerusalem as the "Holy City." During Matthew's lifetime Jerusalem would have been remembered as the 'evil city' where the Messiah had been crucified. None of the other Gospels refers to Jerusalem as the "Holy City," nor does Paul, nor do the other Epistle writers. This is so, despite numerous references to Jerusalem in the New Testament. 'Revelations' has several instances of the "New" Jerusalem, but the author seems to be referring to a glorified future city, not the Jerusalem of Matthew's lifetime. The only references to Jerusalem as the "Holy City" in the New Testament appear in Matthew. [Cf. Mt. 4:5 & 27:53] Both of those references had to be originally composed after the Crucifixion.

One more point can be made here. After the phenomenon at the death of Jesus, the Centurion declares, *"Truly, He was the Son of God!"* [Mt. 27:54 & Mk. 15:39] {Contrast Luke 23:47} Why did the Centurion utter that "Son of God" notion? Scripturally, the Hebrew Deity would never birth a human son by impregnating a human female. That declaration is unconditionally blasphemous; much more so would be the evolved declaration!

No such assertion was made at the Crucifixion. The inscription at the top of the cross read: *"Jesus of Nazareth, King of the Jews."* [Mt. 27:37; Mk. 15:26; Lu. 23:38 & Jn. 19:19] The Jews of the time were expecting the "Anointed One," meaning "the Messiah." [Cf. Acts 10:38] Without question, a Centurion never spoke those unjustifiable words, and no knowledgeable Jew would have made such a profane blunder either. Obviously, a future copyist trying to plant false evidence to prove an equally false assertion added the Centurion's statement; namely, that Jesus was the "Son of God." I don't believe that Jesus, or any of His contemporaries, ever asserted that He was anything other than what He appeared to be, that is, 'a mortal man.' However, they did acknowledge Him to be singularly chosen by God to be the Jewish Messiah. Throughout the Old Testament, the Messiah was never understood to be God Himself, or any part of the Godhood. In the earliest scriptures, the "Messiah" was to be chosen out of the Israelite/Hebrew male population, not born out of a virgin woman.

In Acts, the chief Apostle, Peter, informs Cornelius that Jesus was "Lord of all" and that Jesus was "anointed by God with the Holy Spirit." [Cf. Acts 10:36-38] Doesn't this New Testament passage disprove a supernatural Trinity of Deities with Jesus as the middle deity?

None of the messianic prophecies that I have read ever predicted that the Messiah would be God Incarnate. Dr. Hugh Sconfield, in his book Those Incredible Christians, makes this point much better than I could. He was a biblical scholar who spent most of his adult life studying the Old and New Testament, and the era it encompassed. He declared that no scripturally knowledgeable Jew of Christ's day would ever accept a man as a God, especially not as a co-equal to their Hebrew Divinity! To even attempt to portray God in any form or image, be it of man, of beast, or combination of both, was unforgivable wickedness. Flavius Josephus, a First Century historian of the Jewish race, records the civil disorders caused by Pontius Pilate when he insisted on bringing images of Caesar Tiberius (r. 14 to 37 AD) into the Temple at Jerusalem. (This event occurred circa AD 26, at least four years before Jesus began proselytizing around AD 30)

Whoever first elevated Jesus to the Godhead was merely practicing one-upmanship on the ruling Romans. If Caesar was a Son of a Roman God (as was claimed), then Jesus, whom the deifier considered greater than any Caesar, was a superior Son of the Lord God. Their God resurrected Jesus after His death. No Caesar could provide such an astonishing supernatural authentication!

Reading Paul's earlier Epistles, I am left with the impression that he believed Jesus to have been resurrected in spirit, not in body. In 1 Corinthians 9:1, Paul informs us that he, too, witnessed the resurrected Jesus. Yet the evidence presented in Acts 16:9, and repeated in two other verses, {Acts 18:9 & 26:19} indicates that Paul saw Jesus in a vision, not in His person. Evidently, Paul understood that the Apostles viewed the risen Christ in the same manner, that being via visions! Paul rated himself equally empowered and authorized to preach the "Good News" as were the Apostles. He so states this. [Cf. 1 Cor. 9:1-2] It is the risen (spiritual) Christ, appearing in visions, who conferred the authority to baptize and to preach, as averred by Paul.

The resurrected mortal Jesus didn't inspire the Apostles to go forth and preach just prior to Pentecost; the mystical Jesus did! The memory of Jesus was the real impetus behind the "Tongues of Fire" (Holy Ghost) that imbued the Apostles with the boldness to circulate among the crowds and proclaim Jesus as the long-awaited Messiah. [Cf. Acts 2:1-11] Dwell on this for a moment and you will recognize the perceptiveness of that interpretation.

A Risen Christ doesn't match with the expectations of the Apostles, or with the faithful of the Jewish believers. If Jesus arose from the dead, this could only have signaled the beginning of the Messianic age. Had a resurrected Jesus appeared physically to the Apostles, they surely would have interpreted this as the inauguration of the Messiah's earthly reign.

Here He was, returned from death on the cross, ready to commence the eternal reign of righteousness on Earth. There is little to no justification for Jesus to defeat the corruption of death, if it wasn't to defeat the corruption of the ruling nations of the Earth. If the only result of His resurrection was His ascension into Heaven, why bother to appear to the Apostles at all? Was it: to foster futile hopes; to encourage the Apostles to abandon the Judaic faith; to have them believe that He would shortly be marching on Rome to establish His eternal Monarchy?

No, that isn't what we read. We read that He returned. He said, 'Hello, here I am.' Then He wafted off to Heaven never to be seen or heard from again . . . with the exception of Paul, who supposedly talked to Him in a vision from Heaven a decade or so later.

The logic of this sequence of events eludes me. The conventional rationale for the resurrection is this: Jesus rose from the dead to prove he was the Messiah, the Anointed One, and that He was also the Son of God. Yet, He appeared only to those who knew Him! But I ask why? They (presumably) already knew or believed as much. To them, Jesus had nothing to prove. Why didn't He appear to Caiaphas, the High Priest? 'Or to Herod Agrippa? 'Or to Pontius Pilate? 'Or to Caesar himself? Why didn't He wait several years and appear to Josephus, so that an eventual world-renowned, first century historian, could have verified the Risen Christ? (Josephus was born in AD 37, approximately four years after the crucifixion.) If Jesus wanted the world to know of His Messiahship: being God, He could have done a far superior job than we can verify was done through His disciples, and through the "Good News" proclamations of the Apostles and Paul.

What conclusion can I draw from the narrative as found in the New Testament? The most logical; least debatable ... the answer that best fits the circumstance is this: He never reappeared at all! His followers, believing, trusting, or possibly just hoping He would return, moved out among the Jewish populace and preached His expected return. They prayed for it, and yearned for it so fervently, that some came to believe they had seen Him ... on the highway; in their meeting places; or even in their minds. (As Paul did later)

They wished with all their being that He would be resurrected and return. But alas, He never did ... not in the sense we are asked today to believe! Ponder querulously my suspicions about the Resurrection: Jesus was unrecognized by the travelers to Emmaus. [Cf. Luke 24:11-35] On a hill in Galilee: "they saw him, they worshiped him, but some of them doubted!" [Cf. Mt. 28:17]. If we discount an obvious addenda to Mark (Mk. 16:9-20), there is no post-execution appearance by Jesus. Apostle John has entirely too many post-crucifixion appearances by Jesus. But, in his last appearance [Jn. 21:4]: "Jesus stood on the shore talking to those Apostles who were fishing; yet the Apostles did not know that it was Jesus advising them where to cast the nets."

My belief is that Jesus never resurrected, and never was seen by anyone after the crucifixion. Discernibly, Jesus inspired His followers following His death, but not in the supernatural and literal manner that the New Testament describes. Second generation Christians, especially the Gentile converts, could more readily accept that Jesus was the physical Son of the Living God, for they had been hearing such mystic drivel all of their lives. The Greek Gods lived and walked among men. Several Caesars professed to be fathered by Gods. Many foreigners ensconced in Rome had wondrous tales to tell of gods who trod the Earth in human guise. The cult of Jesus was no novelty to these people.

And the early Christian missionaries were, by comparison, superior to the other religious proselytizers of Rome. The Christians coupled morality (decent behavior) with their mysticism! That was novel! Accepting this analysis, it is no great wonder to me that Christianity flourished in Rome (and elsewhere!), while it foundered and perished in Hebrew Jerusalem.

The Non-Hebrew world had only to accept that the morality most humans yearn to embrace was sanctified and authorized by a Jewish holy man who many asserted was truly a "Son of God." But the Jews of the Holy Lands were being asked to believe that their personal deity, Yahweh, had finally sent the long pledged Redeemer, and that this person (Jesus) was the actual biological "Son of their unique Deity." For a devout Hebrew, no religious teaching could have been more challenging to accept and believe. I don't wonder why the greater numbers of the earliest Christians were Gentiles and not Jews. The real marvel is why there were any Jewish converts to Christianity at all!

CHAPTER 10
Diagnosing

WHY RENOUNCE RELIGIOSITY?

Having progressed thus far you rightly will be asking yourself, "Well, this author has effectively destroyed my previous perception of Heaven, and he has done serious harm to the concept of a personal God, but what has he offered me in compensation?" I admit that this poses a requirement that I am unable to readily meet. What would compensate for the loss of a personal Deity and an eternal reward? Shortly, I will give my reply to the last put question.

Religion, for all its falsity and deceit, undeniably does satisfy a nagging, unfulfilled human craving. If I remove this emotional palliative from your life, what shall I replace it with? The short retort is that I shan't replace it with anything. You are either going to have to outgrow your dependence on religiosity, or forever remain addicted to religion. Primarily, I have to point out the unrecognized harm of that addiction. I also must be able to demonstrate that you will be better situated if you can overcome your innate yearning for divine affection and spiritual succor.

It isn't surprising that religion is often introduced as a substitute for chronic drug dependence. So, for chronic addicts of religion I should be prepared to supplement that dependence, at least in the early stages of withdrawal. The first requirement must be for you to desire to be cured from religiosity, or be willing to accept treatment leading to a cure. For in the end, all I have to offer you is truth, reality, and the ultimate recompense: freedom to question anything and everything objectively! {My answer}

God didn't give us intelligence so that we shouldn't use it. Our questions can't harm God. But they may expose a charlatan who is attempting to deceive us. If we occasionally curse and then damn another human, is God's ego bruised because we have usurped His divine prerogative? No, because God can't have an ego. Ego is the impetus behind pride. Ego is what causes one person to conclude that he is a "better" person than is some other person. God knows He is the best; He doesn't need an ego; He doesn't have an ego. God is God! No other axiom can surpass that factum. If we attempt to add any attribute at all to that declaration we have delimited Him, and thereby, we have diminished His exclusive and unparalleled Godhood.

The previous point isn't apparent, but it is no less valid. For if we attest that our God is a "Just" God, we imply that there is, or could be, an "Unjust" God. If we attest that our God is a Loving Deity, then we concede that God could have been a Deity who harbors Hate! If we postulate that God is All-Powerful, we concomitantly acknowledge that there exists the possibility of a less than All-Powerful God. Is it clearer now why we cannot affix any attribute whatsoever to God?

Yet, every minute of every day, some "holy man" enunciates a praise-worthy attribute attaining to his imagined personal Deity. The fact that religionists feel impelled to continuously tout God's virtuous qualities underscores their own subliminal misgivings over His boundlessness of trait —*indeed, of His very actuality*! In reality, a religionist knows less about the Divinity than a Used Car salesman knows about an automobile he has just received. That doesn't prevent the salesman from attempting to sell you the auto. Correspondingly, the lack of factual knowledge about God doesn't ever deter a religionist from 'selling' God to you either. All I can offer my reader is that eternal caveat: "Let the buyer (of religiosity) beware!"

DREAMS AND THE SOUL

Nowadays, we identify our spirit, or equate our soul, with our sense of awareness. Our awareness seems never to malfunction ... never to die. All during our lives, each time we ponder our awareness, that awareness alerts us that it is still functioning. We think back a few moments, or hours, even days into the past, and we are comforted to realize that our awareness was active then, even though we weren't consciously dwelling upon it. It still existed; it was still operational. Factually, by all that is apparent, our awareness never seems to be inactive or inattentive.

Our dreams tell us that this sense is aware even if the remainder of our body is asleep. Yes, it is true (if you reflect upon it) *our awareness is immortal!* Try to imagine your awareness being turned off. You can't! How can you imagine not having an imagination? Because of this actuality, Heaven was invented; we had to have provided for ourselves a place to relocate our consciousness when we contemplate the demise of our physical body.

Primary logic, the logic that most people identify as common sense, is functioning when we reach such chimerical conclusions. Chimera, here, is defined as an absurd creation of the imagination. That is exactly how I describe the notion that our sense of awareness can't be killed; therefore, it will always exist! Some people have even attached Godhead essence to this awareness, *vis á vis*, our soul. The reasoning generally follows this pattern: The essence of our 'ego' comes from God; perchance it is an atom of the very substance of God; a divine eternal nucleon perhaps. This atom finds expression in the human body, animating it, enlightening it, and ennobling it. Admittedly, God's substance can never be destroyed. It is impervious to death, to debilitation, or even to further division. Once this spark of awareness is activated, it can't be extinguished. This your mind informs you about your mind. But how factual is this rationale?

If you are sufficiently endowed mentally to contemplate the foregoing, then it is evidently true. But what if your mind can be turned off, just as a computer can be turned off? One might only ponder a dreamless period of sleep, or traumatic unconsciousness. Granted, a mind is vastly more complicated than is a computer, but there are still many valid aspects of comparison. Think of this: Does a computer know when it has been turned off? Positively not! Can it perform any functions whatsoever without a power supply? That answer is also "No!" If you postulate that the energy that animates humans is that 'bit' or 'byte' from the Godhead, then reasonably, you could expect that bit of 'energy' to be eternal. But this rationalization breaks down rather easily when we reason through the proposition with a thoroughness of deliberation.

Our soul isn't just an energy source; it is an independent entity. It has awareness, i.e., a spiritual brain. It reasons ethically. It possesses the human senses of sight and hearing along with the ability to communicate with us. It is marvelous in that it retains all the desirable capabilities of a human body, while discarding all the undesirable liabilities. It is impervious to physical harm; it is free of the destructive results of aging; it has no need of rest or repair. Lastly, your soul doesn't need nutrition to sustain it.

Consider for yourself what the beneficial attributes of a spiritual existence are, then ponder all the taxing and limiting restrictions that are obviated the moment we dispense with our human body. Every useful human attribute you can imagine is found to coexist with spiritual living. We can even fly without flapping wings, or without an external means of propulsion. Your imagination grants you every spiritual perk you have ever dreamed. But wait, an unsettling element has just intruded itself into this mental soliloquy; that being, the invocation of dreams.

Dreams, too, emanate from our imagination. In our dreams we are able, at times, to perform inexplicable feats, while concurrently, we are unable to perform simple, everyday physical tasks. Additionally, investigators determined long ago that dream sequences are wholly illogical; but as we try to recall them upon awaking, we tend to sort them into a more orderly sequence than we dreamed them. Yet despite this initial rearrangement, the recalled dream is seldom logically sequential. For this reason, I am unapologetically skeptical when I read in the Bible that God (or an Angel) appeared to someone in a dream. Because of my previous experiences with dreams, if Jesus appeared to me in a dream, frankly, I wouldn't place trust in the celestial origin for that dream without tangible confirmation.

You could dismiss my every assumption about dreams by stating that God and Heaven are of the spiritual world, not of the physical world. But, in doing so, you negate the entire physical world and every physical entity in it. Tell me: Is my brain of the physical world? What about my memories? Are they, too, of the physical world? What of my personal goals? Aren't they related to a material universe? "No! No! No!" can be successfully repudiated, so I will assume that your answers were "Yes!" "Yes!" "Yes!"

Isn't it then true that if you ravage my recollections, if you shatter my aspirations, and you wreck my thoughts, that you have destroyed me?

Unquestionably, this is true. Hypothetically, all that would remain of me is my spirit. So try to imagine my soul without memory of my physical experiences. A soul without a memory of its past is unthinkable. It would be as mindless as is a vegetable. It would be as tenuous as a wisp of smoke. It would be less substantial than a neutrino zipping through space able to react with physical matter only in the most circumspect and inconsequential manner. Is this to be my eternal reward for loving, fearing, or even believing in Almighty God?

Dreams furnish us with the evidence we need to combat the baseless notion of soul; or awareness; or consciousness; or whatever else proponents choose to call the irreducible "I." Dreams prove that our awareness isn't always the logical, deductive, perceptive apparatus that it seems to be during periods of consciousness. Our awareness functions sensibly only when the stimulations it receives arrive in a sensible manner. Normal people become disoriented when the stimulus they receive is gravely distorted.

The "Crazy House" at an Amusement Park, where furniture is attached to the ceiling or where the floor is inclined from level, confuses our brain and causes many people to become nauseous. This confirms the suspicion that our awareness isn't some quintessential essence, but is merely another functional element of our human body. Dreams, insanity, comas, and retardation are all unmistakable manifestations of the human limitations of our consciousness.

Transcendental Meditation, Yoga, et al., are all pretentious yet futile attempts to link our consciousness with a force, or power, or eminence that is imagined to exist on a higher ethereal plane than the human mind inhabits. Narcotic users equate their insipid, confused, befogged disorientation to detached, lofty mental elevation, when in actuality all they have accomplished is the disconnection of many of their sensory nerve pathways within their brain that is the very abode of their awareness! They imagine that they have progressed to a superior level of awareness, when factually they have retrogressed to the perceptual level of an infant.

Persons involved in psychological quasi-religions, who shut out normal physical stimulation (as most meditation-based cults do), can only achieve the same result. They picture their spirit as rising to immeasurable heights, whereas, I view their condition as sinking to the depths of deaf, blind, mutes that reject all attempts to communicate through their senses.

Helen Keller could have exposed Transcendental Meditation for the farce that it is.

I have nothing against the practice as such, only so far as it impacts me. But I am fearful that one day its practitioners may come to power and impose their dogmas on a captive populace. Our governing body should officially denounce any and all practices that are proved substantially self-deluding. The very rules that apply to deceptive advertising should be applied uncompromisingly to all metaphysical beliefs (for example, religion) with the same unrelenting skeptical rigor!

DIVINE INSPIRATION — RARE OR UBIQUITOUS?

If there is absolute truth, then where is this truth to be found? To each person mentioned at the beginning of this book (those who came to believe they had been endowed with divine enlightenment), the solution is apparent; it is embodied in their beliefs! 'Regardless! Religions, taken as a whole, are so mutually opposed and contradictory that they cannot be taken as a whole. One, many, or all of the existing faiths must be false.

If God has shone light on humanity, then, of course, there can be only one true religion if there be but one God. Grant for a moment that a Supreme Being does exist. Grant further that He has enlightened mankind as to the manner we should employ to worship Him. (Theorizing that God does need or want to be worshipped) Does this explain the vast and various assortment of human beliefs? No, it argues invincibly against an assortment of beliefs. If God is unique, then the faith that worships Him must also be unique. Did God inspire a singular, 'true' religion, or did He merely infuse a human proclivity toward religiosity? The dogma of divine inspiration prohibits a diversity of faiths. Yet, we all can witness just how diverse our beliefs are, and concomitant to this, how prolific our disparate, ever-expanding, Christian denominations are!

The growth in the number of the various cults proclaiming Jesus as their inspiration rivals the growth of political parties who allege to 'represent the people' in most of the emerging, nominal democracies. How is mankind to separate the true inspiration from the ubiquitous aggregation? For if we disavow divine enlightenment then all alleged inspiration becomes purely mental delusion, or deception! How, then, can we discover the one, true, infallible faith? 'By miracles? 'By moral behavior? 'By potency of their petitions? 'By the longevity of its existence? 'By the outrageousness of its teachings?

If you can't discern an obvious flaw in each of the above, or any other standard I could apply, then we are evidently reasoning on two divergent cogency paths. (Metaphorically: we are tuned to different wavelengths) The resolution to the above query is that there is no enlightenment, no infallible infusion of divine lore, no pious dialogue of any type, or in any manner between the universal truth and mankind. Even the Bible recognizes that we must labor to earn our bread. [Cf. Gen. 3:19] So, too, must we exercise our mental faculties to earn the sustenance wage of error-free knowledge, namely, universal verifiable truth!

Some denominations would have us believe in miraculous cures as proof of God's reality. Contemplate the miraculous cures that physicians, surgeons, engineers, and scientists are now able to perform? Anyone who is impressed with the miraculous events of the Bible should be truly astounded by the documented accomplishments of this age. The modern counterparts of the ancient miracles are more than impressive; more than amazing; they are astonishing! Hardly a day passes in this Century when a human event, which would have astounded the peoples of two thousand years ago, doesn't occur as a matter of everyday routine. If the necessary time was allotted, and if the required research was undertaken, the summary list you are about to review could have been expanded into dozens of pages.

A CURSORY LIST MIGHT
RESEMBLE THE FOLLOWING:

ANCIENT WONDER	MODERN MIRACLE
World-wide Flood	Melting Polar Caps (potential for)
Calming a Storm	Cloud Seeding
Destruction of Cities	Atomic Bombs, ICBM Weaponry
Multiplication of Loaves	Synthetic Fertilizers, High-Yield Crops
Parting the Red Sea	Constructing Tunnels under Water
Walking on Water	Surfing, Water Skiing, Hydrofoil Craft
Bodily Ascension	Backpack Thrusters, Space Program
Curing Illnesses	Antibiotics, Vaccines, Drug Therapy
Ascension to Heaven	Deep Space Probes, Moon Landing
Dream Suggestions	Hypnosis, Subliminal Messages
Lightning Strikes	Laser Beams, Microwaves, Cruise Missiles
Restoring the Lame	Joint Replacement, Prosthetics, Bone Surgery
Re-attaching Severed Limbs	Micro-Surgery, Organ Transplants
Fire from Heaven	Incendiary Bombs, Laser-Guided Ordnance
Barren Women Conceiving	*In vitro* fertilization, Artificial Insemination

ANCIENT WONDER	MODERN MIRACLE
Driving Out Demons	Psychiatry, Shock Treatments, Brain Surgery
Predicting Disasters	Satellite Radar Pictures, Forecasting Hurricanes
Changing Water into Wine	Creating Trans-Uranium Elements, Synthetics
Raising the Dead	Electrode Stimulation, Adrenaline, Life Support
Omniscience	Live Television, Radio Broadcasts, Spy Satellites
Knowing the Future	Weather, Flood Predictions, Comet tracking
Knowing the Past	Paleontology, Archeology, Books, Films & Tapes

Today's technological advances didn't emanate from Bible study. Without our printing technology, the Bible itself would never have received the widespread ownership it now enjoys. The Medieval Church correctly viewed printing as a mixed blessing at best, and wherever clerics were empowered, they enforced stringent controls over what could be printed. {Confer an encyclopedia: Index of Forbidden Books – Pope Paul IV} During the Inquisition of Toulouse in AD 1229, lay persons were forbidden to read the Bible.

Returning to miracles, let me state that the absence of miracles is just as portentous as is their alleged presence. Primitive peoples are ruled by superstition; they have no miraculous cures. They suffer and die from maladies occasioned by their ignorance of hygienic practices. They do possess forms of religion; what they lack is practical information. If God imparts knowledge to mankind, why doesn't He inspire the backward peoples of the world with a little inspiration on sanitation?

As stated previously, no proposition stands alone. God is judged not only by what He has supposedly done (imbued us with a predisposition toward cultic indoctrination), but also by what He has failed to do, e.g., divulge to humanity the necessary knowledge to control our hostile environment so that humans wouldn't have to rely on trial/failure/retrial to accomplish that which was indispensable for agricultural development. God instructed mankind how to bow, but not how to plow. Evaluated from this viewpoint, God is found criminally negligent in the care and nurturing of the mass of His created offspring. Malnutrition is the number one cause of sickness and death in the world of yesterday, today, and all of the likely tomorrows!

What process does or should mankind employ to ameliorate hunger, privation, and pollution? Obsequious supplication isn't going to solve the world's woes. Intelligent management of its resources, coupled with voluntary or forced reduction of procreation may? Frankly, the anti-intellectual leadership we have had so far may have led us beyond the brink of disaster already. I am not overly optimistic about the chances of humanity reversing some of its more fallacious procedures in time to avert the impending fallout from the fouling of its habitat.

The time for a reassessment of some of our most cherished sanctimonious beliefs is at hand. Within a generation or two we will either have made the right decisions, or we will have turned the corner to irreversible self-destruction, for then only prayer will be all that will be available to us. If that day ever dawns, I earnestly pray that God listens more intently, and acts more compassionately, than He ever has in the past!

RELIGIOSITY IS A HUMAN INSTINCT

Religiosity appears to spring from man's depths spontaneously as a vague, poorly resolved but universal impulse. Compare it with humanity's predilection to cry when sad, or to laugh when happy. Our proclivity toward religiosity then is viewed as just another of man's innate emotions. No one has to teach a child to laugh, that trait develops naturally. Is the natural inclination facilitating religious gullibility, likewise, the manifestation of a basic instinct? The development of specific dogma may then be explained as man's imperfect attempt to partially placate his innate religious propensity.

At first thought, you may be tempted to dismiss the above theory as mere conjecture without proof. But in truth, no one can explain why we laugh. Not only is laughing an instinct shared throughout the human species, but oddly, it is found in the human species exclusively. The instinct isn't present in any other species, not even our closest relatives the anthropoid apes. The instinct responsible for laughing and smiling is active almost from birth, and is definitely well developed before our first birthday. Yet, despite the universality of this instinct, we still know nothing of its origin. We know it exists because we can see it, hear it, and experience it, yet its genesis remains a mystery.

Man's observed compulsion toward superstitious (religious) beliefs is just as universal, and only slightly less evident. We all know that children are fascinated with fairy tales and fables, but has anyone ever questioned why? Children always believe in goblins and ogres, giants and magic, yet we can hardly convince them of the perils of crossing the street without first looking. Isn't this bewildering when you consider the absolute reality of the risk of harm from motor vehicles against the positively non-existent danger posed by imaginary creatures?

Children believe that which they can imagine before or perhaps in lieu of, that which they can see. Apply this oddity to the human predisposition toward belief in the paranormal and man's universal religious propensity becomes somewhat more explicable. It also posits a more satisfactory resolution to the problem of the confusing welter of specific beliefs. Different fables appeal to different children, and different creedal interpretations similarly appeal to different adults. If you accept the foregoing as valid, then revelation becomes irrelevant, and Divine Inspiration becomes inconsequential. Man has an instinct to laugh, so he invents jokes. He, likewise, has an instinct toward mysticism (religion), so he invents gods!

PROVOKING YAHWEH'S RETRIBUTION

You would think that if there were specific actions that we humans could perform that would please God that He would display His preference for those actions in some conspicuous manner. For instance: If it could be proved that no disaster has ever struck a House of Worship on Easter

Sunday morning, I could readily accept that I should attend services there, at least on that Sunday. Or, turn it around: Let anyone who desecrates a Church on Christmas Day; thereafter have some inexplicable malady strike him. There should be at least one reprehensible act that would unfailingly provoke God's disciplinary or retaliatory reaction.

Instead, what we read of are the many cases of gross sacrilege that are acted out during the worship of Satan at Black Masses and the like. Black Masses are where consecrated hosts (purported to be the actual body of God Jesus) are subjected to the most offensive and abhorrent abominations imaginable. If God is ever moved to lash out against depraved humanity, those contemptible acts should invariably be the catalyst. But is this what we observe? "No!" Whenever such revolting exhibitions have become known, religious apologists have dodged recriminations behind a welter of platitudes of which, 'The Lord is long suffering in His mercies and justice,' is a typical alibi. It appears that no amount of deliberate provocation is sufficient to impel God to retaliatory actions. Nor can the opposite reaction ever be enticed. The prayerful petitions of thousands of persons won't elicit, predictably, the slightest beneficial response from God.

If the Old Testament is reliable fact and not religious invention/fantasy, then God can, will, and does intervene in worldly matters. The Egyptians suffered grievously by the hand of Yahweh; we know this from the story of the Exodus. Yet the Romans, whose atrocities against the early Christians far exceeded those that the Egyptians perpetrated against His chosen people, were totally unpunished by "God the Father" (new appellation for Yahweh per Jesus).

Where is God's justice? Was it justice when He agonized the Egyptians with plagues, famine, infestation of various insects, fiery hail, bloody water, frog fallout, boils, continuous darkness for three days and, finally, the death of all of Egypt's male first born, both of man and of beast? Not if He later permitted the Romans to crucify; to burn at stakes; to subject to horrifying and lethal attack by wild beasts; or otherwise to brutalize the Christians —*all without any Divine retribution!* Citing only these two examples (the Egyptians and the Romans) as uneven justice, is to grossly understate the totality of similar evidence existing against God's apparent nonfeasance as the whimsical dispenser of divine "justice" here on Earth.

Pharaoh merely kept the Israelites enslaved, and not all of them discernibly! Exodus informs us that the Israelites took with them "their livestock, very numerous flocks and herds." [Ex. 12:38] By definition: 'Slaves cannot own any commodity of commercial value, particularly livestock.' Perhaps, the circumstances of the Israelites in Egypt weren't as deplorable as later Hebrew generations recounted them. Perhaps, they weren't even slaves. Recall that the idol carved by Aaron was fashioned from pure gold. How did 'slaves' accumulate so much gold? (Verse 22 of Chapter 3, Exodus, may answer that question.) [Cf. Ex. 11:2-3 & 12:35-36]

To commemorate their deliverance from the avenging 'angel of death,' the Hebrews instituted the feast of Passover. Yahweh (inferentially, in person) instructed Moses and Aaron, *"These are the Passover regulations: No foreigner shall eat the Passover meal, but any slave that you have bought may eat it if you circumcise him first."* [Ex. 12:43-44] What is God demanding here? Did the Israelites bring purchased slaves out of Egypt with them? My definition of slavery precludes one slave from owning another slave. Apologists will finesse these verses by interpreting them as referring to future feasts of Passover. Semantically this is possible, but then, I will question if these verses confirm God's evident sanction of slavery? The Bible never demonizes slavery. St. Paul never preached against slavery. *"Slaves, obey your earthly masters with deep respect and fear. Serve them sincerely as you would serve Christ."* [Eph. 6:5]

Perhaps the illogical assertion (patently insupportable) that "God loves us all equally" has validity. [Cf. Mal. 1:2-3 for refutation] For if God loves the cruel oppressors of His divinely inaugurated religion (Christianity) every bit as deeply as He loves His adherents, then He would never punish their fatal excesses against His ardent followers. God loved Nero also! If this hyperbolic rationale makes the tiniest sliver of sense to the current reader, then my book, on this occasion, has been abjectly unavailing. When God failed to act against the anti-Christian Roman Caesars, He proved that He was unmoved by love to act, or that He was incapable of acting. Neither option is commendable.

PHILOSOPHIZING ON VIRGINITY

What merit is there in remaining virgin your entire life? To my mind, no particular kudos should attend that unnatural proclivity. Celibacy, absent biological justification, is nothing but overindulged vanity. If a person has an intrinsic urge to consummate sexual relations, yet sublimates the desire merely to deem himself or herself closer to God, I would condemn that person as an insufferable egotist. If a person lacks the desire (or the capability) to engage in sexual activities, then no renown should be accorded that denatured individual because of this infirmity. Sympathy or commiseration is the appropriate emotional response that should be tendered to these atypical individuals

Conversely, indiscriminate sexual behavior has too many predictable deleterious consequences in human societies to offer a permissible alternative. Accordingly, promiscuity also should be despised without qualification. Many cogent reasons exist for moderating our sexual deportment, but religious sanctification isn't a sensible one of them. A normal woman who seeks to remain chaste her entire life forfeits her right to marry an equally normal man. Contrariwise, the reverse! Human societies function best when they are composed of stable husband and wife units. Any person bereft of all sexual propensities is probably abnormal in other traits as well. Homosexuality is an unfortunate mutation of natural sexuality that should be tolerated for the sake of societal harmony, but should never be endorsed as congruent with heterosexual relationships: fate forbid that it be exalted or glorified in any fashion. [Cp. Lev. 18:22]

In the case of Mary, why did she marry Joseph if not to solemnize and consummate their marriage through sexual intercourse? Was her consent to marry Joseph granted simply to supply Jesus with a normal familial upbringing? I would hardly think so! If He was the "Son of God," Jesus was in no danger of becoming psychologically impaired through lack of a paternal role model. The reason may have been financial? Somehow, that solution begs acceptance also. A wealthy family would have been a wiser alternative to a sexless marriage, and this would have bestowed credence to the desired dogma of Mary's lifelong abstinence from sexual indulgence.

Joseph truly was a saint if, for all the years they were married, he never once shared a sexual interlude with his wife Mary. We can presume that neither Joseph nor Mary masturbated either. This isn't entered into the discussion crudely, or for its shock value. But it does underscore the irrationality of the dogma of 'Eternal Virginity.' 'A dogma that exploits a human idiosyncrasy to attribute virtue to actions which are more aberrant than reverent.

Sexual drives are natural. There is nothing vulgar or demeaning in indulging those impulses provided we indulge ourselves in a judicious and appropriate (socially acceptable) manner. It is the extremes of human sexuality that are inappropriate. Promiscuity is harmful to the human libido. It is likewise offensive to most others, and it is invariably detrimental to any unfortunate offspring of these casual liaisons. Total sexual negation, although more abnormal than promiscuity, is less harmful to the individual, and it doesn't offend public standards; yet, it is utterly lacking in true merit in that it would result inexorably in the extinction of humanity if widely or universally adopted.

So where does that leave this discussion of sexual rejection? Right here: Misguided persons gird themselves with sanctity for rejecting a normal impulse that is more than beneficial to the species; it is vital! Equally misguided spectators often validate this utter and glaring misperception through their public acceptance and acknowledgment of the sexually abstemious person's "holiness." No one should ever be positively or negatively impassioned by such a deviant rejection of human sensuality.

Tell me, who gains by their abnegation? 'Not the individual! He merely substitutes the vanity satisfaction of peer adulation for the physical enjoyment of sexual indulgence. Who knows which pleasures satiate a person most, save that person alone? What we do know is that many persons seek gratification fulfillment in diverse and perverse methods. I don't rule out that there are persons whose greatest enjoyment is obtained through ego stimulation as distinct from sexual stimulation.

Mary's proposed lifelong virginity doesn't add one whit to the greatness of Jesus; neither does it detract from His greatness. It merely tacks on another illogical and implausible event to the mythos of Christianity that can only reinforce a skeptic's suspicions. No theological consideration is served by Mary's imputed ever-chaste condition. The present dogma is more readily dashed with a query than with ridicule. "Why didn't Mary, the wife of Joseph, share physical love with her husband?" A more perturbing question follows. "Why did Mary deceive the people who knew her?" They thought Jesus was the son of Joseph, and she never informed otherwise. Anyone who reads the Gospels knows that everyone believed Jesus to be the son of the carpenter. Neither Joseph nor Mary ever corrected this biblically erroneous, albeit rational, presumption. [Cf. Mt. 13:55; Mk. 6:3; Lu. 4:22 & Jn. 6:42] Similar lack of forthrightness nowadays is known in church parlance as 'acting out a lie' and is considered a serious offense.

Despite this, Mary is credited with being 'without sin' her entire life. This accreditation cloaks Mary in sanctity, but it also robs her of her humanity. No human could ever live their entire life without sinning once, especially if that life span covered almost eighty years. Many human actions that are judged sinful by a stilted ministry arise out of frustration, or anger, or despair, or selfishness, or any number of other mortal emotional reactions. Was Mary completely bereft of these human feelings? Doctrinally: Yes! Therefore, for Mary to be without sin necessitated that she, simultaneously, was without humanity. Does this lack accurately describe Mary the mother of Jesus as we have come to know her through the Gospels? Throughout the Gospels, Mary is forever depicted as a typical emotion-guided mother.

SELF-MORTIFICATION
AND OTHER PIOUS PRACTICES

While reading a book about Ancient Egypt, I turned a page and saw a representation of the Palette of Narmer. This object is thought to date from the period of the initial unification of the Upper and Lower kingdoms of Egypt more than three thousand years before the Christian era. The picture story inscribed onto the stone depicted the victorious Pharaoh with his arm raised as if to strike a defeated foe that is kneeling beseechingly at the king's feet. In Egyptian historical art, indeed, in the historical art of the entire ancient Middle East, this dual theme of Threat/Entreaty recurs frequently.

Artists, early on, employed a kneeling human being to symbolize the subservience of an individual, and concomitantly, to dramatize the dominance of any erect individual who towered over the kneeling man.

Which preceded which? Did a conquered man kneel to his vanquisher first, and then an artist seeing this event merely faithfully represented the scene? Or did a perceptive artist symbolically represent the event, and then have future captors mimic this posture to symbolize their life-controlling power? Whichever! Early on, everyone came to recognize this act as an open admission that the kneeling person submitted to the authority of the individual who was the object of the petitioner, and as the pleading one who sought his mercy as well.

The religious requirement to kneel while praying or importuning a Deity had its origin in this ancient symbolic action. To kneel before a potentially harmful authority figure often placated that figure, and generally worked to the benefit of the kneeling practitioner. It was natural, and probably inevitable, that the same form of subservience should be shown to a potentially vengeful God. Today we call it "worshiping." In truth, we still employ kneeling in prayer for the same reason ancient peoples employed it. That reason being to appease, and hopefully to favorably predispose, a vain conqueror or any entity otherwise unreachable, unrelenting, or vengeful. In the Christian circumstance, to placate God after we have sinned!

Candidly, we need what the Deity has to offer: benefit and benevolence. We feel we can enhance our chances of obtaining His favor if we kneel when we ask for it. The ancient peoples hoped as much. Lest you conclude that kneeling to God is an inborn or divinely imbued trait, consider that throughout the animal kingdom one or another act, performed in the presence of an aggressive attacker, signifies submission to that creature. Most simians assume a position called 'presenting' to demonstrate their servility. Averting the eyes is another act that is widespread in the animal kingdom. Bowing your head and lowering your glance while in Church has always been considered a gesture of reverence. (Extrapolated: "Submission to the Will of God")

Prostrating yourself before someone is an extreme form of the same act of self-abasement. Factually, that is what kneeling is, and all the more so is prostration. Religious zealots and aesthetics use this extreme form of humiliation (prostration) because they equate this act with great worthiness or profound devoutness. Self-mortification is practiced for the very same reason, to obtain some esoteric benefit available only to the mortified person. (That being: self-glorification) The seam of logic intrinsic to these acts seems to be: in order to receive an exceptional beneficence, one must perform some extraordinary act of mortification. This is simplistic reasoning, and can't pass muster as anything other than an immature, banal rationalization at best!

Those who inflict indignity upon themselves, bother me not at all. Those who deem this idiocy as something ennobling or sanctifying, annoy me no end. The latter think that performing acts of masochism is engendered by sanctity, when most often it is motivated by pure pomposity or worse: by devout deviousness. (Egotism unduly coddled) Without delving too deeply into the subject, I will provide an example to that which I am referring. Certain human male individuals are sexually aroused when experiencing pain. The stronger the pain, the more exquisite is the sexual ecstasy. For these individuals, mortification accomplishes the same ends that masturbation does for other individuals. Since both actions are performed alone, or without the cognizance of others, who can determine who performs which action to achieve their own furtive designs?

Most of us are impressed by those individuals who join a strict religious order that requires rigorous exertions from its adherents. We consider that surely these individuals are closer to God at a maximum, or they are more deserving of His love at a minimum. I confess. I believe neither! If it could be arranged, I would administer a truth serum to each one to determine his true motivation for abandoning mankind's normal lifestyles for the wholly abnormal lifestyle in a monastery. Condemn me as an irredeemable skeptic if you will. But if I am wrong, please show me; don't merely tell me! Faith won't sustain me. Just as with the Apostle Thomas, I ask for evidence. I require data that I can validate; proofs that I can touch; results that I can see. Too much misery has been foisted on humanity under the rubric of "faith" for me ever again to become the blind believer that I was as a child and young adult.

The past few observations taken separately do not signify much. But, when added to the total panoply of religiosity, they support the theory that every action we perform had its origin in some inborn natural propensity. Soon, the evidence becomes overwhelming: "God didn't invent religion. Religionists invented God!"

BENDING THE WILL OF GOD

A critical examination of all religiosity will show that belief in any other-worldly force is always expressed in human terms. We are, at base, no more than human. Any concept that we attempt to broadcast or promulgate will be stated or proffered essentially in human terms.

We entreat the Creator in human fashion, for although He is credited with power over forces we humans can't control, we wondrously can exercise considerable control over Him through religious magic. Our use of magic takes many forms. We can cajole, we can beg, we can even demand. Yes, demand! Isn't this what we are doing when we perform a specific ritual with the expectation of a desired result? If the 'Rain Dance' is properly executed, surely, God has no choice but to send rain. Likewise, when the priest whispers the appropriate incantations, God is unable to stop the Communion wafer from changing into the body and blood of Jesus.

Even a non-ritualistic religion as such as Quakerism is invested with power over the Deity. When they all assemble and pray silently together, God is compelled to listen. More so, God is compelled to imbue inspiration into individuals moving them to speak out authoritatively on religious matters. The early Friends (as they called themselves) frequently shuddered and quaked spasmodically while God was 'moving' them. Therein resides the derivation of the more familiar name "Quakers." They (or you) might insist that they are merely entreating God to respond. But an unbiased appraisal would ultimately conclude that this case corresponds more closely with the other two cited examples. (Rain-dance and Communion wafer)

If the proper form is attained (in this instance, group prayer), the Deity invariably will respond in a predictable manner. Again, in the Quaker instance, He will be attentive. Even God, the Supreme Entity, must conform to the group's expectations. Incidentally, the Devil is equally powerless to resist the cajolery of magical gestures and mystical incantations. Any manual on sorcery or black magic will convince you of this. An immutable tenet of every religious (or mystical) belief is the unconditional assurance of a desired result, in certain prescribed circumstances, if the effectuating rituals (or detailed requirements) are exactingly choreographed. God can no more snub the pious ritual "requests" of an empowered holy man (or woman) than can a marionette fail to respond to the manipulative "requests" of a skilled Puppet-Master. When Aladdin rubs the magical lamp, the Genie must appear!

CHRISTIANITY HAS LOST
MOST OF ITS INFLUENCE

Today, the Christian religion has evolved into an avocation. That is, it no longer holds a central position with the preponderance of its adherents. Christianity has digressed into a form of 'Saturday Night Bath' ritual performed once a week to cleanse our soul of transgressional dirt. Most of us go the entire week without beseeching God for any personal benefit. If we desire a nice day, we consult the Weather Bureau, not Almighty God. If we plant a garden, we buy a book that informs us what we must do to grow our flowers or vegetables. To obtain acceptance or favor from our fellow man, we attend classes that teach us how to influence others. When we need more money, we might take a part-time job, or have our spouse find employment.

True, we all, at one time or another, have purchased lottery tickets, or the like. In these instances we may seek Divine intervention for the expedient reason that we know we have no control over the outcome of the lottery drawing. Yet, no matter how earnestly we solicit God's aid, still, only one winner is ever drawn, and often he doesn't even believe in our Deity!

Religionists would attribute the cause of God's apparent capriciousness to the workings of the Devil. But the most plausible explanation lies in the efficacy of petitioning the Deity. Too many times, and for too long a time, God has disregarded our pleas. Pray for clear skies on a day the Weatherman predicts rain and see who is the most potent. Plant two flowering bushes, pray over one, and fertilize the other. Which one blooms first? 'No need to answer that question. Each passing year finds God much less influential in the everyday affairs of modern man.

It is reported that attendance at Mass and other Christian Church services is still high presently. I question that statistic. But, accepting that there may be truth in it, I still insist: "Today, more people go to Church with apostasy on their minds, with sin on their lips, and with fundamental disbelief in their heart, than has ever been the case in all of Christendom."

The Christian Divinity is fast becoming totally irrelevant. ('Except on Sunday!)

MODERN RELIGIOUS ENIGMAS

Are only biblical episodes puzzling in the light of today's knowledge? Has the Christian religion reformed from its superstitious, medieval ways? Is modern sophistication reflected in the views and beliefs of the present-day Church? A religiously significant event of the Twentieth Century is informative. (If intellect prevails; it is definitive!)

In late summer of 1978, the reigning Pope died, and the Cardinals of the Catholic Church, after the official mourning period, met to choose a successor. On the fourth ballot, Albino Luciani, the Patriarch of Venice, was chosen. He was a pastoral-type prelate who was not a member of the Roman Curia. The name he chose was John Paul I, becoming the first to choose a dual name. The dual name was fashioned to honor his two most recent predecessors, Pope John XXIII and Pope Paul VI.

Everyone hailed his selection as an extraordinary choice. They could plainly see that Divine Providence had had a hand in his election. (Then) Cardinal Krol of Philadelphia openly stated that only the Holy Spirit could have inspired so worthy a selection, and in such a short period of deliberation. Personally, I feel that had the Holy Spirit influenced the election of John-Paul I, he would have been chosen on the first ballot, not the fourth. However, he was instantly acclaimed in the United States, and many (including myself) expected momentous enactment's during his pontificate. He seemed to be a person the masses would love instinctively, not dictated by convention. He projected a magnetic, pastoral charisma almost unanimously perceived and admired.

Suddenly, thirty-four days after his elevation, John Paul I expired! The Christian world was thunderstruck. How could this be? The man from whom everyone expected so much was dead before he had accomplished anything. He hadn't written a single official document, and had pronounced only a lone doctrinal position. He hadn't even filled his own vacant Patriarchy. If a person believed in Divine intervention, he could only conclude that the Cardinals had made the wrong choice, and this was the manner the Holy Spirit chose to so inform them. But to an eternal optimist, cheap port wine is indistinguishable from premium champagne if politic sacred requirements so dictated.

How did Cardinal Krol respond to the news of the unexpected death of Pope John Paul? Quoted in a local newspaper (The Philadelphia Journal), he said, "We've had a Pope of great promise but the God who called him to the Papacy, called him to his eternal reward. As much as we are saddened and grieved by the death; we look forward with joy and confidence. Pray for the repose of his soul, and I invite you also to pray to the Holy Spirit, so that the Cardinal electors may again be objects of the Holy Spirit."

If you look intently enough for a cloud with a silver lining, you will find one even on a cloudless day. Human capacity for self-delusion, it seems, is infinite. If the Holy Spirit influenced the selection of Patriarch Luciani, why did it take four ballots for him to receive the required tally? If the Holy Spirit desired him and no other, why is it that nothing was accomplished during his pontificate? His ultimate replacement, a Polish Cardinal (the first non-Italian Pope in 455 years) was present at the initial conclave; accordingly, the Holy Spirit could have inspired his election one month earlier. Why select a man whom God "<u>knew</u>" would die thirty-four days later? More damaging to Cardinal Krol's hypotheses is the suspected fact that the excitement and burden of that very demanding position may well have precipitated the fatal heart attack that killed the sixty-five-year-old Pope.

The only doctrinal position announced by Pope John Paul I, was to reaffirm the previous Pope's stand against birth control. If I were an Old Testament chronicler, it would be facile for me to connect his death with this, his only definitive religious pronouncement. A logical link could also be forged to the death of the previous Pope (Paul VI) who had disappointed the Catholic liberals with his edict reaffirming the prohibition of contraceptives. If these papal events are indicative of the divine actions of the 'Spiritual Pope' of the Catholic Church (the Holy Ghost), then I conclude that those who oppose the prevention or termination of inconvenient pregnancies have misinterpreted God's Will. They may be struck down at any moment!

"Blasphemy," you say? "Evident," I say! Of course, that conclusion is only binding if there is Divine intervention, and if the events just described were influenced by the Third Person of the Trinity. Instead, if you opt to abandon the unprovable, unknowable, and unconfirmed belief in a personal Deity, then all the happenings of this world, including papal elections, are comprehensible to the non-deluded, non-superstitious, and disbelieving rational segment of humanity.

Please don't construe from the foregoing that I wish anyone dead, especially the Pope! I would much sooner convert him than crucify him. Nevertheless, if this was the Dark Ages or the Middle Ages, and if any official of the Church were to attempt to silence me either through execution or imprisonment, then I would strive to reverse his sentence upon himself without remorse and without relent! Only a fool or a mindless lackwit turns the other cheek when struck, and only an equally deficient mind is impressed by such deranged logic. In the real world, anyone who bends over and presents his rump, will surely have it swiftly kicked, and deservedly so!

PROHIBITED ACTIONS

Does God care if you eat meat on Friday? Of course not! If you enjoy eating meat, go ahead and eat it. Will God hate you if you eat pork? Are cows any more sacred than any other animal? Is any creature, particularly man, intrinsically sacred? No! No! No! Does God insist that women cover their faces or their heads, or even their breasts? No!

The measure of honor and respect we humans deserve should be freely determined by those who confer that honor and respect, not as prescribed by divine inspiration or decreed by royal edict, or even as required by government protocol. Communal living requires communal harmony, and therefore, we must have communal laws. Communal laws aren't blessings from on High; mainly, laws are a nuisance! Irrespective! Laws are an indispensable nuisance. They should be kept to a minimum. They should be enacted only on a temporary provisional basis subject to periodic review after a reasonable initial trial period.

Laws that had as their impetus a religious or superstitious root for their justification, would be invalidated and repealed forthwith. Community standards would be enforced only within the community, and everyone in the community would be free to either petition to change an existing law, or to move to another community that had not enacted that law. Nationwide laws could be subjected to national review if enough persons throughout the nation requested this. Nationwide laws should be minimized!

Laws whose primary purpose was to "honor" God would be disallowed with the 'burden of proof' resting on the sponsor of the proposed law. Is God so vain that He would be elated to have a large segment of the human population obeying senseless religious strictures contrary their wills, or by forcing them to bow reluctantly, or with rancor replacing reverence? Is this what God desires? I cannot accept that, and no rationally sensible person would either. Primarily, this section refers to governments dominated by hierarchical legislators. (Example: Hasidic Jews, Fundamentalist Christians, Extremist Muslims, *et al.*) But it is also targeted at the Christian "Blue Laws" once prevalent throughout this nation.

SUPERSTITION RULES THE RELIGIOUS MIND

An important difference between primitive and modern religion is that modern religion supposedly makes sense. Unlike modern religion, which is founded on presumed fact, primitive religions were based solely on superstition. Primitive cults promoted unreasonable concepts. For instance, belief that a pregnant woman frightened by a goat would bear a newborn with vestigial horns, we are told, was superstitious drivel. Today we mock such base ignorance. Yet, we believe that a Catholic who eats meat on Good Friday is doomed to be dispatched directly to Hell when he dies. We also believe that certain days of the year are deemed holier to God than are other days. The utter inaccuracy of the early calendars, coupled with the many adjustments made to our present calendar, curiously, hasn't detracted from this belief.

Another oddity: We celebrate the birth of Jesus in the beginning of winter. Yet, we also read in the Bible that the shepherds were tending their sheep in the presumptively warm pastures. A technical aside will illustrate graphically where this point is headed. Good Friday is not a set holy day. It is determined by the dating of Easter, which is also a movable feast day. Over the early centuries many systems were used to set the calendar date for Easter. Let us run through just a few. Jesus was crucified during the Jewish festival of Passover. As a consequence, Easter is inextricably tied to a Jewish holy day. Passover was celebrated according to a lunar calendar and fell on the evening of the first full moon during the month of Nisan. This event fell on different days of the week from year to year. Early Christians desired always to celebrate Easter on a Sunday. Thence, Emperor Constantine convened the Council of Nicaea in AD 325, which, among other decrees, formulated a method to avoid celebrating Easter Sunday on the same Sunday that the Jews were celebrating Passover in a particular year. Read the following quoted material.

"The council unanimously ruled that the Easter festival should be celebrated throughout the Christian world on the first Sunday after the full moon following the vernal equinox; and that if the full moon should occur on a Sunday and thereby coincide with the Passover festival, Easter should be commemorated on the Sunday following. Coincidence of the feasts of Easter and Passover was thus avoided.

"The Council of Nicaea also decided that the calendar date of Easter was to be calculated at the city of Alexandria, then the principal astronomical center of the world. The accurate determination of the date, however, proved to be an impossible task in view of the limited knowledge of the 4th century world. The principal astronomical problem involved was the discrepancy, called the epact, between the solar year and the lunar year. The chief calendric problem was a gradually increasing discrepancy between the true astronomical year and the Julian calendar, then in use.

"Later Dating Methods: Ways of fixing the date of the feast tried by the Church proved unsatisfactory, and Easter was celebrated on different dates in different parts of the world. In 387, for example, the dates of Easter in France and Egypt were thirty-five days apart. Around 465, the Church adopted a system of calculation proposed by the astronomer Victorinus (fl. 5th cent.) who had been commissioned by Pope Hilarius (r. 461-68) to reform the calendar and fix the date of Easter. Elements of his method are still in use. Refusal of the British and Celtic Christian churches to adopt the proposed changes led to a bitter dispute between them and Rome in the 7th century.

"Reform of the Julian calendar in 1582 by Pope Gregory XIII through adoption of the Gregorian calendar, eliminated much of the difficulty in fixing the date of Easter and in arranging the ecclesiastical year; since 1752, when the Gregorian calendar was also adopted in Great Britain and Ireland, Easter has been celebrated on the same day in the western part of the Christian world. The Eastern churches, however, which did not adopt the Gregorian calendar, commemorate Easter on a Sunday either preceding or following the date observed in the West. Occasionally the dates coincide; the most recent times were in 1865 and 1963.

"Because the Easter holiday affects a varied number of secular affairs in many countries, it has long been urged as a matter of convenience that the movable dates of the festival be either narrowed in range or replaced by a fixed date in the manner of Christmas. In 1923, the problem was referred to the Holy See, which has found no canonical objection to the proposed reform. In 1928, the British Parliament enacted a measure allowing the Church of England to commemorate Easter on the first Sunday after the second Saturday in April. Despite these steps toward reform, Easter continues to be a movable feast." {End Quote} [Funk & Wagnall New Encyclopedia]

If you have successfully waded through that mire of confusion, let us reconsider the Catholic who eats meat on Good Friday. Suppose he is in Greece, which isn't celebrating Easter until the following week? Or suppose he is aboard a naval vessel in the year 387, and is halfway between Egypt and France: Does he maintain his abstinence for thirty-five days, just to be certain? Does God truly care? Is He willing to punish you for an eternity if you eat chicken on some indeterminate day of the year, yet remain unoffended if you eat a chicken embryo (i.e., an egg) on the very same day?

This belief is clearly a case of rigid doctrine devolving from an arbitrary pious practice. In my own lifetime, the belief has changed from abstinence from meat on every Friday of the year, to Good Friday only. God decreed neither commandment. The fact that I chose a Catholic doctrine has no ulterior motivation, and none should be inferred. Non-Catholic Christians should derive no satisfaction from a criticism of the Roman Church because the other Christian denominations have never wielded the power, nor shouldered the responsibilities of so massive an organization. It is a wonder that today this Church (Roman Catholic) is as flexible as it is. My quarrel isn't with any one denomination or belief, it is with the whole mistaken concept of a personal, cognizant, activist Divinity.

THE NAMING OF EASTER

[Extrapolated from Funk & Wagnall New Encyclopedia] Whence came the name "Easter" to celebrate the day the Son of God was resurrected from the dead? Ironically, the name has no etymological connection with Jesus Christ or Christianity. Saint Bede, an eighth century historian, offers the only root foundation I could uncover. He postulated a connection with a Norse fertility divinity named Eastre (Ostara?).

It seems Eastre {*sic*} was a Teutonic goddess associated with the Spring season and rejuvenation. Curiously: with the annual rebirth of Nature at the time of the Vernal Equinox. Many of the distinctive customs of Easter are impossible to link with religiosity, and much less with Christianity. An Easter Bunny distributing decorated eggs being the most recognizable objectification of Easter. The rabbit has always symbolized reproductive vigor; and eggs are the actual manifestations of new life. The juxtaposition of eggs and rabbits is incongruent, but their synthesis has nonetheless become firmly established in the American Christian Easter tradition.

Another suspicious factor associated with Easter is the readily verifiable fact that several ancient mythologies relate physical resurrection tales that occur in the Spring of the year. The Spring season is the time of year when the plant world renews itself, and it is likewise the time of year when many animal species 'resurrect' themselves by bearing offspring. Could there have been a more propitious time of year for God the Father to have resurrected His only begotten Son after His crucifixion? {'Coincidence? Or plotted orchestration?}

CHAPTER 11
Mental Aspects

HOW DID RELIGIOSITY BEGIN?

A comprehensive study of formal religion would show that it too has evolved from simple, uncomplicated beginnings. The exact course of its evolution, just as the exact course of human evolution, can't be known in its totality. However, we can conjecture a broad outline. A detailed review of the religious behavior, and more importantly the religious beliefs, of the few remaining primitive cultures in the world gives us a starting point.

The cargo cults of the South Pacific can provide us with a measuring tool. Imprecise to be sure; yet superior to no tool whatsoever. We know exactly what occurred to stimulate the genesis of these cults following WWII. We can now observe how the true facts were distorted and misinterpreted into erroneous religious dogma. The how and why could lead to a working hypothesis for the birth of our own beliefs. The actual events foreshadowing or provoking our beliefs assuredly are different, but the methods of our formulating those beliefs should be similar. We could then re-examine the biblical tales and deduce their underlying factual source.

With the arrival of the American servicemen on their isolated islands the primitive natives were dragged from their modified Stone-Age culture into the ultra-modern twentieth century. Instantly, there were thousands of wonderful man-made desirables (items) available to the natives through gift or barter, the likes of which they had never even dreamed! The natives were in total awe. In their technologically naïve minds, the arrival of the American G.I's was miraculous. The never-before-imagined accoutrements that the soldiers brought with them were even more miraculous. Then disastrously, the war ended and the American G.I's went home, taking their modern technological trappings with them.

The native shaman (pl.) recognized this eventuality as an opportunity to bamboozle the guileless natives into thinking that, through the magic cajolery of a native mystic, the Americans could be enticed back to the Pacific Islands. The returned G. I's would bring with them even more wondrous paraphernalia. The native shaman (pl.) fashioned elaborate rituals would entice the Americans to return to those South Pacific Islands. First, a monetary payment was required from the artless natives.

Of course, some Americans did reappear after World War II, but not pursuant to the magical incantations of the shaman deceivers. You and I both know why and how the American tourists did visit those Pacific Islands. But many of the native Islanders believed the paranormal deception of the shaman frauds. Thus the "Cargo" cults had their origin.

The more guileless and primitive a person is, the more susceptible that person will be to the fakery of supernaturalism, or its evolved progeny 'religiosity.' It appears that human intelligence is easily countermanded by the human imagination, not only in the case of the juvenile and the unsophisticated, but seemingly with the adult and the sophisticated likewise.

GNOSIS — A RELIGIOUS MIND GAME

Very early in the history of Christianity there formed a cult of secret knowledge called Gnosticism. Gnosis is Greek for "knowledge." Their beliefs were as diverse as are the beliefs of the glut of Christian sects today; therefore, to lump all Gnostics theologically would not only be difficult, it would be in error! Most didn't even consider themselves as Gnostics. That name now seems more to have been an epithet applied scornfully to them, rather than by them.

Nonetheless, they did share a few similar beliefs, and it is on this basis alone that we can discuss them as a group. Patently, they all believed in the availability of an inscrutable infusion of divine knowledge (*gnosis*).

It is unclear exactly how one became eligible for this infusion. What is more, it is self-evident that each beneficiary received his own version of 'true' gnosis. Also, they taught that not everyone could become a recipient of this secret knowledge; only the privileged few could share God's hidden wisdom. The residuum of Christianity was irrevocably excluded from this preferment. A notable proponent of this elitist movement was a man named Valentinus. Most of the writings of the Gnostic authors eventually were destroyed once the Christian Church attained power via the Emperor Constantine (circa AD 313). But, a number of Gnostic writings did survive; additionally, much can be construed about Gnosticism by reading the counter attacks against them composed by the 'orthodox' Fathers of the early Church.

Fortuitously, a collection of Gnostic tractates (books) was found during the year 1945, in a cave in Egypt. Collectively, these are known as the "Nag Hammadi" texts. They constitute up to ninety percent of our direct knowledge of the beliefs of the ancient Gnostic writers. {Author's estimate} Squabbling over who owned those, and thereby who controlled those, kept the tractates from being translated fully until the 1980s.

Most are so esoteric of syntax, and are laced with such obscure verbal symbolisms, that it is problematic to extract any coherent data from them. But the few that are reasonably intelligible today are also quite familiar. That is, they contain a smattering of verses found also in the well-known New Testament texts. However, these are juxtaposed with verses not found in the N. T., which precludes them from being compared exegetically with their more customary renderings in the traditional Gospels. An inkling of the verity of what was just written can be gleaned from a few quoted verses found in the Gnostic Tractate, The Gospel of Thomas (II, 2).

"They showed Jesus a gold coin and said to him, 'Caesar's men demand taxes from us.' He said to them, 'Give Caesar what belongs to Caesar, give God what belongs to God, and give me what is mine.'" [Ibid. v. 100] [Cf. Mt. 22:15-22; Mk. 12:13-17 & Lu. 20:19-26] The previous is an almost verbatim quote of the Synoptic Gospels. Yet, just a few verses further along, the original author of 'Thomas' writes: "Jesus said, 'He who will drink from my mouth will become like me. I myself shall become he, and the things that are hidden will be revealed to him.'" [Ibid. v. 108] This allegorical verse is found nowhere but in the Gnostic Gospel of Thomas.

Even more revealing of the mind-set of Gnostic teachings is an earlier verse in the Gospel of Thomas. *"Jesus said, 'Recognize what is in your* (sg.) *sight, and that which is hidden from you* (sg.) *will become plain to you* (sg.)*. For there is nothing hidden which will not become manifest.'"* [Ibid. v. 5]

Note that the modern translator has added the parenthetical abbreviation "(sg.)" indicating that the personal pronouns "you" and "your" were singular. Perceptively, the original author wanted his readers to recognize that knowledge {gnosis!} was a singular gift, never intended for the common laity. Verse 108, similarly has a singular connotation, implying a personal, reserved, esoteric bestowal of intimate knowledge available only to the select. The 'select' being restricted to those who "drink from the mouth of Jesus." {Paraphrased} "Drinking from Jesus' mouth" would have been impossible for everyone born after the Crucifixion. However, someone who could glean a deeper meaning from the words of Jesus might be metaphorically able to 'drink from His mouth.' 'Or so the Gnostics discernibly believed!

Subliminally, if not secretly, most Christian proselytizers (and all theologians) deem themselves superior interpreters of the fullness of the message Jesus left behind in the body of the New Testament (per the Holy Spirit). This, they believe, is an ancillary benefit of their calling to be one of God's elect. This belief stokes the human vanity, but does it conform to the reality of the situation? I think not! The proofs of my determination can be counted in the various and conflicting interpretations almost every verse in the New Testament has been rendered into. Occasionally a given statement can be correctly interpreted twofold in both kind and degree. But that doesn't establish that all statements are amenable to two or more interpretations. If this were so, then all instruction would soon become that ambiguous as to become administratively unenforceable. {This very thing is happening to our criminal laws due to the legalistic scheming of deceitful defense lawyers and the lethargic senility of dotty jurists, judges and justices.}

If anyone could ever compose a wholly unambiguous stricture, that person must himself be a Deity. God's commands would never be given with double entendre. Yet, there have always been those who believe they can extract hidden enlightenment from the Bible that is effectively concealed from all others. These people must feel that they not only deserve Heaven, but that God has set aside front row, personal reservations for them. These individuals have the gall to characterize atheists as vain. How very pomp-ous, yet hypocritical, these pious pretenders were, are, and always will be! My evaluation of the early Gnostics is that they were extreme egotists. They were also both forgers and plagiarizers. They pilfered the words of the Evangelists and they also brazenly assumed their identities. They were the perpetrators of the most insidious crime mankind can commit against trusting mankind, i.e., they pretended to be authorized scribes and inter-preters for a Universal Divinity.

Surprisingly, there are still those today who consider themselves Gnostics. That is, they deem themselves intellectual heirs to a spiritual infusion. One of the consistent tenets of early Gnosticism was that God had a rival who perpetrated evil upon the world. In modern times, it appears this same demiurge still exists; only now, the powers of the demi-urge are not only comparable to God's, they are identical! This is known philosophically as 'Dualism.' The fullness of Gnostic beliefs is well beyond the scope of this book. I will venture no further.

A mere listing of the Codices recovered from that cave in Egypt (Nag Hammadi Texts) will suffice to give the reader an inkling of the full contents of the Gnostic books. To what extent this listing represents the totality of original Gnostic writings isn't known, and probably never will be known. The book noted at the foot of this page contains Modern English translations of most of the tractates listed, but not all of them. Reading the translations didn't influence this author to alter (or even to question) any of his previously held opinions about the accepted Gospels. Indeed, the reading didn't cause a change in my perception of Christianity, nor of religiosity *in toto*. Mr. Robinson's book truly was interesting, but, for me, not inspiring! In truth, that book is permeated with even more 'mystispeak' than is the entire Bible.

TABLE OF TRACTATES
IN THE COPTIC GNOSTIC LIBRARY

{Nag Hammadi Texts}

The Prayer of the Apostle Paul	The Apocryphon of James
The Gospel of Truth	The Treatise on the Resurrection
The Tripartite Tractate	The Apocryphon of John
The Gospel of Thomas	The Gospel of Philip
The Hypostasis of the Archons	On the Origin of the World
The Exegesis on the Soul	The Book of Thomas the Contender
The Apocryphon of John	The Gospel of the Egyptians
Eugnostos the Blessed	The Sophia of Jesus Christ
The Dialogue of the Savior	The Apocryphon of John
The Gospel of the Egyptians	Eugnostos the Blessed
The Apocalypse of Paul	The (First) Apocalypse of James
The (Second) Apocalypse of James	The Apocalypse of Adam
The Acts of Peter & the Twelve Apostles	The Thunder: Perfect Mind
Authoritative Teaching	The Concept of Our Great Power

PACIFISM AND RELIGIOSITY

Suppose I am able to produce proof of the adverse effects of indulged religiosity? The reverend Jim Jones of Guyana is a reprehensible example of the fatal consequences of mindless obedience to fanatic cultic leaders. Less obvious, but no less tragic, are the events in Iran since the accession of a religiously oriented government. With any form of governance: 'Personal Freedom Exits When Religious Domination Enters!'

Could you imagine our country today if Puritan-minded persons had gained political power after the American Revolution? You would be burned at the stake for merely reading this work. I would never have been permitted to publish it in the first instance. Consider what the present of this nation would be if the Amish, with their rejection of all modern appliances, had risen to power in the 1930s. We would all be saluting a swastika emblazoned flag today. Hitler would have relished their pacifism. The Quaker pacifism of the late twentieth century has crossed the line between noble compassion and disloyalty via "giving aid and comfort to our enemies." Their flaming egotism surmounts their tepid patriotism!

Admittedly, if the entirety of humanity went around clasping hands and greeting each other with a *"peace unto thee, brother,"* we all would be safer in our homes. But, not only is this highly unlikely, it is categorically impossible! All that prevents a villain from enslaving (or worse!) every gentle soul within his dictatorial reach is the certainty that someone else assuredly would defend the pacifists with force. Doctrinally benign people can flourish only in the midst of a society that continually and unfailingly shields and protects them from every militant oppressor.

The oft-propagated dogma that peace-loving men can exist without weapons or violence is both myopic and delusional. This philosophy has the same basis in reality as does the timid man, living in a fort formerly under siege by attackers, who afterward kneels and gives thanks to God for protecting him from his enemies. The reality is that he was protected by the defenders of the fort who were willing to forfeit their own lives to protect his life.

Contrary to what liberals and other compassion-gushing groups preach, there are thoroughly evil people in the world, just as there are patently good people. These evil people must be held in check. They must be restrained, for they view a kindness as a weakness that should be exploited. They will exploit it whenever or wherever the opportunity avails itself or it is seized.

Fortuitously, mankind has a median group that compensates for the two extreme groups. Mistake it not: the 'good' group can be no less detrimental than is the 'evil' group. Cultural progress wasn't achieved through persistent and prolonged prayer. Persons steeped in religious superstitions never added a whit to the advancement of human culture. {Exempting the monk Gregor Mendel & a negligible other few} All new inventions and discoveries, generally, have been looked upon as the work of the Devil by religionists. Hence, all such advancements habitually were discouraged, if not banned outright.

Was bubonic plague overcome through prayer? Did a priest invent the wheel? Hardly! It may be true that ultimately religions come to recognize the value of material progress, but they are always the last to concede this, and often, only after the major portion of their adherents had clearly recognized the attendant benefits of the novel innovation.

CULTIC INDOCTRINATION

The turbulent 'Sixties' (1960s) gave birth to several new denominations and sects; the most visible of these being the 'domination' cults, of which the Hari Krishna's and the so-called 'Moonies' are representative examples. Another short lived yet highly publicized movement was the "Jesus Freaks," a faddish 'in' cult of the period. "Freaks" was an aptly coined epithet for the last mentioned group as most of their converts presented just such an appearance. The major sin one of their members could commit would be to take a bath, or to occasionally comb their hair. Their main 'hang-up' (idiosyncrasy) was an extraordinary dress code in reverse; soiled dungarees and stained tee shirts essentially were considered acceptable formal wear to a sect that eschewed nearly all genuine formality.

Jesus was promoted as a 'hip' guy who gathered together a revolutionary band to attack the establishment. His refusal to honor the religious strictures of His day was paralleled with the counterculture of that decade. (1960's) His scorn for custom was said to legitimize the hippie rituals of pot smoking, illegal drug indulgence, and almost any other form of defiance toward authority. To me, they were nothing more than immature 'spoiled brats' traipsing around the world thumbing their noses at everyone more than thirty years in age. Their philosophies were incredibly shallow, and their logic was fatally simplistic. Any action, however gross or repugnant to adult society, found sanction in their code of praiseworthy behavior. Their behavior code permitted (and even persuaded) everyone to "do his or her own thing", i.e., to reject all accepted morality, and also to scorn all widely practiced social amenities.

Much more could, and probably should, be said about the counter-culture groups. 'Not because they themselves are important; they are not! But many of their juvenile conceived (oriented?) tenets have been espoused, or at least conceded in general, by supposedly sensible adults of today. It is to this latter group that I wish to devote this section of my composition.

I think of them as secular Messiahs. They reject the established Churches out of hand. Jesus is relegated to the position of an inept teacher whose philosophies, although valid, were woefully incomplete. They dis-avow all gods save one: the god of self! They, acting alone or in concert with their peers, form the Godhead. All that can happen, or will happen, flows out from their enlightened actions. Divine intervention is rejected and direct action is substituted.

Each self-appointed Savior sees himself as a potential benefactor for the entirety of mankind. They, personally, recognize all the ills of society and insist that only they and their ideological allies can cure those ills. Without proclaiming it, perhaps not recognizing it, they have usurped God's assigned role on Earth (by believing adults). In religious supposition, the Supreme Deity knows unfailingly what is best for mankind and instills this knowledge in a favored individual, who then leads others onto the proper path in life. Our 'saviors,' without benefit of divine enlightenment, possess this knowledge intrinsically because of their exalted status as mod-ern Messiahs.

Through some inexplicable inner quality that surfaces in their late teen years, these evolving "Solomon" types are moved to impart their wisdom to an ignorant, erring, and resistant adult world. They demonize greed as a cardinal vice (which it can be!), but their antidote for this vice is for everyone who possesses anything of value to parcel out their possessions to the poor, the incompetent, and the indolent. Cause and effect become hopelessly confused in their all-too-naïve pronouncements.

The relative material status differentials between prosperous and destitute people are caused by a multiplicity of actions and attitudes; yet today's messiahs find social remedies that are patently uncomplicated. The Robin Hood recourse, "Take in taxes from the rich and give (via government subsidies) to the poor," is the most widespread of their misguided philosophies.

Our present-day reformers advance similarly mangled philosophies. They expropriate the most quoted maxim of Jesus, "Thou shall love thy neighbor as thyself," yet they ignore the real life observation that this love must be reciprocal to be sustained. The poor don't love the rich; they envy them! The 'never hads' don't love the 'always haves'; they loathe them! The lethargic hate the ambitious. The above ersatz 'commandment' (?) only functions in one direction. Candidly, most 'have-nots' lack the talents of those that 'have.' In some cases it may be applicable that there is no shame to be poor, but conversely, it is seldom justifiable to be proud of being a low achiever. In this instance: Content to be complacently poor and parasitic upon government supplied Welfare at the insistence of the liberal minded!

I have strayed somewhat from religion here, but you will agree when I declare that for Christianity, ethics is embodied in religiosity. The drift of my theme here is that today's social reformers derive their legitimacy from Judeo-Christian ethical tenets, despite the fact that today's "Messiahs" have grown averse to organized Christianity. The most fundamental principle of their secular-ethical credo is that all men are created equal. The originator of that supercilious falsehood should be confined evermore to a hell of unending deception. Open your mind to the world around you. No two entities in life are exactly equal in any two aspects of their existence; that cosmic fact may well be the essence of the divine rationale for the existence of life on Earth, i.e., to develop an intuitive affinity with the cosmos.

Read into that statement what you will, but I cannot believe that God created us as unequal as we are so that we might all attain a comparable level of equality. It doesn't take deep deliberation to discover that the only way possible for all of mankind to be truly equal is for the most brilliant to sink to the depths of the most unintelligent; for the reverse is quite unattainable. In the <u>Wizard of Oz</u> movie, the scarecrow lacked a brain until the Wizard presented him with a diploma; instantly he became a genius! In the Land of Oz this may be possible, but in the non-magical lands of Earth, reality functions otherwise.

Equality is a concept in mathematics and should be restricted there where it performs a cogent operation. Liberals do expound at least one valid maxim, "Let everyone develop his/her talents to their fullest potential." But their implementation of this adage is counterproductive. They would shackle the gifted so severely as to limit their achievements almost to the level of no achievement at all, thus forcing the gifted into near parity with indolent low achievers. If it were within their power, liberal religionists would clone us all into dull little choir members mindlessly chirping rhyming platitudes to a non-existent spiritual egotist: by title, God!

Religionists and liberals (liberal here is defined lightly as a religionist who has committed deicide and seized the Godhood throne himself) have steered us onto a path of mediocrity and strict regimentation. Ignorance is in no wise a virtue. And, for a species whose continued survival is wholly dependent upon intelligence, suppression of our intellect would be (will be!) inexorably and inevitably fatal. I direct one more question at liberals: "Aren't compassionate people, 'better people' than those who are uncaring or less caring?" You liberals know the answer to that question. "Yes, we are all equal." Only some of us (liberals and their allies) are endowed with a higher equality than the common herd. We know who we are! {< − The liberal mind-set.}

Most of the successful sects of this century have stressed mutual love and affection while at the same instant subjecting initiates to a haranguing barrage of creedal philosophies. Neophytes are instructed to openly express this affection by speaking constantly of love, unity, brotherhood, and to embrace loyalty above all else. Impressionable adolescents are prime targets for conversion because of the natural proclivity at this age level to experience love both physically and emotionally. Shortly after pubescence, teenagers are highly susceptible to this form of indoctrination and behavior channeling.

The proof of the success of this type of brain-molding can best be judged by the method used to redeem these duped adolescents who have fallen prey to cultic recruitment. It is called deprogramming, and that word not only best describes the process, it states it as succinctly as it can be rendered! Notwithstanding the previous, the process itself isn't simple. If the initial indoctrinator has been moderately successful, then the deprogramming process will be inversely more difficult. This is especially true if the deprogrammer is ethically motivated.

The deprogrammer could simply use the same tactics as did the original programmer. That is, overwhelm the young adult with love and affection, coupled inseparably and incessantly with goal-directed orientations. That would be effective, but it would leave the teenager with the same dependence on the deprogrammer as he became victim to from the original programmer. The teenager would also be highly susceptible to the trauma of rejection once the deprogrammer necessarily departed from the life of the redeemed teenager.

No! Reversing an indoctrinator's tactics against the indoctrinated would be effective, but it would create the exact number of problems it attempted to resolve. The misled indoctrinees must be intellectually matured to the point where they realize that true love and affection will accept the loved one exactly as they are. If you have to change the way you behave; if you have to change the way you think; if you must alter your very personality to be accepted and loved, then you aren't truly loved! Any person or organization that attempts to mold your mind doesn't love you. They may need you; they surely want you; but candidly, they don't love you. They desire you personally only so long as you accede unfailingly to their sacrosanct credos.

It is regrettable, but true, that most people only feel affection toward us while we are acting in a manner that pleases them. But do not misconstrue. I am not advocating that you traipse around harming, or insulting, or ignoring everyone else in an effort to show your independence. Be sensible in your actions. If your native personality is habitually vexing, then you shouldn't expect very many persons to love you.

We all need someone. Needing someone to have affection for us, however, mustn't be the impetus for joining a cultic group, as this reaction tends only to validate evolution. Love and affection are quite effective survival instincts that were primarily accountable for the dominance of the class of animals called mammals. All primates are born mother-dependent! Mutual affection establishes harmony within a human grouping.

In tandem, that mutuality evinces cooperation, protection, and ultimately a stable, harmonious community. Stated plainly: 'All human beings are gregarious!' We are most contented interacting with like-oriented persons.

THE POWER TO CURE

An acquaintance at work once confided to me that Jesus had appeared to him in a dream and ever since that night, he had the power infused into his right hand to heal others. It chanced at that time that I was suffering from a painful condition in my heel that a Podiatrist had been attempting to treat, without success, for several weeks. After considerable coaxing I finally persuaded my co-worker to touch my aching heel with his divinely empowered right hand. He admonished me to be patient, commenting that God takes His time with such cures. But he confidently predicted that my pain would be ended eventually, if not forthwith.

Well, so as to not drag out the suspense, I will tell you that my heel condition was cured … two doctors and one and one-half years later! In the meantime, I had been diagnosed as having a bone spur (that two widely separated x-rays disproved), and then calcareous bursa was suggested and also was disproved. Gout was proposed, and then discounted because of an absence of high levels of uric acid in my blood. Finally, the third doctor I consulted guessed that I had a bone infection and prescribed antibiotic capsules that cured the condition in a matter of days. That cure thoroughly discredits my co-worker's heavenly dreams!

ATHEISTS

Factually, it is much more demanding to be an atheist than it is to be a Christian. To begin, an atheist must study much more material than a religionist must study. If he is intellectually honest, an atheist must research everything that he can about religion. To arrogantly dismiss someone else's beliefs without knowing them intimately and without proof, will only engender a bigotry of ignorance. Most religious persons I know are intolerably biased against anyone who doesn't profess the same beliefs as themselves. But the identical isn't true of most of the atheists this author has known.

Allow me to distinguish who I mean when I refer to a 'religious' person. My definition: A person who makes a conscious effort to let all those around him be aware of his devotion to religiosity, chiefly through ostentatious posturing and sanctimonious discourse.

Typical of the type of person I am referring to was a newly arrived man I knew from the Air Force while serving in the Philippine Islands (circa 1954). He professed to be a "born again believer." Not long after he had arrived in my outfit, he began coming over to my bunk, sit down, and open a notebook he carried on his person. The notebook contained the names of the men in our outfit that he prayed for daily.

Not long after he first began his semi-regular visits to my bunk I noticed that my name had been added to the list of those he prayed for. I was somewhat embarrassed because, at the time, I still considered myself merely a lapsed Catholic. Yet, inwardly I was also pleased. Several weeks passed, and at each night visit the ritual remained essentially the same. He would come over, sit down, open his notebook, and tell me who he had prayed for, sometimes adding specifically what he wished that man to receive or accomplish, and then letting me know whenever one of his prayers noticeably or inferentially had been answered.

Then one night, quite unexpectedly, he asked if I would help him to pray. He explained that he wanted me to come and sit on the balcony of our barracks building with him and several of his church friends to discuss the Bible while holding hands. I was dumbfounded. All I could do was stammer that I didn't want to be a partner in his group. He persisted until finally I became angry and told him emphatically that I wouldn't participate in such theatrics. Then I ended by telling him that he could do so if he wanted, but to exclude me from his balcony ritual.

Angrily he strode over to his bunk, opened his notebook, and crossed out one of the names in the book. He never spoke to me again, and frankly, I was pleased that he didn't. Over time I became aware of his emotional instability. He would be calm and placid one day; moody and storming on another day. Watching him react was disconcerting to me. His initial presumption that because I was a decent person, I must, perforce, be a religious person, was unwarranted, and also untrue!

The reason I behave affably and courteously toward others is because intellectually I reason this as the proper way to behave, and most of the intelligent people I know appear to think similarly. To this day, I still prefer the company of intellectual people to religious people. Religious people seem to me to be overly dogmatic in all their beliefs, even non-religious tenets. They are intolerant of contrary opinions, and are resistant to even hear anyone else's divergent views.

This shouldn't be construed as an egocentric intimation that I consider myself a super intellect. With deep regret I admit that I am not. My I.Q. is graded somewhat above average and much below genius. If I seem to worship intellect, perhaps I do, but I do so with reasoned cause! Intelligent people are more tolerant of less intelligent people. Further, I maintain that tolerance breeds freedom; freedom encourages expression; expression creates intellectual progress, so that the process becomes self-sustaining, even amplifying! A virtual heaven will be created here on Earth only when we have voluntary harmony among all its inhabitants. Religion recognizes the real illnesses of mankind, but it prescribes the wrong antidote. Harmony, if it is attainable ever, must be maintained by our heads, not by our hearts!

CAN ATHEISTS PROVE THEIR PRINCIPLE PREMISE?

The weakest point in the foundation of atheism is the question "How did the Universe originate?" Every cosmological theorem ever postulated begins with some form of basic matter already present. Religionists, knowing this, then sagely (or slyly) ask "Where did this original matter come from?" With philosophical 'ylem' (theoretical substance)_on their faces, Atheists are thereby coerced into an embarrassing admission. Namely, that they do not know! Religionists, in possession of this concession, pridefully thrust out their chests and begin strutting around cockily assured that their belief in a personal Deity has been irrevocably validated. Would that such a mystery-encrusted query was so easily resolved!

The atheists' lack of a theory to explain the origin of the very first atom of hydrogen doesn't prove the theory of a Divine Creator. More germane to this work: The absence of an explanation for the initial molecule isn't proof of Yahweh's reality! Christians (and religious Jews also) find their proofs for the existence of Yahweh in the Bible. But atheists ask those religionists to verify for everyone that the Bible is irrefutably the 'Word of God.' Now when atheists pose this question to religionists; speculate what their response could be?

The reply of the religionist necessarily will be that one must have faith! Atheists truly do have faith! They have faith that eventually mankind will pierce the cloud of ignorance that presently obscures the knowledge of the genesis of proto-matter; that, atheists believe in! Faith is the aphrodisiac of a religionist; lack thereof is the sustenance of an atheist! The principle premise of an atheist, namely, "There is no God!," is perpetually unverifiable. So too is the proposition, "God is the Creator of All Existence!" Neither proposition can be verified empirically. Christians point to the Universe, and then point to the Bible as their proof. Atheists point to the Universe and then point to verifiable scientific findings. Considering the evidences presented by both sides, this author deems the atheists as having the firmer postulation.

ON ATHEISM AND HUMAN INTELLIGENCE

Atheists have never banded together as have pro-Deity proponents for the practical reason that believing in nothing is less of a reason for forming an association than is believing in 'something.' Something must be protected; nothing can be ignored! If non-religionists ever do come to power, then I believe that mankind with its unrivaled learning capacity will advance culturally in vast strides. The quality of life on Earth would be immeasurably improved; the accumulated knowledge that each generation becomes heir to will expand exponentially; and man's control over the forces that affect his existence should likewise increase in a manifold manner. All this is probable once we shed completely the superstitious constraints of all religiosity and every other mode and manifestation of mysticism and paranormal bigotry.

Atheism isn't, and shouldn't be considered, a negative concept. It is, and should be recognized as, a positive force for unlocking mankind's creativity, unleashing his inquisitive drive, and freeing his mental soul (his imagination), that can only be bound with cords of ignorance. Religion has coerced man's intellect into shutting down completely whenever super-naturalism (that is "talk of gods") is broached.

From the foregoing it might be assumed that I favor a Communist form of government. Do not make that surmise. Communism, as practiced in the former Soviet Union, was not anti-religious. The Communists brazenly substituted worship of the Supreme State, through the Papacy of the infallible Party Head, for the older religions. They were every iota as intolerant of behavioral freedom as any religious sect that has ever existed. The smallest action that merely hinted of political sacrilege or doctrinal blasphemy was ruthlessly oppressed and suppressed. Extermination, excommunication, and exile abounded in Russia, her republics, and in her former satellite nations.

In Russia the state-approved Deity was the State itself. All homage was due the Communist Party, which administered the State. Self-criticism, a healthy practice in all situations, was not only discouraged; it was positively forbidden! The Almighty State was supreme and governed wisely, but firmly! Woe betides the individual who questioned this immutable precept. Communism itself was a religion that would brook no competition from any other religion. The Communist Deity, similar to Yahweh of old, had a chosen people whom it favored to the total abandonment of all other peoples. They were the Party members! The corollary between the religion of Communism and the Christian religion was (& remains) very high.

Drawing an analogy between two differing articles or processes is limited at best. If two things are not identical, then they have differences. Reversing this, if two things are identical, there is no difference between them; thus, they are everywhere the same. Comparing a political system to a religious system generally fits only the first proposition. However, the more one can show points of agreement or sameness, the closer an analogy will coincide. Then, if enough points match one with the other, one can confidently state that they are similar systems that either can be linked together or that can be generally contrasted.

If you compare the practice of Communism to the practice of a religion, I believe you will agree with me that the Communists had merely replaced Marx and Engles' theories of governing for their former religious tenets. One of the most damaging charges one Communist could bring against another was a charge of 'revisionism.' What was revisionism?

It was the changing of established doctrine. Revisionism was heresy! Communism had 'sacred' principles that 'dare not' be challenged, much less be violated. It also had a priesthood to identify and expose every noted violation. This duty was performed by the Party leadership, who were its hierarchy. Contrary opinions were unwanted, unwelcome, and unhealthy. Dissent was anathema.

Capitalism was the great enemy of Communism; a Capitalist was the villainous equivalent of Satan. Anyone who deviated from official dogma could expect severe repercussions. The comparison between the two systems was even more striking if you contrasted Soviet Communism with the clericalism of the Middle Ages. Communism suppressed free thought exactly as the ruling medieval Church repressed non-canonical ideas. The Puritans could attest to this, as could the Quakers, and the other sects that splintered away from their empowered European religionist oppressors, i.e., the Anglican Church.

The Iron Curtain was asserted to have been instituted to keep political heretics out. But its main purpose was to keep their laity in. When the Berlin Wall was razed in 1999, institutional Communism fell with it. This eventuality was the first major defeat of Communism, and this is a calamity that it has not recovered from in Europe. The United States may be the least godly State on Earth, yet people throughout the world are clamoring to migrate here. Total religious freedom encompasses the freedom to reject religion, notwithstanding the attempts of zealots to force their bizarre beliefs on the rest of us. Our coins are stamped: "In God We Trust." How would religionists react to coins stamped: "Trust Yourself, There Is No God"?

Overall, our standard of living is higher here than in any nation on this planet. Did religion bring this about? The fact is: "It did not!" Our lack of a recognized, official religion was the real operational factor. We were free! 'Free to do as we pleased; 'Free to vote for whoever struck our fancy; 'Free to oppose those in authority. But more significantly, we were powerful enough collectively to enforce and sustain those freedoms. (Not that we always have done so)

Most religions advocate obedience to lawful authority where those authorities are congenial to that religion. All religions seek to restrict our freedoms, and to limit the power of the majority to rescind or alter those rules favorable to an ecclesiastical minority. It further seeks to establish laws that perpetuate itself, and that stifle opposition to itself. This same stifling predilection is alive today in dogmatic interpretations of the "Living" Constitution. In his later years, Thomas Jefferson himself warned that our Constitution wasn't a holy, complete, inviolable document written with the blood of patriotic martyrs. He stated with perceptive wisdom that our Constitution was merely a set of propositions that served our nation for the time of its creation. He anticipated that in the foreseeable future it would need revisions, deletions, addenda, and possibly even a thorough revamping.

I concur with his assessment. The Constitution, as is the Bible, is fallible. It is incomplete; it is inadequate; it is imperfect. We should be able to live with it, but not for it! A fuller exposition of the above will have to await another occasion. Here we are dealing with religion in the United States and how it may evolve in the future.

No matter how our society evolves, it can only grow more complex. Our intellects have been fettered with religious shackles for far too long a period of time. We can begin our intellectual emancipation by recognizing the supremacy of brainpower over contra-logical dogma. If we humans are a unique creation, we are unique only in the complexity of our thinking processes. All the higher animals have intellects; most of the lower ones do also. Even certain insects seem capable of a process akin to learning.

Trying to analyze and to specify unerringly how my brain differs from the higher animals is very taxing to do. If I state that I am able to communicate with my fellow man, and that this ability distinguishes me from the lower life forms, I am reminded that dolphins and bees (plus many other life forms) can communicate intelligibly within their respective species.

If I brag that I can fashion tools from natural elements, I recall that Jane Goodall observed chimpanzees preparing a slender twig by removing all the leaf stems, then inserting the stripped shaft into a termite's nest and withdrawing the twig full of clinging termites (which the chimps ate with conjectured relish). Otters use rocks to crack open oysters.

Environmentalists, with emphatic disdain, will agree if I declare that I am able to alter the world I live in, not only by random accident, but by purposeful design also! Yet, what would you call that which beavers do to streams where they build their homes? Chimps at the Yerkes Primate Study Center have even been taught to compose sentences using symbolic computer language. Chimps have been taught to use American Sign Language elsewhere. Incidentally, the high level of intelligence exhibited by chimpanzees argues effectively in favor of evolution and against a separate, exclusive creation for mankind.

How does the Bible account for the closeness of chimpanzees with humanity? It doesn't. It doesn't because the authors of the Bible never saw a chimpanzee: that includes Noah! Had the inhabitants of the ancient Middle East ever seen a gorilla or an orangutan, I am convinced that at least some of them would have deified it. The name Orangutan translates to "man of the forest" in the Maylay language. If that doesn't prove a point, nothing I could write would either. The creation fable in Genesis fails even a cursory examination by a genuinely open-minded person.

Human brains are unmatched, not in kind, but in mental acuity! We can count higher, vocalize more words, build better tools, and invent mystic causes for natural events. The one action the truly intelligent seem totally incapable of is to stop thinking; concomitantly, to cease questioning. Human brains are also dichotomous. We use our brain to conceive a Deity to explain that which we don't understand; then as our understanding expands, we use our brain to nullify the conception of that Deity. I wonder if all the higher animals are plagued with similar perceptual dichotomies.

Maybe, in our intellectual immaturity, we needed the make-believe world of religion just as children seem to thrive on the fantasies of childhood. If so, then perhaps the 'God is Dead' period that began in the middle 1960s was analogous to mankind's adolescence. Extending the analogy, we can expect eventually to reach full collective maturity; i. e., experience a spiritual epiphany that leads us all to convert irreversibly to unambiguous and unqualified atheism.

Just as in life, this maturity shouldn't be measured in years, but in mental and emotional development. For if we are to grow to full intellectual adulthood we must first divest ourselves of all of our superstitions, most especially those that are disguised as religious articles of faith. Next, we would have to accept full responsibility for all of our actions, not credit some to the grace of God, and blame others on the temptation of Satan.

Additionally, we must begin working to provide sustenance to our kindred family. By that I mean we must expand upon the knowledge that those inquiring souls who lived previously endowed us with so that, in the natural progression of humanity, our intellectual offspring will inherit a wealth of fact-proven information to draw from, and in hope, to further expand upon!

Each of us born into this world has a surcharge placed against us. The charge is payable all during our lives in installments rated according to our ability to pay. Of course, you realize that I am not referring to money. Our debt is to society as a whole. The debt we owe our parents is a separate issue; that debt is redeemed with love and respect; provided our parents have earned respect! Merely parenting a child conveys no entitlement.

Religionists, when they preach love and respect, are quite correct. But their exhortations are incomplete. There is more to the equation than just those two requirements. To start, our love and respect must be directed at persons who are deserving of love and respect. That satisfied, we must exert conscious effort, both physical and mental. We have to be willing to contribute, in whatever manner we can, to those who are working resolutely toward the intellectual advancement of human society.

Every living person is indebted to those intelligent persons who lived before us that exercised their brains to expand man's understanding of his environment, or who have in some manner facilitated mankind's intellectual ascendancy, or have otherwise improved human life on this planet. We are all beneficiaries of this inheritance. Our task, each of us, is to add to this inheritance. Be it little, or be it much, is immaterial! We all have limitations. Our personal contribution will vary considerably from individual to individual; but few of us are utterly bereft of any potentially beneficial capability. Appreciating the intelligence of others is a contribution. Low intellect persons can contribute little or nothing.

We must employ whatever abilities we possess; first, toward the support of our society; second, toward its perpetuation; and lastly, toward its expansion. Every single day we should employ our minds toward achieving these goals. Knowledge is the road to the realization of our tripartite purpose. Man's knowledge has barely reached its horizon, his intellectual vista is limitless. His physical body is finite, but his potential for comprehension is near infinite. Can anything stop man from attaining his full potential? Unequivocally: "Yes," man himself! Ask yourself what became of the Egyptian pyramid builders, or the founders of the other great civilizations? The answer can be deduced from a perceptive allegory. 'A jackass secured to a barn can kick it down in a short space of time, but place a hammer, nails, and lumber next to that jackass and you would wait an eternity for it to build a new barn.'

The strong and the many are invariably able to tear a structure down; only the intelligent are able to build a structure in the first place. Unfortunately, mankind is more readily led by a strong man (tyrant) than by a wise man. The reason for this seems tied to our emotional make-up. The mechanics of this emotional conditioning are not specifically understood. But we can see it at work if we know where and how to look.

One can observe it in a football coach exhorting his team to victory, or an industrial manager urging his workers to exceed production targets, or even a rights activist demanding, not that his views be considered, but that they be implemented without further delay!

Try analyzing a political campaign speech the next time you hear one. Is the speaker addressing your intelligence or your emotions? In every successful thrust you will find that the politician is attempting to obtain an emotional response. Political slogans are more blatantly directed at our emotions. Consider these four examples: "All the Way with LBJ!" All the way to where? Or a negative one: "Don't Vote for a Dead Man!" This was directed at Dwight Eisenhower's second presidential campaign after he had suffered a severe heart attack during his first term. What does it mean when black politicians counsel: "Keep the Faith, Baby!"? Or the slogan of another campaign: "In Your Heart, You Know He's Right!" Not in your head. 'Not in your brains. 'Not in your intellect, but in the supposed seat of your emotions: 'In your heart!

Women have been accused of being more emotion driven than are men, and in my observations fittingly so. How often have I heard a mother shopping with an unruly child threaten to leave the child home on the next shopping trip if he doesn't behave? That is an emotional threat. The child instinctively desires to be near his mother. If the child believes the mother, he will probably be coerced into reluctant compliance, at least temporarily!

Child psychologists would presumably advise the mother to sit the child down and reason with him, and you might guess that I would be in agreement with the psychologist. But you would be wrong! I direct my intellectual appeals to mature persons, not children or juveniles … whatever their chronological age! That written, not to denigrate everyone who doesn't agree with me; but to limit those whom I wish to address. Children and adolescents aren't capable of the depth of understanding and experience needed to confirm or rebut my observations. This is exactly where child psychology fails. Children, in the situation mentioned above, may comprehend the words of the mother, but utterly fail to grasp the underlying significance of those words.

If you have ever had an intellectual debate with a child (and lost!), then you know: A child's logic is nowhere near as developed as is yours. All your learned arguments for a proposition can be effectively brushed aside with the trite disclaimer: "But Dad, I won't let that happen." Teenagers are notorious for the dismissive attitude they exhibit toward a parent who cautions them against a real or prevalent danger to which they may be about to expose themselves. Illicit drug experimentation is a tragic case in point.

Now, to finish the illustration: The father who threatens a spanking will invariably get the most lasting results; especially if the child has no doubt that the threat will be carried out forthwith. This is not an endorsement for child abuse. There is a vast difference between a spanking and a thrashing. Many current theories on human behavior modification appear workable when we weigh them emotionally, but thoughtful reexamination, coupled with judicious observation, invariably proves that our emotions are not to be relied upon in the all-important business of living a human life.

Anyone who desires to be an effective evangelist should strive to develop a skill in verbal appeals to human emotions. At its essence, religion is an emotional exercise. We all know the passions that can be stoked by religious conflict. Nothing can generate livid heat faster than a perceived attack against a passionate person's religious beliefs. This is utterly irrational, but it is nonetheless the reality. The elation at attending religious service is likewise primarily an emotional experience.

People speak of having "found God." Yet when you ask them to explain, they invariably begin by describing a feeling or sensation that overcame them, particularly during a period of great stress in their lives! Convicted criminals often turn to religion while in jail. Drug addicts find solace in religion while they are trying to detoxify themselves. 'Similarly with alcoholics. Married persons, who become separated from their loved one either through divorce or death, often lessen their angst (distress) through church attendance.

The examples of persons using religion as an emotional analgesic run the entire gamut of human experience. However, religion isn't the only occasion in life that plucks our emotional chords. Competing in sports can have the same effect, as can music and singing likewise. If you ever have wondered why most Christian religions employ organ music and group singing when there is no doctrinal or scriptural requirement (or precedent) for it, now you know! It is principally used at religious functions and during religious ceremonies to heighten the psychical experience, that the 'pastors will convince their audience is "spiritual."

From my own recollections, I can testify that the self-same sensations that used to pass through my body during religious services when I was a youth, later were similarly induced by popular music. I have never been on a sport's team that won an important championship, but I witness that this exhilaration seems to match or surpass the stimulus of the most solemn or joyous of religious ceremonies.

Sexual matters are also highly psychical as well as physical, but it isn't my purpose to examine such in this exposition. What I do want to expound on is the fact that religiosity does evoke strong passion. So if you are going to evaluate my theses candidly, then you will have to judge each proposition on its intellectual merits, and not by the sentiments (feelings) it arouses. By design, some of my arguments have been phrased emotionally, rather than intelligently. My purpose for this was twofold. First, an entirely logical presentation could become tedious. Second, I purposely choose to rouse emotions in you, my reader!

I stated earlier that mankind could progress technologically and intellectually by leaps and bounds if we could shed the shackles of religious indoctrination. Well, how best to impel you to action than to employ the time-tested method of arousing emotional passions, then channeling the resultant energy onto a desired goal? If telling you so lessens the impact, then so be it. It is true, and if I am sincere when I ask you to use your intelligence when making your evaluation, then I should expect that you long since would have learned to differentiate between an emotional appeal and an intellectual assertion.

DISPROVING A CONCEPT

Proving that a concept such as 'religion' is in error is exceedingly difficult. (Perhaps this is impossible categorically?) A concept can't be seen, felt, or tasted, it can't be struck and heard, nor can it be physically weighed or measured for it has no substance. An explanatory concept (theory) can only be promoted by accounting for past occurrences, and can be 'proved' only by accurately predicting future events. The validity of Christianity specifically, but apropos too all religions generally, rests solely on the prophetic concept that God in Paradise awaits all human beings. However, only after they die! The lone method of proving or disproving that proposition is to die! Yet, provably, deceased persons cannot converse with the living to either confirm a supernatural Divinity and a splendiferous Heaven, or to refute both of those otherwise unprovable avowals.

The Old Testament is peppered with purported predicted events that reportedly eventuated after the fact! There is no way to disprove these alleged confirmed 'predictions.' The New Testament, notably "The Acts of the Apostles," references many 'predictions' that are alleged to have been fulfilled always, "after the fact!" But the New Testament's most significant prediction has never come to fruition. To wit: The speedy return of Jesus to establish His 'Everlasting Kingdom.' Almost two thousand years have passed and that prophecy remains unfulfilled, despite the immediacy stated or implied in verses that echo the prediction of the 'Return of the Redeemer.' [Cf. Mt. 16:28, 24:34, 26:64; Mk. 13:26; Lu. 9:27; 1 Thes. 4:14-15; Jas. 5:7-8; 2 Pet. 3:12 & et al.]

"Knowing the future" may be the greatest contradiction of all, particularly in the context of human events. Human societies have grown so complex that virtually every eventuality results from the interplay of countless actions both of human intrusion and of Nature. No religion has ever successfully passed the test of predicting unanticipated future events that could be empirically proven to have eventuated precisely as predicted.

Many people would take exception to the last statement; so I will defend it. Further, I will challenge them to prove their case by accurately predicting future events that I can verify. The perceptive axiom that 'hindsight is always more accurate' fits this matter perfectly. Pseudo-scientists avow that particular individuals have a capability called extrasensory perception: "ESP" for short. But whenever impartial investigators have controlled the testing, the claimant's ESP has predictably vanished. Miracles, and other religious marvels, exhibit the same singularity. They can never be predicted. Please don't dispute this by offering as proof, an event that has already transpired. You could assert that the 'proving' miracle was an act of God, and I would counter by alleging the proffered miracle was a manifestation of the natural order.

Besides, why would God perform miracles for some persons, and not for others? If an unambiguous miracle from God could be demonstrated to me; I would immediately, and forthwith, renounce all that I have written and believed; to thereafter devote the remainder of my life to whatever I deemed would foster belief in miracles, and concurrently, belief in the miracle Maker. No sincere person would do less. But let us assess precisely what this entails.

If you give me a thousand dollars for some slight service I have performed, I can do no less than call you generous. But, if I am only told that you have given someone else a thousand dollars, then I won't be convinced with certainty that you are generous. My point is this: If God has shown a miracle to someone, there is no innate merit if that person believes in God. This recipient has been favored by God over practically all others. Indeed, he would be foolish to deny God. On the other hand, if this same person only heard of the miracle, and didn't witness it, how could he reasonably be expected to believe the miracle took place? He would have only another human being's word that a miracle took place. In the latter case, he would be unwise to accept that a miracle has taken place absent unambiguous tangible proof.

Perfect justice stipulates that everyone receives equal treatment from the justice dispenser. Failing this, we must be judged with the same measure of inequality as we were disfavored with through the inequality. The non-believer, who has never been shown physical evidence of a God-enacted miracle, should not be condemned for his disbelief. This is at variance with Christian teaching. Jesus is said to have rebuked Thomas the Apostle for not believing the other Apostles who averred to have seen the risen Messiah. *"Blessed are they who have not seen and yet have believed."* [Jn. 20:29] An all-knowing Deity should have commended Thomas for demanding proof. Anyone who could foretell the future in those times would have counseled His followers to demand verification for everything they were told concerning the Resurrection; the descent of the Holy Spirit at Pentecost; the Ascension into Heaven, to list only three suspect events.

Therefore (by my evaluation), who was the greatest Apostle? Doubting Thomas was —*barring all doubt!* When he was told something fabulous, he demanded proof. When told of the appearance of Jesus to the assembled Apostles during his absence, Thomas declared, *"Unless I see the scars of the nails in his hands and put my finger on those scars and my hand in his side, I will not believe."* [Jn. 20:25] 'Kudos to Thomas! If today's religionists had even a modicum of the skepticism Thomas exhibited, we would have had considerably fewer apostate religionists proselytizing us down through the ages. But then, perhaps we did have a fair number of doubters? One of the inevitable results of pampered skepticism is theological heresy. Of them, there have been ever so many.

There were more heresies the first two hundred years after the death of Jesus than there were up to the advent of the Protestant Reformation. (This development became the impetus for the never-ending differentiation of Christianity that has expanded exponentially every year thereafter.) The most serious early controversy revolved around Jesus Himself. Was He created at the conception, or was He always an uncreated Deity? [Cf. Arian Heresy] That dispute was settled by debate, not through divine enlightenment. The belief that is central to Christianity was resolved by the Council of Nicaea in AD 325 with only 220 of the approximately 1,800 eligible Bishops in attendance. The Bishop of Rome, Pope Sylvester, didn't attend, but he did send two presbyters. Jesus of Nazareth's Divinity within a Trinity was decreed by far less than a true majority vote. That fact alone taxes my credulity into total incredulity.

In conclusion: Can the concept that Jesus was the second person of a Triune Godhead be disproved? No. How could such be definitively disproved? How would one even attempt to controvert such? But neither can any mortal prove that Jesus is the middle personage of a Tripartite Divinity. God (in the guise of the Father, the Son, or the Holy Ghost) could prove such if He so chose. But, by all that was and is apparent, God chooses not to reveal Himself unambiguously to mankind. Unless and until He does … our earthly abode will be riddled with skeptics in replication of Doubting Thomas. That is as it should be!

POINT — COUNTER POINT

<u>Argument:</u> Angels don't exist because they are non-corporeal. (Abstract)

<u>Counter:</u> Does beauty exist? Beauty is non-corporeal.

<u>Rebut:</u> Beauty does exist, but only in the perception of its beholder!

<u>Argument:</u> Angels exist because the Universe would be less perfect without them.

<u>Counter:</u> This is omnibus reasoning. Every entity, whether real or imagined, can be verified with this logic. The reverse makes the point. Bad angels don't exist because the Universe would be less perfect with them. Bad angels detract from the perfection of the Universe; ergo, there are no bad angels!

THE ONE TRUE CHURCH

The author of a book, <u>You've Got a Point There</u>, by Dr. Rest, addresses the question of which church is the "One True Church." Of necessity, his answer is evasive, simplistic, and inconclusive. However, that question is intrusive, and it is a thorny one for all Christian denominations. Dr. Rest's explication is as valid as any ever presented and superior to most in that he doesn't endeavor to tout his own denomination exclusively as the authentic "Church of Jesus Christ."

Without identifying it by name, he disavows the Catholic Church's claim to primogeniture by observing that infants crawl before they can walk, which hopefully leads you to conclude that walking is preferred to crawling. The full inference being: Although the Catholic Church predates all Protestant sects (metaphorically is the "first born"), they are not the "true church" because they are immature "crawling infants." He then dismisses all objective criteria, such as size, piety, theology, beauty of services, and even moral or ethical standards.

Having dispensed with any measurable quality, he then provides what he deems is a definitive response to this unsettling question. His solution: "No church is true in the sense that all others are false. Some churches are more mature than others in Christlikeness." He proposes "maturity" and "Christlikeness" as the measuring tools. He, thence, narrows the field to only Christian Churches. Then, he offers a subjective yardstick that has the miraculous property of proving that the sect taking the measurement is the more mature and the most Christlike. However, it does allow that other Christian denominations can be a little less 'mature' and a little less 'Christlike' without being condemned as heretical, schismatic, or false.

I can't help but recall an ad in a pulp magazine for inexpensive panty hose. The large, bold-faced banner informed, "One Size Fits All." Dr. Rest's definition can make the same assertion for discerning the 'one, true church.' Would any Christian sect ever grant that it was immature in its Christlikeness? What is Christlikeness? Is a man who deserts his separated-divorced-widowed mother a Christlike person? We don't know what became of Joseph; neither do we know how Mary supported herself in her presumed widowhood. What we do know is that Jesus didn't provide for her during His public ministry. In the non-canonical Protevangelion [Cf. Lost Books of the Bible], as a child Mary was fed by angels. Perhaps, the angels returned and again nurtured Mary after Joseph had disappeared from her life.

Similarly, would it be Christlike to break the windows of the many businesses that derive their livelihood by supplying goods and services to Christian churches? Many firms engaged in such transactions are no less culpable than were the moneychangers of Christ's day. Which is to observe: they charge whatever the traffic will bear! In the year 1980, the television show <u>Sixty Minutes</u>, exposed a religious organization that paid one of its administrative officers two hundred thousand dollars a year in salary. This would have been bad enough, but we also learned that the man (born a Jew) wasn't even a Christian until long after he was employed.

The television show alleged that the man established a financial interest in virtually every concern that did business with the vast religious organization of which he was treasurer. This is a conflict of interest, which probably led to a 'compounding of interest' for him. Accordingly, is Mike Wallace "Christlike" because of his exposé? He was seeking to expel a modern-day moneychanger! [Cf. Jn. 2:14-16; Mk. 11:15 & Mt. 21:12]

Christlike, defined piously, is an unwarranted glorification, and is an unjustified exaltation of certain of the acts of Jesus, coupled with de-emphasis or suppression of other less dignified acts as judged by today's standards. Does being Christlike mean we shouldn't do anything Christ didn't do? Of course it does! Jesus never married; accordingly, a celibate is more Christlike than is a non-celibate. And, logically, you could extend this and decide that if all men remained celibate and all women remained virgin, then humanity would have reached a perfect state of maturity in "Christlikeness." However, that isn't the only result of the foregoing scenario! Humanity would soon become extinct and we would hasten the end of the world, for there would be little point in delaying the final judgment once all of mankind expired. (If this line of reasoning appears to be heading toward the improbable, then keep reading; it progresses to the ridiculous!

There isn't one instance of Jesus bathing or cleansing Himself recorded in the Gospels. The bathing of His feet by the sinful woman is the lone example of Jesus being washed. [Cf. Lu. 7:36; Lu. 11:38; Mk. 7:2 & Mt. 15:2] Where and how Jesus accomplished His toilet is likewise never divulged. This can be rationalized as prudent editing, but what about the sleeping arrangements of the group? There is no polite reason for not mentioning where Jesus and the Apostles slept. Did they sleep out-of-doors every night? Were they houseguests of believers? There were many caves in the hill country of Galilee; did He and His band utilize these? Some of the everyday necessities of mortal life are never revealed, not even as accompaniment to the stories of His earthly experiences. This is especially quizzical if two of the Evangelists were intimate companions, and were privy to every event that transpired during His public life.

How does the previous fit in with the current topic of Christlikeness? Well, the answer to that is another question: How should a Christlike person handle his daily toilet? Daily bathing wasn't deemed necessary or even desirable at the time of Christ. The washing of hands was required as a ritual, not for hygienic reasons. Underarm deodorants hadn't been invented yet; nor was the use of a toothbrush universal *per se*. After forty days and forty nights in the desert, Jesus must have been quite a visual sight and an olfactory intrusion as well! How often should we, "Christlike" emulators, sojourn in the desert? After returning from the desert, should we bathe or not?

The whole concept of Christlikeness, as with all other facets of religiosity, becomes foolhardy whenever it is applied in anything other than a superficial and significantly selective manner. 'Christlike' has no denotative meaning whatsoever, but it is brimming over with connotative implications. Vague, imprecise, ambiguous the word "Christ-like" may be; yet, the connotation attending it is ever favorable.

Academically, we can extol the story of the life of Christ. But as a practical matter we can never even approximate His life, nor should we try! A query: how did Jesus support Himself and His followers? Luke reports that female followers used their 'personal resources' to support Jesus and the apostolic band. [Cf. Lu. 8:3] Or was there a miraculous appearance of manna for them to eat? 'And think of money? Did the Apostles collect tithes from their followers? Dr. Rest, in his book, encourages the payment of tithes despite the fact that there exists no New Testament justification for it. Saint Paul felt that a true herald of the Messiah should earn his own support and not be a burden upon the community. Then again, I have never heard of anyone admonishing Christian Churches to become more Paul-like. [Cf. 1 Thes. 2:9; 2 Thes. 3:8; Acts 18:3 & 20:34] Did God inspire Paul to work for his own support? If so, then why are all current Christian denominations now predominantly supported through the collection plate?

Jesus cursed a fig tree, and it withered and died. We know this because the Bible records so. [Cf. Mt. 21:19; Mk. 11:13-14, 20-21 & Lu. 13:7-9] But suppose the incident was never recorded for us. Wipe the account from your memory, and then pretend none of the extant scriptures mentioned it. Further, imagine that last year someone found a buried scroll that contained nothing but the story of the barren fig tree. Would anyone accept this find as scriptural? 'Positively not! Every Christian religious leader in the world would denounce this scroll as a fraud, or they would attribute the fig tree incident to the inspiration of Satan. That report would be universally decried as 'unchristlike.' The story is out of character for Jesus, if we compare it with the sanitized concept of the life of Christ we have had foisted on us by proponents of the divine compassion of the Messiah.

The sanctified and highly polished version of Christ's personality, that is held up for display at Sunday school, loses some of its brilliant sheen when it is scrutinized with the first-hand knowledge available to those who read the Bible with their skepticism fully engaged. We have eulogized Jesus so thoroughly that the historical Jesus can't measure up to His own piously exaggerated stature. Incidentally, cursing the fig tree isn't an isolated example of 'unchristlike' behavior by Jesus.

The story of the "would-be follower" causes Christ's apologists discomfiture when they try to harmonize His remarks with the glorified persona Christians have fashioned for Him. It seems a man offered to come and follow Jesus after he buried his deceased father. But Jesus spurned his offer and, in so doing, mocked the Commandment: 'Honor thy Father and Thy Mother.' He told the man to *"let the dead bury the dead."* [Mt. 8:21-22 & Lu. 9:59-60]

Moralists are forced to perform Herculean feats of ethical prestidigitation with this damaging, albeit enlightening, pronouncement. Damaging, in that it commands an impossible task: the dead can't bury themselves! Attempting to explain this event as an allegory isn't viable either. This wasn't a parable or a hypothetical situation; both Evangelists present this as an actual event. What Jesus indicated to the young man was that He (Jesus) was more important than was the burial of the man's dead father. This inferred declaration is edifying. In similar secular situations, most humans would deem this utterance as a manifestation of megalomania, and with justification, would revile and rebuke the person who spoke it.

Grant the premise that Jesus is the Son of God! Viewed in that aspect, perhaps He rightly should come first. Several passages in the Bible insinuate that Jesus was deemed 'special.' The anointing of His head and the washing of His feet are illustrative examples. But with His own words, elsewhere, He denounced this type of egotistical declaration. He said, *"If any man desires to be first, the same shall be last of all."* [Mk. 9:34, 10:31; Mt. 19:30, 20:16 & Lu. 13:30]

It isn't easy to be Christlike after reading some of the requirements set by Jesus. Luke provides this example: A great multitude began following Jesus, so He turned and addressed them. *"If any man come to me, and hate not his father, and mother, and wife, and children, and brethren, and sisters, yea, and his own life also, he cannot be my disciple."* [Lu. 14:26 & Mt. 10:37, 19:29] These verses can, it is true, be construed (excused) as bombastic rhetoric not to be taken literally. But once you allow one section of the Bible not to be taken literally, then you open every other section to that identical interpretation at the whim of the interpreter.

Exactly this has been done repeatedly, with the observable, as well as predictable (and maybe even inevitable) result, that almost anyone can twist and pervert the Bible into an authorizing document for their own self-declared dogmas. Protestants have long felt the stings of this lashing criticism. The Catholic Church, early on, realized that possession of the sacred scriptures alone, without the guiding light of tradition, and without the stabilizing leadership of an unquestioned central authority, would never suffice to ensure orthodoxy of beliefs.

And then we have the biblical command of Saint Paul to the Corinthians, who reportedly had begun devising their own interpretation of the meaning of the "Good News" he had given them. *"By the authority of our Lord Jesus Christ I appeal to all of you, my brothers, to agree in what you say, so that there will be no divisions among you. Be completely united, with only one thought and one purpose."* [1 Cor. 1:10] Allow me here to emphasize Paul's dictate (via the Holy Spirit's inspiration!) to the faithful in Corinth: *"agree"; "be united"; "with only one thought and one purpose"; "so that there will be no divisions among you!"* Pardon my bluntness, but doesn't the ever-increasing fractionation of Christianity violate that unambiguous command of the Holy Spirit as relayed to us through Saint Paul? The essence of Paul's message is unity! Obviously, Paul was ignorant of Dr. Rest's rendition of "Christlike."

[Exploring a definition of "Christlike."] In the scriptures (as we have them today), Jesus exhorts us to serve God's purposes with all our hearts, and to love one another without reserve even as God loves us all! [For example: Jn. 13:34 & 1 Jn. 4:11, et al.] His sentiments are so lofty and so ennobling that I find myself unable to present them into my words precisely. In my mind, I comprehend His message. Yet, it is impossible for me to convey this understanding to anyone else with unambiguous clarity.

But Jesus, Himself, couldn't live by His own guidelines, and neither can anyone else. They cannot be applied literally. He hated the Scribes, the Pharisees, and the Sadducees, not to mention the High Priest and the elders of the Temple. The only ones Jesus seemed to have held deep affection for were little children and those who followed Him. The evidence is sparse, but that which we have indicates He had little regard for His mother and His brothers and sisters. This is a formidable accusation to accept, and I don't submit it to you on faith in my words. I ask you to test its veracity yourself. Read the four Gospels yourself; they convict Jesus!

Open your Bible to Matthew 12:46-50, Mark 3:31-35, and Luke 8:19-21 where Jesus disowned His mother and His brothers. Why shouldn't He disavow His family? [Cf. Lu. 14:26] Further, read in all three Gospels where Jesus lamented: *"A prophet is respected everywhere except in his home town and by his own family."* [Mt. 13:57; Mk. 6:4; Lu. 4:24 & Jn. 4:44] John is more explicit: *"Not even his brothers believed in him."* [Jn. 7:5]

In this same episode Jesus lied to His brothers. Yes, that is correct, Jesus lied! Quoting John: Jesus spoke to His brothers, *"You go on to the feast, I am not going to this feast —After his brothers went to the feast, then Jesus also went. He did not go openly, however, but went in a secret way."* [Jn. 7:8-10] Is it a lie, or is it not a lie, to state you are not going to do a thing that you know implicitly and unconditionally that you are going to do?

Luke's tale of the boy Jesus in the Temple doesn't show that He regretted the anxiety His mother suffered while He was missing for three days. [Cf. Lu. 2:41-47] Jesus hadn't seen His parents for all that time. Wasn't He aware of their distress? As God the Second, He knew of their apprehension, why did He cause them such parental anguish? When Mary finally located Him, did He apologize for His thoughtlessness? No, instead he ungraciously rebuked her. His near desolate mother asked Him plaintively, *"Son, why did you do this to us? Your father and I have been terribly worried trying to find you."* Did Jesus acknowledge her mental torment? Here is His reply; you decide. *"Why did you have to look for me?"* [Lu. 2:48-49]

Frankly, there was no excuse for His utter lack of empathy. His further retort, *"Didn't you know that I had to be in my Father's house?"* had already been answered. [v. 49] If she had known where He was, she wouldn't have taken three days to locate Him. His question was specious, and His actions were indefensible. If Mary and Joseph were worthy parents, then His treatment of them, in this instance, was shabby; what's more, it was cruelly inconsiderate! One could (should?) describe His attitude as un-Christlike!

At the wedding feast of Cana, Jesus publicly chastised His mother. [Cf. Jn. 2:1ff] She told Him that the wine was all consumed. His response was disrespectful no matter what inflection you assign to His words. *"You must not tell me what to do, woman."* [Jn. 2:4] {Note: Every translation varies}

The examples cited so far all tend to show a callous disregard of His mother's feelings. The only kind (?) words He directs to her are recorded only by John at the crucifixion. *"Jesus saw his mother and the disciple he loved standing there; so he said to his mother, 'Woman, here is your son.' Then he said to the disciple, 'Here is your mother.'"* [Jn. 19:26-27] Those pronouncements aren't bristling with filial affection; but they are the nearest Jesus ever came to exhibiting concern toward His mother.

One final word on the topic of "Christlikeness" and I will return to Dr. Rest. It may surprise some, but Jesus never appeared to His mother after His resurrection. The confirmation of the last statement may be had by reading the final chapters of the Gospels. In the Acts of the Apostles, Luke recounts (ambiguously) a visitation to the Apostles by the risen Jesus, which culminated in the Ascension from the Mount of Olivet. After returning from Olivet, the Apostles returned to Jerusalem where, *"They gathered frequently to pray as a group, together with the women, and with Mary, the mother of Jesus, and with his brothers."* [Acts 1:14]

From this we could infer that Mary was present at one of the visitations of the resurrected Jesus before He ascended to Heaven. However, this is only an inference; therefore, I repeat my allegation: "Jesus never appeared to His mother after His resurrection." In the Synoptic Gospels, she isn't present at the crucifixion. Even John fails to record a post-resurrection visit by Jesus to His undoubtedly bereaved mother. To me, this is the most damaging evidence condemning (convicting) Jesus of my accusation against Him.

Dr. Rest cannot deny any Christian sect its legitimacy for they all offer the Bible as their license to practice Christianity. If he denies any one denomination their claim, thereby he denies them all; even his own! Therefore, he substitutes an elastic measure that can shrink or stretch to match the dimensions of an equally ambiguous blueprint for erecting the "One True Church."

But is the Bible the only test of the legitimacy of a Christian denomination? The evidence in the New Testament itself weighs heavily against that proposition. There isn't sufficient evidence to convict Jesus of willfully originating a new religion. Even accepting that He did intentionally accomplish this, no one can sensibly postulate that He founded more than one (Christian) religious denomination. Consult John's tenth chapter, verse sixteen. (Jn. 10:16)

The Bible repudiates the commonly conceded conclusion that Jesus began a new faith. Yet, in the New Testament, we read that He sought only to bring His chosen religion, Judaism, back to its moral foundations, and to redefine the worship of Yahweh (the vindictive) into the acknowledgment of God (the benevolent) Father. After the death of Jesus, the Apostles remained practicing Jews (until the Sanhedrin expelled them from the Temple, and assumedly from the synagogues also). The Apostles became Christians by default, not by design.

The first proof of this is that not one of them visited His sepulcher on the Sabbath, which would have been a violation of that holy day under Judaism. More convincing proof is found at the end of Luke, *"And {the Apostles} were continually in the temple praising and blessing God. Amen."* [Lu. 24:53] Notice that the Apostles aren't praising Jesus. Also, the Acts records the Apostles as proselytizing in the Temple or in a synagogue. [Cf. Acts 2:46, 3:1 & 14:1] Further proof can be found in Matthew's Gospel. He relates that Jesus sent out His twelve disciples by two's to reform Judaism. That He only intended His message for the Jews is undeniable. His words were: *"Do not go to any Gentile territory or any Samaritan towns. Go, instead, to the lost sheep of the people of Israel."* [Mt. 10:5-6]

Apologists can gerrymander the implications of that unequivocal statement to the dimensions of their devious designs, but the final analysis must deal with the rock-bound sentiment inherent in that directive. 'Return the lapsed Jews to the religion of Judaism.' Jesus didn't proclaim a new faith. That eventuality seems to have been the accomplishment of Paul. Jesus wasn't a 'Christian!'

A more ominous, almost militaristic, declaration is found later in Matthew. There, Jesus states openly: *"Do not think that I have come to bring peace to the world. No, I did not come to bring peace, but a sword."* [Mt. 10:34] I have never heard a propagandist's sanctimonious rationale for that undeniably bellicose pronouncement, but it must be a contorted marvel.

Continuing with the search for the 'One, True Church': If the Gospels are the authorizing document that grants a denomination legitimacy, then I ask, why didn't Jesus keep a diary, or ensure that an authentic record of His teachings was kept? Why wasn't one of His disciples a scribe? Jesus could then have instructed the scribe to report accurately all that He wanted future generations to know. Jesus was God the Second; He should have foreseen the doubts the differences in the Gospels have generated.

Why inspire conflicting stories of His life when He could just as easily have kept a reliable, complete, and official record while He was alive?

If Dr. Rest is correct, then there is no "One, True Church." What we have are many, greater or lesser, 'True Churches.' Is that what Jesus left behind; a welter of partially accurate faiths? Or did Jesus only intend to reform the religion of Judaism, which was itself fragmented in His day? Did Jesus allow that the divisions of Judaism were all acceptable to His Father? No, He didn't! What He said was that they all had strayed from the True Faith, and if they didn't reform their ways, they all would be damned from the sight of God. Now, if that was true in His lifetime, how much more unerring is this conclusion today, when we have hundreds of divisions in the Christian religion? No, Dr. Rest, your definition will please man (appease is more apropos), but it would offend Jesus! His desire was that we all honor the one, true God, in the one, true manner, and through the One, True Church, that being, Judaism as then headquartered in the Jewish Temple in Jerusalem.

EFFECTS OF A RELIGIOUS EDUCATION

The nostalgia of our childhood and early adolescence provides us with the fondest memories of our lives. Regrettably, when a born-and-reared Catholic renounces his religion, he necessarily renounces a major portion of those fond memories. By this, I am not intimating that Catholics enjoy some exceptional predilection for nostalgic reverie. But a Catholic child, in his eight years of Elementary School, is so enmeshed into the activities of his Church that it later becomes impossible to separate his secular education from his religious indoctrination. The two are interwoven so as to create the illusion, but not the reality, of being contiguous and inseparable. Perhaps this proposition needs to be explained for those who have never attended a Parochial school.

In a Catholic school every activity is directed at, or governed by, religiosity. Religious dogmas are daily drilled into young minds during a programmed period of teaching Catholicism. But additionally, during other non-religious periods, Judeo-Christian ethics are invoked or biblical examples are cited to illustrate secular teaching. The twelve Apostles formed a dozen; thence, when Judas hanged himself only eleven were left. That is subtraction. During Health periods I learned that Moses commanded the Israelites to wash before eating; therefore, it was both sensible and moral to wash before meals. In order to grasp Civics, we were taught about Herod Philip II the Tetrarch and Pontius Pilate the Procurator. {Pilate's actual title may have been "Prefect of Judea."} Indeed, God confers all authority; hence, representatives of the government must be obeyed with the same deference as is shown the Bishop.

The school play, in effect, was staged by the Nuns, and quite often it had a religious theme. In Geography, I learned where the "Dark Continent" was located. But I was also given the erroneous impression that everyone in Africa dressed in loincloths and lived in grass thatch huts. Presumably, their only contact with the outside world was through the kindly missionaries from America. How happy I was to give my pennies to help these vital emissaries of the Catholic Church.

Yet here I am sixty plus years later, rejecting all that was taught to me. Alas, when you reject the teaching; you reject the teacher as well. This fact was brought home most dramatically when I attended the one hundred and twenty-fifth anniversary of my boyhood parochial school. Everyone was so delighted to see everyone else. A childhood sweetheart of mine came up from Atlanta, Georgia, and I was thrilled to see her. The Nun who supervised the altar boys was there (yes, I was an altar boy!); Sister Mary Ethel remembered me. We hugged. For me, the affair was truly memorable.

What would have been that Nun's reaction if she had known what I was committing to writing during this time? I still felt affection toward her even though I realized that she was partially liable for the fear I had of the consecrated hosts. (The consecrated hosts are purported to be the actual body and blood of God Jesus.) I absolved her for misleading me. Would she have accepted me if she knew how "misled" I am now? 'Certainly not! I would have been anathema at that affair had I openly expressed my views. Had this book been in print at the time, my request for tickets would have been denied, and I would have been barred at the door had I attempted to enter. I would have been branded an 'anti-Christ' and an outcast at an affair that I had as much right to attend as did any other graduate of that Grammar school.

Why should this be so? Can't someone have an opinion contrary to a religionist's and still be welcomed graciously to what was, in reality, a reunion not a religious ceremony? No! Religion is such an emotional exercise that only emotion can sustain it. Emotionalism evokes more passionate emotionalism!

By now, non-Catholic Christians should have a sharper focused picture of their fellow Christians. Protestants, in general, do not operate a network of schools. So they compensate for this lack by creating a deluge of religious tracts, and by staging one hundred (or more!) religious events a year. Christianity isn't unique in its attempts to totally dominate not only a person's actions, but more insidiously, to condition his very thought processes. This is the crime of all Religiosity; it enslaves the mind! One may query Plato's theories of democracy with immunity, but God damns those who question His ever sacred biblical precepts.

Ask any Ayatollah in Iran if he knows what pleases Allah. Ask any Televangelist what pleases Jesus. Ask a Buddhist Monk in Vietnam, or a native shaman in Micronesia, and all will know unerringly what pleases the Universal Deity. God (the Universal Divinity) has been successfully psycho-analyzed by every self-ordained or seminary educated cleric who has ever lived. What massive egos these religious protagonists have! Don't wonder why they defend their God so ardently. Without appended or perceived divine approbation and affection, even the 'holy' men shrink to the mundane level of "brightest of the primates," which is quite complimentary to all of mankind! Yet to egotistic religionists, it is far below their exalted status as 'Generals' leading Heaven-destined humanity. Their position of imagined confidante of the 'Ultimate Presence' is much more honorific than that of a clever ape. How uncomplimentary it is to picture oneself as just another wave in the global ocean. When we peer behind the pious frontage of Christianity (and all other religions of mankind) we find, not humility & sanctity, but rampant pride, vanity & conceit!

In the United States today there are more organizations formed to accomplish some noble or worthy cause than anywhere else on the planet. What did each of these organizations have in common at their founding? It was a person who believed himself or herself to be the one best able to head that organization. 'Ego' impels more persons to acts of religiosity and charity than any other human trait. (Fear is an emotion)

So, in ending this segment I will express these sincere thoughts: My Catholic education was both enlightening and exhilarating. Overall, I have the fondest memories of my childhood experiences as a pupil in the Parochial school system. I doubt that today I could say the same if I had had a Public School education. Notwithstanding, I also recognize that I had been successfully indoctrinated into a near unshakable belief (and fear!) of the supernatural. To this day I cannot prove that God, His angels, His adversary Satan, et al., factually aren't otherworldly entities. This is a lasting legacy of my religious upbringing and education. My mouth declares that I am an unwavering atheist. But deep in the remote recesses of my mind, I probably will everlastingly harbor clandestine uncertainties. I sincerely desire this not to be so. But it is so!

CHAPTER 12
Spirit Essence

MUSING ABOUT SPIRITS

[Before proceeding: a disclaimer.] All things spiritual are non-existent, exempting neither God, the Angels, the Demons, Heaven & Hell, nor human souls! Spirits are a human mental conception that in truth serves no purpose other than to masquerade as an opposite to that which is real, tangible, and verifiable. However, and because the reality of just such ethereal entities is so generally accepted, here I will attempt to showcase the improbability, if not the impossibility, of spiritual matter. As I often do, the discussion will proceed at times as though spiritual matter was an unchallenged fact. With that caveat presented, I proceed.

At this juncture it could be helpful to reflect on the essence of spirit, and on the properties (or lack thereof) that spirits exhibit. First, spirits have bounds; they have limits; they occupy space, even if that space likewise is spiritual. Why do I state that spirits occupy space? Simply because this is the way we conceive spirits. Will your soul diffuse throughout the limitless Universe at death? Not according to conventional Christian theology. Mentally we perceive the soul's shape and bounds as replicating the shape and bounds of our human body. The spirit of a person is always pictured as a gossamer replica of the human person. That we do this bespeaks even more about spirits, but we needn't examine that perception just yet.

Undoubtedly (in human discernment), our soul retains at least the general appearance and silhouette of our human body.

In our cognition of spirits or angels we theorize that each is a separate and identifiable entity. We know instinctively that one spirit differs from another, if in nothing else, via ownership. My spirit is distinct from your spirit. In a specific instance, our spirits may be likened to a can of shelled peanuts. All peanuts seemingly are interchangeable, yet upon searching examination, each peanut is slightly different and individual. What makes them individual? The answer is that some discernible or measurable quality is the basis for our ability to particularize an individual peanut. With spirits, our method of identification is by possession alone.

The differentiation of souls is of paramount importance. How complicated it would be if my soul and your soul could overlap and coalesce in the manner of two puffs of smoke blown into a transparent balloon. No one would ever be able to extract and reconstitute unerringly each individual puff of smoke. Providentially, this doesn't happen when our souls are brought together in Heaven. In theory, they continue their separate existence. This postulate requires that a soul be more substantial than is a puff of smoke. Therein resides the cause of a soul's destruction. Contemplate thus: A soul, if one did exist, would be made entirely of spirit matter, which is the same as saying non-matter. Non-matter is the conjectured opposite of matter, and accordingly, can't have measurable or recognizable properties, not even ownership or personality. Academically, all things do have an opposite, but in this case, we wouldn't have physical matter counterbalanced by spiritual matter. The opposite of existence is non-existence. Hence, the opposite of matter is the absence of matter, meaning nothingness!

Spirit matter may be equated to one of the three main states of physical matter, viz., solid, liquid, and gaseous. The total individual could then be thought of as a combination of flesh and blood (i.e., solid and liquid) animated by a soul (i.e., the gaseous state). At death, the solid and liquid components begin to disintegrate, while the gaseous state retains its coherency, yet is freed of the constraints of the imprisoning body. Now liberated, the soul can waft off to Heaven, or perhaps more likely, be shunted off to Hell to suffer punishment for the sins of the flesh. This theorem seems plausible enough to be true. But is it? 'Not a sliver of a chance!

What you have just read is a seeming possibility camouflaged as a plausible reality. Gaseous matter is every bit as real as is solid matter or liquid matter. All three are subject to detectible laws of physics. Gaseous matter can be measured, weighed, confined and manipulated at the whim of man. The state of matter that we call gaseous could only seem 'spiritual' to the superstitious, the dim-witted, or the ignorant (uneducated).

God is a pure spirit also, but is His essence the same essence as is soul spirit? It can't be for the simple reason that God is eternal and everlasting. Human souls are created at the conception of that human being whose ownership is assigned by God, so it would seem that soul spiritual matter differs just as physical matter does. The spirit essence of God had no beginning and shall have no end. The spirit essence of a human soul begins at the birth of a human being. Doesn't this belief demand two different types of spirit essence? This is a baffling concept to comprehend: different types of nothing! In truth, this discourse on spirit essence becomes more and more laborious to sustain. How can anyone talk about nothing cogently? A religionist might attribute my difficulty to the inability of the human mind to grasp the concept of spirituality, but this is merely a semantic ploy. Discussing spirit is stressful because no such endowment exists. God and all other spiritual entities are only mental specters seemingly participating in, or reacting to, mankind's mental life adventures.

Theology's first task is to render the irrational intelligibly!

WHAT IS SPIRITUAL ESSENCE?

God created the Universe *ex nihilo*. What does this statement mean? The image this opening sentence tries to evoke is that of a resplendent Being suspended in a complete void that stretches forth His hands and miraculously causes an endless Universe to appear from nothing. Can you picture this in your mind? How do you conceive the initial act of creation? If it was possible, I would want to amass all the different mental scenarios that imaginative persons have formulated to enable themselves to visualize God's initial act of creation.

The reason for this aspiration is so that I can evaluate for myself the seeming accuracy of their mental depictions. Personally, I find it very taxing to imagine an actual instantaneous Creation of so vast a cosmos. More succinctly, I should say that I am unable to conjure up a satisfactory scenario for the origin of the Universe. The difficulty doesn't arise at the initial premise. There is a known and provable Universe extant; all that my mind has to supply is a unique being who has mystical faculties that are accountable for the existence of the Cosmos. A powerful, masculine, authority figure forms readily in my musing.

The problems commence when I continue to fantasize about the Creation. The tangible Cosmos is obvious and unquestioned. My senses can easily perceive the physical. It is the spiritual that inevitably haunts my thoughts. What is spirit essence? Of what are angels made? What comprises my spirit? If I own a soul, what endowment differentiates this entity from nothingness? I will examine definitions here. What is nothingness? Nothing is the total absence of something. Fine! That I accept. If the concept of nothing is valid (it must be if God created, because nothing existed prior to the Creation), then spirit matter must be something! Whatever spirits are composed of, that essence is something! For if spirit matter is nothingness then spirit matter doesn't exist. It isn't facile to render this more lucidly for, in fact, we are discussing an absurdity. Spirits are absurd!

Proceeding: God created spirits also, consequently, where there was once nothing, God fashioned something. This something religionists call spirits. So spirits truly are something. Spirits aren't "nothing." What is the something of spirits? What properties constitute spirit essence? What dimensions shape spirit entities? Does a spirit have any qualities that distinguish it from nothing? How can we define a spirit apart from a total lack of anything substantial?

You see, we reason around and around, but we always arrive back at the same conclusion: Spirit and 'nothing' are precisely the same thing; they are identical. Spirits and nothingness share the same description. There is a theorem in physics that states "If two things are equal to the same thing, then they are likewise equal to one another." If, as I have just stated, the description of spirit and the description of nothingness are identical, then, as a result, nothingness and spirit are identical. Leading inexorably to the conclusion: "Spirits don't exist!"

Now answer the most pertinent question of all: "What is the substance of God?" God, too, must be composed of something, for He can't be composed of nothing. Nothing is the absence of something. We declare that God is a pure spirit, but we know this isn't so, for God has a spirit Himself. Can a spirit have a spirit? No! If God exists, then He has substance. If He has substance (which He must if He isn't nothing), then God is something. For if He was made of nothing then He wouldn't exist. Even spirits must consist of a substance. Consequently, it doesn't matter what substance we postulate for God, whatever that substance, the inevitable question intrudes concomitantly: "How did the substance of God originate?"

Religionists are stymied by the same dilemma that confounds an Evolutionist. Where did the original substance in the Universe come from? The substance of God in this instance! If you clear away the clutter of religiosity, then your mind's eye will recognize that what we term spirit essence is, in reality, only invisible physical matter. God is an invisible human being, as are angels and demons. But, is there such a reality as invisible human beings? No, there isn't! Spirit essence only exists for those who have permitted their fascinations to overrule their intellect.

What we call God is only a highly speculative theory that endeavors to account for the origin of the Universe, and the creation of all living matter. The theory has great aesthetic appeal, but is wholly lacking in any proofs whatsoever. By its very nature, substance has bounds. Only nothingness is infinite, and only in the abstract. It is small wonder then that theoretical religionists have resorted to the mysterious in their efforts to explain God. Yet, their pious speculations are no more valid (or logical, or even essential) than are an Agnostic's confession of ignorance, nor an Atheist's disparaging rejection of all theology. Objectively, no single theory of the origin of the Universe holds incontestable credibility over its several rivals.

To a religionist, a creator-less Universe is unthinkable. For an Atheist an uncaused 'Cause' is an absurdity. While an Agnostic throws up his hands and disregards the entire issue. Obviously, the premiere question in all of cosmogony is unanswerable now and for all time. For instance, if it could be proved that physical matter materializes spontaneously wherever a total vacuum exists, religionists could still undauntedly ask: "Who causes matter to generate spontaneously?"

If biologists working in a laboratory could repeat the entire sequence of evolution from the first inert atom of hydrogen, through the formation of self-replicating bio-molecules (DNA) until one-celled micro-organisms were produced, would this prove God doesn't exist? No! The Creator could still be postulated as the Architect (Designer) of the Universe, instead of its Manufacturer. God may well have dictated the properties of the elements, and charted a course for the development of evolved matter after His initial creation of the hydrogen atom. I certainly can't prove otherwise.

In order to test the hypothesis of an uncreated Creator we must move away from square one (the existence of the Universe). Once we do, all the weight (proof) begins to shift toward the Atheist's position. The question: "Does God have essence," can only be answered "Yes," by a religionist. However, an Atheist will immediately ask: "Who made God's essence?"

Every facet of the Godhood can be challenged by Atheists with the same result. The verifiable evidence favors Atheism. Fundamentalist Christians, accordingly, reject all contrary facts and place their entire credence in the Bible. This has the convenient faculty of relieving its proponents of the fruitless labor necessary to defend the indefensible. For example: When the Bible records that 'Jonah was swallowed by a great fish,' then he truly and simply 'was swallowed by a great fish.' [Cf. Jon. 1:17 into Jon. 2:1] The modern apologist searches for a fish that conceivably is identifiable as the culprit of this inane fiction. The scientific objections to this fish tale (cetacean tale?) are overwhelming. In truth, an unreserved belief in the literal veracity of the Jonah myth amounts to nothing less than wishful, willful or witless bibliolatry.

WHAT IS THE ESSENCE OF GOD'S SPIRIT?

When we state that God is a pure spirit, what do we mean? Is the essence of God's spirit the same essence that comprises our spirit? No, it can't be because then our spirit would be the equal of God's spirit. That premise is theologically intolerable; accordingly, human spirits must be composed of an essence that differs from God's essence. Now, ponder the question of angelic essence. Angels are pure spirits; yet, as with humans, their essence must surely be different from the Creator's. Consequently, we have no fewer than two different types of spirit essence; the spirit essence of the Divinity, and the spirit essence of angels and men. This supposes that angel essence and human spirit essence are the same. There is no revealed enlightenment that this is so, and summary examination of the premise indicates that it isn't so.

Angels possess many faculties that we humans lack, even after death when our spirit is released from the constraints of the flesh. If this is factual, then the essence of angels must be different from the spirit essence of man because angelic essence is more potent; as a consequence, there must be three separate essences of spirit.

Likewise, devils and demons are spirits. And, because this is stated, it must be asked: "Does demon spirit essence differ from the three other spirit essences?" Not surprisingly, the answer is that, in theory, demon essence is different. Demons can perform feats of their own volition, whereas angels can perform only that which God directs them to perform. Also, demons are evil, but angels are saintly! How do we account for this difference? If both angels and devils are comprised of nothing but spirit essence, then any difference between them must, perforce, be intrinsic to their sole essence, which is spirit. This argues for an essence count of four. God's spirit essence, Angel spirit essence, Devil spirit essence, and man's spirit essence.

Yet, is four the final count? Probably not! For, you see, there are nine choirs of angels. Each choir must somehow be different from all other choirs. For the same reasons listed previously for angels and devils: If nine separate choirs exist (theologians say they do!), then each choir must consist of a different essence. This raises the total of spirit essences to twelve. That is a significant figure in biblical numerology, but is it the complete tally? 'Maybe not!

Both Heaven and Hell are spiritual places and, without argument, neither is the same destination as the other. This forces us to consider each as a separate spiritual entity; which, in turn, points to the conclusion that the spiritual essence of Heaven is a different spiritual essence than that which constitutes the spiritual essence of angels, or any other spiritual essence. The different essences can be classified as animate (active) and inanimate (passive).

If I would continue to search I might eventually discover as many as ninety-two spiritual essences, paralleling the ninety-two naturally occurring basic elements found on Earth. In that situation, a new science must be founded: <u>Spirit Chemistry</u>. Mankind could then proceed to discover what it is that causes the spirit world to be so fractionated.

If this spectral soliloquy seems to have led down a primrose path, then my point is made. Spirit essence is "turtle wings!" That is, it sounds plausible, but is intrinsically impossible. Spirit essence is a contrariety (borrowing one of St. Augustine's terms). Essence is matter; while spirit is the absence of matter. To declare spirit as unimaginable won't suffice either; for spirit has been imagined, and by my reckoning, spirit exists only in mankind's imagination.

It would be remiss on my part if I neglected here to question another facet of a Trinity of Gods totaling one. Here I am not debating the count, but only the essence. Does the essence of God the Father differ from the essence of God the Holy Ghost? Those two: does their essence differ from the essence of Jesus? Doctrinally, No! The question has been resolved by Church Council. All Three are of one essence. Yet each is a true individual (homoousios). How can this be so?

An analogy readily presents itself to a piously thoughtful person, namely, triplets born from a single zygote. All three have a single gene complement and are identical, and will continue to be identical, barring only environmental intrusion. Curiously, the Church rejects this analogy. It seems the Triune Godhood must share a single will also. No matter how close, triplets do not think with one mind, nor do they act with one will, nor do they possess a communal memory. This is crucial for religionists. God the Son must possess the same knowledge, at the same instant, as the other two Entities of the Trinity. Alas, no triplets have ever exhibited this communal memory attribute. This strands us with the already stated proposal that the Godhood consists of one essence, permanently split into three personalities. They are so unified that they have a single memory pool and a single essence, yet the three remain so separate they can speak, act and travel independent of one another and appear to be three independent entities. Defying the previous, when the Christian Church counts the Trinity it arrives at one for a total!

What purpose does all this contorted numerical theology serve? It seemingly preserves the devolved premise that only one God exists. This premise was never espoused by all Jews before the advent of Jesus. The Old

Testament is replete with examples of the Hebrews worshipping foreign gods while they were professing Yahweh as their lone Divine Benefactor.

In modern times, Mankind has refined the doctrine to the point where God the Father, Allah, Buddha, Brahman, Quetzalcoatl, Zeus, Jupiter, et al., are all human attempts to name (identify) the one, true, lone creative essence in the Universe. To a Christian, the doctrine has great appeal; it satisfies the requirement that only one Divinity (God) exists. What Christians fail to appreciate is that with Jesus, they invalidate every religion but their own. Christianity believes it has been granted, through the Incarnation of Jesus and the inspiration of the Sacred Scriptures, what most other extant, Non-Christian religions have been denied: Intimate affinity with the Supreme Being, and written witness (biblical proof) to that relationship. Most other religions possess something akin to "sacred Scriptures." Islam's Koran is an example.

WHEN DID GOD BECOME THREE PERSONS?

"In the beginning God (etymologically 'the Gods') *created the Heavens and the Earth."* [Gen. 1:1] Halt here! What was happening before the general Creation? Imagine now what existed before the Creation mentioned in Genesis. We must suppose that angels, and consequently devils also, had already been created. Now, think back before the introduction of the angels. God exists alone in all the cosmos. Ponder these queries: "How many divine persons were present? Was there only Yahweh? Was Jesus there also? Was the Holy Spirit a separate personality, if not a separate entity? If all three existed, why don't we just admit that there are three Gods, by name, Father, Son, and Holy Spirit?"

The question is this: Before anything or anybody was created, did a Trinity exist? If it (or they) didn't exist, who created the Trinity? Religionists are forced by their own dogma(s) to believe in the eternal existence of all three manifestations of the Godhead. Because this is so, I am forced to ask how, or in what manner, the Holy Spirit differs from the Father or from Jesus. What difference is there between the Father and Jesus? Jesus was true man, i.e., He was flesh and blood. Was He always flesh and blood? If we could peer back into the endless (timeless?) time before the creation, before the advent of the angels, would we see Jesus in the form of a mortal man? I hardly think so! But then, rejecting a pre-creation human Jesus, we must infer a human beginning for Jesus in Mary's womb.

Is there a difference in the space these three Gods occupy? We state that God is everywhere, but are we referring to God the Father, God the Son, or God the Holy Spirit? Are all three present simultaneously? Are all three spatially congruent? If God the Father isn't the same person as God the Son, how is He different? When the Holy Spirit appears on Earth as a dove, is God the Father also in the dove? Is Jesus in the dove additionally? When Jesus was crucified, did God the Father feel the pain of the nails in His wrists? Does God the Father have wrists? Does the Holy Spirit experience pain?

I could continue, but the questions would get sillier and sillier, and so too would the answers. There is just no way to squeeze three persons into one God. The need to attempt it arises through an imperative Christian tenet (namely, that Jesus was/is a God). If a personal God exists, then He exists alone, unequaled, unparalleled, and unique. Even God can't create another God because a "God" must, perforce, be uncreated! Truly, this feat is an impossible contradiction universally and everlastingly!

The Old Testament errs in its belief in a God and His Spirit. Analyzed: the Old Testament chroniclers believed in ghosts. Everyone had a ghost, even God. Early on, God performed His acts in person. Later, as doctrine-formulating religionists became somewhat more sophisticated, when God wished something done, He sent His Spirit to accomplish the task. Also, and perhaps more significantly, the belief evolved that death would strike anyone who looked upon God's visual self; thus, when God appeared to man, He manifest Himself in spirit form so that the person so favored wouldn't instantly expire.

The Old Testament notion of a Supreme Being and His Spirit isn't too difficult to accept. Essentially, a man's spirit is almost the same essence as is his person. The whole notion collapses, however, if as I conclude, no such entity as a spirit exists either in man or in God. Nonetheless, the ancients did believe in ghosts: spirits that is! Each person had one, God included.

This bizarre notion that God had a spirit engendered another erroneous postulate professed by the early Hebrews. They theorized that

God Himself was more than a spirit. They imagined a vibrant, substantive entity that, indeed, did possess a powerful arm. [Cf. Job 40:4] And, indeed, did sit upon a throne in Heaven. [Cf. Rev. 5:1] He was ever vigilant of their Semite ethnicity, provided they worshiped Him exclusively! The Israelites worshiped the "living" God. Their God was "real." In fact, He was so real that He, as all other living beings, possessed a spirit ... a Holy Spirit. [Cf. Eph. 4:30]

But the appearance of Jesus introduced a new and wholly unexpected aspect for the Jewish Christian community. Where was the Messiah's place in the universal scheme? Was Jesus a 'God' hiding in the guise of man? Jesus Himself said no. He stated He was the 'Son of God.' Yet, what did 'Son of God' truly signify? Sons are generated during an act of sexual passion between a man and a woman. Could God be a partner to such convulsive antics? No, God must be infinitely above the petty lusts of man. In Hebrew theology, Yahweh is never associated with females, nor is He ever even whispered about in terms with sexual connotations. Judaism disdained virtually all heavenly (spiritual) sexuality.

Frankly, the more thought I give this issue; the more I am convinced that Jesus never claimed to be the actual biological Son of God. If He had, no one (not even the Apostles) would have accepted His claim. The thought is unthinkable in Hebrew theology. The attribution of true divinity to Jesus was a pagan contribution to the Messiahship claims of the first Christians. Reading the scriptures academically, *sans* blinding reverence, conjures pictures of Jesus as a reformer of Judaism, not as the founder of a competing faith. It was Jesus himself who told the Canaanite woman, *"I have been sent only to the lost sheep of the people of Israel."* [Mt. 15:24]

At the conclusion of Matthew's Gospel we read: *"Go, then, to all peoples everywhere and make them my disciples."* [Mt. 28:19] Was the Risen Jesus thereby commissioning His Apostles to institute a new religion? I wonder if the translation shouldn't read thus: 'Go, then, to all *"the people"* everywhere and make them my disciples, with *"the people"* indicating the Jews of the Diaspora. This seems to coincide more closely with the entirety of the Gospels. Namely, that Jesus the Jew was first chosen by Yahweh, and then commissioned to reform the practice of Judaism.

Jews, throughout history, have been dispersed among the nations. Most, however, maintained their ties and loyalties to the Temple in

Jerusalem; those that never forsook their Jewish heritage, that is! During His lifetime, Jesus attempted to reform the ecclesiastic hierarchy (especially targeting the Temple) and failed. Isn't it logical that He would then attempt to reform the secular body of believers, thereby forcing His reforms on the priests?

Anticipating your objection that I am altering the meaning of the passage by adding the word 'the'; I offer in defense of my addition, the Jerusalem Bible's rendering of the very same verse. *"Go, therefore, make disciples of all the nations."* [ibid.] The wording of the passage is considerably different from the Good News for Modern Man version previously quoted. My addition does change the sense of the passage somewhat, whereas the Jerusalem's translation doesn't. However, this is no real obstacle for the tiny article 'the' could very well have been accidentally dropped from the text in the very first copy, and no one today can prove otherwise. Also, we know that the emphasis placed on a spoken word can alter its meaning too. We will never know what inflection Jesus placed on the word 'peoples' in His charge to His Apostles.

Matthew's Gospel especially reinforces the belief that Jesus thought of Himself only as the promised Jewish Messiah. He, likewise, believed He was witnessing the fulfillment of the ancient prophesies predicting the advent of the 'Last Times.' The Messianic Age was soon to dawn, and He was God's chosen deliverer. Jesus perceived the imminent arrival of Heaven's hosts to defeat the enemies of Israel, and to install Him on the new Davidic throne. Must we speculate when later, the crucified Jesus cried out in despair, *"My God, My God, why hast thou forsaken me?"* [Mt. 27:46 & Mk. 15:34 –citing Ps 22:1?] These words resonate with clarity and discernment once we concede that Jesus never expected to factually die on the cross.

More than a thousand years previous, God had commanded Abraham to kill his beloved son only to delay until the last moment before countermanding the order and sparing Isaac's life. Jesus knew the same result would ensue in His circumstance. God was testing Him, testing His faith, testing His obedience to God's Will, just as He had tested Abraham of old. [Cf. Gen. 22:2-12] In Jesus' case, however, the last minute reprieve never came.

Jesus hung there quiescently despite the excruciating pain, while ignoring the shame and the degradation of His nudity. (Public crucifixion was designed to humiliate, as well as to execute.) Yet, even the faith of Jesus flagged and eventually failed. After three hours of debasing exposure before a horrified (titillated?) mob, Jesus despaired. He ceased raising Himself up (which is the only way crucifixion victims can breathe), voiced His utter desolation at the God of Israel, and expired!

Incidentally, one of the convincing evidences of the authenticity of the Shroud of Turin is the fact that the crucified person pictured on the Shroud was completely nude. Christian artists have always depicted Jesus as wearing a loin cloth on the cross. Had a pious Christian wanted to counterfeit Christ's burial shroud, he likely would have sanctimoniously covered the lower torso of Jesus conforming to common Christian modesty. Militating against this indicator is the observable fact that the corpse on the Shroud has his hands judiciously placed over his groin area shielding that portion of his anatomy from future prurient inspection.

PONDERING DEVILS

The dogma of the Fallen Angels presents skeptics with additional fuel to fire their skepticism. The first log into the fire is the question: Why did God create angels if He knew in advance some of their number would rebel against Him? Next: Why does He permit demons to continue to exist? The logical posers emanating from this initial improbable event (the creation of angels) are countless. Progressing: Why weren't Lucifer and his followers perfectly content in Heaven basking in the Beatific Vision? Specifically, the Beatific Vision is the unfiltered, unobstructed, undiminished entirety of God's singularly ineffable person.

Also: "Who tempted Lucifer?" More exacting: "Did God create evil or did it spring to life of its own volition?" The Bible discloses one revolt in Heaven. Will there be another? To amplify: Why isn't it possible for some of the remaining angels to start a second revolution, overthrow God, and install Satan as the Ruler of the Universe? Logically, granting the premise that the angels have free will and can still rebel against God, we agnostics and atheists (and certain-to-be-damned doubters also!) could hope that this eventuality might come to be. And, if so, we may be liberated from Hell on that day and thence undeservedly slip into Heaven despite our iniquities.

Without contradiction, I know that God wouldn't permit Himself to be overthrown or deposed. He only permits Himself to be contended with up to a safe limit. For a few moments, repress your infused bias favoring the Bible. Instead, reason out the supposed sequence of the Creation. Mentally, I have done this.

I began by visualizing God existing as the solitary Entity in an endless void. He looked around and He thought to Himself: "I am all alone, why don't I create someone to adore Me? He then proceeded to create the Angels … nine choirs of them. Now He had company, but somehow He still wasn't fulfilled. So He reflected again and discerned the reason why. The angels were all respectful and loving, but they had no alternate choice; who else could they worship? Only God in His goodness existed. So God had another idea. "I will create a Devil," He thought. "He will be almost equal to Me in abilities. However, as I am all goodness, I will invest him with all wickedness; thereafter, the angels will have a choice of adoring him or Me."

God then permitted the angels to have free will and an independent intellect. But, as to their intellect, of necessity, He had to limit their cognitive powers. If they had perfect intellects, then no way would they choose following Lucifer over remaining steadfast with God. Had they deduced in advance that Heaven was infinitely superior to Hell; and had they reasoned that they could never succeed in their rebellion; then assuredly, they would have remained loyal to God without end. This would have foiled God's master plan. No, God would have to impair their wisdom, or else His initiative would fail its objective. We all know the result of God's plotting.

Lucifer, divinely duped into believing he could contend successfully with God for the fealty of his fellow angels, led the uprising designed to dethrone God. He failed because God hadn't given him sufficient capabilities to win the rebellion. Afterward, God created Hell and cast the mutineer angels into its torments because they had bumbled into a snare God Himself had set for them.

Once more God looked around and was discontented. Admittedly, the loyal angels loved Him. But why wouldn't they? They knew for a certainty now that God was all-powerful. They knew beyond a doubt what another rebellion would bring. So, God conceived another plan. "I will create human beings," He beamed with anticipation. "And I will make them even less intelligent than the angels. I won't allow them to view Me. I will permit the Devil to tempt them incessantly. He will have the craftiness and the determination to constantly confuse mankind. I will endow My creatures with a nature that is weak, and I will imbue mankind with near irresistible yearnings (particularly sexual passions) that will aid the Devil in his skullduggery.

"I will afflict them with sickness and death. I will bestow great favor upon some of My creation, regardless of how undeserving. I will saddle others with heartrending misfortune their entire lives, despite their personal worthiness! However, I will first create a Garden in Eden and forbid Adam, the father of all humans, to eat from the most desirable tree … the one in the center of the Garden. The Devil will be dispatched to practice his wiles on Adam. And, to aid the Devil, I will create a woman who will be the immediate cause of Adam's downfall. Man, with his irrepressible urge to possess woman (implanted by Me!), will be easily seduced into sin.

"Once I beguile Adam into disobeying Me, I will then severely burden him and his offspring with adversity. [Cf. Gen. 3:16-19] This is the only way, despite My omniscience, that I will ever know if I am truly exalted for what I am, and not just because I am God and I created humanity expressly to have many of them worship Me. Then, to doubly ensure that mankind venerates Me through personal volition, I will saturate the Earth with evidence that refutes My personal existence. Also, I will plant sham evidences that seem to validate evolution, while invalidating creationism. To be fair, I will endow a few individuals with intuitions of My Divinity. I will inspire those to write about Me. They will call this composition 'the Bible.' The Bible will tell of Me in such a dubious manner that all those with intelligence of a median level will be enticed to question the veracity of my book. The inquisitive will doubt My existence and I will thereafter consign all those doubting cynics to Hell, confining their human body ceaselessly in tormenting fire along with those already damned rebellious angels.

[Continuing My plan] I will split Myself into two persons. No! 'Make that three persons. I will have mankind picture Me first as a peevish, vengeful, unpredictable Sky Deity. Then I will have My second self impregnated into one of the females of the human species. He will grow into manhood, and when He is around thirty-something, I will induce my chosen people, the Jews, to cause Him (Me, that is) to be crucified. This will atone for the trick I played on Adam. In the meantime, My third self will appear on Earth as a dove (or water, fire, wind, oil, rain, a voice, a seal, or even as cloven tongues) to mysteriously infuse people with ephemeral hints of My existence. Of course, I first will have to be certain that none of My falcons are circling above, I wouldn't want one to make a meal of Me while I was in the physical form of a dove.

"After the Romans kill Me (My 2nd Persona) at the insistence of the Jews, I will switch My allegiance to the Gentiles, especially the ones in the Roman Empire. Lastly, I will permit so much confusion to surround the belief in Me that not just one Christian faith will worship Me, but thousands of different individuals will read my book, interpret it to their own designs, and splinter off into endless groupings of 'Christians.' I will permit these factions to denounce, defame and make war among each other over Me; thereby have them appear ludicrous to the more intelligent of the humans I create. By so doing, no one will ever be entirely certain if I am real, or just a sanctimonious delusion fashioned in the minds of vainglorious men. To those who reject the misleading clues that I have permeated the Earth with, I will grant eternal life in Heaven. To those who fall prey to My deceptions by accepting all the planted delusive evidences of My non-existence, I will lock them into the fiery Hell with Lucifer for all eternity!"

The foregoing is a grandiose fairy tale. It is stark nonsense. Not a word of it should be believed. Yet, essentially, this is what Christian theologians (and their propagandists, the religionists) ask us to accept as 'gospel truth.' Not that a religionist would phrase his pre & post Messiah era suppositions as I have. Theologians encrypt their tenets in sanctimonious verbiage. They thereafter express those mystified tenets in pious homilies that suggest the most virtuous rationale for their promulgation.

Today's advertising copywriters do exactly the same thing. They choose positive words with favorable connotation that generate pleasing mental images. 'This is effective! All too many persons are influenced by the implications, or implied qualities, of the names of products and services. The reality is, however, that if a product or service is truly that much better than its competitor, it won't need to be advertised. After a favorable trial, word-of-mouth will cause its purchase to eventually become universal. Religionists exploit the frailty humans have of being swayed by the connotation of words, often ignoring the contrary factual evidence, to inculcate religiosity through sanctimonious speech and pious posturing.

Notwithstanding their efforts, reverent rhetoric can never transform fables into fact for the intellectually cognizant.

As stated previously, the same rules that demand evidence that supports the assertions of consumer products should be applied to religious assertions. For instance: 'God loves you!' How do you know God loves you? Your reply: "Because He made me." But didn't He also make the viruses, bacteria, and other microbes that attack you, that sicken you, and even kill you? Didn't He create the crotchety old neighbors who cursed you and chased you as a child? Didn't He also make the bully who used to intimidate and strike you every day in school? Didn't He create all the people who have hated and despised you throughout your life? For example, people whom you never have harmed; yet, who persisted and delighted in causing you misery. He can't love them, if He truly loves you. Was Hitler, at his worst, loved by God?

Mindful of all of the above, the Christian teaching insists that God loves everyone equally and always. If so, God isn't very discriminating with His affections. In candor, there is no virtue in loving everyone all the time. God should hate someone. [Cf. Deut. 32:39-43 or Amos 9:1-4] If not, His love is cheapened by its commonness and its unwarranted, indiscriminate universality.

If God's affection is so all-embracing, why doesn't He love Satan? We postulate endless love from God until His forgiveness ends with our death. God will only love and forgive you while you are alive. His solicitude is only available while you live. But where is the proof? There hasn't been any empirical evidence provided since the Apostles passed away. Unlike 'Doubting Thomas,' we must take the word of another human being that God loves us. All who accept the word of another as a foundation for their beliefs should refrain from attending a meeting of U.F.O. enthusiasts. There are thousands of them! Some have seen aliens, and some have even been abducted by aliens. Ask any of the abductees about extraterrestrials and they will tell you sincerely, emphatically, and persistently "I believe!" With that, some parting words to all believers in the witness of another human being: *"For false Messiahs and false prophets will appear in order to deceive even God's chosen people.... Be on your guard!"* [Mk. 13: 22-23 excerpted]

THE ATTRIBUTES OF LUCIFER

You are aware, and I am aware, that God knows every language in the world. This includes even an invented language such as Esperanto, or the local patois of a small, isolated community. But, have you ever stopped to consider that the Devil, Lucifer, Satan, Beelzebub, or whomever it is that commands the legions of the spiritual Underworld, has that same ability? The Devil also knows all languages, and reads all thoughts, just as God can. Both are creative. God created the Universe, while the Devil creates delusion and folly.

Lucifer is similarly an intriguing entity. He, too, can change himself into a human being (always a male?), but when he takes human form it inevitably is to deceive man, and never to assist him. [Cf. Job Chap. 1 & Chap. 2] When evil man is assigned his earned niche in eternal damnation, he can be assured of at least one companion, viz., the Devil; who god-like is everlasting and eternal.

Now to make my point I am going to ask these questions: "Does Lucifer possess unique powers? How did the Devil (Lucifer), obtain such powers? Can all the Fallen Angels perform the same deceptions that Lucifer can? Are all angels, good or bad, infused with paranormal capabilities almost equal to the powers of God?"

Lucifer, in our religious mythology, is a proficient opponent of God. But where did he obtain his almost limitless abilities? From God, of course! No other source has the omnipotence to bestow such powers. God created a being who is an imperishable rival to Himself. In retrospect, one must ask oneself what faculties God has denied to Lucifer. After thoughtful reflection, you will inevitably discover that Lucifer has every evil ability imaginable. This, dear reader, is the resolution to all the questions framed around Lucifer. He has all the powers we can imagine; not because God granted those powers to him, but simply because we imagine he has them!

His capabilities derive from the same source as does God's powers; by identity, human imagination! Lucifer has every evil power we can conceive simply because we concede him those powers. But, can this be proven? I think so. We are taught that we shouldn't tempt God, nor put Him to any test, for this is a sin. Moreover, you will find that if you do put God to a test, He will fail that test every time. Yet, if Lucifer is the antithesis of the Godhead, then he should be opposite in every way. Applying this same one-dimensional rationale, Lucifer should pass every test. Let us then pray to Lucifer for some evil manifestation. Perhaps, we should seek a personal appearance from him. After all, since His Resurrection, Jesus has appeared publically many times; more so has His Mother, Mary. Why shouldn't we witness a materialization of Lucifer?

The idea of praying to Lucifer may seem grotesque, or even frightening to a devout Christian, or any other believer in the spiritual or the mystical. Still historically, in occult records, many attempts have been made to do just this. That being: To communicate with the personification of Wickedness! To my knowledge, the effort has met with the same success as attempts to commune with the Personification of Holiness; that being, no success whatsoever! We are as impotent at calling up Satan as we are at calling down God. It seems that Satan is as elusive as are all other phantasms of the spirit world. Our imaginations can produce visions, but they can't produce one solid iota of matter, including spirit matter. Satan, too, is securely locked within the psychological boundaries of our human brain.

Long ago mankind invented "gods" to account for all good fortune. It didn't take much more time to imagine "demons" that were answerable for all misfortune. This mirrored image notion of good and evil covers the extremes of the human experience. But isn't there a middle ground? Whose actions determine the mundane events that dominate the average existence? Wouldn't it beat all irony if there chanced to be a spiritual entity superior to both God and Satan? This Ultimate Deity would be accountable for all nondescript occurrences. (Forgive the masculine bias, but …) 'He' would be honored as the Divine Patron of Mediocrity. Thus, every single act in the drama of life could be perceived as the choreography of one of three Deities. This 'Trinity' would be far less inscrutable than the one we now accept!

Did a given occurrence benefit me? Then God, the Father, caused it! Did that occurrence harm me? If so, then the Devil, Lucifer, caused it! Was the occurrence wholly pointless or insignificant? Then the Ultimate Deity, Mediocrity, caused it to befall me!

So, all eventualities are accounted for as the deliberative action(s) of one, two, or three deities secreted in the inscrutable climes of the unfathomable heavens.

SATAN ISN'T ALL-POWERFUL

Is Satan literally the originator of all sin? I doubt it! The evidence fails to corroborate this pervasive religious doctrine. Someone lies, and we alibi that he has succumbed to the wiles of the Devil. A woman commits adultery and the priest or minister admonishes her for permitting the Devil to commandeer her body. A normally placid husband has a poor night bowling, comes home to his wife in a stifled rage and proceeds to wreck the kitchen. Again, the "Evil One" reaps the blame for this ill-tempered behavior.

Superficially the supposition would seem to have substance. A closer look dispels the notion. Is there anyone who is an incorrigible sinner? Is there any identifiable person who epitomizes sinful man? Does any human being exist who has so given himself over to villainy that he is irreversibly denied redemption? No, without stipulation! Still, I ask why not? There are many persons who are undisguised (professed) atheists. This action violates God's first commandment, which, according to conventional Christian reckoning, should lay oneself open to complete domination (subservience) by Satan. Yet, it doesn't!

Catholics teach that attendance at Mass, and keeping the commandments earns a believer specific rations of sanctifying grace. Sanctifying grace is a mystifying spiritual infusion from God that assists the recipient in resisting future temptations. Protestants don't teach of sanctifying grace, but they hold a similar belief that by your acceptance of Jesus as your personal Savior, you are saved from sin permanently. Proclaiming Jesus to be "Lord" protects you from Satan. The formal theologies of Protestants may be different from Catholics, but the result of their disparate beliefs is the same, 'believe in the Lord, and Satan is defeated!'

This aphorism is truly ego-inflating, yet it is nothing but the risible rhetoric of religion. We neither succumb to temptation, nor can we overcome it. What we do is pamper our individual whims, or we don't! No external force is powering our actions. Any honest evaluator can see this if he will only examine his actions without preconception. It is impossible for one person to know what transpires in the mind of another person. In this sense, no one can say for certain if a demon has or hasn't tempted anyone other than himself. Still, we aren't entirely clueless in this consideration of the origins of temptation.

We can all note that no matter how depraved someone may be generally, specifically, he will have some laudable qualities. Facetiously, we could point out that Hitler's dog loved him. So did Eva Braun. In sorry note, many otherwise decent persons admired him at one time. Hitler wasn't exclusively wicked. He neither smoked nor drank, and in later life he became a vegetarian. A thorough inquisitor must ask why. Why is the Devil successfully able to tempt a person to commit one type of sin, yet fail when tempting him to commit another type of sin?

Why do certain prostitutes accept money for one abominable sex act, yet steadfastly refuse to participate in some other equally ignominious sex act? Why is it that cold-blooded killers are sometimes the gentlest of parents? Some of the most worthless of idlers have become social activists promoting meritorious ecological prohibitions. There must be some cogent reason for these irrefutable paradoxes. I believe the answer to these relevant posers lies in personal preference. The Devil (Satan) doesn't have a thing to do with our indiscretions. We all do that which pleasures us most. And, because each of us is psychologically different, the sins we are prone to, and the sins we shun, are all matters of individual predilection. This is why we have swindlers who might return a lost wallet. They gain more pleasure out of cheating you than stealing from you. Your author has heard of trollops who regularly attend church services on Sundays.

The Devil has no input into these human idiosyncrasies. There is no such entity as a Devil. There is no such condition as temptation. Only personal motivation exists. Study animal behavior and you will soon learn that every living entity is, indeed, an individual. Pedigreed animals are very closely interbred to enhance some admirable or desirable canine trait. Yet, even long line pedigreed animals show marked variability in their degree of inheritance of specific attributes. So, too, is it with microbes who move, or are moved by reflex, rather than reasoning. Even these lowly creatures are individuals. Individuality is the prime cause of differences in behavior: mostly to the detriment of the species (extinction); occasionally to the benefit of the species (evolution).

We are all different. Our foibles are as diverse as are our faces. This is another proof of the postulate of evolution. That is why and how the life forms on this planet diversified. That is also why most species have become extinct. In the broadest of scope: Plants evolved first that subsisted on inert chemicals. Then animal life evolved that subsisted on plant life. Finally predatory animal life evolved that thrived on other animal life. 'Not to gloss over plant/animal symbiosis that is an integral factor in the natural scheme of all life! This, and other bio-interactions, aren't specifically germane here. The sustenance of most life forms is the ingesting of other life forms. Factually, the preponderance of life forms are predatory on other life forms.

This is how life is, and was, and will be! You can be assured that no instantaneous multifaceted creation ever took place. The creation scenario recounted in Genesis 1 would have taken billions of years to have evolved naturally. Every scrap of evidence we have been able to discover reinforces the hypothesis of a protracted evolution for all biological life forms. There isn't a trace of physical proof indicating an instantaneous creation, not a scintilla!

There is absolutely no evidence of talking snakes either. Consequently, we have no proof of the existence of the Devil. The differences we exhibit in our proclivity to sin arise not from the intrusion of a demon, but from our natural inclinations that are the accumulation of millions of years of evolution! Once we forsake the puerile notion of satanic temptation, we can get on with the imperative need to codify morality so that we can arrive at a societal consensus of tolerable human behavior based upon intelligence, not upon emotion or scriptural directive.

The need for reasonable justice in the affairs of mankind far outweighs our propensity to seek spiritual solace from the vagaries of life. The best possible solution to the vexations mortal man faces is the intrusion of a Divine Rectifier in Heaven. This isn't to affirm that such an entity exists. It merely observes that such would be the simplest solution to the natural and social tribulations we humans face. The second best solution is to have an actual Fairy Godmother. The third best is that one might find a ring that grants a single wish to its owner. My wish would be for a ring that granted all my wishes!

You can discern that once you give free rein to your imagination, anything does become possible! Invoking the "possible": Why isn't it possible for Lucifer to recognize the error (and futility!) of his ways and to ask

God for forgiveness? If this could happen, God could close and secure Hell, and we would all be redeemed. We could all enjoy eternal bliss in the magnificent majesty of the Resplendent Presence, i. e., the Beatific Vision. So let us all begin petitioning immediately for the repentance and repatriation of the former Archangel, Lucifer. The last happy chapter in the saga of mankind could be written into the historical annals of the Universe once the Devil forsakes his rebellion. All together now, let us pray aloud, "Repent Satan!" "Repent Satan!" "Repent Satan!"

If you have lost the point of this present segment because of my waggish rambling, it is this: Religiosity is a simplex solution to the bafflement of the Universe. A Personal God is a juvenile reply to the question of all existence. Every question that begins with a 'why', can be answered simply, 'because that's the way God ordered it.' All inquiry is thus rendered superfluous. "Glory be to God in the highest: Amen." Thereafter, the brain of religious man closes on the only exalting attribute mankind possesses: an inquisitive mind probing to discern universal truth through acquired knowledge.

Satan's corpse can be placed in the same coffin as the dead Divinity (God!). We must bury the memory of both, disregard all literature that glorifies superstition, and we then should forge ahead with explorations that lead toward true enlightenment. Never again look back to the Bible or any other artifact from our ignorant past. Force your eyes to look forward continually. True knowledge is always accumulated; it is never supernaturally infused!

CHAPTER 13
A Mélange

MANUSCRIPTS OF THE NEW TESTAMENT

Few adherents of the supremacy of the Bible as the foundation of authority in matters pertaining to Christian doctrine and belief are aware of just what a muddled mess the Bible is in actuality. The New Testament is just as muddled as is the Old Testament, but for my present purposes I will restrict examination here to the Four Gospels exclusively.

To begin, none of the original documents exist, only fragments of early copies. How early? No one is certain! {AD 150?} Yet, as far back as can be traced, no single copy stands out as authentic. That is, even the earliest copies have rivals that vary textually from one another. How much they differ, I can't define authoritatively. But the fact that variations occur arouses my suspicions that the original texts (if original texts ever existed as such!) have been altered to reflect the beliefs of individual copyists, almost from the outset.

St. Jerome noted that there were almost as many variations of the Gospels as there were copies, and there were versions in languages that he wasn't even aware existed. Everywhere, the Gospels required frequent recopying by hand, if only to accommodate the growing numbers of Christians. Studied copies of the Scriptures wore out through continuous use. In the point of an odd fact, it is fortuitous to my contention that so numerous are the number known, for their variety evidences their falsity!

One such diverse document was known as the <u>Diatessaron</u>. The word "diatessaron" originated as a Greek musical term meaning: *harmony of four parts*. That is generally what the <u>Diatessaron</u> was, an attempted harmony of the four Gospels. An Assyrian Christian named Tatian (later condemned as a heresiarch) compiled it before AD 170, and his efforts were well received for more than two hundred and fifty years. Had his harmony remained unchallenged, many of the objections to the veracity of the four Evangelists would not have come to light. Tatian, who became an Encratite (eschewed animal food, wine and matrimony), injected his own partialities into his compilation. An example: According to the Diatessaron, John the Baptist ate only milk and honey; not locusts and honey. Encratites forbade eating locusts.

This is the very essence of biased editing that must have occurred in many other places throughout the Gospels. Still, lacking the original manuscripts, how will we ever know the extent of the tampering? Religionists are becoming increasingly sensitive, even apprehensive, at the burgeoning knowledge of the extent of the divergence in the translations of the "approved," "official," "authentic," "infallible," "original," or whatever other appellation these ego-tarnished translators christen their work with. Below is another example of precisely the brash arrogance that attended some translations.

An editorial testimonial found on page forty-two of <u>An Introduction to the Revised Standard Version of the New Testament</u> by F. C. Grant states:

"It will be obvious to the careful reader that still in 1946, as in 1881 and 1901, no doctrine of the Christian Faith has been affected by the revision {RSV} for the simple reason that, out of the thousands of variant readings in the manuscripts, none has turned up thus far that requires a revision of Christian doctrine."

How can the man make such a misleading statement? By Mr. Grant's own counting "thousands of variant readings" existed. Of course, no doctrinal revisions were required! The revisers wouldn't permit it! They would simply manipulate the interpretation of the variant texts so that they didn't contradict established doctrine. They would contend with potentially dissenting passages in the manner that politicians do when they are caught accepting money or favors from lobbyists, that is, they finesse the truth until it seems to exonerate them. Whenever a variant text was encountered, the editors merely reworked the passage until it no longer conflicted with current beliefs. {This author's assumption}

Here is a familiar quotation that will make this point. In Luke's Gospel, just before He dies, Jesus speaks to the 'good' thief, *"Verily I say unto thee, today thou shall be with me in paradise."* [Lu. 23:43] Christian doctrine teaches that immediately after Jesus died, He descended into Hell [Cf. Acts 2:24, 27] and remained there until the resurrection; He rose into Heaven sometime after Easter Sunday. Now a skeptic might assert, 'If Jesus was in Hell on Good Friday, then He broke His promise to be with the good thief in Paradise on that day ("today!").' But any translator, of modest accomplishment, could just as easily render the self-same passage as: *"Verily I say unto thee today, thou shall be with me in paradise."* Therefore, Jesus is making the promise today, *"I say unto thee today"* [v. 43], but the fulfillment of the promise can come later. My effective day modification of this verse required only the re-positioning of a comma.

Saint Jerome, when he was commissioned to research and rewrite the Gospels from their earliest sources, well realized the perils and pitfalls of attempting to standardize the extant Latin Gospels. Everyone possessed of a New Testament had their pet verses, or their favored interpretation of a section of the Gospels. Accordingly, Jerome proceeded cautiously & discerningly with his task. A true believer would have to presume that the Holy Spirit guided Jerome in his work. The evidence, some of it supplied by Jerome himself, is arrayed against this presumption. But, because this conjectured assistance from the Holy Spirit is an article of faith, all contrary indications should be overlooked. Why diminish a grand story by pointing out its logical flaws?

If anyone harbor doubts that the Holy Spirit aided Jerome in his re-translations, let the pronouncement of the Council of Trent dispel those doubts. The Council decreed, *"The same holy synod, considering that no small advantage may accrue to the Church of God, if out of all the Latin versions of the sacred books in circulation it make known which is to be held as authoritative, determines and declares that this same ancient and vulgate version which is approved by the long use of so many centuries in the Church herself, be held as authoritative in public lectures, disputations, sermons and expository discourses, and that no one may make bold or presume to reject it on any pretext."*

The Church, thence, put her official stamp of authentication on Jerome's Vulgate translation; this, despite the well-publicized fact that Jerome's original work has disappeared, and notwithstanding the manifest knowledge that later copyists reintroduced renderings of verses that Jerome had purged from his personal translation. So, in 1546, the Vulgate became the official Roman Catholic translation of the Bible, and remained so until the year 1943. But, during the intervening years, a damaging eventuality befell Jerome's Bible on its way to everlasting infallibility. The Protestant Reformation occurred and generated a renewed impetus to find the original letters (and meanings) of the New Testament Scriptures. 'Not out of pious inquiry, but for the practical consideration that the Protestants were searching for texts to refute the authority of the Roman Church, and hopefully to find texts to legitimize their schism.

None were found supporting either goal; consequently, Protestants had to settle for the less compelling argument that possession of the Scriptures alone conferred legitimacy. Moreover, Protestant scholars didn't sit back and wait for ancient discoveries; they actively searched for them. Gradually the breadth and depth of the inconsistencies of the Biblical manuscripts became known. The European community must have been shocked to learn that they weren't the sole heirs to God's inspired words. Versions of the Bible were found throughout the Near East. They were found in many languages and these could trace their roots back not to the Latin translations, but to the Greek, and perhaps even to Aramaic originals.

Admittedly, what they found wasn't a single, authoritative version of the Gospels. The Gospels of the Near East were as corrupted (conflicted?) as were the Latin Gospels. Still, this gave scholars the hope that now they might deduce the original meaning of many obscure passages through critical comparisons; that they might resolve the obvious contradictions found in the four Gospels; that they soon might be able to excise material that had been blatantly inserted by revisionist copyists. The hopes of those pious biblical scholars have never been realized, but the task of textual criticism continues. To my mind, all that can ever be accomplished, barring some unanticipated eventuality, is a consensus of agreement, not reconstruction of the original texts.

All that has resulted thus far is to dull the aura surrounding Jerome's work, for his translation has proved to be as variant as any other Latin translation. Jerome knew this himself. Yet, in the face of the certain knowledge that Jerome's work was later tainted through questionable re-translation and willful forgery, the Council decreed: *'Let no one be so bold as to presume to reject Jerome's translation under any pretext.'* {Paraphrased}

The above decree remained in force for the next four hundred years; that is, until a reigning Pontiff of the Roman Catholic Church presumed to be just that bold. In his encyclical, <u>Divino Afflante Spiritu</u>, dated 30 September 1943, Pope Pius XII retreated as far as he prudently was able from the extreme position of the Council of Trent. Pope Pius wrote: "This authority of the Vulgate in matters of doctrine by no means forbids; nay, today it almost demands; the proving and confirmation of this same doctrine from the original texts as well, and the calling into aid everywhere of the same texts, that by their means the right significance of the sacred writings may throughout be more clearly brought out and explained." {Author's version}

In effect, what the Pope said was this: 'Jerome must prove his version of the Bible is correct.' Whereas, what the Council of Trent said was: 'No one can reject Jerome's translation on any pretext.' The Pope's Encyclical is carefully worded (hedged) to avoid the appearance of contradicting the Council's decree. But, in actual fact, it does just that! Allow me to bring to your notice the most significant phrase in the encyclical: "today it almost demands." In the year of 1943, the Ecclesiastic mandamus of 1546 is reduced to merely a provisional endorsement.

Don't fault Pope Pius, and don't fault the Council of Trent. They both acted in the best interests of their Church, as they determined those interests! Yet both did grave harm to the proposition that the Holy Spirit doesn't permit the Pope to err in his official enactments on matters of faith and doctrine. The history of Christianity proves undeniably that the Holy Spirit has been absent from the affairs of the Church since the first Christian Pentecost (conjectured to have occurred between the years AD 30-33). The inspiration of the Bible ended two thousand years ago (if it ever existed?), and God the Third has been remiss, and thereby negligent, ever after.

Not everyone would agree with me in this conclusion. One who surely would have denounced me was a high prelate who assumed the incongruous sounding style of Pope Sixtus the Fifth (r. 1585-1590). Recognizing the indefensibility of widely divergent readings of scriptures whose authorship was declared to be solely inspired by God, he undertook to recompose an updated Vulgate edition. You see, by AD 1585, there were all too many differing versions of Jerome's Vulgate translation circulating throughout Christendom. Once again there would be a commendable, yet frustrated, attempt to purify (standardize) the texts of the New Testament.

How much success attended the reigning Pontiff's efforts can be gleaned from Mr. F. F. Bruce, the author of <u>The Books and the Parchments</u>. He writes, "Sixtus showed a confidence in the authority and finality of his work unbefitting a scholar." Pope Sixtus claimed otherwise for he pronounced, "By the fullness of Apostolic power, we decree and declare that this edition, approved by the authority delivered to us by the Lord, is to be received and held as true, lawful, authoritative and unquestioned in all public and private discussion, reading, preaching and explanation."

The use of the editorial pronouns 'we' and 'us' might have had a deeper significance to Pope Sixtus than to his audience; perhaps he was alluding to the joint authorship of himself and the Holy Spirit. Undoubtedly that would render his translation "unquestioned." Was his decree "ex cathedra"? That is, was it made from the Chair of Peter, and was it a ruling of faith or morals? If it was, then the decree would have rested in the category of Papal infallibility, notwithstanding the fact that the doctrine of Papal infallibility hadn't yet been promulgated. If such an attribute truly resides in the Papacy, it has resided from Saint Peter's reign onward! (circa 30-33 A.D.)

Still, no one inspired Popes Gregory XIV and Clement VIII, successors to Pope Sixtus V, with such grandiose notions. They undertook to correct the three thousand "real textual variations" in Sixtus' edition. If the Holy Spirit does intervene in the affairs of the Church, then someone must rationalize this quoted fact from Mister Bruce's book: "But Pope Sixtus died a few months after the publication of his edition, and his enactments were never enforced."

THE GENEALOGY OF JESUS

Two of the Gospels, Matthew and Luke, provide us with a list of the male forbearers of Joseph, the foster father of Jesus. Rather, I should say these Gospels provide us with two separate lists of the male forbearers of Jesus through Joseph, for the lists are vastly dissimilar. [Cf. Mt. 1:1-16 & Lu. 3:23-38] Neither Gospel purports to delineate mother Mary's antecedents!

In the notes at the end of Luke's Gospel in the Catholic Family Edition of the Holy Bible, the editor states: "Both Evangelists give the genealogy of St. Joseph but according to different relationships." More truthful, this editor should have admitted he couldn't explain why the Gospels contain conflicting genealogies. The Hebrew custom was to trace one's lineage back through the male antecedents. Unless it is possible to have two fathers in every generation, all ancestor lists plotted on the male parent alone should be identical, as each of us has only one father! Also, Matthew omits three generations of Hebrew kings (disputing divine inspiration?) between Joram and Uzziah. {Ahaziah-Joash-Amaziah} [Cf. 2 Chr. 25:25-26 & 26:1]

The lists in Matthew and Luke aren't even the same length. Matthew names twenty-seven generations from David to Joseph (thirty, if the inadvertent {?} 'three King' omissions are respectively slotted), while Luke names forty-two male progenitors.

MATTHEW 1:1-17	LUKE 3:23-38	LUKE (cont.)
(1) David	David	-
Solomon*	Nathan	Semei
Rehoboam*	Mattatha	Mattathias
Abijah*	Menna	Maath
Asa*	Melea	Naggai
Jehosaphat*	Eliakim	Esli
Joram*	Jonam	Nahum
Uzziah*	Joseph	Amos
Jotham*	Judah	Mattathias
Ahaz*	Simeon	Joseph
Hezekiah*	Levi	Jannai
Manasseh*	Matthat	Melchi
Amon*	Jorim	Levi
Josiah**	Eliezer	Matthat
Jechoniah	Joshua	Heli
Shealtiel	Er	(42) Joseph
Zerubbabel	Elmadam	-
Abiud	Cosam	-
Eliakim	Addi	-
Azor	Melchi	-
Zadok	Neri	-
Achim	Shealtiel	-
Eliud	Zerubbabel	-
Eleazar	Rhesa	-
Matthan	Joanan	-
Jacob	Joda	-
(27) Joseph	Jasech	-

* = Kings of Judah

** = Last King before Babylonian captivity

The only possible solution to this discrepancy is for one or the other list to be a fabrication. What is patently more probable is that both are fanciful inventions of over-fertile imaginations. What would you calculate the odds to be against any one family maintaining accurate records of all male children descended down from David through twenty-seven (thirty?) generations? How about forty-two generations? Keep in mind that no one knew beforehand exactly which male sibling in each generation would be the descendant leading to Jesus.

The first divergence between the lists comes in the first generation after David. Luke informs us that Jesus was descended from David's son Nathan, while Matthew writes that Jesus descended from son Solomon. You remember Solomon: the man with seven hundred wives and three hundred concubines! He, alone, is a genealogist's fright.

There is another problem intrinsic to both lists which is occasioned by human nature, and it is this: Although most of us can be reasonably assured of who mothered us: not all of us can be just as certain who our father was! Human nature and the frailties of the flesh combine to create this ubiquitous veil of uncertain paternity.

If we had no knowledge of any of the ancestors of Jesus, we could dismiss the last objection foregoing all doubt. But knowing of them through the Bible forbids this instant dismissal. All too many of the female ancestors of Jesus were all too venal to have been regarded as near saints. They were human beings in the fullest connotation of that term. We could presume (and I am certain you thought of this also) that God inspired all of the female antecedents of Jesus to remain ever faithful to their spouses: Bathsheba included! But when we presume this, we must likewise presume He inspired the two Evangelists to accurately record those ancestors. Yet, we know that in at least one instance, God's inspiration failed. (The lists are different, and Matthew omitted three generations of Hebrew kings.)

If, as Christian apologists aver, the lists proceed through different relationships, why didn't the Evangelists tell us this? Why present two markedly conflicting lists without resolving the conflict? Didn't Matthew know what Luke had written? Or Luke, hadn't he ever read or talked to Matthew? The obvious and inescapable response is twice "No"!

What relationship might the variant lists have traced: friends-in-law? (The previous sentence was written facetiously.) Luke writes that

Joseph's father was named 'Heli.' Matthew provides the name 'Jacob' as Joseph's father. Why didn't the Evangelists simply ask James, the brother of Jesus? [Cf. Ga. 1:19] Surely he knew his grandfather's name, if anyone did! Barring some miracle of dual paternity, one of the Evangelists must be wrong. If one is wrong, who can state with certainty that the other isn't also mistaken? Either way, the unproved avowal of infallibility for the Bible receives yet another setback. Inspiration didn't write the Bible, imagination did!

Finally, it must be asked: Is there something to be learned from the enigma of two genealogical lists that are so disparate? If intellect prevails, there are two conclusions that should be drawn *apropos* the lists. An initial premise must be that the author of Matthew, and the author of Luke, weren't in collusion with one another when they compiled their respective lists. Neither were they singularly or jointly in communication with God. Each Evangelist wrote separately, even though both authors borrowed heavily from Mark for other "Jesus" events. (Mark's Gospel contains no genealogical list)

Where, then, did the lists originate? If we discount the presumption that both lists are total fictions, and we agree that both lists can't be factual, then the question of their origin becomes imperative. Who enunciated the litany of the ancestors of Jesus for the two Evangelists? It is conceivable that Matthew, being a Jew, had access to the genealogy of the kings of Israel. Luke, born a Gentile, would have needed assistance from a scripturally knowledgeable Jew.

Here let us interpose a second proposition. Inasmuch as at least one of the lists must be fictitious, why not consider that the ancestor lists are later additions to the basic witness of the original author(s). This could explain the dissimilarity. Perhaps the lists were appended to the first and third Gospels long after their initial composition. The problem with this theory is that, then, it would seem they should be in substantial agreement. This is refuted by their perusal. No, this proposition, viz., that the lists were added after the Gospels had been recognized as sacred, creates more objections than it satisfies.

Much more cogent is the inference that the lists were composed independently before "Luke" knew of "Matthew" and vice versa. This argues for an early date of composition. The disparity in the lists, however, indicates that they were composed after the brethren of Jesus were no longer available for consultation. This also could indicate they were composed outside of Jerusalem, after its destruction. The dating of the lists (likewise, of the entirety of the Gospels) is a vexing nettle. This composition never intended to resolve the N. T. dating issue.

The only solution I can offer (and I do so timorously) is that Jesus was the type of person about whom heroic and wondrous tales are fabricated. In the Old Testament many of the epic heroes have genealogical lists of their forbearers provided. Any scripturally knowledgeable Jew who wished to authenticate the Davidic ancestry {i.e., Messiahship} of Jesus would have been moved to create a similar ancestor list for Him. In the New Testament we have had two such motivated individuals. The lists may even be authentic genealogies; just not the genealogy of Jesus! My intuition suggests to me that both lists were lifted from a non-scriptural source that the authors felt confident would never be compromised. (They haven't!) Perhaps they were contained in some obscure apocryphal Old Testament manuscript(s) similar to Chronicles. We will never know, unless by some fortuitous circumstance the ancient manuscript(s) is/are recovered.

In concluding this segment, allow me to point out that Matthew's list contains, in their proper chronology order, the names of most of the Kings (three are not) that succeeded David. This stratagem, although highly unlikely, renders the 'Messiahship of Jesus' postulation incontrovertible. Jesus was not only descended from King David, but through all the 'right' descendants of David as well. Incontestably, Jesus was born to the role Matthew ascribed to Him. Jesus was no usurper. He was a true and legitimate scion of the lineage of David.

By the time Jesus was born, a sizable portion of the population of Judea, Galilee and even Samaria could claim some Davidic blood. Luke wasn't aware of this; Matthew would have been. Matthew, by including the Kings of Judah in his genealogy, strengthened the cause for the Messiahship of Jesus to a fortress beyond rebut. Paul, in his Epistle to Titus, offers the best resolution to the disparity between the ancestor lists. Paul advises: *"But avoid stupid arguments, long lists of ancestors' names ...."* [Tit. 3:9 & Cf. 1 Tim. 1:4] Let us all heed Paul's prudent counsel.

MATTHEW IDENTIFIES THE MESSIAH

You will recall earlier, my hypothesis of how Jesus became deified almost accidentally by the Gentile converts to the new faith. Re-read Matthew's Gospel now and you will recognize that Matthew's central theme isn't the Godhood of Jesus, it is His Messiahship.

Throughout, Matthew sets himself the task of proving Jesus to be the long-awaited Messiah. The Messiah was to be the final and everlasting King of Israel. Meaning: His reign on Earth would be endless. There never was an imperative for the Messiah to be a divine person. That interpretation originated with the Evangelists, chiefly John. Pre-Christian exegetes interpreted the Hebrew Scriptures as heralding an "anointed" one. To anoint someone was to invest that person with authority to rule or minister over the Hebrew people. Surely Jesus, as God the Second, needed no one to convey authority to Him. Hailing Jesus as the awaited Messiah, concurrently (should have) precluded Him from the Godhead, i. e., divinity!

How, then, did Jesus come to be deified? 'Rather circumspectly. Matthew, in his zeal to identify Jesus as the Messiah, culled Isaiah's ancient verse of a virgin giving birth from the Old Testament and appended this prediction to his version of the Nativity. [Cf. Isa. 7:14 & Mt. 1:23] How was it possible for a virgin to give birth? The people of those times were lacking in some fields of knowledge, but they surely knew how human babies were conceived. If Mary couldn't have a human (male) consort, then Matthew would provide a spiritual consort for her. Mary became pregnant through the Spirit of God. Note that God didn't impregnate her personally for that would have been lewd. His Spirit came upon her. [Cf. Lu. 1:35]

Now we can see, Matthew wasn't proclaiming Jesus as "God" in the Nativity. He was showing how it became possible for a Virgin to give birth to a human baby without the participation of a human father. God willed it, and it happened! On a technicality, Jesus could be considered to be the 'Son of God.' He was still merely a human being. More unerringly, Jesus was the unfathered son of a virgin. The distinction was clear to Matthew's immediate audience who had been taught the doctrine of one God, and who believed in divine miracles. Later, when former polytheists became the sole heirs to Matthew's Gospel, this distinction was lost. They pictured

God, not as a passive conjurer of Mary's impregnation, but as an active participant in that miraculous biological event.

There is a repellent lesson to be learned from the Messiahship of Jesus coupled with His association in the Godhead. It is this: The Old Testament scholars and Rabbis never predicted God would come to Earth as a human being. Instead, they were awaiting a man who would bridge the chasm between mortals and God caused by Adam's sin; accordingly, if Jesus is truly God, then all the Old Testament scholars and rabbis were mistaken. To a person: the ancient holy men had all misinterpreted the Old Testament scriptures before the advent of Jesus!

Inverting that argument: If Jesus isn't factually a member of the Godhood, then we of the New Testament have misinterpreted the Scriptures. Somehow, the Bible loses much of its legitimacy when it is known that bogus dogmas can arise so readily from its pages and persist for more than twenty centuries. The ambiguity of the Bible, manifest by the many divergent philosophies spawned from its pages, is all the proof anyone should need of the Bible's exclusively human origins.

Returning to Matthew's Gospel, consider this: No sooner does Matthew announce the divine conception of Jesus, than he introduces the Magi who inquire, *"Where is he that is born king of the Jews?"* [Mt. 2:2] They never ask "Where is God Incarnate?" They discernibly never suspect a Trinity of Gods. The Magi obviously were acquainted with the Hebrew messianic prophesies. Yet, they sought out a human being (a babe?), not a God. It is also highly probable that the Wise Men were expecting a grown man. To wit, the messianic passages we know of today all referred to an adult, not to an infant! (A virgin mother being the lone exception)

How the Magi knew enough to look for a newborn baby is never divulged in the Bible. The Magi were well informed about the Jewish Messiah, more so than all of the contemporary Jewish exegetes. The one thing they didn't know was precisely where to find baby Jesus. The star led them to Jerusalem, not to Bethlehem. Once there, Herod learned of their presence and their mission. Herod was informed by the Jewish chief priests and scribes that the birth city of the Messiah would be Bethlehem. It is curious that the Jewish chief priests knew the expected birth location of the Messiah, yet failed to recognize the astral harbinger in the night sky heralding His actual birth. [Cf. Mt. 2:9-10]

Notwithstanding this, the story proceeds. Herod summoned the Magi and sent them to Bethlehem to locate the Messiah so that, *"I, too,* {Herod} *may go and worship him."* [Mt. 2:8]

How odd it was that the Magi knew so many of the messianic prophecies, yet didn't know of this verse: *"And thou, Bethlehem, of the land of Judah, art by no means least among the princes of Judah; For from thee shall come forth a leader who shall rule my people Israel."* [Mt. 2:6 via Mi. 5:2]

The tale of the Magi is inconsistent, and the inconsistencies don't end after their departure. After the visit of the Magi, Matthew writes of the flight into Egypt to escape the 'Slaughter of the Innocents.' The sojourn into Egypt lasted an unspecified length of time before Joseph, in a dream, was informed by an angel that King Herod was dead. (Herod died in 4 BC) The Holy Family returned to Israel, but Joseph was warned, again in a dream, that they would be safer outside Judea for Archelaus (r. 4 BC – AD 6) had succeeded his father, King Herod, as Ethnarch of Judea, Idumea, and Samaria.

At this point, and not for the first time, Matthew flatly refutes Luke. In his dream, Joseph was given instructions to go up to the Province of Galilee to settle for the first time in Nazareth. [Cf. Mt. 2:22-23] Herod Antipas (r. 4 BC – AD 39), another son of King Herod, ruled over Galilee as Tetrarch. You will recall how Luke (confuting Matthew) wrote that both Mary and Joseph came down from Nazareth and traveled to Bethlehem only to comply with the Census requirement. [Cf. Lu. 2:1-4] Matthew (confuting Luke) knows nothing of a census, which is puzzling. Matthew, a tax collector, should have known more about census history than Luke, the Gentile physician.

The next recorded event in Matthew is the Baptism of Jesus. After He emerged from the water, the Holy Spirit, in the form of a dove, alighted on Jesus and a voice from Heaven spoke, *"This is my own dear Son, with whom I am well pleased."* [Lu. 3:22; Mk. 1:11 & Mt. 3:17] The very next sentence informs us that the Holy Spirit led Jesus into the desert to be tempted by the Devil. To what end was Jesus tempted? As with all other mortals, Jesus was tempted to sin. Is it possible for God to sin? No! How can God offend Himself? If God could sin, then to whom would He pray to for forgiveness? John the Evangelist (Apostle) does not record a desert sojourn.

Did Jesus lose His Godhood when He came to Earth? The Devil thought so. Jesus demonstrably thought so. Matthew positively thought so. Satan asked Jesus to worship him. Imagine that, Satan, who never accomplished anything of note asked the Creator of the Universe, the Supreme Intelligence, a Being who could have anything He wished simply by wishing it. 'Satan asked that person to worship him? What did the Devil offer as an inducement? He offered the Earth to Jesus. Didn't he know that Jesus already owned the Earth, and the stars, and the galaxies? The Devil, in this instance, was befuddled beyond excuse to have made such an illogical proposition to Jesus.

Jesus, for whatever reason, didn't tell Satan here that He was God. Instead, He fostered the mistaken notion that He wasn't God by deriding Satan's request with an innocuous retort. The gist of His reply was 'Only God should be worshiped.' [Cf. Mt. 4:10] Why didn't Jesus tell Satan that He was God in the Second Person? Why didn't He say here what He said on a different occasion in John's Gospel? (*"I and the Father are one."*) [Jn. 10:30] Jesus didn't say it because Matthew, who wrote the story, didn't know it. "Son of God," to Matthew, didn't indicate the precise literal meaning early Christians interpreted from that phrase. Matthew probably likened the birth of Jesus to a fetal developmental process known as parthenogenesis, i.e., development of an embryo from an unfertilized ovum. {'Disregarding the gender impediment}

Everything that follows in Matthew's Gospel is less puzzling after you grant the previous amendment. Hypothesizing that Jesus was only a man greatly favored by God obviates many of the difficulties raised by the teaching that He was God incarnate. If nothing else, it solves the enigma of Christ's dying words: *"My God, my God, why have you forsaken me?"* [Mt. 27:46 & Mk. 15:34] Much more is explained by that concession. Read again Verse Nine of the Sermon on the Mount: *"Blessed are the peacemakers; for they will be called the sons of God."* [Mt. 5:9] Jesus worked for peace among men. Was that Matthew's basis for styling Jesus the "Son of God"?

Matthew's theology also clashes with Paul's teachings about the Hebrew "Law" both in the Epistle to the Galatians 2:19 (q. v., and throughout Chapters 2, 3, 4, 5 & 6), and as reported by Luke in Acts 15:1-21, (q. v.). Paul told his Gentile converts to flout the "Law." Belief in Jesus Christ as the Redeeming Savior was the essence of Paul's theology. Matthew taught the reverse. *"Therefore, whoever breaks even the smallest of the commandments, and teaches others to do the same, will be least in the kingdom of Heaven."* [Mt. 5:19]

{A brief aside} Doesn't the above quote indicate a 'hierarchy' in Heaven? Those who "break the smallest of the commandments" … "will be least in the kingdom of Heaven," implies to me that some non-breakers of the Law will 'be the greatest' in Heaven. St. Paul taught others to break the Law (by ignoring it). Is Paul one of the "least" in Heaven? Is Paul even in Heaven?

Unless God made a mistake when He inspired these diametrically opposed theologies, one or two of these three contributors to the Bible (Matthew, Luke, or Paul) was falsely inspired. Even this statement is conditional. The statement hinges on the unverifiable premise that any portion of the Bible was inspired by God. The premise itself isn't verified by any unambiguous evidence. The overwhelming prevalence of evidence refutes the theory of divine inspiration. The theory of a Personal God rests alone on hope and faith, not on evidence!

We all hope that there is a personal God. Yet, our faith is nothing but pious repression of the physical proofs that dash that hope. Faith isn't a laudable trait when, or if, it blinds us to the reality of our cosmologically insignificant existence. Faith in our personal importance to the (imagined) Creator of the entire Universe implies a significance for our existence that wholly lacks even a sliver of authentication, excepting only the biblical declaration that God, the Creator of the Universe, 'knows' us individually. Paul writes in Galatians, *"But now that you have come to have knowledge of God, or more truly, God has knowledge of you…."* [Ga. 4:9]

The 'Calming of the Storm' offers another proof that Matthew didn't recognize Jesus as God, but rather, as a man who held great favor with God. Here is the scene: Jesus is asleep in the boat being operated by the Apostles when a fierce storm strikes over the Sea of Galilee. The Apostles are fearful of being drowned, but Jesus sleeps on. In desperation they awaken Jesus and entreat Him to *"Save us Lord … We are about to die."* Jesus chides them for their lack of faith, and then proceeds to calm the storm. The Apostles are amazed and exclaim, *"What kind of man is this? Even the winds and waves obey him."* [Mt. 8:23-27]

Stop here and reflect. Would you be amazed that the "Son of God" could calm a storm? No, for God that feat was nothing remarkable. But for a human being, even the Messiah, quelling the turbulent forces of nature was a prodigious accomplishment. It was amazing!

Matthew's version of the healing of the paralyzed man makes the same point. *"Jesus said to the paralyzed man, 'Get up, pick up your bed, and go home.' The man got up and went home. When the people saw it, they were afraid, and praised God for giving such authority as this to man."* [Mt. 9:6-8] Note that the people gave praise to God, not to Jesus! It was God who gave such authority to men. The man who received that authority was Jesus. Matthew would have us anoint Jesus as the Messiah; it was the first pagan converts who declared Jesus a God consubstantial with the Divine Creator of the Cosmos, i.e., "Son of God." Early pagan misinterpretation of a Hebrew idiom elevated Jesus from the Messiahship to the Godhood.

ANTI-DIVINITY TEXTS
FROM THE ACTS AND EPISTLES

[Acts 17:31] The scene describes Paul in Athens discoursing before the Areopagus. *"For he {God} has fixed a day in which he {God} will judge the whole world with justice, by means of a man {Jesus} he {God} has chosen. He {God} has given proof of this to everyone by raising that man {Jesus} from death!"* [Braces { } enclose this Author's insertions]

Paul's entire homily this day relates to God, yet he never mentions that Jesus is an integral part of a Trinity. In fact, nowhere in the Epistles can we read of a Trinity. If Paul thought Jesus to be (a) God, then this episode demands that he inform so explicitly. He doesn't! What he writes is that God raised the man, Jesus, from death. Just a few lines previous Paul reproves the Athenians for their counterfeit religious notions. His words: *"We should not suppose that God's nature is anything like an image of gold, or silver, or stone, shaped by the art and skill of man."* [Acts 17:29] Here was an appropriate, almost imperative, opportunity to introduce Jesus as the middle personage of a Triune Godhead. Why didn't Paul tell them that although God wasn't made of gold or silver or stone, God Jesus was made of flesh and blood at the Incarnation?

Do you know why I say Paul didn't? Because he didn't know it! Had he been told such, he would have rejected this assertion. Note the phraseology of Paul here: *"... by means of a man he has chosen ...."* [Acts 17:31] The operative word is "chosen." Paul could have used, and should have used, another term if Jesus was literally the Son of God. The term "chosen," however, is correct if we understand the true expectation of the Messiah. The Messiah was to be the chosen King of the Jews, not the divine biological Son of the singular, exclusive Hebrew Deity! Read and learn what St. Paul taught: *"Because he hath appointed a day wherein he will judge the world in equity, by the man whom he hath appointed; giving faith to all, by raising him up from the dead."* [Acts 17:31]

The conception of a deified human being would have been sacrilegious to a devout Pharisee, which is precisely what Paul had been! Paul's word (as reported by Luke) was carefully chosen, and he chose the word "chosen," not any other term that would have been less in conflict with today's doctrine of the divinity of Jesus. Paul reports that God "appointed" Jesus and "raised Him up from the dead." This line of discussion doesn't even touch on the matter of inspiration. God's choice of inspired words won't be addressed here, although that postulation certainly should always be raised.

If you continue on to Chapter 22 of Acts, you will encounter another example of wording that repudiates the divinity of Jesus. The setting is the Fort in Jerusalem where the Roman soldiers were garrisoned. The Commander of the Fort had just rescued Paul from a gathering of observant Jews who sought to kill him. Paul, while proselytizing amongst the Gentiles, had absolved converts to the new faith from the requirements of the Mosaic Law. The angry mob viewed Paul as a schismatic Jew and a heretic. Furthermore, to their mind, he warranted death; a sentence they would have promptly carried through themselves had the Romans not intervened. Paul, presumably inspired by God or the Holy Spirit, sensed an opportunity not only to mollify the crowd, but possibly to win additional converts to his novel teaching.

Well, Paul was perilously mistaken on this occasion, for the attempted conversions ended abruptly when the people started shouting at the top of their voices, *"Away with Him! Kill him! He's not fit to live."* [Acts 22:22] Christians of the future espoused identical sentiments for a schismatic, and sometimes for much lesser offenses. But that exceeds the present point. The pertinence of this next quotation is, once again, Paul's choice of words.

Just before the assembled group had shouted him down, Paul was telling of his conversion from prosecutor of the faith, to his divine promotion of Apostle to the Gentiles. (Disputing Acts 15:7, where Peter is to instruct the Gentiles.) After Ananias cured Paul's blindness in Damascus, he explained to Paul: *"The God of our ancestors has chosen you to know his will, to see his Righteous Servant* [alt. *"Just One"*]*, and hear him speaking with his own voice."* [Acts 22:14]

Jesus, here, is referred to as the servant of God. Now you must understand that the term translated as "servant" in the Bible is a euphemism for a slave. Throughout the New Testament, whenever the word "servant" appears, read "slave" and you will have a more accurate understanding of the original texts. We interpret a servant as a hired person who is paid wages, who has the freedom to quit one master and subsequently to offer his services to whomever he may choose. This decidedly was not the lot, or the prerogative, of the "servants" of the Scriptures. What is more, a biological son could never be a servant in the household of his father. The servile condition was intolerable for so close a relative, as can be discerned handily in the parable of the prodigal son. [Cf. Lu. 15:11-32] How could Jesus, the Second Person in the Trinity, be a slave or a servant to the First Person in the Trinity?

The wording of the quote is only consistent with the assumption that the author, Luke per Paul, viewed Jesus as someone less than God. Jesus was glorified by God through His elevation to the Messiahship. But God didn't deify Jesus; that misconception must be assigned to mystically inclined human beings. In the Old Testament, God occasionally appeared on Earth in the guise of a man. But that is all His appearances were: a guise!

In fairness, it should be pointed out that there are numerous places in the New Testament where Jesus is titled "Son of God." Notwithstanding, only in the Nativity accounts is it imperative to understand the term literally. Even at the Baptism, we could infer figurative 'sonship' without distorting or diminishing the import of the occasion. How can anyone wholly discard the suspicion that scribal deifiers haven't penned in proofs of their personal beliefs, just as Tatian did in his Diatessaron? Every biblical scholar concedes that intentional alterations of the texts have been made at various (numerous?) times in the past.

In the preface to the <u>Inspired Version of the Holy Scriptures</u>, we read the quote of a man named Dupin, author of <u>Complete History of the Cannon and Writers of the Books of the Old and New Testaments</u>: "It is mere superstition to assert, as some authors do, that the Hebrew text which we have at present is not corrupted in any place, and that there is no fault, nor anything left out, and that we must indisputably follow it at all times. This is not only to speak without all evidence, and contrary to all probability, but we have very good proof to the contrary."

Dupin's quote was referring specifically to the Septuagint (Greek O. T.), but the same sentiment is applicable to the New Testament. Perhaps even more so in the case of the N. T. inasmuch as the early Christians, by and large, came from the less educated segment of the population. No less so, because they hadn't initiated a tradition of trained scribes whose primary task was to accurately transcribe the Scriptures. The Hebrews had a long history of skilled biblical transcribers, still errors entered into their Sacred Texts. Every new copy presented an opportunity for a mistake, a deletion or an alteration, and there was frequent need for new copies. This isn't calumny; it is human nature! Under these conditions, a paucity of errors would be a greater wonder than is the Bible's purported divine authorship.

From a Twentieth Century perspective even more indicative of the pitfalls in sanctifying the Scriptures is the problem of translating the ancient writings. On a previous page I coincidentally pointed out a significant difference in the Revised Standard Version translation and the Catholic translation of Acts 22:14. The former renders "Righteous Servant" and the latter reads "Just One."

Had our scripturally smug religionists been diligent enough to compare the various translations side by side, their confidence in any single translation would be far less resolute. Imprecision permeates every Bible rendering. Uncertainty is no stranger to an honest exegete. Speculation, not inspiration, guided many a translation. Further complicating an already muddied situation is the matter of punctuation. The Bible's authors didn't use punctuation. Now if the reader doesn't appreciate the potential ambiguity of sentences without punctuation, then closely examine the sentence below.

The religionist said the atheist is an ignorant fool. {Do you agree with this statement?}

Now add a comma and quotation marks. *The religionist said, "The atheist is an ignorant fool."* {Who is the fool?}

Or add a comma; reposition a comma and the quotation marks. *"The religionist," said the atheist, "is an ignorant fool."*

{The fool, it devolves, is the one who places unquestioning trust in scriptural interpretations.}

Can this happen in the Bible? Can God's very own words be misconstrued? There is little need (indeed none) to respond to these two queries. I am positive the reader already has divined the answer. Even more devastating to the proposition of biblical inerrancy is the matter of sentence structure and location of the parts of speech. The Hebrews didn't follow our standard format of subject, verb, and object. Quite often the ancient writers formed their sentences: subject, object, adjective, verb; followed by modifiers tacked onto the end.

The best of translations can only hope to present the gist of each sentence, not the precise thought! When fundamentalists insist on an uncompromising, strict & literal interpretation of any Biblical translation, they are committing bibliolatry. They are worshiping a man-made conversion of foreign arcane words into a modern language; (in hope) without distorting or misinterpreting the sacred thoughts as they putatively were inspired by God. Add to this, the fact that many of the words used in the Bible aren't precisely defined, or can't be translated exactly into English, and you will necessarily hesitate before you trumpet "truths" from any Bible translation. Faith can never be an acceptable alternative for intelligent inquiry.

PAUL'S THEOLOGY

"Ask the God of our Lord Jesus Christ, the glorious Father, to give you the Spirit, who will make you wise and reveal God to you … This power in us is the same as the mighty strength which he used when he raised Christ from death and seated him at his right side in the heavenly

world. Christ rules there above all Principality and Power and Virtue and Domination …." [Eph. 1:17-21] (Principality, Power, Virtue and Domination – four of the nine choirs of angels)

"God has put all things under the authority of Christ and has made him head over all things for the benefit of the church." [Eph. 1:22] As elsewhere, it is clear here that Paul not only didn't teach the partnership of Jesus with God the Father, rather, he preached of the elevation of the man Jesus to a ranking above even the highest order of angel, namely "Lord." [Cf. 1 Cor. 8:6; Eph. 6:23; 1 Thes. 1:1 & 2 Tim. 1:2] In Paul's theology, Lord Jesus is the pinnacle of all creation. Jesus occupies the most exalted spot in the Universe: the seat at the right hand of God! Jesus is the most efficacious Intercessor between God and man. When we pray to Jesus, God unfailingly grants our petitions, for Lord Jesus is the promised "anointed" Messiah.

After the Fall of Adam and Eve, God promised to send a Rectifier who, by His sacrifice, would reconcile the rift between God and mankind. Jesus was that person, according to Paul. He was, and is, the Messiah (the "anointed One" promised by God). In Paul's theology no one can ever be as intimate with God as is Jesus. But Paul never taught that Jesus and God were one and the same Entity. Paul wrote that the Father was the God of Jesus just as "The Father" is the God of all who exist in the Cosmos. This is Paul's theology. Paul's teachings have been perverted into a sacrilege. Judging by today's evolved theology, Jesus has usurped a portion of the sacred divinity that belongs exclusively and eternally to mankind's Creator (God).

I could, and perhaps I should, here launch an assault on the very notion of a Personal Divinity, or any other sentient otherworldly entity proffered as the uncaused, *'prime cause.'* The effort would prove fruitless as well as pointless. Religionists, through their own definitions, have rendered God unknowable. We offer that God is a pure Spirit. Upon deep reflection, He is in reality less than this. Angels and Devils are spirits, yet they were created. God, because He was uncreated, can have no substance what-soever, not even spirit substance. Pondered with dispassionate objectivity, God must be nothing: absolutely and positively nothing!

Truthfully, we can only know God by inference. We can recognize the acts of God, although we can never observe Him personally performing those actions. Every act of God is an inference. We witness an event and we postulate God as the actuator who caused the event. As any inquisitor can see, God is truly only a theory that attempts to explain the physical Universe. In essence, what the theory states is this: 'The Universe is here; The Universe can't have created itself; therefore, 'Someone' created the Universe!'

The stilted logic in this theory (presumption) is patently biased in favor of a personal Deity. Pure logic would alert any unbiased theorizer that an uncreated, ever-present Universe is just as logical (or illogical!) as an uncreated, ever-present Creator. A Super Person (God) is simply much less complicated for a human being to perceive than is an impersonal universality (eternal cosmic material existence).

If we have ever laughed at primitive peoples who imagined malign spirits as the true impetus behind the destructive actions of nature (by name, hurricanes, earthquakes, droughts, or sickness), then we can stop laughing now! They didn't know any better. They hadn't learned of tropical depressions, plate tectonics, precipitation and evaporation, or viral infections. We have learned! We have disguised their unenlightened beliefs, but we haven't forsaken them.

We are every bit as superstitious as was the most gullible person who ever lived. The only difference being that we express ourselves with words and ideas more abstract than theirs. Our abstractions effectively insulate our intellects from the practical implications of our beliefs. The Trinity is just such an abstraction. Our belief is that three separate and distinct individuals are only one singular Divinity. This postulate is so absurd that it is ridiculous. Yet, we have the audacity to ridicule an Eskimo who returns to the ocean a small portion of a harpooned whale in order to appease the whale's spirit. What is so illogical about a spirit for a whale? If we grant the idiocy of God's Spirit flapping around in the form of a dove; subsequently, how can we defame any other absurdity?

If we are ever to reach species maturity we are going to have to renounce all superstitions, even Western man's most pervasive credulity: Christianity! The adulthood of the human race has been impeded by religious beliefs. Let us all awake now and face the true facts of life. We can begin by taking our Bible and placing it on the bookshelf between the Greek Mythologies and a Treasury of Science Fiction stories. Once we renounce religiosity in all manifestations for the delusion that it is, we can proceed with our maturation. Racially, we are at a chronological point in our development that parallels the early teen years for human beings. We are beginning to experience most of life's major problems, but we still expect a universal parent (God) to favorably resolve those problems for us.

The only way for us to reach our potential as racial adults is for us to shed all of our juvenile superstitions. Religiosity denigrates intellect. Humility sops initiative. Ritual replaces resourcefulness. Piety places blinders on our curiosity. Overall, the practice of religion stultifies our racial growth. Despite the obstacle of religiosity, still, we are on the threshold of another remarkable milestone in the epic of mankind: The Age of Intellectual Adulthood! But we will never reach that milestone on our knees. "So Stand Up! Unclasp your hands! Raise your head and open your eyes!" [Author's declaration] We won't ever exploit the total potential of our human species by assuming the postures of worship, supplication, or of penitence.

In the early 1960s, when John F. Kennedy made a commitment to land an American on the Moon by the end of the decade, many scoffed. But mankind, working in concert, can accomplish prodigious feats. All that is needed is a leader with wisdom whose orders are followed by underlings. Reduced to its basics, this is how all human accomplishments were achieved. But be cautioned! Think and recall! Have all our leaders led us in the best possible (most beneficial) direction? I am thinking of Alexander the Great, Napoleon, and even Hitler. In our own day, we have had all too many invidious leaders such as David Koresh in Waco, Texas.

No, the world hasn't lacked for leaders. What it has lacked is intelligent leadership to guide us (or order us!) in the most favorable direction for aggregate mankind. Decisions affecting all of the human family must be made intellectually. We must foreswear all emotionalism. But most importantly, all religiosity must be abandoned, for its end goal will prove, ultimately, to be irredeemably detrimental to human society. What is religiosity's never wavering final objective? It is the total and unremitting enslavement for all time of the human body through the willful enslavement of the human mind via interminably tyrannical religiosity.

Are my words here nothing more than idealistic, impious rhetoric? Religionists would say yes. But they are wrong! I don't advocate the end of the world. They do! I advocate a heavenly life for the living, not the dead! My heaven would be physical, not spiritual! All that a religionist can offer is mindless hope, predicated on unsubstantiated faith, achieved by self-denigrating denial, supported by adopted ignorance, and attained through groveling ennui.

GOD'S PROVIDENCE

An obvious anachronism struck me while reading Paul's Epistles. In several of his missives he solicited alms from the newly established convert groups to be conveyed to the Judean Christians. After thanking them for their anticipated generosity, he promised them that God would bless all who shared their possessions with others less fortunate. He further assured them that they needn't fear poverty or want for themselves because God will see that they will always have whatever they need through His divine providence. 'God will reward generosity,' is Paul's theme. His assurance is comforting; but is it factual? How could it be? If God does provide for His own, why were the Judeans in need of aid? The reason for their plight was an extreme famine that must be presumed to have been caused by God Himself.

My words don't adequately convey the sense of the Epistle, so I will supply Paul's. *"And God is able to give you more than you need, so you will always have all you need for yourselves and more than enough for every good cause ... He will always make you rich enough to be generous at all times."* [2 Cor. 9:8-11] The refutation of Paul's assertion is contained within his request. The fact that the Judean Christians needed outside alms is all the proof required that Paul's declaration is nothing more insightful than pious, deceptive, self-serving cant.

THE HEMORRHAGING WOMAN
AND THE PROTEVANGELION

Quirky behavior, such as covering feet, or covering face, or covering head, is said to please God. To me these actions appear suspiciously akin to some of the rituals that sexual deviates practice. The same can be said for the wearing of crosses, medals, and similar religious exhibitions. In a book detailing sexual aberrations {title long forgotten}, I read of a man who was futilely impotent unless he was fingering his mother's wedding ring during the sex act. The cause of his impairment was mental, not physical. This aptly (yet ominously) illustrates the ability and propensity of the human mind to affect the functioning of the human body.

Most healing miracles are accomplished through the same agency, the power of the mind. Reread the story in Mark of the woman who was cured of hemorrhaging by touching the hem of the cloak of Jesus. *"There was a woman who had suffered terribly from severe bleeding for twelve years, even though she had spent all her money, but instead of getting better she got worse all the time."* Then she heard about Jesus. Soon thereafter, she managed to be in a crowd that Jesus was passing through. *"If I touch just his clothes,"* she said to herself, *"I shall get well."* She reached out and touched his cloak as He went by and her bleeding stopped at once, *"and she had the feeling inside herself that she was healed of her trouble."* [Cf. Mk 5:25-34; Lu. 8:43-48 & Mt. 9:20-22]

This is an example of the mental delusion that lends credence to formal religions. Definitely this 'miracle' never took place outside the imagination of its originator despite the observation that it is found in all three Synoptic Gospels. How, in actuality, was the miracle verified? Did the Apostles conduct an examination of the woman afterward? How can we know that she indeed did suffer from 'severe bleeding'? Did she walk around leaving a trail of blood wherever she went? I hardly think so! The conclusion of the episode is likewise unverifiable and contains an implicit repudiation of the divinity of Jesus. *"At once Jesus felt that power had gone out of him. So he turned around in the crowd and said, 'Who touched my clothes?' His disciples answered, 'You see that the people are crowding you; why do you ask who touched you?' But Jesus kept looking around to see who had done it."* [Mk. 5:30-32] Jesus didn't know!

Curiously, Jesus' healing power seemingly is functional without His purposeful activation. The healing power just flowed out of Him and cured the woman without His willful intention, or His conscious direction. Does God's power act of its own volition? Our author conceives Jesus as a type of storage battery. Jesus is full of curative energy that He can discharge at will to perform miracles, or the power may be stolen by anyone who connects with His potent person. Such things are possible only in fairy tales where magic lanterns and flying carpets and all sorts of enchanted objects perform their sorcery unfailingly, yet totally independent of a 'sorcerer.'

How did the Evangelists know that 'Jesus felt that power had gone out of him'? Oh yes, that is right, God inspired them, so the story must be true! If so, then it must be equally true that Jesus didn't know who touched Him, for the Evangelists tell us this also. Perhaps God only knows most things; not all things! That observation may be flippant, but is it untrue? If it is untrue, then all three Evangelists were mis-inspired. Can God not know everything and yet remain God? One theory of the Godhood requires that God be "omniscient." If we deprive God of any knowledge at all, we deprive Him of His divinity in tandem! Frankly, the New Testament is littered with similar incongruities (*in lieu* of calling them outright discrepancies).

The earliest New Testament stories were verbal traditions written down as they were recalled. When they were compiled they were pieced together as intact units much in the manner of a painting of the Last Supper. Each artist would design his own scenario, yet the pictorial theme of every artist's work would be near identical. Saint Jerome, when he re-translated the Gospels admitted candidly that he had, "Used my pen with some restraint ... I have allowed the rest to remain as they are." Similarly, the initial redactors of the Gospels acted cautiously, correcting only that which (to their minds) had to be emended.

Notwithstanding the above, almost every glorifying tale relating to Jesus found a home in the Gospels. The Apocrypha of the New Testament (Extra-Canonical books eventually rejected by the Church), which today have no standing with Christians, had a widespread following among the Church's first Fathers. During the second century there were extant gospels by Peter, James, Thomas, Philip, Mary and others, all eventually rejected! Rejected not because of their internal fabulosities, but because their authorship, thus their authenticity, was suspect.

To illustrate how similar they sometimes were to the accepted books of the New Testament, allow me to summarily chronicle an unapproved 'gospel' called the <u>Protevangelion</u>. This book is attributed to James the Lesser (Just), son of Mary, brother or cousin (?) to Jesus. The book opens with the story of Mary's parents Joachim and Anna. It seems that Anna was barren {familiar theme?} and Joachim was scandalized by his fellow priests because the couple was childless. Joachim, in his yearning to father a child, swore an oath to remain fasting for forty days and forty nights {familiar theme?} with neither food nor water till the Lord God would send him an heir. The threat is effective; for God sent first one angel, then two angels to inform Anna that she would conceive and bear a child. Joachim is so overjoyed that he sacrificed 10 she-lambs, 12 calves, and 100 goats, all "without blemish" for he, too, had been visited by an angel and had been informed that his wife would conceive.

The text isn't explicit, but it seems to convey that Anna conceived without Joachim's participation. This certainly would have been biblically consistent! The future Virgin Mother could hardly be expected to be conceived in the usual manner. Alas, no later assertion of perpetual virginity was ascribed to Anna; consequently, we may presume that Anna and Joachim strove for and attained parenthood in the fashion of all other human couples. Meanwhile, Joachim, who is a priest himself, consults a priest. The object of the consultation is to discover if the Lord is charging any unredeemed sins against Joachim. Below are the texts verbatim.

> <u>Chapter 5, verses 1 to 4</u>. *"And Joachim abode the first day in his house, but on the morrow he brought forth his offerings and said, 'If the Lord be propitious toward me let the plate which is on the priest's forehead make it manifest.' And he consulted the plate which the priest wore and saw it, and behold sin was not found in him. And Joachim said, 'Now I know that the Lord is propitious to me, and hath taken away all my sins.'"* A footnote explains the plate on the forehead of the priest: 'such an instrument God had appointed the high priest to wear for such discoveries.'

In due course, the time was fulfilled and the fated couple was delivered of a child. Anna asked the midwife the gender of the child and is informed it is a girl; whereupon Anna promptly named her Mary (Miriam in Aramaic/Hebrew). It is mildly surprising that the angel didn't forecast the gender of the child at Anna's Annunciation. But no matter, I proceed.

The narrative then relates a pointless trio of nines. Mary, at age nine months, takes nine steps, both being preceded by nine months' gestation period. If the ancient author was making a point here, then that point is lost on me. Anna speedily gathers up her toddler and vows not to allow Mary to walk again until after she was presented to the Temple.

On her first birthday Joachim ordered a great feast and invited the priests, scribes, elders, and all {*sic*} the people of Israel. At the feast, Joachim solemnly offered Mary to the service of the Temple; after which, the chief priests blessed her, and they predicted her name would be famous and would be remembered throughout all generations.

At age three, Mary was taken to the Temple and was given, along with other undefiled tiny girls, to live and serve there. Once again a priest was moved (by God?) to proclaim: "Mary, the Lord God hath magnified thy name to all generations, and to the very end of time by thee will the Lord shew his redemption to the children of Israel."

Mary remained in the Temple until she was twelve years old. Nothing untoward seemed to have happened during those nine years, save for the revelation that during this period she "received her food from the hand of an angel." This should have led the priests to recognize that Mary was unique among their charges. But conspicuously it didn't, for it was at this time that they met together to discuss a potential embarrassment.

They queried one another: "Behold, Mary is twelve years old, what shall we do with her?" They feared that the Holy place of the Lord might be defiled if she remained. We never learn which it was they feared most, Mary's commitment to chastity; or their own lechery! Eventually they decided the safest course of action would be to marry her off to some worthy bachelor. However, first they would consult with the Lord to ask His assistance.

The high priest, Zacharias, entered the Holy of Holies to petition God for guidance. Yahweh never seems to have disappointed the biblical personalities, and this instance was no exception. An angel had Zacharias set up a complicated scheme whereby widowers from all of Israel (all?) competed for the right to house Mary. The text relates that the chosen widower was to be the husband of Mary. Yet, when the entire section is read, much doubt remains as to precisely what the status of the winner really should have been. To render this interjection more clearly, I must skip ahead in my reportage.

As we all know, Joseph was the man eventually chosen to be Mary's husband. Yet he was a reluctant winner. No sooner did he fetch her to his house, than he departed to ply his carpenter's trade. Curiously, when Joseph learned that Mary was pregnant, he complained bitterly to her that his reputation was now permanently blighted in the community because everyone would think him the father. I am puzzled by this report. Why did he agree to compete in the selection of a husband for Mary, if not to be exactly that … a husband?

What did the Temple priests expect of him? If they wanted Mary to remain a lifelong virgin why not continue to shelter her in the Temple? But no, they raffled her off among middle-aged widowers. Shouldn't they have foreseen that a teenage virgin living in the same house with a healthy, virile, unattached male would have posed an irresistible temptation? Having an alcoholic safeguard a bottle of whiskey doesn't adequately depict the latent potentiality of this placement situation. The grace of God may have surrounded both Mary and Joseph, but who instilled the idiocy into the priests to contrive such a hazard laden arrangement?

But enough of such foolish religious folderol! The story is a venal effort to alibi Mary's invented virginity. Once Isaiah's prophecy of a virgin bringing forth a child became enmeshed in the messianic predictions, and Jesus became identified as the Messiah, then ancient authors were compelled to weave a story that fit both criteria. As anyone can witness, their result is pure twaddle. The Extra-Canonical books exhibit the very same flaws as their more acceptable brethren, the Gospels. That is, they reek with the aroma of male bovine fertilizer.

On that non-ambrosial note, I will resume with the selection process that the angel delivered to Zacharias. As per God's instructions, all the widowers turned their rods over to the high priest so he could examine them for a sign from God. At first, no sign was manifest. But after the rods were returned to their owners, a dove proceeded from Joseph's rod and alighted on his head. This was seen as an unmistakable sign of God's choice. 'The widower Joseph was to be the guardian of Mary.' Incidentally, Joseph had adult children who apparently still lived with him. The Protevangelion doesn't elaborate on this point, but his son, James, would have been older than Mary at the time of the marriage. In all probability, James was in the prime of his manhood.

The tale proceeds through to the angel's announcement that Mary was to conceive through the power of God. She visited her kinswoman Elizabeth; was found to be pregnant (much to the distress of Joseph who reacted as a typical cuckold); traveled to Bethlehem to give birth; was visited by the Magi; learned of Herod's attempt to find and kill her child, and hid Him in an ox manger, "because there was no room for them in the inn." [ibid. Chapter XVI, verse 2] By skimming through the last portion of the gnostic book as above, the story seems to match alternately with Matthew's and Luke's version of the Nativity.

Additionally, the last section of the Protevangelion is much more expansive, contains many incidents not recorded in either Matthew or Luke, and even refutes them in sequence, intention, and result at times. Among the additions in the story, as compared with Matthew and Luke, is the trial-by-ordeal of Joseph. He is made to drink "bitter water" and if he became ill or died, he would have been adjudged guilty of violating Mary's virginity. The described ordeal seems to be an adaptation of Moses' rules for discovering female adultery recorded in Numbers. [Cf. Num. 5:11-29]

Another addition involves Elizabeth, Mary's cousin. She feared Herod will kill her son, John, as well as baby Jesus and she sought to escape the King by scaling a mountain. Ominously, due to her advanced age, she was unable to climb to safety. Then miraculously, the mountain opened and hid her and the infant John (the future Baptist). Zacharias was both Elizabeth's husband and a High Priest; therefore, when King Herod learned that Elizabeth had hidden her child, Zacharias was killed for not revealing the hiding place. In the Protevangelion, Herod was as anxious to kill John as he was to kill Jesus. However, Herod was inept in both instances, and only managed to slaughter the innocent children of other parents.

It is perplexing to imagine how Herod the Great could have been baffled so. With all the notoriety that accompanied the births of both John and Jesus, I find it problematic to believe that Herod would have had much difficulty at all locating and identifying the searched-for infants. Likewise, he surely would have been informed that the sought after pair had escaped, obviating the need for a massacre. Murdering helpless babies could only have brought down his throne ... not eliminated rivals! In any case, he hardly could have fretted over the immediacy of the baby Jesus seizing his throne. Herod was in his late sixties at the time! Rationally, incurring the wrath of the Romans could have provoked his swift and certain removal as King of Judea.

The Slaughter of the Innocents has a superficiality of truth about it, but when all the facts are known, Herod's actions seem politically suicidal. Only the Roman authorities could legally sentence someone to death. Herod had all too many enemies for the Romans to have been kept ignorant of the King's murderous rampage. Infanticide is a heinous crime in all civilized cultures. If, somehow, Herod's orders could have escaped the notice of the Romans, there is no way possible for his blood-stained orders to have escaped the notice of historians of Herod's reign. Such outrages are impossible to secret, and they would have been just the sort of ammunition Herod's detractors would have used against him. The able and comprehensive Jewish Historian, Flavius Josephus, knew and reported many scurrilous deeds perpetrated by King Herod. But he knew not of 'The Slaughter of the Innocents.'

That ends my interpretive reporting of the Protevangelion, and also ends this segment that had as its theme the observation that other 'Jesus' stories abounded that may well have been included in the Bible. By and large, they were substantially equal to our declared and enumerated N. T. Canon. In instances, they were superior. But they had this in common with all Divinity stories: They are utterly unbelievable; they are wholly false; and they are all the exclusive handiwork of mankind's mystically attuned imagination.

THE ASSUMPTION OF MARY INTO HEAVEN

Throughout this book religious proselytizers and theologians have been the major recipients of my attack ... and deservedly so! They are the major deluders in the matter of religiosity. Yet, they haven't perpetrated their fraud unaided. One of the most culpable of their confederates has been the artists. In the interest of comprehensiveness, include sculptors and other image makers in our discussion of artists.

Artists can grasp the most abject fantasy and portray it into a seeming reality. They can begin with a quaint, abstract notion, such as holiness, and depict it so graphically that it can be visualized. For instance: How can we tell the saints from the sinners in religious paintings? Rather easily. The saints all have a halo called a nimbus surrounding their heads or an aureole encompasses their entire body. Quite often, sinners will have small goat-like horns protruding from their heads. I have been in the personal company of at least one of the above mentioned categories (saint or sinner), and I haven't noticed either such appendage. The Devil, as anyone can witness, is readily identifiable in any depiction. Yet, no one has ever seen the Devil. At least, no one brags of having seen him. Perhaps he only appears to artists and their kindred.

Discussing angels: How do we know what angels look like? I am certain your reply is the same as mine. We both have seen depictions of angels. The Bible reveals there are nine choirs of angels. Accordingly, artists have developed separate portraitures to represent the ascending classes of angels, by name: Angels, Archangels, Principalities, Powers, Virtues, Dominions, Thrones, Seraphim, and Cherubim.

My favorite representation is of Michael the Archangel. He is tall, athletic, and attractive (in a feminine perspective), and he is unmistakably Caucasian! He has an impressive pair of five foot wings firmly attached to his back. He always wears a full length gown belted at the waist with a silken cord. The garment covers him from the shoulders to the ankles. Altogether he is quite handsome and well-built. Perhaps, that explains why the men of Sodom were so attracted to the Angelic pair who forewarned Lot of the coming destruction of the cities of Sodom and Gomorrah. Michael may well have been one of that stimulating pair of Angels. Did God have a dual purpose in dispatching those comely two? The first purpose was to alert Lot, the second was to entice the Sodomites? Obese, unattractive angels could have served the first purpose adequately.

I wonder, also, what an engineer of aerodynamics would think of an angel's aerodynamic design. Personally, I don't think an angel would get off the ground with those ungainly wings. Besides, why does an angel even need wings? Birds need wings to beat against the air that surrounds the Earth. I doubt that Heaven is suffused with an atmosphere. Perhaps one of our recent back-from-death resurrectees can enlighten us on that aspect of Heaven.

My chief complaint, however, revolves around Mary, the Mother of God Jesus. Catholic doctrine teaches that she was assumed bodily to Heaven at her death. (Referred to as "The Assumption") Christian artists have piously recorded the event for us on canvas. Thoroughly absent surprise, not only do they portray her being divinely raised to Heaven on a cloud, but she is also miraculously restored to an approximate age of twenty-five again. Which of the two artistic depictions denotes the greatest miracle? Mary's death is traditionally ascribed to have occurred in the year, AD 66. If Jesus was born in 7 BC, and if Mary was sixteen years old when she gave birth, then Mary was eighty-nine years old at the Assumption. Traditional or otherwise, what evidence is there that Mary, in AD 66, looked different than any other eighty-nine-year-old woman?

There is no evidence, and no need of any evidence. Artists are manifesting an age bias in favor of young women when they depict her thus. There is indeed no theological necessity for Mary to remain ever-youthful. But, has their deception been successful? Answer me! Have you ever seen a depiction of an aged, care-worn Mary? When the Blessed Virgin appeared to the children of Fatima (and elsewhere), how did she appear? 'Exactly as artists have continually portrayed her; she was young and beautiful. Aren't there any unsightly, wrinkled old women in Heaven?

I become hyper-suspicious when God abets human prejudices. I suspect the hand of man at work, not the hand of God! Then, again, why hasn't God inspired an artist to paint a true likeness of Mary, or Joseph, or Jesus, or anyone else from that generation? Conceivably, artists and sculptors could make grievance with God for being slighted in the issuance of inspiration. Granted: the thought is impious; but it is not irrational. The explanation is that the Jews of the time of Jesus forbade all images or representations of any human being. Despite Christian yearnings to the contrary, Jesus, Mary, Joseph, and the Apostles were all Jews both by birth and by religious persuasion.

Non-Catholics may not be moved much by a discourse on the Assumption of Mary. Still, my point is not to discredit one denomination in deference to another. All religions are founded on unproved speculations;

therefore all are fake and delusive by my assessment. I think that mankind would be infinitely more motivated to act kindly if all religions were renounced forthwith. Religion is the most divisive invention mankind has ever concocted. Nationalism runs a close second. For me, the only cause worth rallying around is intellectualism. Brain Power is humanity's salvation. What a different world we would have if only we could shed all of our superstitions, including religiosity, along with our other contra-intellectual biases.

No belief stands entirely on its own; not even a bogus belief. If "A" is true, then "B" and "C" must follow and so on. That is the real tragedy of religiosity. If there is a personal God, then certain other propositions must be true also. As each added proposition is embraced, they, in turn, spawn new propositions, and so on, until eventually we stand right where we are today. We are a discordant, intolerant, bellicose assemblage of ignorant, bigoted individuals roiling with enmity and vituperation toward all who espouse differing supernatural imaginings (beliefs) than our own.

I am not, however, preaching universal love. That sanctimonious precept is as idiotic as is universal hate. What I do advocate is mutual respect for all those who can demonstrate they deserve the respect of their fellow human. The isolated or incidental act of being born entitles no one to respect. Respect should be earned. Perhaps this is why the concept of universal respect hasn't yet gained wider acceptance. All too often in the past, respect has been conferred on persons patently unworthy of the honor with the inevitable result that he who conferred the respect later regrets his unwarranted or unwise bestowal. Our guidelines for conferring respect are faulty due mainly to our being misled by spurious Christian doctrine.

Is a pious man more deserving of honor than is a kind man? The answer depends on a precise and accurate definition of what is a kind man, and that definition needn't entail sanctity. Is a chaste woman more deserving of esteem than is a promiscuous woman? Yes, she is, but not for reasons of piety or religiosity. A promiscuous woman doesn't offend God. After all, He supposedly endowed her with her carnal passion. Without doubt, she offends the man who has affection for her if she permits intimacies with another man; or equally with another woman!

For the same reasons, a promiscuous man offends the woman who holds affection for him. There are many factors that militate against promiscuity, not the least of which is venereal disease. Confidence of paternity is another. But, perhaps, the greatest factor is simply that it does offend. For this reason alone, no one should betray the trust of one who loves them.

Many of the virtues of religiosity become more laudable when they are espoused through personal conviction rather than being imposed by pious decree. Their value to society is enhanced and magnified absent endorsement, because they are embraced intellectually. A consciously adopted virtue has an inherent merit that is intrinsic to itself. It is not, and never should be, dependent upon pleasing/appeasing a non-existent spiritual fabrication!

CHAPTER 14

The Doctors

UNINSPIRED THOMAS OF AQUINA

Thomas Aquinas (AD 1225-1274) arguably was the Catholic Church's greatest theologian. But, without quibble, he was the most abstruse. Very little of his theology will be discussed in this work. Yet, because of his exaggerated stature as a theological formulator, he can't be wholly discounted. St. Thomas is revered as both a philosopher and a theologian. Above all else, what I believe him to have been was a polemicist arguing the faux notion of a personal Deity. Whatever one may think of him though, no one can deny that he was an accomplished 'Wordsmith.' Aquinas could make the most mundane situations bend to his theological persuasions. He took his examples from the commonplace, yet by the time he finished, the commonplace was no longer mundane. Unquestionably, his example itself became more broadly understood than when he began. He was a man who could prove that clouds were made of clamshells if he so chose. First, however, he would proceed to 'prove' that clams could fly; this to explain how they inhabited the sky in the first instance.

Words were his *raison d'etre*; consequently, it is befitting to attack him with his own words if one wishes to debunk him. As a first premise, St. Thomas, too, is credited with being inspired by God in his writings. Is it possible to prove that a given work was or was not inspired by God? No, at least not as an absolute! There is no way to either prove or disprove inspiration. We accept inspiration on faith, or we reject it on intuition. Logic is only a minor consideration, at best. Yet, a nagging thought recurs in my mind about supposedly inspired writings. The thought has been cited previously. Here it is presented again.

"Writings inspired by God should be entirely free of all error." This statement is axiomatic. God can only tell the truth. God doesn't lie. [Cf. Tit. 1:2] As an inevitable consequence, every literary work that God inspires is, and must ever be, absolutely true, although not necessarily embodying the totality of truth. In other words, God is permitted to infuse the truth only partially, but that portion of knowledge that He imparts to us must be completely accurate.

So far, what I have written agrees with approved Christian theology. But I again ask; suppose an inspired writing can be shown to contain untrue information? Doesn't this prove that there was no divine editing in its composition? Yes, it does! No intelligent religionist should reject this conclusion. Notwithstanding religionists' ardent prayer; provable errors are contained in the Bible. And, as you will read, they are found in the "inspired" writings of St. Thomas also.

How do religionists reconcile this with their beliefs? Rather easily, they simply deny the errors, or they do as the magazine Immaculata suggests. The quote embedded in the following is taken from the November issue, 1981, page 13, "Are the Gospels True to History?" The article states that St. Augustine (an earlier theological apologist, AD 354 – 430) kept two principles uppermost in his mind: "(1) There exists no error in the Bible. (2) What seemingly appears as contradictory to a truth must be thoroughly studied to discover the means by which the statements at odds with each other can be harmonized."

The article continues: "Catholic faith has consistently maintained these two principles down through the centuries: because God is the author of Sacred Scripture it can contain no real contradictions or errors of any kind."

Dogmatic (as distinct from fundamentalist) Christians preach that although the Bible, in places, may not contain the literal truth, in every place, it does contain veritable truth. The overall tenor of the article seems to be an attack against modern theologians who excuse the errors in the Bible by declaring them to be allegories. Worse, by far, are those who admit that a few inconsequential errors are contained in the Bible. The author of the quoted article (Reverend G. H. Wilhelm S.T.D.) is determined to take these 'misinformed' revisionists to task. {Author's interpretation} Reverend Wilhelm writes they have been "led astray by rationalistic prejudices." What he utterly fails to recognize is his own anti-rationalistic prejudice.

Factually, religious faith is only pious bias. Reverend Wilhelm has an abundance of faith; accordingly, he is abundantly biased against anyone who doesn't share his faith-based, bible-confirmed beliefs. What proof has anyone that God inspired any part of the Bible? Absolutely none! The witness of the Bible is all hearsay at the secondhand ... or even further removed from an original source!

Who verifies Genesis as God's words? Who can authenticate Exodus, Leviticus, Numbers, or Deuteronomy? Who approved Joshua, Judges, and Ruth? Who legitimized the two Samuels and the two Kings?

Whom should we believe when we read the next two books of the Bible? Catholics call them Paralipomenon, whilst Protestants call them Chronicles. Which name was the one inspired by the Holy Spirit? Who was the recipient of this inspiration? Who posits that Tobias and Judith should be omitted from the sacred canon? Pause here and reflect on this last question. Protestants omit books that Catholics believe were inspired by the Holy Spirit. Who is correct? Assume that Martin Luther was solely responsible for the Canon of the Protestant Bible. How did he know that God didn't inspire Tobias and Judith (and other Protestant rejected books)?

You could postulate that Luther was the object of God's inspiration also, but this is unconvincing. The Apostle John is the only Evangelist to write of the Wedding Feast at Cana. The Holy Spirit inspired all four Evangelists, yet their Gospels differ. Because they are different, are they accordingly seen as contradictory, hence false? No, of course not! The Holy Spirit merely caused each Evangelist to recount the events in the life of Jesus in his own individual fashion and sequence, and complete-ness! This is accepted theology. God didn't inspire Mark with the story of the Wedding Feast, but He did inspire John; therefore, the Wedding Feast, although not part of Mark's inspiration, is still fervently purported to be historical.

The same may be said of Martin Luther and the Council of Hippo. Both were inspired, but in a different manner. The observation that Martin

Luther excluded Tobias from his Old Testament Canon doesn't prove that this book is uninspired. Have I made my point?

If I have, then please explain the point to me, for I think the previous rationalization is pure hogwash! If the Holy Spirit had inspired John the Evangelist, why bother to inspire three others who seemingly disagree with him? What need had we for four Evangelists? One complete narrative would have been sufficient. Two similar stories would have been redundant. Three or four identical stories would have been completely superfluous. Four different, but compatible, stories would have been convincing, although still open to skepticism.

But what do we observe? We look and we find four stories that agree in part, disagree in part, while at the same time each contains some unique material. This fact (it is a fact notwithstanding Christian protestations to the contrary) can best be reconciled by the following contrivance: If, instead of inspiration, we postulate that glorified stories about Jesus began circulating shortly after His death. Also, that these magnified stories varied from one locale to another. Further, if we postulate that in some areas local legends became enmeshed with the Jesus stories. These stories became unique to that area. If we make these logical postulations, then we can discern the truth. What is the truth? The truth is that we just don't know what transpired during the lifetime of Jesus, and we never will. That is the truth! Everything else is sanctimonious extrapolation, or intentional dissembling!

Perhaps Jesus was born in a stable. But if He was, it happened through the untutored progression of random happenstance. Perhaps Jesus was born of a virgin. But I ask why? Throughout the Old Testament, God favored women who were promiscuous. It would have been more biblically consistent for the possessed Mary Magdalene to have been selected to be the mother of the Messiah. Perhaps Jesus was tempted by Satan. But why did Satan wait until Jesus was thirty years old? My first temptation came long before my thirtieth birthday. What the honest skeptic finds in the Bible inspires him or her to dismiss the entire notion of divine inspiration.

Now, after this wordy digression, let us return to Thomas Aquinas with an aside concerning him. St. Thomas Aquinas is listed among the twenty-six Catholic 'saints' who were purported to have had the ability to levitate.

The writings of St. Thomas have long been revered as inspired. If this aggrandizement was proven factual, then one would search in vain for an error in his writings. At my left hand as I write this paragraph I have a pocket-sized book titled <u>The Pocket Aquinas</u>, edited by Vernon J. Bourke. On page sixty-nine, St. Thomas is arguing one of his religious theorems, and in so doing he makes a distinction between an elementary object and a compound object. His example for the latter is the human hand, which is composed of fingers and a thumb, flesh and bone, and several other separate, identifiable, constituent parts.

Against the hand, he contrasts an object that has no differing parts and which any small fragment thereof is identical to the whole. This is the correct definition for a basic element. However, he errs grievously when he chooses his example. His words: "But an element is not divisible into parts that differ in kind; water, for example, each part of which is water." Water is not an element. Water is a compound of two atoms of hydrogen joined with one atom of oxygen. (H_2O in the shorthand of chemistry)

If St. Thomas had used iron as his example he would have been correct. He erred because he wasn't inspired by God, but by the flawed science of Aristotle. Aristotle believed the entire world to have been built up from four basic 'elements': Wind, Earth, Fire, and Water. St. Thomas erringly chose the least diversified of Aristotle's four elements "water." Why didn't St. Thomas use copper or tin for his example? Why did he use a substance that God knew was not an element? Can God's inspiration contain demonstrable errors?

The biblical errors that I have pointed out in this book prove convincingly that divine inspiration is a Judeo-Christian 'wish myth.' Please do not undertake to make a counter-argument that the Bible is one thousand or more pages long, and my criticisms, if concatenated, would only occupy a few dozen pages or so. In the first place, I have in no wise exhausted the number of verifiable, substantive errors that the Bible contains. The arguments for refuting a proposition always require more space to delineate than the proposition itself. To have covered all the contradictions I alone have found in the Bible would have necessitated a book larger than a college-level dictionary, and I am far from being accredited as a biblical scholar. A serious critic with a scholarly bent could easily fill a small library with his commentary. I not only lack the faculty for such an undertaking, but I lack the motivation as well. Further, I doubt that many readers would have the forbearance to read such a ponderous tome under any circumstance.

What I have done is to pick up the Bible frequently, just as anyone might have done, and I have read it with a questioning mind-set. No attempt was made to read sequentially from cover to cover. Factually, there are sections I have never read, and other sections that I have re-read many times over. I have covered the Bible extensively, because I have done so for a period of more than thirty years. This book was begun in early 1978. It is almost five years later as I compose these words. Yet, I am still not finished. What I have striven to achieve is to write a book that the average person might have written. The arguments presented (in hope) are clear, concise, and comprehensible to almost everyone.

I believe religion to be a hoax on the average person. The victims of religious fakery have always been the common folk primarily. My desire is to expose both the conscious and the accidental deception contained in the Christian Bible. All religion is a scam. Consider me as a want-to-be "debunker of religiosity." The appellation may be wanting in accomplishment, but not in purpose. Religion is harmful to your human development. St. Thomas was a brilliant man, but he was a mistaken man as well. He first formed a conclusion, and then assigned himself the task of proving himself correct. The intriguing truth is that in his day, his writings were attacked as unorthodox, bordering on the heretical by two separate Archbishops of Canterbury. His detractors never ceased their assaults on him until the year 1323, after the Church had canonized Thomas. [Cf. The Age of Belief] Thomas had been dead forty-nine years by that time. {Deceased AD 1274}

St. Thomas' most notable work was his Summa Theologica, which incidentally, was never completed! An obvious inference can be drawn from this fact, vis-a-vis, the inspiration for the composition of his magnum opus. (Greatest Work) But, because it is so evident, I won't elaborate here. What I will dissect here is perhaps his greatest theosophical query: Does God Exist?

Unsurprisingly, St. Thomas argues the affirmative. He gives five 'proofs' for his belief, all of which are outwardly logical. I point this out for a very sound reason. The reason being that logically, there is no God! Belief in a Supreme Being is a mental determination as to which of two opposing illogicalities (absurdities) that one chooses to affirm. Empirically, no cosmogony ever conceived has any more evidence to substantiate its validity than any other cosmogony, including the theory of a Supreme Being.

I will return to this discussion after listing the five proofs for the existence of God enunciated by St. Thomas. {Paraphrased and much simplified from <u>The Age of Belief</u>}

The first proof is motion: 'All things in motion must have a Mover.'

The second proof is cause: 'Every existence must have a cause. The cause must be separate and superior to the existence. The cause of all existence is the Creator.'

The third proof is impermanence: 'All entities had a beginning; consequently, they must necessarily have an end. Somebody (*more cogently,* 'Something') must have always pre-existed and must never cease existing; thereupon necessitating an "uncreated" Creator.'

The fourth proof is the superlative: 'Everything hot must have a hotter, and must eventually end at the hottest. Good must have a better, and better must have a best. The apex of goodness is God.' St. Thomas dismisses the opposite of "goodness", namely, "evilness." I suspect that St. Thomas believed this thesis would verify Satan as God's reverse Equal. {The fifth 'proof' will be revealed shortly}

St. Thomas argues persuasively. Yes, there would seem to be a 'prime mover.' Also, on the surface, one could look for a 'first cause.' Less compelling is the argument that all things are impermanent, hence, some 'permanent entity' must exist. His fourth argument is probable, but not inevitable. Good and bad, hot and cold, are all comparative. Theoretically, hotter can proceed on indefinitely, and cold might not stop at absolute zero, but may continue on into minus absolute zero values just as dividing by one-half never ends, or the fact that one-third has no exact decimal equivalent (mathematical infinities).

The weak link of the five proofs St. Thomas offers, however, is his last. His final argument is that '*all events happen for the best;*' hence, some "intelligent being" must be directing those events. This really isn't an argument. Plainly and simply, it is an unambiguously subjective platitude, and it is a patently biased postulate by Thomas Aquinas.

Contra Five: That the Universe 'acts' is incontrovertible; that it acts purposefully benevolent is intrinsically questionable and observably false. Misfortune is ubiquitous. Calamity abounds. The Universe is in constant conflict with itself wherever we peer with our space telescopes. For humans, pain and suffering are with us all the days of our lives. These are incontrovertible facts. St. Thomas here resorts to wishful thinking, not to intellectual reasoning.

Contra Four: The argument here is that all things have a maximum. St. Thomas states, "Fire, the maximum of heat, is the cause of all hot things." Forgive me, Dr. Aquinas, but fire is not the maximum of heat. Nuclear interactions, such as fission/fusion, are much hotter. "The Big Bang," in all probability, was the maximum of heat.

In actuality, when we discuss superlatives we really are discussing potentialities of a median. Hot and cold are deviations from a central comfortable temperature. Good and bad both proceed out oppositely from neutral. St. Thomas looks to the extreme for God and finds Him on the "good" side. What would he find if he looked to the "bad" side? If you state that he would find Satan, then you must concede that Satan is equal (albeit opposite) to God.

Logically, it wouldn't seem possible simultaneously to have two completely opposite Gods: one a God of Goodness, the other a God of Evil. Intrinsically they would be an anathema to one another. Hot and cold present a simpler example. If extreme heat comes in contact with extreme cold, they cancel one another and the result is neither hot nor cold. The same would be true of God and Satan. No amount of Evil can exist in the presence of perfect Goodness. For even the slightest bit of evil to exist would require God to be just that bit short of perfection. My conclusion is that the Universe isn't "good," neither is it "bad." It is neutral.

Contra Three: Here St. Thomas critically departs from objective reasoning. Why is an ever-present Being more logical than is an ever-present Universe? Once again his bias that all events in the cosmos are intelligently directed, and aren't random, compel him to postulate a Supreme Being. The Universe revealed to us by today's astronomers is everywhere chaotic. To argue otherwise would be to exchange advocacy for objectivity.

Religionists have a grossly exaggerated sense of self-importance to believe that a Universal Deity cares if they are sexually aroused by a smutty photo, film, or illicit situation. On a cosmic scale, human beings are infinitesimal. Religiosity fosters conceit. The pious practice of religious ritual is self-indulgent. We pretend to be seeking God's favor. The reality is that we receive nothing but our own redounded veneration when we practice religion.

Contra Two: God is the prime cause. This argument arises solely from galactic ignorance. No one knows the cause of the Universe, but this doesn't prove the existence of God. An impersonal 'cause without cause' may seem absurd to a religionist, but it is no more and no less absurd than is a comprehensible Entity who exists everywhere at once throughout all time, without either beginning or end. Is this logical? Is it even possible?

Answer this: How large is God? You opine that He is infinitely huge; He has no end. Wonderful! Now respond to two ancillary questions: How vast is the Universe? Does the Universe have an end? If the Universe has an end, then what lies beyond it? If the Universe has no end, then the Universe and God are identical. The Universe must therefore be God, or God must be the Universe. The Universe is everywhere!

Ignorance shouldn't be the genesis of religious disputation, but obviously it is! We instinctively mystify that which we can't comprehend. The notion of a God is a metaphysical connivance for a lack of comprehension or knowledge about Nature and the Universe.

Contra One: All motion derives from the 'prime mover,' i.e., "God." This proposition is difficult to rebut because it is so uncomplicated. Our own cosmogonists have had to deal directly with this same dilemma. Their solution is the "Big Bang" theory in which all the primal matter was set in motion in one explosive nano-instant. No theory has ever been tendered as to how this initial clump of matter originated. There never can be a presumptive theory for the creation of matter until scientists can learn to create matter themselves. Is that requirement achievable?

Scientific theorizers begin their cosmogonies with matter already existent. Religionists sneer and haughtily ask how this original matter was created. Then they brazenly pronounce their own solution. 'Someone who is nothing (God) created something (the Universe) from more nothing.' {Author's extrapolation} But is this a solution? No, it is meaningless claptrap. If God is nothing, then He, She, or It doesn't exist! If God is something, then I ask: Who created the something of which God is composed? Further I ask: What is the substance of the "Who" that created God's substance?

As you should now see, both solutions, the ever-present Universe and the ever-present Creator, are equally dumbfounding. St. Thomas avers that all entities have a beginning and have an end, save one. He calls this entity "God." Scientists state that matter (or its alter identity as energy) can neither be created nor destroyed; consequently, the need for a creator is obviated. Energy-Matter, itself, is the ever-present emanation in the Universe. The second alternative is repugnant to religionists who insist that a 'person' had to have formed the Universe. Still, I ask that you refrain from considering both theories equally plausible. They aren't!

Scientists can demonstrate the conservation of matter and energy. They can even prove the conservation of angular momentum (spin motion). Scientific theories must be, and are, tested continuously, and the test results are invariably the same regardless of who the tester may be. Religionists forbid the testing of God. Should anyone have the audacity to force a test on God, the result is almost always the same — *unremitting failure!*

I am convinced that in this world more people are praying for peace than are agitating for war. I believe this has always been so. Yet, we have always had wars. I am certain that we always will have wars. Wars are caused by power-hungry men seeking ever more power. Ambition is the prime cause of all strife. We have in our natures an ingrained trait that prods us to attempt to dominate others. This drive is part of our human nature. If God made us, then it is He who is accountable for our deplorable 'domination' penchant. My guess is that our desire for power is an extension (and a perversion) of our instinct to nourish ourselves. Human beings don't learn aggression. Rather, we have to unlearn aggression in order to maintain our civilizations. The suppression of our aggressions is what we term morality.

Returning to St. Thomas Aquinas: Let me offer here that had he been born seven hundred years later, he probably would be a world-renowned cosmogonist, and a dedicated atheist! St. Thomas was a deep thinker. He rejected blind faith as a foundation for belief. He sought to prove the tenets of Christianity empirically, rather than aesthetically. To me, he seems to have been the type of individual who would have formulated a workable theory for the origins of the Universe utilizing today's scientific facts as his starting point just as convincingly as he used Aristotle's scientific deductions in his own day.

Thomas of Aquina was burdened by a dearth of dependable scientific knowledge. He was led astray by the inaccuracy of Aristotelian physics. Everything considered: St. Thomas produced a remarkable work when we recognize the extent of the flawed (inaccurate) data he had to work with. Before re-consigning Aquinas to history, I shall lay bare more Thomist errors.

[St. Thomas discoursing on "light"] The first sentence on page eighty-seven of my source (The Pocket Aquinas) reads thus: "It is impossible for light to be a body." Was St. Thomas right? The most widely accepted theory, by far, of the nature of light is that it is composed of discrete little packets of matter (quanta) called photons. Apparently, St. Thomas was wrong about light.

Inasmuch as this isn't unquestioned fact (some experiments indicate that light may be composed of rays; the exact nature of which aren't comprehensively understood), you may be inclined to grant St. Thomas exculpation due to disputed fact, and not charge him with making an erroneous statement. If so, then consider an undeniable misstatement in the very same paragraph.

Discoursing on the speed of light, St. Thomas informs: "But illumination is accomplished instantaneously." Without quarrel, this is wrong. Light moves very rapidly, but it isn't instantaneous. God knows the precise speed of light. (If God lives!) Why did God inspire St. Thomas falsely? Why did God inspire St. Thomas inaccurately? Was St. Thomas inspired in any way by God?

On the very next page (eighty-eight), St. Thomas, still arguing that light has no substance, coincidentally exposes his belief in geo-centricity. He speaks of the Sun rising and moving around the Earth. We know, and we can prove, that the Sun doesn't revolve around the Earth. Fewer than three hundred years later, Nicholas Copernicus would correctly describe the motion of the Earth around the Sun. God could have inspired St. Thomas with this knowledge before Copernicus discovered it. What would have been the harm?

Thomas's entire dissertation on the nature of light was incorrect. In no way could a Universal Creator have been inspiring St. Thomas in this segment of his work. You might once again excuse God's apparent ignorance of scientific fact by postulating that God only inspired the theology of St. Thomas, not his technology. If you are comfortable with this, fine and okay! But I feel that the least an inspiring Deity should have done is to induce St. Thomas to refrain from presenting arguments that were certain to be refuted in the future.

St. Thomas never completed his <u>Summa Theologica</u> ("A Treatise on Theology"). He did, however, complete his discourse on <u>Nature and Philosophy</u>. There are indications in this observation that are not easily disregarded. To a skeptic, as with your author, the most obvious is that St. Thomas and I both received the same sum of inspiration from God, that is: zero!

I could spend much more time with the Tomist writings, but I would only belabor the point. St. Thomas wrote with the hand of man —*period!* I arrived at this conclusion through a process that St. Thomas himself proposed. Read his words first, and then you decide whether eternal truth truly does reside in the writings of Thomas of Aquinas.

HOW TO FORM AN OPINION
ON A DEBATABLE POINT

{Composed by Thomas Aquinas}

"However, in the acceptance or rejection of opinions, a man should not be influenced by love or hate for the person who has the opinion, but rather by the desire to ascertain the truth."

"Yet, we should be open to conviction by the more certain side: that is, to follow the opinion of those who have arrived at the truth on a more certain basis .…"

Clarified, what St. Thomas said is to believe the person who presents facts, not mysteries. 'Proof, not piety. Beliefs contrary to the evidence are less credible than are conclusions coherent with the evidence. St. Thomas, whatever his failings (as I see them), did have redeeming qualities. He correctly reasoned that "truth" dependent upon faith is merely blind acceptance of superstition. If you re-examine his five proofs for the existence of God you will confirm that not one of them is dependent upon faith. Each is supported by observable facts, as St. Thomas interpreted and applied those facts!

Most Christian and Jewish religionists of today (and probably of all past yesterdays) would argue that the Bible professes that God exists, and because the Bible is the 'Word of God,' then this itself is incontrovertible proof of God's reality. St. Thomas was scant convinced by this self-verifying, circular proposition. He sought empirical proofs for the existence of a living Deity. He thought he had found them in his five propositions just disabused. However, any one of us can be misled through our failure to correctly discern between a fact, and our interpretation of the implications attendant to every fact.

The erroneous conclusion that the Sun revolves around the Earth was gleaned from the obvious 'fact' of our observation that the Sun does, seemingly, cross the heavens each day. Certain sections of this book couldn't have been written one-hundred-years ago. Had I lived in St. Thomas' era, I could not have successfully repudiated his arguments.

Allow me to restate here with added emphasis "We are living now in a Golden Age of Enlightenment." We haven't reached the zenith of knowledge. Yet, we have left behind many of our immature presuppositions. Currently, we stand at the adolescence of our intellectual attainments. The future beckons us enticingly. But be cautioned! Progress isn't inevitable. The Dark Ages prove this. Civilization, which is co-dependent upon intellectual development and acquired knowledge, has progressed at times, and has retrogressed at other times. Absolutely no one can guarantee that we humans won't someday return to the caves with clubs and spears as our only weapons. No one person can ensure that we won't bomb ourselves into oblivion before we learn how best to utilize our technological warfare accouterments. Don't infer from the previous that I wish to promote universal pacifism. Universal disarmament is as likely as is a single universal religion, or as is universal atheism, for that matter.

Now to end this segment critiquing St. Thomas Aquinas: My goal herein was to demonstrate that God didn't inspire the writings of Thomas Aquinas. I opined that any single proven fallacy renders the whole premise of his divine inspiration as false. The counter-argument that I have only highlighted a few examples shouldn't be construed as evidence that this was all there was to be found. That wasn't the case. In actuality, my sources contained only a smattering of Tomist philosophy. Yet this smattering was littered with inaccuracies. A book length treatise could have been composed by anyone with the same intentions as me.

No, it should suffice my premise to provide one valid example of error in his work to demolish the imputation of divine inspiration of St. Thomas. I evaluate myself as having more than accomplished this. You are now in possession of much of the same information as this author. What is your conclusion? Did an all-knowing Deity inspire St. Thomas? Or was he limited to his own unaided speculations, as are the rest of us? Did God imbue St. Thomas with knowledge that He denied to you and me? Was Thomas Aquinas the victim of his own misinterpretations?

There is no option for opinion waffling here. Either God instigated St. Thomas to write unerringly, or there is no divine inspiration. (Consequently, no Divine Inspirer!) Any conclusion that attempts to circumvent the above is, and can only be, contrived rationale. Why is God's very existence dependent upon faith for proof? The notion of a Supreme Creator began as a philosophical explanation of cause. Man originally was encompassed with mystery. Everywhere he looked he saw something he didn't understand and couldn't control. In his species ignorance he groped for simple answers. Man groped and groped, and finally his groping was rewarded. He found the resolution to all his questions. "God" is a religionist's metaphor for the Universe. God is the resolute, final, inarguable solution to every query!

Why did that tree fall? Because God wanted it to! Why am I beset with some enervating illness? To serve some hidden purpose of God! When a rogue dictator invades my homeland and enslaves me and all my countrymen, this also is God's will. He is testing our loyalty to His teachings. God is the answer! Why frame the question? Is the above admirable faith? Or is it a simplistic pandering to our superstitious propensities?

This world functions exactly the way it would if no benevolent Deity was intervening. Imagine today that God decided to take a vacation from the affairs of man. Reasonably considered, what would change? 'Absolutely nothing; because we are already living in a wholly arbitrary world. St. Thomas was wrong in his noblest precept. The Universe isn't intelligently governed.

Mayhem, violence, and catastrophic happenstance abound in the cosmos. Human existence on this planet is just as hazardous overall as was the expectancies of those who lived near Mount St. Helens just before it last erupted. Only the time frame differs. The Sun is a natural bomb with a long fuse. No one knows for certain how long the fuse is. But we can all rely on one immutable reality. The fuse is lit!

AUGUSTINE OF HIPPO

If the Gospels are found to be too corrupted to have been inspired by God in their present form, perhaps we can look back to Four Great Latin Fathers for inspired theology. (St. Clement, St. Athanasius, St. John Chrysostom, & St. Augustine of Hippo) It would, however, be too lengthy to examine all of their writings here, so I have culled several paragraphs from the works of the man acclaimed the greatest of the early Fathers, St. Augustine (AD 354-430). First, his writings appear to have survived the centuries basically unaltered. Second, he is specific enough in some areas that his beliefs can be scrutinized and evaluated in depth. From his book, "City of God," I have excerpted some Augustinian Theology.

[From City of God — Book XIV, Chapter 18]. {The entry is sub-titled, 'Of the shame that attends all sexual intercourse.'} In this exposition, St. Augustine grasps a generality and propounds it into an absolute. He maintains that all sexual activity is relegated to the obscurity and anonymity of darkness, even the lawful intimacy of husband and wife. His point seems to be that all sexual gratification is shameful. Although he doesn't specifically mention this next principle, it is unambiguously implied: 'celibacy and virginity are virtuous because they are exhibited in the light of day.'

How very sanctimonious is his observation. His thesis has an apprehension of truth in my cognition. But are his words unquestionably true, or do they only provide an apparent truth? Does mankind collectively hide the satisfaction of its natural sexual lusts under the shroud of night, behind locked doors, or in other secreted places? No, emphatically and demonstrably not! Only the more civilized members of the world's citizens suffer to conceal this normal impulse. But the underlying 'why' should be considered first before anyone critiques these civilized amenities. Our exhibited morality isn't morality that was infused by God at our conception. The generally accepted sexual customs and sexual mores of a society have more influence over our practiced sexual behavior than do our inherited inclinations.

Many primitive tribes had considerably fewer sexual inhibitions before association with Christians. They learned the 'shame' of nakedness from those with Augustine's persuasions, not as an inborn or inevitable development! Civilization, which fundamentally is community living, necessitates concessions from its citizens. One such prevalent concession is the requirement for discreet sexual indulgence. But this concession isn't imperative, nor is it biologically compulsory. Examples that mock the notion of the universal infamy associated with sexuality have been numerous in the past, and are on an upswing in today's Western world.

The best examples can be seen in our permissive society. The vast breadth of the sexual revolution in America hasn't fully penetrated the collective cognizance of the general adult population. Perhaps not everyone is yet aware that magazines are published that print an actual photo of individuals and couples advertising their perverted sexual preferences, while seeking others to share in their fulfillment as a group. We can deplore the inclinations of these persons, but we cannot deny their existence. Contrary to religious "wish fulfillment," the opprobrium attached to physical desires is neither inherited nor infused. It is learned! {Today's television dramas and motion pictures are relentlessly attempting to 'unlearn' us our morality!}

Augustine is far from accurate in his supposition. The overriding reason why married couples don't copulate openly is because the sight of this act is stimulating to human beings, and could be the impetus for uninvited and unwanted intrusion by others. Anyone who has observed a troop of baboons will understand this readily. Operators of pornography shops are well aware of the commercial potentialities of visual sexual arousal. The physical stimulations we call sexual are pleasant, hence we tend to gratify them more often than is essential, or even prudent, to requite our hereditarily implanted copulative impulse.

It is religious bigots who pervert an intelligent prudence in the conduct of sexual activities into shame at the act. The ability to stimulate others, especially those of the opposite sex, has very broad implications for civilized humanity, and is the root cause of much of both our joy and of our grief. Formerly, women riding on public conveyances kept their knee-length skirts down and their thighs pressed tightly together. This was termed modesty, but it was also common sense. Men are easily aroused to sexual fervor. The mere sight, or near sight, of the female genitalia is greatly stimulating to men. This also is the basis of the popularity and ubiquity of well-above-the-knee skirts worn by today's women. I suspect the sight of nude men, or the intimation of a sexual encounter with a desirable man, stimulates women no less (amplified or diminished only by her monthly hormonal cycle). That is our nature!

There has always been a market for sexually oriented material. Not because mankind is universally sinful, but because Nature made sexual stimulation pleasurable. (Even mildly addictive) Sexual reproduction is the handiwork of God (if anyone!), not the Devil. Sexuality is a manifestation of successful evolution. Bi-gender reproduction multiplies the possibilities of evolutionary diversification (often beneficial) to a greater extent than does asexual reproduction; thereby, we are here. Religionists interpret divine planning in this fact. But, as always, they peer into a mirror and mistake the reflection for reality. As with Alice, they, too, wish to step into the world behind the looking glass. The emergence of man from the primate family lineage required no more planning than the formation of "Natural Bridge" in the state of Virginia.

Did God purposely plan the Grand Canyon? Or is this geologic feature the result of the erosive effect of rushing water over long eons? If God carved the Grand Canyon, why are many of the proofs of geo-evolution found in its exposed layers? The Grand Canyon provides firmer evidence against the creation scenario in Genesis more profoundly than can the written or spoken words of man. Yet, religionists persist in ascribing supernatural machination into the random actions of impersonal natural forces.

In St. Augustine's "City of God," he points out the nonsense of believing that humans can walk on the underside of the flat Earth just as they do on the upper flat surface. He concludes that this is "utterly incredible." ["City of God," Book XVI, Chapter 9] Augustine tries to picture people walking on both sides of the flat Earth, and decides this isn't possible. He was wrong in this belief twice. The Earth isn't flat! And people can walk on the earth's surface half a globe from other people walking antipodal on the earth's surface!

Why didn't God enlighten Augustine? The knowledge that the Earth was a globe wasn't unknown in his day; it just wasn't espoused by very many scholars. Augustine himself knew of the belief that the world was a globe. But he dismissed that idea as nothing more substantial than "scientific conjecture." The absolute fact that Augustine was never so inspired by God to know the actual shape of our planet is indisputable evidence against the very notion of Divine Inspiration. Implacable religionists can't accept this evidence. But then, neither can statues and, perhaps, for the same reason, because both are equally impervious to all proffered evidence.

THE ORTHODOXY OF AUGUSTINE

A Catholic who has heard so often of the contributions of St. Augustine to the orthodox theology of the Catholic Church would be incredulous upon learning that not all of his views are today considered orthodox. Verily, our Catholic simply wouldn't believe such an assertion. Nonetheless, it is true! Incredibly, not one person in the history of the Church has ever been acclaimed one hundred percent orthodox. Does this surprise you? It shouldn't! After all, what is orthodoxy?

Orthodoxy is, as orthodoxy says it is. By that is meant: Whatever the ruling faction of the Church declares is orthodox, becomes orthodox only because the current hierarchy states that it is so. Over the years, that which is considered orthodox will vary with the changing of the pastoral leadership. Any organization with a history as lengthy as the Catholic Church will have passed through many leaders, thus through many orthodoxies. That the Roman Church has been rift many times over by theological controversy is inarguable. The Great Church Councils provide irrefutable witness to this assertion. Demonstrably, orthodoxy isn't an absolute. There never has been, and never will be, a definitive and unalterable template of Christian orthodoxy.

Reading St. Augustine's "City of God," I was at first impressed with his seeming modern orthodoxy. But slowly, almost imperceptibly, a realization began to form within my comprehension that some of his convictions were tangential to the articles of faith I had been taught as a child of the Parochial School system. The nuances of difference were subtle, but they were there despite their obsequiousness. I couldn't help speculating how Catholic Theologians of this age reacted when they read the "City of God." If a lay person (such as me) could discern small deviations from orthodoxy, surely they (as experts) could discern radical departures from what today's Roman Catholic Church deems orthodox.

Many of the deviations would be difficult for the average reader to fully appreciate. Yet, there is one section, which is both plainly stated and readily understood, that exposes one of Augustine's unorthodox beliefs. It concerns St. Jerome's translation of the Bible, known as the Vulgate. Recall that the Council of Trent in 1545-63, (long after Jerome's death in AD 420) declared the Vulgate as "authoritative and inarguable." Well, it is evident that Augustine knew of Jerome's work, but he thought much less of Jerome's version, than he did of the Septuagint version. If Augustine spoke for the Church of his day (and by his own declaration, he did!), then the Septuagint translation rendering was more accurate and more authoritative than was Jerome's. Read Augustine's words below and you will witness the verity of the preceding statement.

"There have, of course, been other translations of the Old Testament from Hebrew into Greek. We have versions by Aquila, Summachus, Theodotian and an anonymous translation that is known simply as the 'fifth edition.' Nevertheless, the Church has adopted the Septuagint as if it were the only translation. ….

"From the Septuagint a Latin translation has been made, and this is the one that the Latin Church uses. This is still the case despite the fact that in our own day the priest Jerome, a great scholar and master of all three tongues, has made a translation into Latin, not from Greek, but directly from the original Hebrew.

"The Jews admit that his highly learned labor is a faithful and accurate version, and aver, moreover, that the seventy {Septuagint} translators made a great many mistakes in their version. Christ's Church, however, thinks it inadvisable to choose the authority of any one man as against the authority of so many men." [City of God, Book XVIII, Chapter 43]

As you can plainly see, either the Church was mistaken in Augustine's day, or it was mistaken at the time of the Council of Trent. Augustine's deviation from modern orthodoxy exceeds this one example. His teaching on the Eucharist has been interpreted in a non-Catholic sense. [Cf. The Evolution of Medieval Thought, by David Knowles, page 33.]

Augustine's belief's concerning statues are an embarrassment to the Church who champions some of his other beliefs. You will know why I declare this after you have read the following: "Why have the Romans, like other pagan races, dishonored him (Jove, the chief Roman Deity) by making a statue in his likeness? Varro himself {an apologist of Roman Pagan religiosity} objected to the practice, so much so that, though he had to yield to the force of perverse custom in so large a state, he did not hesitate to declare and write that those who introduced statues among the people 'robbed them of reverence, and put error in its place.'"

Augustine perceptively fully agreed with Varro that making statues of God is an error. Protestant Christians (in general) have purged themselves of this ancient sin, while the Roman Catholic Church has become awash with statuary. All Christian faiths rely on pictorial representations of Jesus, the Apostles, and even of God the Father, to stimulate the imaginations of their pious followers. Moses would order the stoning of the entire brotherhood of Christianity on charges of gross idolatry if he was alive today. Protestant artists would be assaulted with the same number of stones flung at Catholic sculptors.

THE LONGEVITY OF METHUSELAH

[Refer to the "City of God," Book XV, Chapter 11] St. Augustine's copy of Genesis gave the chronological ages of the antediluvian ancestors of Noah inaccurately. His Bible recorded that Noah was born when his father, Lamech, was 188 years old. Lamech was born when his father, Methuselah, was 167 years old. If Noah was 600 years old at the time of the Flood [Gen. 7-11], then Methuselah must have been 600, plus 167, plus 188 years old; that is, 955 years old. This would have been Methuselah's age at the time of the Flood. We all know that Methuselah lived 969 years, so this would mean that he lived beyond the Flood by 14 years. [Cf. Gen. 5:27] Yet the Bible states that only Noah and his family members survived the Flood. Augustine's Bible was in error. Either the ages of Lamech and

Methuselah at fatherhood are wrong, or Noah's age at the time of the Flood was wrong, or the longevity of Methuselah is overstated by 14 years.

Augustine argues for a mistake in translation between the Hebrew texts and the Septuagint translation. My argument is this: If God didn't permit errors in the original texts, He would not have permitted errors in the translation texts either. Any other explanation is specious, if not an outright evasion of an inevitable extrapolation of the doctrine of divine inspiration. I can picture an analogy wherein a guard is posted to protect a household. He stations himself at the front door and vigilantly bars the entrance to thieves. Yet he complacently permits robbers to enter through the visible nearby front window and burglarize the home. Should such a guard be commended for the perfect watch he performed guarding the front door, or should he be excoriated for permitting burglars to enter the house unhindered in full view of his post? Didn't God know that His sacred words were being corrupted?

There is no satisfactory reply to this doctrinal dilemma except to cast out the doctrine. The doctrine of infallible inspiration must be scrapped. The doctrine itself is beyond proof under any conceivable circumstance. How can anyone know if God inspired anyone else unless God Himself inspires that person also? Inspiration can only be proved if God inspires the inquisitor (doubter) as well. God should know this. Discernibly, He doesn't!

My main point here is slightly different; accordingly, let us move on before I become hopelessly bogged down in pedantic hyperbole. My reference material has been emended to correct the apparent discrepancy in Methuselah's age and the dating of the Flood. Current Bibles have Methuselah's age at fatherhood listed as 187, not 167 years old. Lamech's age is listed as 182, not 188 years old when he fathered Noah. These changes make Methuselah's age at the Flood add to 969 years and resolves St. Augustine's dilemma.

Now for my point: How was this discrepancy resolved? The resolution is obvious: the texts were purposely altered! We could argue till doomsday without resolving the question of whose version of the Bible reflected the original texts. The truth is beyond knowing at this date. Hope and faith both desert us here. Hoping that something is so, won't make it so. Faith that something supernatural has happened won't cause this to become factual no matter how convincingly an advocate implores us to believe it has occurred.

All we have to guide us in this matter of inspiration is trust. Trust that the many authors of the Bible, along with a full multitude of copyists and translators, were kept from serious error in their labors by God's power. We already know for an absolute certainty that their translations aren't completely error free. We can't personally know of God's intervention, so our trust lies not in God, but in men. Did the compilers of the Bible accurately transcribe the thoughts and words of God? For proof, we have only the word of the authors' themselves, not God's word!

Trust those words if you will. But I see far too many errors and inaccuracies (and human imperfections) for me ever to believe that the O. T. is anything other than the unenlightened suppositions and superstitious biases of ancient Jewish holy men as chronicled by exclusively human scribes. To cherish the O. T. is to embrace both ignorance and deception. God Himself, through Jeremiah, informs that His words have been "changed." "*How can you say that you are wise and that you know my laws? Look, the laws have been changed by dishonest scribes.*" [Jer. 8:8] Once you reject the sanctity of the Scriptures, the Bible loses much to all of its value. Candidly, it is neither historically accurate, nor is it motivationally inspiring to those who have outgrown the fascination of propitious fictions.

[City of God — Book XIX, Chapter 25] "That where there is no true religion there are no true virtues." St. Augustine's argument here is flawed and circular. He states that virtue in the absence of religion ("God") is nothing more than pride inspired by demons. Yet, we know that God doesn't exist, neither do demons. Both are fictions of religionists. A single atheist practicing sincere virtue renders Augustine's axiom disproved. By actual count, there would be an equivalent number of ethical atheists as there are ethical religionists. Naturally, there would be a comparable number of unethical persons in both classifications also.

Religionists would desire us all to imagine that pure evil would stalk every locality on our planet were it not for the condemnation provided by Christian holy men. This just isn't so. Idyllic personal relationships existed throughout the Pacific Archipelagos long before the Christian missionaries arrived and taught the guileless natives there that nudity offended God.

Morality is an outgrowth of familial affection, not a divine infusion from God. The forlorn desire to be loved and respected by others, likewise, originates in our infancy. We are born needing the maternal care of another. We never outgrow the desire to regain that bestowed affection, even though we do outgrow the necessity of physical care from another in order to survive.

What is the strongest selling point that Christianity offers ('as does every other "personal" Deity theology)? Answer: That God Loves You! God is your eternal parent, your eternal guardian, and your eternal nurturer. Religiosity is selling intellectual dependency. Unwisely, most of us are buying!

THE AGE OF THE EARTH, ETC.

[City of God — Book XII, Chapter 10] {St. Augustine discoursing on the age of the Earth} "They {those who believe the world to be older than the Bible permits} are deceived, too, by those highly mendacious documents which profess to give the history of many thousands of years, though, reckoning by the sacred writings, we find that not 6,000 years have yet passed." {The subtitle of this quote is: Of the Falseness of the History Which Allots Many Thousand Years to the World's Past.}

Did God imbue St. Augustine with the knowledge that the Earth was fewer than 6,000 years old in his day? If the Bible is accurate in chronological references, then Augustine is much closer to the actual age of planet Earth than are our present day scientists. Scientists propose the Earth to be 4.5 billion years old. Both can't be correct. Who is most grievously in error?

Augustine also believed in the literal resurrection of the body at the Second Coming, not a spiritual or supra-physical resurrection as some of our modern revisionists propose! Below, Augustine postulates how physical bodies can counteract the pull of gravity so as to ascend into Heaven following a physical resurrection. Augustine, while rationalizing physical resurrection and ascension, coincidentally exposes his mistaken notion of the central position of the Earth in relation to the Sun and the Planets. For me, this unequivocally rules out any divine inspiration of his resurrection premise (and the remainder of his sanctimonious writings as well).

Did Augustine directly allege such a distinction? Throughout his books, he frequently asked for God's enlightenment. And, at least on some questions, he writes that God had "given me to know …." This raises the question: Did God inspire Augustine's writings? Postpone answering the question until you have completed this section.

"Let not the philosophers, then, think to upset our faith {in bodily ascension} with arguments from the weight of bodies; for I don't care to inquire why they cannot believe an earthly body can be in heaven, while the whole {flat} earth is suspended on nothing. For, perhaps, the world keeps its central place by the same law that attracts to its centre all heavy bodies." [City of God, Book XIII, Chapter 18] {Partial quote}

As we now know, Augustine was wrong in his presumption that the Earth was the center of the Universe. So what about his other contention? Will there ever be a resurrection of the body? Sadly, it must be acknowledged that he is in error here also. No deceased person has ever yet had his physical body reconstituted, and none ever will. *From dust art thou come, and to dust shalt thou return.*" [Gen. 3:19] I have no idea who first penned those words and credited them to the inspiration of God. But whoever: his words echo an eternal truth! Ironically, these words are found in the same Bible that informs us of bodily resurrection after we have returned to dust!

First, God told Adam that from dust man was formed, and to dust all men will return. Later God told us, through Jesus, that our bodies will be resurrected. The only revealed truth I discern from the foregoing is proof positive that the Bible is nothing more than a jumble of disjointed Semite history interwoven with fabulous Hebrew deity myths. That some factual material is found in the Bible is coincidental and inevitable; for truly, there is no such composition as absolute fiction.

Several pages later, Augustine qualifies the physical resurrection by comparing it with the resurrection of Jesus. In his words, after the resurrection: Jesus was "spiritual, but yet real flesh." How did Augustine become saddled with such a self-contradicting absurdity as spiritual flesh? Rather easily, he read it in the Gospel of Luke! Jesus, materializing from nowhere, stood in the midst of the Apostles and asked, *"Do you have anything to eat here? They gave him a piece of cooked fish, which he took and ate before them."* [Lu. 24:41-43]

In order to defend the physical incongruity of spiritual flesh, Augustine enlightens us with the unlikely and irrational proposition that not the power and ability to eat, only the need, is lost after a bodily resurrection. Then must I wonder if all other human biological functions remain operational after our resurrection. Alas, Augustine never elaborated on this obvious corollary.

Similar to most 'good Christians,' he only labors to buttress Church doctrine, not to seek after total truth. He courageously extracts a spoonful of broth that he deems is truth from the 'Mulligan Stew' of religious beliefs. He, thereafter, nonchalantly discards the remaining stew that he alleges is untruth, and happily announces that the meal is over, and that no more food exists. Actually, much food for thought remains. Augustine simply ignores its presence!

[City of God — Book XVI, Chapter 7] St. Augustine while attempting to rationalize why different animals are found in remote locales throughout the world after 'The Flood' exposes his erroneous information about the genesis of the lower life forms. He wrote, "A question arises how wild animals, propagated by ordinary mating like wolves and the rest, can be found on the islands far at sea, unless those which were destroyed by the flood were replaced by others descended from the animals, male and female, which were saved in the ark. (There is no problem in regard to domestic animals or to those which, like frogs, spring directly from the soil.)" St. Augustine's belief: The higher animals needed parents, but all the lower forms, like frogs, did not! Soil unaided generates frogs, et al.

[City of God — Book V, Chapters 3 & 4] St. Augustine discourses on the rapidity with which the celestial sphere revolves. He is referring, of course, to the 'fact' that the Earth is stationary in space, whereas the heavenly globe above the Earth revolves around it. Ironically, in this book Augustine is scoffing at the notion of horoscopes and fortune telling that the "mathematicians" {astrologers} of his day employed to deceive the gullible. Augustine ridicules the "emptiness of the talk of the mathematicians." All the while, he blindly overlooks the emptiness of his own religious volubility.

With that observation, I commend St. Augustine back to the ages. In his later life he was a decent man. By then, he had become indoctrinated with his mother's beliefs, and had sought to share her (mis)information with those contemporary with him. Consequently, to mislead all who followed after him! The world would have been better served if Augustine had espoused atheism, and afterward sought to convert all of humanity through his demonstrated cognitive and literary talents.

POPE CLEMENT AND THE RESURRECTION BIRD

Clement I (r. 88-97 A.D.?) was a successor to St. Peter, the chief Apostle. The Catholic Church credits him with being the fourth Pope historically (some record him as second after Peter). Although never revered as extensively as either St. Thomas Aquinas or St. Augustine, Clement nonetheless was held in very high esteem by the early church. Traditionally, he is titled, "An Apostolic Father." Two of his Epistles (instructional letters) to the nascent Christians were honored and disseminated just as fervently as were St. Paul's Epistles. It would not be totally false to state that the two missives of the first Pope Clement were deemed equally by the early church to be "scriptural." That is, likely to have been inspired by the Holy Spirit.

Funk and Wagnall's New Encyclopedia has the following to inform about St. Clement: "Little is known of his life, but it is believed he was one of the Apostolic Fathers of the Christian Church and that he may have been the author of the Clementines, the celebrated early Christian writings."

One may ask quizzically, why is Clement included in this segment of my work? Clement is included in this chapter for only one reason. He is the person most responsible for the spread of the legend of the "Phoenix." Almost everyone knows of this mythical creature, but few know where the fable originated. St. Clement introduced this impossible bird to us in his first Epistle. Clement, wishing to authenticate a future resurrection for the faithful began his Chapter XII (XXV?) with the story of the Phoenix arising from its own ashes. Below his words are reproduced from "The Lost Books of the Bible."

CHAPTER XII

"Let us consider that wonderful type of the resurrection which is seen in the eastern countries; that is to say, in Arabia.

"2 There is a certain bird called the Phoenix; of this there is never but one at a time; and that lives five hundred years. And when the time of its dissolution draws near, that it must die, it makes itself a nest of frankincense, and myrrh, and other spices into which when its time is fulfilled it enters and dies.

"3 But its flesh putrifying {sic}, breeds a certain worm, which being nourished with the juice of the dead bird brings forth feathers; and when it is grown to a perfect state, it takes up the nest in which the bones of the parents lie, and carries it from Arabia into Egypt, to a city called Heliopolis:

"4 And flying in open day in the sight of all men, lays it upon the altar of the sun, and so returns from whence it came.

"5 The priests then search into the records of the time; and find that it has returned precisely at the end of five hundred years.

" 6 And shall we then think it to be any very great and strange thing for the Lord of all to raise up those that religiously serve him in the assurance of a good faith, when even by a bird he shews {sic} us the greatness of his power to fulfil {sic} his promise?"

It is obvious that Clement believed (& propagated) the tale of the Phoenix. As late as the ninth century, the official church still thought highly of his epistles. Of those theological scholars who were skeptical, most attacked Clement's writings, not because of the myth of the Phoenix, but because Clement wasn't clear about the accepted unique relationship of Jesus to God and His Holy Spirit. Nowhere does Clement define an orthodox 'Trinity.'

But there is one other quote from Clement that I wish to share with my readers. Clement makes the very same point that I do many times in this work. From Chapter XII, verse 11: "For nothing is impossible with God but to lie." (In another source, Chapter XXVII) With that statement I agree wholeheartedly. 'God cannot lie or deceive'; therefore, if one finds errors in any writing, then God had no part in its composition. [Cf. Tit. 1:2] Throughout this work I have exposed error after error found within the Bible. Not because God lied to us, but because mankind, in his ignorance & in his arrogance, falsely attributed his own human words to a Divinity. The grand deceiver of the universe isn't God or even Satan; it is superstitious and deceitful man himself. Every last supernatural philosophy (i.e., 'religion') has been man-made!

CHAPTER 15

Smatterings of Religiosity

MAN, EARTH, GOD AND PROBABILITY

Any reasonably intelligent person should, upon reflection, be able to perceive the comparative non-essentialness of man. Contrary to early Christian doctrine, Mother Earth isn't the vortex or hub of the Universe. Our planet is considerably less than a cosmic granule of matter dispersed among a myriad of both dark and incandescent, highly compacted, gigantic masses of matter that are themselves inconsequential when contrasted to the entire universe.

In terms of universal importance, man is insignificant, approaching sans-significance. Yet, in his own eco-system, he is supreme among all living entities. Mankind's innate worth has different values depending upon that which it is contrasted against. We inflict a great injustice upon humanity in general when we insinuate human beings into the cosmos. Man's proudest accomplishments shrink to near nothingness just as surely as does his physical stature. We are a tiny bio-quark in a microscopic molecule (Earth). If we insinuate ourselves and our planet into the limitless space that is the Universe, we become totally lost and obscured in its vast milieu.

Why did God create the Universe? Did He have anything more in mind than to test mankind's penchant to sin? Was this the Almighty's sole reason for creating? Why create an unclassifiable profusion of living entities on the Earth if all that is consequential in the Universe is a tiny iota of life called humanity. God went to great lengths to fashion a vast, panoramic stage for mankind's exhibition of morality, or lack thereof! Why are so many countless bit players (non-human bio-forms) so hidden that only God is aware of their contribution to the overall drama? Today, mankind is discovering previously unknown life forms almost daily.

I have treated on this theme before. But ponder this query now: Who is the audience to our earthly show? Only God and the Devil will ever review our performance. Does the Almighty need every creature of the deep? Is Satan conniving with the air-borne microbes to subvert mankind's (self) decreed mandamus to serve the Universal Deity's morality purposes?

Why can't religionists recognize the sublime stupidity of their indulged ignorance? They denounce the discovery of the emergence of living matter through the process of evolution by observing that the odds are hopelessly against it. They maintain that the inert elements, which abound on Earth, could never have coalesced to form the complex life-form called mankind. Their argument is framed so, because it seems to render the entire premise of evolution so improbable as to brand it an actual impossibility. Yet, I know that in their cognitive core they covertly acknowledge evolution as the singular cause of the assortment of life's bio-entities.

If a High School football team were to be scheduled for a game against last year's Super Bowl winner, there would be no doubt whatsoever of the outcome. That wouldn't keep some fans (sobriquet for 'fanatics') from rooting for their High School team. Loyalty is seldom, if ever, dependent upon cognitive appraisal. Still, the High School loyalists would cling to the fruitless hope that somehow, in some miraculous circumstance, their team might prevail. But they hope against practicality. In similar manner, religionists are ever loyal to their "home-team" Divinity. Evolutionists have a preponderance of mankind's intellectual heavyweights backing them. Our studied intellectuals propose to us that life began as a result of the chance union of several of the correct elements at a fortuitous time, in a suitable place and in the proper setting.

Religionists scoff and conclude that the odds against such an event are beyond astronomical. I have read that the chance of the twenty amino acids needed in the manufacture of living protein combining to form any one specified protein is ten to the one hundred and thirty-ninth power

(10139). This truly is a prodigious number. But it isn't an impossible number! If we concede that any protein matter is ever formed from free-existing amino acids (it is!), then we have conceded the unrestricted possibility of chance biogenesis. What are the odds against breaking the bank at a gambling casino? They are very great indeed. Yet, it has been done!

Religionists invert the logic of probability. They maintain that when the odds are very long, then a given event will not take place. Whenever one spins the wheel of fortune, someone wins each and every time. Is this mathematical fact clear? Winning the top State Lottery is a virtual impossibility. Still, the very act of repeatedly holding drawings ensures that eventually someone will win. The very fact that amino acids can and do form various proteins guarantees that all proteins will be formed eventually. In nature, any event that isn't impossible ... is possible! Anything possible is thence eventually probable. And any event that becomes probable becomes a certainty if enough time and repetition is allotted for its occurrence.

Ponder this scenario as an allegory: You have one hundred pairs of dice, and you want to roll them out so that every top die face shows a three. You might cast them out for an eternity and never meet your requirement. Suppose, however, you set the condition that whenever the die nearest your hand showed a three, that die would remain on the board, and only the remaining dice (descending from ninety-nine and one-half pairs) would be subsequently thrown. Now you have not only removed the impossibility of rolling all three's, but you have made it a certainty that eventually all die faces will show a three. With your lone stipulation, you have changed the wildest improbability into an absolute inevitability. (Amino acids are formed naturally)

If you are intimidated by odds, then consider this: What are the odds against the existence of an Ever Living/Never Dying; All Powerful/Seldom Acting; Super Being called God? What are the odds in favor of three persons only constituting one person? On the basis of adverse odds alone, no one should ever deny any eventuality. Only contradictions are impossible. God is a contradiction. God is something; however, He is really nothing! He is everywhere; yet visually, He is nowhere! God has always lived; still, He died on the cross! Are any of the foregoing contradictions logical? What are the odds against the existence of a living, loving, vibrant Deity whose perception spans the totality of both time and the Universe?

There aren't longer odds against any actuality. God is the acme contradiction; thereby God is the supreme impossibility!

VANITY IS A SIN

One of the most frequent and most damning charges hurled against non-believers is the sin of vanity. Religionists accuse atheists of harboring undue pride in their own persona. They aver that the proof of their accusation is that atheists credit man with the works of God. Religionists, in their feigned humility, inject God into all that occurs, infrequently even to deleterious happenings. Not that God Himself performs unwelcome evil. He does, however, suffer it to happen. If He chose, individual evils could be rectified, recompensed or eliminated.

In the end, if a man denies that there is a God, then he must credit something/someone else with responsibility for each occurrence. This alternate motive force must be either Nature or man himself. Religionists disagree; they assign every act of "Nature" as an act of "God," also any act of man that produces beneficial results as the impetus of God. Therefore, their recrimination of vanity against atheists seems merited. But is the anti-deity accreditation of atheists based on pride? 'Or is it on necessity? Atheists have no option but to credit or blame man for all that happens in life that can't be charged to nature. The verity of a religionist's indictment is superficial. Ironically, it happens that vanity is a factor in this dispute, but the culprits are the religionists themselves. Recall the germane definitions of 'vanity': Undue pride in oneself; unjustified conceit in one's person; an over-inflated sense of one's worth.

Now, reflect on these inquiries mentally. Who states that God loves man, Atheists or Religionists? Who states that man is made in the image of the Almighty? Who states that every man is a child of God? Who states that man is the greatest of all God's creatures? Who states that man will never die? Who proposes man's conditional reservation into blissful Heaven for the remainder of eternity? It isn't atheists who glorify humanity beyond all reasonableness; it is religionists who elevate mankind to a degree of magnificence unparalleled in creation. If we can believe religionists God, Himself, vies for man's respect and affection. The epitome of vanity is expressed in the doctrine of the immortal soul. Atheists attribute no such preeminent worth to mankind. It is religionists who are overawed by mankind's self-identified, self-appointed significance. If vanity is a sin (it usually is!), then religionists are far more besmirched by that sin's taint than atheists can ever be.

THE VANITY OF RELIGIONISTS

To a religionist, the human race is the quintessence of creation. God's most endeared work was the creation of Adam and Eve. This belief is truly ego-inflating, but it deprecates and deeply depreciates the rest of creation. The only entity of value in the Universe is man's immortal soul. How very demeaning to the other species and kingdoms it would be if only they were cognizant of their total worthlessness in the assessment of religious mankind. A Mayfly is born, mates, and dies, all within twenty-four hours, yet no one cares. Some species of sea turtle are born, mate, and don't die for two hundred years; still, who cares? Surely, not God! He has granted eternal life to man alone. All other life forms perish without hope or realization of resurrection. 'Reflect on those extinct species. They didn't even live on through their progeny. That is truly pitiable.

Religionists place mankind on a pedestal so elevated that the remainder of creation shrinks into unrelieved irrelevance by comparison. That is egomaniacal! Atheists espouse no such grandiose delusions. However, religious dogma concerning the exaltation of mankind isn't without its paradoxes. While human beings in the aggregate are the apex of creation, individual man, in solitude, is deemed wholly unworthy of divine approbation. Common man is a lying, cheating, thieving, lustful wretch more deserving of God's disdain than His love. On the other hand, if a person (a religionist, for instance) could believe that he neither lied, nor cheated, nor stole, and was free of lust, then perhaps this individual not only would merit God's respect; even more, he could demand it!

The fact that almost one hundred percent of all religionists I have known have been absolutely certain of God's love for them informs me as to which grouping of mankind they slot their persona within. Pride finds a welcome home in the mind and in the heart of a religionist. Their love of

God is surpassed only by their love of self. The depth of their self-esteem can be measured by the persistence (and volume!) of the love they declare that God has for all of us.

The practical truism "The louder he proclaimed his honesty, the faster I counted the silverware" has a parallel application to religionists concerning God's love for everyone. "If God has constant love for the least of us, then surely He has even more affection for those who announce His divine love the loudest!" Why else would one become a minister for Jesus Christ? Why expose one's self to the rigors and hazards of evangelism, when the same eternal reward awaits those who merely lived a decent, Christian life? The unadorned reply is that there is no glory in unobtrusively leading a decent, Christian life.

{All would-be heroes need a 'cause' to champion.} What is more vital, they must assemble a 'coterie' of submissive devotees to their professed creed to validate their purportedly divinely sanctioned, yet self-appointed, 'vocation!' Christianity is the 'cause.' Converts are the 'coterie.' The 'vocation' is evangelizing. Their subliminal motivation is ego-requiting self-glorification. The Leader (hence the one who will reap the greatest honors for any success) is the proselytizing evangelist. There is no more prideful person in the Universe than a Christian evangelizer.

When the seventy-two disciples returned from evangelizing in the Holy Lands, Jesus said to them, "... *rejoice because your names are written in heaven.*" [Lu. 10:20] Human vanity seeks admiration leading toward eventual veneration. Plainly, there is no adulation to be garnered in the advocacy of atheism; hence, there is no priesthood of commissioned proselytizers preaching and teaching non-belief. There should be!

MOODS & HUMORS OF GOD

Religionists, speculating on God's motives for creating our planet and the calculating beings that inhabit it, have modeled the Deity after the first City or State ruler-kings of the initial civilizations. Historically this is amply attested or readily researched, so I won't expand on this aspect further. I will expound on a few pertinent thought-provoking introspections here.

Proselytizers assert that our sins offend God, which is a logical assumption. But I ask: "Is this true?" Can the Master of all Creation experience offense? Think about this deeply. Can God in the Highest have His moods altered by the actions of man? Can the all-seeing, all-knowing, all-powerful, ever-present 'Subsistence of the Universe' be happy, sad, or indifferent, modulated solely by human deportment?

Statistically, at any given moment, some fraction of the human race is celebrating Mass, while another fraction is committing murder, and still another sizable portion will be performing some vital, yet innocuous, function such as using the sanitary facilities of a lavatory. Taken separately, we can assign the appropriate Divine reaction to each of the foregoing. But not simultaneously! Theoretically, nothing is impossible for God. Yet, I can't conceive of the Essence of Divine Majesty smiling, weeping, and holding His nose … all at the same time. {Jocular, but not immaterial}

Religious theoreticians are so expansive in their theses that they cast an aura of reflective insight onto their speculations. This reflective insight is often mistaken for verity. Yet, if I take any one of their devout theories and examine it closely, I find that our sacrosanct theoretician may begin with a simple premise, but he invariably ends with an involved and unwarranted extrapolation of that premise. If one were to strip away the intimidating veneer of their sanctimonious rationale, their theses are exposed as mere verbal imagery concocted to emotionally placate our ever-active need to be entertained by favorably concluded fairy tales, fables, or some other fabulous mental concoction.

Once more, let us return to the eternal virginity of Mary for an example. All Christians know the story of the Annunciation almost by heart, so there is no imperative here to rehash it *in toto*. The angel Gabriel has just announced to Mary that she is to be the Mother of God's Son. What is Mary's response? "How can this be, for I have not known a man?" [Lu. 1:34] 'And so the tale progresses! You have listened to, or read, many a pious expansion of this virginal scenario. It would take many pages for me to recount the delineations and the extrapolations I have been subjected to concerning this mystical myth. But, if you will sit down and reflect on the situation as presented in Luke's Gospel, you will quickly realize that no religionist has ever dealt honestly with this illogical gospel fiction.

First, ask how Mary knew that a man was necessary for her to become pregnant. One answer is obvious. A betrothed young maiden surely would have been instructed by her mother on the expectations of a wife. Whatever the source, Mary already knew about sexual relations. Of that, we are assured. Now, if you can picture the day her mother first explained the facts of life to her, a not-impossible verbal exchange could have transpired thus:

Mother: *"... now those are the duties of a wife."*

Mary: *"But, mother, I want to remain a virgin all my life."*

Mother: *"Then why did you agree to the betrothal to Joseph?"*

Mary: *"Even virgins have to eat. You don't expect me to earn my own keep, do you?"*

Mother: *"What does Joseph think of your intention?"*

Mary: *"I haven't told him yet ... that is going to be my honeymoon surprise for him."*

Mother: *"I think you should tell Joseph before the marriage. His intentions may be praiseworthy, but know this: he wasn't conceived without sin as you were."*

Mary: *"Of course you are right, Mother, but I'm sure he will understand I am only marrying him for his security and his financial support —not to have sex with him!"*

As we all know, Joseph did respect Mary's wishes. Or do we know? Does the Bible tell us that Joseph never engaged in physical intercourse with his wife? No! All that is stated is that Joseph and Mary hadn't 'come together' before Mary was rendered pregnant with baby Jesus. Nowhere will you find mention of eternal virginity for Mary. Mary's life-long chastity is pure speculative attribution (pious poppycock) on the part of religionists. It is an unsupported, unwarranted, fanciful attribution on its face, and most assuredly in reality!

One could just as readily formulate the doctrine of the eternal dryness of the ankles of Jesus. If Jesus could walk on water, then surely He never got His ankles wet. Any puddles He encountered He must just have walked across, rather than into. Nowhere in the New Testament does it report that He did get His ankles wet; accordingly, I propose devotions to the 'Perpetually Dry Ankles of Jesus.' Roman Catholics can maintain their veneration of His 'Sacred Heart.'

Don't read tactless mocking into the above. The intention is merely an illustration of the selectivity of devotional extrapolations. The biblical support for most devotionals is just as tenuous as is my 'dry ankle' fabrication. The only real difference in accepted extrapolations and my offering is in their respective appeal to human aesthetic predisposition. The human heart is the purported focus of our emotion of love; hence, it evokes pleasant humors. The same can't be said for the human foot. As a consequence, my objectification is repugnant to religionists; perhaps to mankind in general?

Of the two devotionals, heart or ankles, which has the greatest validation in the Bible? In my estimation, the ankles! Candidly, I can't locate where, in the Gospels, the Roman Church finds the basis for their 'Sacred Heart' devotionals. Jesus' exhortation to His disciples to love one another as He loved them isn't empirically documented in the New Testament. The love that Jesus felt for His followers is inferred. It isn't demonstrated!

During His lifetime Jesus cured uncounted ill persons. Yet, His greatest proselytizer, Paul, suffered a painful, unrelenting ailment for the duration of his ministry. [Cf. 2 Cor. 12:7-10] Why didn't Jesus exhibit His love for Paul by curing him? Should we credit the 'calming of the storm' as an act of love by Jesus toward His Apostles? If so, then to whom do we assign responsibility for generating the storm? Ostensibly, Jesus was asleep! We can extrapolate on and on.

All of God's moods and humors are an inference concocted by our imagination. The O. T. Prophets hectored the rulers of the Hebrews incessantly. Did the amoral or idolatrous actions of the kings truly irritate God? Or, more simply, did the prophets merely set themselves up as the moralists of the Hebrew nation? Invoking Yahweh conferred on the prophets a respectability, and an authorization that they otherwise would have lacked. Today's preachers invoke God's authority to impose their own values under the same reasoning and effect. Who can disregard, or even quibble, with a precept relayed directly from God?

How is it that so many religionists can know the temperament of God so unerringly; yet be so totally ignorant of His reactions? They pretend to be privy to His every emotion; yet His actions forever remain a mystery. The religionists may be deluding themselves, but they aren't fooling me. Actions do speak louder than words. The existence of a Personal Deity is all mental speculation. Religiosity is all "talk." The revelation of toilsome, unpredictable human history echoes more thunderous than the sanctimonious bombast of the entirety of religionists.

Why religionists never attempt to predict God's reactions is because God never predictably reacts. This assertion can be verified. The reason religionists always pretend to know God's moods and humors is because this portentous assertion can never be verified, consequently it cannot ever be discredited. The ubiquitous declaration that the Almighty is offended by our sins and that we should pray for His forgiveness after we have sinned is simply an unverifiable presumption. Therefore, I write: "Renounce your credulity; reactivate your incredulity; discontinue your prayers; end your posturing and your importuning: God is a hoax.

MODERN SUPERSTITIONS

Presently, we believe that we are much less credulous than the peoples of the Bible. Sophisticates: we smile slyly at one another when we read many of the Bible's paranormal events. Exorcising demons from mentally disturbed persons is an example. Yet, today I see syndicated columns purporting to know a person's horoscope. A horoscope is obtained by a study of the motions of the planets correlated to the zodiacal constellation that was most prominent during the month of your birth. This belief (in the validity of horoscopes) dispenses with several knowable truths that would expose the utter foolishness of astrological charts.

First, constellations are not groups of stars; they are apparent groupings of stars. Grammar School astronomy would so inform anyone who wished to know the truth. Second, the Earth, being a sphere, faces all the constellations simultaneously so that the longitude and latitude of your birth as well as the date and time should be worked into your horoscope (if the stars did exercise potency over your life). Not surprisingly, this type of exacting horoscope is available for a pecuniary presentation.

Third, the constellations of the Zodiac follow roughly the plane of the celestial equator; consequently, persons born far north or far south of the Earth's equator are likely to have a non-zodiacal constellation directly overhead at the moment they emerge from their mother's womb. The previous statement was phrased thus because it seems to me that if the stars or planets could have an effect on a human being's personality traits and future fortunes, then that influence would be operational from the moment of conception, not from the moment of birth. However, so few of us (if any!) know our precise moment of conception that most of us would be unable to obtain a horoscope predicated on the actual moment of our conception.

Another obvious conclusion, derived from a belief in astrology, is that all Eskimos born above the Arctic Circle have Ursa Minor (the Little Dipper, including Polaris, the North Star) as their astrological sign and, consequently, would have identical horoscopes, identical personalities, and identical destinies irrespective of their actual birth date. There are many factual considerations that unmask astrology, but the foregoing should suffice to make the point. 'Superstition lives on in the Twentieth Century.' We have palm reading, phrenology, good luck charms, black magic, yoga, transcendental meditation, and even bio-rhythms, to identify only a few of our superstitions. Still, the most prevalent, the most persistent, and the most pernicious of our embraced deceptions is "Religion" ... all religions, not just Christianity.

No "Religion" can ever be debunked dispassionately. I can scoff at palm reading and no one cares. I can scorn phrenology without comment. All other forms of superstition may be debated intelligently, deemed deficient, and discarded without arousing the slightest animosity. But, shine even the narrowest beam of critical light on the concept of a personal God, and you will have roused a human maelstrom that will refuse to be quieted. That inevitable outcome is harmful to, never supportive of, those who preach a personal God.

Why is there such fervor for defending Almighty God? Why do adherents display such zealotry in repulsing an attack on the Supreme Being hypothesis? Why do believers evince such intensity, such passion, and such vitriol in combating non-belief? If their theories are valid, then disbelievers will earn from God the utmost punishment ... eternal damnation! No punitive action of man can even approach this irreversible, unconditional, and eternal finality.

A parallel observation will illustrate the thrust of this latest point. No one would come to the aid of a muscular weight lifter if he were challenged to a wrestling match by a six-year-old. The outcome of the match would be known before it happened; yet if a reversed situation unfolded. 'What then? Suppose instead, that a bully menaced the timid youngest son of a family of a dozen very rough men. All the brothers would rally to defend their vulnerable sibling who otherwise would be helpless.

Apply these two illustrations to an attack against an all-powerful Deity. Does God need to be defended against puny man? Not in any manner, or under any circumstance! But, if God isn't all-powerful, and if He factually is the impotent mental fabrication of mankind, then it urgently behooves His adherents to marshal their forces to repel all assaults against Him. There is no way a delusion can repulse a truth. The observation that believers are such ardent defenders of their faith plumbs the depths of their underlying doubts. If the innermost recesses of their consciousness could be extracted and displayed on a video screen, the picture it would reveal would be of a distracted, deceitful, and physically defenseless Deity.

True believers are always fanatical in their defense of their Deity because without this fanaticism their Deity would be easily exposed as a devious, craven, powerless, spectral phantasm. If pious respect and specific worship for your Deity earns you earthly benefits, such as success in battle (for one), then why doesn't public disrespect, especially blatant sacrilege cause that Deity to strike out against that malefactor personally, such as the fate of the sons of Aaron who offered "profane" fire to Yahweh? The resolution of that question is so obvious that it inevitably blinds all religionists to the eternal truth. God doesn't act, either in "Reward" or in "Revenge."

Religionists extrapolate the entirely random natural happenstance of life on earth, or the unpredictable results of actions by mankind, and contort that happenstance into "the actions of God." Whatever happens on earth, either naturally or via the intrusion of humans is always credited to the "Will of God." This ubiquitous tenet of immutable faith promoted by all religions is impossible to debunk for it is impossible to verify or authenticate in any manner whatsoever.

HUMAN GENESIS

Religionists are deceived by the believability of a Universal Creator in the same manner that the earliest sky-watchers were deceived by the stars, the wandering stars (planets), the galaxies, the comets, and exceptionally by lunar eclipses in the nighttime heavens. Superstitious man observed the complexity of the Universe in bafflement. 'How can such immensity have gotten here,' they wondered? The answer probably came quickly. Some enormous "Person" must have created it. How else could it have been formed? Only living entities can create. Bees construct hives; Birds build nests; Man can fashion many edifices. But none of the living builders has the ability to construct this that is the mother of all living creation: Mother Earth!

It didn't take early man long to deduce that all bio-entities were (and likely always have been) dependent upon this planet for sustenance, either directly or indirectly. The earth itself, i.e., the physical soil, observably had the power to both generate and sustain life. Yet soil, obviously, had no life of its own. Soil could not create more soil. Dirt was inert! Still, soil itself seemed to be the mother of many smaller life forms. Not just plant life either. Soil could create tiny vermin also. Those who looked close enough could see that the dirt of the Earth contained both plant and lesser animate life. To be sure, larger animals needed individual mothers. But the smaller life forms could be generated spontaneously by Mother Earth. Many intelligent philosophers, St. Augustine among them, made this very observation erringly.

Nonetheless, close examination of the Earth indicated that the soil itself was dead. How can a lifeless element generate life? This was a puzzler. Yet, one thing was certain: Females are the custodians of life, and, because of this, the planet that gave birth to all life must be female also; ergo, 'Mother' Earth. Yet, ancient man was not totally ignorant. He knew one other immutable fact: Females couldn't conceive independently. They first had to be impregnated by a male. But who was this male? Where was this male? How did he manage to impregnate Mother Earth?

The ancients searched for clues. What was the seminal fluid that caused the earthly life forms to grow? Long before man ever became a farmer, he must have fathomed the answer as rain. "Rain" was the fecund fluid that caused the plants to grow. Mother Earth was impregnated from the sky through the medium of rain. Clever man turned his attention skyward. Who up there was the cause for the rain? The sky, as a whole, is generally innocuous. The nighttime sky was truly interesting. The nighttime Sky has a yearly procession of constellations; the monthly gyrations of the Moon; and the nightly wanderings of the erratic 'stars' (planets) to stoke interest.

But the stars were too tiny and too disinterested to have an effect on the earth. The Moon would have been a likely suspect as the consort of Mother Earth, except for the fact that the moon seemed more mischievous than potent while changing size and shape nightly. Moreover, life forms generally slumbered at night ignoring the antics of an ever-changing Moon!

So mankind looked into the day-lit skies. How obvious the suspect was when man lifted his face to the illuminated heavens. The Sun, truly, must be the cause of the generation of life on Earth. The plants of the Earth recognized the Sun as their benefactor, and always turned their faces to "him" in silent homage to "his" paternal dominion.

Another consideration was this: When vegetation was shaded from the life-giving rays of the Sun, or when it was uprooted from the life-sustaining breast of its mother (the Earth), it soon withered and died. Man, however, was not a plant. He could thrive in prolonged shade. His feet weren't rooted in the soil, so his attachment to Mother Earth wasn't as direct as was a plant's. He was, nonetheless, still vaguely aware that he, too, sprang from Mother Earth. The Bible declares that man was formed from the clay of the Earth.

"Then the Lord God took some soil from the ground and formed a man out of it; he breathed life giving breath into his nostrils and the man began to live." [Gen. 2:7]

The significance of this speculation shouldn't be minimized. Admittedly, there arose problems with this theological proposition. But, generally, imagining the Sun as the Creative Father of all of mankind was a rather facile explanation for the enigma of our own genesis. The theory of the Sun as the 'Father God of All' is unsatisfactory in many ways, and this probably accounts for its eventual demise. Yet, our current theory of an invisible Sky God is unsatisfactory also, and probably for the same reason. Because it too is wrong!

Similarly, Atheism isn't entirely satisfactory in that it doesn't supply a determination for our origin; it merely postulates that there isn't a purposeful or personal resolution as to why we human beings are here. This may be true, but it is hardly reassuring, plus it is far removed from ego enhancing. For this reason alone (there are others), don't look for a massive defection of religionists to Atheism soon, or at any time in the predictable future.

CREATIONISM IS ANTI-INTELLECTUAL!

The miscellany of life forms abounding on this planet is a philosophical enigma to any religionist. What purpose could God have had in mind when He created so profusely? From the tiniest virus, to the enormous blue whale: why did God go to all this inconvenience if all of creation is nothing but backdrop for the drama of humanity? God wasted a prodigious amount of energy on life forms that have absolutely no relevancy to the major (sole?) theme of creation, that being, human behavior amidst the vagaries of human existence.

Supposedly, the Earth was created for the enjoyment of Adam and Eve alone. Adam never "knew" Eve until after the expulsion, so one can presume that God never intended Adam to have children. [Cf. Gen. 4:1] You will recall that the creation of Eve was an afterthought. This fact (if any portion of Genesis, Chapters One to Five can truly be denoted as fact!) raises a vital question: Was it part of God's original plan to create all humanity, or was it God's design that only Adam would roam this vast planet? This question, initially, seems altogether spurious. Not so! The question is relevant (and vital), and is forced by a judicious reading of Genesis.

Examining Chapter Two of Genesis I find: First, God created Heaven and Earth, then Adam, then the Garden of Eden, then trees and other plant life, and then four rivers. The narrative interrupts here for God to give Adam the command not to eat of the Tree of Knowledge. It is also at this point that God notes that, *"It is not good that the man should be alone; I will make him a helper fit for him. "* [Gen. 2:18] But God doesn't create Eve just yet. First, He *"formed every beast of the field and every fowl of the air,"* and then He had Adam name them all. [Gen. 2:19] Knowing now how plentiful is the animal world, how prolific are birds, and not considering the insect world, one wonders how long this naming process took?

'Regardless! The naming of the animals was secondary to the real purpose of examining the beasts and the birds; that was to find a fit mate for Adam. *"... but there was not found a helper fit for him. "* [Gen. 2:20] Finally, after all this rigmarole, God thought to fashion Eve out of Adam's rib. Only after the entire menagerie of animals had been rejected, did God decide to create a woman. [Cf. Gen. 2:21-22] What is this section of the Bible imparting to us? It is telling us that Eve wasn't essential to God's original plan! Discernibly, Eve was meant to be a helpmate to Adam. Read Genesis 1, 2, & 3 for yourself. The creation of Eve was an afterthought. Am I dissembling or distorting? No, I am not! But am I shedding illumination? Please open your eyes and observe for yourself that which is plainly visible for all to see.

EVOLUTION VERSUS CREATIONISM

Whenever the topic of evolution arises religionists smugly opine that evolution hasn't been conclusively proved. Then, they will proceed to point out that the theory can't explain unerringly how each and every nuance of species change came about, or exactly when it occurred. Finally, with thinly disguised elation, they add that this or that famous person has openly expressed doubts about the absolute validity of evolution, or some portion thereof!

Am I to conclude from their puerile contention that they think that no one of consequence seriously questions the biblical account of the creation of man? Aren't they aware of the numberless multitude of observant persons who laugh at the religionists' wholly unbelievable, wholly unproved, wholly illogical fable of Adam and Eve? Not only does this fable lack one iota of proof (in itself this is conclusive!), additionally, every shred of evidence, every hint of a clue, and every speck of verification tends to validate evolution, and tends to disprove the prodigious conception of instantaneous creation. Likewise, ponder the paradisiacal conception of a "Garden of Eden."

Irrefutable data that will convince all religionists of the reality of evolution can never be presented. Religionists accept Creationism on faith alone, and faith resides solely in the imagination of the believer. Imagination isn't bound by the rules of logic or evidence. In truth, if proof is present, then there is no need for faith. Faith is required only where all evidence is lacking. If a demented person came to believe that water was air, and if he had faith that if he remained under water long enough he would be able to breathe in water just as fish do, how could I prove otherwise? Should I hold his head under water until he drowns?

This analogy isn't too fantastic if applied to religious beliefs. How can I prove to a resolute Christian that Jesus isn't waiting in Heaven to welcome him personally? The final truth in that belief can only be determined by dying. The incontrovertible truth or falsity of afterlife postulations is only knowable to those whose life has ended. (If anyone ever learns such!) However, this doesn't place the concept of a personal God into equivalence with the concept of an impersonal universal impetus. Those uncompromising opposites are far distant from equal!

COSMIC QUESTIONS

Why does the physical Universe exist? Why are there planets in our Solar System? Does this compromise the enlightenment God supposedly shared with us in the Bible? What purpose do any of the myriad manifestations of the physical Universe serve? (Supernova explosions, as one example) If the Bible is a complete cosmic encyclopedia, what can we learn from the immensely vast vault of the created galactic entirety? What relevance does the immeasurable Universe hold for man's relationship with its imputed Creator?

It was noted earlier that naive persons could easily become suitable converts to formal religions. They need supply nothing other than their unquestioning submission to cultic beliefs along with a steadfast adherence in the cult's canons and rituals. Then why does the totality of creation contain so much excess potential knowledge for mankind? Why is man the only known creature in creation capable of grasping any, possibly all, of the observable intricacies of nature? Man is unique among all identified living matter, but not in the manner religionists cast him.

Chimpanzees are capable of kneeling and bowing. They, also, are formed in the likeness of man; therefore, they can't be very deviant from the image of God: who shares man's likeness. [Cf. Gen. 1:27] (This comparison relates to the anatomical appearance of the apes, i.e., anthropoids) Myna birds, among others, can imitate the human voice, and theoretically could be taught to praise God, and mimic the other vocal religious requirements. As any owner can attest, Dogs are capable of exhibiting love, shame, and many other human emotions. Termites can build large structures that superficially resemble miniature cathedrals.

The point here is that many of the basic activities we perform as religious ritual could be approximated in the non-human kingdoms. If God had desired creatures that simply mimicked postures, imitated voices, feigned love, or were controlled by instinctive behavior patterns that predisposed the creature to construct certain edifices, then man was unnecessary. Lower life forms would suffice this purpose with much more punctuality, much less deviation, and what should be more important to an egocentric Deity, unreservedly without sacrilege or blasphemy!

But wait, you aver that man is exceptional because he has an immortal soul. A soul that is invisible, has no substance, and can't be detected in any manner whatsoever. Such an entity would not only be unaffected by the physical world, but conversely, it would be unable to have effect on anything in the physical world. If such an entity couldn't be known through the senses, then it couldn't have an effect on those senses. It is fortunate indeed for the soul (and its formulators) that it can't be located, for I am certain that some inquisitive human would have found it, measured it, listened to it, smelled it, and eventually tasted it … all to learn more about it! This isn't stated out of irreverence; it is simply familiarity with our intrinsic human nature.

The standard description of the soul is just too religiously convenient. All cultic items that can be disproved empirically are thereby consigned to the spirit world. Thenceforth, they constitute matters of faith, interminably relieving their proponents the impossible task of proving the existence of things that don't really exist. Is there anything "real" (i.e., tangible) in religion? "Yes," devout advocates chant in unison. "Look at the Universe around you!" But as soon as man begins to understand that Universe, and to control or alter it even in a minuscule way, the chorus changes to, "If God had intended man to fly, He would have given him wings!" This is the single-most imbecilic axiom that sentient mankind has ever been assaulted with.

If the soul is what is important to God, then why all this folderol with the positioning of the body, the use and misuse of parts of the body, and all the other corporeal aspects of religion? No action, whether physical or mental, would have an effect on a pure spirit. If the existence of a human soul has validity, then every other mental conception of humanity can allege that same validity. If a soul is possible, then truly, nothing is impossible!

Mankind can, and is, learning more each day how nature functions; what the properties of combined matter are; even where Heaven isn't. The what, the when, the where, and the how are all generally recognized, though not comprehensively understood or defined. Only the enigmatical "why" continues to baffle us. But the answer to that baffler need not entail a personal God.

One: We may not be the final (uppermost) rung in the evolutionary ladder. If that is the case, then we can expect no more affection from the Deity than we now suppose the lower animals receive from God. Two: A Universal Creator, who always existed, is just as incomprehensible as is a Universe without a Creator. Neither option is more logical than is the other. Or is it that both are equally illogical?

The only verifiable difference between mankind and the rest of the life forms on Earth is man's intellect. He is alone in his ability to know of God's existence. Or oppositely, to perceive that God doesn't exist! If God does exist, then mankind doesn't need His assistance to come to recognize Him. Man can divine the supernatural without the Supernatural revealing His Divinity. Unquestionably, not everyone who has averred enlightenment from God has spoken the truth. This despite a personal conviction that the claimant's beliefs are factual! One can readily deduce this from the plethora of beliefs, practices, dogmas, tenets, creeds, expectations, opinions, convictions, doctrines, denominations, sects, factions, and religious cults extant today.

One of the clearest misinterpretations of the biblical texts occurs with the Ten Commandments. [Cf. Ex. 20:1-17 & Deut. 5:1-21] Number Six reads: *'Thou shall not kill.'* Yet Moses, returning from Mount Sinai and finding the people worshiping a golden calf, cried out, *"Whoever is for the Lord, let him come to me!"* All the Levites then rallied to him, and Moses told them, *"Thus says the Lord, the God of Israel: Put your sword on your hip, every one of you! Now go up and down the camp, from gate to gate, and slay your kinsmen, your friends and neighbors!" The Levites carried out the command of Moses, and that day there fell about three thousand of the people. Then Moses said, "Today you have been dedicated to the Lord, for you were against your own sons and kinsmen, to bring a blessing upon yourselves this day."* [Ex. 32:26-29]

How should the Sixth Commandment of the Bible be translated with biblical accuracy and fidelity, 'Thou shall not kill,' or 'Thou shall not commit murder'? Both Ex. 20:13 & Deut. 5:17 now generally read in the modern English language, "Do not commit murder." {q. v.} The difference being that civil or ecclesiastical executions were lawful, but unsanctioned murder was unlawful. If anyone on Earth knew the divinely imparted intent of that Commandment, surely that person was Moses; yet, he killed three thousand Israelites within hours after receiving the Sixth Commandment directly from God {Yahweh}.

Shortly afterward, God personally ordered Moses to slay an entire city of non-Israelites. The Bible reads thus: *"The Lord said to Moses, 'Do not be afraid of him* {King Og of Bashan}. *I will give you victory over him, all his people, and his land. Do to him what you did to Sihon, the Amorite king who ruled at Heshbon.'* {All were killed} *So the Israelites killed Og, his sons, and all his people, leaving no survivors, and then they occupied his land."* [Num. 21:34-35]

Further scrutinizing the true meaning of the Sixth Commandment against murder: King Hezekiah of Israel was about to be attacked by Sennacherib, king of Assyria. Hezekiah was frightened, but Isaiah advised the king that the God of Israel would protect him. The Assyrians were prepared to attack when …. *"That night an angel of the Lord went to the Assyrian camp and killed 185,000 soldiers. At dawn the next day there they lay, all dead! Then the Assyrian emperor Sennacherib withdrew and returned to Nineveh."* [2 Ki.19:35-36 & Isa 37:36-37] Noticeably, God's Angels also are exempted from the Sixth Commandment.

Consider also, the Eighth Commandment, *"Thou shall not steal."* In the very next chapter of Exodus after the Commandments were given, God told Moses, *"You and the people whom you have brought up from the land of Egypt, are to go up from here to the land which I swore to Abraham, Isaac and Jacob I would give to their descendants. Driving out the Canaanites, Amorrites, Hethites, Pherezites, Hevites and Jebusites. I will send an angel before you"* [Ex. 33:1-3] Did God say, 'buy them out'? Did He say, 'bargain or barter with the inhabitants'? Were the Israelites instructed to reimburse the Canaanites for their loss of homesteads and property? No! No! No! The Israelites were told to 'drive them out!' 'Steal their lands by force of arms ... an angel will assist you.' [Cf. Joshua, including Jos. 11:23] So how, then, should the Eighth Commandment *'Thou shall not steal'* be interpreted? [Ex. 20:15 & Deut. 5:19]

All of the Commandments, at one time or another, were violated by leading personalities in the Bible. I am not referring to the fact that we are all sinners. What I am averring is this: "The Ten Commandments never hindered the Israelites from any action that benefited their group, regardless of how disastrously those actions impacted their fellow (non-Hebrew) human beings."

ON MICROSCOPIC LIFE

What position in the cosmic scale of importance, or even relevance, do the microscopic and submicroscopic life forms hold? If, as religionists believe, all that matters on Earth is the manner in which man deports himself under the scrutiny of the Creator: why does such an abundance and admixture of life exist? Surely there is no cogent reason for the unimaginable and almost unknowable proliferation of bio-forms existing on, above, or under the Earth.

Conceding that many minute organisms do affect human lives admits concomitantly, that many more have no impact whatsoever on mankind. In Nature, man is born, thrives, and expires without ever interacting with many equally oblivious species of minuscule animals and plants. The argument that all life forms are dependent one upon another, *ad infinitum*, is generally true, but specifically false. The indisputable fact that some pre-existing life forms are now extinct proves the last statement.

In all probability whole phyla of soft-bodied bio-entities have been generated, evolved, thriven for millennia, and eventually departed without leaving a single fossil trace of their past existence.

How should we interpret this from a religious perspective? The Bible doesn't even know of most of the existing phyla of life forms. Don't look for enlightenment there. In a religionist's mind the most worrisome event in the mind of the universal Deity is whether or not man barks out an expletive after he stubs his toe on a rock. My thinking is that such fatuous reasoning on the part of religionists is the real sin by any god's reckoning. Religionists would have us believe that the 'Sublime Intellect of the Cosmos' is pleased with man when he grovels in ignorance. Did God deign to set a snare of knowledge to catch unwary humanity? Has He endued sentient man with the very curiosity that draws him to the trap that will doom him? 'Yea, verily' intone the religionists. Yet each day, seemingly, new discoveries in the microscopic world reveal a diversity of bio-forms that previously had been unsuspected, even by the men of science.

On television one evening I was discomfited to learn of a tiny worm-like creature that lives its entire life at the roots of my eyelashes; similar examples (though not necessarily similar organisms) of parasitic, or quasi-parasitic organisms, that derive their sustenance in or on the human body could be cited. All life forms must tolerate uninvited visitors or unloved boarders. At all times, this tolerant mutualism is either beneficial or detrimental to the entities involved. Which is which, depends entirely on one's perspective. Athlete's foot fungi think it is just dandy that people wearing shoes have sweaty feet!

Did God purposefully create each and every life form that exists? There are so many that I can't even guess at the number. I am alluding here to species, not individuals. But now consider each individual in every species, genus, family, order, class, phylum, and kingdom until the entire domain of the active has been encompassed. Does God manipulate each and every one? Let's not overlook plant life! Many plants are liable for both the life and the death of mankind. Who all share in mankind's gift of free will? Do animals have free will? Do microbes? Do plants? Or is every action of every individual organism the action of a performer dutifully following his world script? Is God the writer, the producer, and the irresistible director of all the world's players performing in some cosmological drama? Are all things inanimate merely props on the world stage designed solely to create the illusion of reality? Religionists would have us believe that God is the only reality in the Universe. The exact opposite is the unmodified truth.

The point of this latest discussion is this: The range of life forms is evidence against a personal Creator. The more that knowledge of life is learned, the less viable the belief in a Divine Script Writer becomes. Not only because of the undeniable unlikelihood, and the evident impossibility of God staging every occurrence, but more so because of the ridiculousness of such an actuality. Yet religionists, because of their erroneous initial premise (the existence of a personal Deity), are compelled into professing just such theological tripe. 'False premises beget more false premises.' Understand "more" here as denoting both number and degree!

DIVERSITY OF LIFE FORMS

If (the fact of) Evolution is nothing more than a sophist daydream, how do you explain the diversity of creation? This world is literally teeming with life. The tiniest microorganisms complete with the largest vertebrates for the essence of life, viz., nutrition. Everywhere man searches, he finds bio-forms thriving. What does this all mean, and what is man's true place in this extensive labyrinth of existence? The explication of that query is as elusive as is an uncontained bead of mercury. 'More so, really!

Religionists, philosophers, humanists, and others, have all pondered that question, yet no consensus has ever been attained, nor is one likely in the future. The question presupposes that an answer does exist, and only remains to be discerned. This may well be the genesis of this mystery. If life, which simplistically is just a distinctive state of inert matter, is the result of a cosmic spin of the universal wheel of fortune, then basically, the reason we exist is because it was possible for us to exist. Given enough time and enough energy all things possible will evolve. The cosmos has had an abundance of both of these commodities (time & energy). Thereby we corroborate an inconceivable miscellany of life-forms, and thus we eliminate the requirement for an 'uncreated' Creator who fashioned that monumental flux of life-forms.

ANIMAL INTELLIGENCE

Without minimizing the profound degree of intellectual disparity between the animals and mankind, here follows a factual illustration of the innate cleverness of the simians. Simians, of course, are monkeys, and they are almost unanimously recognized to be not-too-distant genetic relatives of the great anthropoids (chimpanzees & apes); hence, near relatives of mankind also.

To better study a troop of macaque monkeys in the wild, scientists introduced the animals to a small uninhabited Japanese island. Inasmuch as the monkeys weren't native to the island, and because the scientists wanted to keep the troop under surveillance as much as possible, it was decided to provide food for the monkeys. This stratagem not only proved to be a success, but also became the occasion for an unanticipated revelation.

Each morning the scientists would deposit a small pile of sweet potatoes on the moist sands of the beach. The monkeys quickly learned to do their 'dining' at the scientists' convenient 'larder.' The arrangement worked to the advantage of both the scientists and the monkeys. The monkeys didn't have to forage for their sustenance, and the scientists had little difficulty observing and photographing the monkeys while they were feeding on the open beach.

However, there was one small problem encountered by the simian assemblage. Fresh sweet potatoes are naturally gritty, and when placed on moist sand, they become even more so. This, understandably, renders them somewhat less delectable; a fact not overlooked by a certain female monkey. One day, without prompting, she took her potato over to a small pool of rainwater and washed the grit off before she ate it. From that day henceforth, our bright little cousin never failed to cleanse her potatoes before she enjoyed them. Soon the whole troop adopted the practice. Predictably, the scientists were overjoyed to have witnessed this intelligent innovation on the part of the monkeys. But their surprise didn't end there. Shortly thereafter, one of the human experimenters reasoned that if the monkeys' diet was changed from sweet potatoes to rice; the monkeys would spend more time at the feeding area; thereafter, be under observation for a longer period of time. This tried, monkey ingenuity again manifest itself.

The rice, likewise, became coated with sand, but the resourceful monkeys applied the same solution as with the potatoes. The monkeys scooped up a couple of handfuls of the donated food, ran to the nearest pool, and threw the sand-coated rice into the water. The sand sank, but the rice floated. 'How providential! There was a slight modification in procedure between the rice and the potatoes. With the potatoes, any convenient water pool would suffice. But with the rice the monkeys invariably chose pools of salt water, rather than rainwater. Could it be that the bland rice tasted more delectable when rinsed in salt water than it did in fresh water? This was the deduction of the scientists.

Yet, for all their ingenuity, monkeys remain monkeys, and mankind maintains first place by a wide margin in the rankings for intelligence. How we evolved intellectually so perceptively over our kin, the primates, is still an unanswered question. But we needn't look to the spirit world for a solution. Intelligence flourishes throughout the mammalian order. Indeed, it seems to permeate the entire spectrum of the coherent bio-forms to a greater or lesser degree. Only the plant world (and the microbial world?) is predominated by the non-sentient. Invariably and unanimously, the observed 'facts of life' reinforce Evolution, not Creationism!

CHAPTER 16
Conflicts, et al.

JESUS RECRUITS APOSTLES

Saint John (Apostle cum Evangelist) contradicts Saint Mark (Evangelist) about the recruitment of the Apostles. You can learn this in a few moments' time; but most religionists aren't the slightest bit cognizant of this fact. They read the words of the Bible, but they absorb only the propaganda of religiosity. It doesn't matter who the preacher is, if you listen closely to his words, you will find his message more presumption than enlightenment. Interpreting the Bible convincingly requires at least three talents: Misinterpretation, Extrapolation, and Invention.

The Old Testament is nothing more than a patchwork of subjective Hebrew history, intermingled with superstitious ancient deity myths (Yahweh-Eloi). Several of the Books in the Old Testament are all-but-proven frauds in that scholars propose to declare them written by a person other than the attributed author (e.g., 2nd half of Isaiah). These books weren't inspired by God. They were inspired by a desire on the part of sham prophets or wily religionists to deceive the gullible. Incredibly, their deceit somehow became glorified into "sacred scripture." So now, along with all His other imputed offences, God (via the purported inspiration of the Holy Spirit) is guilty of complicity in a Bible deception. That crime, supplementing His additional misdemeanors, felonies, murders, and mass exterminations as recorded in the Old Testament.

Please don't misconstrue my rhetoric here and elsewhere. God isn't factually guilty of any crimes or other offenses, because there is no God. The fraud and deceit in the Bible can all be laid at the feet of mankind. Man is the deceiver, not the fictitious personage titled 'God.'

Mark (an Evangelist, but not an Apostle) reports that Jesus was at the Sea of Galilee when he selected Simon, Andrew, James and John to be His followers. *"As Jesus walked along the shore of Lake Galilee He saw Simon and Andrew. 'Come,' He said. At once they left and went with Him. He went a little further and saw James and John. They went with Him."* [Mk. 1:16-20] (Paraphrased for brevity) Mark reputedly writes for Peter, so here we have the words of a (presumed) totally reliable eyewitness.

Now read the Apostle John's account of the call of the first followers. *"All this happened in Bethany on the east side of the Jordan river where John was baptizing."* [Jn. 1:28] (Bethany is on the west side of the Jordan; However, Bethabara is on the east side of the Jordan.) Is the Holy Spirit deficient in geography?

Before continuing I must expose a contradiction in the sources used for this book. The "Good News Bible" locates the calling of the first Apostles in Bethany, a town just south and east of Jerusalem. Other translations consulted name the town as Bethabara. [e.g., KJV] This town is far north of Jerusalem just south of the Sea of Galilee on the east side of the Jordan River. Bethany is in Judea. Bethabara is in Perea. Herod the Great ruled all of the Holy Land when Jesus was born. After Herod died in 4 BC, his kingdom was divided. By the time of Jesus' ministry Pontius Pilate administered Judea, the southwestern portion of the Holy Lands. Herod's son, Herod Antipas ruled only in Galilee and Perea, the northern and eastern sections of the Holy Lands. John the Baptist performed his baptismal rite from Perean territory, the eastern side of the Jordan River, which placed him under the suzerainty of Antipas. Jesus, being a Galilean, also came under the authority of Antipas, not Pontius Pilate.

John the Evangelist composes a tale different from Mark when he writes of the call of the first Apostles. Apostle John writes that John the Baptist was performing his ablutions with a couple of his followers present when Jesus 'walked by.' The Baptist identified Jesus by announcing, *"Here is the Lamb of God."* [Jn. 1:36] The narrative continues: *"The two disciples heard him say this and went with Jesus."* [Jn. 1:37] Cryptically, only one of the two who originally were disciples of the Baptist is later identified. He was Andrew. Inasmuch as John the Evangelist never relates how he came to be an Apostle, one may (should?) presume that John was the other follower who deserted the Baptist in favor of Jesus. Andrew finds his brother Simon and recruits him to be a follower of Jesus also. Jesus immediately renames Simon as "Cephas." The text explains that the meaning of that Aramaic name is 'rock,' which in Greek is 'Peter' {Petra} the name so familiar to all of us.

Enigmatically, this "call of the first followers," according to John the Evangelist, took place near Bethany almost 50 miles south of the Sea of Galilee. There was no place for a fisherman to ply his employment in that locale. The other three Evangelists, Matthew, Mark and Luke record the call of the first followers as occurring at the Sea of Galilee. [Cf. Mt. 4:18-22; Mk. 1:16-20 & Lu. 5:1-11; Compare Jn. 1: 28, 1:35-42]

The next day Jesus went to Galilee (He had been in Perea previously) and said to Philip, *"Come with me!"* [Jn. 1:43] John's description of the call of the first Apostles essentially ends with this sentence: *"Philip found Nathaniel and told him, 'We have found the one of whom Moses wrote in the book of the Law, and of whom the prophets also wrote. He is Jesus, the son of Joseph, from Nazareth.'"* [Jn. 1:45]

However, John continues this episode with Nathaniel asking: *"Can anything good come from Nazareth?"* [Jn. 1:46] Your author asks: Can any Gospel texts inspired by the Holy Spirit be so replete with contradictions, ambiguities, and errors as we have them today? Even the identities of the chosen twelve are compromised by imprecision. Matthew, one of the Apostles doesn't know of Nathaniel. John, also one of the Apostles, who reports the call of Nathaniel, doesn't know of Bartholomew identified by Matthew as an Apostle. The Evangelist Luke, inspired by the Holy Spirit to write a gospel, identifies the tax-collector Apostle as "Levi." Peter's spokesman, Mark, also inspired by the Holy Spirit to write a gospel, likewise identifies the tax-collector Apostle as "Levi." Yet Matthew, inspired to write a gospel by the Holy Spirit, contrariwise identifies himself as the Apostle "Matthew" who collected taxes, not as "Levi."

I am confused, and I know of three other persons (at least) who are similarly confused. The other three persons (Evangelists all) have been dead for almost two thousand years. Yet the confusion continues into the present era. The honest, observant reader of the New Testament will find fifteen (15) Hebrew men identified as Apostles, Simon/Peter; Andrew; the brothers James & John, sons of Zebedee; Philip; Bartholomew; Thomas; Matthew; James, son of Alphaeus; Thaddeus; Simon the Zealot; Judas, son of James; Levi; Nathaniel & Judas Iscariot. 'Count them!

WHITHER THE APOSTLES?

The only record we have of the post-Ascension lives of the eleven Apostles comes from Luke, who was a companion of Paul. Paul was not one of the original twelve Apostles. Paul wasn't converted until AD 37, several years after the Crucifixion. Regrettably, Luke doesn't tell us how he knew the movements and experiences of the Apostles immediately after the death of Jesus. How did Luke come to know what transpired in Judea before he became a disciple of Paul? If you read Luke with your mind opened as wide as your eyes, you will be doubt-filled. Elsewhere I have opined that John's Gospel reads most as an eyewitness account. How, then, does Luke's Gospel read? Below are some excerpts, you may decide for yourself.

"One time Jesus was standing ...." [Lu. 5:1]

"Once Jesus was in a certain town ...." [Lu. 5:12]

"One day when Jesus ...." [Lu. 5:17]

"On another Sabbath ...." [Lu. 6:6]

"Some time later ...." [Lu. 8:1]

These are indefinite time references. Most of Luke's chronology is ambiguous. In a "Basic English" translation of Luke's Gospel the phrase, *"And it came about..."* is found sixteen separate times. Undeniably Luke is repeating stories told to him. He isn't recording events he personally witnessed. His source wasn't a personal witness either. In Luke's Gospel the Apostles aren't depicted as real persons. They are stage personas acting out their assigned roles. They speak and act only when it serves the purpose of the immediate narrative.

Moreover, even if we accept all that the Acts of the Apostles records, it tells so little about the chosen band that I am fairly bursting with curiosity.

What became of John? Likewise: his brother James? What became of Matthew after he wrote his history of the ministry of Jesus? What happened to Thomas the doubter? Did he eventually lose his faith? Or did he cast his seed ("Good News") upon rocky soil where it failed to germinate?

Before they met Jesus, Andrew fished with his brother Simon (Peter). Did they have a dispute after the departure of Jesus? Why is it we seldom hear of Andrew after his call to be a *"fisher of men"*? [Mt. 4:18-19 & Mk. 1:16-17] What became of Matthias? Who was Matthias? Do you know? He was the man formally chosen to replace Judas Iscariot to restore the Apostolic band to the symbolically (in)significant number of 'twelve.' [Cf. Acts 1:25-26] Curiously, when Paul first met with Peter three years after Paul's conversion from prosecutor of the new faith, to proselytizer of the new faith, only James the brother of Jesus was currently in Jerusalem with Peter. Paul remained with Peter (and James?) for 15 days. Yet Paul states unequivocally, *"But other of the Apostles, I saw none."* [Ga. 1: 18-19]

For a fact, we don't know scripturally what became of Paul, for he is still alive when Luke ends the Acts of the Apostles. What became of Luke? What did the complete band of followers do after the Resurrection? What happened to those who are absent from Acts and the Epistles? Why isn't there some record of their fate? Why did Jesus choose twelve Apostles, if only three of them ever accomplished anything recorded in the Bible? The significance of "twelve" Apostles is belied, even negated, by their collective absence of N. T. inclusion.

In Matthew's Gospel, Jesus informs the twelve Apostles that they will sit on thrones and judge the twelve tribes of Israel. [Cf. Mt. 19:28] Judas was one of those spoken to by the living Jesus. Will Judas the traitor sit in judgment over anyone? He committed the most heinous crime possible. He was an accomplice to deicide. Not even the Fallen Angles were able to execute God. So I ask again: "Will Judas 'sit in judgment' as Matthew's Gospel states?"

If Judas isn't going to judge, then Jesus lied! 'Or the Evangelist lied! 'Or the New Testament copyist lied! Judas isn't going to judge anyone … ever! He is the only man in the Bible of whom we can be certain of his fate. Judas is an esteemed resident in Hell. Jesus informs us it would have been better if Judas had never been born. [Cf. Mt. 26:24 & Mk. 14:21]

Of course, even this seemingly unequivocal statement can be qualified. The logic here is slightly devious, yet quite valid ... by accepted theological apology! Jesus didn't declare that it would have been better if Judas had never been conceived; therefore, the almost immediate remorse of Judas may have spared him from eternal damnation. The justification for this postulation proceeds thus:

If a newborn baby dies, he/she goes directly to Heaven because it has committed no sins. Continuing: What becomes of newly conceived fetuses that miscarry? Obviously, they aren't consigned to Hades, for they too haven't sinned. They go to Heaven. (Catholic theology postulates a virtual heaven-like place called Limbo for unbaptized infants.)

If Judas had never been born, but had been conceived, he would have gone to that place where unborn fetuses go when they die. So, if we make a distinction between never being conceived, and never being born, then maybe the Holy Spirit didn't intend us to interpret the passages under examination as the damnation of Judas. Perhaps suicide is the appropriate penance for deicide. Perhaps, Judas didn't go to Hell, notwithstanding his heinous sin. If that is the case, then Judas very well may judge one of the tribes of Israel after Doomsday. The Bible affirms that he will judge!

So, after much murky theological manipulation, I have arrived at the conclusion that Jesus didn't lie when He told the original twelve they would sit in judgment over the descendants of Jacob. But have I convinced you? If I have, then this entire book has been a waste. Traitor Judas isn't going to judge anyone; nor is Doubting Thomas! Neither Apostle will ever judge me. Thomas was a witness to the daily miracles of Jesus; still he doubted! I have never witnessed a single miracle. I certainly haven't placed my fingers into the wounds of Jesus either. My doubts are well founded. The doubts of Thomas cause me to doubt the entirety of the Gospels. If Thomas can be absolved despite his reservations, then no one should ever go to Hell for doubting. As for Judas; forget it! If Judas ever sat in judgment of me, I would denounce him to his face. I have never caused anyone to be crucified, much less, the incarnate divine Son of God!

Returning to the theme of this segment: After the conversion of Paul, the other Apostles all but disappear. Biblically, they do just that. They disappear! Luke, in his Acts of the Apostles, focuses exclusively on the life and works of Paul after Paul's conversion. The Acts and Paul's Epistles evidence Paul as the chief recruiter of nascent Christianity. According to Luke, Paul is the acknowledged Leader of all Christendom. Let me qualify that. Paul was either the *de facto* first Pope of the new Christian faith, or he was its first schismatic! In Galatians, Paul denounces Peter "to his face." [Cf. Ga. 2:11]

If, as I contend, Jesus was a reformer of Judaism, then Paul is the real architect of the Christian Faith we witness today. If you believe Jesus intended to begin a new religion that welcomed Gentiles, then the Apostles were apostates. After the Resurrection, we learn from the Gospels, the Apostles taught in the synagogues and only evangelized Jews. They, likewise, insisted that their Jewish adherents (converts) observe all of the Jewish religious Laws. The Apostles were seeking to prove the fulfillment of the ancient Jewish Scriptures. Paul was intent on negating the Mosaic Laws. [Cf. Ga. 2:19-21]

Of all the Apostles, I would have anticipated that Thomas would have been the most ardent and the most effective recruiter (propagandist). He knew beyond challenge that Jesus indeed had defeated death. What became of Thomas? Why didn't more of the twelve leave behind some witness of the divinity of Jesus? Why must we trust and believe the manifestly unsubstantiated testimony of two Evangelists who never even saw Jesus?

The almost total lack of verifiable knowledge of the fortune or destiny of the Evangelists, and the Apostles (include Paul) is damning evidence, deductive though it may be against the Godhood of Jesus, and is especially damaging to the reports of His resurrection. Everyone who was a witness to that unparalleled wonder should have broadcast that marvel unceasingly shouting, 'I have seen the crucified Jesus; He lives!' Jerusalem would have been abuzz with that startling news. Everyone would have been gossiping about that unprecedented spectacle. (Historically, the revivification of deceased Lazarus is recorded only in John's Gospel.) [Cf. Jn. 11:43-44] Every publicity seeker in Jerusalem would have made false avowal to being one of the favored persons who had observed the risen Christ. Instead, the city and historical records are silent. Only two eyewitnesses ever committed their testimony to writing, and they differ considerably in their accounts! (John, and possibly Matthew, witnessed the death of Jesus.)

The mainstream of Christianity wasn't Jewish at all; it was Gentile. The Jews of the "Holy Lands," (God's <u>chosen</u> people) were crushed by the Romans and driven into a nineteen-hundred-year exile. The cause of the destruction of Jerusalem wasn't the spread of Christianity; it was the rise of Jewish nationalism. Jesus, who died only a few decades before the Jewish Revolt of AD 66-70, doesn't even comment on the nationalistic agitation of His day. Reading the Gospels, one fails to discern the intense Jewish nationalistic fervor of those days. Surely Jesus was opposed to the subjugation of His race by the Romans, but you would never apprehend this when perusing (studying) the Gospels.

Jesus is most notably mute about the suzerainty of the despised Romans. The Gospels dwell on the undue pride and haughtiness of the empowered Jews (Pharisees, Sadducees, Scribes, *et al.*) to the exclusion of all others. There is little doubt who the Evangelists recognized as the real enemy of the nascent Christians. The rulers of the Sanhedrin were affixed that damning distinction. At every opportunity, the Pharisees are made to fulfill their historic role as the villains in the drama of the Gospels. The Gospels read all too suspiciously anti-Semitic to have been written by two apostolic Jews, and to contain the literal recollections of other Jews.

John's Gospel is noticeably biased against 'the Jews.' In his first chapter John writes: *"This is what John* {the Baptist} *said when the Jews in Jerusalem sent priests and Levites to ask him 'Who are you?'"* [Jn. 1:19] Why was John so persistent in his apparent motive to impress upon his readers that those who opposed Jesus were Jews? Only the opposite was necessary. Jesus was a Jew, living in a Jewish nation, populated overwhelmingly by Jews. Only when Jesus was interacting in the presence of non-Jews should John have noted the ethnicity of the participants. It requires no scholarly effort to conclude that the bona fide author of the Fourth Gospel wasn't a Jew. And, if 'John the Evangelist' wasn't a Jew, then neither was he a personal witness to the events described in the Fourth Gospel.

Other proofs indicating that the author of the Fourth Gospel wasn't a Jew are the instances where a Jewish term is translated. [e.g., Jn. 5:2, 19:13, 19:17 & 20:16] This is evidence that the author was writing primarily to a non-Jewish audience. That could hardly be John the Apostle. Perhaps this was the genesis of the tradition that John's Gospel was written in Ephesus (now a city in western Turkey).

Wherever the words of Jesus were received poorly, the author of the Fourth Gospel specified that the listeners were Jews. Likewise, whenever the crowd contended with Jesus, or was hostile to His preaching, the author identified them as Jews. Approximately fifty times, when the designation was uncalled for, John the Evangelist named those who opposed Jesus as "Jews." Only in Chapter Eighteen (which describes Jesus before Pilate) was it necessary to differentiate between the Roman authorities (non-Jews) and the Jewish authorities.

Whenever Jesus was well received, or was acclaimed, no mention is made of the nationality of the "acclaimers." They are simply referred to as 'the people.' The inference is unmistakable: the allies of Jesus were 'the people,' and His enemies were 'the Jews.' Chapter Seven of John's Gospel provides a fundamental example: *"There was much whispering about him {Jesus} in the crowds. 'He is a good man,' some people said. 'No,' others said, 'he fools the people.' But no one talked about him openly, because they were afraid of the Jews."* [Jn. 7:12-13] Who were these people who accepted Jesus, but feared retribution from "the Jews"?

Even Jesus is made to distinguish His followers from the contentious Jews. Speaking to the Apostles about His death and ascension, Jesus said: *". . . I shall not be with you very much longer. You will look for me; but I tell you now what I told the Jews. 'You cannot go where I am going.'"* [Jn. 13:33] What, pray tell, were His Apostles if they weren't Jews? The author of the Fourth Gospel had an evident bias against those he referred to as 'the Jews.' No hint of this nationality prejudice can be found in Matthew, Mark, or Luke; not even where the same incidents are related! Yet, if John the Apostle didn't write the Fourth Gospel … Who did? Why did he try to represent himself as an Apostle? And, how can I not ask this question: "If he lied about his identity, what else did he lie about?"

PETER'S DREAM (VISION)

There are many instances of dreams related in the Bible. The incident involving Peter recorded in Acts reads closer to an actual dream than many of the others. Here is a recounting of Peter's dream from <u>The Acts of the Apostles</u>:

"The next day, as they were on their way and coming near Joppa, Peter went up on the roof of the house about noon in order to pray. He became hungry and wanted to eat; while the food was being prepared he had a vision. He saw heaven opened and something coming down that looked like a large sheet being lowered by its four corners to the earth. In it were all kinds of animals, reptiles, and wild birds.

A voice said to him, "Get up, Peter; kill and eat! But Peter said, 'Certainly not, Lord! I have never eaten anything considered defiled or unclean.' This happened three times; and then the thing was taken back up into heaven."
[Acts 10:10-16]

Peter awoke from his 'vision' and was perplexed. What could be the meaning of the vision? Soon thereafter, the servants of the Roman Centurion, Cornelius, arrived and asked Peter to visit the home of their master. For a devout Jew, entering the home of a Gentile would have rendered Peter unclean. Now the meaning of the vision became apparent to Peter! God, by means of a vision (aka 'dream'), was informing Peter that associating with Gentiles was not defiling.

To me, this appears to be an actual dream. The sequence of events, as chronicled in Acts, is seemingly incredible, even supernatural. Yet, all we must do to reconcile the chronology dilemma is to suppose that Peter had received Cornelius's invitation before his mystic dream vision. If we make that time sequence adjustment to the story, then the event becomes not only more logical, but also much less supernatural. The impending meeting with the Centurion was troubling for Peter. He may have been less than fervent about Judaism, but Peter was still not an open apostate. Consorting socially with Gentiles, most especially with Romans, could result in total ostracism for him from the Jewish community. 'His mind conflicted thus with disquieting thoughts, Peter nodded off and had his revelatory dream (vision).

At the time of Christ's death, or before, a practicing Jew socially visiting with a Gentile would have been beyond consideration. Now, however, time and circumstance had changed. True, the first "Christians" were exclusively Jews. But the conversion and proselytizing of Gentiles by Paul began to change that. After initial success, the conversion of Jews into Christians began to ebb. By the start of the Jewish rebellion against Rome around 66 A.D. Jewish conversions to Christianity were increasingly rare and their scarcity threatened to become a positive drought.

The reason for the paucity of Jewish converts is readily comprehended. In Jewish eschatology there was no mention of a dead Messiah. The sacred texts foretold a conquering Savior … a hero king who would return His people to their lost position of power in their Promised Land! The Jews longed for the 'anointed one' who would redeem them from the degrading consequences of their former sins. Roman subjugation was only possible because Yahweh was angered with His 'special people.' The arrival of the Redeemer (foretold in sacred O.T. scriptures) was the long awaited beacon event that Yahweh had finally forgiven His delinquent children. The Messiah that the Jews of Christ's day were awaiting was to be the rebirth (reincarnation) of David, the conquering King, definitely and decidedly not the mild-mannered morality philosopher-commoner, named Jesus. {Yeshua}

EVOLUTION OF CHRISTIANITY

Did the Resurrection of Jesus prove that He was the "Anointed One?" The resurrection of Jesus only made sense if He rose from death in some now indestructible body that the despised Romans, and members of the Sanhedrin, could no longer harm. But if He had indeed returned triumphantly from the depths of Hades, where was He now?

The only proselytizing point the Apostles could advance was to postulate His imminent return. Jesus was gathering the heavenly hosts for the final assault upon the foreign forces of subjugation of the Hebrews. The forces of that wickedness were generally understood to be any nation in a position of world authority other than the Jewish Nation. The Jews hadn't waited a thousand years for a murdered Messiah. The resurrection of Jesus and His subsequent departure back to Heaven was only temporary. His return was only weeks, months, or at maximum, a few years in the future. Surely many of those listening to the Apostles (hesitant Jews by and large) would live to see His victorious reappearance; or so the Apostolic teaching proclaimed! [Cf. 1 Thes. 4:16]

This belief sold readily at first. But as the weeks, and months, and even years began to pass with no sign or notification of the return of Jesus, interest in His cult began to flag. It should evoke no astonishment at the reluctance of the scripturally knowledgeable Jews to accept the Messiahship of Jesus. Why was the promised Redeemer to come from the House of David? What qualities did David possess that would be reborn in his worthiest descendant? David had no praiseworthy attributes, at least none with religious import. The Jewish people revered the memory of King David for his military exploits. Candidly, he was never a paragon of sanctity! David, least of all, was no model (or practitioner!) of sexual or social morality as was Jesus!

The only praiseworthy heir to the House of David would have been a warrior and a conqueror, not a religious reformer. The Magi came to Jerusalem looking for a king, not a moralist. Religiously, David was a scandal to the Jewish people. Do you think the Jews of those times were expecting the 'Anointed One' to arrive merely to redefine their Judaic religion more strictly? They were not! The scriptures they read told them that a son of David was coming to re-establish Jewish sovereignty over the Holy Lands. This was the Promise the scriptural Messiah was to redeem.

Anyone who would verify my last premise need merely skim through the Psalms. They tell us what role the Anointed One was to fulfill. You can begin with Psalm Two, attributed to David.

> "The kings of the earth set themselves ... against the Lord, and against his anointed ... Yet have I set my king upon my holy hill of Zion ... the Lord hath said unto me, 'Thou art my Son; this day I have begotten thee. Ask of me, and I shall give thee the heathen for thine inheritance, and the uttermost parts of the earth for thy possession. Thou shalt break them with a rod of iron.'" [Ps. 2:2-9] The Messiah was to 'break the heathens with a rod of Iron.'

Knowledgeable Jews knew the scriptures well, perhaps superior to the apostolic band; nowhere did the texts tell of a crucified, then absent, Messiah. As fewer and fewer ethnic Jews subscribed to Christianity, the embryonic Church leaders had to look more and more to Gentiles for converts. In this endeavor the Apostles and their immediate heirs were successful beyond expectation. Whole communities of non-Jewish Christians sprang into existence. The Christian cult was growing rapidly, but it was straying increasingly from its Hebrew origins. This occurrence may have been the stimulus for re-identifying the new faithful as "Christians."

The ethnic Jewish Christians saw their formerly unchallenged leadership roles in the newly burgeoning sect come into question. A belated attempt to re-impose Jewish ritual predominance failed. James, the first accepted leader of the newly established sect, had to compromise with the Gentile converts and their new spokesperson and champion, Saul of Tarsus (St. Paul), to stave off potential schism. Rabid Judaizers refused to accept this compromise, and from that day forward, they dogged Paul's steps countering his relaxed version of Judaism, now called Christianity. [Cf. Ga. 2:4-6] Paul's Epistles to the various communities frequently, though disparagingly, verify this observation. Several times Paul speaks of opposition from "false Apostles" [2 Cor. 11:13] also "false Brethren." [2 Cor. 11:26 & Ga. 2:4] Whom does he mean by this description? Is he referring to any of the Twelve? Possibly! But if not, without doubt, he is referring to influential Jewish leaders. [Cf. Jude 1:4 & Titus 1:10]

How could Paul's message differ from the message of an Apostle? Both were inspired by God; both were infused with the Holy Spirit. Paul had access to eyewitnesses to Christ's ministry. So too would any non-apostolic leader of the infant Church, even if he himself wasn't a first-hand witness to the ministry of Jesus. How could distortions, errors, falsehoods and sham doctrines have been introduced so early into the Christian faith, if the Holy Spirit personally was guiding that Faith? The answer is evident; the answer is undeniable! Neither God, nor anyone allied with Him, was spiritually infusing the first missionaries of the Christian Faith.

The life of Jesus was something memorable. He inspired a cast of loyalty in His followers seldom witnessed before or since! This loyalty transcended His death on the cross. The recognition of Jesus as the promised Messiah never crystallized until after His crucifixion. In what manner could the Apostles honor this man who had so diametrically altered their lives? In the same manner that all epic heroes are honored: Exaggerate their noteworthy attributes to the point of glorification, or take a momentous event in the life of the hero and expand it into a wondrous, even miraculous, event. Super heroes always perform superhuman feats, and thereby, the miracles came. Those who knew Him intimately needn't have been the actual authors of His deification; still they must have been the commencing point of the basic stories that eventually led to His immortalization.

The narratives of the virgin birth are mythical; that is why Luke's version differs so substantially from Matthew's. Early Christian doctrine differed because no such thing as the doctrines of Jesus Christ ever existed. Jesus taught the reform of Judaism, not the founding of Christianity. The problem with Christian doctrine is that Jesus didn't live long enough to fully expound and define such. Three years isn't enough time to delineate a new religion. Had Jesus lived longer, and had He formally broken with Judaism (which He inevitably would have), then an authoritative and comprehensive Christian creed could have been fully formulated prior to the crucifixion.

Uncertainty and confusion plagued the early Church. Too many questions arose that Jesus, in His recorded lifetime, never addressed. Should Christian men and women marry? Paul didn't know. He guessed that everyone should remain as they were "... *as the Lord has called them.*" [1 Cor. 7:17] If not married, you were to remain unmarried. If married, then remain married. If a person's lusts were such as to lead toward sin, then the unmarried should marry as the lesser of two evils. *"There is not much time left ... married men should live as though they were not married."* [1 Cor. 7:29] Paul's instructions here prove conclusively that his inspiration, whatever its source, told him the advent of the return of Jesus was imminent. [Cf. Rom. 13:11] Two thousand years beyond, we can attest to his irrefutable error.

By the way, Paul often is very explicit when expounding doctrines. Some of the dictates Paul lays on his followers are his alone, while others are decreed from "the Lord." *"I tell you this not as an order, but simply as a permission."* ... *"For married people I have a command, not my own but the Lord's"* ... *"To others I say (I, myself, not the Lord)"* [1 Cor. 7: 6, 8, 12] *"What I am now saying is not by the order of the lord"* [2 Cor. 11:17]

Paul takes particular precautions not to commingle <u>his</u> dictates with the dictates of God (Yahweh) per Jesus. Why? Answer: Because so many important behavioral strictures were never enunciated by Jesus. Obviously, Paul felt no obligation to consult with Peter before issuing his personal directives. There is a refuting inference against Peter's apostolic supremacy arising out of this readily verifiable observation. But you, my reader, must reconcile Paul's dictates for yourself. The following point is incidental to the main theme of this segment, but can you see here that Paul didn't know he was being inspired by the Holy Spirit? If he didn't know this (and he didn't!), how did the generations that were born after him come to know that all of Paul's writings were divinely inspired? Paul recognized that many thorny questions were unanswered by the known teachings of Jesus. Paul had to personally interpolate certain 'Christian' teachings by surmise.

If we could cull from the Bible only those dogmas that Jesus fully enumerated personally while He was on Earth, we would be without a Christian religion. What we would have would be an inconclusive and rudimentary philosophy of meekness and submissiveness.

{Examples follow} *"Take everything you have and give it to the poor...."* [Mt. 19:21; Mk. 10:21 & Lu. 18:22]

"God takes care to see that the sparrows are fed. You are more important than sparrows; therefore, God will take even better care of you." [Mt. 6:26] [Cf. Mt. 10:29-31]

When Jesus said, 'You are more important than sparrows'. He was speaking to whom? Did He mean 'you,' the Apostles? Did He mean 'you,' His listeners? Or did He mean, 'you,' all the people in the world? (As we interpret His words today) I will present just a few more examples, and then present my point.

"If your eye causes you to sin, pluck it out and throw it away." [Mt. 5:29]

"If someone slaps your cheek, turn your face so he may slap the other one as well." [Mt. 5:39]

"If someone forces you to carry his load one mile, carry it an additional mile." [Mt. 5:41]

"Let the dead bury their own dead." [Mt. 8:22]

"The Sabbath was made for man, not man for the Sabbath." [Mk. 2:27]

What does the last example mean? If ten separate theologians responded to the last put question, ten different answers would be rendered. The conclusion of this entire segment is this: The Holy Spirit didn't inspire the early Church leaders. Each recalled or heard the events in the life of Jesus and extrapolated them as best he could. So much was left unresolved that each leader became an authority unto himself. Given this circumstance, it isn't surprising that there were conflicting instructions being tendered to the perplexed converts from the very outset of the Christian indoctrination (proselytization).

Paul's First Epistle to the Corinthians exposes divine inspiration for the deceit that it is. *"For some people … have told me quite plainly … there are quarrels among you … each one says something different. One says, 'I am with Paul;' another, 'I am with Apollos;' another, 'I am with Peter;' and another, 'I am with Christ.' Christ has been split into groups!"* [1 Cor. 1:11-13 – with irrelevant deletions] Where was the divine inspiration? Was it with Paul; with Peter; with Apollos? Who can reply with absolute certitude? The confusion has continued unabated for two millennia. Witness the Councils of the Church: the revisions: the retrenchments: and most especially the endless schisms; not to invoke the outright reversals of previously defined doctrines. An all-knowing Deity should have, would have, been more explicit with His instructions. Jesus didn't propound a new religion; He proposed that the Jews return, with sincerity and with humility, to the only religion that He recognized. {By identity: "Judaism."} Jesus didn't define a new religion, because He had no intention of inaugurating competition to Judaism.

Paul told the Corinthians unequivocally that a woman must have her head covered while at public worship. *"And any woman who prays or proclaims God's message in public worship with nothing on her head disgraces her husband; there is no difference between her and a woman whose head has been shaved. If the woman does not cover her head, she might as well cut her hair, she should cover her head."* [1 Cor. 11:5-6] The Christian Church, in deference to modern liberal revisionism, has rescinded this 'God inspired' edict.

Why has virtually every Christian denomination flouted this unambiguous command from Paul? Perhaps it is because they similarly want to disregard Paul's rationale for his edict. *"On account of the angels, then, a woman should have a covering over her head to show that she is under her husband's authority."* [1 Cor. 11:10 – Good News Translation] What preacher of today would want to stand in the pulpit and proclaim this message to a congregation predominated by hatless women? (Very few indeed!) Paul also forbade long hair for men. [Cf. 1 Cor. 11:14] But then, how long does he mean? Jesus' hair probably reached to his shoulders. In America before the turbulent 1960's, that length of hair on a man would have caused eyebrows to be raised, and would have provoked disapproving sideways glances at most Christian services.

Actually, what we read throughout the Epistles aren't the Laws of God, but merely the jaded edicts of opinionated early Christians. Don't read into this statement sniping criticism of Paul. Paul's motives were highly commendable. He wanted everyone to find the salvation he found in the belief that the resurrected Jesus was the promised Messiah. He was wrong; but he was sincere. I applaud his sincerity. I deplore only his mistaken presumption.

Why do you suppose that Paul absolved his Gentile converts from the strictures of the Mosaic Laws, when he felt obliged to keep them himself (while in Jerusalem)? Preponderantly, the 'Law' was burdensome. Secondly, the return of Jesus was imminent. Once Jesus reappeared, the old order would be repealed and a new Messianic order would be inaugurated. Paul knew this intellectually (instinctively), not through divine inspiration! (Intuited) This is why he imposed so few Judaic strictures on his Gentile converts.

All through his life, Paul was a champion. First of Pharisaic Judaism, afterward of Christianity. Once he espoused a cause, he gave over his life unstintingly and unreservedly to that cause. Had he been born a Greek and not a Jew, the Western world might still be importuning Zeus for favors instead of Jesus. Paul recognized that each of us possesses a different talent (from God?), and he correctly identified his chief asset as a herald of the return of Jesus … echoing Mark & Luke. '*The kingdom of God is at hand – Prepare the way!*' [Mk. 1:15; Lu. 10:11, 21:31 & Mk. 1:2]

Did Paul rate himself the equal of the original Apostles? Yes, he positively did. We, today, accord him the identical elevated status. Paul asked the Corinthians, "*Am I not an Apostle?*" Then he answered his own question. "*You, yourselves … are proof of the fact that I am an Apostle.*" [1 Cor. 9:1-2] Now read how Paul ranked the 'gifts' of the Holy Spirit. "*In the Church, God has given the first place to Apostles.*" [1 Cor. 12:28]

What I am highlighting here is the fact that Paul was also a proud man. Pride and vanity are the twin impulses necessary to any successful leader. Lacking them, leadership is impossible. A highly-developed ego is a must for every charismatic leader. Paul was a remarkably capable leader; consequently, we know his ego was more pronounced than that of most others. Yet, even in his own exalted evaluation of himself, he never stated that God whispered into his ear as he composed his Epistles. [Cf. 1 Cor. 16:21]

This raises a pertinent question. Did any of the authors of the New Testament know God was inspiring them as they wrote? Read the

456

New Testament and you will clearly recognize that with the exception of Revelations (Apocalypse), the reply is undeniably and emphatically "No!" Then I ask: "How does anyone else know the texts were inspired?" They can't know! This is why it took so long to sort out the Canon of the New Testament. Everyone had their own presumption of which writings were inspired, and which weren't. The greatest of the early Church Fathers were divided. The Holy Spirit didn't mandate the result of the deliberations that finally delineated the codified Canon of the New Testament. The New Testament, in its present form, is nothing but the best evaluations of a majority of the presiding Catholic Bishops deliberating more than three hundred years after Jesus died. [AD 397 – Council of Carthage]

The above assumes that such issues were resolved by majority vote. The history of the great Church Councils gives inarguable evidence that this wasn't always the case. Power politics has ever been an operational factor in the administration of the Church. Examined from another angle: Majority voting would seem to rule out divine inspiration of the Bishops in council. In every biblical instance of purported Old Testament inspiration, the recipient of the inspiration was an individual, never a group. More often than the reverse, he (the inspired) opposed the opinions of the majority. I believe our current 'Christian doctrines' are the precepts of Christianized Gentiles, not the faithful reproduction of the beliefs and teachings of the Jewish followers of Jesus (Apostles, and other Hebrews).

A QUESTION RAISED BY PAUL'S EPISTLES

Mostly, Paul refers to Jesus as separate and subordinate to God, not co-equal. Yet, he also clearly infers that Jesus is divine in a few isolated yet debatable instances. In the main his references portray Jesus as an intermediary to God. If Jesus was an alter ego of God, why didn't Paul know this? Several places he explicitly affirms that God raised Jesus back to life. If Jesus was God, then He resurrected Himself. [Cf. 1 Cor. 15:15 & Acts 2:24, 32] It is grossly misleading to phrase Paul's statement as it is recorded, when and if, Paul knew that Jesus participated in the Godhead. But, of course, Paul didn't know this!

And then we have the ever-present consideration of the copyist who added a few subtle verses of his own composition. How can I make this accusation when I have no more proof of this than a religionist has that nothing has been added to the scriptures? The answer, thankfully, is that those who edited the New Testament were human. Consequently, they made mistakes! Noticeably, God didn't enlighten them as to what or where these mistakes were. An example: In 1 Cor. 15:5, the Catholic version (Douay) reads Christ appeared to the "eleven." The New Jerusalem Bible (plus all Protestant translations) informs that Christ appeared to the "twelve." In the notes at the end of the Catholic version the editor explains that most manuscripts (MSS) read "twelve." He points out that "the twelve" is a euphemism for the Apostles regardless of how many were intended.

He is conditionally correct. The condition being that the story of Christ's life had to be well known to everyone before the euphemism would be intelligible as such. Also, he admits that some pious scribe had changed the word 'twelve' into 'eleven' (or vice versa) at some previous time. Our editor doesn't realize it, but he makes a discrediting admission when he informs that the sacred word of God was changed arbitrarily by a meddling scribe.

Take the epistle where Paul writes that Christ died for our sins, *"in accordance with the scriptures."* Paul continues and adds that Christ was buried for three days, and then He was resurrected, *"in accordance with the scriptures."* [1 Cor. 15:3-4] (Some translations here read: *"Writings,"* which unmistakably refer to the Old Testament texts.) My question: Which "scriptures" was Paul referring?

The only texts that mention Christ's death and resurrection are the Gospels. The author of the phrase did, indeed, think of the Gospels as 'sacred scripture.' But I can find no evidence in Paul's Epistles of any personal knowledge of the existence of the Gospel narratives during Paul's lifetime. To Paul, only the Old Testament narratives were deemed 'sacred scripture.' Paul is thought to have died between the years AD 64-67. Mark's Gospel, theorized to have been the first gospel composed, was written sometime between AD 57 and AD 63. The other three gospel narratives date later, with the last, John's, generally being dated as advanced as AD 90. Paul appears virtually ignorant of the four Gospels.

FIVE VERSIONS OF THE RESURRECTION

Briefly, let me highlight the five versions of Jesus' postmortem activities (the four Gospels & the Acts) and you will see that none of them match with Paul's post-Resurrection version in his Epistle, which becomes a sixth version! [Cf. 1 Cor. 15:3-8]

In John's Gospel, Jesus first appeared to Mary Magdalene; then to ten Apostles; then again to those ten plus doubting Thomas; finally at the Sea of Tiberias to Peter, Thomas, Nathaniel, the sons of Zebedee (James & John), along with two unidentified Apostles. No ascension into Heaven is recounted. [Cf. Jn. Chaps. 20 & 21] {End of John's version}

In Luke's Gospel, Jesus first appeared to two disciples on the road to Emmaus. One of the men was named Cleopas, the other isn't identified. However, when the two returned to report to the Apostles, they are informed that Jesus had already appeared to Simon (Peter). Then, just as everyone was discussing the appearance by Jesus on the road to Emmaus, He appeared among the gathered disciples. After speaking with them briefly, He led them to the outskirts of Bethany and ascended into Heaven. [Cf. Lu. Chap. 24] {End of Luke's version}

Mark's Gospel reports that Jesus first appeared to Mary Magdalene and a few other women at His tomb (an alternate ending does not mention the site of the occurrence). Then Mark informs us that Jesus appeared to two disciples in the country (road to Emmaus?). Next, Mark refers to a visit to the eleven, where Jesus instructs them to go out and *"proclaim the Good News to all creation."* [Mk. 16:15] Mark ends thus: *"And so the Lord Jesus, after he had spoken to them, was taken up into heaven: there at the right hand of God he took his place."* [Mk. 16:19]* {End of Mark's two versions}

*A note at the conclusion of Mark reads: "Many MSS omit vv 9-20 and this ending to the gospel may not have been written by Mark, though it is old enough." {Author's asterisk}

Matthew writes that Jesus appeared to the two Mary's after they had left the locale of the sepulcher. (Magdalene and the 'other' Mary) Then Jesus appeared to the eleven on a pre-arranged Mount in Galilee, where He gave them instructions. [Cf. Mt. Chap. 28] The final two verses of Chapter 28: *"Go then, to all peoples everywhere and make them my disciples: baptize them in the name of the Father, the Son, and the Holy Spirit,* [v.19] *and teach them to obey everything I have commanded you. And remember! I will be with you always, to the end of the age.*" [v. 20] The Gospel of Matthew concludes without mention of any ascension into Heaven. {End of Matthew's version}

In Acts: He showed the Apostles, *"by many demonstrations"* that He was alive over a period of forty days. Then at the conclusion of the forty days, *"a cloud took him from their sight."* [Cf. Acts 1:1-11] {End of Acts' version}

As can be seen, none of the Resurrection narratives fits Paul's description, 'according to the scriptures.' [Cf. 1 Cor. 15:3] Without doubt, some devout, but identifiably deceptive, copyist added these words. In his zeal to authenticate those words, this copyist has Paul refer to 'the scriptures' (of the New Testament) before they were written. Later, when second and third generation Christians assumed the leadership posts vacated by the deceased first generation Christians, the stories of Christ's life would have begun to be sanctified into the sacrosanct category of 'scripture.' But not during Paul's lifetime! Read Paul's Epistles. Nowhere within them will you find Paul advising his converts to 'read the scriptures' (Gospels). They didn't exist publicly as such until after Paul's death (c. AD 64-67).

SPECULATIONS ON THE RESURRECTION

Here follows a brief account of the actions of the Apostles after the Crucifixion as they may have transpired. {Author's suppositions}

Because they feared the authorities, none of the Apostles was present at the Crucifixion (excepting John putatively). The female followers, however, did witness the death of Jesus. Upon hearing of the rumored resurrection of both Lazarus and the daughter of Jarius, the authorities decided to keep secret the location of the tomb selected for Jesus' burial. Joseph of Arimathea, an influential man, offered the use of his personal burial cave. The women among Jesus' band followed the burial group and noted the location of the tomb. Unfortunately (perhaps fortuitously), they were observed by the burial detail, and this fact was reported to the Jewish authorities. The Jews appealed to the Romans to place guards at the tomb to prevent His followers from retrieving His body. The Jews, themselves, couldn't provide security for the corpse of Jesus because of Sabbath restrictions.

During Saturday afternoon, Pilate decided that neither the Jews, nor the followers of Jesus, should know the location of the body of this Jewish religious agitator. He, therefore, sent a cohort of troops to move the cadaver to a new burial site. This was done late Saturday, just after the general populace had retired for the night. The soldiers rolled back the stone and entered the tomb. In the flickering light of their torches, they removed the burial cloth(s) from His body. One compassionate soldier had the decency to fold the large cloth neatly. They then carried the corpse to a wagon parked near the entrance. The lifeless body was subsequently transported to a Roman garrison somewhere outside Jerusalem for reburial in a common, unmarked grave; perhaps to Caesarea, the official residence of the Roman Procurator. The road to Caesarea runs alongside Golgotha. This detail of soldiers never returned to Jerusalem.

At first light on Sunday morning, Mary Magdalene and several other women arrived at the tomb only to find it empty. Frantically they searched for someone to question as to the whereabouts of their slain master. Presently, they found a gardener who could give little information. Annoyed at the persistence of the women, the gardener sarcastically remarked that perhaps Jesus had revived from death and had left the tomb under His own power.

The women returned to the Apostles, who by now had reassembled at the Inn (?) where the Last Supper had been held. The women excitedly told them of their experience at the gravesite. Peter and John raced to the burial grounds and found the stone seal rolled back and the tomb vacant, just as the women had reported. They also found the burial cloth(s). They did not see or speak with the gardener.

Before the middle of the day, word of the disappearance of the body of Jesus had reached the ears of the Sanhedrin. The Elders gathered together and discussed the matter. Soon a deputation was formed and sent to the Governor's residence to inquire as to the disposition of the Roman guards. Pilate feigned ignorance. 'The guards were needed elsewhere and had been withdrawn from the still sealed vault,' may have been his reply. The Jewish delegation left as bewildered as when they had arrived. The Jewish authorities eventually concluded that the followers of

Jesus had bribed the guards, and had removed the body themselves. This is the explanation they offered to all who inquired.

When the women first reported the disappearance of Jesus to the Apostles, the women were not believed. However, when the apostolic band, through informants, had learned of the bewilderment of the Jewish hierarchy the Apostles concluded that maybe Jesus had somehow been miraculously revived. Later that day, two of Jesus' occasional followers met a man on the road to Emmaus who also had been in Jerusalem during the Passover Festival. At first this stranger pretended not to know of the fateful events of the previous days.

Soon the three were discussing Jesus. The stranger scolded the disciples for doubting the conjecture of the faithful women that Jesus had arisen. (Obviously, the two didn't believe Jesus to be resurrected, or they would never have left Jerusalem on Sunday.) Before departing, the stranger shared a meal with the disciples. During the meal the disciples became suspicious that this man might have been Jesus himself in an altered guise. [Cf. Lu. 24:13-35]

Throughout the day, the Apostles pondered the mystery of the missing corpse. If Jesus was alive again, why hadn't He contacted them? Could it be that He had? But they had failed to recognize Him in His revivified body? The Apostles now re-questioned the women. Did the gardener bear a resemblance to Jesus? Did he have any of the mannerisms of Jesus? Did he hint of a resurrection? Three times the women answered "yes."

Now the Apostles were beginning to understand. Jesus had appeared to Mary and the other women disguised as a gardener! No, the gardener probably wasn't Jesus, but he might have been an Angel left behind to inform His followers that He had, indeed, arisen. Opinions were divided. Because there was division among the gathered group they turned their attention to the now returned disciples from Emmaus. 'Tell us about this man,' they ordered the two. When the disciples reached the point where the unknown man broke bread and offered it to the disciples, the Apostles cried out in instant recognition. Jesus had performed this exact ritual during His last night with the Apostles. This information was conclusive. Jesus had appeared to the two disciples in a disguised form. But, He had given them a clue as to His real identity by breaking the bread.

Now they all recognized the clue. Jesus had appeared twice since His death. Of this, the Apostles were certain. This self-conceived revelation gave them the courage to go forth and proclaim Him as the expected, now risen, Messiah. With unaccustomed bravery, and led by Peter, the Apostles preached to the crowds. 'Jesus is the promised Messiah and He proved this by His Resurrection.' {Author's conjecture}

However, still unexplained are the gospel reports of Post-Resurrection visitations by Jesus. Constrained by fear and trepidation, the reassembled Apostles remained indoors for several days. Then one night (perhaps Sunday, the very first night) one of the Apostles had a dream entailing the appearance of Jesus among the Apostles. Could Thomas have been the dreamer? In the dream, one of the Apostles asks Jesus if he can place his hand in the wounds of Jesus. Upon having the dream sequence described to them in the morning, the Apostles concluded that perhaps the resurrected Jesus had appeared via a vision to the dozing Apostle. One or more of the other Apostles also may have dreamed about Jesus due to the trauma of His crucifixion. Presently, most of the Apostles came to believe that the now mystical Jesus had appeared to them via a vision or a dream, *'but some of them doubted.'* [Interpolated from Mt. 28:17] This surmised resurrection scenario could additionally explain the different locations of the Ascension as reported in the Gospels.

After Pentecost, more Jews were recruited, but most remained skeptical. 'If Jesus had been resurrected, where was He now,' they asked? Obviously, He wasn't with His faithful band, so He must have been with His Father in Heaven. Yes, that was the answer. Jesus was in heaven preparing for His triumphant return. The reports of the Ascension itself were an addendum by the original redactors of the four gospels. 'How soon would be His return? No one knew for certain, but His recruits were confident it wouldn't be long. Their mission would be to prepare as many of the Jews as would accept His message: "The kingdom of God is a hand, Repent ...." [Cf. Mark 1:15 & et al.]

At first the conversions came readily, but all too soon they began to wane. Even before this, the Apostles had been expelled from the Temple. The priests had hired Saul of Tarsus to root out these latest messianic agitators who had spread (or fled?) to Damascus. [Cf. Acts 9:1-2] It was at this time that the apostolic band began to disintegrate. From the Acts we learn that the original leaders of the incipient religion were headquartered in Jerusalem. But we also read of their continued fidelity to Judaism, and their respect for the Jewish Temple and Jewish religious customs.

{A few examples} At Pentecost, Peter addressed the crowd: *"Fellow Jews and all of you who live in Jerusalem ..."* [Acts 2:14] *"Listen to these words, fellow Israelites!"* [Acts 2:22] *"About three thousand people were added to the group that day."* [Acts 2:41] *"Day after day they met as a group in the Temple."* [Acts 2:46] *"One day Peter and John went to the Temple ... for prayer."* [Acts 3:1] Do these examples witness the founding of a new religion? Or do they provide evidence that the Apostles were proclaiming the advent of the fulfillment of the predictions of ancient Judaism? After his conversion, even Paul (the actual founder of present-day Christianity) was compelled to make an insincere display of his submission to Judaic strictures whenever he journeyed to Jerusalem. [Cf. Acts 21:17-26] Inside Jerusalem, Paul was an observant Jew; Away from Jerusalem, Paul was a non-observing Christian. Undeniably, Christianity is the offspring of Judaism. But it is illegitimate progeny inasmuch as its parent has consistently denied it.

The Apostles began a movement that ultimately became self-propagating. They initially preached the fulfillment of Judaism. Paul, the persistent activist, turned the fledgling sect from an offshoot of the old beliefs, into a totally new creed that competed with other religions for believers. Religious man had detoured down yet another bogus path. The quest for knowledge, truth, and social justice will forever elude mankind so long as he searches among the supernatural. There is no Deity. There are no angelic helpmates. There are no hidden byways. Nor is there a road map to guide us to a chest full of gems of wisdom. Lastly, there is no Redeemer!

Man has continually stumbled along the paths of life searching for an elusive destiny. He (and she!) has been perplexed throughout the entire journey by questions of purpose. Why am I here? Where am I going? How do I get there? And, even more perplexing, are the questions: Why me? Why anyone?

WHAT IS 'SCRIPTURAL'?

How did any writing come to be classified as scriptural? The process isn't instantaneous; it evolves! Gradually, over a span of time (in some cases centuries), a composition gains increasing respect and hallowedness until it eventually reaches the plateau of sanctity and reverence defined and accepted as scriptural. A portion of the aura of sanctification is generated solely by the passage of time. A similar process creates the value of an antique, which often far exceeds its initial or intrinsic value.

There were many priestly writings produced during the Old Testament era. Why and how did some compositions come to be considered "inspired" while other compositions did not? My research has revealed that throughout biblical times the same book(s) may have been deemed both apocryphal and scriptural concurrently, although respectively by different authorities.

Strictly speaking, there never has been a universal Canon of the Old Testament; not in Judaism, nor in its rejected progeny 'Christianity.' The Old Testament Canon of the Hellenized Jews of Alexandria was different from the Pharisaic Old Testament Canon at the time of Christ. The Essene sect, that we know of through the Dead Sea scrolls, had a Canon of Sacred Writings that differed considerably from both the Alexandrian and the Palestinian Canons.

The New Testament encountered the same confusions in the early years of the Church. Gospels appeared whose authorship was attributed to various Apostles. All of these spurious writings were ultimately rejected. Catholic theologians are quick to quote the defined doctrines of the Early Church Fathers, and to declare those doctrines as unquestioned tenets. Yet, those very same Early Church Fathers fervently revered many of the New Testament era writings now excluded from the Canon as apocryphal or pseudepigraphical.

The forward in a book titled, The Lost Books of the Bible, (Bell Publishing, New York) provides an example. A Mr. Solomon J. Schepps wrote the foreword to the 1979 Edition. He opines: "Peter's Gospel (apocryphal), which was once held as highly as those of Matthew and Mark, and more highly than those of Luke and John, was ultimately rejected because it differs too much in its details from the three chosen synopses. The Gospel of Thomas (apocryphal) was rejected for a different reason. It opens by declaring that he who "understands" the words of Jesus will be saved. This, of course, is in direct contradiction to the chosen Gospels and to Paul's Epistles, which read that it is he who "believes" will be saved.

Paul is, of course, the primary interpreter of the Gospels, and all of the letters in the Bible by persons other than Paul are in thematic agreement with his letters. That is because, by the time of the Fathers, Paul's authority was so firmly entrenched that any apostolic letters differing from his own, even without contradicting them, were rejected. The three Books of Hermas, for example, were recommended for use at one time or another by Tertullian, Origen, and Jerome" {Tertullian: AD c160-c250; Origen: 185-253; Jerome: 331-420}

Deciding which books to include in the Canon, and which to exclude, was no simple matter. The problem came to a partial resolution after two major Councils in North Africa. The first was held at Hippo in the year AD 393, and the second at Carthage in AD 397. The New Testament, in its present form, dates no further back than the year AD 397. (Cf. 'The Council of Carthage') That is, almost four hundred years after Jesus was born. By the way, the disputes with the New Testament Canon didn't end until almost two hundred years later, i.e., in AD 600. If that studied historic fact doesn't expose the ruse of "divine inspiration," then nothing can!

Many of the rejected writings were lost after the ascendancy of the Church under Constantine (beginning around AD 313). The Church of the fifth century and afterward, up until the advent of the Middle Ages, actively sought after, suppressed, and destroyed any composition that even hinted at contradicting 'the holy words of God' … as the Church authenticated His 'words.' Historians refer to this period as the Dark Ages, and aptly so. But the Church wasn't a victim of the Dark Ages; it was a facilitator of the Dark Ages. More so: The Church was an accomplice!

Books on medicines and chemistry were declared diabolical, and then destroyed. Sanitation and cleanliness were seen as sins of vanity, and were disdained. All skepticism within the Church was ruthlessly dealt with. Dissenters who refused to recant were executed cruelly. Disbelief was intolerable, and doubters were harshly punished with imprisonment, torture, and mutilation until as the malefactors "received the Holy Spirit" and performed public penance for their transgression. Clerical intimidation was ubiquitous. Much learning was repressed and lost.

The Renaissance brought a reawakening and a revival of scholarship. But in truth, we will never know if some vital knowledge, previously available, hasn't been permanently lost. The rise of Christianity precipitated the fall of Western Intellectualism. The Germanic barbarian hordes are often blamed for the fall of the Roman Empire. In actuality, they were no more culpable than a river is chargeable for the actions of the man who commits suicide in its waters.

The retrenchment of Western Civilization during the Dark Ages abetted the expansion of the Muslim faith, which had its cradle in the same geographic area that gave birth to Judaism and Christianity. At that time, fortunate it was that the kindred Islamic faith not only didn't fear learning, it cultivated learning. Greek philosophy survived in Arab libraries. Roman bureaucracy was incorporated into the religious structure. Much of the accrued knowledge of civilized man was preserved in Muslim learning centers throughout the Dark Ages.

Meanwhile, the Christian Church led Europe into barbarism. The most barbaric city of the period was Rome itself. Filth and squalor were everywhere; disease was rampant; plague continually decimated the urban populations. The people were prisoners of the Church, and the wardens of the faith were ever vigilant against backsliders or irreligious idlers. Intellectualism, unless thoroughly Christianized, was perniciously suppressed.

Catholics and Protestants alike imagine the Canon of the New Testament forming spontaneously as if by divine infusion. Nothing could be further from the actuality. There are doctrinaire references in the works of the early Church Fathers to manuscripts that no longer exist. What happened to these 'divinely inspired' works? Did they lose the backing of their 'Divine Patron' (the Holy Spirit, that is), or did they merely lose their 'inspiration' at the whim of the successors to the earliest Church Fathers?

Why do the facts always support the wrong conclusions? If one sits down and rationally deduces the origins of the Judeo-Christian religiology myth as the invention of man, and not as inculcation from God, then all the inconsistencies, improbabilities, inanities, and all else … evaporates! What remains is a thoroughly human saga replete with all the aspirations of man, yet consistently tempered by the inherent foibles of mortal beings. The Bible, seen as the work of man, is consistent with its incongruities; whereas the Bible viewed as the handiwork of God raises insurmountable obstacles, and generates nothing but incredulity in the minds of the quizzically intelligent.

As anyone can verify, the same story covered by two different reporters will never read the same. Different individuals will view the same event from a different perspective, and so their reports of the event will differ. Most proponents of the Bible offer this as an apology for the differences in the four Gospels. What must be reckoned with, however, is the proposition that God inspired all that the Evangelists wrote. This isn't their intention: but they thereby make God liable for the discrepancies in the Bible. As they would describe, the human authors were nothing but robot scribes penning in the dictated words of God. Theologically, this renders the Bible unassailable, as was the intention of the doctrine formulator(s). Yet, for anyone who investigates the implications of that doctrine, its unassailability unfailingly vanishes.

I have already pointed out some of the abject contradictions in the New Testament, such as: Was Jesus born in a house or a stable? Did Mary and Joseph live in Nazareth always? Or did they move there after the return from Egypt? Did they go to Egypt? Or did they present Jesus at the Temple for Simeon and Anna to proclaim Him as the Messiah? Reprising only a few controversial scenarios!

The Old Testament is just as flawed. But for me, its most blatant inconsistency is the method the Hebrews used to gain possession of the Promised Land. In Joshua, we read of victorious battle after victorious battle wherein the Israelites completely annihilate all opponents. Still, subsequent books (Judges, 1 Samuel, & 1 Chronicles) inform of a gradual infiltration of the Israelites into Canaan. The filtering-in never seems to have resulted in complete Hebrew predominance until the time of the kings Saul, David, and Solomon. The city of Jerusalem (Jebus) was inhabited by the Jebusites until David captured it. Even then, non-Israelites controlled much territory in the full span of the entirety of God's 'Promised Land.'

Clearly and demonstrably, we have two differing versions of the conquest of those lands that Yahweh promised to the descendants of Abraham in perpetuity. First, we have the epic and the miraculous. Then we read of the less wondrous, but far more accurate, slow annexation of Canaan. Until the time of David, the Israelites were more 'emigres' than 'conquerors.' I doubt that the Israelites ever attained a numerical majority throughout the entire lands of the 'Promise.' Even if they had, that majority was lost after the Assyrian Captivity (circa 740 BC), and never has been regained, even to the present day. History proves that God reneged on His promise to Abraham and his heirs ... if we interpret the Old Testament literally!

At the time of Christ, the Jews dominated only Judea. After the Jewish Bar Kochba revolt (AD 135), they lost even that. I see only two paths out of this scriptural contradiction. Either God is a liar, or man is a liar. If the Bible is inspired, then God deceived Abraham and all his descendants. The other alternative is for man to have lied to his fellow man when he alleged to have been inspired by God. Moses told the Israelites that Yahweh had made a covenant (pact) with Abraham promising the Israelites eternal possession of the "land of milk and honey." Was Moses mistaken or was he deceived? Did Abraham lie? Someone lied!

The Israelites may never have controlled all of the Promised Land. God's promise to Abraham set the boundaries from *"the border of Egypt to the Euphrates River."* [Gen. 15:18-21] The 'promise' included lands now a part of Jordan, Syria and Iraq. The Israelites never ruled in those areas. At best, the Israelites ruled a portion of the "Promised Lands" for perhaps a century. For the last nineteen centuries, their descendants scarcely controlled more than a few villages. Furthermore, in 1948, when they finally returned (*en masse*) to a much-diminished division of their Promised Land, it wasn't Yahweh who facilitated their return. The Jews regained their land through the benign indulgence of two nominally Christian nations: Great Britain and the U. S.

Search your Bible for the prophetic texts that foretold this eventuality. You won't find any. The reason you won't find any is because no one could even imagine beforehand this ironic inversion of history. By observation, it is ironic that Christians should facilitate the reacquisition by the Jews, of a small portion of the lands God promised they would own 'in perpetuity.' [Cf. Gen. 48:4 & Ps. 105:11] [Ps. 104:11 in Catholic translations] It appears that 'Scriptural' doesn't always translate into 'Factual.'

ORIGEN — THEOLOGIAN OR HERETIC?

Origen (AD 185–254?) was a Christian scholar and a theologian. He is considered to be the first theologian of the early Christian Church. During his lifetime, Origen was much respected by the Church hierarchy of his day. However, after his death his writings were considered heretical and Origen was anathematized by a subsequent Church Council. Thereafter, most of his written theology was destroyed.

[Second Council of Constantinople in AD 553] At this Council the following denunciation of Origen and others was formally decreed: "If anyone does not anathematize Arius, Eunomius, Macedonius, Apollinaris, Nestorius, Eutyches and Origen, as well as their impious writings, as also all other heretics already condemned and anathematized by the Holy Catholic and Apostolic Church, and by the aforesaid four Holy Synods and all those who have held and hold or who in their impiety persist in holding to the end the same opinion as those heretics just mentioned: let him be anathema."

I was somewhat surprised to learn that Origen, a third century exegete and Christian apologist, taught that many of the Gospel narratives should be interpreted allegorically, rather than historically. One example: The cleansing of the Temple, although described by all four Evangelists, never happened. [Cf. Mt. 21:12-13; Mk. 11:15-17; Lu. 19:45-46 & Jn. 2:13-16] This event was incorporated into the gospel texts merely to expose the corruption then rampant in the Jewish Temple. The purported actions of Jesus purified the Temple. {The rationale for the above supposition is this author's, not Origen's.}

A modern corollary might be made thusly: Imagine a modern day reformer attending a present day Revival, and further imagine our zealous fanatic rushing to the front of the Meeting and disrupting the collection of donations to the preacher. I am certain that this zealot would have been forcibly ejected from the Meeting long before he could effectively halt the collection of money from the congregants. To my mind, Origen pictured the Temple cleansing episode as an invented instructive example, not to recorded fact.

The Temple incident isn't the best example I could have chosen of Origen's belief that many of the Gospel narratives are allegorical. In reality, I personally believe that the Temple incident may well have transpired generally as recorded in the four Gospels. However, I also believe that all of the miracles recorded in the Gospels should better be received as allegorical instead of as factual. Assuredly, the virgin birth of Jesus, which is beyond proof in any manner, is symbolic not historic.

By my reckoning, Origen's exegetic errors were numerous, still grudgingly I must confess that I admire him. Origen was a deep thinker, not simply a blind believer. He was a firm proponent of the inspiration of the Holy Spirit in the writing of the Gospels. Yet, he denied the reality of the Holy Spirit's appearance in the form of a dove at the Baptism of Jesus. This may seem to be an incontestable contradiction. It is! 'Unless you happen to be a devout theoretician ... as Origen undoubtedly was.

If, indeed, the Holy Ghost truly descended from Heaven as a dove, then we have added a novel dimension to the Trinity. For just as Jesus is promulgated as "True God and true Man," so too must the Holy Ghost be promulgated as 'True God and true Dove.' Ridiculous, isn't it? But perhaps no more ludicrous than is the totality of all religiosity ... without exception!

PROVERBS TO PONDER

"The innocent believe every word; the discreet man considers his steps."
[Pr. 14:15]

'Gullible people believe anything, but the thoughtful are careful where they place their trust.' {Author's paraphrase of the above biblical quote}

"No man is free from pollution, no —not though he should live but one day!" [Job 14:1-4 paraphrased by Clement in 1 Clem. 15:20]

"Who can make him {man} *clean that is conceived of unclean seed? Is it not thou* {God} *who only art?"* [Job 14:1-4, Cf. Catholic version]

"Who can bring a clean thing out of an unclean? There is not one." [Job 14:1-4 RSV]

Was it Job's text above that prompted the doctrine of the 'Immaculate Conception'? Could Jesus have been born of an unclean woman? No! Mary must have been conceived without 'Original Sin.' Only thereby could her seed, Jesus, likewise be conceived sinless.

As this book attempts to prove: All religiosity, and all religions, constitute "the greatest deception ever perpetrated upon humanity." Yet, the persistent question remains, "Can we live together harmoniously without the invoked moral authority of an entity superior to man himself?" Only God Himself can know! That is, if there is a God?

CHAPTER 17
An Inspired Bible?

THE BIBLE IS A HUMAN COMPOSITION

The Bible is a composite book admittedly written by a miniature mob. Each person wrote in his own style, with places where two different authors report the same incident, yet important details of that incident disagree substantially. This is entirely in accord with what you undoubtedly could expect from human beings. But never when the Supreme Being (the all-knowing Creator) was inspiring the author and professedly keeping him from written error.

Discrepancies of even minor magnitude and import can only have occurred if the person writing was spiritually unassisted, was human, and thereby was fallible. Working with the limited knowledge they possessed; reporting on events that they did not witness; inconsistencies are both understandable and pardonable. Yet, once you admit one inaccuracy in the Bible, then the entire book is liable to re-inspection. Compare Genesis 12:10-14 to 26:7-10 and Genesis 19:1-11 to Judges 19:11-27, and you will discover a single myth/legend repeated in a slightly altered form in each of the compared sets above. Both sets are variant accounts of the same story.

Then, there is what I term, 'mythic fabulosities.' Was there a flood that engulfed the total surface of the Earth? Archaeologists have unearthed fossils of identifiable sea creatures buried on the crests of mountains. Fundamentalists were quick to advance this as proof of the biblical

Flood. They were either unaware or purposely disregarded the fact that these fossils are found throughout layers of sediment that are thousands of years apart in time. The accepted interpretation being that the mountains weren't always mountains. That in a remote eon, the present-day mountain summit lay at the bottom of a body of water for thousands of years accumulating fossil specimens. This is many times the calendar year that the Flood is recorded to have persisted.

Having invoked Noah, I now ask: Do you believe he took onboard two of every kind of animal found on Earth? Visit your local Zoo; talk with the attendants; imagine the immensity of that undertaking; then decide for yourself! There has been a concerted effort by zoologists for the past hundred years and they haven't even finished cataloging the known existing animals. How does the 'Ark' fable account for the utterly unique animal population of Australia? Let us consider the extinct species. How does the biblical apologist explain the appearance and disappearance of the dinosaurs? There is no prudence in continuing along these lines here. Suffice to observe; the Bible proves itself to be in substantial error. No amount of rationalization can reconcile the discrepancies noted between the "inspired texts" and the contradicting scientific evidences, much less the incompatible historic evidences.

There never has been a worldwide flood … at least not in the lifespan of mankind! Noah never built an ark that could hold two of every animal, even if we limit that aggregation to only those animals Noah knew personally. {Although there are today a minimum of religiously oriented scholars who conclude that Noah's Ark could have contained twenty-five thousand pairs of ground animals with room left over for storage of their feed.} (An advocate's exaggerated hyperbole) Regrettably, the words "never happened" are applicable to every other mythic fabulosity similarly contained in the Bible.

Then again, if you aren't thoroughly convinced by now, reply to these queries: What became of the ground dwelling insects (beetles, gnats, bees, ants, and numberless others) that would have perished without progeny during a worldwide flood? How did Noah feed his menagerie? Did he gather two of each plant form also? Did he provide extra prey animals to feed the carnivores? If you propose Divine assistance; I will ask why God didn't just exterminate all the human beings that He wished destroyed in the same week's time that it took Him to create the entire universe. Why utilize a yearlong Flood when a mere thought would have sufficed? God truly does 'work in mysterious ways.' Less mysterious is the explanation that every event on earth is a "natural" event, caused by "natural" happenstance, and serving no grander purpose than "this is how the natural world functions." Mystery solved! — God is obviated!

WORD OF GOD OR WORD OF MAN?

The 'Word of God' demonstrably is merely the 'Word of Man.' Whenever we scrutinize the concepts of religionists, again and again, their tenets are found lacking in empirical or rational verification. Always, their mystical beliefs contradict all that our intellect confirms to us. Why must all miraculous beliefs run counter to the 'Laws of Nature,' if God enacted those laws? Religionists offer that God contravenes the natural laws in order to prove His existence. This may be so, but He only proves it to those who personally behold the contravention. Hearing or reading about a miracle is not proof that it has occurred!

If we must rely on the word of another human being to be convinced of God's reality, then God has made a grievous blunder. There are entirely too many false witnesses out there, all professing to perform miracles. 'Or to relay heavenly messages. 'Or to have been graced with divine or angelic visitations, for us to sort out the total charlatans from the possible prophets. (Assuming there may be even one of the latter!) Human witness is the least reliable source of error-free information on earth. Every grouping of mankind in the world has some supranatural story to relate. We call them legends, and remark how quaint is the native folklore. But is it folklore? We accept the Gospels of four men on the identical "evidence" that we invoke to reject the deified mythologies of Greece; that being, the recorded words of fellow human beings.

Luke says that God impregnated Mary, and we believe him. Homer says that Zeus impregnated many mortal women, but we don't believe him. Matthew writes that Jesus walked on water … and that is truth! Homer writes that Poseidon lived in the sea … but that is mythical! Three Evangelists testify that Jesus told us to drink His blood in order to gain eternal life. Yet, when Bram Stoker wrote that Count Dracula drank human blood in order to sustain his vampire existence, we scoff and ridicule the story as superstitious humbug. Bram Stoker's story was written as fiction, but the inspiration for the tale existed in real life. His name was Count Vlad. How can any of us be confident that the Gospels weren't written as fiction, likewise inspired by a real person, "Jesus"? We can't! All that we should do is accept or reject individual stories on their individual merit. The Gospel stories have no more proof of their verity than does any other fabulous composition.

What is it that recommends the Old Testament over the tales of King Arthur and His Knights of the Round Table? Is a fire-breathing dragon any less believable than is a talking ass? [Cf. Num. 22:28] Logically, both are highly improbable, and both are utterly bereft of confirmation. Only mental set (bias) renders the talking ass more believable to a religionist than are fire-breathing dragons. Religionists predispose their intellect to accept the stories of the Bible, while simultaneously, rejecting equally unbelievable tales from secular sources.

Tell me: "What is a myth?" Do all human groupings have their own myths? It would seem so. I am not aware of any race or division of mankind that doesn't profess its own unique folklore. The Hebrew are no exception if we concede a lone caveat. The Hebrews placed much of their creation mythology into the first chapters of the book of Genesis. Having created a beginning, the Hebrews then incorporated their mythical, semi-mythical or possibly actual predecessors, e.g., Adam, Cain, Noah, Abraham, Lot, Isaac, Jacob, ending with Joseph of the multi-colored robe, into the last chapters of Genesis.

Thereafter, the early racial mythology of the Hebrews gradually evolved into "Sacred Scripture." The subsequent Old Testament chronicles grew out of the Genesis myth. Most Judeo-Christian religionists insist that Genesis isn't myth, but is incontrovertible truth! How very suspicious it is when we read the Old Testament intellectually, dispassionately, and especially skeptically only to discover how similar are the 'truths' of Judaism to the 'fictions' of other folk tales and ancient racial semi-myths.

As recorded in Babylonian Mythology, The Epic of Gilgamesh (ancient Babylonian poem) recounts a flood story that is similar to the biblical flood story. Add to this the knowledge that the Jews were taken in bondage to Babylon, and must have known of this legend. Given this knowledge, one must honestly question which story inspired the other, or if either are true and not just outgrowths of a single historical, albeit, ancient regional flood disaster. Other peoples had folklore floods.

Read of Deucalion, a legendary character from Greek mythology. [Funk & Wagnall's New Encyclopedia]

> *"Deucalion was the son of the Titan, Prometheus, and the father of Hellen, the mythical ancestor of the ancient Greek race. Deucalion was king of Phthia in Thessaly when the god Zeus, because of the great wickedness of men at that time, decided to destroy them by flood. For nine days and nights Zeus sent torrents of rain upon the earth; the rivers overran their banks and the sea crashed over the land until all life was drowned in the dreadful deluge. Only Deucalion and his wife Pyrrha were saved. They alone, of all the people on earth, had led good lives and remained faithful to the laws of the gods. Having been warned by his father Prometheus of the approaching disaster, Deucalion had built a boat, which carried him and Pyrrha safely through the flood and finally came to rest atop Mount Parnassus."*

What an amazing similarity to the story of Noah and his Ark! But is it amazing? 'Not necessarily! Once belief in a personal Deity is embraced, the remainder of the story becomes almost automatic. First, believe that there is a personal God. Then posit that mortal behavior influences His humors. Imagine that His creatures are wicked in His sight. This isn't very difficult! Further, imagine that God decided to destroy those people for their wickedness. What method might He choose? Probably some natural disaster, such as: fire, flood or earthquake. But wait! God doesn't want everyone to die; that would eradicate the very creatures He needed to honor and worship Him. No! Some method must be employed to destroy most of mankind, but not all of mankind.

There doesn't seem to be any natural way to survive a worldwide fire. Worldwide earthquakes might miss killing everyone that God wanted to die. But a worldwide flood could be survived if the intended survivors were forewarned to build a sturdy boat (an Ark). Therefore, the decision was made by God to destroy the world by flood. He would first inform those He wished saved. This would enable them to survive via the Ark Noah was commanded to build, while the remainder, those wicked mortals, perished. And so it was!

The flood raged, but the elect few were safe in their watertight craft. Eventually the storm ended and the waters began to subside. Now where do you suppose this vessel might first make land? If you guessed on top of a high mountain; you chose the obvious! For that is precisely where both Noah and Deucalion landed, although not on the same mountain. After all, the Deity who saved them wasn't the same. What necessity was there for the mountain to be the same?

Has the point been made? Even if one story is a direct steal from the other, or both are imaginary, or both are founded on real events … a worldwide flood is refuted by the geological evidence! At the very time that the Bible states that the world was flooded, an Egyptian dynasty was flourishing. Perhaps the Bible is erroneous in its time references, but if so, then perhaps the Bible is likewise incorrect in other conceded facts detailed in the narrative. Perhaps the entire story of the flood in the Bible is fictitious; hence, we should read it as a local folk tale, and not as the "Word of God."

It should come as no surprise that the Egyptians have no flood myths (to this author's knowledge). In this case, in the minds of the ancient Egyptians, the yearly flooding of the Nile was seen as a blessing from the gods, not a disaster from Heaven. If angered, the gods would have reprimanded the Egyptians by not sending the Nile over its banks. So geography, most likely, is responsible for the lack of an Egyptian flood legend. Yet, the Egyptians didn't lack for other divine folklore. As already stated, all groupings of mankind have their own racial mythology, including the Hebrews. The Hebrew myths are known collectively as the Old Testament. All we need do is recognize those tales for what they are, and we will have freed ourselves of more than three thousand years of superstitious thralldom.

Ignorance binds the intellect; only knowledge truly liberates the mental soul. Christian religionists predict that not all of mankind will attain Heaven. Through knowledge, I believe we can all romp in the Elysian Fields. Perhaps with sufficient knowledge, we can learn to scale the ramparts on the Mount of Olympus. Once there, we would proceed to the banquet halls of Valhalla where we could feast on the roasted flesh of a bison fattened in the Happy Hunting Grounds. Satiated, we could have a nap in the Garden of the Hesperides, and thence achieve the blissful state of Nirvana. {'Beg pardon, if I have missed anyone's "Paradise," familiarly known to Christians as "Heaven."}

THE BIBLE WAS INSPIRED?

The purported inspiration of the Bible, upon analysis, is seen to be nothing more than the exaltation of a reasonably historic account of the origins and travails of an ethnically related grouping of Semites. Then, prefaced to a questionably historic account of one of the descendants of that group (Abram), the whole agglomeration being allied through an egotistical bias that the Israelites were "chosen for exceptional elevation" out of the collective human stock by the Semite God, Yahweh.

The Bible is not only riddled with inaccuracies, even more damaging to those who would glorify and extol it, is the fact that it is also over-blown with triviality that has no significance to anyone other than its authors. The whole of the Bible could be proffered as proof, but here in deference to concision, only two items will be offered. The two examples are: The creation of the Universe in six days, and the walking on water by Jesus. {The immediately following excerpts are all from Genesis, Chapter One, and are concatenated for brevity and occasionally paraphrased. No intentional distortions have been included; and in hope, none were created.}

First, ponder the Creation. [Refer Genesis, Chapter 1, Verses 1 through 31] Disregarding the obvious miscalculation that it would take God six days to create something from nothing, we read in God's inspired words that on the first day, "God said, *'Let there be light'* and there was light." (The source of that light isn't revealed, but we can know it wasn't the sun.) Continuing: *"God separated the light from the darkness calling the light Day and the darkness Night. And there was evening and morning, the first day."* That ended the first day's work of creation.

On the second day God created the firmament. The firmament was the crystal dome upon which all the stars (and planets) would be affixed. It also served to separate the *"waters that were below … from those that were above … And God called the firmament Heaven."*

On day three, God said, *"Let the earth bring forth vegetation: seed-bearing plants and all kinds of fruit trees that bear fruit containing their seed. And so it was."* (Is this the day that bacteria were created? Bacteria exhibit both plant and animate characteristics.)

Day four: *"And God said, 'Let there be lights in the firmament of the heaven to separate day from night; let them serve as signs and for the fixing of seasons, days and years' ... God made the two great lights, the greater light to rule the day and the smaller one to rule the night, and he made the stars."*

There we have it from God's own mouth; He created light on the first day, but He didn't create the Sun until the fourth day! Picture that if you can: daylight on the first day of creation without the light of the Sun! Picture, too, if you will: forests and trees and all manner of plant life growing on the third day before the Sun was created to activate the chlorophyll through the process of photosynthesis!

Contemplate the second day's accomplishment: Where is the 'firm' dome of the sky today? What water was above the dome? Rainwater, of course! The ancient author of Genesis, Chapter One, wondered 'where came rainwater'? He didn't know about evaporation, water vapor, cloud formation, and eventual precipitation. Just how did the rain water get up in the sky? Obviously (to the ancients), God created it there. However, God protected us in the beginning from being inundated immediately (i. e., the "Flood") by positioning a dome between the waters above and the waters below. (The Oceans, Seas, etc., are the 'waters below.') There are numerous, verifiable facts that condemn the biblical sequence of creation for exactly what it is: A juvenile, anachronistic fable that should have been consigned to a child's fairy tale long ago. To call the creation story unenlightened would be to state the obvious much too trivially. That story is the result of simplistic, uneducated ignorance.

The proof of the creation story's falsity doesn't end there. The final proof that the creation didn't take place as the Bible relates is the accumulating knowledge acquired by our scientists of how the creation of the Earth might have taken place (did?). Today's scientific knowledge has long since disproved Genesis, and that knowledge is systematically disabusing the subsequent superstitious folderol of organized religions. The evolution of mankind, the evolution of life, and the evolution of the Earth and the formation of our Solar System, all have evidences that anyone can inspect. Evidences that are intellectually plausible, that aren't reliant upon faith to sustain the conclusions formulated from an intelligent interpretation of those evidences.

To me, one of the simplest, yet one of the profoundest clues of human evolution from a lesser life form, can be observed in our newborn babies. Note how tightly an infant clenches its tiny fists. Even its toes are turned under almost continuously as if to grasp something. What is this something that infants instinctively attempt to grasp? Well, in case you haven't already theorized it; the answer is fur! Any infant who could hold on to its anthropoid mother's fur while her hands were occupied, as when she was moving through trees or scampering to safety while running on all fours from a predator, would have a decided survival advantage over an infant who couldn't cling to its mother. Advantageous instincts are invariably passed on to future generations in greater numbers than are disadvantageous instincts.

The proofs of man's descent from a hairy, ape-like ancestor are much more direct, and much more detailed than the example given. It is offered as one small piece in the jigsaw-like puzzle of life. What makes the theory of evolution so convincing is that each year new puzzle pieces are found that fit neatly with the pieces already placed within the frame. Admittedly, the puzzle isn't complete as yet, and may never be completed. Some of the pieces have been scattered, and we can't know if we will ever find them. Yet, enough pieces have been found (deduced) and placed into the mosaic to assure us that we are on the right track. Enough pieces so that we can speculate on the gist of the creation picture; if not know what its exact replication would look like.

A bible-sized book could be written outlining the proofs of evolution. However, if it were written, I doubt that anyone could get religious dogmatists to read it. Religionists ridicule the labors of scientists, and scorn the factual evidence they present to us. But what do the scorners offer in rebuttal? They present a fable that insists that the Earth had light before the Sun existed; a fable that insists that plants and trees grew without the aid of the Sun; a fable that states that God the Creator was seen *"walking in the Garden"* He had just created. [Gen. 3:8]

First, I will repeat the statements I made earlier. Namely, that the Bible was riddled with inaccuracies. The Creation fable illustrates only one of its inaccuracies. I then stated that it is likewise riddled with triviality. My example for this will be the fabrication of Jesus walking on water sometime after midnight, preceded by the afternoon feeding of five thousand spectators. [Cf. Mt. 14:22-26; Mk. 6:45-52; & Jn. 6:19-21] Luke knows nothing of Jesus walking on water. Why?

To begin, let's examine the walking on water: Why did Jesus perform such a senseless wonder? The only reason I can discover is so that Matthew's version can end with the doctrine-affirming exclamation of the disciples, *"Truly, you are the Son of God."* [Mt. 14:33]

This episode takes place on the night of the afternoon feeding of the five thousand in all three Synoptic Gospels. However, "Walking on Water," is not found in Luke. In John's version the final result of Jesus walking on water was that the disciples reached their destination. It seemed that a strong wind was preventing the disciples from rowing to the far shore. Then, after Jesus joined them, they *"immediately reached land at the place they were headed for."* [Jn. 6:21] Any reasonable person should ask why the feeding of the multitude and the walking on the water took place in the sequence that the Gospels detail.

Specifically, why did Jesus miraculously feed the gathering? [Cf. Mt. 14:21; Mk. 6:44; Lu. 9:14 & Jn. 6:10] Two reasons are evident. One: Because he felt compassion for the crowd who must have been hungry after listening to Him most of the day. This is possible, but it isn't probable. If one boy had seven loaves and two fish, surely out of that throng of five thousand, others had food with them also. Besides, no one would have starved to death, or have suffered great privation, by missing a single meal.

No, the only logical explanation for the miracle was to exhibit His divine power to the multitude. But the impact of this miracle would be diminished greatly merely because of the size of the crowd. In the end, who would know for certain that Jesus had only the seven loaves and two fish? A miracle of this type is unrecognizable by such a huge gathering. Still, it is the only solution we can conceive. Jesus performed the multiplication miracle to prove to the crowd that, factually, He was the divine "Son of God."

Next, Jesus sent the disciples out in their boat while it was still daylight. He then dismissed the crowd. [Cf. Mk. 6:45] Why dismiss the crowd before performing His more spectacular miracle? Why did He fail to exploit the opportunity the lake furnished to dramatically demonstrate His supernatural powers? Jesus could have walked out on top of the waters in full sun-lit view of five thousand astonished onlookers. Skeptics could have attempted the feat themselves, just as Peter reputedly did in Matthew's version exclusively. When the skeptics sank, as Peter did, Jesus could have admonished them all to have more faith in Him precisely as He scolded Peter. *"How little faith you have! Why did you doubt?"* [Mt. 14:31] This would have been a spectacular miracle that would have reaped spectacular conversions.

This is how it might have been, but this isn't how the Gospels report this episode as having unfolded. Instead, Jesus sent the disciples away in their boat while He secluded Himself on a hill to pray. Then, in the middle of the night, ["fourth watch"] between three and six in the morning, He decided to rejoin the Apostles. Or perchance He was just out for a moonlit stroll on the water? I raise this possibility because Mark (inspired by the Holy Ghost!) told us, *"He was going to pass them by."* [Mk. 6:48] Why would He pass them by? Do you suppose that He didn't know they were still in the middle of the lake, and He was hurrying to join them on the far side? Or maybe Jesus just didn't want them to observe that He could walk on water, and He, therefore, was endeavoring to sneak past them unnoticed?

The disciples had rowed 'three or four miles' (25 or 30 furlongs) onto the lake. [Jn. 6:19] Consequently, Jesus necessarily had to have walked briskly across the water so as to reach the far side before morning. If so, then the time reference given would fit. The Evangelists agree that it was between three and six in the morning. Perhaps it should read: 'from three until six in the morning,' because it would have taken about that length of time to walk that distance, especially on water! Don't ask me why He either didn't fly out to the boat, or didn't appear instantly in the boat. I don't have the answers to those two cogent posers.

Neither do I have the explanation as to why Jesus performed this miracle during the obscurity of night. Only the Apostles witnessed this wonder. Ask yourself 'why.' If the multiplication of the loaves and fish was wrought to prove His divinity, why not demonstrate an indisputable paranormal feat (walking on water) in view of the entire five thousand in bright sunlight? How many of those astonished viewers would have recognized Him instantly as a mighty wonder worker? More convincingly, He may have been recognized as the Old Testament prophesied "Messiah"?

Allow me to return now to my discourse on religionists: fundamental religionists in particular! They attack scientists and scholars and all who expose their unfounded assertions. They damn any who dare question one of their cherished teachings. Yet, I have never read where Charles Darwin ever ridiculed anyone who didn't accept his Theory of Evolution. Copernicus never threatened to harm anyone who expressed doubt about the Sun centering the Solar System.

Atheists don't band together to ostracize believers. The Christian martyrs weren't put to death by non-believers, but by believers in a different religious persuasion (paganism). As soon as Christians gained power they immediately began to punish and exterminate anyone who didn't embrace their beliefs. Atheists and Heathen alike had to hide from the Christians. Atheists have had to flee from all religionists perpetually. Even the indifferent were at lethal risk.

How can the verity of the proposition be proven that the writers of the books of the Bible were inspired by God? The only response that acknowledges the actuality of this proposition is that the proposition is not provable. Expositors of religious apology usually admit this actuality themselves. They invariably instruct their followers that this belief rests solely on faith, not on proof! Although moments later, they will often commence rationalizing their scripturally based tenets as though they were unchallenged facts beyond any question or doubt whatsoever.

Religionists vouch that God inspired every word in the Bible. Yet, when scholars examine these writings they find differences in style, syntax, spelling, and other objective dissimilarities in the various books. Religionists alibi these very real differences by proposing that God only inspired the thought, not the word. The transparency of the foregoing argument isn't readily discernible. It should be! In actuality, many thoughts are first formed as pictures in the mind. Thereafter, these images are transformed into words. For instance: When you are thirsty you recall something wet and refreshing in your mind, you then phrase the thought verbally. Contrarily, when a religionist reflects on the Trinity, he can't readily visualize it. What he does is merely verbalize the formulary concept that three persons constitute only one God. A three-leafed clover is sometimes used to depict the Trinity, but not to my discernment. God is everywhere and He is a spirit. Can He be three separate spirits (as leaves of clover) without becoming three separate Gods?

The rhetoric above isn't the easiest argument to express. But think about this: Did God inspire the words that name the descendants of Jesus (per Matthew & Luke), or did He inspire the thought? Undoubtedly, He inspired the actual names (if anything!), and not just the idea that Jesus was descended from King David. Religionists are playing word games with us, whether they realize it or not. Much of the prophetic material contained in the Bible (if not all) had to have been inspired word for word, and not thought by thought.

Pause here to read Chapter Four of Judges. If God inspired the writing of this chapter, did He similarly orchestrate the actions of the personalities described therein? The Kenite heroine of this Gothic tale had a name that was an amalgam (purposely?) of the two names for the Semite God, Yahweh and Eloi. Her name was Jael. This woman took a tent peg and a mallet, and drove the peg through the head of Sisera, Captain of King Jabin's military forces. [Cf. Judg. 4:21 & 5:24-26] Her story is twice told. What an astounding woman she was. It is puzzling that she hasn't been immortalized for her lethal sectarian valor.

When I first read of this Old Testament heroine I envisioned Evangelist Billy Graham armed with a sub-machinegun blowing away the enemies of Christianity. Don't scoff! When the Church wielded temporal power, all her enemies fled from her disfavor. Anyone who dared defy the Church was well advised to remain beyond its reach. Yet, does this characterization only apply to Christians? Indubitably no! All religions have been sullied by the most heinous of all crimes, genocide, incited solely by superstitious arrogance; i. e., the belief that God looked down favorably upon assassins that were murdering detractors of His exclusive system of worship. (as that system was delineated by the murderers themselves)

THE "INSPIRED" VERSION OF THE BIBLE

In the preface to the Inspired Version – The Holy Scriptures (per Joseph Smith Jr.), there are quoted many early critics of the accuracy and completeness of the Bible. These early religionists decried the differences, deletions, omissions, addenda, and confusions noted in the manuscripts of their day. Joseph Smith highlighted these emendations, presumably to contrast with his own "inspired" (by God!) version that corrected those erring human textual alterations. 'Great! So now we have a modern, supposedly complete and trustworthy, version of God's Holy Scriptures. But behold and contemplate: what do we find at the end of the preface to the "Revised" edition of Joseph Smith's inspired version, but an apology from the revisers for some necessary corrections required in the original transcripts of Joseph Smith's "Inspired" translation of the Bible. Does the irony of this confession strike you as it did me? God inspired Joseph Smith to rewrite the Bible for the stated reason that inaccuracies were contained in the then extant versions of the Bible of Joseph Smith's day. Fine! Concomitantly, didn't God's prescience alert that Joseph Smith's "inspired" version would also contain transcription errors? 'Evidently not!

Read the preface to the 1944 edition, page six. "The committee found some words and phrases transposed or improperly placed in the work done by Joseph Smith, Jr. These errors, together with others involving spelling, punctuation, and typographical or other omissions, were corrected, particularly in those instances where the meaning of the text had been affected. Few other corrections were required." So now we know: God doesn't supply punctuation, for the earliest manuscripts had none. God doesn't inspire correct spelling. God doesn't edit His inspiration for omissions or careless copying of His infusions. On page two, the committee admitted "errors in grammar," so we may also suspect that the Holy Ghost isn't articulate in English composition. Do you wonder now at my doubts?

To summarize the intent of this section I will restate it thus: Joseph Smith, Jr. must have puffed expansively when he exposed the venality of the prior biblical copyists down through the ages. Then, swollen with pride, he presented his own testaments. How smug and confident he must have felt to have so presumptuously titled his work "Inspired." Yet, in the aftermath, Joseph Smith becomes a victim to an occupational malady that strikes most (all?) writers. Namely, someone follows after you and uncovers your blunders. Why is it that none of us can discover every one of our own errors? Because we are not perfect, nor are any of us enlightened confidantes of an infallible ghostlike divinity. (Holy Spirit God)

Joseph Smith's mistakes are all the more significant because adherents to his creed found them. If bias colored their efforts, that coloration was surely less intense than would be the case had a detractor scrutinized his translation. Yet, even his staunch advocates had to admit that sometimes "the meaning of the text was affected." We should all heed the unarticulated implication contained herein and lay to rest the corpse of 'inspired texts.'

While I have Joseph Smith under scrutiny, allow me to offer another proof that God did not inspire him as he claimed while composing his "Inspired" Bible. The follow excerpt comes from a book titled: <u>99 Reasons Why No One Knows When Christ Will Return</u> by B. J. Oropeza, InterVarsity Press, 1994, page 120.

"AD 1832 Mormon founder Joseph Smith prophesied under 'divine revelation' the gathering of the saints and the coming of the New Jerusalem, the temple of which would be built in Missouri, and 'reared in this generation.' Joseph Smith added: 'Pestilence, hail, famine, and earthquake will sweep the wicked of this generation from off the face of the land, to open and prepare the way for the return of the lost tribes of Israel from the north country ... there are those now living upon the earth whose eyes shall not be closed in death until they see all these things which I have spoken, fulfilled.'"

Pardon my burgeoning skepticism, but every last person alive in 1832 have 'closed their eyes in death.' But Joseph Smith's prophesy remains unfulfilled. Someone has falsely reported the actuality. Is it myself? Was it B.J. Oropeza? Was it the Holy Spirit falsely inspiring? Or was it Joseph Smith brazenly indulging his own ego? You decide!

THE BIBLE SHOULD BE REVERENCED

If God required that we reverence His words, He would have carved the entire Bible in stone, not just the Ten Commandments. The fact is: God carved the Commandments twice. Moses smashed the first pair in anger, so God obligingly prepared a second set of tablets. [Cf. Ex. 34:1 & Deut. 10:1-4] This religious 'fact' however, causes the skeptic to wonder. The wonderment of the 'fact' arises when you ask yourself "Why?" Why did God inscribe replacement tablets? He must have deemed those Commandments so important that they had to be preserved for the future. He could have prevented Moses from destroying them in any number of ways. He even could have caused all the pieces of the original tablets to reassemble miraculously. But He didn't! What He did was re-inscribe another set of tablets. {< – Using Moses' hands?}

Consequently, one must conclude that God wanted the Israelites to heed the message on the tablets; likewise, He wanted the people to have the physical tablets as well. Then why did God permit the tablets to be lost, stolen, or destroyed? What became of these replacement tablets? They vanished more than 2,500 years ago! [Cf. 1 Sam. 4:4-22]

These tablet questions are somewhat askew from the main theme in this segment. But they are no less pertinent. What the current segment queries is this: "Was the Bible truly inspired by God?" In corollary: "Is it infallible?" If the Bible itself can't be relied upon as infallible, what credence can we give to doctrines that aren't based on scriptural readings? Are these doctrines founded exclusively on misguided extrapolations of pietistic religious leaders?

The prohibition against eating meat on Friday was one such doctrine that since has been rescinded. Another is the doctrine of the lifelong virginity of Mary, the mother of Jesus. Not only isn't this last doctrine supported by the scriptures, it is explicitly refuted by the scriptures. How then can anyone believe in this doctrine after having read the New Testament? Frankly, I am bewildered, other than to observe that some very intelligent people apparently have believed that Mary remained chaste (virgin) her entire life. Many people still do believe!

The Gospels and Acts refer unambiguously to the brothers and sisters of Jesus. [Cf. Mt. 12:47-50, 13:55; Mk. 3:31-32, 6:3; Lu. 8:19-20; Jn. 2:12, 7:3, 5, 10 & Acts 1:14] Even Paul informs us that Jesus had brothers. [Cf. Ga. 1:19] Were all the children of Mary fathered without Joseph's participation? In other words, did the Holy Spirit conceive them also? No, of course not! That would crowd the Trinity into a small mob, and would further confuse that already muddled issue. No, the Christian explanation is direct, but without proof: 'The "brethren" that the scriptures refer to are the cousins of Jesus, not His brothers and sisters.' Their proof for this postulate is the statement that the Aramaic language had no word for "cousin." Perhaps this is because the Aramaic people used the term "kinsman" to indicate "cousin." I believe that in Aramaic "brethren," referred exclusively to "brother." Additionally, I have read that ancient Aramaic did have a separate word for "cousin." 'Sister' in Aramaic, meant 'Sister'! The New Testament declares that Jesus had 'sisters.'

In the modern world we sometimes employ the word "brethren" in the context that persons sharing common beliefs are brothers in a figurative sense. However, there is no evidence that the word brethren in the texts referenced above meant anything but literal 'brother.' The sense of the texts is this: *"Is not his mother called Mary? And his brethren, James, and Joses, and Simon, and Judas? And his sisters."* [ibid.] If 'brethren' meant "cousin," what does 'mother' mean, "Aunt"? Even in biblical times 'sister' meant "sister," not female cousin! [Cf. Mt. 19:29 & Mk. 10:30]

No, Joseph wasn't recruited as a subterfuge father, for that would subject God to a charge of willful deception, which is inadmissible. Further, we must ask, "Did Joseph ever kiss Mary?" Exactly how intimate was he with his wife Mary? Think about Joseph's humanity! Was he entirely human with fully masculine emotions and natural masculine drives, and all the other traits that attend masculinity? It has never been promulgated that Joseph was sinless, so I ask, "What were his sins?" We have no enlightenment on this subject. Instead, we are mollified with the sanctimonious blather about Joseph being the patron Saint of those who die a happy death. Why? Because Joseph died a happy death! How do we know this? Because ancient tradition says so! 'A tradition completely bereft of even an iota of substantiation!

Could that tradition have been broadcast by the same persons whose other traditions were rejected as uninspired by those who decided the Canon of the New Testament? The inference here is to the (pseudepigraphical-apocryphal – deuterocanonical) non-canonical writings, which contain many such pieties. We haven't the slightest inkling of how, or when, Joseph died because God never inspired anyone to inform us. So we will never know if Joseph died happy, or if he died sad. In fact, there is no N. T. proof of when he died. It is possible that Joseph and Mary were divorced or separated during the ministry of Jesus.

But God did inspire the Nativity story! If He wanted the world to know that His Son was born to a virgin, He could have done so more convincingly without Joseph. Mary could have been praying in the Temple, and God the Father could have opened the skies and had the baby Jesus descend down from Heaven into the waiting arms of Mary. He then could have sounded the phrase, *"This is my beloved Son in whom I am well pleased."* [Per Mt. 3:17] Thus proving what God wanted the world to know, i.e., His Son wasn't fathered by a human male!

Accepting the two Nativity stories exactly as they are written refutes two other cherished beliefs. First, that Jesus was true man. Second, that Jesus was true God. If Jesus was born of the union of Mary and the Holy Spirit, then He was a hybrid. Speaking impiously but accurately, He was half-human and half-divine. Beyond that, if Mary was truly the mother of Jesus and not merely the vessel for His fetal delivery on Earth, then Jesus didn't exist until the moment of His conception in her reproductive system. This reasoning may contradict accepted theology, but it agrees perfectly with verifiable obstetrics.

The dilemma for a theologian generated by this thesis is that Jesus (God in the Second Person) is forced to have had a beginning. That, to them, is intolerable, and they can't abide its corollaries. To them, God always was, and He can't have had a beginning, not even if He splits Himself into three personalities! 'Why? Why can't God create a clone of Himself? Doesn't He have the power to accomplish this feat? I find the belief that He could cease being God, and that He did become a mortal being, immensely more perplexing to embrace.

By accepting the divinity of Jesus we are forced to accept a host of other dubious dogmas; the first of which is the unlikely, untenable, and indefensible multiplication of God into three entities. This opened the early Christians to a derisively mocking charge of polytheism. This charge they would have been passionately motivated to rebut. Yet, here they were elevating Jesus to second place in the Godhead, when Jesus Himself believed in only one God. The problem arose initially because of too literal an interpretation of a Jewish idiom. 'Son of God' to the average ancient Jew simply meant a man well favored in the judgment of their singular God. It was a term of high praise toward the man who was its object. But to Gentile ears, the phrase meant precisely what it stated, namely: "God's Son."

In the Greek deity myths the Gods habitually sported with human females and they frequently fathered a child through them. To postulate a true 'Son of a Deity' was no heresy to a Roman, as it would have been to a devout Jew. The Jewish Deity (Yahweh) had no peers among the extant 'Gods.' How, then, could the Jews espouse God's equal among men?

No, the first of those to deify Jesus couldn't deny the charge of polytheism, so they brazenly and audaciously contorted the arithmetic intrinsic to a Trinity. Yes, there were three persons, but those three persons constituted only one God. One plus one: plus one more: equaled three in all cases except when you were counting gods. Then, and only then, the sum added to one.

The entire elitist argument dissipates completely when, and if, we subtract the supernatural and minus the mysterious. Make Jesus a man, and make Yahweh a myth, then all that remains is the question of how so many people could be duped into believing in Christian supernaturalism. The manifest response is: they wished to believe! They strove so mightily that in most cases they were successful, especially when other believers supported them. More crassly, they succeeded when the belief was reinforced by those who had something to gain through someone else's gullibility. Patently, the latter group is the priestly hierarchy of the Holy of Holies and its successor and ancillary artifacts: Synagogue, Church, Congregation, Pastor, & Ayatollah, Imam, and more!

WHY WAS THE BIBLE WRITTEN?

Did God inspire the Bible's authors so that His words could be referenced for all time? In places, this could seem to be the case. Nonetheless, there are just as many passages where such an interpretation is inappropriate or inapplicable. Balaam's talking ass and Jephthah immolating his daughter are prime examples. [Cf. Num. Chap. 22-24 & Judg. 11:30-40]

No, the most cogent reason for the existence of the Bible is to prove that God acts! This is the real impetus behind every story. If God doesn't act, then it doesn't matter if He exists. If God exists, then He must do something to prove it. Even religionists recognize this. The Bible, therefore, is primarily a written account of God's alleged actions. The Bible claims that God acts, and as an irrefutable corollary, it testifies that He lives!

The perennial difficulty for all religionists is establishing that God is extant. By providing prior proofs of God's activities, the Bible does just this. On the other hand, atheists and scoffers strive to demonstrate that God doesn't (or hasn't) intervened in mortal sagas, and thereby, He is proved non-existent; or if extant, then irrelevant. Yet, is it possible for me or anyone to prove that Abraham (father of Judaism) never spoke face to face with Yahweh? [Cf. Gen. 18:22-33]

God's essence exists only in mankind's imagination. God's being is the construction of man's fancy. God has as much substance as does a transient thought. His spirit is as alive as is a secret wish. Whenever we cease dwelling on His presence, He fades away. Heaven forefend that we question His reality intellectually; for when we do, He vanishes evermore.

UNASSAILABLE BIBLE

Jesus Himself repudiated the doctrine of the incontrovertibility of the Bible, and in so doing He repudiated its divine origin! Reflect on this: *"Some Pharisees coming up asked him, testing him, 'Is it lawful for a man to put away his wife?' But He answered, and said to them, 'What did Moses command you?' They said, 'Moses permitted us to write a notice of dismissal, and to put her away.' But Jesus said, 'By reason of the hardness of your heart he wrote you that commandment.'"* [Mt. 19:3-8 & Mk. 10:2-5] [Ref. Deut. 24:1]

As you can see, Jesus stated categorically that Moses himself initiated this easement, not God. Then Jesus proceeded to define just what God's actual decree on divorce was: *"But from the beginning of creation God made them male and female. For this reason a man shall leave his father and mother, and cleave to his wife, and the two shall become one flesh. Therefore now they are no longer two, but one flesh. What therefore God has joined together, let no man put asunder."* [Mk. 10:6-9]

Which other ordinances from Moses are his alone, rather than God's? Many of the directives of Moses to his people are clearly of his own uninspired authorship. This can be discerned readily by almost anyone. Reading the extensive legislates of Moses exposes their mortal origins. Yet, the next logical conclusion, i.e., that the entire Bible was authored without mystical guidance, and was composed with human credulity, and with susceptibility to error. That determination is adamantly denied and is collectively controverted by all of the Bible's adherents. For those who hold that every word in the Bible issued from God's own mouth, can't they discern that they are quarreling with Jesus Himself because of their mulish refusal to see that which is plainly apparent before their very eyes?

Did God inspire Moses to codify the treatment of, and behavior toward, slaves? [Cf. Ex. 21:1-6] If so, who inspired Abraham Lincoln to free the Negro slaves? Was that the work of the Devil? Moses even imparted God's rules governing how a father should sell his daughter into slavery. [Cf. Ex. 21:7-11] Imagine that! God regulated the procedure for selling your daughter into slavery. Note this also: The rules that Moses set for the Hebrew (Israelite) slave owners only applied to their Hebrew slaves. What you did with your foreign-born slaves was your own business, and (perceptibly) was of no concern to the God of Moses (Yahweh). *"Give the Israelites the following laws: 'If you buy a Hebrew slave, he shall serve you for six years. In the seventh year he is to be set free without having to pay anything.'"* [Ex. 21:1-2] *"If a man sells his daughter as a slave, she is not to be set free, as male slaves are."* [Ex. 21:7] Who knew, back then, how abhorrent such an instruction (commandment) would be to future believers? God would have known, but His mind was occupied elsewhere.

God was busy formulating the entirety of sacred instructions detailing the construction of an ornate 'ark' to house His Ten Commandments, plus an enclosure called the Holy of Holies to encompass that ark. [Read Exodus, Chapters 25, 26, 27, 28, 29, 30, & 31] To describe these instructions as 'elaborate' is tantamount to gross understatement. The pomp and ritual must have been a sight to behold. But didn't Jesus teach that it wasn't the outward signs of religiosity that pleased God; it was your inner worth? What God saw in the depths of your heart was paramount to any overt action you could or would perform. It should be obvious to everyone that what Moses wrote came from man (Moses), not from God! Jesus recognized this, and so should you!

READ THE BIBLE WITH A PROBING SPIRIT

More than once the reader has been invited to study the Bible with an open mind. Permit me to alter that. Here I am going to exhort you to do more than that. Now I ask that you read the Bible with a probing spirit. I will guide the way. Begin with Mark. Jesus discourses to all the Apostles:

> *"Don't you remember when I broke the five loaves for the five thousand peo-*
> *ple? How many baskets full of leftover pieces did you take up? 'Twelve,'*
> *they answered."*

> *"And when I broke the seven loaves for the four thousand people,' asked*
> *Jesus. 'How many baskets full of leftover pieces did you take up?' 'Seven,'*
> *they answered."* [Mk. 8:19-20 & Mt. 16:9-10]

You could simply reject both miracles summarily and mentally close your mind to anything and everything the Bible states. You could, but then you would be no less inflexible than the most intractable religionist! Don't be a blind disbeliever thinking you are counteracting the slavish devotion of blind believers. Both extremes are an outrage against intelligence.

Examine the words of Mark. Did you notice that when Jesus started with five loaves, He fed five thousand people? Yet, when He started with seven loaves He fed only four thousand people. Did you also note that from the five loaves there remained twelve baskets of leftovers, while an initial seven loaves yielded only seven baskets of leftovers? Did Jesus become more efficient at 'catering to a multitude' the second time He performed the multiplication miracle?

What became of the bread remnants? Without knowledge of preservatives, the bread either had to be consumed quickly or become waste. How was the miracle accomplished? Was each piece miraculously replaced as it was broken from the whole loaf? If so, then the remainder should have been the same figure as was begun with. Start with seven loaves; end with seven loaves! Just as in the second feeding, but not in the first feeding.

What were the sanitary conditions at the feedings? Presumably, the crowd was far from the city. After a lengthy period of listening, where did the people wash before eating? Were the twelve baskets of fragments miraculously sterilized so as to prevent the spread of disease? You will concede that Jesus, the miracle worker, attracted a large percentage of the lame, the blind, and the diseased to His gatherings.

Incidentally, where did the twelve empty baskets come from? Do you suppose twelve people just happened to be carrying empty baskets with them? How many other relevant posers could be asked? Indeed, many!

Can you see now that it isn't just me who refutes the story of the multiplication of the loaves, but it is the deficiencies in the story itself that expose it as a fiction? If Jesus was God, and as God, He knows all things, surely He knew exactly how much bread would have been required. In that case, no fragments would have remained.

Were these two examples the only large crowds Jesus attracted when He preached? This is surprising if you believe His ministry lasted three years. Were there other large crowds that Jesus didn't feed? In three of the Gospels, the multiplication miracle takes place early in the public life of Jesus; did the crowds begin to diminish after His wonder-working became more widely broadcast? The exact opposite should have been the reality. Mark informs us this was the reality. Jesus cured a leper of his affliction, and charged him not to tell anyone. In direct disobedience, the leper told everyone. That concluded predictably! Mark reports, "*Jesus could not go into a town publicly.*" [Mk. 1:40-45]

If, as Matthew reports, "*Jesus healed them all,*" [Mt. 12:15] then the crowds would have grown to such magnitudes that the assortment of the illnesses the crowds harbored would have been the cause of increased deadly infections. [Cf. Mt. 4:24] Sanitation would have become impossible, and the multitudes seeking after Jesus would have grown exponentially, with potentially calamitous health consequences to all present!

Just as devout religionists dwell and reflect on the Bible assiduously and invent all manner of pious extensions (extrapolations), such as the Immaculate Conception, or the Assumption of Mary into Heaven, so too, ought we to probe beyond the bare words of the Bible to discern the untruths embedded therein. Every section of the Bible should be subjected to the same sort of searching scrutiny and detailed examination.

One more example will be given before I conclude this thought. This isn't the best example available, but because of my lifelong fascination with astronomy, it is significant for me. The example is the Star of Bethlehem. [Cf. Mt. 2:2, 9-10] Did such an aerial singularity ever occur? Manifestly, no confirmation can be found outside the pages of Matthew's Gospel. Questions arising out of this celestial manifestation are plentiful.

Was it a comet? Was it a supernova? Was it a conjunction of two or three planets? Or was it precisely what Matthew writes: a peculiar star in the sky that guided the Magi toward Bethlehem? Whatever it was: how did it guide anyone? Due to the rotation of the Earth, only Polaris (the North Star) and a few nearby circumpolar stars appear to be relatively fixed in the sky. All other visible stars first appear generally across the entire sky at dusk, and then seemingly move slowly, but inexorably, toward the west where they disappear behind the horizon, or until sunrise fades them from view.

As might be expected, this is the recorded direction of travel the Magi took. There is nothing miraculous about a star that traversed the sky from east to west. How did the Magi know this particular star signaled the birth of the king of the Jews? Grant that a wondrous star did appear and stood motionless in the sky over Bethlehem: How did the Wise Men know this was the omen proclaiming the birth of the long-expected Jewish Messiah? The Hebrew priesthood either failed to see the wonder, or failed to grasp its import. Yet, foreigners (the Magi) knew precisely the cryptic message of the star. This is curious! No one is certain who the Wise Men were, but it is likely that Matthew was identifying Persian soothsayers who were both astronomers and augurs (forecasters of future events).

The chief problem of the story of the Magi emanates from the fact that no one else in history knew of their visit, and no other source mentions the phenomenon of a star heralding the birth of the King of the Jews. How could any alert astronomer overlook such a signal beacon in the nighttime sky?

The Magi, being priests of a heathen religion, would have been the object of deep suspicions from the Pharisees and Sadducees, if not targets for outright enmity! Their mission, however, to find the promised Messiah king should have triggered keen interest from all eschatologically minded Jews. After stopping and divulging their mission to Herod in Jerusalem, afterward, the Magi could neither conceal their presence, nor their pursuit. Every gossiping tongue in the city would have spread the word of their extraordinary objective. Yet, only Matthew, of all the reporters of that age, knew of the portentous Star of Bethlehem and its attendant visitors. That scriptural 'fact,' alone, is more incredible than the mere appearance of a stationary star over the town of Bethlehem. Why didn't the other three Evangelists learn of that unforgettable signal star? Why didn't Flavius Josephus report such a highly visible wonder?

No spiritually guided event can be fully evaluated until we examine its aftermath. What was the result of the visit of the Magi? The result was this: The infant Jesus was adored by fortune-telling ministers of a pagan persuasion. That is so, but this isn't all that occurred because of the Magi's visit. The slaughter of the innocents was the revolting ultimate outcome of their visit. [Cf. Mt. 2:16]

'The Lord moves in mysterious ways, His wonders to perform.' No religionist would ever append the previous axiom (apologetic!) to the slaughter of the innocents, or to the adoration by the Magi. But the axiom is as relevant here as it is anywhere else. However, this inference isn't laudatory; consequently, religionists would surely reject applying this adage to the wanton slaughter of the infants of Bethlehem.

The point of this segment is now essentially complete. Nonetheless, before concluding I will pose some review inquiries that may more fully illuminate my current objective.

1. Why did God create the 'Star of Bethlehem'?

2. How did the Magi come to know its significance?

3. Why isn't there any other record of this highly unusual Star?

4. Why didn't the Jewish priesthood interpret the Star's message?

5. If the Magi were inspired, why did they go to Jerusalem first?

6. Did God desire Herod the Great to know of the birth of Jesus?

7. Did God know beforehand of Herod's murderous reaction?

8. Did God approve of the 'Slaughter of the Innocents'?

9. Could God have prevented this detestable infanticide?

10. Rationalize specifically God's role in Matthew's Nativity story.

In concluding, let me urge you to read your Bible. Not so that you may be convinced of its truth, but rather the opposite. Whenever some misguided religionist begins to pontificate from its pages, you may silence his prattling with logical queries relating to his subject matter. The only response to your probes will be: 'With God, all things are possible.' Your retort will be: 'Is it possible for God to err?' If the reply is "No," then one thing is impossible to God. If the reply is "Yes," then suggest that in the instance of the miraculous star and its attendant butchering of a score or more of innocent infants, He did err!

PROVING THE BIBLE

Several books have been produced that purport to prove the accuracy of the Bible, *vis-a-vis* written history and archeological discovery. One that I personally enjoyed is The Bible as History – by Werner Keller.

The book is interestingly written, scholarly, and was diligently researched. To fail to read this book would be to deprive oneself of an informative historical exposition. Yet the main thrust of this writing seems to be to authenticate the Bible in its mystical entirety, and in this aspect the book fails utterly. Not because of lack of effort or dedication, nor is there a lack of vital information! Quite the reverse is the case. Enough evidence is presented to condemn the untrue and unjustified surmise that a Supreme Being orchestrated the Nativity scenarios in the Gospels of Matthew and Luke respectively. This never happened, therefore, when all the facts are presented, rather than supporting the premise, the facts refute the premise. It couldn't be otherwise!

The stories in the Bible are coincidental to the essence of the over-riding theme. This being: That the God Yahweh chose the Hebrews as His special people, and from that point on, He alternately either favored them or punished them. God relied solely on their allegiance and fidelity to Him as the determinant. If this isn't true, then the Old Testament tales are nothing more momentous than a confused account of the political memoirs of one small branch of the Semite racial family.

The excitement in Mr. Keller's book comes in verifying the ancient facts, not from the facts themselves. In one chapter he tells of a man who discovered a hidden tunnel leading from an underground spring of water back into the city of Jerusalem. To me, it isn't exciting to know that fortified (walled) ancient city dwellers had hidden paths to water. But finding the actual path is aesthetically stimulating.

The book informs of a sap excreted by the tamarisk tree when a certain insect pierces the skin of its leaves. The liquid secretion rapidly solidifies into flakes that are sweet and nourishing to eat. This substance, when supplemented by other sources of nutrition, such as quail meat, will sustain human life marginally for an indefinite period. The author (Mr. Keller) interprets this solidified leaf sap as the 'manna from heaven.'

This book also writes of the twice-yearly migration of quail that, exhausted after their extended flight back from Africa, can to this day be caught by hand during Spring season in the Sinai Peninsula. But here, even Mr. Keller can see the flaw in his argument. The Bible records that God provided this food miraculously for the Israelites. If it can be proven (and it can!) that anyone who happened to be where the Israelites were, would have reaped the same benefit absent divine input, then the Bible is disproved! This is the fact unerringly. The manna from Heaven and the miraculous flight of quail are both natural occurrences, not unnatural logistics that were divinely provided solely to succor Yahweh's chosen people.

Throughout his book, Mr. Keller unintentionally, but inevitably, makes the same point. The glories and the miseries of Israel are the result of natural interactions, not divine dalliance! In those days, every grouping of peoples thought that one or more Gods or Goddesses were controlling the destiny of their community. Thanks to Mr. Keller, this point can be detailed also.

He writes of the land of Sheba, an area of the Arabian Peninsula in present day Yemen. It has been found that the peoples there built a gigantic dam that blocked the River Ad hanat {sic} that provided irrigation, hence fertility, to the entire region. Many spices were grown there and traded with Israel, and with other nations. For 1,500 years the Shebans enjoyed prosperity; but then, in the year 542 BC, the dam burst. The Koran says the dam burst because "the people turned their backs upon God." [Refer: The Bible As History – page 233]

It would seem from this pronouncement that the Sheban God is no less vindictive than is the God, Yahweh, when his anger is provoked. Carrying this causation theory forward, one should question today which God (or Goddess) was angry with the inhabitants of Washington State because one of the Earth Deities caused Mount St. Helens to explode in 1980, killing a score of people, a small boy among them. You don't suppose this is a prelude to the final destruction of the Earth by fire, do you?

Perhaps we should all begin running toward the nearest cave shouting "the sky is falling." I am sure this would be the advice of 'Chicken Little.'

Accept my apology for the last few sentences. They are specious. However, they were inserted intentionally to graphically expose how very childish are the imputations of divine retribution (in the form of natural disasters) so liberally provided in the Old Testament.

You, of course, can discern where my hypothetical is leading. There is no divine input into history. God neither punished nor prospered the Israelites or their contemporaries. Each event that befell the Egyptians, Babylonians, Sumerians, Assyrians, Hittites, Jebusites, Ammonites, Israelites, and all the rest of that superstitious aggregation, was the result of natural happenstance or mortal contrivance, not supernatural orchestration!

If God is truly just, then the fairest course He could follow would be to leave us entirely to our own peculiarities. The tiniest interjection of Heavenly interference does grave harm to the proposition of 'free will' as well. The fixing of responsibilities and the application of culpability are hopelessly clouded if we accept the promulgated principle of any 'god' meddling in our lives.

Contemplate this simplified example: If both Jack and Jill had cancer and God cured Jack but killed Jill. Is this fair? A fair Deity would kill Jack also, so that he too could enjoy Heaven immediately. Pardon, but which is the favor we mortals most seek? 'The killing; or the curing? Even religionists agree: Curing a person is what we pray for. That is the favor we seek. Dying and going to Heaven is the second choice, or is it the third, or the fourth? Any continuation of living seems to be preferable to dying, even if attaining Heaven is deemed assured when death threatens. You wisely may deduce how atheists interpret this almost universal preference for life over death!

Religionists, as with everyone else, want to continually enjoy this life, not the afterlife! Heaven is taught to be a place where we will continue to live a life that is far superior to mortal life. But given a choice, everyone chooses this life instead of Heaven. Bravo for them; the point is made! Religionists hope that some reward beyond this life exists, but they don't really believe that it does. All the evidence attainable is arrayed against the reality (actuality) of Paradise. Self-delusion and prayerful 'wish fulfillment' are all that support the notion of a 'Heaven.' The Bible is reasonably true only if we delete every reference to a Supreme Spiritual Being, and reject *in toto*, every fancied 'otherworldly' contravention of natural or mortal happenstance.

Mr. Keller's book makes the point that some of the fabulosities contained in the Bible could, indeed, be factual. But, by proving them to be natural events and not paranormal interventions, he has simultaneously removed them as articles of faith. He should be commended for this, despite this not being his intention. Faith is naught but the glorification of willful ignorance in all instances where religion requires it. In every incident that Mr. Keller proves the Bible to be factual; he concurrently proves that God is fictitious. His original intention is defeated by his very accomplishment.

If God is a myth, then so too are all the other impedimenta with which religionists have burdened our imaginations. Gone are the Guardian Angels, Messenger Angels, Vocalist Angels, Companion Angles, and every other angelic career as well. Gone also are the Bad Angels, Devils, Demons, talking serpents, body-napping spirits, and all manner of malevolent manifestation.

Also lost is Heaven, all seven of them! Limbo, Sheol, Hades, Hell, Gehenna, the Bottomless Pit, and the abode of Darkness, are all consigned to the ash heap of faux history and folk legend. Of course, Lucifer loses his legitimacy as well.

The Nether world is really the Never world. It Never was! It Never will be!

THE BIBLE ON THE BIBLE

In the preface to the R.S.V. of the Bible, we find this academic disclaimer: "If, in the judgment of the Committee, the meaning of a passage is quite uncertain or obscure either because of corruption in the text or because of the inadequacy of our present knowledge of the language, that fact is indicated by a note. It should not be assumed, however, that the committee was entirely sure or unanimous concerning every rendering not so indicated. To record all minority views was obviously out of the question."

Frankly, it isn't obvious to me why all disputed passages aren't clearly indicated. Was the number of such disputes so huge? Was the depth of divergent rendering that deep and that controversial so as to preclude unanimity? The almost numberless multitude of intransigent Bible brandishers extant today should be made to memorize that most previous quote from the R.S.V. I have lost count of the individuals whom I have personally heard bragging how perfectly they can interpret the scriptures. How favored they must be to be able to understand and interpret the Bible more precisely than the scholar-laden Committees that translated it.

The actuality is, of course, that the confidence of these ego-driven verse interpreters far outstrips their actual abilities. Only an intellectual featherweight could so mislead himself. Before they spout their next scriptural platitude, they should be forced to recite this verse from scripture: *"Of course, what I am saying now is not what the Lord would have me say. Such boasting is not from the Lord, but I am acting like a fool."* [2 Cor. 11:17]

Here is Paul himself warning us that he is writing contrary to what God inspired him to write. Is Paul a liar? Or are we fools to think that God inspired Paul to write this verse? Advocating that God inspired this verse is an assault on rationality, and it likewise refutes the precept of God's prescience. An 'all-knowing' Divinity would not have inspired Paul to write those words!

Superstition is the father of all religiosity; and ignorance is the nursing mother. All religiosity owes its genesis to this unenlightened pair. Furthermore, Christianity is, perhaps, the most illustrious child born of this irrational, though highly pretentious mating. By name: 'Superstition conjoined with adopted Ignorance.'

THE BIBLE CONTAINS FALSEHOODS

Still, another reason why we should exercise restraint when we are tempted to venerate every word in the Bible as an issuance from the lips of God, is because certain passages contained therein can be proved false. Now we all know that God wouldn't lie to us; consequently, if falsehoods are found in the scriptures, we can confidently assign these discerned falsehoods to the fallible authorship of man.

What provoked the foregoing paragraph was a two-verse declaration in the Acts of the Apostles. These verses predicted an impending worldwide famine that, purportedly, occurred not long after the famine was first forecast. *"About that time some prophets went down from Jerusalem to Antioch. One of them, named Agabus, stood up and by the power of the Spirit predicted that a great famine was about to come over all the earth. It came when Claudius was Emperor."* [Acts 11:27-28]

Claudius reigned from AD 41 to 54. Historical records from this period do not confirm such a worldwide famine. Josephus mentions a difficult period for Judea throughout the years AD 44 to 46, which does seem to validate the relief mission undertaken by Paul and Barnabas to the Judeans, also recorded in Acts. [Cf. Acts 11:29-30] Yet, how were Paul and Barnabas able to gather alms for the Judeans if the entire world was in the throes of a famine? It should be obvious that the Christians of Antioch weren't experiencing deprivation or starvation. Provably, they were experiencing a period of relative abundance.

The Bible at this point, as in many others, is self-contradicting and ambiguous. But let us not indict God on this score. Instead, let us extract from the Bible those passages that are practical and moral, apply them if we can, and confer mental accolades on the human being(s) who wrote them. As for the silliness, the supernatural, and the rest of the hokum, treat this as just so much jetsam and flotsam littering the Sea of Life. Trash it whenever the opportunity arises. At all other times, avoid it or disregard it.

Please don't feel repelled by my rhetoric here. Even if it were within my wherewithal to become a second Nero, I would forswear that role. I have no desire to feed Christians (or other religionists) to the lions. Neither would I set all believers before an Inquisition, as the Christians did during their suzerainty. Rather, I would prefer that the philosophies to which I ascribe would prove to be so accurate, and so enticing, that everyone of average and above intellect would become converts. I would hope that the remainder of mankind would join us. Yet, I don't foresee any great calamity befalling either grouping if unanimity isn't achieved, providing, of course, that the prerogative to govern is reserved for the 'untainted by religiosity' intelligentsia! Here, intelligentsia doesn't mean snobbish pseudo-intellectuals who judge that proximity to learning has rendered them "superior" to the vast multitude.

The truly intelligent know that everyone is most apt to prove fallible when they are most convinced of the infallibility of any conviction. Consequently, persons who granted credence to stories of miraculous benefactions, devious malfeasance, or the slightest interposition of deities into the tableau of human history, would be barred evermore from all leadership positions. Not that I advocate instituting a pogrom against speculation. Speculating on the supernatural is a colossal waste of time; but it isn't philosophical treason.

The Twenty-First century needs the absolute truth, not the truth according to the mythical scriptures. We delude ourselves when we deify the words of the Bible. Was Agabus the instrument of the Holy Spirit when he predicted a worldwide famine? No, and you and I both know this. Then why do we permit others to exalt or lionize themselves by parading around with Bible in hand (or <u>Koran</u>, for that matter), mouthing inconsequential abracadabras, and posing pompously as worthy deputies of a universal omnipotence. We err when we tender obsequious reverence to those who harbor self-glorifying pretensions. We mustn't encourage their delusion; much less, we mustn't pamper it!

If we scrutinize the biblical verses that inspired this segment, we will note that the prophecy of Agabus is recorded after-the-fact, as are all the miracles and wonders in the Bible. That is, the Bible hasn't predicted anything. It merely grasps an accomplishment and then reports that someone previously predicted it. In cases where the New Testament did make predictions of the future, those predictions have proved false. The prime example: The Christ (Messiah) didn't return before all the living witnesses to the ministry of Jesus had died! [Cf. Mt. 16:28; Mk. 9:1 {Mk. 8:39 D-R} & Lu. 9:27]

Read the two Books of Kings in the Old Testament and it will become obvious that what was written just previous concerning prophecy is true. The scriptures only chronicle those prophets whose predictions were fulfilled. The kings of Israel and of Judah each had many soothsayers, whether as part of their entourage or as consultants. Also, there frequently abounded self-appointed critics in the guise of reformer prophets. Those prophets whose predictions came to pass were honored by being named in the Bible. Those prophets whose predictions & warnings failed went unnamed and unrecorded in the Bible.

"Then the king of Israel assembled the prophets, about 400 men, and said to them: 'Shall I go to Ramoth-Galaad to fight, or shall I forbear?'" [1 Ki. 22:6]

"Jezebel, the wife of king Ahab, was causing the death of the king's prophets so Obadiah hid 100 of them from her." [1 Ki.18:4]

Prophets, Seers, Soothsayers, and their kindred weren't a scarce commodity in Old Testament days. In Deuteronomy, the Israelites ask Moses how to distinguish between sham prophets and true prophets. Moses answers, *"... if his oracle is not fulfilled, or verified, it is an oracle which the Lord did not speak."* [Deut. 18:21-22] To this I add, "Forever, Be So Guided!"

Reading the Bible reverently (meaning with unquestioning acceptance), one is led to believe that the prophets were solitary figures who presented their prognostications unbidden, at the instigation of God Almighty. This was seldom the case. Prophets were ubiquitous, and most were in the employ of the Hebrew kings. Superstition flourished, and those soothsayers prospered who were most talented in exploiting (deceiving) the gullible!

BLAME THE HOLY GHOST!

Here follows another exposition of fact that assails the sanctimonious error of declaring the Holy Spirit as "ghost author" of the Bible. As everyone knows, there are an abundance of early copies of the New Testament manuscripts. So many, indeed, that the later codices are numbered rather than named. One such group is known as the 'minuscules.' The minuscules vary as much from one another as they do from the more ancient uncials. But the minuscules do share one notable irregularity that is edifying for our era. The minuscules place the story of the woman charged with adultery (*"He that is without sin ... cast the first stone."*) just after Luke 21:38, instead of in the traditional location of John 8:1. (Refer: <u>A History of the Bible</u> – Fred Gladstone Bratton, page 225)

Is this a trivial matter hardly worth noting? 'Or is it significant? The reader will have to be his/her own authority. For my part, I see it as another proof that the Bible is solely the work of man. God Himself could never be so slipshod or so bumbling either. The story of the adulteress is plainly and simply an addendum to the life of Jesus appended to an extant Gospel. In one area to Luke, and in another area to John at a time after those Gospels had been composed and widely disseminated. There are manuscripts that exclude altogether the incident of the woman caught in adultery. Perhaps those MSS are less deceitful. (A side question: What punishment was proposed upon the male person who participated in the adultery? On this, the Gospels are silent.)

After reading of the misplacement of the story in Luke, I consulted the notes at the end of John's Gospel contained in the Catholic Family Edition of the Holy Bible (©1953). Below is what I found printed there: "7, 53 – 8, 11: [Jn.]. This passage is wanting in many Greek MSS; in some others it is found in chapter 21 [Lu.]. It is well supported in both the Old Latin and Vulgate MSS. There is no doubt of its right to be included among the Sacred Writings." [Page 137]

Excuse my contrariety, but there is a doubt! The Old Latin manuscripts were peppered liberally with extra-canonical passages and extrapolations. This was the very reason that Pope Damasus commissioned Saint Jerome to research his Vulgate edition. Despite his written intention to consult the original Greek manuscripts, in actuality, Jerome relied chiefly upon Latin sources, which probably explains why the story of the adulteress appears in the Vulgate also.

The "Good News" version of the New Testament places verses John 8:1 through 8:11 in brackets without comment. Most other translations I have consulted afterward also bracket or parenthesize these verses. Altogether, I conclude, the evidence points against the inclusion of this anecdote in any part of the New Testament!

Another of these well-intentioned, but fraudulent, additions can be found in the early English translations of the Bible. Read now, Chapter Six of Matthew's Gospel that contains the "Lord's Prayer." When you reach Verse 13, see if your Bible continues: *"For Thine is the kingdom, and the power, and the glory, for ever. Amen."* [Mt. 6:15 Inspired Version (Mormon) Bible]

If your copy of the Bible doesn't contain that ending to the Lord's Prayer, then you are probably reading from the Revised Version of the Protestant Bible, or from a Catholic version of the Douay-Rheims translation. Is the most previous quote the actual wording from Jesus as He taught the Apostles to pray? How can it be if it isn't found in the earliest manuscripts available? Can you see now why I charge the Holy Spirit with negligence? If He inspired the Evangelists faithfully, why didn't He inspire the copyists also? There are entirely too many discrepancies in the manuscripts we possess. In this instance, to credit the Holy Spirit as the divine author is to <u>impugn</u> Him simultaneously as being negligent "after the fact."

Allow me to present an enlightening instance. A quote from the <u>Catholic Family Edition of the Holy Bible</u>: "… [W]*hen delivered up by the settled purpose and foreknowledge of God, you have crucified and slain* {Jesus} *by the hands of wicked men.*" [Acts 2:23] Now read the editor's note concerning that verse at the end of the book of <u>Acts of the Apostles</u>. {Begin Quote} "2:23, *Crucified:* According to the Greek and most Latin MSS, *affigentes*, 'fastening to (the cross).' The *affligentes* ('afflicting') of our Clementine Latin Bible appears to be a corruption of *affigentes*, attested not only by the original text but by good Latin texts." {End Quote}

Obviously, a past copyist erringly added the letter "L" to the word "AFFIGENTES" changing that word to "AFFLIGENTES" and thereby changing the sense of the verse. Are there any other instances of miscopied texts in the Bible? Resolve that question via your intellect.

The Bible lacks perfection because it was composed in its entirety by human beings. The Holy Spirit is no more accountable for the Bible than I am; less so in truthfulness, for there is no such entity as the Holy Spirit. It would be a near impossible task to identify every questionable verse contained in (or for that matter omitted from) our present day Bibles.

More has been written about the man we know as Jesus (Yeshua) than about any other person who has ever lived. This alone has probably made Him immortal in the sense that He will never be forgotten as long as sentient man exists. Philosophies attributed to Him are among the noblest ever conceived; His ethics are impeccable. The endless extrapolations of His not-so-numerous ethical pronouncements are seemingly unimpeachable. He is a philosophical beacon to us all. (The present tense is appropriate.) We have glorified His person to God-like dimensions, deservedly or erroneously isn't germane here! However, we still must apply His sentiments to the circumstances in which we live. My retort: Yes, we must love our neighbor as ourselves. But first, we should choose most carefully who we consider to be our neighbors!

"Honor thy father and thy mother!" Does this commandment permit me to hate my parents as long as I don't dishonor them? Suppose I love, honor, and obey them while they are teaching me to murder, or to sin otherwise? No one, not even Jesus, can propound a generalized moral principle that will be applicable to every conceivable human situation. This, too, is an impossible contravention of reality. Sooner or later, every religious sect becomes a victim of their own dogmas. The same is true of our past and present laws. Future religiosity will be no different, unless we can forsake all sanctimonious (supernatural) dogmatism!

There is no human action that should positively be forbidden under every conceivable circumstance. Likewise, there is no action we could perform that would be fitting to every possible situation. The particular circumstance should always dictate the appropriate response. 'Turning the other cheek' [Cf. Mt. 5:39 & Lu. 6:29] can be just as inappropriate as is 'an eye for an eye.' [Cf. Deut. 19:21 & et al.] We can't use the Bible as a guide for living, because we would cease living if we interpreted it too dogmatically. Turn the other cheek in today's world, and you will never cease having it slapped!

Adolph Hitler presents a fitting example, especially if we apply the commandment against murder to the circumstance of Hitler's racial philosophies. You undoubtedly are aware that Hitler believed the German race to be superior to all other races. What is more, he advocated that all the inferior races should be made slaves of the superior 'Aryans,' plus, for the most inferior races to be exterminated forthwith. With this in mind, picture how successful Hitler would have been if all other nations had espoused the doctrines of the Quakers who unequivocally eschew all war and all killing. Where would we "sub-humans" be today if no one had actively opposed Hitler? I dread even pondering that retrospection.

Why pursue this point any further? In actuality, the commandment doesn't forbid killing. It forbids unlawful murder. Moreover, God didn't inspire this commandment; Moses propounded it in order to maintain harmony amongst the discordant Israelite tribes. Moses also promulgated "a tooth for a tooth." [Cf. Ex. 21:24 & Lev. 24:20, et al.] But even this stricture was never intended to be applied categorically. Many offenses could be redeemed with a monetary offering. Expiation could be obtained via 'sin offerings' in all but the most heinous of violations.

Religionists avow that God inspired Moses to write the Pentateuch (the first five books of the Bible), but this can be positively disproved. The final book of this series describes the death of Moses and goes on to relate events that transpired after his death. [Cf. Deut. 34:1-12] This narrative, too, was written from a third person perspective, as was the entire Pentateuch. No, Moses didn't write the Pentateuch; he was written about in those five books. To believe otherwise is to discount the clearly evident, and to pervert the overtly obvious. How many of the 'laws' of Moses apply only to infractions that a settled community can commit? The Egyptian-born followers of Moses became roving nomads! Ever and always, when the Bible is read without pious preconception, the humanity of its authors is evident beyond reconsideration. The same is true of the Gospels. The Gospels tell about the Apostles and obviously weren't written by verifiable eyewitnesses.

EDITORIAL AGAINST BIBLIOLATRY

Alas, for anyone who humbly searches for truth in religion, no validation is to be found in the Christian Scriptures. Not only are there scant facts to support the 'divinity' assumptions of Christian apologists, there are ample facts that confute those assumptions. The substance of the Christian faith is the Bible. Yet, I maintain that the Bible thoroughly disproves itself. Even the Roman Catholic Church, which argues its legitimacy chiefly on unbroken continuity and direct inheritance, not on the Bible, is disenfranchised because its verbal traditions produced the written Bible. All religions are the creation of the human imagination. Still, an active imagination may be turned toward either the extreme of 'good' or the extreme of 'evil'; this is and ever was the root cause of both our laurels and our infamy.

The invention of the weapon is the prime reason for man's dominance over all other life forms. ('Weapon' here is used in the broader sense of any device or artifact that multiplies our human capabilities.) Yet, more often than was necessary, we have turned our "weapons" upon our fellow human being. Now we have constructed nuclear weapons! What an ignominious epitaph it would be for the human race to have exterminated itself, should this eventuate!

Christianity purports to have an alternative to this potential self-annihilation. Yet, we have had Christianity for two thousand years and we haven't ever had a sustained peace. Evidently, something is wrong with Christianity's solution. What is it that is deficient in the Christian formulary? Well, the Christian solution may be compassionate; it isn't compulsive! While it may be aesthetically enticing; it isn't mandatory! With mankind, peace must be imposed because the invention of the weapon permits one individual to dominate many others. If any individual was the sole possessor of a lethal weapon, he would eventually rule all the remaining individuals. This is truly regrettable, but it is also the proven historical reality. We must be guided in all of our societal determinations cognizant of this inerrant actuality.

Every human society has religious beliefs. Those that possess an alphabet have written enlightenments purportedly received from a personalized divinity. Religiosity is ubiquitous; it is endemic; it is boundless. Yet, is it factual? If you (the current reader) give your reply in the affirmative, then you, too, are personally guilty (via extended designation) of the discernibly grievous 'Sin' of divisive, discriminatory, destructive and delusive Bibliolatry!

CHAPTER 18
More Dogma

FAITH AND DEATH

Every facet of religion is dependent solely upon faith to sustain it. The case would be identical if one were to seek to prove the Greek Deity myths factual. Even after they have grown to adulthood, subconsciously humans love to play 'let's pretend.' Isn't it grand to imagine that the greatest personage in the cosmos (God) loves us personally? How provident it is that He provides us with a guardian angel to ensure that no harm befalls us. Aren't we fortunate when we pray to God that He hears our every word? We are so flattered after He has given us the fortitude to resist temptation that we fairly radiate with self-adulation. Isn't it positively magnificent that God will take us with Him into Heaven after we have experienced a long and mostly happy lifetime? (The woeful or deplorable eventualities in a lifetime are never ascribed to God.)

Then, following a personal welcome in Heaven, we will learn that the nasty old bogeyman, the Devil, won't ever again be able to work his wiles on us. God will see to that! Heaven will be such fun 'no work, 'no schedules, and 'no early morning reveille.' The Christian religion promises (ambiguously) every idyllic benefit the human heart could desire. Regrettably, the fulfillment of the promise is invariably withheld until we die. The most outrageous lie that Christian proselytizers assault us with, and the most egregious, is the patently bogus assertion that we must die before we can live evermore! The stark truth is that death kills the mind (consciousness/awareness) as permanently as it does the body.

Death is finality; death is not a transition. But fear death not! Death is the cessation of living. You will never know that you are dead after you have died. Once you attain that inalterable state, you will never again be unhappy; you will never again experience deprivation. In truth, you will never again experience anything! One day we will all attain this real Paradise, Saint and sinner together. Absolute death is our inevitable, our universal, our eternal completion of life forevermore, misnamed as our "Heaven!"

WE NEED A GOD

Obeisance to an invisible sky God is just as scorn-worthy as is obeisance to a visible stone idol. The latter is truly the creation of the hand, while the former is just as truly the creation of the mind. Christians and Jews have fashioned a counterfeit god out of words, i.e., The Old Testament Scriptures and The New Testament Scriptures. This god has proved to be much more durable than have been the other gods of old, but he is no less of a deception.

So far this book has persistently renounced the existence of a Personal God. Would it surprise, if now, the author did an about-face and stated that we presently need someone to act as God? Well, we do! Some God-like decisions have to be made, and, if the results are to be conducive to the retention of humanity, those decisions must be made soon. The most propitious time for these decisions may already have passed. If not, that time soon will expire.

Our most immediate danger arises from the proliferation of nuclear arms technology. Only slightly less urgent, but eminently more destructive, is the proliferation of human beings. The food supply problem probably can be solved. However, the consequences of human pollution are categorically insoluble, at least at current population levels. This is why a God-like decision is needed. Some governing body has to decide 'who can have children' and 'who cannot.' This responsibility is awesome; but the inevitable repercussions from shirking this responsibility are even more fearsome.

Voluntary birth control won't work. Only the wise could be expected to cooperate. The foolish and the dimwitted would continue to reproduce in indiscriminate numbers with an inevitable outcome. Our collective reproductive gene pool would become overwhelmed with ova & sperm from randy dullards.

Can we depend upon religion to save us from this impending retrograde calamity? Obviously, if you have been awake for the past couple of decades, you are aware that now is the time for God to act, if He is able. God waited until the last moment before He countermanded His own order to Abraham to murder his son Isaac. [Cf. Gen. 22:12] Should mankind wait until the first stroke of midnight preceding Doomsday before they realize that there is no God? Heaven help us if this happens! {'Heaven' metaphorically}

Why should we, of the physical world, wait for assistance from the spiritual world when we can, and we should, devise our own Doomsday solutions in the here, and in the now. The time for a resolution is at hand. We can't all stand around listening to the population time-bomb tick. While we dawdle, it could explode!

GOD LOVES ME

Everyone knows that God loves him/her. Yet, how can we know beyond ambiguity? Does God dislike anyone? How about the Fallen Angels? Does God hate them? We humans can commit the most heinous of crimes and still, God forgives us. Why, then, hasn't He forgiven the Angels who rebelled but once against Him? Can't they be forgiven? Where is the proof of God's forgiveness of us, or of His implacable condemnation and irreversible expulsion of the mutineer angels? What heavenly revelation do we have that explains this seemingly biased and discriminatory application of Divine Justice negating Divine Mercy?

Rationale, which would merely point out differences in the circumstance attendant to the rebellion of the Wicked Angels as compared to human rebellions against God, is pointless here. In matters as consequential as rebellion, conjecture won't suffice. Either unambiguous revelation or demonstrable evidence must supply the denouement to this apparent inequity in Divine forgiveness.

A rather facile excuse (albeit a faux one!) for the disparity between the punishment inflicted on the Fallen Angels and the endless forgiveness proffered to mankind, is to postulate that the Angels' sin of rebellion was more abominable and more heinous than are the transgressions of man. This postulation is true upon cursory examination, but is utterly false upon deeper reflection. The lapsed angels committed the most grievous sin they were capable of committing. We humans do exactly the same, namely, we commit the most grievous sins we are capable of committing! There is no difference whatsoever in intent. If our evil achievements fall short of those of the mutineer angels, it isn't because we are slack in effort, only that we are deficient in ability. We don't lack the will to sin that grievously, we lack only the capability.

In the face of this, religionists still insist that God loves us; after all, He made us didn't He? Didn't God make the angles also? If God did create all humanity, then He also made the quadriplegic child; the encephalitic child; the Mongoloid child; and the child born addicted to illegal drugs. The dope-besotted mother of the addicted baby is never liable. The fact is: She didn't make the baby; God did! If God hadn't made her pregnant, then the child would not have been born. Besides, God is all-powerful. Why didn't He cause the baby to be born perfectly healthy? Doesn't He love this child? Why punish the child? The child hadn't committed any offenses —*yet!*

A question for the deeply religious: If God loves me, and if God made me, how do you explain (alibi) the incidence of conjoined twins? This isn't a uniform abnormality. The variations in the body location and in the extent of the conjoining are myriad. There have been such "twins" joined at the head, and various other positions on the human body. More bizarre cases have been documented of a partially formed "twin" that consists of just extra legs and feet of a second entity attached to a fully formed first human entity. There have been cases of two heads attached to a single body. These wildly abnormal conceptions are often stillborn, or the child dies shortly after birth. Only a small percentage of such deformed infants live long enough to be known outside of the immediate family. Can all such cases of birth anomalies be credited (or charged) to God's willful action? Can what we observe in the natural world be assigned to the inscrutable machinations of a 'Perfect Deity'? Or can they all be accurately ascribed to 'Imperfect Nature,' rather than to an inexplicable Supernatural Being? Aren't we all, "the children of God"?

Understand: a parent who lavished gifts on one child, but cruelly burdened another child in the same family, would be liable to both a charge of favoritism and a charge of child abuse, with just cause! So, when we attribute all events to God (include imperfect human conjoining), we subject Him to the same charges. Granted, the charge of physical abuse isn't true. Moreover, if the charge of abuse isn't true, then neither is the charge of favoritism. My understanding of Christian theology mandates that God orchestrates every eventuality, and that every action of God is reasoned. His actions are never arbitrary. Meaning: If we honor God for granting our blessings, then we must also account Him with causing our woes!

Why can't religionists see that their pro-God propositions are untenable? They tell us that God watches over us and keeps us from harm; yet, when I slip and fall, it is my own fault for not looking where I am walking. They opine that God provides my food; yet, if I starve, I have only myself to blame. If I am well, I should thank God. If I am sick, I should consult a doctor. If I experience prosperity, I should praise the Lord's beneficence. Conversely, when adversity strikes me, religionists shake their heads and declare that my luck has turned bad.

Can't they see that God is neither creditable for my fortunes, nor culpable for my misfortunes? By unbiased observation, we should conclude that God isn't a factor in anything that transpires on Earth, or in the Universe! The 'creative principle' of the entire cosmos transcends the personal. The 'uncaused cause' can in no way be equated with anything human. Not in the most minuscule manner can 'the cause' be limited to mortal dimensions. The creative principle can't have any limitations whatsoever. God, the Ultimate Being, must be illimitable! Is God contented when we love Him? Is He dismayed when we wrong Him? In order to be pleased, one must also be capable of being displeased. Can God change? Can He vacillate from happiness to anger? More to our point: Can God love anyone, if God is unable to hate anyone? Conversely, can God be indifferent to human kind for even a split second? What exactly is the full breadth of God's emotions? No one knows; nor can one ever know unerringly ... arguing that God is existent! (He isn't!)

KNOWING GOD?

Intellectually, every concept we as humans are able to verbalize or visualize has bounds. What we try to grasp when we conceptualize a creative god is utterly beyond our human cognition. Mortal man can only conceive that which is conceivable. Anything inconceivable is beyond our reality; ergo, it can't be imagined. Inconceivability doesn't seem to exist for us. The very notion that we can perceive of a God, places a measurable dimension upon Him, thereby negating His total, 'illimitable' Godhood.

This line of argument is inherently abstruse. But it is nonetheless valid. Agnostics hold a similar, if not identical, view. To them, God was/ is unknowable. Regrettably, agnostic theology (atheists cannot have a "theology") contains little magnetism for the average man. There isn't hope in its teachings, only responsibility. The faith it requires is faith in one's self. Agnosticism tells you to trust only that which can be tested and found trustworthy. In a capsule, what agnostics teach is for man to use his intelligence, not his imagination. Unfortunately, not all people can reach this level of purely neutral intellectual reasoning. But, it seems we all have the propensity to fantasize about the mystical (e.g., gods).

The previous remark about intelligence versus imagination wasn't inserted derogatorily. Intelligence is a variable quality, as is strength. Whenever we devise a human variable, quite naturally, some persons rate low on the scale; while others rate high. This is intrinsic to the act of measuring and calibrating. However, the results of measuring are often controversial. If I say that John is stronger than is Mary, this is noncontroversial. Whereas, if I say that John is smarter than is Mary, I will have initiated a heated imbroglio. We humans are very sensitive about our intelligence quotient. This factor broached, let us proceed.

To my knowledge, no one has yet devised a method to measure imagination; although imagination may well be the fountainhead of intelligence. In our imagination, anything is possible. We imagine ourselves able to swim through space to the Moon, but our intelligence brings us back down to Earth. Our intelligence is pragmatic, thankfully! We would perish without it; especially if we gave free rein to all our imaginings.

A pathetic example of the potential tragedy of an unbridled imagination comes from a 1980 newspaper story. Similar stories recur all too frequently! A group of religious extremists in a Southern State had formed a weird cult that practiced poisonous snake rituals. Adherents were told not to fear snakebite because, "The power of the Lord will protect you from harm." {Ubiquitous tenet of religiosity) [Cf. Mk. 16:18, extrapolated] Well, something went wrong with 'the power of the Lord,' for a snake bit one of the adherents of that cult and that person died.

How should this group be dealt with? Should intelligent authorities put a stop to this unenlightened, injurious cult? This will be very difficult because they invoke the same authority as do all other Christian religions, to wit, the Holy Bible. The story of Paul being bitten by a viper on the island of Malta grants them legitimacy. [Cf. Acts 28:3-6] Who can dispute with the 'Word of God?' Jesus Himself (as quoted by Mark) conveyed to the Apostles that His believers, *"will pick up snakes in their hands"*; inferentially 'without harm.' [Mk. 16:18] It is now known that every time a poisonous snake bites it does not inject venom. In Luke, we have yet another example of Jesus declaring that 'believers' will have power over poisonous snakes: *"See, I have given you power to put your feet on snakes and evil beasts, and over all the strength of him who is against you: and nothing will do you damage."* [Lu. 10:19]

Notwithstanding the Bible, can prudent men stand by and let the foolish destroy themselves? Are we obliged to be our brother's keeper in this particular circumstance? The least we can do is expose the foundation of their ignorance. We, who recognize the truth, must speak out and proclaim it. Closet atheists must cease condoning the superstitious antics of all religionists, and likewise of all religions. Not that we should burn all Bibles (or Korans); this would be counter-productive. But neither should we stand around posing reverently while some self-deluded holy man (priest, minister, ayatollah, or shaman) intercedes with God for us. We should make it a point to religiously renounce all religiosity!

When someone says to us "May God bless you," answer him: "There is no God, and if there was, then He already has blest me with the intelligence to know that I don't need you to ask for my blessings. I can do that for myself." Now if your intended benefactor hasn't already left the vicinity you could add this: "If you must pray for me, then please ask God to send me a million dollars soon, as I have many worthwhile enterprises I wish to initiate with that money." If, by now, your startled religionist is too stunned to move, you may want to add the final clincher: Tell him you are going to pray that God promptly grants your potential benefactor's prayerful petition to send you a million dollars!

We have a hazard-prone potential problem brewing in the world. Formerly, when nation and religion were relatively isolated from other nation and another religion, the disparate groupings could ignore their irksome counterparts elsewhere. Today the situation has changed drastically. Specifically, we may not be our brother's keepers; but we are all, rapidly and increasingly, becoming one another's neighbor. Today, with the advent of world-wide news organizations, and instantaneous satellite communications, each of us who can and do avail ourselves of these services is aware of what people around the world are doing, frequently at the virtual moment they are doing it!

How does this fact fit into an exposition about religion? In this manner: All religions have taboos. Generally, taboos are prohibitions against, or restrictions on, specified actions. Private thoughts can be objects of a taboo as well, but there is no way to independently detect those violations, so we can disregard them temporarily. A problem arises, however, when one man's taboo is another man's indulgence.

You can imagine what might happen in India if a television documentary there would broadcast the events in an American cattle slaughterhouse. Here in our own country, legitimate researchers utilizing wildlife subjects experimentally are continually harassed by Animal-Rights advocates, when/if their intended beneficial experiments with subject animals are broadly reported.

The frantic antics of some of these 'Animal-Rights' advocates are more hysterical than heroic. Surely, mindless cruelty to animals is socially unacceptable; but not for the reason that all life is sacred. It isn't! Roaches are alive; yet no one hesitates to kill them by whatever means their personal squeamishness permits. No one agonizes over the swatting of a bothersome fly. Are flies any less alive than we ourselves are? These so-called animal lovers are exceedingly selective in which life forms they choose to love and to protect. What they do is to attempt to force others to love, hence protect, the same life forms that they expend affection toward. They don't, and can't, champion all life forms. The glow from their self-attached halos dims noticeably when you realize this.

Every member of the plant world is alive also. Those dandelion weeds that we poison so diligently each Spring are just as alive as is the family pet. But, then again, dandelions don't lick your face, or purr when you stroke them, or chirp when you feed them. Animal lovers' most heated passions are generally reserved for selected higher animate life forms.

Basically, any human being who would wantonly maltreat a non-threatening creature is a despicable person who should be castigated for violating common human standards of conduct. Human communities have the right and an obligation to set standards of acceptable human behavior and to punish violators. Present day lawyers, abetted by all-too-liberal Courts, don't seem to think so, but viable society requires societal harmony. We can only have harmony when most of us are acting in a manner that doesn't disturb that harmony. Those who disrupt the attunement of a community are guilty of breaking the first law of communal living: "Thou shall not antagonize thy community!" If the community, in general, has no complaint, then a splinter special interest faction shouldn't have any complaint either. Animal rights provocateurs, take heed.

This isn't to declare that someone can't go and form their own community, or that community laws and mores are etched in titanium steel; therein, they cannot be rewritten. Every law should be liable to amendment, rescission or repeal. With religious beliefs, this is often difficult; sometimes impossible. Thereby arises our problem. Religious taboos are all too frequently irrational, unenlightened and even ludicrous. They are based primarily on Bible-inspired misinformation, compounded by superstition. Saint Paul was a victim of just this when he preached the resurrection of the body. As a Pharisee, he had already espoused the superstitious precept of bodily resurrection. Then, when he heard of the Resurrection of Jesus (the misinformation), he now felt his previous Pharisaic belief had been confirmed.

If you have noted that resurrection of the body isn't a taboo, you are correct. Nonetheless, the belief in bodily resurrection has caused the Catholic religion, as well as some other Christian sects, to forbid the cremation of dead bodies. This prohibition is puzzling if we believe that God can reconstitute cremated bodies with as little effort (for an Omnipotent Deity) as is required for restoring decayed and disintegrated bodies. Yet, the taboo against cremation remained in force for Catholics until early in the year 1983.

In most instances, because taboos are founded on superstition and are cherished on faith, not on logic, they are not amenable to compromise or accommodation. This is the very essence of the incompatibility of diverse religions within pluralistic societies. Now, because of worldwide social as well as economic interactions, our Earth is becoming one, immense, unwieldy, and inherently contentious mega-society. Intelligence alone, in the form of learned and adopted unemotional common sense, is the only guide that can direct us safely through the partisan minefields sown by biased religious extremists of whatever paranormal persuasion. Yet, national governments worldwide have seldom been observed behaving "intelligently"! {'Religions – even less so!}

LAMB OF GOD

The allusion of Jesus to a lamb is an apt one if we can believe the passion narratives of all four Evangelists. Jesus submitted resignedly to the violence and to the indignities wreaked upon Him by the authorities in Jerusalem. One envisions the quiet tranquility of a noble French Monarch being led to the guillotine by a mob that the king knows is beneath his dignity, when we visualize Christ's passion. Jesus answers the soldiers' blows and taunts with an almost majestic silence. If Jesus did cry out when the nails were driven into His hands and feet, that cry was not heard by the Evangelists. [Cf. Mt. 27:35; Mk. 15:24; Lu. 23:33 & Jn. 19:23]

Of course, the intention of the Gospel writers was to portray Jesus as a heroic figure. A problem arises, however, when the writer wishes to convince the reader that Jesus was also a Supreme Being with the power to rescue Himself at any second. Jesus could have been very smug and sneer at His captors as they mockingly performed their sadistic actions upon Him. But this scenario doesn't evince the sympathetic emotion that a religionist desires. The analogy to a lamb, however, evokes just the right response. Lambs are herded; Lambs are shorn; Lambs are led to slaughter. Everyone but the executioner and his despicable comrades feels compassion for the lamb.

Mindful of this, is it noble to be a lamb? Positively not! A lamb is rather dim-witted when contrasted with mammals in general. The meekness of a lamb isn't a virtue. But then, neither is it a defect. What it is – is a successful evolutionary technique. Animals whose survival is predicated on the herd instinct can't be individually aggressive, for then the herd would disperse and all individual animals would become more vulnerable to predators.

If you reflect how one shepherd, and perhaps a dog or two, can control an entire flock of sheep (ultimately to the sheep's doom), then their docility is seen as disadvantageous for them, not a noble trait. The God of the Old Testament was no lamb. I believe both Moses and the Israelites would have forsaken a pliant, timorous, lamb-like Deity. Yahweh was to be feared. He needed no one's sympathy or empathy. The God of Moses was mightier than was any monarch on earth. Even the Jews of Jesus' day were looking for a warrior Messiah, not a moral pacifist. Depicted as a lamb, Jesus in no way matched the expectations of the messianic-minded Jews. The scholars of the Jewish Scriptures never embraced Jesus. Only ignorant fishermen and a reformed tax collector could believe that the son of a carpenter was factually the Son of God.

Doesn't it make you wonder about our religious leaders of today when you realize how mistaken the 'experts' of Jesus' day were? They studied the Old Testament; they kept the letter of the Law; they followed the traditions and avoided the taboos of their faith with a fidelity that should have been admired. They traveled hundreds of miles to be in God's Holy City for the religious festivals. They wore the prescribed robes on the appropriate holy days, and intoned the correct incantations upon hearing the reading of the sacred scrolls. Despite all this, they were wrong! All their piety availed them naught. They dedicated their entire lives to God's will as revealed in the Old Testament scriptures. The underlying message of the New Testament is that the Old Testament is valueless. The first Rabbis had misinterpreted the ancient scriptures.

Jesus, through His spokesmen Apostles, led everyone to disregard those Old Testament laws and formularies. Paul, who admittedly was taught the Hebrew Scriptures by Gamaliel, a "Doctor of the Law," [Cf. Acts 22:3 & 5:34] told his converts to disregard the Old Testament. All the pious men who lived before Jesus were mistaken. No one predicted a Messiah that mirrored Jesus. Before Jesus, no one anticipated a meek lamb; they all envisioned a roaring lion.

Paul's missives simply instruct us to believe that Jesus was the Messiah come to save the world from its sins, and this belief alone would spare us from the torments of Hell. If you believe in the message of Jesus as expounded by Paul, then go now, take your Bible in hand and rip out the Old Testament. It is without any merit! Especially worthless are all those prohibitions and strictures that God imparted to Moses. Moses must have composed those rules himself, for Jesus repudiated most (all?) of them. We know this from Paul who personally repealed 'The Law' for his converts. *"Now, it is clear that no man is put right with God by means of the* Law, *because the scripture says; 'Only the person who is put right with God shall live through* Faith.'" [Ga. 3:11; Cf. Hab. 2:4; Rom. 1:17 & Heb. 10:38-39]

Disregard Matthew, who reports that Jesus said He wouldn't change a single item of the Law. Matthew writes: *"Do not think that I have come to do away with the Law of Moses and the teachings of the prophets. I have not come to do away with them, but to make their teachings come true. Remember that as long as heaven and earth last, not the least point nor the smallest detail of the Law will be done away with – not until the end of all things. So then, whoever disobeys even the least important of the commandments and teaches others to do the same, will be least in the Kingdom of Heaven."* [Mt. 5:17-19]

What could Matthew know? He only traveled with Jesus; unlike Paul, who had visions from Heaven to direct him. While you still have that Bible in your hands, rip out Matthew.

Mark can also be excised, but for a different reason. Virtually everything Mark wrote is repeated either in Matthew or in Luke. This raises a very poignant question of why God inspired Mark to write at all if his Gospel wasn't going to contain any unique material. The first six chapters of Luke can be cut out because they contain too many incidents that Paul was unaware of, or that he repudiated. John's Gospel is 80% unique, thereby questionable, and the 20% are repeats of the Synoptic Gospels. Remove John's Gospel. The Acts of the Apostles can be trimmed up to Chapter Thirteen where the Holy Spirit elevates Saul (Paul) and Barnabas to the (effective) rank of Apostles. [Cf. Acts 13:2] Your New Testament is considerably thinner now.

With only conjecture to guide me, for there is no unequivocal outline, I would remove everything in the New Testament that doesn't come directly from Paul. Not because Paul was ever chosen as the premier

Apostle. He wasn't! But simply because the Christianity we practice today is primarily (exclusively?) Paul's handiwork. So, here we are with only Luke's abridged Gospel, Acts from Chapter Thirteen onward, and the first thirteen Epistles. That is the extent of our "Christian Bible." Surprisingly, we still have enough for a Christian religion to be inaugurated and promulgated. This is basically all Paul had to work with also. But he succeeded in founding a world-wide belief in a "Just" Heavenly Father and in an "Anointed" intercessor, namely, Jesus, who effectively petitions the Father to temper His Justice with forgiving Mercy, 'Lest we all perish! [Cf. Lu. 13:5]

FROM COMMUNISM,
TO ABORTION, TO DEFORMITY

It was written previously that communism isn't merely a form of government. It is a modified form of religion. And, so it is. Yet, what is religion, if it isn't a form of governance? The United States preaches separation of Church and State as if they were two objectively separate entities. They aren't! What we have are many small, weak religious governments operating under the protection of the powerful and paternalistic secular government. The Church in the U. S. is granted the privilege to tell its congregants what they should or should not do. But only the civil government can compel its constituents to perform in a prescribed manner, or face civil prosecution! This observation applies to all religions functioning in the U.S.

This subservient status is tolerated by religionists, but only because they presently are powerless to change their status. The current Pro-abortion/Anti-abortion battle is evolving into a test of just where the Church's authority to impose its beliefs on non-believers extends. Personally, I am against abortion. Abortion is infanticide! I am still waiting for the first Pro-Choice (a euphemism for 'pro-abortion') activist to stand up and declare "Women have a right to kill their unborn babies." Yet, facing the realities of life, I can envision situations where someone may be self-justified in terminating a pregnancy through abortion. My views are a tat ambivalent in the practical utilization of abortion. On one point, however, I am adamant. No religionist has the right to tell me what to do on the authority of any Deity unless he (or she) can demonstrate, not merely assert, that a God has appointed him that authority.

Let these hypocritical miscreants look to their own behavior before condemning anyone else's actions. They are quick to parade the Ten Commandments, but mighty slow to follow the rest of the Mosaic Laws. Pointedly, if childbirth is such a gift from God, then why were women declared unclean for forty days after the birth of a boy, and for eighty days after the birth of a girl? Yahweh mandated the previous to Moses. [Cf. Lev. 12:1-5]

One of the reasons for seeking abortions is the fear of the birth of a deformed child. Religionists say we shouldn't let this be a reason for abortion because God loves us all the same, deformed or not! But this is a blatant falsehood, as anyone can learn from God's own words.

> *"The Lord said to Moses, 'Speak to Aaron and tell him: None of your descendants, of whatever generation, who has any defect shall come forward to offer up the food of his God. Therefore, he who has any of the following defects may not come forward: he who is blind, or lame, or who has any disfigurement or malformation, or a crippled foot or hand, or who is humpbacked, or weakly, or wall-eyed, or who is afflicted with eczema, ringworm, or hernia. No descendant of Aaron the priest, who has any such defect, may draw near to offer up the food of his God. ... he may not approach the veil, nor go up to the altar on account of his defect; he shall not profane these things that are sacred to me, for it is I, the Lord, who make them sacred.'"* [Lev. 21:16-24] [Cf. Mal. 1:8, 13]

Look into your Bible; these words are a direct quote from God to Moses. 'Crippled people, Sick people, even Dwarfs profane the altar of God!' Don't state that this prohibition was invalidated with the coming of Jesus, because God declares otherwise. He said, "Of whatever generation." (Another translation: "For all time to come.") Besides, the coming of Jesus didn't invalidate the Ten Commandments. 'Did it? The present-day Christian Church is highly selective in choosing which of the Mosaic Laws to repeal, and which to retain. Yet, Moses presented them all as inviolable divine writ.

Elsewhere, putatively writing for God, Moses commanded: *"This shall be an everlasting ordinance for you: On the tenth day of the seventh month every one of you, whether a native or a resident alien, shall mortify himself and shall do no work. Since on this day atonement is made for you to make you clean so that you may be cleansed of all your sins before the Lord, by everlasting ordinance it shall be a most solemn sabbath for you, on which you must mortify yourselves."* [Lev. 16:29-30; 23:26-33 & Ref. Num. 29:7-11] (Yom Kippur, for observing Jews)

The last time I looked, most Christian sects were fastidiously ignoring this 'everlasting ordinance.' I am aware that today we deem the death of Jesus on the Cross as atonement for our sins; but where does Jesus tell us that the Mosaic Laws have been rescinded? He doesn't! Paul does when he excuses his converts from the Law. Paul, who wasn't a companion of Jesus; who never heard Him preach; who didn't even know of Jesus until several years after the crucifixion; is who repealed the Laws of God (per Moses). Paul began a religion based on a myth about a Man (Jesus) who believed, and who followed, many of those laws. That is irony at its zenith.

Anyone can see that issues such as abortion will increasingly be the cause of discord in the world community. We can't let ourselves come to the point where an archaic, bigoted, ambiguous and misguided book dictates the laws of the world. Permitting this would be developmentally retrogressive. This is why I urge all non-believers to speak out and denounce the very essence of religiosity. Never mind all the actual or potential harm that religionists are capable of inflicting. The greatest disgrace a mortal man can bring down upon himself is the charge of confounding his intellect. Don't reject your own common sense when confronted with an irrational tenet. It is no disgrace to be slow-witted. But it is unforgivably damnable to reason illogically under the pretext that this pleases a reputed super intelligent deity.

MATTHEW'S "NAZARENE" QUOTE

Matthew's quote, *"He shall be called a Nazarene,"* is not found anywhere in the Old Testament. [Mt. 2:23] The identified verse begins, *"He did this to make come true what the prophets had said"* and it is counted as one of Matthew's many 'fulfilled' messianic prophesies. This fact, trivial in itself, has consequences that ripple out and affect all other parts of the Bible. The most obvious question provoked by its absence is this: If this verse didn't come from the Old Testament, where did it come from? The number of answers to this poser is very limited, and none of them reinforces the proposition that God inspired every verse in the Bible.

First to mind is the proposal that a portion of the Old Testament has been lost. This is a distinct possibility, and there exists some evidences that buttress this speculation. Once we embrace this solution, however, we must question why God inspired mortal scribes to write passages in the O. T. text that didn't survive into N. T. days. This constitutes a Divine waste of time. Could there be inspired thoughts from God that were so inconsequential that it mattered not if they were lost between the days of Moses and the days of Jesus? An affirmative reply here would be demeaning to God. So, responding for the religionists, I will reject this solution.

Of course, it is possible that Matthew only made up the quote to delude his would-be adherents. This makes Matthew a deceiver, and invites doubts into everything he wrote. Without further comment, we can all reject this solution.

What other solution can there be? In frankness, none! Yet, for someone who believes God has been sitting on a throne in Heaven for all eternity (except when He turns Himself into a dove), some other solution must be possible. Why not this one: The only verse missing from the Old Testament is the quote Matthew referenced. Therefore, because God inspired Matthew to re-insert this verse, the Bible was once again complete.

This solution isn't overly imaginative, and I am convinced that an able theologian can concoct several alternates that would be much more ingenious. In this actual instance, Matthew is probably quoting from an apocryphal source lost to the early Christians. (Possibly 'Source "Q" — a conjectured, semi-mythical, unattributed early Gospel.) The most likely of all solutions, i.e., that the entire Bible, excepting only some incidental historical material, is nothing but human fiction would never occur to a religionist. Thereby, this option is seemingly beyond consideration. Still, this is the solution that best resolves every anomaly in the Bible. Anyone with a modicum of objectivity must ultimately come to the same conclusion. If only he or she will unshackle their intellects, and rein in their gullibility while examining the Bible.

MODERN RELIGIOUS VENALITY

If Jesus returned to the Earth tomorrow, the first location I would want Him to visit would be a church fund-raising Carnival. The open thievery that passes itself off under the guise of entertainment there would appall Him. Not that all other religious money-garnering schemes would be acceptable to the Man who drove the moneychangers out of the Temple. Carnivals just aptly epitomize the commerciality of today's churches.

I, personally, could do without carnivals for all of my life. But my family enjoyed them; adventitiously, I attended them rather frequently. One memorable Carnival we attended had a golf ball challenge that was nearly impossible to conquer. At a dollar per attempt, someone was raking in a considerable amount of ill-gotten money. Predictably, the Church isn't the sole beneficiary in this "Rip-Off" enterprise. The operator of the Carnival entourage pockets most of the cream (*and all of the skim!*). But the Church must accept culpability for commissioning this unconscionable fleecing of the neighborhood residents. Carnivals disguise themselves with a façade of respectability by appearing to 'help the Church.' Frankly, the moneychangers of Jesus' day were no greater leeches, than are today's Carnival operators. The description: "money-grubbing scoundrels" fits both groupings snugly.

Holding Flea Markets, selling lottery chances, and presenting Bazaars are only slightly less amoral. Television has opened a whole new vista for religious fund-raisers. Not always jokingly, Bingo is spoken of as the eighth Sacrament of the Catholic Church. Yet, how should the Church raise money; by begging for alms or a handout? Collection plate donations, on balance, are precisely that: 'something for nothing.' Disregard people who profess to receive peace of mind, or some other esoteric benefit from the Church's ministrations. The secular law punishes this form of induced delusion; they call it quackery. Honey-tongued charlatans selling mineral water they purport to cure lumbago are arrested for fraud. Yet, a priest anointing a dying man with consecrated oil is promoting the same article. 'That being deception! While I do recognize a moral and motivational distinction in the two contrasted examples, I find no functional dissimilarity.

Religionists state that their benefits are spiritual; thus, they can't be seen nor tested. If so, then why can't we pay them for their services with spiritual cash that can't be seen nor spent? Yes, I am being ludicrous. But, the doctrinal point I am offering to my readers isn't whimsical, neither is it facetious.

SPECULATIONS ON THE DIVINE

I have told you that there isn't a Personal God, and this statement alienates me from all religionists. Then again, I have written that there must be some impersonal creative force (no capital letters), and this probably renders me an outcast among atheists also. So where will you stand if you heed my words? Well, wherever we are, we will be standing together. We will be searching for eternal truth together in motivational solidarity. If such an element as divine inspiration exists; we should all be personal recipients of it. There is no theological impediment that forbids anyone from being inspired by God. I can't think of the slightest reason why God can't inspire me right this moment to do His Will. Joyously, I would perform whatever acts God requested of me. If He exists, then He knows this. I have always felt this way, long before I discerned that the God notion was a fallacious mental conception.

When I was a devout young altar boy, I longed to be led by God to accomplish something worthwhile in life. Why didn't God hear my prayers? I didn't ask for Heaven. I didn't ask for any reward at all. I would have been content with far less than eternal life in Paradise. All I wanted was that my being born would be recognized as having added something beneficial, however negligible, to this world. The aspirations of most (all?) religionists are identical to mine. They proceed further, however. They postulate a God who loves them as the proof of their worthiness. But this is nothing but foundationless self-indulgence.

A honeybee has much more utilitarian value to the world than do most human beings. Worth and value are relative terms. They must be rated by a cognitive entity who determines the utility of another entity. Invoking a god into any argument renders all future discussion tautological, thence, redundant. 'God can do anything!' Accordingly, any argument that interposes the Deity ends all further debate. God doesn't have to prove Himself! God doesn't have to be logical! God ends all inquiry!

Did God create me because He loves me? Or does He love me because He created me? What does it matter if God created all things? And, if He created all things, did He create all things equal? No, He didn't! Mount Everest is manifestly much higher than is Bunker Hill. A Redwood tree is many times more massive than is a mulberry bush. Leonardo da Vinci may have been mentally keener than was anyone else who has ever lived.

If we are all equal in the eyes of the Lord, then the Lord must have severe vision impairment. God, Himself, makes distinctions between us. Some of us are tall, and some of us are short. Some of us are sharp, and some of us are dull. Some of us are healthy, and some of us are sickly. Some of us are Christians, and some of us are not. But most divisive of all, some of us have been inspired (*sic*) by God, but the overwhelming ninety-nine point ninety-nine percent (99.99%) majority of us haven't.

God must know that anyone who is favored with a personal inspiration from Him is surely going to believe in Him. Contrarily, if a devout person prays continually for inspiration and forever is denied that favor ... in time that person is going to reach the conclusion that, A: God doesn't love them! Or B: There is no God! Answer this query: "Why wouldn't God appear to every person once during his lifetime?" (Theophany) Or at least send an angel to bolster belief in God's inspired religion, if such inspiration has ever occurred?

Permit an aside here. As the present segment was originally being composed, I paused and spent time reflecting on God and inspiration. Here are the words I wrote at that time: "As I sit here and write, it is the wee hours of June 1, (1981), and I am alone in the back bedroom of my home. If God so chose, He could appear to me right now. No one but He and I need ever know. If this would happen, I would immediately take all my writings, and burn them forthwith. But, it hasn't happened. So, therefore, it must be God's Will that I complete this manuscript.

"Perhaps, what I am doing is following the will of the Devil. In that case I will pause here and pray for an appearance from him. You see, I have as little confidence in the reality of Satan as I do in the reality of Yahweh; God the Father, Allah, et al.

"Several minutes have passed since the last two paragraphs were written, and I am still as alone as I have been all night."

Alas, the spirits weren't favorable to me. I could summon neither gods nor demons. But, then, no one else can either. I have much company in my inability to successfully beckon spirits. Human beings are in fact quite alone with their intellects on this planet. While it is true that our intelligence is only a step above the brightest mammals' intelligence, that step is a giant stride! The factor that bars all creatures, save humanity, from immortality is the mental acknowledgment of any god. Animals have no conception of a Deity; consequently, there isn't an animal heaven, and there are no animals in humanitiy's Heaven.

It is common knowledge that some people are very fond of animals. For them, a Heaven without their favorite pet would be a depressingly lonely place. Or, in the case of the opposite destiny, does Satan welcome pets? My guess is "No," for this would permit some measure of enjoyment for the condemned soul. Decidedly, God couldn't allow this.

Yes, you read correctly, I wrote that <u>God</u> would bar anyone from bringing a pet into Hell. In case you haven't discerned it yet, God created all things; this includes Hell. Furthermore, it is He who determines the regulations governing your confinement there. God also decided exactly how you would be tormented in Hell. He lit the fire. God is the actual ruler of Hell. Satan (the Devil) is only its disloyal resident manager. If you never have thought about this aspect of Hell: 'Think about it now! If the Devil had his way, Hell would be a place of boundless iniquity. What could bring God more anguish than to be forced to view His damned creatures replicate their most grievous sins for all eternity? Rape, incest, and murder should all be rampant in Hell.

Wait! Back up! There wouldn't be murder, for spirits can't die. There couldn't be rape either; sinners that they are, they would all enjoy endless fornication. It is quite impossible to rape someone who is gleefully willing to participate. 'How about incest? No, I am afraid that offense is obviated also. Remember, Jesus Himself taught that there wouldn't be husband and wife in the afterlife. [Cf. Mt. 22:30; Mk. 12:25 & Lu. 20:35] One would presume from this that even blood relationship likewise would be abolished. Sinning while confined to Hell may be impossible on pragmatic as well as on moral grounds, or upon divinely dictated statute. The one sin that may be possible in Hell is endless hatred for the entity that (who?) confined the damned to such an excruciating destination.

It is repugnant to contemplate this, but, theologically considered, Hell must be regulated by God. Could the Devil be relied upon to follow rules that were less than compulsory? Does Satan fight God fairly? The forces of darkness are engaged in an all-out battle to win men's souls. Having lost his rebellion, will Lucifer now be content merely to embarrass God by encouraging wholesale defections of the human race from the community of the Almighty?

No, Lucifer can only be coerced into appropriate behavior by God's incontestable commands. Accordingly, only God can possibly be the absolute overlord of the place called Hades. This proposition is reinforced, perhaps verified, by every logical presumption congruent with the concept of Hell. The previous is (apparent) fact. However, we are dealing with religiosity here. 'So who needs facts? Faith and piety, not fact or reality, rule the religious intellect.

Here, let us imagine how Hell came into existence. Right now, trade places with Lucifer mentally. In these imaginings, you are the Devil. But first you were the Archangel, Lucifer. Whatever possessed you to think that you could depose the Infinite Being who created you? If God had no beginning, and will have no end: how could you ever hope to conquer Him? Suppose you and your followers did manage to overcome God and the faithful Angels. What, then, would you have done with Him?

You couldn't kill Him! You couldn't imprison Him because He is all-powerful and invariably would have escaped any confinement of your conception. You couldn't banish Him, for He is omnipresent. There just wasn't any way you could harm Him. 'Or bind Him. 'Nor do anything else to Him. In actuality, all He had to do was desire that you cease to exist, and that would have been the end of you. You foolish Angel into Devil! There never was even the slightest chance of you succeeding. God, as you must have known, is omniscient. He knew of your plan to rebel against Him before you were created. Didn't you fear God's wrath if your pitiful plan failed? Who tempted you to such folly? You were tempted, weren't you? Or did those insurgent thoughts just foment in your consciousness from nowhere? Can Angels devise a sinful action independent of an evil "Tempter"? I surmise not!

Human beings need you (Lucifer/Satan) to teach them to sin. Without you, all of mankind would be sinless. If mortals needed a Fallen

Angel to corrupt their wills, then I ask: "Who corrupted your will?" Was it a Fallen God? Could it be that originally there were four Divine Persons in one God? Did one of those personages rebel against the other three? This is a more reasonable hypothesis than conjecturing that a mere Archangel would dare oppose all three manifestations of God.

Yes, this makes more sense logically. In the beginning there were four Gods: The Father God called Yahweh; the Son God called Jesus; the Spirit God called the Holy Ghost; and lastly, the rebellious God whom I shall name "the Renegade." Only another God could entertain hope of defeating God Almighty in battle. Another God would be able to conceal His thoughts from the other three Gods. Only He would be brash enough to challenge Yahweh.

The Renegade God would not have feared the Holy Ghost. The Holy Ghost never seems to do anything but change Himself into a dove, or occasionally into a tongue of fire. The second God, Jesus, would forgive Him if He failed. Jesus forgives everyone who repents his transgressions. But does Yahweh? No, Yahweh was a vindictive God. He punished people severely for even minor infractions. If one were wise, one wouldn't try to depose Yahweh, unless that one had a reasonable hope of ultimate victory. Would you, Lucifer (a lowly Archangel) ever possess that much confidence? No, I don't think you would; not unless you had inside help. (Perhaps from the Renegade God?) This also explains how Lucifer became that powerful as a force for evil in the affairs of men. The Renegade God infused Lucifer with that capability. {The reader is Lucifer in this mental ploy}

Now you can see how one false premise can generate an equally false premise. There is no Renegade God; nor is there a Holy Ghost God; nor is there a mortal God (Jesus); and, finally, there isn't a personal God. (Neither Yahweh, nor God the Father, et al.) The force or forces that generated the Universe, and all that abounds within it, isn't human or even superhuman. The logicality is that the creative force must be universally and perpetually inconceivable in human cognizance. Scrutinize the totality of bio-life on this planet, and the previous statement's corroboration will become pro-foundly more obvious. You, the reader, may herewith return to your status as a mere human being.

This segment is ended. "Pax vobiscum!" (Peace be with you!)

DISTINGUISHING BETWEEN
REALITY AND APPARENCY

Several times in this book, a distinction has been made between apparent reality and actual reality. What is the difference, and can anyone know as a certainty which is which? Often the difference is only a matter of opinion, and in those instances one must decide the case for oneself, or accept the conclusions of a trusted advisor or confidant. In other cases, facts are available, or can be garnered from collateral sources. Whenever proofs are available, these should be weighed into your evaluation of the actuality of the situation. A few examples will render this proposition clearer, or at a minimum, shed some illumination in that direction.

In Sports, how many times have we been misled by the untested observation that a team won their championship because of the camaraderie of its players? We have all heard this a hundred times or more. But is this true? Can we test this theory? I think so. To begin: Has a team of comrades ever lost a championship game? Of course it has. And the reverse: Has a team riddled with dissention ever won a championship game? Yes, it has. Consequently, on the surface, the axiom that affection and mutual respect between teammates is a guarantee of winning, and that enmity or hatred precludes victory, is shown to be misapprehended.

Yet, there is an apparent observation that seems to vindicate the congeniality axiom. Winning teams are often effusive with brotherly love after an important victory. Meanwhile, on the losing side, often we read of acrimony by one team member directed against another team member. Does this prove the axiom? Not at all! What is happening here is the application of rationalized hindsight. After an event is over we all tend to look back and rationalize the result. The victorious team is happy and full of love. The defeated are full of rancor and ill feelings, especially if the defeat was particularly humiliating. These feelings are exhibited by a release of invective, often applied against a teammate, or even against the aggregate team, for some real or perceived failing.

My conclusion is that camaraderie is the result of winning, not its cause. The causes of victory are much more complex than a single axiom can express. The prime ingredient in all sports is talent, blended with luck!

An increasingly pertinent factor today is the officials. Their decisions, laden with a complex set of rules, have singly decided many a contest. Another overrated attribute in winning is desire. Notice I said overrated. Desire is a necessary ingredient surely, but desire will never supplant talent, all other factors being in equilibrium.

Up to this point, have I presented facts (?), or an opinion (?), to buttress my case against the sports' truism extolling camaraderie? If you chose opinion, you are correct. To prove my contention I would have to gather many statistics together, and present them in a comparable and clear format. Being somewhat of a sports buff, I feel comfortable and justified in my opinion; but I haven't proved my point. Ultimately, each of us must do that for ourselves.

Another truism from life in general is that persons who persevere and persist will invariably succeed. We all know that this is true. 'Or do we? We have only the word of those who have already succeeded to guide us. But is their testimony fact? Once having succeeded, each of us may look back and recall the early failures that didn't dissuade us from our goal. Yet here again, a thoughtful inquisitor should ask: Has anyone ever searched and found someone who has striven time and time again, yet continued to fail? If so, then this truism is now under suspicion. Should our inquisitor search further and find someone who has succeeded with almost no effort on his part whatsoever, then the truism should be considered disproved, and from then on it should ceaselessly be disavowed.

As in the previous example, hindsight has again misled us. Naturally, most persons will fail the first time they attempt something difficult. If they continue to come up short of their goal, they will give up the quest eventually. Few goals in life will ever be accomplished merely through pertinacity. Life is much too complicated for that. There just isn't any simplex formula for any of life's enigmas, religion included. Placing God at the master controls of life's complexities is a glaring oversimplification. God isn't beyond all human conception. Rather, He is a concept that anyone can readily conceive. (Barring only the mentally defective!) The concept of God only becomes complex when we try to define and rationalize the concept.

We aver that God is good, and everything He made is good; still we recognize that evil exists. How was evil created? Did evil self-generate? If it did, then Evil is a Deity also. Did God create all things neutral, that is, with the potential to be used either for good or for evil? Who is it then that alters a neutral event into a good event? Is it mankind? Or is it God?

If it is God, then He likewise must be the one who alters neutral matters into evil matters. This we cannot accept, so we must absolve God of responsibility for either good or evil. For, if we propose that only God can accomplish good, then we must propose an equal entity who alone can accomplish evil. This because we recognize that evil exists. Is the Devil the equal of God? That, also, is insufferable. The fact is that man alone is the architect of both good and evil. He is also responsible for neutrality.

The reason for this is because all three concepts 'good' 'evil' 'neutral' exist only in man's perception. God, too, exists only where man imagines Him. This may be opinion, but it is opinion predicated from verifiable facts. Did God create all things? Did He create disease bacteria and viruses? Do they infect and kill mankind? Are 'good' men murdered as often as are 'evil' men? Is God accountable for earthquakes, thunderstorms, floods, famine, plague, and all other forms of malady? Do the previously stated maladies adversely affect the pious as persistently as the perverse? Do birth defects occur? Do accidents occur? Do carnivores exist? Does misfortune strike all of humanity indiscriminately?

You would be exceedingly perceptive to believe that misfortune is no stranger to any one of us. Why is this so? Is it because God is playing inscrutable little dramas with our lives? How altogether naive is such an explanation. Yet, this is the only alternative that doesn't positively repudiate the personal God hypothesis. So, only if we reject this hypothesis, do the facts begin to make sense.

Allow me to rephrase the last paragraph. Is the God who wishes us to thank Him for our meals, the same God who created ptomaine bacillus? Is the God who wishes us to attend Church every Sunday, the same God who cripples us with arthritis so that we can't walk? The God who loves to hear our praises, is He the same God who caused us to be born mute? When you burn incense to God, does He enjoy the aroma? When lightning strikes a house causing a fire with everyone inside being burnt to death, does that aroma please Him?

The foregoing isn't a crude attempt to denigrate the universal Divinity theory unfairly. It is intended to magnify the dissonance between the positive attributes we cloak God with, and the concomitant negative corollaries that enshroud Him. The discord between the traits we wish God to possess, and those associated traits that must necessarily accompany, should be evident to everyone. But it isn't!

In religion, as in other subjective areas, humans fastidiously discount the unfavorable, while concurrently they magnify the favorable. One result of this is the flagrant distortion of truth and reality. But another result is a comforting sensation of self-appeasement. It is eminently more rewarding to reflect on Nirvana, than it is to contemplate oblivion. Which is more satisfying: That a universal God knows, protects, and loves you? Or that no one or no entity anywhere in the universe cares whether you are unhappy, sick, or even dead? If no one loves you, why does it matter that you are alive? Now can you understand why it is so vital to humanity that an Omniscient and Loving Creator must be created?

SEXUAL RELATIONS ARE A SIN!

Before eating of the tree incorporating the knowledge of Good and Evil, Adam was sinless and innocent. No one can sin that doesn't know what sin is. It is said that Adam disobeyed God, yet in his pure state, he was as blameless as is a newborn babe. Genesis informs us that Adam and Eve knew it would be wrong to eat from the forbidden tree. If so, then they already had some knowledge of Good and Evil. The tree, then, was nothing more than an alluring enticement, planted in the center of the Garden by someone who wished to tempt Adam and Eve. We all know whom that Creative someone must have been. Satan simply exploited a *de facto* situation. It wasn't Satan who planted the tempting "Tree of Knowledge."

Then after eating the fruit, how did our original progenitors manifest their knowledge of 'Good and Evil'? They covered their naked bodies! Why? Is it because naked bodies are evil? 'Apparently so! So, likewise, must coitus be sinful because Adam never knew Eve until after their expulsion from Eden. Now in the stilted minds of religious dogmatists, sex and nudity may seem noxious. Their jaundiced view of all things related to carnality might seem disgraceful to a deified personage who, via scripture, is indicated to be asexual. But normal, intelligent people have no such revulsion toward nudity. Sexual attraction is an evolutionary development. Sexual repression is merely an accommodation to cultural harmony within community environs. Celibacy is an outrage to the God who allegedly fashioned our bodies, and imbued us with our copulative impulses. God's reproductive gift is flung back in His face and told that it is lewd and immoral! Even Paul glorified celibacy over sexuality. [Cf. 1 Cor. 7:8, 7:29 & 7:34]

HUMAN SUFFERING — HOW DID IT ORIGINATE?

On a New Year's weekend one year, a television show aired in Philadelphia that could almost wrench your heart out of your chest. The program showed starving children from Asia, Africa, and Latin America. The scenes were graphic enough to induce discomfort & nausea, but I had no doubt they realistically portrayed actual living conditions in those areas of the world. The camera focused in on kids who were as listless as a soft licorice stick. Flies congregated at their nostrils siphoning a seemingly endless stream of nasal mucus. Other flies jostled for position at the inside corners of the children's eyes to lap up a cloudy discharge trickling down the side of a nose. One child sat passively on her mother's lap while a small swarm of these flying pests busily explored even the lips and inner surfaces of her slightly open mouth.

I reflexively had the urge to shoo those flies away, even though I concurrently knew that the effort would have had no effect. No one could have watched this show without experiencing a jarring assault on his/her human sensibilities. The flies were far from the worst maladies afflicting these children. The viewer saw walking skeletons whose skin appeared to have been applied by some super-efficient shrink-wrap method. Every bone in these miniature human bodies showed in three-dimensional outline (bas-relief).

The horror of such suffering and misery is literally beyond perception. We look; we strain our imaginations; but we fail to comprehend for to experience such conditions is to anesthetize your brain from the comprehension. This is paradoxical, but true. No one can feel total empathy in these situations without living them personally. Yet, living them destroys our capacity to reflect on the very conditions that we wish to contemplate. If you imagine that such misery is unimaginable, then you have probably approached as near to understanding as you will ever attain without having experienced these conditions personally.

The narrator, with constrained emotion, enumerated the diseases ravaging the starving children of these Third World countries. He identified them as pneumonia, measles, rickets, polio, and a medical dictionary of others. (And now, endemic AIDS!) The children were unwilling hosts to all manner of parasites. Tiny human bodies were the hospice and sustenance for a miniature menagerie of dependent life forms, and always to the detriment of the child. The purpose of the program wasn't merely to showcase the plight of these hopeless waifs. Its purpose was to solicit contributions to alleviate the suffering of the children. The sponsors of the show never identified themselves particularly, but one could conclude that they were Christians of a Protestant persuasion. Their identity isn't an issue here. But there is a point to be made.

Toward the end of the show, viewers were exhorted to pledge money for the ongoing care and feeding of these children. Then, in the midst of a particularly lengthy appeal, a female solicitor urged her audience to "show these children the love that Jesus Christ has for them." This minor reversal of reality startled me back to my senses. What this person was portraying by unequivocal declaration was: "You provide sustenance to these needy children, and we will tell them the aid comes from Jesus Christ." I am aware that any reasonably accomplished semanticist could argue just such a proposition successfully. But to my mind, never legitimately or honestly!

This declaration is blatantly misleading and incomplete if we overlook where the misery originated. Where did disease originate? Who created it? What method of distribution did this Creator devise when He parceled out suffering? Why is the Third World overburdened with poverty? Is this Divine design? Or is this human ineptitude? While man himself may be partially culpable in some of mankind's afflictions, most of the physical maladies, and all of the natural disasters, must be assigned to God. Jesus Christ, as God, created the pneumococcal bacterium that is killing these innocent children. Why is He acting so perversely? Because Adam and Eve ate the fruit of the forbidden tree, that is why! God has been killing countless hundreds of millions of innocent people for thousands of years because of the sin of two people. God's Garden of Eden retribution, in this instance, is frightful and appalling to contemplate. ('Reprehensible fits!)

I wonder: Does anyone ever tell these guileless natives who made their children sick in the first place? I rather doubt it. In the New Testament, Jesus only cured people. We are never told who caused their illnesses. I ask, 'Who killed Lazarus?' [Cf. Jn. 11:13-14] Who caused the blind man to be born sightless? If it wasn't the sins of his parents: whose sin caused his blindness? [Cf. Jn. 9:1-3] Who caused Peter's mother-in-law to develop a fever?' [Cf. Mt. 8:14; Mk. 1:30 & Lu. 4:38] Nothing occurs just as a matter of course; at least this is what religionists affirm. Every eventuality has a cause. That is, every eventuality except God, who is the Uncaused Cause of everything. This is a religionist's reasoning, not mine!

Evolution posits that events follow a pattern, but not necessarily a plan. Religionists refute this vehemently. They state that all events follow God's plans. Yet, frequently, they disregard, at a minimum, half of the contradictory evidence. Scientists have to forgo this philosophical evasion. They must offer incontestable proofs to substantiate their hypotheses. They must account for contrary indications in the same hypothesis. This is as it should be.

It is ironic today that we are asked to believe on faith alone, the presence and providence of God the Father. The Israelites asked for, and received, multiple signs from their God, Yahweh, to prove His existence. Yahweh acceded to their insistence unfailingly and provided many wonders. Yet, several of the miracles that Yahweh worked for Moses, the Egyptian priests were able to replicate. Today's religionists totally discount the revealing implications of this biblical admission.

The credulity of religionists throughout the ages is astonishing. They pray so ardently for a Personal Creator to comfort them that they succeed in creating Him in their imaginations. Jesus deluded Himself into believing He was the chosen Messiah. He believed He was ordained by God Almighty; His Father, and the Father of all, to serve as the eternal Melchisedech. [Cf. Ps. 110:4 (Ps. 109:4); Heb. 5:6; 5:10; 6:20; 7:1, 10, 11, 15, & 17] Melchisedech, also, had a miraculous birth & life. *"He is without father or mother or genealogy, having neither beginning of days nor end of life, but resembling the Son of God, he continues a priest forever."* [Heb. 7:3]

Recall how Jesus once told His Apostles, *"You can buy two sparrows for a penny; yet not a single one of them falls to the ground without your Father's consent. As for you, even the hairs of your head have all been counted. So do not be afraid; you are worth much more than many sparrows."* [Mt. 10:29-31 & Lu. 12:6-7]

Did this affirmation apply only to the Apostles? Was it limited to the seventy-two disciples? Were all of the followers of Jesus included? Or, as religionists insist today: Every member of the human race is encompassed in this pronouncement by Jesus. If no sparrow dies without God's consent, then similarly, no human suffers without God's knowledge and concurrence. How do you suppose the religionists working for the conversion of the impoverished from these Third World countries would react if I went among those people informing them that their miseries were caused by Jesus? Yet, according to a proselytizer's very own Christian scriptures, God is culpable! And Jesus is an integral part of the Godhead.

Justifiably, the Creator of disease viruses and harmful bacteria should be charged with causing the prevalence of sickness on Earth. We hold Chemical Companies liable for the safe disposal of their toxic wastes. The Occupational Safety & Health Administration of the United States declares that the employer is solely responsible for the safety of the employee. Even in the case of willful negligence on the part of the employee, such as refusing to wear safety goggles. The Company is liable for failing to enforce safety regulations. In almost every instance the onus is on the employer to protect the employee. Who, then, is chargeable for the natural accidents that befall us in life? Shouldn't the Creator (God) also be held accountable for His actions (or lack of action!) when natural or physical disasters strike us?

If you examine our interaction with the Deity objectively, you will soon discover that we do, indeed, treat God exactly as we would a capricious and vengeful Monarch. Would any prudent subject be so foolhardy as to suggest to a despotic Monarch that he shouldn't jail everyone who criticizes him? No! For this very act of questioning a despotic Monarch might well excite his anger against the impudent subject. The Almighty's actions are also beyond inquiry. We praise Him for even the slightest of favors; yet we dare not even frown at His most outrageous outbursts. Consider a devastating earthquake or, perhaps, a merchant ship sunk in a violent storm with all hands lost. There are countless examples that could be cited. Imagine a meteorite striking a nursing home for elderly Christians that exterminated all within? Could God be held directly accountable for this tragedy? By any sensible standards He could be.

However, religion isn't an act of sensibility; it is the ungoverned indulgence of our superstitious idiosyncrasies, coupled with our tendency to mystify poorly understood natural phenomena. We have learned our lessons well, for indeed we do, 'Render to Caesar the things that are Caesar's' {condemnations, criticisms, and vituperations}, 'and render to God the things that are God's' {praise, admiration and acclaim}. [Cf. Mt. 22:21; Mk. 12:13-17 & Lu. 20:20-25]

CHAPTER 19
Analysis

THE MIND OF JESUS

Devout Christians will be more than slightly disconcerted to learn that some less-than-devout scholars have undertaken the task of analyzing the mind of Jesus. Not that these scholars are chargeable as being deliberately impious. Rather, their innate curiosity has compelled them to consider the mental state of Jesus during His public life. Not entirely unexpected, several have diagnosed Jesus as a paranoid, or have posited some other mental aberration as the impetus for His actions and His philosophies.

It is entirely outside the scope of this book to critique these authors and their theories. But, inasmuch as this information was unknown to me and only came to my attention after I had begun this work, I thought it may be informative to my readers also. Evidently, much of the analytical work on the mental state of Jesus was done around the turn into the twentieth century. Many of the references cited in the two books I read referred readers to papers composed by German authors in the German language. Most, I would imagine, were written by scholars, for scholars, and would be heavy laden with scholarly analyses. If this is so, then the general reader needn't lament never having read this psychological hypothesizing.

Some benefit, however, may accrue to those who reflect on the implications attendant to a cursory analysis of the thought processes that convinced Jesus that He was in fact the long awaited, often referenced,

"Messiah." The four Gospels will provide our groundwork material; although the pseudepigraphical 'gospels' do contain more intriguing stories! Together, let us identify and dissect the major incidents in the life of Jesus that may have been the catalyst around which His Messianic aspirations and beliefs formed.

John's Gospel is much too evolved theologically to be of help. But the Synoptic Gospels should provide ample breadth for our analysis. Matthew's account is especially suited to our purposes, and will be our chief citation. We will begin, however, with the Gospel of Luke, for his is the only narrative to tell of the boy Jesus astounding the elders of the Temple with His knowledge of the ancient scriptures. [Cf. Lu. 2:46-47] At that time, Jesus was twelve years old. If the significance of His chronological age eludes you, permit me to give my explanation.

Male Hebrew children weren't held accountable to the strictures of the Law until they reached puberty. Attendance at, and participation in, the rituals of the local Synagogue wasn't obligatory until the onset of maturity. Jews of the day reckoned this to be at age twelve. What Luke is informing us is that Jesus knew the contents of the sacred writings at a very young age. This is not to say that juvenile males weren't exposed to the Scriptures before reaching the age of accountability. Jewish fathers began schooling male children in the revered writings as soon as they were able to recite them.

This incident of the boy Jesus in the Temple, in its context, appears wholly legendary. Yet, it isn't inconceivable that a person, who in later life was steeped in religiosity, was well versed in the Torah at age twelve. Singularly, the incident neither confirms nor rebuts the Messiahship of Jesus. It merely indicates to Luke's readers that Jesus was a precocious child, drawn at an early age to individual interpretation and disputation of the Hebrew sacred texts. Youthful prodigies of the Christian Bible aren't unknown, even in today's age. This indicates more about the psyche of the child than it does of the authenticity of the philosophies the child may espouse. Hitler's Youth Corps bred many fervent devotees of National Socialism. This doesn't legitimize the teachings of the Nazis. In the same vein, a child reciting nursery rhymes doesn't render 'Old King Cole' historical or ideologically relevant.

The next point of reflection is the baptism of Jesus. Here Matthew and Mark agree completely. After His baptism, Jesus saw the Spirit of God descend upon Himself in the form of a Dove. Note that neither author states that anyone other than Jesus observed the Dove. Then they both agree that Jesus, not the onlookers, heard the voice from Heaven. Essentially, Luke concurs with one indicative, if not actual, exception. Luke records in one paragraph that John the Baptist was imprisoned by Herod Antipas. [Cf. Lu. 3:19-20] Then in the next paragraph, he states that Jesus was baptized *"after all the people were baptized."* [Lu. 3:21]

Is Luke reporting that someone other than John baptized Jesus? It would seem so. Yet, as stated previously, Luke does otherwise reaffirm the testimony of Matthew and Mark. Luke reveals that as Jesus was praying after His baptism, the Spirit came down upon Him in the form of a Dove, and then Jesus heard a 'voice from heaven' intone, *"You are my own dear Son, I am well pleased with you."* [Lu. 3:22; Mk. 1:11 & Mt. 3:17]

Can you grasp the interpretation the 19th Century German analysts' imputed to this episode? To their minds, Jesus had a personal vision of God's Spirit visiting Him. Plainly, they concluded that Jesus had hallucinated this entire event. The three Synoptic Evangelists don't contradict this interpretation. They all report the incident as a personal experience of Jesus. John's Gospel doesn't specifically refute this interpretation either. John, however, writes that the Baptist was a witness to the descent of the Spirit on Jesus.

Yet, John's account isn't more enlightening. It is more baffling. John never records unequivocally that the Baptist performed his rite on Jesus. Instead, John writes that the Baptist was told by God that, *"You will see the Spirit come down and stay on a man."* [Jn. 1:32] John the Evangelist then quotes John the Baptist as saying: *"I have seen it and I tell you that he* (Jesus) *is the Son of God."* [Jn. 1:34] The Baptist bears witness to the appearance of the Holy Spirit on a day subsequent to the baptism, not on the day of the event.

What was the Baptist doing when the Holy Spirit appeared? From John's account we can only conjecture that Jesus was being baptized, and that John was the one who baptized. When was it that John the Baptist became cognizant that Jesus was truly *"the Lamb of God"*? [Jn. 1:36] My understanding of this incident is that the Baptist gave his witness sometime after the baptism. What did the expression, 'Lamb of God', signify to those who heard the Baptist make his belated declaration? Also, John the Evangelist's version of the descent of the Spirit forbids the understanding that those present at the Baptism heard or saw anything supernatural. Present day extrapolations of the Baptism of Jesus are simply unfounded. If you are now, or have ever been "a Christian," please consider the next question thoughtfully. Weren't you led to believe that everyone present at the Baptism saw the Holy Ghost in the form of a Dove? Also, that all those present heard God the Father proclaim Jesus to be His beloved Son? With few exceptions, you were. We all were. But this is not the witness of the four Evangelists.

Progressing: The next incident warranting our reflection is the 'temptation in the desert.' Immediately after the Baptism (in the Synoptic Gospels), the Spirit leads Jesus into the desert to be tempted by the Devil. (The Evangelist John knows not of the sojourn in the desert!) Without argument, only Jesus witnessed this travail. Were the events "real" as recounted by Matthew, Luke and by Mark (barely!)? Or were they imagined? We can never know this, as the entire sequence is beyond corroboration. Fasting for forty days in desert conditions could induce almost any mental delusion. [Cf. Mt. 4:1; Lu. 4:1-2 & Mk. 1:12] How can anyone other than the recipient know that a 'spirit' led someone somewhere? All I can personally add is that I have never seen, nor communed with, an evil or benevolent spirit being. I have misgiving that Jesus did either. How can a dove lead anyone anywhere? This story is preposterous.

What might in truth have happened was that Jesus was moved emotionally by the intimidating exhortations of the eccentric mystic, John the Baptist. Jesus felt an impulse to aid the Baptist in his preparations for the arrival of the Messiah; whoever He might be! At this time (the time immediately after His Baptism), Jesus retired to the desert to contemplate the entirety of the Messianic prophecies, and His role in the enfolding thereof. In the course of fasting, it was to be expected that Jesus would experience hallucinatory visions. The Plains Indians of North America induced hallucinatory visions in the same manner by fasting while resident at length alone in the wilderness. The specifics of the Devil's temptations fit this scenario much more snugly than a scenario wherein Jesus is declared part of the Godhead. Permitting His Person to be so manipulated by the Devil would have been overly accommodating to grossly understate the actuality of this fantastic anecdote!

Before His desert retreat had ended, Jesus had conjectured His niche in God's scheme for the redemption of His Chosen People. Jesus himself was soon to be exalted to the Messiahship. Jesus wasn't yet certain of how or when, only that it would happen soon. The full revelation of His mission on Earth probably didn't crystallize in the mind of Jesus until after His self-imposed ordeal in the wilderness. We know from two of the Gospels that Jesus, from thenceforth, (in essence) repeated the cry of John the Baptist, *"Repent! The Kingdom of Heaven is at hand."* [Cf. Mt. 4:17] Two thousand years afterward it still hasn't arrived.

Curiously, Mark's version changes the word "Heaven" into "God," and then adds: *"and believe the gospel."* [Mk. 1:15] What gospel? They hadn't been written (compiled?) yet. 'Gospel' here obviously means "Good News"; the good news that the age of 'the Kingdom' had commenced. Still, I am suspicious. Luke doesn't report this phrase, but in several verses he does use the word 'gospel' (i.e., 'Good News'). [Cf. Lu. 4:18, 7:22, 9:6, & 20:1] [Cf. Isa 61:1] {Note: The word "gospel" appears in the N. T. almost 100 times!}

Next Jesus made several exploratory journeys to both Galilee and Judea airing His newly conceived theology. Quick and lasting results, however, weren't forthcoming. The crowds came; they listened intently; then they returned home to resume their persistently mundane secular lives. {My presumption} Fanatic devotees of whatever persuasion are always dismayed by the collective lethargy of the unresponsive masses. They can't comprehend the lack of fervor exhibited by those whom the devotees favor with their wisdom and their insight. After the success of the French Revolution, people were executed for merely a lack of enthusiasm toward the revolutionaries. Activists abhor apathy; they detest disinterest. Jesus taught, and the people listened. But did they learn?

Soon, Jesus theorized that His 'anointing' was fast approaching. He recognized all the signs of the 'Last Times.' The scriptures said that Elijah would return first, followed speedily by the arrival of the Messiah. If John the Baptist was the reincarnation of Elijah, as deduced by Jesus, then John's death foreshadowed the Messiah's imminent appearance. [Cf. Mt. 11:13-14]

Jesus vacillated at first. When He performed His curative miracles he admonished the beneficiaries to tell no one. [Cf. Mk. 1-44] When He asked His companions who the people thought Him to be, they answered, "the Messiah." [Mt. 16:16] But Jesus cautioned His followers not to confirm this presumption. [Cf. Mt. 16:20] By now, Jesus had persuaded Himself that He was God's promised Redeemer. Yet, how could He convince the people? Time was running out; Jesus knew He must act decisively. He, personally, could never get the 'Good News' tiding to all the Jews of the Promised Land before the ever-awaited Messiah was revealed as Jesus Himself!

With this in mind, Jesus sent out the disciples in pairs to spread the message throughout Judea and Galilee. But not in schismatic Samaria! The time was short; but so, also, was the message they carried. Jesus forewarned the disciples that they wouldn't complete their vital mission *"before the Son of Man comes."* [Mt. 10:23] Jesus believed Himself to be that person. He believed that in some fashion known only to God, He would be manifest to all the Jewish people as the 'Anointed One.' (Aramaic = Messiah; Greek = Christos)

The Gospels don't reveal how long the disciples remained on their mission. But we do know they did conclude their commission, and returned to find Jesus still not publically revealed as the Messiah. Whatever spectacular event Jesus had envisioned would visually transpose Him never did materialize. Discernibly all necessary requisites hadn't been discharged. Jesus, puzzled and dejected {inferred}, initiated a period of retrospection. Throughout His last autumn and winter, Jesus pondered His delayed Messiahship.

Ultimately, He perceived that He had found the missing element. That element was His death! What more positive and convincing sign could God give to His chosen people that there was, in actuality, a life beyond this life, than to retrieve and revive God's chosen Messiah from the unrelenting and inexorable grip of death? Jesus would prove to the people that there was a bodily resurrection by being resurrected Himself. The sign of Jonah would be the sign of the Messiah. After three days of death, Jesus would gloriously be returned to life; the Golden Age of Hebrew religious (and civil?) hegemony would reign for ever and ever. That is how Jesus must have pictured the future. But as we know, this isn't exactly how events unfolded.

The arrest, the sentencing, and the crucifixion probably occurred much as the Gospels relate. There is more agreement here than anywhere else in the four discrepant accounts of the life of Jesus. True, there are glaring and worrisome inconsistencies between the gospel crucifixion narratives. But we won't examine those here. Our next consideration will be the Resurrection.

All the Evangelists agree that Jesus was resurrected, so we should proceed conceding that something indicative of a resurrection did take place. The varied accounts of the events after the Resurrection, however, do seem more conjectural than historical. Each narrative contradicts the others. They can't be reconciled without raising serious charges of defective inspiration by God; selective amnesia by certain Apostles; or some otherwise Apostolic or Divine failing. I believe something did happen that convinced the Apostles (or at least some of them) that Jesus had been released from the unyielding maw of mortal death.

Matthew informs us that not all of the Apostles believed in the Resurrection. In Matthew's Gospel, Jesus only reappeared twice after His death. Once, on Sunday morning, He appeared to the women who visited the sepulcher. Lastly, on a predetermined hill in Galilee. Matthew writes that all eleven disciples were present at the pre-selected Galilean site. *"When they saw him, they worshipped him, even though some of them doubted."* [Mt. 28:17]

A few modern translators render the word 'doubted' as 'hesitated.' I am not qualified to dispute their rendering, but my intuition tells me that their translation word-choice was dictated more by subjective and indulged reverence, than by judicious and intellectual scholarship. It is unfortunate that Matthew doesn't tell us what the Apostles doubted about the Resurrection, or why they doubted, nor even who doubted. But then, if he had, perhaps today there would not be a Christian faith to discuss. Nonetheless, some of the disciples doubted. So, if today we doubt also, why couldn't God find it in His Mercy to forgive us? If there is a God!

For if God exists, He lied to Jesus. Jesus read the sacred scriptures and came to believe that He was to be the Messiah. Even more damaging to the credibility of Jesus is His failed prophecy recorded in Mark's Gospel. *"And he {Jesus} went on to say, "I tell you, there are some here who will not die until they have seen the Kingdom of God come with power""* [Mk. 9:1 {Mk. 8:39 D-R Bible}; Mt. 16:28 & Lu. 9:27] Was Jesus wrongly inspired? Or did His inspiration issue forth from His own self-delusion? I say it was self-delusion. I say it, I trust, with ample justification. Read the Gospels side by side. Even the three Synoptic Gospels are different and contradictory! Where the stories are in agreement, often they are so similar that anyone can see that they come from a single source. It isn't as though different witnesses were viewing the same event, but more in the manner of three persons writing separately about an original story they all had been told. That is how all the Gospels read, as orally learned stories being graphically recorded, not as eyewitness accounts.

Each story, each event, each teaching when examined individually can be made to appear reasonable, and often inspiring through the wiles of a skilled extrapolator. But if you step back and examine the entire mosaic from a dispassionate distance, all you will see is a confused welter of misapplied religiosity. No religionist, however skilled, has ever been able to make a complete and coherent picture of the life of Jesus. The facts and the fictions surrounding Him have been so interlaced that no one afterward can ever unravel the actuality from the misreported truths.

If we believe parts of the Gospels, then Jesus must truly be a God in His own right. Yet if we believe other parts, then Jesus must have been entirely and exclusively human, consequently subject to all frailties attendant thereunto. The dilemma of the early Church Leaders (some of whose beliefs were ultimately deemed heretical) continues to plague us into this very age.

Those who would try to analyze the mind of Jesus must contend with both scant information and misinformation. Their study is hampered by a lack of direct communication with Jesus. Still, there must be some factual matter contained in the Gospels. If we adhere to just that which seems factual, then Jesus doesn't appear paranoid. By my evaluation, Jesus had an exaggerated sense of personal mission. He believed in the Father God as strongly as any Jew in history. But Jesus was an activist. Belief in the ancient scriptures alone couldn't damper His religious zeal. Jesus found no solace in solitude, or in mere contemplation.

When Jesus heard the Baptist tell the populace that the 'Final Times' were upon them, Jesus interpreted this as God's inspiration for Him to begin His ministry. A less insistent Savior might have paused and waited for God to unveil Him before the people. But this wasn't the Jesus of the

Gospels. He was self-assured of His divinely assigned mission to reclaim for God all the 'lost sheep of Israel.' [Cf. Mt. 15:24] (Read Mt. 15:26-27 about Canaanite "dogs")

If you scrutinize the Bible closely, you will discover that Jesus never proselytized anyone other than the Jews of the Holy Lands. John's Gospel discloses that Jesus' disciples baptized in a Judaic fashion. Does this indicate to you that Jesus was intent on starting a new religion to compete with Judaism? No, it doesn't; and He wasn't! Jesus taught in the Temple because He was a devoted Jew. Jesus was not the founder of Christianity!

Do the Gospels contain any factual matter? Yes! But most of the true facts are obscured or distorted by an overlay of sanctimonious hyperbole. The truths in the Gospels must be mined, for they are deeply buried under an edifice of deceit, misinformation, and ignorance. Faith won't unearth the truth; honest inquiry might.

CRITIQUING THE NATIVITY AND THE RESURRECTION

Was Jesus truly born as two of the Gospels report? Because neither Mark nor John mentions the birth of Jesus, we can learn nothing from them. Luke's account is so obviously bogus that we can disregard it also. Still, before we consider Matthew's Nativity story, I will critique Luke so that the reader will know my reasons for dismissing him so unhesitatingly.

Luke begins his Gospel with the tale of Elizabeth and Zechariah and the miraculous conception of John the Baptist. If Luke's account was true, then Jesus and John the Baptist would have been kinfolk. Every version of the baptism of Jesus refutes this. More than that, when Elizabeth is first greeted by the pregnant Mary, she instantly knows the child in Mary's womb was the Lord, that is, the Messiah. If Elizabeth knew this, then surely she would have conveyed this knowledge to her son John. Accordingly, John the Baptist would have known about Jesus long before the Baptism. This, also, is disproved by the other Evangelists. In Luke's own version, the adult John the Baptist sent messengers to ask Jesus if He was the Messiah, sometime after the baptism rite had been performed on Jesus. [Cf. Lu. 7:18-23]

Also, Luke records that the Angel Gabriel appeared to Mary. How did he (or anyone else!) come to know the name of the announcing angel? The angel who appeared to Zechariah identified himself as Gabriel. But the angel who appeared to Mary never did give his name. Luke assumes it was the same angel who appeared before Mary. Later, when another angel of the Lord appeared to the shepherds in the fields, Luke doesn't identify this angel. There are all too many angelic appearances in Luke's tale. Scripturally, he has a multitude of angels singing God's praises to the shepherds. Moreover, as already pointed out, Quirinus didn't become Governor of Syria until AD 6. But Luke can be forgiven this error; Quirinus was probably present during the census begun in 7 BC, he just wasn't the then Governor of Syria. [Cf. Lu. 2:2]

Luke's version has much imagination, and very little (if any) inspiration. The final straw, and that which indelibly brands Luke's Nativity as a fiction, is the incident with Simeon and the Prophetess Anna. According to Luke, at the 'Presentation' these two set about proclaiming within the Temple itself that the baby Jesus was the promised Messiah. [Cf. Lu. 2:25-38] Imagine this if you will: Two Galileans, living in a stable in Bethlehem, presenting their child in the Temple with a two dove offering (this is the set offering of poor people), and then having this humble child hailed as the future King of the Jewish Nation? [Cf. Lu. 2:24 per Lev. 12:8]

Any other religious body might have laughed themselves silly at such a preposterous contention. But the dour old Jewish authorities most assuredly would have shrieked, 'Blasphemy,' and would have promptly accosted everyone involved. No! All that Luke proves with this fable is that he wasn't a Jew, and that he knew little about Jewish beliefs and customs.

Luke's ending to the Nativity segment is in direct disagreement with Matthew's Nativity. Luke concludes: *"When they {the Holy Family} had finished doing all that was required by the Law of the Lord, they returned to Galilee to their home town of Nazareth."* [Lu. 2:39] Luke not only doesn't know of any flight to Egypt, he doesn't leave room for anyone else to squeeze in any such indefinite excursion.

For me, this eliminates all but Matthew's first two chapters as our sole source of information about the birth of Jesus. This assumes further that some facts are contained in Matthew's arguably fanciful tale. In this account, an Angel of the Lord appears to Joseph, not to Mary. Matthew, an ethnic Jew, subordinates Mary's role in the Nativity, and has the Angel(s) interact exclusively with Joseph throughout. ('Women's Liberation' would have been an anathema to the author of the first Gospel.)

Matthew's Nativity version is sparse. His only purpose seems to be to attribute the prophecy of Isaiah concerning a virgin giving birth to the nativity of Jesus. [Cf. Isa. 7:14] Inasmuch as all prophecy is attributed after the fact, there is a possibility that Mary did become pregnant without Joseph's participation. There existed an apocryphal story that proposed a Roman soldier as the real father of Jesus. This makes sense evaluating the few details Matthew provides. If, as the Protevangelion {Apochcryphal} records, Joseph was a middle-aged widower, then it is entirely possible that his marriage to Mary was an arranged affair, not a love affair.

Pregnancy out of wedlock was a serious infraction under the religious strictures of that day. Mary's family would have been most anxious to hide her youthful indiscretion. Yet, what self-respecting Jewish man would have stepped forward to accept responsibility for an unwed woman with child, especially a child fathered by a Roman or a Gentile? An elderly man, with an established family, might just consent to marry a sixteen-year-old, slightly pregnant, maiden. Probably, their marriage would have been the ideal scenario for both Joseph and Mary. He acquired a young female to oversee his household, and she was spared the shame of out-of-wedlock motherhood. This also would explain why Joseph wasn't around during the Ministry of Jesus. He probably was dead! This life concluding eventuality overtakes older people much more consistently than it does younger people.

Mary's young life could have transpired in this manner: As a newly flowered maiden, Mary became enamored with a young man of whom her family disapproved. Any Roman would surely have been a pariah to even a less-than-pious Jewish family. In order to forestall inevitable disgrace, her family arranged to have her betrothed to the elderly widowed (?) Joseph. This may or may not have occurred before Mary was found to be pregnant. Whichever! Joseph was persuaded to marry Mary, but not before both families learned of Mary's blossoming condition.

The Protevangelion reports that Joseph had grown sons. One of them was James (the future head of the apostolic band?). Joseph could have discussed his predicament with this son, or James may simply have counted the months and calculated that Jesus wasn't Joseph's child. In this circumstance, it is likely that Jesus could have grown up knowing that he was chronologically illegitimate. If Mary kept her own confidence, then no one needed to know who the father of her child was. The very question soon would have become *verboten* in the Carpenter's household. Not that the question was forgotten; it was merely unspoken. Jesus Himself may have invented the 'Spirit of God' as the agent of His birth. Or any of His early followers could have fabricated this mystical exoneration. The observation that both Evangelists felt the need to expound on the Nativity raises an inquiry. Was there an unresolved and lingering question in Nazareth as to the identity of the biological father of Jesus?

Before I proceed, permit this short digression: Charles Manson had a childhood similar to the instance just postulated. Manson's mother became pregnant out of wedlock. Later, she met and married William Manson, and he gave his last name to young Charles. Manson never learned who his real father was. As an adult, he used his uncertain paternity to proclaim that he was the 'Son of Man,' an impious wordplay on his adoptive last name. His flagrantly delinquent followers claimed him as the Second Coming of Christ based in part on this sacrilegious pun.

I don't compare Charles Manson to Jesus. What you should extract from this last bit of information is this: "If no one knows who your father is, you can select anyone you fancy." Most illegitimate persons chose royalty, or a movie star, or some other famous (or notorious) personage. A deeply religious person might just choose the Spirit of God, especially if that person saw himself as a creature with a divine mission or a sacrosanct destiny.

The story of the Wise Men may contain a nucleus of fact also. Matthew informs us they 'studied the positioning of the stars.' [Cf. Mt. 2:2] People who study the stars don't require spectacular heavenly manifestations to trigger their prognostications. The occurrences of truly spectacular phenomena are so few in number, and generally are so distant in time, that astrologers could go a lifetime without ever observing anything extraordinary or sensational. Conversely, a super-bright star could have been seen and interpreted by everyone. Who needs astrologers, when the celestial event is visible to every observant person?

No, there was no 'Star of Bethlehem' as such. Rather, there was (may have been) an unusual configuration of the known celestial bodies that intrigued the Magi. Factually, that is what they studied: the positioning of the visible stars and the "wandering" stars (planets). A modicum of knowledge about astronomy would be helpful here to the reader. My next point will be made as clearly, and as simplistically, as I am able without providing technical explanations.

The constellations on the celestial equator (the zodiac) complete one full circuit of the skies in approximately one year and six hours. 'Not that the constellations move at all as distinct entities! The imperceptible orbiting of the Earth around the Sun creates this apparent motion. The Earth also revolves on its own axis causing night and day. Combined, these motions facilitate the practice of astrology, i.e., fortune-telling from the stars. But these two motions aren't synchronous; hence, midnight in Jerusalem, on June 1st of the year 1, won't show the same overhead constellation and planetary locations as the exact time and place one year later.

In actual observation, it would be many future years before essential re-positioning is observed. The planets move independent of one another (in the main) and independent of the motions of the Earth or the background stars, which makes exact repositioning virtually impossible when we include them into our determination. The ancients didn't recognize the planets for what they are exactly. They explained them as 'wandering stars.' These unpredictable 'stars' meandered through the zodiacal constellations in such a willy-nilly fashion that no one in those times could ever predict their future locations.

This never-repeating positioning of the wandering stars is what renders astrology viable, for it allows an endless variety of interpretations of star positioning. The Egyptians calculated the time for planting crops from the Spring rising of the star Sirius at daybreak. This, however, is a simple observation that recurs yearly and thus served the Egyptian purpose faithfully.

The calculations of astrologers are much more complex, and are thereby open to many more and varied interpretations. According to one theory, the position of one or more planets in the constellation "Virgo the Virgin," possibly just before an autumnal sunrise, may have been the heavenly sign interpreted to presage the birth of an extraordinary person. In this case there is little to wonder why only the Wise Men knew of the implications of the 'Star of Bethlehem.' It also could account for the inclusion of a virgin within the Nativity narrative. The story of the Magi coming to Bethlehem may be fanciful embroidery, without denying that their prediction of a Jewish World King being born was in general circulation in Palestine for Matthew to learn of their astrological prognostication.

Matthew, as we all can readily verify, was a prolific reader of the sacred O. T. scriptures. He also was fairly adept at matching present events with past prognostications. All Matthew would have needed was the hint of a prediction concerning the Jewish Messiah, and he would have pounced on that conjecture. By the time Matthew wrote about Jesus, however, at least forty years had passed. The Magi, if they ever had visited Bethlehem, must have long since concluded that their star-based divination was erroneous. The gospels and history both confirm that Jesus never did become the King of the Jews; not even two thousand years after the Wise Men made their fateful interpretation as indicated to them by the stars and the planets.

There is no quick way to make the overall point of these last few segments, if it wasn't already discerned. The point is this: The gospels aren't total fiction. By and large, real events begat the origin of the stories contained therein. What I am attempting to show is how those fanciful stories still may have been fact based. Anticipating that here you may conclude, justifiably, that there is no absolute proof for my extrapolations either, I concur! However, what I am offering is scant proof against no proof. In point of a fact that even religionists must concede: Most religious premises are not only without proof, but they often are contrary to the evidence. Their support is found in faith, not in knowledge. 'Not always in rational hypothesis either.

The 'Star of Bethlehem' is just such an item. At the time of Jesus' birth there were many learned astronomers charting the heavens. The Magi weren't the only sky watchers. Yet no astronomer anywhere in the world reported the 'Star of Bethlehem.' We do not know of this wondrous heavenly anomaly from astronomers. Matthew, the Tax Collector, is the sole source of this scintillating manifestation. If the astronomers of Egypt, or Persia (home of the Magi?), or China didn't record this event; how came Matthew to record it? Why didn't Josephus, or any other contemporary (to Matthew) historian, record this intriguing aerial event?

Josephus wasn't born until after the appearance of the Star. But then, neither was Matthew, if his traditional age is accurate. Why didn't the other three Evangelists inform us of this spectacular star? This star was visible in the homeland of the Magi; was it invisible everywhere else? This postulation is too preposterous to even consider!

Do you concede the point? There is no proof whatsoever (outside Matthew's Gospel) of a 'Star of Bethlehem,' yet there are indications aplenty that no such star ever emblazoned the sky over Bethlehem. Is Matthew thus to be branded an outright liar? No! If my intuitions are correct, he is just a misinformed reporter. He heard of an unusual positioning of the wandering stars centered in or near the constellation Virgo. The conjecture involving the King of the Jews' birth needn't have been Matthew's fiction. He may have just misapplied a circulating story of the Magi's astrological Messiah forecast in the town of Bethlehem to the birth of Jesus.

Wrapped up, here is what these last few paragraphs propose: One of the many speculations concerning the coming of the Promised Messiah was that some portentous celestial event would accompany His birth. A legend abounded that a spectacular comet flashed across the sky the night Alexander the Great was born. Matthew, upon learning of the expectation of a portent heralding the Messiah's arrival, either invented the Star of Bethlehem, or he may simply have borrowed an extant astrological reality (the conjunction of several planets in Virgo) and applied it to the birth of Jesus. A 'true believer' never questions any story that exalts his hero. Matthew, alone, wrote also that ominous aerial events accompanied the death of Jesus. The author of Matthew's Gospel believed that portents from the sky conclusively verified the Messiahship of Jesus. A representative example of Matthew's predisposition pertaining to the crucifixion follows:

> *"At noon, the whole country was covered with darkness which lasted for three hours."* [Mt. 27:45; Mk. 15:33 & Lu. 23:44] *"Then the curtain hanging in the temple was torn in two, from top to bottom. The earth shook, the rocks split apart, the graves broke open, and many of God's people who had died were raised to life. They left the graves; and after Jesus rose from death they went into the Holy City, where many people saw them."* [Mt. 27:51-53 – exclusively]

Isn't the previous an event that would have been reported many times, in many different fashions, by many different people? Undeniably, it is. Suspiciously, it wasn't! Matthew fabricated the multiple resurrections addenda, just as he also did via the 'Star of Bethlehem' story!

The Jesus' Resurrection narratives, in a less obvious instance, could have had a reasonable explanation. Here Matthew's account fails us. It is entirely too sparse. A sudden appearance to Mary Magdalene and the other Mary, and then another appearance on a hill in Galilee: whereupon Matthew abruptly ends his narrative. If all we had to convince us was the first Gospel, the Resurrection of Jesus would have been relegated to the classification of probable folk legend. Throughout Matthew's story of the life of Jesus two vital ingredients are always missing. Those ingredients are personal insight and personal involvement by Matthew.

Again, in the Resurrection narrative, Matthew records the story from a third person perspective. Why doesn't he tell us how he felt when Mary Magdalene told him Jesus had arisen? What did Matthew say? What did he do? What was the consensus among the Apostles? Did some of them believe the body of Jesus had been stolen or hidden? Recall that Matthew is the Evangelist who reveals that some of the Apostles "doubted." [Mt. 28:17] Then there is the next to the last statement in Matthew's Gospel. Jesus instructs the Apostles to baptize, *"in the name of the Father, and of the Son, and of the Holy Spirit."* [Mt. 28:19]

The Readers Edition of the Jerusalem Bible adds a footnote here that is worth repeating. "This formula is perhaps a reflection of the liturgical usage of the writer's own time." [Page 79] To that I will add my own footnote: "These are obviously not the words of Jesus. Nor do I believe they reflect the sentiments of Jesus." Matthew's narrative, at this juncture, is highly suspect of being a sanctimonious editorial addendum, meaning a later inserted 'forgery'!

My guess is that all of the followers of Jesus dispersed after His arrest. By the time they regrouped, no one knew where Jesus was buried. Because Joseph of Arimathea is never mentioned before or after the death of Jesus on the cross, I believe that the Apostles never knew him beforehand. It is quite possible the Apostles never did learn where Jesus was buried.

Mark and Luke both write that Mary Magdalene and another Mary followed Joseph of Arimathea and noted where the tomb was located.

Discernibly Joseph didn't know the female associates of Jesus, or he would have invited them to learn the tomb's whereabouts. Even more would have been expected of a devoted believer in Jesus. This exposes John the Evangelist's contention that Joseph was a secret disciple of Jesus as nothing but *ex-post-facto* revisionism. [Cf. Jn. 19:38, also Mt. 27:57] John's Gospel is so obviously out of harmony with the Synoptic Chroniclers, especially in his version of the events after the Resurrection, that we are forced to disregard it here.

Yet, when we come to consider Mark's post-Resurrection narrative, we encounter a different obstacle. Mark has two disparate endings to his Gospel, neither of which appears to be particularly authentic. Of necessity, we should peruse both endings and see what conclusions can be drawn from the accounts as we now have them. The debatable section begins after Mark 16:8. The shorter ending contains only two subsequent verses.

> *"The women went to Peter and his friends and gave them a brief account of all they had been told. After this, Jesus himself sent out through his disciples, from the east to the west, the sacred and ever-living message of eternal salvation."* [Mk. 16:9-10] {End of Mark's shorter version}

It isn't apparent here, but if this version is both complete and correct, then we have no compelling proof of a Resurrection from Mark. I haven't detailed it yet, but immediately preceding the two above quoted verses there are two paragraphs that, all combined, comprise the whole of Mark's shorter Resurrection segment. The two paragraphs merely report that the women who witnessed His burial returned early Sunday morning to an empty tomb. ('Not entirely empty!) Inside they saw a young man wearing a white robe who caused them to fright.

> *"'Don't be alarmed,' he said, 'You are looking for Jesus of Nazareth, who was nailed to the cross. But he is not here —he has risen!' Now go and give this message to his disciples, including Peter; 'He is going to Galilee ahead of you, there you will see him, just as he told you.' So they went out and ran from the grave, because fear and terror were upon them. And they said nothing to anyone, because they were afraid."* [Mk. 16:6-8]

From this version of Mark's ending all we know for certain is that the body of Jesus was missing from the sepulcher and in His stead sat a young man announcing, *"He has risen!"* {Excerpted} This is hearsay evidence, not proof. If this was all the evidence we had, we could discount the resurrection of Jesus as a probable fable or fraud. We don't even know who this man in the white robe was. We surmise that he is an Angel; but this isn't confirmed in the narrative

There is, however, another ending to Mark's Gospel, and we will examine that now. The notation is Mark 16:9, but should logically be enumerated Mark 16:1, for it is really a variation on the entire chapter. In this version, Jesus first appeared to Mary Magdalene. But no details are given as to where the appearance took place. Neither can we read what, if anything, Jesus said to Mary. All we know is that when Mary told His "companions" (the Apostles?) that Jesus had arisen, and that she had seen Him, *"they did not believe her."* [Mk. 16:11]

Next this ending mentions, just briefly, that Jesus appeared, *"in a different manner to two of them"* {Disciples?}. But when these two reported the incident, *"They* {the Apostles} *would not believe it."* [Mk. 16:12-13] Obviously, doubt was endemic among the Apostles! Lastly, Jesus appeared to the gathered eleven as they were eating. First, He scolded the Apostles because some of them had no "faith," and they refused to believe those Disciples who claimed to have seen Jesus "alive." Contrary to Luke's Gospel, in this version, Jesus doesn't partake of any of the food. He does, however, order the Apostles to *"Go to the whole world and preach the gospel to all mankind."* [Mk. 16:14-18] To me, this wording is also suspect. There is no way eleven men could ever preach the Gospel to the whole world, even if we limit our geography to the world the Apostles knew. No matter what effort they expended, they could never accomplish such a vast mission. Not to overlook the biblical 'fact' that none of the 'Gospels' had yet been written. Mark's Gospel ending reeks of after-the-fact insertion multiple decades (even a century) after the Resurrection.

Luke's Resurrection story generally follows Mark's version except that Jesus only appeared twice. Initially: To the two disciples on their way to Emmaus. Finally: To the assembled Apostles in Jerusalem. Also, Luke provides incidental details not found in Mark's post-crucifixion account. An example: The Risen Jesus asks for food during His appearance. *"Do you have anything to eat here?"* [Lu. 24:41]

Logically, Mark, who is postulated as the voice of Peter, would be expected to know most of the particulars concerned with the full ministry of Jesus. 'Not so! The opposite is the observed case. Yet Mark, who never even knew of Jesus until long after the Ascension, provides more post-resurrection data than does Matthew; who was an eyewitness after the resurrection! This reversal of expectation must direct heedful persons to conjecture that Mark's expanded version [Mk. 9:20] is embroidery after-the-fact, rather than factual exposition. More about this after you have read my extrapolation of Luke's rendition.

Luke reports not one, but two men in bright clothes informed Mary Magdalene, Joanna, and Mary the mother of James, that Jesus had arisen. [Cf. Lu. 24:4] As Luke's Gospel informs: 'When Mary Magdalene told the Apostles of her experience with the two angelic men at the sepulcher, they thought she was speaking *"nonsense."'* [Lu. 24:11] Luke then adds: *"But Peter got up and ran to the grave, he bent down and saw the grave clothes and nothing else."* [Lu. 24:12] Curiously (and damaging to its credibility), Luke completes the above verse thus: *"Then he {Peter} went back wondering at what had happened."* {A number of translations of Luke 24:12, read "he (Peter) went back to his home"} Several translations read: "He (Peter) went away." No translation reads that Peter went back to the assembled Apostles.

Why should Peter wonder? Hadn't Jesus told all the Apostles He would arise again on the third day? All four Evangelists report that Jesus predicted His Resurrection to the Apostles. [Cf. Mt. 17:22-23; Mk. 8:31; Lu. 9:22; Jn. 12:32-33 & 14:18-19] During Mary Magdalene's visit to the sepulcher, one Angel (?) reminded her of Jesus' revelation. Mary *"remembered his words ... and told these things to the eleven disciples."* [Lu. 24:7-9] On several occasions, Jesus told Peter that He would arise after His death. [e.g., Lu. 18:33]

Luke then informs us that, *"On the same day"* [Lu. 24:13], Jesus appeared to two disciples on the road to Emmaus, but *"they somehow did not recognize him."* [Lu. 24:16] How could they fail to recognize Jesus' wounds? Why would Jesus hide His identity one moment, only to reveal it a short time later? Following the story, they never recognized Him. Weren't His hand (wrist) wounds visible? What happened was that the unrecognized Jesus broke bread and gave it to the two disciples. It is at this point that they perceived Him (possibly) to be the 'Jesus' who had just been crucified.

I believe there is a germ of truth in the resurrection story. On Sunday morning Mary Magdalene searched the burial grounds, but only found an empty sepulcher. Did Mary find the correct burial tomb? Joseph of Arimathea knew precisely where Jesus was buried. But I don't believe he told anyone! If he was a secret convert of Jesus (as Matthew & John inform us, and the other two Evangelists do not textually contradict), then he may well have acted thus to later foster the rumor that Jesus had truly arose from death. The gospels describe Joseph as a man who either was "waiting for the kingdom of God" or was a "secret disciple of Jesus." [Cf. Mk. 15:43; Lu. 23:50-51; Mt. 27:57 & Jn. 19:38] It is curious to me that this Joseph didn't come forward and give witness to the fact that his donated sepulcher was now empty. After the burial of Jesus, we never again read of Joseph of Arimathea. The rumor of the disappearance of the body of Jesus was instigated by Mary Magdalene. Did Mary visit the correct grave location?

Advancing this skein of deduction: When the two traveling disciples met this stranger who spoke to them about Jesus, and knew of the predictions about Jesus' death on the cross, they still didn't recognize Him as their recently executed Master. But their eyes were opened when He broke the bread!

What may have happened is this: After this unknown man had departed and the two disciples had mulled over His words, they concluded He must have been the rumored risen Jesus in disguise. They then returned to the Apostles and reported their conjecture. The result was a typical instance of mass confusion wherein everyone soon came to believe they might have seen the risen Jesus also. Implanted (false) recollections aren't unknown today. Witness the plethora of recalled childhood molestation's currently being broadcast. It is well-nigh proved that some of those "recollections" never happened. (Ruefully, many of these coaxed recollections also were/are true, but that unforgivable outrage isn't the object of this work.)

This scenario is proffered only to accommodate the reported appearance of Jesus in the midst of the Apostles. There is total disagreement between the Gospels as to when and where the resurrected Jesus first did manifest Himself to His chosen band. Matthew, who would have been present in Jerusalem when Jesus appeared to the eleven, doesn't even mention an appearance in that city. He states that the Apostles went to a hill in Galilee where Jesus appeared to them. Why doesn't Matthew, who had to have been there, know of the appearance in Jerusalem? Yet, we are asked to believe that Luke, who learned of Jesus through Paul, who ostensibly knows more details of Jesus' life and death than two of His chosen Apostles, Matthew and John. But then, Luke doesn't know of Jesus' appearance and Ascension in Galilee. Luke records that Jesus ascended from Bethany in Judea. [Cf. Lu. 24:50-51]

Another oddity in the New Testament already mentioned, sketchily, is the lack of personal insight in the reporting of the life of Jesus. Only John's Gospel contains any insights. Yet, even he inserts them obliquely. Plus, there is an additional problem with the Gospel attributed to John. The fourth Evangelist never directly identifies himself! His frequent reference to the 'Apostle Jesus Loved' (which we infer to be John) is all the evidence we have. Neither imputation is confirmed. We really don't know if the 'Apostle Jesus loved' is the author of the Fourth Gospel, or if the Apostle so indicated was John the Evangelist.

Skeptically, granting that John the Apostle was the author does serve the purpose of imbuing the Fourth Gospel with authority, and provides a shield against an attack on its veracity. But then, a parallel question can be framed as to who wrote the pseudepigraphical Gospel of Peter? The Church ultimately declared this gospel uninspired. But, how did they determine so?

Another difficulty with John's Gospel is that he centers Jesus' ministry in Judea, and he makes it last for up to three years. [Cf. Jn. 2:13, 6:4 & 11:55] The Synoptic Gospels (Matthew, Mark, and Luke) center Jesus' ministry in Galilee, concluding in only a single year. As a final point (and not the least injurious), John has almost everyone who meets Jesus proclaim Him the 'Son of God.' Whenever Jesus isn't proclaiming it Himself, that is! {Note: Eleven citations in John} How could this be true? How could Jesus have survived approximately three years without running afoul of the religious authorities? Many times, Jesus brought Himself to their notice in the very Temple in Jerusalem. This should stretch everyone's credulity to the point where it rebounds. There is no way possible that the Jewish priests would have tolerated so blatant a blasphemy repeatedly, within the very walls of the holiest site in all of Judaism. Viz., the Temple in Jerusalem!

At the very outset of His Ministry (according to John), the Baptist calls Jesus the *"Lamb of God."* [Jn. 1:29] Why does the Baptist call Jesus a lamb? Did he know of Jesus' future sacrifice? Or is this another *ex-post-facto* addendum penned in by an unknown redactor after the death of the

562

Baptist? At this point, the Baptist tacks on the blasphemous statement: *"Who takes away the sins of the world!"* [ibid] Every Jew knew that only God could forgive sins. Surely this arrogant blasphemy would have been promptly reported to the religious authorities; after the ear witnesses had run out of stones, that is! Furthermore, what Jew would have known that the Messiah had come to redeem the entire world, not just to reward the righteous Jews exclusively?

Several days afterward, Jesus personally drove out the moneychangers from the Temple while announcing boldly and authoritatively: *"Do not make my Father's house a market place."* (Also reported as a *"Den of Thieves"*) [Jn. 2:16; Mk. 11:17; Mt. 21:12-13 & Lu. 19:45-46] According to John, this happened during the first year of Jesus' public life. Didn't anyone see or hear Him assume proprietorship in the Temple? They must have, for His audience asked Him to perform a miracle to prove He had divine approbation to roust the Temple merchants. But Jesus ignored their request and instead, uttered this cryptic sentence: *"Tear down this house of God, and in three days I will build it again."* [Jn. 2:19] This is what is suspect (questionable) with John's Gospel. Too many audacious things are said and done by Jesus, yet the Jewish ecclesiastic authorities never move against Him until a couple of years later.

Despite all the above, John's Gospel still reads somewhat as an eyewitness account, rather than as a story retold. His Gospel is also the most paradoxical. Chapter Three begins with the discourse between Jesus and Nicodemus, *"a leader of the Jews who belonged to the party of the Pharisees."* [Jn. 3:1] During this conversation, Jesus declares Himself to be the *"Son of Man"*; *"God's only Son"*; and *"Savior"* (of the world?). [Jn. 3:13-18] Does Nicodemus shout "Blasphemer"? Does he fume indignantly and demand that Jesus retract his scandalous, sacrilegious remarks? No. He does nothing.

In the subsequent verses of John's Gospel we read that Jesus, thereafter, went about openly competing with the Baptist for converts. Hardly worth noting: Jesus is more successful at winning converts to His baptism (performed by His disciples) than is John the Baptist. [Cf. Jn. 4:1] Still, the guards sent to arrest Jesus are, instead, captivated by Him. Incredibly, as the Pharisees are discussing this eventuality, Nicodemus speaks out, *"According to our Law we cannot condemn a man before hearing him and finding out what he has done."* [Jn. 7:51] [Cf. Jn. 7:32-52]

The Pharisees and their cohorts were the most inept adversaries anyone could provoke. This could answer the prompted question of how Jesus was able to proclaim his blasphemous theology for three years before the authorities finally acted. This is a weak argument. A stronger one would be to postulate that Jesus (as God —not as Man) orchestrated His Ministry so as to have it continue for three years. A serious charge of tampering with mankind's free will would then have to be raised. The question of culpability, likewise, would be compromised by this postulation.

No! If Jesus directed His own life's script, then the entire New Testament would necessarily have to be renounced as a divine contrivance. This is a typical case where the side effects of the remedial medicine are more injurious than is the medical malady itself. We will have cured an ingrown toenail by amputating the foot. Once again, the best solution is to postulate that the Fourth Gospel, as it now reads, was never written by John the Apostle. Who, then, did write this Gospel? The question is forever unanswerable. The internal evidence points toward a Jew who was familiar with Jerusalem and Judea as the basic author. The theology, however, is much advanced, and probably was redacted by an unidentified editor long after the crucifixion. If we scrutinize the Fourth Gospel closely, it becomes obvious the author was an educated Judean, not a Galilean fisherman. [Cf. Acts 4:13]

None of the Gospels can be definitively credited to an individual simply because there has been so many addenda appended to the basic stories. Furthermore, all the Gospels have been embellished upon. {My speculations follow} At first, the stories of the public life of Jesus were circulated orally. Then, as most of the first-hand witnesses died off, the remaining followers recognized the need to preserve those oral testimonies in writing. All the "Jesus" narratives were born thus. The first century prelates sorted through the welter of stories collected and afterward selected three composite compositions that they held to be basically authentic. Later, John's Gospel was added because his account also glorified Jesus, but more enticing than that, theologically his account was superior to the Synoptic Gospels. Thereafter, the Gospel stories granted credence to the myth; the myth granted credence to the religion; and the religion granted credence to the nascent Church.

THE BRAIN IS THE MEANS OF REMEMBRANCE

What is the affinity between soul and memory? Soul is ill-defined because soul is ill-understood. Religious theorists seem to entwine our memory with our soul as if the two were a unit. Soul doesn't exist, but religionists hold that it does, so of necessity here I will discourse as if souls were a reality.

Why do I declare that soul and memory are interchangeable? Because when you examine what a soul is you will have to concede that a soul must, indeed, have a memory. Picture this scenario: At the final judgment God opens the "Book of Life" [Cf. Phil. 4.3 – found 7 times in Rev.] and announces the sins committed by the deceased body of the adjudged soul. Can you suppose that this soul has no recollection of the indicting sins? No, you can't, for the very practical reason that if no memory of the sins remain; no stigma of guilt can be applied. Consequently, no just punishment can be imposed. One of the benchmarks of human justice is that the accused must be cognizant that his actions were criminal. A soul that had no recollection of the sins of the body could not be held accountable for the consequences attendant to those sins.

Likewise, the soul must be personalized to the body that committed those sins. It would be misapplied justice for someone else's soul to be punished for my body's sins. If we deemed our souls as distinct entities utterly dissociated from our human body, then the soul becomes purely an innocent bystander to sin. No, the only theoretical construct that is viable is for the soul and the body to be deemed one contiguous entity, or for the soul to be the motive force intrinsic to the actions of the otherwise dormant body.

That affinity can be likened somewhat to the association of automobile and driver if we correlate the auto with our body, and the soul as the vehicle operator. If this be the case (and I can readily visualize no other), then the soul is our consciousness, our awareness, *in toto*, our very mental essence. Do you agree? If so, then ponder this: Brain damaged persons lose the memory of past events. How can this be if memory resides in the soul? Does the soul suffer impairment when the body is injured? The soul is a pure spirit. Spirits can't be harmed by physical accidents. If they can, then they must consequently be liable to suffer death just as the corporeal body is destined to die.

Consider also, persons who have experienced comas. They recover from the coma with no memory of the events that occurred in their presence while they were comatose. Why not? Was their soul comatose also? We must all concede that soul was soporous (asleep) during that coma if we posit that soul memory does exist. Evidence abounds refuting each and every proposition that religions affirm. All an inquisitor needs to do is accept the contradicting proofs that are found strewn everywhere before the very eyes of the faithful. Self-induced mental blindness is all that keeps the gullible from recognizing the 'actual truth' from the 'sham truths' proffered by religionists that deceptively attempt to legitimize all religiosity as valid and factual.

THE QUINTESSENTIAL ME

How can I convey to you, my reader, the monumental delusion of the proposition that God inspired the entirety of the Bible? The ten obscene examples expounded in Chapter 7 of this book prove to me that a God who admired and desired morality had no involvement in writing those salacious episodes. The silliness of events such as Balaam's talking ass further precludes the possibility of an intelligent Deity. The superstitious gullibility of the Bible's authors fairly leaps off the printed pages of those now glorified Hebrew Deity legends at every reading.

The Bible, without the endorsement of heavenly inspiration, loses most of its credibility, even as a historical document! This is not to say the Bible is total fiction. In the main, what the ancient authors have done is to glorify and spiritualize their secular history. An author who writes that the Sun stood still in the sky for twenty-four hours is not worthy of the trust we are required to grant a historian. [Cf. Jos. 10:13] We are asked to believe a woman was turned into a pillar of salt for merely turning her head, while her husband and her daughters engage in frolicsome incest; yet no heaven-directed retribution strikes them. [Cf. Gen. 19:30-38] Doesn't God forbid incest? This particular story may be true, but only if we remove God as an author, and especially as the sole script writer and director. Once we ascribe Divine impetus to the biblical narratives, then God Himself is shorn of His credibility, and in tandem, of His holiness.

In the depths of their heart, everyone knows there is no personalized cosmic Being; no Super Father; and no all-seeing/all-knowing/all-just Spiritual Force. If I were absolutely certain that there indeed was a Christian God; that His message to me was contained in the Bible, and that this book was entrusted to the management of His earthly Church: then I would vow to limit my sins henceforth! The universality of sin in the human race tells me that mankind in its collective intellect knows beyond amendment that there is no God!

By and large, they hope He exists. Many sincerely desire Him to live, just as many are willing to participate in varying degrees of officious religiosity in optimistic anticipation of prolonging their own existence beyond death. Any mind capable of grasping the concept "I am," must reject the coincident deduction that one day "I am," will no longer exist. It isn't logical that an entity who unquestionably flourishes today will ever cease to exist in the future. This doesn't make sense to man's ego, so damn all contrary evidences; there must be some form of mental (and hopefully physical) presence beyond the grave! Those are the pampered persuasions of the bulk of the everyday religionist.

Yet, this reasoning is less than profound. More perceptive is the question: "Did 'I am' have a beginning?" If the answer is 'yes,' then the logical continuation would be that 'I am' will have an end. In the interest of disputation I might reply to the previous question in the negative, thence denying my conception in my mother's womb. I could fantasize myself as a vagrant soul wandering aimlessly through the ages, now inhabiting one body, then inhabiting another body. But how does this avail me? I have no recollection of any event before my present birth. If the 'I am' that I recognize to be me can't recall even the tiniest sliver of pre-existence, what benefits accrue to me from that posited pre-existence? My reply: Positively none!

If my soul does survive death yet I am just as bereft of memory of my previous human existence, then the reward of eternal life profits me to the same extent: nil in the absolute. I remember no life but this one I am presently living; therefore, this is the only actuality that will ever exist for me. If I begin a post-mortem life and retain memory of my former mortal life, I will attempt to communicate this eventuality to still living persons (if possible); so that they can realize solace through this most welcome revelation. Yet many problems arise when I give absolute freedom to this transient reverie.

First, no one has ever communicated with me from the afterlife. Why not? I would have welcomed it, as they must have known. 'Had anyone so desired; had anyone been thus empowered. If communication is impossible between the spirit world and the physical (real) world, all will be greatly disappointed.

I have always been strongly motivated to assist people whom I have deemed worthy. I am pleased when helping certain others, even to the possible disadvantage to myself. (I am not looking for personal accolades here. Please read and evaluate this idiosyncrasy at a purely academic level.) If you deny me this pleasure, you have diminished my Heaven. The only way to alleviate my frustration would be to alter my emotional make-up. That leads into my second problem. If God, or death, or whatever alters my emotions: Am I still me? Fully, what I am elucidating here is this: "I am the sum of my thoughts and emotions. At what point during any alteration would I cease being me and become someone new?" Dogmatically, any change in my make-up, however slight or covertly insignificant, changes me.

In a capsule, here are my conclusions. Without remembrance of a human life, a spiritual life is as original and unique as is this life. Without remembrance of a human life, the present consideration of a future existence is an unmitigated inanity. With remembrance, but lacking the ability to communicate or interact with the physical world, that very memory becomes a disconsolate absurdity.

The murky concept of an ineffable life hereafter is the greatest irrationality. If God desires to reward any of us, why doesn't He do so right now, in the present? If He simply ensured that worthy people lived a little longer; had a bit more joy in this life; and suffered less misery; that would be compensation enough for most persons. Forgo an eternity of Heaven. Never-ending bliss is far too grand a reward for saying "Gosh darn it" in substitution of "God damn it." Why not resolve 'that which I deserve', reward or punishment, on this Earth while I am still alive? Why must I die before I can live forever?

Here, as always, every thoughtful inquiry is best answered by denying the existence of a personal God. Why is this ever so? Is God an even greater deceiver than is Lucifer? If the witness of Christian theology is 'fact despite the contrary facts,' then why do such contrary facts exist? Has the Supreme Being seeded the Universe with forged apparent truths that seem to refute revealed truths, so as to mislead His most intelligent creatures? Fundamentalists and their brethren, confute the conclusions of scientists and able scholars with a contemptuous charge of coddled vanity. But I ask: "Was it vanity or knowledge that enabled man to travel to; land on; and return safely from the Moon?"

The Bible insists the Moon is nothing but a "light in the sky" to separate the night from the day, and for the "fixing of seasons." [Gen. 1:14] The Moon, as everyone should know, isn't a 'light in the sky.' It is an astronomical body, one-quarter the size of the Earth. It has no light of its own, but only reflects light from the Sun. Yes, man has ascended into the heavens, but not through the inspiration of the Bible. He accomplished this feat through the determined application of his remarkable (collective) intellect. Someone might counter with the almost weightless question, "So what does the voyage to the Moon prove?" My rejoinder would be, "If the value of the space program isn't self-evident, then no editorial of mine can penetrate that person's bias against intellectualism and human technological advancement."

The World Health Organization, in 1979, announced the total elimination of smallpox (since rescinded). Who is responsible for this modern miracle? Is it 'Science or Spirituality? If you believe that all human lives are sacred (all believing Christian do), then render due homage to the persons of science whose dedicated research efforts wrought this life-saving miracle.

Ascribing that cure to God in the advanced nations doesn't apply, unless you also credit Him with the invention of the Atomic bomb. Both marvels had their genesis from the same foundation, the ingenuity of mankind. Professedly, it was God who endowed humanity with its nimble wits. By sanctimonious reasoning, God is responsible for "all that occurs!" God is the initiator of all Goodness; then necessarily, He is the cause of all Evil. We mortals are blameless! Well, aren't we? Result follows Cause; God is the Cause.

In the same vein: "Should I kneel down and thank God when I pluck an apple from a tree and enjoy it?" If so, then why shouldn't I get up and revile Him when I am set upon by robbers and beaten? Why didn't He prevent it? He gave even robbers free will. God is a perpetual 'innocent bystander' to all the misfortunes in our lives. I am sorry if you believe this, because I believe otherwise. I believe God fails to act because He fails to exist! That is saddening; yet it is true. The sooner more of us admit this unwelcome truth, the better it will be for most of us collectively. Evaluate the following statement candidly.

The world's food supply was dramatically increased when:

A) The farmer offered a pleasing holocaust to Yahweh.

B) Scientists developed inorganic fertilizers.

If you answered "A" above, then begin reading this book again. You obviously have missed the paramount premise of this endeavor. I am not alone in my condemnation of God's lack of concern, exhibited by His inactivity during the distressful and perilous periods in our lives. Saint Paul was troubled by the same observation. He eventually devised an exculpatory rationale; but not through inspiration, for his solution is hardly inspiring! What Paul theorized can be gleaned from his Epistle to the Romans. [Cf. Rom. 9:14-21]

'Who are we to question the motives of God?' asks Paul. 'God grants His grace when and where, and to whom it pleases Him.' [Inferred by Rom. 9:18, 21; extrapolated Hosea 2:1] Man is so inherently sinful and unworthy that nothing he can do would earn God's munificence. Therefore, God's grace is an undeserved gift that can be bestowed as He deems fit, and not as man presumes to dictate to Him. Paul explains that God's choice of recipient is determined by mercy, not on acknowledged worthiness. 'For none of us are worthy! In Romans 9:15, Paul quotes: "*I will show mercy to whom I will; I will take pity on whom I will.*" [From Ex. 33:19] Mercy, unlike justice, isn't granted on either merit, or entitlement, but upon the caprice of the grantor (God). {Author's extrapolation}

Paul's hypothesis is wrong; still it appears to resolve an apparent enigma. If we attribute God's favor to every beneficial occurrence, and scale the deservedness of the individual to the extent of the beneficence, what other answer is there? There is no other solution! Paul's thesis isn't insight; it is rationale! His hypothesis is a partisan's advocacy, even when critiqued via the most accommodating interpretation. Or perhaps, it was inspiration from the Holy Spirit? That being the case, one can go out and sin freely; it doesn't matter here on Earth. We still may "get lucky" and we may have God reward us with good fortune or good health, at His whim.

Paul, himself, suffered much because of his beliefs, yet never was he personally rewarded. Quite the reverse was the case. Unnamed "false brothers" (one translation: 'Special Apostles') attacked him scripturally. [Cf. Ga. 2:4 & Jude 1:4] He was calumniated incessantly by observant Jews. He was whipped. He was stoned. He was afflicted by an unidentified physical ailment that caused him great pain. [Cf. 2 Cor. 12:7] Paul was a prime example of the capriciousness of God's questionable mercy. Yet, He never forsook God the Father, or His saving Messiah Jesus. (-As far as we know?) Paul had unshakable resolve that in the end, i.e., the imminent Parousia (Second Coming) of Jesus Christ, he would receive the most precious gift of all; everlasting life!

Not only did Paul expect this reward, he expected it within his lifetime. This inference is clear in his first letter to the Thessalonians. The question arose as to the disposition of the "saints" (converts) who died before Christ's return. Paul wrote, *"We believe that Jesus died and rose again; so we believe that God will bring with Jesus those who have died believing in him. This is the Lord's teaching we tell you:* <u>we who are alive</u> *on the day the Lord comes will not go ahead of those who have died."* [1 Thes. 4:14-15 & Ref. 1 Cor. 15:23] {Underline added}

Paul fully expected to be alive at the 'Second Coming.' *"We who are alive,"* was Paul's phrase. Paul lived in hope. It was apparent there would be no settling of accounts until the return of Jesus. Paul's theology here doesn't spring from inspiration unless that inspiration was deceptive. (Paul envisioned himself still alive at the Second Coming.) Rather, Paul is moved to profess this eventuality because it was evident! Everyone could see that neither divine mercy nor divine justice was being administered here on earth while awaiting the advent of the Parousia. As every Christian can attest, ever since Cain jealously slew Abel, injustice has reigned unrecompensed on this planet virtually unabated!

MENTAL STATE OF A SOUL IN HEAVEN

The physical aspects of a heavenly existence have been discussed previously. Here let us consider the mental aspects. Pointedly, will our present emotions and affections accompany us into Paradise? This question is perhaps more significant than the survival of our human body. Resurrection of the body doesn't strike me as all that essential in a mystical environment. Revival, or more correctly, survival of my consciousness, seems to me to be the indispensable requirement in the promise of Paradise.

An awareness of this requisite isn't new, as we can discern from the Gospels. The Synoptic Gospels all record the question of the Sadducees to Jesus regarding the often-widowed woman who eventually married seven brothers. [Cf. Mt. 22:23-33; Mk. 12:18-27 & Lu. 20:27-40] Their query to Jesus was this: Whose wife will she be when all are reunited in Heaven? Jesus' response was that men and women in Heaven will not remain married; *"they will be as angels in heaven and will not marry."* [Mt. 22:30; Ref. Mk. 12:25 & Lu. 20:35]

This little vignette has ever expanding implications for the proposition of resurrection and eternal life in Heaven. The first that comes to mind is: What will be our emotional state? Will we experience love? Will we love God alone and become completely impassive to every other spirit, or body, or to whatever alternate form our existence is manifested? Will each entity in Heaven love every other entity in Heaven equally? Will they then hate those whose destination is Hell? Will they pity the Hell-tormented souls, or will the saved reason that the damned are justly reaping their deserved punishment? Will they even be aware of those in eternal damnation?

The recollection of my boyhood religion lessons recalls to me that families will, indeed, be reunited in Heaven. Yet, the words of Jesus seem to repudiate this teaching from my youth. Somehow the thought of the loss or absence of all familial bonds dims the luster of Heaven for me. Moreover, I fully recognize that if I love someone more, then as a direct consequence, I must love another less. Perhaps this logic questions the grandest supposition of Heaven: we will all love one another with sublime equanimity! At first thought, this notion is spirit ennobling. Still, a nagging contradiction intrinsically attends this notion.

Doesn't perfect love imply the presence of unmitigated hate also? Anyone, or anything, excluded from that perfect love would make that point. Worse still, would be the thought of an endless array of mesmerized robot-like persons bumbling aimlessly through Heaven hugging perfunctorily anyone they chanced to collide with. Simultaneously, their mouths would continuously voice the phrase "I love you," in soporific monotone.

What I am attempting to define is the pointlessness of boundless love. How can you express love to another spirit? Although an emotion is a state of mind, any emotion can only be communicated to another being through verbalization, facial expression, or physical posture. Take the example of a statue: Does a statue possess emotions? No, of course not! Still, can a statue express emotion? Undeniably, yes! A statue of the Blessed Mother, smiling with her palms open and her arms extended slightly forward of her body, surely conveys the idea of welcome friendliness, even affection! The statue of a black man with a grimace on his face, and a clenched fist raised high above his head, imparts a perception of defiance and rage. The world famous sculpture "The Thinker" accurately projects the notion of a deeply thoughtful person, and therein, resides the genesis of its renown.

How is it that an object incapable of experiencing emotion can convey the implication of an emotion? The answer lies in the depths of mental perception, which (conjecturally) predates the evolution of vocal language. One can readily verify the communicative capabilities of species far removed from the human evolutionary line. Any life form capable of recognizing another life form as a separate entity can communicate on an elementary level through a phenomenon known as body language. Certain actions performed under specific circumstances produce intelligible information to all cognitive observers. We needn't delve too deeply into this matter here, so long as you agree that essentially this is true.

Concerning statues, manifestly, there can be no actual action performed. Yet, no matter how we posed our statue, some action would be implied. It is the implied action that fosters the intimation of an emotion. In Heaven, how will the idea of love be conveyed? What action, or implied action, will God perform to manifest His love? More importantly, how will our souls, or spirits, or resurrected bodies manifest our love for God, and for one another? Will we all be caught up in some communal act of mental telepathy? Right this moment; try to conjure up feelings of love or happiness. The thought is impossible to sustain, or perhaps even to form, without relating the feeling to a past or to a projected future joyful event, or to a revered person.

Openly, what I am stating here is that even mental attitudes, i.e., our emotions, are dependent upon physical stimuli to maintain their existence. An actual spiritual world is not only unquestionably beyond the attainment of human beings, it is beyond their ken. It is beyond ever knowing short of truly being spiritually present in Heaven! Previously, I believe that I demolished the preposterous notion of a physical resurrection. Now I believe I have likewise demolished the equally preposterous notion of a mental resurrection. So what is left; the liberation of the soul? Pray tell, what is a soul? That which is popularly described as a soul is nothing more than our awareness, which is a function of our physical brain! Souls can't be defined, nor can their presence be confirmed because in reality, Souls don't exist!

Withal, in this discussion of our affections and our emotions, it isn't the broad all-loving/all-encompassing concept that troubles me most. Instead, I ponder the natural affections of human relationships. Do they survive physical death? If husband and wife will no longer be married, does it inevitably follow that mother and father will no longer reserve special love for their children? This must be so if everyone shares a common and identical love for one another. This notion neutralizes the commandment that admonishes us to honor our parents. Honor is defined as respect, and conveys the idea of unique distinction; that is, deference shown to one person that exceeds that shown to all (or a majority) of our other acquaintances.

A place where parents lose the personalized affection for their children (and *vice versa*) seems to me, to be an emotionally barren environment. It isn't a happy place, but merely a neutral place stoically devoid of all sentimentality or emotion. Jesus said that men and women wouldn't be united in marriage in Heaven; will they remember to whom they were married? Will they recall any of the happier moments of their shared life? Returning to mothers and fathers: Will Heaven-bound children know who their parents were while they lived on earth?

Another specific question about souls in Heaven involves the case of a human being who dies in infancy. At what emotional level will the infant's soul enter Heaven? Will the soul reach Heaven with infantile intelligence? No, surely the soul is created fully matured, or else Heaven would need soul baby-sitters to watch over a deceased infant's soul until it reached adulthood. Conversely, is it possible to conceptualize an adult soul saddled with a child's mind for eleven or more years of human mental maturation?

Comprehend this: The closer we scrutinize Heaven, the more bizarre and grotesque the entire concept becomes? In actuality, Heaven lies outside the realm of any experience we humans can envision. The nature of existence in Heaven is entirely foreign, and to me, it is an inscrutable abstraction. It is really silly to discuss living in Heaven for there is no comparability between the meaning of 'living' as applied to Heaven, and the meaning of 'living' when relating to human earthly existence. The muddled theology (religiology?) that embodies the compost of Christianity is mind boggling. The full spectrum of sacrosanct (religious) beliefs is so multifaceted, so profuse, so diverse, so confused, so ill-occasioned and adolescent that it virtually confounds intelligent rebuttal.

The tenets of bodily resurrection and the existence of a soul entity are prime examples of the incongruity of religiosity. A resurrected body only makes sense in a physical world, and an immortal soul only becomes intelligible in a spiritual world. Which are we destined for? We positively can't have both! The concept of 'spirit' is irreconcilably opposed to, and a negation of, 'body.' A squared circle is a familiar metaphor. Less familiar, but equally contradictory is the elevation of a mortal man (Jesus) to the Supreme Godhood.

Theologians wisely postulate 'God' as the uncreated, ever-present entity responsible for all of creation. They couldn't do otherwise. God can't ever have been absent from the Universe. The dogma declares that God always was and always will be. No one should quibble with that postulate; it is impeccable. If God exists today, He must have existed always. What this book offers is the conclusion that the creative impetus of the Universe isn't a personal Divinity. Christianity proffers the opposite, and they offer Jesus as proof. Yet, Jesus was a man; He was made of flesh and blood; He had a mother, and her body produced an ovum that became impregnated, multiplied, and diversified into the human being we call Jesus. Jesus, therefore, had a beginning! This reality, all other arguments notwithstanding, precludes Jesus from the Godhead. We can hypothesize; we can philosophize; and we can allegorize; but in the end we must all realize; Jesus cannot be an actual Son of God!

MORE ABOUT THE SOUL

A soul, if such existed, would be unknowable, inconceivable, and unsuspected! Yet, we all know we possess a soul. Don't we? How do we know each of us inherited a soul at birth? We know of soul only because philosophers, through the ages, have told us we all own a soul. Perhaps more accurately, I should write that a soul possesses us, for that seems to be more the case than the reverse. The concept of soul appears to have existed before the advent of written history. Indeed, primitive cultures that lack writing do have vague notions about the existence of soul. However that may be, the breadth of the soul notion isn't my point here.

What I will dissect, once again, is the manifestation of a soul. How did man come to know of the existence of a soul when a soul has no tangible attributes? Was Divine inspiration the impetus for the ubiquitous incidence of awareness of a soul? The Egyptians knew of soul. So did the American Indians. The natives of Oceania have always had a conception of soul. Historically, the supposed knowledge of soul reality permeated Asia for the past three thousand years at a minimum. Ironically, it is this almost universal perception of a soul that fuels my suspicions that no such entity exists.

As stated previously: As we conceive it, soul is nothing more than singularizing and individualizing our sense of being. Our brain allows us to know ourselves. This awareness is a function of the human mind. Soul isn't a separate entity with a dissociated will of its own. But this is precisely what we try to make it when we extemporize about soul. Linguists tell us that all peoples have a concept of soul. Perceptively, this is so. Yet, I wonder: is it so? If a soul is truly only our recognition of personality, then surely we all possess a soul for we all are aware of our own uniqueness and individuality. But this isn't how the Greek philosophers have defined soul for us.

Primitive people, and all people for that matter, recognize individual persons. They look and see that others are vigorous and cognizant, just as they themselves are. Then one tragic day this other person ceases to interact. Why? How can this happen? One minute a person is vibrant and warm; the next moment he or she is cold and dead. This isn't logical! Especially when the observer looks and notes that the deceased person still has an intact body. How can eyes that once saw, stop seeing? How can a mouth that once talked, lose this ability so mysteriously? How can a loving mother so caring in a yesterday, be so lifeless today? Death is, and will ever remain, as perplexing as it is frightening. Even to an untutored mind, the absence of life where life once existed compels elucidation, if not comprehensive explanation.

Obviously, some invisible essence, which once animated the living body, is absent from a dead body. This thought makes sense, and only this hypothesis makes sense. We call this invisible essence by the name of soul. The theory of soul is intriguing. But then, too, so is the theory of a personal God. Both theories, however, are mistaken. Anticipating an objection here, I will ask myself what proof have I that the theory of soul is false? The reply: None that would satisfy an ardent religionist. But I think I can demonstrate that there is no proof for the existence of a soul either.

Now I ask: what proofs have we that humans are actuated by a soul? As with all facets of religiosity, soul is not a fact, but is a premise. We surmise soul. A book excerpted from the writing of selected medieval religious philosophers will provide an example of the utter foolishness of any attempt to delineate the functioning of a soul. The author of the book, The Age of Belief, quotes a Father Christopher Devlin, S.J., who has made a "brilliant comparison" {sic} between St. Thomas Aquinas and Duns Scotus. (These two are medieval religious theoreticians.)

The following are quotes from Father Devlin's observations. [London Aquinas Society, March 15, 1950] "There is a power of the soul which is below understanding, but which has better evidence of the soul's origin…." What does Father Devlin mean when he states that a power of the soul is below understanding? What is this power of the soul which has better evidence of the soul's origin? How do souls originate? The man is babbling intellectually. The conclusion of the above quote is similarly rendered unintelligibly, "… and there is a power of the soul which is above understanding and which is more in touch with the soul's destiny."

From my studies, I have concluded that the only possible destiny for a human soul is either Heaven or Hell. But not both! Father Devlin declares that an unspecified power of the soul is more in touch with either Heaven or Hell. Wonderful! How does a power keep "more in touch"? A power is a potential for activity, and not directly an action in or of itself. Is he saying that your soul extends its boundaries right into Hell or Heaven? Does it touch both destinies simultaneously? Or does the individual soul merely keep in touch with its predetermined destination? If the latter were so, I would suppose my soul to be in constant touch with Hell. Yet, I can't factually aver this for Father Devlin has stated that such a power is above understanding. What is the difference between a power that is "above understanding," and a power that is "below understanding"? What affinities do the above have to a power that is 'inside' understanding; or 'outside' understanding? Or even 'astride' understanding?

Here is still another pedantic inanity culled from Father Devlin's 'brilliant comparison.' {sic} "The human soul is not co-extensive with reason or understanding …." The definition of the word 'co-extensive' follows: "Extending through the same space or time." Father Devlin is telling us that our soul isn't the same faculty we call reason. It is pertinent that he thought it necessary to make this distinction for, by his observation, he indicates that many people do equate the soul with the functioning of the mind. He, privy to some secret repository of knowledge, disabuses us of our erroneous assumption.

The soul is the repository of our ethical standards, as Father Devlin would declare. Can't he see that all he is accomplishing is inserting an intermediary where none is required? If the soul is separate and distinct from the mind: Who am I? Where (or what) is the ineffable essence that comprises selfness? My mind tells me that I am me. My reasoning and my understanding are the source of my awareness of self. If my soul is other than a reflection of my mind, then my soul must be likened to some parasitic appendage attached to my mind. The soul then becomes only an advisor to my brain, and an inept one at that.

Expounders of religious mystispeak, such as Father Devlin and his idol, St. Thomas Aquinas, are the real Grand Masters of Deceit. Their metaphysical prose is more akin to science-fiction writers than to supernatural expounders. If one shields his mental gaze from the dazzlement of their misapplied words, then their speech comes up barren. "Above understanding" and "below understanding" both have the same meaning. They translate to "beyond understanding." When you say something is beyond understanding you are saying that it can't be understood. Yet, Father Devlin would have us believe that he fully understands the powers of the soul. What Father in effect is saying is that intimate knowledge of the soul is beyond the powers of discernment of the vast doltish majority. He fully understands soul. But for the remainder of humanity the knowledge of soul confounds our intellectual infirmity; therefore, his enlightenment is tendered!

The author of the book wherein Father Devlin's quotes are contained describes his words as "brilliant." The word brilliant has several meanings, one of which is 'blinding.' This is the sense of the word I would apply to his exposition on the soul. The brilliance of his soul postulates is so intimidating that we daren't admit that they don't contain a shred of intelligible data. The only way one can possibly evaluate his thesis is to first shade your mind's eye from the overall glare of the totality. Once we are able to examine the components of his postulations separately, we can begin to denounce them individually. Only in this manner can we arrive at the reality (or lack thereof!) of soul. The brilliance of Father Devlin's dissertation doesn't shed enlightenment; instead, it only creates a loquacious maze that is nearly impossible to navigate.

His words bewilder our intellect. How can a spirit entity be "in touch" with anything? The man is prattling obliquely with language. His definition of soul exactly parallels the explanation of a surrealistic artist's painting; i.e., 'Much ado about nothing!' There is a story extant about an artwork that was fashioned by a chimpanzee that won a prize at an exhibition. After viewing some of that which passes as art today, I can believe the story.

On a trip to the University of Oklahoma during the 1970s, I was fortunate enough to arrive in time for a student art exhibit. One especially large canvas appeared to have had six different colors of house paint poured (or splashed) onto the canvas in a rather haphazard manner. The artist, standing proudly nearby, was asked how his creation was fashioned. His reply didn't amaze anyone: He took house paint and poured it onto the canvas. But, he explained in utmost solemnity, the pouring wasn't done without forethought. The flow of each color was in a different direction. (Each color was allowed to dry before the next was added?) The painting had a subliminal meaning that artistically represented the flowing of life's gravitational pulls on a human being, first in one direction, then in another. The painting was a symbolic icon of the artist's life. How unenlightened of me not to have discerned this myself!

No doubt Father Devlin could likewise explain his "above" and "below" understanding of soul. Perhaps one day he did tell us just what this power of the soul is, which has "better evidence of the soul's origin." The more I study his elucidation on the soul, the less sense he makes. His statements are brimming over with inference, yet are absolutely devoid of truly sensible meaning. Frankly, I don't have the vaguest specific understanding of what he is averring. But I am forced to grant that he has presented his exposition profoundly. Without further comment I think we can dismiss Father Devlin's speculations about the soul.

Are you convinced that no such entity exists? If not, ask yourself just what a soul is? What does it do? What role does it play in your life? Why do we have a soul? Why don't all living creatures have a soul? Is soul responsible for good behavior or bad behavior? Is soul an advisor or an observer? Is my spirit the same entity as my soul? Did Jesus have a soul? Is the Holy Spirit the soul of God? What is my soul doing while I am asleep? When was my soul born? Can my soul leave my body while I am still alive? Why or why not? Are there souls in Hell without bodies? Are there such in Heaven? Does an infant's soul have an adult awareness of life, or an infantile awareness? At what age does a soul become accountable for the sins of its owner? Does a soul exercise any control over a brain? Is a soul a complete confidante of the brain? Does a soul know everything the brain knows? When a person forgets, does his soul forget also? When a person becomes drunk, does his soul remain sober? When an old person becomes senescent, does his soul remain lucid? What affinity exists, if any, between a soul and the mind? Can a soul be more knowledgeable than the brain? Can souls communicate with one another? Do you know any more about soul now than you did previously? "Neither do I."

This segment is herewith ended.

FINAL THOUGHT ON SOUL

Indulging in religiosity is somewhat akin to participating in a giant lottery. In his/her 'heart,' everyone knows there is almost no chance of winning a Million dollar lottery. But 'why quibble'? If the cost isn't too high, they take a chance. The alternative, to refuse to pay the ticket price, only guarantees that you won't win the millionaire lottery.

Perhaps there is a third alternative in life, and if so, that is what this book should be presenting. Maybe we humans can achieve Utopia. But if I am correct about the falsity of a life hereafter and the fabrication of a personal Deity, then our Garden of Eden will have to be found here on Earth. We are going to have to search for it with our intellect, not with our imagination. Supernaturalism and religiosity have detoured mankind in its quest for Arcadia. (An imaginary place) We have opened our eyes to the faux light of spirituality; or rather the opposite! We have closed our eyes to firm reality, and permitted our imagination to entice us into embracing fantastic longings.

The real instigation toward religiosity is a subliminal compulsion to recoup the recalled security and carefree happiness of our early child-hood. Heaven represents the haven that was our early home. God is the Invincible Father who shields us from all harm. Young children visualize their home as an impenetrable fortress, and their father as an all-powerful protector. So long as this supposition remains untested, the illusion can be maintained. Adults pleasure their fancies with the same mendacious day-dreaming. The (imagined) protective power of the Shroud of Turin gives an example. Good luck charms and bad luck taboos are also representa-tive. Does one literally "break his mother's back by stepping on a crack"? How do such beliefs come into vogue? The resolution of the last presented question can be an important step toward understanding the origins of religiosity, which is only 'superstitions about gods.'

First, I ask: Do broken mirrors cause bad luck? Please answer "yes," for the sake of developing an argument. How can a mirror affect any external occurrence? Does God act in retaliation for the mirror? Is it the Devil who avenges the mirror? Who, then, or what, is the impetus for the misfortune imputed to shattered mirrors? Okay, you can change your response to "No" now, for the truth is that broken mirrors cause no more misfortune than do open umbrellas, spilled salt, or meandering black cats.

Yet, it isn't the nature of the superstition, but its cause that con-cerns me. How do groundless superstitions arise? If God doesn't imbue us with these false notions and neither does the Devil, then who does? I believe those notions are formed unaided in the imagination of man. All superstitions are man-made, and can only flourish in a growth medium of adopted ignorance. The notion of soul is a superstition!

Originally the soul was inferred to be the life-sustaining force within a human body. Later, it was pictured as the spiritual essence of self. Today we talk of soul as if it was an invisible internal organ of the human body that exudes moral principles into our consciousness. Yet, if the soul is the source of our morality and ethics, why then does acceptable behavior vary so greatly between one person and another person? Why are our children completely without ethics until first we propagandize them, and then indoctrinate them? Are there different types of soul just as there are different types of people? The closer one looks at a soul, the less distinct it becomes. And, if one looks more searchingly, a soul completely disappears!

CHAPTER 20
Rationalizing A Deity

QUESTING INDIVIDUALS
REQUIRE A CREATOR GOD

The Universe is proposed by some and accepted by others to be proof of a Creator God. The majesty and incomprehensibility of the universe would seem by many to insist upon an equally majestic and incomprehensible Creator. Yet, is there wisdom in this view point? "No" with resounding emphasis! The Universe is neither majestic, nor is it incomprehensible. Perhaps I should qualify this last statement.

The universe is vast and encompasses many diverse aspects, but majesty, to me, implies dignity, authority and splendor … these the universe undeniably lacks. The universe is decidedly impersonal. The chaos of matter that comprises the universe is anything but dignified. The splendor of its appearance resides only in the perception of a euphoric beholder. For mankind, the reality is that the universe is nothing more than an endless profusion of lights in random disarray, sprinkled ubiquitously throughout its visible entirety.

The dearth of knowledge about the universe is awe inspiring to a religionist, while to an astrophysicist that dearth is an intriguing challenge. What is the present state of knowledge about our universe? It is considerably greater than religionists would wish, and considerably less than our questing scientists would be satisfied with. Our preliminary knowledge is quite comprehensive, while our total knowledge is tantalizingly incomplete.

For those who have reservations about accepting the most previous statement, allow me suggest that they visit their nearest magazine store and ask the clerk for the latest publications dealing with theoretical astronomy. I'm certain they will be shockingly surprised at the recent advances in this field. The Universe is becoming minimally less incomprehensible every year.

Another supposed proof of a Creator is the beauty and symmetry of a wild flower. 'Truth equals Honesty' – 'Honesty equals Truth.' Many of the life forms in the plant kingdom are indeed beautiful, and part of their beauty is caused by their color and their symmetry. Yet, isn't the splendor of the plant world tempered by the grotesqueness of an overgrown impenetrable jungle? Some plant forms are undisputed eyesores. Florists know that not all plant forms are beauteous, but choosing intelligently which to offer for sale can be lucrative.

Having spent fifteen days at sea crossing the Pacific Ocean I can personally attest to the magnificence and silent sublimity of ocean view sunsets. Each night's solar descent surpassed the previous night's panorama. What a spectacle to behold! Was a personal Creator responsible for this meteorological elegance? If He was, then He was equally responsible for that rainy, overcast day when the sun didn't shine through even once. He can also be faulted for the violent midnight storm that tossed and slammed our ship so fearfully that almost everyone aboard became disgustingly ill. Attributing kaleidoscope-like sunsets to an artistic Creator is nothing but selective attribution of human aesthetics, applied to dispassionate nature personified into a beneficent supernatural being (God).

The viability and apparent balance of nature in the animal world is often advanced as proof of a watchful and provident Creator. Is this ascription factual? Once again the lamentable yet truthful answer is negative. The apparent balance of nature is only that, apparent! On a random day or during a limited observation period, nature in the animate category may appear to be in balance. However in long range, the very opposite is the actuality. Each organism strives to meet its own needs to the total disregard of its neighbor, whether the neighbor is a competitor or an ally, or a disengaged third party.

Environmental changes that favor one species or flora invariably disfavor another species or flora. This is a causal factor in evolution that has resulted in elimination of some life forms and proliferation of other life forms. Nature at work is an inscrutable taskmaster; therefore, when we personalize nature into the aspect of a deity (God) we are enormously taxed to reconcile nature's impersonal harshness, with a loving Creator's fancied benevolence. The dilemma created by personalizing nature is that no sense can be made of nature's arbitrary actions; whereas all of God's actions are presumed (professed) to be sensible, intellectual, and beneficial!

What other proof have we that a personal Creator exists? Well, we have the written words of God found in the Bible. We know that the Bible contains the words of God because the word of man states that this is so. Make no mistake about this; even if the Bible is one hundred percent (100%) truth, it isn't the "Word of God," it is merely the words of man purported to be the words of God. This may be a bit confusing to grasp at first reading so I will restate. God never wrote anything Himself save the tablets recording the Ten Commandments. The Bible informs us (indirectly) that these two stone tablets disappeared eons ago and no longer can be proffered as proof. This raises the engendered question of why God provided the tablets at all. But that's another matter.

Jesus never personally composed anything, consequently we don't have any writings of His either._We can and do postulate divine inspiration of the Bible's content, but how can we prove divine inspiration? We can't! We must accept the word of man that the entire Bible contains only the words of God. Our assent to that declaration requires that we absolve the multiple authors from all deceit, delusion, error, and self-intrusion. The human author becomes solely God's automaton; anything less will tarnish the hallowed image of the Bible. Written otherwise, 'we must have faith.' Not faith in the absence of evidence; but faith contrary to the evidence. Now that you have read thus far into this composition, you are aware of the vast array of evidence which refutes the Bible's claim of supernatural inspiration, plus its allegation of divine truth.

Objectively weighed, the only substantive proof of the existence of a Creator is the number of persons who believe in Him. Unquestionably, this evidence is decidedly circumstantial and totally subjective. Here, I'll deal with the number factor, not because I myself am impressed by the tally, but because so many others are swayed by this actuality. In reflection, who can deny that a majority of his contemporaries disagreed with Columbus about the shape of the earth? Throughout the world, Christians are outnumbered by non-Christians. Does this prove that Jesus the Hebrew Messiah was false?

The opinions of the many aren't validated simply by their number. Historically, the opposite often has proved to be the case. Sometimes a majority will form an opinion on a debatable subject; then later, their consensus is discovered to have been faulty. Religiosity is mankind's most pervasive and most pernicious fiction. The quantity of adherents to a belief indicates only the extent of the propagation of that belief, not its verity. What disturbs me personally is not the quantity, but the quality of some of the believers in supernaturalism (deities). More than one religionist was an exceptionally intelligent person. How can this be if intelligence dispels superstition, while ubiquitous religion embodies only ritualized superstition?

The answer to this conundrum isn't facile, but I've given this matter a great deal of reflection. I have reached a provisional resolution. The solution involves the interplay of emotions and intellect. Whereas no one is completely devoid of emotion, contrariwise, no one is completely endowed with flawless intellect. Intelligent people can be blinded by their emotions just as readily, if not as often, as are median level intelligence individuals. It requires a modest intellectual attainment to even grasp the intricacies of religiosity above its primary level.

Mysticism (aka religion) endues believers with reliance beyond self to attain personal goals ostensibly not readily attainable otherwise. For this reason many intelligent individuals are attracted to transcendental meditation and similar mind-straining disciplines. They disdain that which comes easily (for instance, everyday human activities), and direct their energies to the more difficult undertaking of achieving mental 'Nirvana' through rigorous religiosity.

My mind recalls an accomplished debater bragging once that he could argue either side of any proposition and prevail each time. I believed him. Yet, what does this convey toward the validity of either argument? The super intelligent probably choose a contestable position on the basis of loyalty or convenience, and then champion that position to the best of their enhanced mental capacity.

A Sports fan engages his loyalty similarly. Few fans profit from the fortunes of their chosen team because League championships are decided by elimination of all teams but one. Therefore, the perennial fan is many times more apt to back a losing team than the winning team. This doesn't deter faithful followers. It just may 'fire' their desire to 'back' the home team more devotedly. What I am saying here is this: intelligent proponents of religion may not be the ardent supporters that they appear to be at first. They may instead only be exercising their talents to spur their chosen team toward victory irrespective of the worthiness or deservedness of that team (his or her religion, is an alternate advocacy).

The intellectual person is mentally self-reassured, thereby invigorated, while defining and defending his chosen beliefs. It's not so much that the type of individual under dissection is intellectually dishonest. But rather, he is conventionally practical. After all, you lose nothing by believing in a God who doesn't exist. However, the reverse is quite another matter. If this isn't reason enough, then there are other, more immediate, compensations for active participation in religious organizations. For one, there is the camaraderie of the group; prestige positions to be held; and the esteem of the group for services rendered to the group.

High intellect individuals are generally high achievers in whatever their endeavor. Institutional religions offer a convenient vehicle for social advancement. Atheism has few honorific positions to award. Overall perhaps, intellectuals in their superior wisdom recognize that organized religion "elicits public respect," … socially considered. There is an undercurrent of hypocrisy within this hypothesis. Yet, I propose a lack of willful deceit in my explication, and propound instead merely expedient opportunism. Gifted people have something to offer to humanity, and if humanity chooses the gift of a personal deity (a Creator), why not give this to them? Where's the harm?

I think they are wrong to pamper the essentially juvenile wishes of the nondescript majority. I think they should speak out and denounce the sham notion of a personal God. I think they should utilize their mental prowess to expose religiosity for the farce that it is. I reason that the world would then begin moving toward cultural adulthood, and commence establishing our rightful niche in the universe. "I reason." But I am not positive! Who can be certain of a celestial future that hasn't had a comparable past that informs?

The world needs intelligent management. If we offer the management positions to the gifted, I think they'll accept the offer and provide the depth of perception missing in our present-day leadership. The problem of enticing mental heavyweights into leadership roles belongs in its own book and won't be pursued further within these pages.

The one thing that mortals can depend upon is that they must learn to depend upon themselves. 'Heaven help us' is an oft expressed plaint, yet if we can learn from past experiences, we'll realize that Heaven must be stone deaf. Time spent praying should be more profitably spent pondering, and then doing!

It matters little what the magnetism of religiosity is that attracts and binds demonstrably intelligent persons. What matters is that we all permit an open and frank exhibition of the "cons" refuting the possibility of a cognitive creative entity. We all have been overwhelmed with the "pro" side of this proposition. All the atheists in the world, mobbed as one, would be no match for a living, acting God. But if God truly is dead, then let's bury Him. Decent people should do no less.

There is an unarticulated bevy of benefits awaiting mankind if we can only shed our anti-intellectual bias. There isn't a doctrine propounded on earth that is too sacrosanct for intelligent scrutiny. This of course doesn't grant license to those who senselessly disrespect and dishonor all that others cherish. I'm referring to the level of mentality that causes someone to sew an American flag onto the seat of their pants, and similar types of petulant behavior.

Not that the flag is intrinsically superior to any other cloth object, but because we do pay homage to objective symbols. More importantly: so do most others around the world. Disrespect for the symbolism of Americanism can only foster disrespect for our nation throughout the world. My goal is not to abolish respect for all national symbols, but to redirect much respect onto worthy objects and deserving national symbols. We always must consider how a given action, or lack of an expected action, is interpreted by others.

For me, there is no personal God; consequently, all personalized religions are false. Nor do I believe in philosophies dependent upon mind exercising gymnastics to give them an aura of reality. Still, many others hold dear those disciplines. What is accomplished if I ridicule the beliefs of others? Would I win many adherents to my position? Never! Ridicule and scorn are emotional responses, just as worship and adoration are. If mankind is ever to develop to full intellectual maturity, we are going to have to suppress many of our human emotions, never indulge them.

All acts of obeisance have their origins in emotionality. Professing God as our father concomitantly places us into the category of dependent children. The father/child analogy is misapplied anyway. If it was valid, we still should be striving to accomplish on our own, all that our biological father did for us during our inabilities as a child. The objective of parenthood isn't to imbue permanent dependence; but rather, to guide toward total independence. Adults should be able to think, and to act, entirely of their own volition.

Fervently held convictions which dictate priggish social behavior, create cultural invalids. The pious regimen of Judaism was stifling to Paul, and may well have been the impetus for his simplistic requirements for his Gentile converts. Believe that Jesus was the Christ (Messiah) whom God resurrected, and you will be resurrected in Christ. The first Christian converts, Jews primarily, may have been disaffected from the leaders of their Jewish religion; but few were ready to disavow the religion of Judaism. Paul's liberal doctrines led to a showdown with the head (leader) of the infant Christian church organization; James, the brother of Jesus. Ultimately, James conceded that the only impositions on Paul's converts be to refrain from immorality; not to eat food that was offered to idols; not to eat the flesh of an animal that had been strangled; to forbid consuming 'blood'; and lastly from "fornication." These modified "Laws" are recorded in The Acts of the Apostles. [Cf. Acts 15:20, 29]

FAITH DOCTRINES INDISPENSABLE
TO CHRISTIANITY

I sometimes wonder what the result would be if all Christian leaders were asked to compile a list of ten faith doctrines that they deemed indispensable to Christian belief. Each individual leader's list would then be exchanged with a peer, within his own Christian sect, for approval or disapproval, or for emendation. What would be the result of this exchange?

My point is this: once one gets beyond the basics of belief in the divinity of Jesus, His Resurrection, and a scant few other dogmas, the individual beliefs would become so irrational and exotic that a moderator would be strained to find any two leaders in total agreement. Further, a composite list of all those enumerated beliefs would be so incoherent and irreconcilable that the whole would be risible. All "Religion" could then be defined as 'Human confusion, expressed as an illusion, to honor a delusion.'

Returning to Origen (discussed in Chapter 16), he earns my respect for his studied beliefs. The story of the demons and the herd of swine, according to Matthew, Mark & Luke took place in Gadara ("territory of the Gadarenes"), in Gerasa ("territory of the Gerasenes"), or Gergesa ('territory of the Gergesenes"), but not respectively. [Ref. Mt. 8:28; Mk. 5:1 & Lu. 8:26] Depending on which translation version one consults all three of those towns are mentioned by each Evangelist interchangeably. To elaborate on the confusion of location, read a footnote in Matthew from The New Oxford Annotated Bible, New Revised Standard Version.*

*Other ancient authorities read Gergesenes; others, Gerasenes. {Mt. 8:28 reads "Gadarenes"}

The Catholic Confraternity edition emends their gospels (erringly according to Origen) so that all three read "Gerasenes." (John does not report the incident of the demons and the swine.) Origen trusted that the Evangelists knew the topography of the area of the swine incident. He believed that those writers hadn't lied or become confused. His research disclosed the following: "Gerasa is a city in Arabia in the vicinity of neither a sea nor a lake; likewise, 'near Gadara there is neither a lake nor a cliff." Origen, presumably from his own findings, corrected his copies of the Gospels to read "Gergesa," a town on the Sea of Galilee with a nearby cliff. In the Good News version of the Gospels only Luke locates the expulsion of the demons in Gergesa. So, factually, we cannot verify exactly where the demons were expelled into a herd of swine by Jesus.

Origen's investigations seem to indicate that he felt faith alone shouldn't authenticate the Gospels. Origen attempted to personally verify those portions of the Gospels that were liable to proof. But alas, Origen stumbles all too often as he tries to carry Jesus' cross for him. Defending the inaccuracies and the demonstrable falsehoods in the Gospels is a hopeless task. Making allowance for copyist's interpolations, the gospels are still recognizable for what they truly are, viz., imperfect human recollections copiously glorified by overzealous proponents of the cult of Jesus. Their zeal may be commendable, but their accuracy is reprehensible. Origen's attempts to rectify the disparity between the Evangelists' accounts is commendable, and as in Gergesa, successful at times. Still, more often he trips. This fault lies with the stories however, and not with Origen's efforts.

An Early anti-Christian writer, Celsus, author of "True Discourse" pointed out, among other things, that God Jesus could hardly have suffered pain in the Garden of Gethsemane, or via His maltreatment by the Roman soldiers, or on the cross. Origen, in his refutation titled 'Contra Celsum," replies that "Jesus assumed with the body also its pains and griefs." Origen's argument sounds plausible. But the Evangelists themselves refute him.

Didn't Jesus know He was the Son of God? Did he ever lack the ability to instantly extricate Himself from any situation? [As in Jn. 8:59] Wasn't He aware of the full extent and duration of His suffering? God's reputed omniscience erects a barrier between mortal and immortal that is insurmountable. Pain suffered in assent, even if hesitantly or grudgingly, doesn't approach the trauma of pain inflicted upon us against our will. The curative torments wrought upon patients in a modern hospital are no less excruciating than is the involuntary agony of a street mugging. Yet the perceived difference is enormous.

God in the Second Person suffering death is in no way comparable to a human being suffering death. The dogma of Jesus Christ's purported Godhood is indefensible, even for a scholar of Origen's competence. A millionaire who chooses to live a few weeks in the slums doesn't experience the same desolation as the true derelict. Nor can he ever, so long as he remains an actual millionaire. The identical reasoning applies to God Jesus. Deprivation without despair loses much, if not the entirety, of its empathetic impact. The key differences being: personal control, and precise foreknowledge of the future.

If Christianity is truth, then Jesus knew unreservedly that His death on the cross wasn't death as we humans perceive it. Our fear, not to invoke the ineffable terror of death that continually haunts us, originates precisely because we do not know what lies beyond this life ... if anything? I believe I do know, and the finality of this knowledge induces in me the emotion of maudlin despair. If I ponder death, my senses tell me that my body will decay, including my brain, and that no one alive will ever be able to communicate with me again. 'Not my loved ones; not my enemies; not the Pope; not the President; not the world's greatest scientist, nor even the world's most adept psychic.

A religionist, reading the preceding paragraphs, would be volatile with his solution to my dilemma. 'You've got to have faith' would be his insistent rejoinder. Yet it should be obvious that I have no faith. Nor do I believe it would avail me if I did. Castles in the sky (i.e., heaven) can be imagined, but never lived in.

WHY MUST WE HAVE A DEITY?

Does God exist only because we want Him to exist? Grant that there is a personal Divinity. 'Proving what? What does the existence of an invisible otherworldly being prove to you and me, or to anyone? Absolutely nothing; unless His existence has an impact on our lives!

A distant, unreachable, impersonal cosmic Deity who can only be perceived esoterically is relevant only to theologians, scholars, pedants and the self-deluded. The average person couldn't care less contemplating a Spiritual Being that, through personal preference, remained 'incommunicado' for all eternity. An intellectual Deity, having once defined all the laws of nature, that kept Himself wholly aloof from interactions with His created entirety, would induce nothing but indifference from mankind (not to discount scorn and disbelief!). His inaccessibility would have been (and frankly continues to be) the genesis of beliefs now classified as polytheism, pantheism, absurdism and even atheism.

For a god to have any measure of relevancy, He must be close. He must be approachable. He must be manageable. That is, one must imagine he is able to alter the temperament and influence the actions of his personal Divinity. We don't often speculate on the negative aspect of a proposition, but here, we should! Every positive has a negative. For example, take prayer directed to our Heavenly Father. We all know that God hears the prayers of those who petition Him unselfishly. But what of those who don't petition God for their needs? Does God simply take no notice of their presence on Earth? Or problematically: does He afflict them with misfortune, or thwart their every plan? Have you ever heard a preacher expound on what 'The Heavenly Father' does to those who refuse to pray? I have never heard such!

Once, on a U.H.F. television outlet in my city, I heard a televangelist soliciting tithes from his audience. (A tithe being understood as a tenth of a person's wealth or wages) This minister was emphatic in his declaration: "If you will pay your tithes faithfully, God will reward you one hundred-fold." How magnanimous of God to be so extravagant. (If this was factual)

Just then a toll-free number was superimposed at the bottom of the screen for the viewers to call in their pledges of support money. As I watched and listened, a scampish thought formed in my brain. (At the instigation of the Devil, undoubtedly) Suppose I called and instructed that minister to send ten percent of his collections to some other preacher so that God could return his ten percent investment one hundred-fold? Thereafter, the recipient preacher send his ten percent to a third preacher, each preacher sends his ten percent to another preacher, and continuing until all preachers receive 100% of their monetary needs from the provident Universal Deity. What a bountiful way to accumulate funds for God's work! I dismissed the impulse immediately, for I have no desire to ridicule any religion specifically. This television preacher wasn't an abject liar. The probability is that he believed his own preaching as deeply as he believed in the Bible. But again I ask, "Why is there belief in a personal God?" Obviously and exclusively: because humanity universally wants one to exist!'

Why send money to some stranger about whom you factually know almost nothing? The apparent explanation is: "If God truly exists, this will please Him!" We all hope that our good deeds do earn us some beneficence from the Universal Ruler in Heaven. Emotionally, we are joyous over our persona when we convince ourselves that God admires us personally!

On that night, the preacher's chief concern was the current impasse in the matter of abortion. He made an eloquent appeal on behalf of the right of an unborn child to life. His arguments were unassailable until he progressed onto the proposition that God creates each of us as a purposeful act. The counter argument is that a woman who knows she is going to birth a piteously deformed child should have the right to abort that child.

He, arguing the opposite point, noted that many outstanding and accomplished persons were born with physical imperfections. 'How deprived the world would have been without these future artisans,' he noted. Yet, another of the postulates favoring abortion posits cases of rape or incest. If, however, God disapproves of both of the aforementioned offenses, why does He initiate the birth process in such instances? The preacher's anti-abortion rebuttal was extraordinarily weak in this case. For God provably sanctions incest and rape if He utilizes these depraved sexual occurrences for the creation of ultimately laudable individuals.

Worthy Christian couples sometimes can't conceive children, and this is credited as God's Will. Well then, so too is the unwanted conception of children in other circumstances. This corollary must be valid, if the preceding premise is true. If it is God's Will that a woman remain barren, then it is likewise His responsibility when any woman becomes pregnant. God creates all of us wittingly and purposely! The rapist should be applauded for abetting God's Will. The incestuous adult should be held in high esteem as the chosen instrument of God's inscrutable designs.

Let this stupidity be damned out of existence, I say. What you are witnessing here is the projection of a fanciful general doctrine (albeit, a pseudo one) onto the exceptional case where its intrinsic absurdity can be readily discerned. The proposition that God is specifically liable for every birth, renders Him specifically accountable for every action that individual performs throughout his lifetime. (Contemplate Dr. Frankenstein's monster!) The growth of an embryo isn't a singular, isolated event. How strong we will be; how tall we will grow; how timid or how aggressive we will be, are all determined by the unique mixture of genes we receive at conception from our two progenitors.

We aren't born as blank pages ready to be filled in by some itinerant preacher or by some sly demonic personage. Scientists can demonstrate that at least fifty percent of our personality is determined by our genes. My own observations indicate to me that the actual figure is closer to eighty percent varying from individual to individual. Throughout history infinitely more men than women have committed wanton murder. Is this because women are holier than men? Or is it because women are less prone genetically to perpetrate violence? No, not holier! But Yes, less violent! Women commit just as many sins (crimes) as do men. But the type of sin they are wont to commit differs from the sins of their male counterparts.

Religionists, in their zeal to credit God with the responsibility for all that eventuates, are forced to contrive the Almighty into becoming a co-conspirator to rape and incest. Everyone concurs that the conception of an especially gifted person is a rational act by God. There is less agreement when one postulates that God is chargeable for the birth of a malformed person who never achieves notoriety, or more detrimentally is a lifelong burden upon society. It should be obvious that God is either wholly responsible for all_occurrences, or He is responsible for none! If man's free will isn't operative at all times, then how is one ever to know when a given result was caused by man's free will, or was caused by God's cryptic manipulation?

A religionist's response is decidedly subjective. They know that if an outcome is detrimental, then Satan masterminded it. If the reverse occurs, then credit is piously attributed to God. The pro and the con of this proposition could probably find a notable consensus. But the vast gray area inherent within this premise is enormous, and it is overwhelming. Indeed, all Christian sects diverge from one another in the indeterminate area of scriptural interpretations. All agree that the Bible is the word of God; their disagreements arose over the precise meaning of His words, which incidentally, witnesses silently yet tellingly against the dogma of the Divine Authorship via Inspiration of the Bible.

This segment began with the question: "Why is there a God?" The answer was: "God is," because man desires Him to be! Here, I ask you to try to visualize a personal God, if you will. This is done quite effortlessly, isn't it? Why is it so easy to picture God? It is so uncomplicated to call up a mental image of God that it causes religionists to regard atheists as pathetically dimwitted. The conceiving of God is so facile for believers that they find it impossible to empathize with non-believers. Yet, this absence of empathy is the barrier that shields religionists from the recognition of their own biased self-delusion.

Atheism isn't founded on ignorance of the arguments that foster the notion of a Superior Entity. I would undertake a wager that ninety-nine percent of all atheists were once at least nominal religionists. Atheists know all the arguments advanced to buttress a Divine Presence. But have you or anyone else ever paused to question why the ever-present, omnipresent, and ever spiritually present Creator of the limitless vastness of the endless Universe, is so readily conceived by humanity? Conceiving God should be impossible. Yet, even small children can visualize God with little to no complexity!

But what is it that believers envision when they conceptualize God? The reply is: "They picture a loving 'Father' capable of protecting His 'children' from every hazard." He is ever capable; but not always willing! No one can state why unequivocally. So, if your real father punishes his children for disobedient behavior, then perhaps the Father God has identical parental instincts. Still, it was/is always comforting to know that no matter what our chronological age, all of us still possessed a loving (though appropriately stern) Spiritual Father.

The 'Father' doctrine is unimpeachable; only the reality dismays us. Cultures differ in many and divers refinements; yet with confidence, I will state that all civilizations have prayed for peace and serenity more often, and more fervently, than any other heavenly gift. Still, this is the petition most frequently denied by God. All things are possible for a Universal Deity. All things save that which His creatures most desire. Namely: "peace on earth!"

What is the most likely rationalization for God's apparent rejection of our most repeated petition? That God is uncaring? That God is perverse? Or, that God is non-existent?

GOD THE ALL-GOOD

If the social conditions that exist today can be credited to a Good Samaritan God, then contemplating what the world would be if a 'Bad God' administered the Earth, sets me awash with dread. Christianity depicts Jesus as a Good Shepherd, and that is reassuring. Yet, this generalization is unsupported by any evidence. Present world conditions belie this reassuring canard. You can forget the past! World history is the greatest single proof extant that exposes as bogus the universal religious doctrine of a benevolent Deity directing or overseeing all human eventualities.

A current fringe extrapolation which postulates that the Devil rules the Earth, while God rules the heavens, is much more palatable to only a less discerning believer. God is thereby absolved of His excesses, and is chargeable simply as disinterested, or as physically impotent. His super powers are restricted exclusively to the spiritual realms. This apologetic is more in agreement with the observations, but is concurrently much less supportive of the indispensable postulation that God cares about us individually, and that He frequently acts benignly on our behalf.

If Satan has unrestricted governance on Earth, then it might behoove the shortsighted to actively court his favor. Logically, it should follow that the Devil will repay homage to himself with material rewards. But this, too, is repudiated by historic retrospection. Satan worshippers have been as beleaguered as have religionists, and by kindred foes: superstition, ignorance, and bigotry!

Gullibility is the greatest sin we mortals can indulge. Believers in the supra-natural are the most persistent of the oppressors of humanity. Logically, realistically, patently: The only way to resolve the discrepancies in the theory of a universal 'Benevolence,' in contradistinction to a universal 'Malevolence,' is to disavow both premises. There is neither Goodness nor Badness in the endless multiplicity of natural occurrences. Nature, not God, is indecipherable, and for a very cogent reason. Nature exploits possibilities randomly; Nature doesn't act consciously. Nature positively doesn't act benevolently, either willfully or accidentally. Nature just happens naturally.

We state that God is All-Good. Why? Isn't it just as likely that any universal Creator will be wicked? Why is it mandatory for God to act philanthropically? Statistically, God could have been evil, or even neutral. How can we be assured that what we perceive as God's actions are unreservedly beneficial? How would a malevolent Deity have acted? God created disease, famine, calamity, and catastrophe. He created an animate world replete with predators, and yet, we insist that this personification is "good." How would an evil God have created? My reasoning tells me that a villainous God would be an opposite of a virtuous God; hence, His manifestations would be reversed. It would be clever to outline here an inverted scenario of human existence on Earth, but I don't feel this is necessary. I am confident you have perceived my gist already.

Intellectually reasoned, a perverse God would have created a planet similar to the one we live on, if not the identical. Our presumption of the Goodness of God is as deficient as is every other laudatory surmise we make about our unseen and unverified Creator. After having read the fore-going, a person may be motivated to ask if God isn't really evil because of the ubiquity of maladies that abound on the Earth, along with an endless profusion of predators. Allow me to save you the bother of resolving this question yourself. I have done this; the facts won't support that conclusion either. What religionists are prone to call the "acts of God," are factually the events of Nature. Nature is neutral. This conclusion is consistent with the facts. Sometimes it rains on your parade, and sometimes it doesn't. 'Why?' You ask. The uncomplicated explanation is because Nature doesn't notice when a parade is staged, or who stages that parade. Nature is totally oblivious of mankind; formerly, now, and forever!

GOD THE SUPERLATIVE

In our reverent musings we imagine a Supreme Being possessed of the ultimate of all superlatives. God is All-Knowing; God is All-Loving; God is All-Everything! In theory, this is as it must be. Yet, when we examine the theory intellectually we find that not even the Creator of our Universe is categorically omnipotent. Undeniably: One limiting condition that even the devout must concede is the creation of a contradiction. God can't reconcile opposites. This answers why He can't create a light that is dark. It also explains why God could never exchange personalities with Satan. Such would be the ultimate of all contradictions! Some situations are impossible, even to God!

But there are other, less obvious, contradictions that are also impossible to the Almighty. Re-consider the proposition that God is omniscient. We grant that the Father God knows everything, even the future. No one else can foretell the totality of the future, but God can! Or can He? The future is determined, not by an individual, not by a small group, not even by a single nation; but by natural or human happenstance. The entirety of what we will experience in the future is the result of a vast interplay of countless natural and humanity-initiated events impinging one upon another, in vast multiplicity, and in unpredictable profusion.

Human beings, by religious definition and by practical observation, have unencumbered free will. So, too, do all animate entities! I don't know where I will be next Friday for two very sound reasons. For the first, I don't know what eventualities will befall me in the meantime. My existence is influenced by natural occurrences and by 'independent-acting' bio-forms. Secondly, I haven't made up my mind yet! This last fact is the emergency stop switch that halts the workings of God's omniscience. Not even the most intelligent creature in the Universe can know what my actions will be until I decide those actions myself. God doesn't know whether I will eventually go to Heaven or to Hell because I, myself, haven't made an irrevocable decision, even as I write these words! If God already is aware of everyone's final destination, the point of having a human existence is lost on me. The truth is that absolutely no one, not even a god, can know the future. Pre-knowledge of arbitrary events is an impossible contradiction unless the events aren't random; in which case, they must have been scripted and orchestrated! (Staged!)

In our humble speculations, we impute to God abilities that are mutually incompatible because they are contradictions. The reason God can't create another god greater than Himself is because we posit that God is already the greatest entity possible. The same considerations, applied to omniscience, make that every bit as contradictory. If all human, non-human, or natural actions are wholly free of His direction; if all humans have the wholly ungoverned prerogative to act in any manner that they themselves choose; further, if these choices are made at the caprice of the individual, then God in the Highest can't know how that individual will react until this individual has finalized his own course of action.

God can't know the unknowable. The future is unknowable; thereby, God doesn't know the future. If free will is a fact, then omniscience is a contradiction. The weather affects my actions. Does God control the weather? 'All of the time? 'Some of the time? 'Once in a while? Fungus affects my life. Does God influence all plant life? 'All of the time? 'Some of the time? 'Once in a while? Sunlight affects my life. Gravity affects my life. Cosmic radiation from outer space affects my life. The stars affect my life. (When my niece visited, I took her to a Planetarium!) The spacecraft fly-by of the Planet Venus affected many lives. There was a local population explosion nine months after the great blackout in New York City many years ago. Was this a natural accident, or a dubious scheme of some Master Manipulator Deity?

In the computer programming sciences, they have an axiom: "Garbage In – Garbage Out." What this means is that a poorly designed program won't yield sensible results. This is precisely what happens with our pious suppositions. We say that Yahweh is God. We say that He has a separate and distinguishable spirit that is also God. Then we say that Jesus is the human Son of God, yet at the same time is part of the One, True Godhead. This forces Jesus to be His own father. This is pious garbage! If we have three separate entities in the Godhead, then we have three separate Gods: not one! The real mystery inherent in the Trinity is that anyone accepts this irreconcilable, total contradiction as cosmic fact.

How can Jesus be God and man at the same time (even at separate times)? This is a divine mystery too. It is also an incontestable contradiction, and this renders the postulation impossible; thereby, false. There are laws of nature that are unconditionally inviolable. Today we not only know more of these laws than all of our human predecessors did, but more cogently, we understand why many natural laws are operable. This really makes a difference!

We live in a Golden Age of Enlightenment. If you believe this is so (and I can't conceive that you wouldn't), then the age that preceded our present age must have been the 'Sullied Age of Ignorance.' Applied to religiosity exclusively, this is an appropriate classification.

St. Augustine had great deductive capacity, yet he was wrong in almost all that he taught about religion. How can this be if I admit that he was much more perceptive (intelligent) than I am? The answer to this seeming paradox is that St. Augustine was confounded by false information. As an example, read the following:

In his "City of God," St. Augustine informs us that in Cappadocia, mares are impregnated by the wind. [Book XXI, Chapter 5] Now that is a lot of wind, and we all know this. How could such an intelligent man become so thoroughly duped as to believe the wind could father baby horses? In the same paragraph he writes of a fountain in Epirus that can re-light quenched torches. How preposterous!

Still, interwoven in the above chapter, and in other chapters, he relates further "wonders" that, in reality, are factual. One example: He was aware of the reaction of water and lime, although he was unable to explain that phenomenon. [Book XXI, Chap. 7] The mare story may be the capstone of St. Augustine's gullibility, but his religiosity laid the foundation for it. If bread and wine can be changed into flesh and blood by a few mumbled words (St. Augustine fervently believed those two items could be transmuted), what is impossible? Absolutely nothing!

Augustine admitted that he personally couldn't verify that the mares of Cappadocia became impregnated through the wind. He himself never witnessed the re-lighting of quenched torches in Epirus. His belief was bestowed solely on the basis of trust. The men who vouched for the above events were honorable and trustworthy, or so Augustine thought. That is why Augustine believed them, and that is why he included such in his book.

The same is applicable to the entirety of the Bible. We trust that the authors were telling the truth when they wrote their stories. If any one of the authors of the Sacred Scriptures is proved false, then the entire compilation is reduced to human imagination or conjecture. Would God, via the personality of the Holy Spirit, have permitted His Holy Writ to be comingled with fictive scriptures composed by mankind? I cannot accept that scenario. The divine inspiration of the Bible is an illusion. It is no more than pious self-delusion to aver God as the impetus behind every biblical passage. I have written it before, and I will repeat it now: "Read your Bible!" Any sensible person who examines the scriptures with an objective eye must see that what we erringly call sacred is anything but!

Take Joshua as our example here. Did God explicitly tell Joshua to kill all of the male inhabitants of Canaan (many of the women and children as well) in fulfillment of His covenant with Abraham and Moses? The Bible reports He did. *"The Lord had made them {the Canaanites} determined to fight the Israelites, so that they would be condemned to total destruction and all be killed without mercy. This was what the Lord had commanded Moses."* [Jos. 11:20] Joshua's murderous rampage in the Promised Lands was every bit as heinous as was Hitler's extermination of the Jews and other Europeans three thousand years afterward.

How can any decent human being countenance Joshua's slaughter of the innocent Canaanites whose only 'offense' was defending their own homesteads? Joshua's bloodstained memory should be repugnant to the righteous. But is it? Joshua isn't depicted in the Bible as a villain. Rather, he is revered as one of Israel's greatest military heroes. Mary, the immaculately conceived of Yahweh, was so infatuated with the exploits of Joshua that she named her first-born Son after him. (Joshua –"He Saves"– is the same Hebrew name that the New Testament redactors later rendered as "Jesus.") God's only begotten Son was named in commemoration of a mass murderer! If this isn't enough to cause a holy man to gag on his next supplication, then I don't know what is. We should remember, however, that Mary was the handmaiden of the Lord; she lived to serve God. {An unverified presumption}

According to the Evangelists Matthew and Luke, it wasn't Mary and Joseph who selected the name Jesus. Mary and Joseph merely obeyed the instructions of Gabriel. The Archangel Gabriel, we must suppose, carried this message directly from God the Father. Accordingly, it was God Himself who wished His Son to be named after the genocidal Israelite, Joshua. [Cf. Mt. 1:21 & Lu. 2:21] To me, it is questionable why God wouldn't pick a unique name for His unique Son. Why did He choose Joshua? {"Yeshua" in the Aramaic Bible translation) Joshua is nowhere depicted as a particularly devout person, but rather, as a successful military commander. (A merciless one!) Jesus was destined to become known as the 'Prince of Peace.' There is an unarticulated conundrum embedded within this current paragraph. Let he who is amenable to cogency, discern it!

Many pages ago I told you that all religiosity, from start to finish, is false. So it is! Not because I claim so, but more fundamentally, because it was birthed and structured in ignorance. Religiosity was conceived out of gullibility, and has been perpetuated and expanded by those who have suspended their inherent powers of reasoning, and have disengaged their innate inclination to skepticism.

Even Judaic morality is tainted because it was only enforced parochially. Those outside the covenant were likewise beyond Yahweh's mercy. In verity, the Israelites were no more and no less barbaric than was any other ethnic grouping of those times. Yet, we can all attest: the Israelites were barbaric! Historically, this charge isn't particularly defamatory. However, when we note that this is the nation that the God of Mercy and Kindness chose as His emissaries on Earth, then the barbarity of Joshua and his cohorts must be condemned ever more harshly.

Once you embrace the commandment of God: 'Thou shalt not covet thy neighbor's belongings' and 'Thou shalt not covet thy neighbor's wife,' then the universal crimes of pillage and rape become much more odious. [Cf. Ex. 20:17 & Deut. 5:21] Genocide is murder! There can be no justification for the Israelite slaughter of the Canaanites. Joshua and his minions murdered the Canaanites because they coveted their land, and their women. Joshua could have borne personal witness that God Himself told Moses (and scribed into a tablet): *"Thou shalt not kill."* [Ex. 20:13 & Deut. 5:17] Or did God (Yahweh) so command? {A debatable question}

Religiously inclined apologists of the Bible would probably excuse the genocide of Joshua not as a moral lesson, but as a recitation of the venal history of the Israelites. This proposition is untenable. Reputedly, Moses was inspired by God to guide the Israelites into the Promised Land, and to choose Joshua as his successor. [Cf. Deut. 34:9] If Moses wasn't inspired by God to select Joshua, then how do we know Moses was inspired at all ... or ever?

This brings us back to God's imputed Omniscience. Didn't He know in advance of Joshua's murderous excesses? If God knew beforehand and did nothing to prevent the carnage, then He is as guilty as is Joshua. Is the Bible accurate when it states that God approved and even instigated the annihilation of the Canaanites? This isn't nit picking, and I am not carping over trivial matters. There is more at stake here than the culpability of Joshua. The very existence of a moral Supreme Deity is called into question by the queries raised here. If anything, that which was illuminated in this segment is a contradiction.

The Lord of all Gods, Yahweh, is the complete opposite of God the Father whom Jesus exhorted us to revere. Jesus, whom we honor as a veritable co-extensive person with God the Father, is also the moral opposite of Yahweh. The Israelite God (Yahweh) stiffened the will of the Canaanites to resist, thereby ensuring their destruction by Joshua. [Cf. Jos. Chapter 11, especially Jos. 11:20]

Did Yahweh ever 'turn His other cheek?' No, Yahweh punished every infraction. If we are to believe the scriptures, He punished the entire nation for the sins of the few, or even the oversight of an individual. Jesus taught us to 'love our enemies.' Yahweh instructed Moses to order the Levites to kill their kinsmen (the Israelites) for violating His first commandment. [Cf.

Ex. 32:27-29] Jesus forgave even those who executed Him. [Cf. Lu. 23:34] Yahweh inspired Joshua to murder unknown and unlamented thousands merely because they chanced to live on real estate the Israelites coveted. [Cf. Book of Joshua] Jesus charged the men of His day with fornication if they so much as entertained a salacious thought. [Cf. Mt. 5:27-28] Yet, Solomon was given the wisdom (and opportunity) to indulge his lusts with no fewer than one thousand women. [Cf. 1 Ki. 11:3] Additionally I ask, "Who was a greater fornicator than was King David?" [Cf. 2 Sam. 5:13]

Are these isolated examples? Do this and discover for yourself: make a list of all the praiseworthy teachings of Jesus. Now open your Bible to the Old Testament and begin reading. Compare the revealed actions of Yahweh with those reactions you would expect of Jesus. You will find them to be utterly irreconcilable. Jesus and Yahweh could never be partners in the Godhead for one is the antithesis of the other. Any person who avers otherwise must be suffering a paralysis of their objectivity. The evidence of the Bible itself is conclusive. The vengeful tribal God of the Israelites in no way was/is related to God the Benevolent Father of Christianity. Read your Bible, "Yahweh is a man of war." (KJV) Alternately, "The Lord is a warrior." [Ex. 15:3] Quite obviously, Yahweh and God the Father are two radically different Deities!

A RATIONALE AGAINST THE EXISTENCE OF GOD

If someone was to ask me if the existence of God could be either proved or disproved, what would be my answer? It would be 'No' for either option. What this book attempts specifically to refute are the alleged 'actions' of God. A Supernatural Being, to whom all things are possible, is eternally invincible. He is also eternally invisible. Further I deduce, He will remain eternally intangible unfathomable, and without proof for all time; consequently, the attempt to prove His existence, or lack of existence, hinges on speculative reasoning, not on verifiable fact.

As an example: You say there are angels flitting about the sky. I say there aren't any angels because I can't see them, hear them, smell them, or touch them. Have I proved angels don't exist? 'No,' you answer, for angels are pure spirits that can't be perceived by human beings. Have you proved angels do exist? No! Neither can the ablest philosopher prove or disprove the existence of anything in the realm of the spiritual. Moreover, the philosophical arguments for the existence of God are so pedantic as to become meaningless, even I suspect, to the very brilliant. The deep logic required to fully comprehend the proposition of a Deity is so convoluted that it becomes confounded with ludicrousness.

The sage (albeit reversed) axiom, 'I perceive, therefore I am,' is transmuted by religious philosophers into, 'I can conceive of a Supreme Being, therefore one must exist.' Yet, if the latter corollary is proved in error, which it is, then the former axiom falls with it. Do I exist because I can think? Or can I think because I exist? It is only because I am alive and possess a highly evolved brain that I can reflect on my existence. {Cf. Rene Descartes} For the same reason, God doesn't exist merely because I can conjure up His attributes.

If He exists, His reality is wholly independent of human discernment. Humans have conceived of ogres, gremlins, leprechauns, and the like; thereby, are they all real? No, they are not! Concomitantly, no one outside the discipline of microbiology can conceive of the literally undreamed of variety of microscopic life. Yet, these prolific little creatures have been happily propagating for billions of years. We never even dreamed of their existence, yet, they have existed in countless profusion for uncounted eons despite our ignorance.

The human mind is truly creative. But this doesn't insinuate that all, or any, of creation had its origins in the human brain. A thought, independent of an action, cannot create. Think through the proposition of an 'uncaused cause' ("God" for a religionist). What is God made of? God is made of nothing! For if God is made of any matter whatsoever (specifically spirit matter), then God must have bounds and limitations. Even spirit matter must begin somewhere and end somewhere. Yet, God cannot be spatially limited. The Deity, to be God, must be composed of nothing at all. Consequently, God doesn't exist because nothing is the absence of something.

We glibly speak of God as a spirit, without ever thinking through all the ramifications of that proposition. My reasoning: If angels are composed of spirit matter, and if God created angels, then spirit matter didn't exist before the angels were created. If God has any type of substance whatsoever (spirit substance, invisible substance, or any other substance), then my question is this: Who made the substance of which God is made? The very notion of spirit matter is delusive. A spirit is nothing more and nothing less than the mystified, though hazy, perception of an invisible animate ethereal being.

Do spirits, whatever their essence, just wisp out endlessly as a puff of smoke? Under most circumstances smoke, air, or any gaseous matter will disperse and intermingle with other gaseous matter. But there is a practical limit to the dispersion of gaseous matter. There are an immense though ultimate number of molecules comprising any real substance.

God's spirit must be everywhere at once, yet it must maintain its integrity perpetually. Accordingly, it can never mix with other spirits and become inseparable from them. Remember that devils are spirits. God's essence can't intermingle with any universal entity, or with any other cosmic essence. God must ever remain distinct from all of creation. Conclusion: God must be composed of no essence whatsoever. He is emptiness: a void. God is the absence of essence. But can we worship nothingness? No! Our minds won't permit us to revere the barrenness of space; nor can we abide the loneliness of endless time; nor will our egos contemplate the finality of death. We infer God! Our imagination is the only essence of His existence.

The God concept is a simplistic answer to the exceedingly complex question of where, when, how, and why the Universe came to be. Mankind merely invented a 'Who.' Why not postulate a 'What,' instead of a 'Who'? The only reason this is so is because we humans prefer a 'Who' to a 'What.' We desire a person, and disdain a principle. What is even more salient is that we can't prove that the Universe did have a beginning. Perhaps it didn't? Perhaps the Universe is the ever-present reality of itself. All speculations about the Universe begin by presuming that "an intelligence" created it. But the Universe doesn't need intelligent guidance. Frankly, it doesn't seem to function "intelligently." It does function systematically (thence somewhat predictably), but nowhere does it function logically.

Human bias for a man-like God is the lone reason for humanity's depiction of the Creator in the spiritual form of a man. We personalize the Universe, and thereby create a Creator. Does this conception spring from divine inspiration? No! It arises through a process of superficial deduction. The earliest men personified each separate aspect of nature, therein hypothesizing a pantheon of mystical beings accountable for every manifestation of nature.

The Israelite deity formulators merely simplified and particularized the ancient notion of the existence of a host of otherworldly human beings. From them, we have inherited a legacy of ignorance, not a legacy of inspiration! If you would take a searching look at Yahweh, you would see a thoroughly (vain) human being; not a transcendent Deity. More than that, they have endowed our God with the temperament of a man also. Through the Israelites we have learned that God is pleased when we flatter Him; God is angered if we disobey Him; when we commit sins, we sadden Him. It is only fitting that He should sit upon a throne, for our God truly is our king.

Beneath His divine exterior, God exists as a totally human person. Try imagining God without eyes. You can't! Try imagining Him without a human face. You can't! If you are of Caucasian ancestry, try to picture God with Negroid features, or Oriental features. This isn't readily accomplished! Now do you recognize the pervasiveness of your human biases? God can't be imaged in our minds as anything other than a supranational {quasi} human being of our own ethnicity. This is so, even though we know that He can't look anything like a human being of any ethnicity: if He did exist. The same considerations dash the notion that God has human emotions such as anger, pity, pleasure, or vengeance. All of us would find it equally awkward to envision God as a female. In theory, we must deduce that God has no gender. In actual practice, we all see 'Him' as an invincible, authoritative, powerful male being.

Human anthropomorphic predilection perverts our reasoning when we ponder the nature of the Godhead. In this generalization, exclude scholars, who should have no difficulty imagining an asexual, genderless Deity. Having just written this, I now ask "Can anyone who believes in the actuality of a Supreme Being still be deemed a scholar?" My response is, 'Yes!' No questing individual labors under a dictate that all of his conclusions be absolutely without error. Asking the difficult questions ensures that ultimately some of your answers will prove false. Re-examining a position in the light of new evidence should eventually correct most past errors. That is, if one has the fortitude to abandon cherished beliefs that later are indicated to be unfounded or false. This almost never happens with religion. Religionists may occasionally reformulate, but they never retreat.

The dogged tenacity to believe in an activist Deity is a religionist's downfall. No proposition exists in isolation. Proposition "A" invariably leads to Propositions "B" and "C," and on in progression. Therefore, if we have reached Proposition "G" and find it deficient, we not only have to re-formulate "G," but further, we should re-examine Proposition "F" which led us to Proposition "G." Religionists are averse to doing this. They will expediently declare "G" a divine mystery, and proceed to Proposition "H." The "H" proposition, which rests on the false foundation of "G," thereby is many times more susceptible to error than otherwise would be the case.

The evolution of religious proposition is self-sustaining. A proposition soon becomes a belief; every belief eventually is sanctified into a dogma. Then the dogma, in its turn, spawns a new proposition. In the case of religion, Proposition "A" is false, for there is no Personal God. Consequently, all the subsequent corollaries dependent upon Proposition "A" are rendered untenable, thereby false. An example: Can God love you if there is no God?

Notwithstanding all of the above, perhaps the profoundest proof against the existence of a personal Deity is the undeniable fact that we have had, and continue to have, so many alternate bizarre supernatural beliefs. Ironically, the very fact that mankind has always conceived a surplus of gods proves to me beyond all rebut that no such entity exists. My rationale for the last presented contention follows. Suppose, in fairness to honest inquiry, that a personal creator/god does exist. Concede, also, that He (masculine solely for facility of consideration) created humans as a unique act of creation, and further suppose that He desires us all to know and worship Him. Would such an entity passively allow us to merely fumble and stumble through the ages guessing at His attributes, humors, personality, needs, and His very existence?

To me, that makes as little sense as does any other inanity. No! If God exists, and if our personal deportment is a concern to Him, then He must somehow enlighten us. He must unambiguously communicate to us how we should honor Him; how we may serve Him, or how we may please Him. If the form and substance of our worship of Him does matter to God, then He would be instigated by His prescience to so inform us. This rationale is only operable if a personal all-knowing (omniscient) Deity exists. Yet, if He always has been extant, and if He hasn't yet enlightened us, then it matters not how diverse our veneration of Him evolves. That being the case, we wouldn't presently require any religious organization(s) whatsoever!

Accordingly, concede that He has enlightened us. Which of the thousands of worship formularies that have been practiced by humankind is the one and only enlightenment? A singular, intelligent deity would not have tendered thousands upon thousands of differing "enlightenments" to mankind. No, if God acts, He acts sensibly and consistently. If He has shed enlightenment, then that enlightenment is true, it is singularly uniform, and it is immutable! Would God charge us to name him "Buddha" in one age, "Jehovah" in another age, and "Allah" in still another age? Would He instruct us to sanctify a cow in one part of the world, but have us immolate a cow in His honor in another part of the world? Can God be that whimsical? No, it isn't God that is inconsistent. It is mankind that is so bewildered as to the true nature of the universe that he errs each and every time he strives to explain that universe by articulating an immaterial, arbitrary and frivolous Creator.

In closing this segment I will re-state my argument against the existence of a personal deity. The undeniable fact that we have formulated so many differing religions and beliefs is proof well beyond reasonable misgiving that no enlightenment has ever been inspired upon us by any supreme being. There just is no such entity now, nor has there been one in the past; consequently, there can be none such in the future. Yes, there is a universe. Yes, there is a question as to how it came to be. But the mystery of the universe does not prove the existence of an erratically motivated deity who implants diverse "enlightenments" into the minds of disparate individuals throughout all recorded time. The incomparable miscellany of religiosity is the prime proof of its falseness. There isn't anything simpler, yet more potent, that I could offer the reader as substantiation against any sort or form of "enlightenment" from any god; or from any 'goddess' either!

Mankind has experienced thousands of "Divine" revelations. Not from a Divinity, but from thousands of religious charlatans. Whether these charlatans were self-cognizant or self-deluded is a pointless inquiry. Intentions aren't a factor in differentiating between fact and fiction. That conclusion is a fact! The god notion is a fiction!

OLD TESTAMENT ETHICS

It is difficult to reconcile the Old Testament ethics with today's religious tenets. Similarly, it is difficult to harmonize the pronouncements of Jesus with many of the events recorded in the Old Testament. Our religious leaders forbid the harming of anyone. They legitimize their prohibition with a quote from Jesus: *"Love Thy Enemies."* [Mt. 5:43]

We have already discussed how Moses became a mass murderer shortly after receiving the Ten Commandments from God. According to the biblical text, the career of Moses as a Jewish champion began with an act of murder. [Cf. Ex. 2:12] However, Moses was a unique person in the sight of God {*sic*}. For this reason, a religionist may defend the crimes of Moses by arguing that he obtained a singular dispensation from the Supreme that allowed him to execute anyone who rejected his authority. Yet, even if this was the case, the remaining Old Testament heroes would still be damnable by Jesus' words, *"Love Thy Enemies."* [Mt. 5:44] Jesus did utter those words, didn't He? [Cf. Lu. 6:27]

After you have verified those quotes in your New Testament, read the third Chapter of Judges (from verse 11 forward) and tell me why Ehud assassinated King Eglon of Moab. The following is my synopsis of this episode: The hero of this sordid epic was a left-handed man. This is appropriate, for the heroism depicted in the story is 'left-handed' also. Ehud went to the palace of King Eglon of Moab ostensibly to pay the tribute that is demanded from a conquered people. Beforehand, he had secreted a small sword on his right hip. Textually, the Moabite guards only searched the left hip of visitors, presuming everyone to be right-handed. Ehud gained entrance to the king under the pretext of having a secret message to impart. The message came from God. 'Or so Ehud said. He lied? Then, having contrived to position the king alone, he proceeded to bury his sword in the unwary king's stomach. Ehud then wisely quit the scene. Judge Ehud, whom the Bible calls a 'deliverer raised up by the Lord' {paraphrased}, then rallied the Hebrew people and attacked the now leaderless Moabites, slaying ten thousand of them. [Cf. Judg. 3:15-30] {End of synopsis}

How fortunate it was for God's chosen people in those days. When they conquered other nations, our pre-Christian brethren slew every man. Yet, when the neighboring peoples subdued the Israelites, all they did was to extract tribute. How truly stupid the Canaanites were not to repay the Jews with an 'eye for an eye,' and a 'tooth for a tooth.' [Cf. Deut. 19:21; Ex. 21:24 & Lev. 24:20] But then, they didn't have Yahweh's Holy Writ to instruct them in manslaughter. (Murder)

Was Yahweh complicit in this plan of deception and murder? Ehud would have said, "Yes." His ruse to clear the room of the king's attendants was to pretend he had a divine message to deliver to King Eglon. Once alone, Ehud declared, *"I have a message from God for you."* [Judg. 3:20] After this subterfuge, he proceeded with his murderous deed. Inasmuch as the Bible is the incorruptible 'Word of God,' can we assume that God did inspire Ehud to commit murder? If this incident is factual as presented, then Yahweh truly was an instigator, a co-conspirator and an accomplice in a political assassination.

KING SAUL, THE PROPHET SAMUEL, AND YAHWEH

In 1st Samuel (1st Kings in Catholic translations), Samuel relays Yahweh's message to King Saul to destroy Amalek and kill all his people. Samuel's words: *"Now go and smite Amalek and utterly destroy all that they have and spare them not; but slay both man and woman, infant and suckling, ox and sheep, camel and ass."* [1 Sam. 15:3] No person and nothing alive were to be spared. King Saul attacked and did kill every human Amalakite, but Saul spared King Agag. He also spared the choicest animals.

Because Saul disobeyed the commands of Yahweh to spare no one and no animal, God sent Samuel to inform Saul that the Lord no longer wanted Saul to be King over Israel. After more conversation Samuel said: *"Bring ye hither to me, Agag the king of the Amalekites. And Agag came to him cautiously. And Agag said, 'Surely the bitterness of death is past.' But Samuel said: 'As your sword hath made women childless, so shall your mother be childless among women.' And Samuel hacked Agag in pieces before the Lord."* [1 Sam. 15:32-33] Thus, at the command of Yahweh, the prophet Samuel became an unrepentant murderer also."

If the God of Israel's Judges and Kings (Yahweh) was guilty of as many deaths, including women, children and infants, as He is credited with in the Old Testament, He should be hauled forthwith before a world tribunal; tried in court; found guilty; summarily dispossessed of his imputed Divinity, and destroyed. Yahweh was a much more accomplished murderer than even Stalin or Hitler became later. The only mitigating circumstance in Yahweh's favor is the fact that He personally didn't commit the murders. But then, neither was Charles Manson present when Sharon Tate and the others were murdered. Manson only ordered the murders. This, in effect, is what Yahweh did. He directed the Israelites to murder the rightful inhabitants of the Promised Land. [Cf. Deut. 20:16; Deut. 2:30-31 & Num. 21:34; et al.]

Now can you see how grotesquely we pervert biblical history when we credit God as its author? In truth, a human hand wrote every page in the 'Sacred Scriptures.' Yahweh is a Divinity of ignorance, not of inspiration. All religiosity is the subversion of human intellect.

ON THE ORIGINS OF TEMPTATION

Is the Devil the cause of all temptation in our lives? If so, how can we know, for he is such a clever deceiver? Religionists know! Whenever they are tempted to commit sin, they know it is the Devil enticing them to his evil ways. The urge to do something pleasurable, if immoral, originates with Satan who implants all urges in us. This is self-evident to religionists.

Man doesn't initiate his own temptation. Isn't this what religionists have always taught? Aren't we all hapless servants of that master manipulator, Beelzebub? We are, and you can prove it yourself. At least, you can prove it to yourself! I doubt that you could prove the intrusion of the Devil into anyone's life other than your own. This is because the acts of Satan can only be perceived in the mind of the perceiver. The Prince of Evil is a spirit entity, just as God is a spirit entity. Unlike God, however, the Devil's actions are only perceptible to the person being acted upon. To explain: Imagine yourself in a circumstance where it would be possible for you to have sexual relations with a desirable member of the opposite gender. Imagine further that such relations would be sinful. Does the fact that this intimacy would be illicit enhance the appeal of the potential liaison? It frequently does!

Why? Because the Devil makes it more seductive, that is why! The same would be true if the temptation involved money, or fame, or even good fortune. Do you remember the popular axiom: "Everything I enjoy always turns out to be illegal, immoral, or fattening"? This maxim proves the Devil constantly tempts us. At least, two-thirds of this maxim is provable. However, the final item in the axiom invites scrutiny.

It is likewise true that the fatter a person is, the greater the impulse to eat becomes. The temptation to eat is every bit as insistent as is the urge to copulate. Is the Devil at the root of overeating also? Not likely, for being obese precludes many sins a thinner, more sexually attractive, human has the predisposition (or opportunity) to commit. No! If the Devil leads us into obesity, he concomitantly leads us away from many other mortal sins. Consequently, we should conclude that the impulse to overeat is a natural trait, not a supernatural incursion! Surely, the impetus to consume liquids on a hot day is an inherently human impulse not chargeable to Satan. Restated: There are certain bodily functions that originate within the body itself that aren't activated by some external paranormal force, such as the Devil.

Therein lives the germ of truth that will eventually grow and consume the myth of evil temptation. There is no such impetus as external (spiritual) temptation. There is no such person as the Devil. When we ascribe to the Devil our own evil or mischievous faults, basically, we are only transferring reproach from ourselves. Religionists always will excuse their own imperfections by declaring themselves to be the victims of redoubled efforts by Satan. The standard alibi proceeds thus: 'Because I am closer to God, the Devil tempts me more insistently than he does less godly individuals!' How vainly ego exalting! In theory, there are (and there must be) limitations to the strength of the temptation the Devil is permitted to apply against us. But this theory is nothing but pious rationale. (And a proselytizing caveat!)

Theologically (sacramentally), if the Devil had the power to make temptation irresistible, how could we be held accountable for our sins? We couldn't! So the theory always supplies us with enough sanctifying grace from God to repulse the Devil's inducements. The theory works perfectly as long as it remains just a theory. When we test it, however, it invariably falls on its theoretical rump. Some people are continuously and predictably more susceptible to one type of sin than to another type of sin. We have had murderers who wouldn't think of cheating anyone; pedophiles who otherwise have led exemplary lives; also kleptomaniacs with just that single imperfection in their behavior. These singular idiosyncrasies disprove the omnibus of satanic temptation. All individual deviations from the societal norm prove that indeed we are individual. Just as our physical strengths vary from individual to individual, so too, our moral strength (fortitude) to resist temptation varies from individual to individual.

Differences in our metabolic make-up account more for the variations in our libidinous activity than does our attempted sanctity. A small percentage of people are born asexual; that is, they lack either the ability or the desire to copulate. Some people, as we all know, are attracted sexually to their own gender. Most of our erotic aberrations are avowed to be intrinsic, although some do seem to be acquired. Perchance, opportunity whets a predisposition already present, while concurrently diminishing any moral resistance to the indulgence of the proscribed activity.

Do you grasp the intent of this segment now? The gist is this: Our predilections are internal, not external. Our temptations arise within our human psyche; they aren't implanted by the Devil, or by any other entity. The temptation to eat or drink to excess needs no external cause to activate it. Neither do our sexual impulses. The Devil resides not in Hell, but within our mind … just as God does. Both are phantasms created by the human imagination in a futile attempt to disassociate our deeds from our philosophies in the case of the Devil, and as a clarification for the mysteries of nature, including our own existence, in the case of God.

IGNORANCE IS NOURISHED BY RELIGIOSITY

We should look back on the misrule of the Roman Catholic Church with understanding, and conceivably, with compassion also. The early Church was beleaguered by ignorance. They opposed the findings of scholars because they refused to accept those findings. The Bishops possessed the Bible; what need had they for books containing findings that explained nature without the intrusion of God? Why bother to think or to question anything? God had provided all the answers anyone ever needed to know. Besides, questioning the acts of God could be hazardous. Disobey God's will and you, too, may be swallowed by a large fish, [Cf. Jon. 1:17; alt. Jon. 2:1] or turned into a pillar of salt, [Cf. Gen. 19:26] or worse!

Recall what God did to Nadab and Abihu. [Cf. Lev. 10:1-2] He burnt them to death, and they were the sons of Aaron, Yahweh's first High Priest. Any person who dared to violate the directions of God would surely expose himself to God's frightful retribution. God was vindictive toward those who injured His pride. If only everyone could accept that every event that occurs is a manifestation of God's inscrutable volition, mankind could dispense with all those senseless queries about nature and happenstance. This simplistic philosophy thrives into the present day. Not only is it uncomplicated. It is also quite idyllic! The provincial belief in an all-encompassing Deity is generated with only a small expenditure of forethought, and is subjected to almost no afterthought.

One needn't ponder long to discover why the religious authorities of the Dark and Middle Ages persecuted intellectuals so mercilessly. These inquisitive philosophers could have raised doubts in the minds of 'true' believers. The Church taught that the events in the life of man were central to all that otherwise occurred in the Universe. Yet, here was Galileo advocating that the Earth wasn't even the center of the Solar System, set aside the Cosmos. This was out-and-out heresy. These teachings must be actively suppressed without abatement. What would the common man conclude if he was informed that humanity wasn't the top-billed performer of God's universe? Could the Church hierarchy allow such a sacrilege to be broadcast? No! Man was the apex of creation; accordingly mankind must occupy the center of the universal stage!

For a thousand years (AD 400-1400) the Christian Church was empowered to repress contra Christian learning. Yet, what was accomplished during those centuries? Did mankind wax closer to Nirvana during this millennium? Was this forced piety a boon or a bane to those who lived under the Church's intrusive domination? How did the mass of humanity fare under the tutelage of the Church? Have you ever read the history of Christianity during this period of clerical domination of the body and of the mind? Some of the blackest pages of history were written during the political governance of the Christian Churches throughout Europe. This isn't discussed here merely in an effort to defame. Christianity disgraced itself during that period, and in the process it exposed the odious absolutism of all religiosity. Not that the Christian faith was any more domineering and intolerable than the world's other religions of that era.

No, a God who loved truth and despised ignorance would have smote the Church in its infancy. But not so! Christianity was never smitten as such. It merely has been decaying slowly from within for nearly two millennia. Today's bible-trumpeting fundamentalists are attempting to rouse a mortally wounded Goliath. But an insignificant 'David' (the relatively low number of questing intellectuals and insightful skeptics/doubters) has aimed his pebble accurately. This pebble's composition was crafted through scientific investigation. The day may come when this 'David' obtains total communion with his God. That God is factual knowledge. To the first religionists, 'God was Wisdom.' In reality, **'All Wisdom is godly!'**

EDITORIAL POTPOURRI

A well-researched expose of the obvious errors in the Bible should be enough to start it on its way to the fiction department, where it most assuredly belongs! The Old Testament isn't a record of the glories of God; it is a testimony to the ignorance of man. Our sanctimonious reticence grants credence to the untoward teachings contained in, or derived from, the Bible.

Once again, let me state emphatically: "I am not referring to moral issues." Morality is a necessary virtue, but its value is intrinsic. No external entity is needed to legitimize morality. Morality is an oil that keeps the inter-workings of civilization lubricated. Without morality, too much friction is generated for men to live together in harmonious societies. Religionists blend morality with theology and history producing an amalgam of ritual, superstition, and incidental fact that thereafter is difficult to disassemble or disassociate.

The Gospels do the same. We read of the Sermon on the Mount wherein Jesus expounds on the virtue of meekness and submissive behavior. Throughout the Gospels, Jesus acts deferentially toward almost everyone, even gross sinners. Next we read that Jesus was "Transfigured," or that He performed some spectacular miracle. Then we are told that Jesus is God Incarnate and that the Bible is the not-to-be-questioned 'Word of

God.' Where does that situate us? It places us in the position wherein the rejection of the divinity of Jesus is a rejection of His morality as well. Conversely, if we accept His ethical doctrines, we must in tandem accept His theology and His divinity. These two concepts are independent of one another. 'Jesus the moralist' could have been correct in all His ethical pronouncements. 'Jesus the God' could be (and frankly was) entirely the invention of His adherents.

Permit a short digression here: We lionize Albert Einstein for his theories on Relativity. Rightly so! Yet his Cosmological Constant equation that posited that the Universe was "static" (neither expanding nor contracting) was patently incorrect. Einstein himself called it "his biggest blunder." Many of the 'truths' of the Bible are likewise misconceptions erringly elevated to the status of absolute 'fact.'

The evidence in the Bible supports this accusation. Read from Matthew: *"Whoever does not take up his cross and follow in my steps…"* [Mt 10:38] The other Evangelists echo identical sentiments, and they, too, record those sentiments as coming directly from the mouth of Jesus. [Cf. Mk. 8-34 & Lu. 14:27] The fact is: Jesus never carried a cross! Luke records that Simon from Cyrene was forced to carry the cross for Jesus. [Cf. Lu. 23:26; Mk. 15:21 & Mt.27:32] John also reports that Jesus carried a cross. [Cf. Jn. 19:17] Remember, John gives written testimony that he was an eyewitness to the execution of Jesus. Yet, I repeat my repudiation: "Jesus never carried a cross!" The Synoptists have Jesus talking of carrying a cross long before He was crucified. This alone should raise the hackles of suspicion in prudent human beings. Before anyone accepts the Bible as 'gospel truth,' he or she should study the Gospels objectively. Here, then, is why I believe that Jesus never carried a cross:

The historical fact is that the vertical portion of the cross (the stipes) was a permanent fixture on Calvary (aka Golgotha) hill. No condemned person had to carry the stipes, as this was left in place between executions. Persons slated for crucifixion were only required to carry the crossbeam (patibulum) to the site of execution.

The Shroud of Turin (contributing to its authenticity) confirms this little-known fact. The impression on that linen cloth shows bruises across the upper back of that victim (whoever he was). These bruises are indicative of a single beam being carried across the back. A finished cross would have left bruises on the top of a shoulder, and on the upper chest of the same side. No such bruises can be found on the man imaged on the Shroud.

Crucifixion was exceedingly common during the period of the Roman occupation of Palestine. Jerusalem, being a principal city of the day, was the site of many of these crucifixions. A Jewish disciple of Jesus would have been familiar with the procedures associated with death by crucifixion. Whoever wrote the quoted passage(s) of the Gospels wasn't. The Gentile converts to Christianity assumed that Jesus carried the entire cross. Which He did not! When they belatedly began to record the life of Jesus from the quasi-historical verbal stories extant, they perpetuated their error for time immemorial. Many of the errors in the Bible are unintentional in that those who recorded the errors believed them to be factual. The deception arises when we ascribe the Gospels to eyewitnesses instead of admitting that the original verses were written by persons long removed from the events they recorded.

The incident of the 'walking on the water' can provide another example. [Cf. Mk. 6:48-50; Mt. 14:25-26; & Jn. 6:19-20] Mark, the spokesman for Peter, simply relates that Jesus walked out to the boat in the middle of the night and frightened the dickens out of the Apostles. Matthew adds the incident where Peter spoke up and said, *"Lord, if it is really you, order me to come out on the water to you."* [Mt. 14:28] Jesus did so. But once on the water, Peter doubted, and began to sink. Jesus reached out, however, and rescued Peter. He then reproved Peter. *"How little faith you have! Why did you doubt?"* [Mt. 14:31]

There is a lucid and unmistakable message in Matthew's addition to the midnight jaunt of Jesus across the lake. The message is this: 'Have faith in Jesus, and impossible things will become possible.' What happened that night on the lake? Did Peter forget to tell Mark (His imputed reporter) of this frightful, yet inspiring, event in his life? Or, what is infinitely more likely: did the author of Matthew's Gospel make up this tale to instill faith in its readers?

Minor indoctrinating vignettes, similar to the above, are sprinkled throughout the New Testament. Yet, be alert! It is only where the same tale is repeated in an altered form that we can readily detect these addenda. Bearing this in mind, we shouldn't allow ourselves to be naive dupes for the entirety of our lives. Jesus proved through miracles, wonders, and all manner of other marvels, that He was God. If the Gospel stories were (are) true, then the people of that day had no occasion to doubt Jesus. Yet, we know that almost everyone, including some Apostles, did doubt Jesus. His own brothers doubted Him! [Cf. Jn. 7:5]

Why did they doubt? We are asked to believe in His divinity and we can only read of the proofs. If those who reportedly personally viewed the miracles had doubts, we would be fools to place unreserved trust in such improbable events. John's account of the walking on the water is different still from the other two accounts. (There is no 'Walking on Water' in Luke's Gospel.) John writes that the Apostles were out on the lake and the wind was preventing them from reaching the far shore. However, once Jesus had walked out and entered, *"immediately the boat reached land at the place they were heading for."* [Jn. 6:21] What is John telling us? Was the boat, with all its occupants, instantly teleported to the shore? That is quite a miracle in itself. But is this the fact?

If Jesus could move a boat instantly from one location to another location, why didn't He have the boat appear on the shore where He began His walk, then enter the boat, and move it instantly to the far shore? This would have been a lot less strenuous than walking on water. Try walking three miles on a motionless sandy beach and you will have a keener discernment of just how arduous it is to walk on a totally uneven surface. Then imagine how much more so would be a continuously undulating uneven surface, such as the bounding waters of a lake.

What truly happened that night? Today, no one knows! The tale could have originated in this manner: After the Sermon on the Mount, Jesus sent His disciples away. Or perhaps they weren't His disciples yet. They simply had returned to their boats to resume their occupation. After some midnight fishing, the future followers of Jesus rowed to shore at a point other than their point of departure. Upon arrival, they found Jesus already there. They marveled as to how He had arrived ahead of themselves. Maybe one of them even remarked in jest, "Perhaps, Jesus had walked across the lake?" {Author's speculation}

In truth, other fishermen may have ferried Jesus across. Or He may merely have borrowed an animal and ridden around the lake. Or simply, He could have walked through the night to be alone with His thoughts after His previous day's triumphant sermon. We don't know what distance was covered during the night by either the Apostles or Jesus. Nor do we know how long it took to traverse that distance. {Bethsaida to Gennesaret = 5 miles approximately.}

So here then, capsulated, is the sense of this latest segment. After the disappearance (ascension?) of Jesus, the recalled incident of His unexpected appearance at a shore point other than the place He was last seen became glorified into the 'walking on the water.'

Notwithstanding, even with this miracle appended, the story is rather mundane (for a God), and without discernable point. I can imagine the ancient listeners asking themselves: 'What purpose was served by this peculiar miracle?' I can further imagine the earliest proselytizers being stumped for an answer. All proselytizers save the one who later had his stories credited to Matthew the Apostle. You will recall that Matthew is the lone source of *"Thou art Peter and upon this rock I shall build my Church."* [Mt. 16:18]

If Matthew's Gospel does nothing else, it does this much: It reinforces the improbable assertion that Peter was more than just another Apostle. The primacy of Peter benefits Rome alone, and only in the long term. By my reasoning, there wasn't any immediate need for a chief Apostle (Pope?). If the return of Jesus as the Messiah was imminent, as the first proselytizers taught, why appoint a leader? Or, for that matter, why have a Church organization?

No, the need for an ecclesiastic hierarchy arose after it became apparent that the return of Jesus wasn't going to be a near-term occurrence. The growth of the structure of the Church was evolutionary. Reading Paul's Epistles informs us of this. Reflect back on those days two thousand years ago. Imagine yourself as a new convert to Christianity. What was the message your mentor would have presented to you? The message would have been, "Repent . . . ." [Cf. Acts 2:38, et al.] With this artless command the Apostles went forth to alert the Jews of the advent of the Messiah. Each Apostle was a 'pope' unto himself. This explains how Paul could challenge the authority of the "very special 'apostles'" who opposed him. [Cf. 2 Cor. 11:5] Read Paul's words: *"for in no way was I less than the chief Apostles, though I am nothing."* [2 Cor. 12:11-12] Does this sound like a man who considers himself subject to the authority of a chief or special Apostle?

Theologically, Paul should have held a subordinate position, not only to Peter and the other Apostles, but even to the disciples of Jesus. 'All seventy-two (72) of them! [Cf. Lu. 10:1] The disciples were eyewitnesses to the ministry of Jesus. Paul wasn't! Yet Paul's doctrinal position was this: 'Anyone who proclaimed the true message of the 'Christ' (i.e., the Messiah) was an Apostle!' Peter was no 'Pope' in the estimation of Paul. Recall the incident where Paul berated Peter for withdrawing {dissimulating, q.v.} from Gentile converts whenever he was under the scrutiny of Jewish adherents? [Cf. Ga. 2:11-14]

At question is not the appropriateness of Paul's rebuke. What this commentary is exploring is whether or not Paul recognized the primacy of Peter. Would a subordinate so criticize the highest official in his organization? Especially if that official had been given the authority to set the criteria for entry into the 'kingdom of heaven' by God's very own Son? To wit: *"whatsoever thou shalt bind on earth shall be bound in heaven: and whatsoever thou shalt loose on earth shall be loosed in heaven."* [Mt. 16:19] This is the strongest endorsement anyone can receive short of being personally transformed into a god. The appointment of Peter as the judge of permissible or prohibited actions on earth and in heaven is not found in Mark, Luke, or John.

More puzzling is a further passage from Matthew wherein he seems to inform that Jesus empowered all the Apostles to set binding rules: *"And so I tell all of you: what you prohibit on earth will be prohibited in heaven; what you permit on earth will be permitted in heaven."* [Mt. 18:18] A similar, though not identical, quote from John might be advanced to refute the primacy of Peter which is exclusively promulgated by Matthew. After the Resurrection, Jesus came and stood among the Apostles. *"... He breathed on them and said, 'Receive the Holy Spirit. If you forgive men's sins, they are forgiven; if you do not forgive them, they are not forgiven.'"* [Jn. 20:22-23] But it is obvious here that Jesus is referring to sins alone, not to binding doctrine. Incidentally, the Apostle Thomas was not present for this empowerment.

The overall evidence won't support the elevation of Peter as the first Pope. The Gospel of Matthew is the lone source of Peter's primacy. Paul doesn't seem to have ever known Matthew, or to have read his version of the ministry of Jesus. In truth, he seems to have been ignorant of any of the Gospels. Paul, in his letter to the Galatians observes: *"James, Peter, and John, who seemed to be the leaders...."* [Ga. 2:9] He evidently feels all Apostles are approximately equal, including Paul himself! If one studies only the Acts and the Epistles, these argue that, if anyone, Paul was de facto 'Primate' of the nascent Church organization. The inchoate Christian Church was grounded on Paul's interpretation of the teachings of Jesus.

Demonstrably, Paul didn't attain his authoritative position through apostolic appointment alone, nor through democratic acclaim. Rather, it was through dogged determination and lengthy perseverance. Paul forged an organization out of what had grown to be a loose and basically leaderless profusion. Yet, if this conclusion is as accurate as it appears to me to be, then a contradiction exists in the Scriptures. Further, the Bible itself suffers a bruising rebuke whereby many present-day assumptions and extrapolations must be re-examined; if not renounced! Paul rejected the (Judaic?) teachings of 'special' Apostles. He wrote: *"Those men are not true Apostles—they are false Apostles."* [2 Cor. 11:13 & Cf. Rev. 2:2]

Specifically, who were these 'special' persons whom Paul called "deceitful" Apostles? [Cf. 2 Cor. 11:13 D/R] This query is intriguing. Unfortunately, it has no answer. Paul never elaborates in any other of his Epistles, although several contain similar denunciations. If Paul is referring to members of the original eleven (minus Judas) this would be highly significant. If not, then the question of how these unnamed persons came to be held in 'special' esteem also beggars an answer.

Paul levels some serious charges against his antagonists. Paul writes, *"They lie about their work and change themselves to look like real Apostles of Christ."* [2 Cor. 11:13] Then he in effect accuses them of being subservient to the Devil. He charges, *"Even Satan can change himself to look like an angel of light! So it is no great thing if his servants change themselves to look like servants of right."* [2 Cor. 11:14-15] As can readily be seen, Paul harbored a bitter animus toward his detractors.

The underlying pertinence of this current discourse is the question of authority. Who authorized these sham Apostles? The second century historian, Hegesippus, is recorded as having information that a man named Thebuthis, resentful at not being the successor to James (the brother of Jesus per Galatians 1:19), became the instigator of a heretical movement. Thebuthis denied the divinity of Jesus. Josephus reports that James was stoned to death in the year AD 62 or 63. Jude, the brother of James the Just (James the Lesser) and also a relative of Jesus (?), became the second Bishop of Jerusalem. In Jude's Epistle, he reports: *"For certain men have stealthily entered in … who turn the grace of God into wantonness and disown our only Master and Lord, Jesus Christ."* [Jude 1:4]

Is Jude referring to Thebuthis? Whom might Thebuthis be that he would have the audacity to contend with relatives of Jesus? In John's Third Epistle, he rails against someone named Diotrephes who *"does not receive us."* [3 Jn. 1:9] Who could deny the authority of John, the beloved Apostle? What do you make of this statement found in John's Second Epistle? *"For many deceivers have gone forth into the world who do not confess Jesus as the Christ coming in the flesh. This is the deceiver and an antichrist."* [2 Jn. 1:7]

In John's First Epistle, we find another exhortation against false teachers (and another apparent false prophecy of the 'last times'). *"Little children, it is the last time; and as you have heard that antichrist shall come, even now are there many antichrists; whereby we know that it is the last time."* [1 Jn. 2:18]

The Challoner-Douay text of the above quote reads, *"… it is the last hour … whereby we know that it is the last hour."* [ibid] Apologetically, we could accept the latter quote as the more accurate in that the term 'last time' is immediate; 'Now!' the present! Whereas the 'last hour' could be explained in the light of the quotation, *"One day is with the Lord as a thousand years, and a thousand years as one day."* [2 Peter 3:8; Ps. 90:4 & Ps. 89:4 Catholic] With twisted logic we could conclude that if a day is a thousand years, then an hour would be approximately forty-two (42) years. Either translation is proved in error by history. Two thousand years later, the 'last times' ('last day') still hasn't arrived. The obvious conclusion is that John's previously quoted text is exposed as human misinformation, not divine inspiration.

Another nettling puzzler arose while contemplating this current segment. How could there have arisen so many bogus prophets, heretics, and anti-Christ's in so short a period of time? One confirmation of this accusation, among many that could be proffered: *"For many false prophets have gone everywhere."* [1 Jn. 4:1] The logical answer indicated by the foregoing is that more than one charlatan learned of the story of Jesus (with His miraculous Resurrection), and saw an opportunity to garner a dutiful following by preaching their own version of this newly popular cult. If each opportunist hadn't been acquainted personally with Jesus, it is likely that his knowledge of the teachings of Jesus would soon vary from that of the actual Apostles. This could well explain John's complaint/warning.

Examined questioningly, the Bible in its entirety is seen to be an utterly human artifact. God in the Third Person is no ghostwriter. What need would the Creator of 'All That Is' have for imperfect human scribes? If God wanted us to read the story of His Son's life, He could have simply and directly given a written Gospel to Luke, just as He purportedly gave Moses the Commandment tablets. For God, how laborious would it have been to cause an accurate, biographical book (scroll) to be received by Paul?

Why did God require four separate Evangelists to tell the singular story of the life of Jesus? This is nothing less than redundant. Also, what of the non-canonical narratives of Christ's ministry? Who inspired them? Who verifies that the rejected pseudo-gospel texts were not inspired by the Holy Spirit? How do we know? How can the average person know the truth? Assuredly not on faith! Bestowing our faith hasn't led us to God. What it has done is abetted the endless proliferation of diverse, obverse, bellicose Christian denominations.

The Bible itself is the cause of almost every schism the Church has suffered, especially after the advent of Martin Luther. I submit that today, bibliolatry (slavish adherence to selected biblical texts, along with enforced neglect of biblical rejected texts) is the anti-Christ that the earliest Christian proselytizers so adamantly feared, and additionally, so frequently cautioned against.

All religiosity, from Alpha to Omega, is false. There is no God! Without Him, all religions become nothing but indulged sacrosanct mythology. Religion doesn't solve our problems; it merely renders many tribulations more tolerable. Granted, this does seem to be a desirable outcome in instances. But is it truly? I don't think so for the following reason: Bogus information ultimately results in bogus conclusions. Religiosity is strewn with the bodies of persons brutalized by cultic zealots. The perpetrators of the Inquisition thought they were furthering the work of God. During the Reformation, the Lutherans of northern Germany were over-zealous in protecting their beliefs. The current religious leaders in Iran see themselves as saviors of the Islamic people. They view themselves as God's emissaries on Earth. Yet, each day their despotism further tyrannizes the Iranian populace, especially harrowing their females. In Iran religious oppression dominates their culture unabated! Over the past half century, Islam has distended dictatorially and murderously.

Where is God? Why isn't He acting today? Does His inactivity give silent assent to the social barbarities rampant in Iran, and throughout the Middle East? I hope not! Those Mullahs must have their head scarves wrapped too tightly if they think Allah approves of their actions. If God made us, then He must love us. If He loves us, why does He permit us to suffer under an ever and always recurring religious tyranny?

For the overwhelming mass of humanity, life is a continuing ordeal. Lady Luck favors some, but her perverse daughter, 'Miss Fortune' (misfortune), plagues all. Why did God allow Jack the Ripper to live? If God has the power to intervene, then why doesn't He? If He knows in advance whether my conduct will earn me Heaven or Hell, why does He insist that I live out the full span of my life? If I am predestined to go to Hell; or if God has foreknowledge of my final destination; why go through the futile charade of an earthly life where, theologically, I have the option of altering my actions, thereby re-directing my final destination from Hell to Heaven?

The whole theological premise for our existence is pointless. If God didn't want evil to exist in the world; why did He create evil? If He created me merely to shut me into eternal damnation, then He is a sadistic Deity. If what I do is displeasing to God, then why does He suffer me to do it? If I have made God cross through my sins, will He then become joyous once I am cast into Hell? Will God rejoice with glee every time my body is racked by the torments of Hell? What reaction stirs in God's breast each time some new, forlorn soul is flung into the everlasting fire? What emotion is evoked in God as this endless procession of the damned is turned over to God's all-too-successful adversary, Satan?

I could go on, but why? By now you have gotten the point, or it has eluded you for all time. The bases for our religious concepts are juvenile and nonsensical. Discerning, intelligent persons should expose religious bigotry for the scourge that it is. We should do all in our power (non-violently) to combat the spread of the contagion that is religion. All superstition, most especially religious superstition, must be refuted with vigor and perseverance everywhere it is encountered. Our colleges offer classes in theology. Why not institute a continuing course in Atheism? I am sincere! If non-believers would study the Scriptures as earnestly as a Bible-Belt preacher, we could put an irretrievable end to the deception of the "Inspired Word of God." The Old Testament is nothing but a compendium of human superstition and folk fable mythologizing the ultra-vain-but-ever-vengeful fictitious sky God of the Semites, Yahweh.

MENTAL MEANDERING

The following verses were culled from Exodus describing the driving out of the Canaanites. God informs the Israelites: *"No one will try to conquer your country during the three festivals,"* [Ex. 34:22-24] (The Festival of Unleavened Bread, the Festival of Weeks, and the Festival of Tabernacles). [Cf. Deut. 16:16] Was this divine assurance ever realized?

God created angels. Angels are pure spirits. Therefore, one could say that God created angels out of nothing, into nothing. The implication here is profane (and a bit sardonic), but nonetheless, it is accurate in that it faithfully states a widely embraced belief. There was (and is) no mystical or supernatural impetus behind the evolution of mankind. The human animal is nature's most complex creation. Collectively, we are also the most inventive, and the most destructive. What criterion (criteria?) should a universal creator (a creative Universe?) apply to rate our cosmic worth?

Do we evaluate a bird on how well it walks? No, a bird's prime attribute is its ability to fly. Man's glory is occasioned by his intelligence. Man's universal stature should be graded on his development of this faculty alone, never on his adherence to otherworldly religio-cultic prescriptions. The day that mankind engages his intelligence exclusively will initiate Armageddon of all religiosity. Which raises the ultimate question: What is religion? Religion is the public expression of super egotism utilizing mysticism in the belief that it can manipulate the imagined supernatural. Deception Induces Delusion!

CHAPTER 21
Curious Questions

QUESTIONING CREATIONISM
AS METICULOUSLY AS EVOLUTION

The very first verse in the Bible reads: *"In the beginning 'the gods'* [Elohim is plural] *created the heavens and the earth."* [Gen. 1:1] What proof is there that the Universe ('heavens') was created at the same instant as the Earth? None! But is there proof that the Cosmos came into being long before the formation of the Earth? Yes, there is! Also, those proofs don't emanate from a single source. Nor are they confined to a single learning discipline. Theoretical astronomers presently are gathering the accumulating knowledge obtained through radio and visual telescopes (including the Hubble Space Telescope), and they are attempting to organize the revealed evidences into a coherent explication of the entirety of the Universe (cosmogony).

Meanwhile, geologists study the Earth and conclude from their data that the age of the Earth is great (4.5 billion years?), yet it isn't comparable to the age of the Universe. All the evidence gathered since the invention of the telescope indicates an immense age for the Universe (13 to 15 billion years?). At the same time, anthropologists, archaeologists, physicists, botanists, and a multitude of other studied men and women contribute their knowledge, and always the overall consensus is the same. The age of the Earth is so much greater than the author of Genesis reckoned it to be.

The sequence of events described in Genesis is wholly at odds with all the scientific facts! No single shred of verifiable evidence supports the creation scenario as outlined in Genesis. Rather, the accumulating evidences totally discredit the Genesis scenario.

Einstein proposed that E=MC2, which defines matter and energy as interchangeable. He also theorized that man could construct an atomic bomb. Was Einstein wrong? Is the Atomic bomb nothing but a figment in the imagination of some deluded scientists? No, the bomb and millions of other inventions of science are real. Today, more than ever before, our learned academics (scientists) have proven that they not only comprehend much of the physical world, they often can manipulate the intrinsic properties of combined matter to perform desired tasks.

Can clerics demonstrate the same capabilities by importuning God to perform in a faith-confirming manner? Even intractable religionists would admit that all they can do is lean back and observe the natural, though cryptic, orderings of nature, and the unpredictable machinations of man. Thereafter, *ipso facto*, they credit God for every propitious or momentous eventuality. Some religionists credit God for whatever transpires on Earth or in the Heavens, beneficial, detrimental, or even malicious.

To religious man, all happenings are due to the indecipherable mental deliberations of the unfathomable Creator. No explanation for His actions is deemed required; therefore, none is tendered. Yet, how can a religionist know his speculations have any validity? Well, he has the Word of God in the Holy Bible; that is how! Notwithstanding, can anyone prove that the Bible is the Word of God? No, so don't ask for proof; just accept all that a religionist preaches on faith alone.

Asians have a book called the Bhagavad-Gita. They believe this to be an 'inspired' work. Muslims have the Koran; this also, is the 'Word of God' (Allah). All the major religions of the world preach that a Deity inspired their beliefs. Many fanatics profess to have been inspired by a Spiritual Being. All of these can't be true, because they are unquestionably contradictory and undeniably incompatible. Which religion, of all those extant, embodies the actual inspiration of the Universal God? Can there be more than one God? Can one discern beyond question that there is even a singular god?

If by Faith, then define what faith is. My definition: "Faith is trust bestowed without proof, despite the evidence." What, then, is Truth? Truth isn't a proper object of faith. Truth is that which is incapable of being proved false. Truth doesn't need the pretend security granted by faith. Truth should be able to withstand the most extensive searching (the most probing scrutiny) that man can devise. Has any religion ever withstood this sort of exhaustive and comprehensive test? 'Not to my knowledge!

No deity, whether Christian or any other, has ever survived even a cursory testing. In the Old Testament, Yahweh was tested often. If we can believe the witness provided therein, He always passed each test. Yet, who parts the Red Sea today? Who smites the Philistines? Who grants us invincibility in the face of our enemies? Where is God? What has become of His protective Love? Why are His most ardent followers always in such dire need of funds? Pardon my cynicism, but why must religionists constantly be soliciting (begging) the money to 'do God's work'? Doesn't God 'provide for our every need?'

If God's work is chiefly to convince us of His reality, then I see a very straightforward and effective way for God to accomplish His aims. Why doesn't He inspire us with the proof of His existence? Why doesn't God just appear privately to each and every one of us and exhibit His universal benevolence personally? This doesn't happen because God doesn't exist. God never appeared to anyone. God never inspired anyone. God is the creation of the superstitious mind, and I suspect, many devious personalities. From the beginning, 'God' has been the provident provider (meal ticket) of those ardently professing and preaching the belief in Him. Paul was an exception.

Candidly, we humans don't need God's Love. We, contrariwise, don't need Heaven. What we do need is justice here on Earth during our limited span of life. Children need forgiveness for their sins. Adults recognize that punishment should attend wrongdoing, and reward should follow exemplary behavior. This is the essence of true justice. Universal and Absolute Justice is the verifiable 'heaven' that we all seek after so assiduously.

Sincere religionists may not be aware of it, but this is what they, too, are in search of: justice! But they transfer responsibility for administering justice to God, instead of to and by themselves. God is made responsible for the final and everlasting administration of justice. Yet I ask: Would an intelligent Deity be angry at His creatures if they were to administer their own justice? I don't see why. If God is truly the Father of us all, He shouldn't resent our maturing to the point where we can manage entirely for ourselves. This should be the ultimate destiny of all children, even children of God: to mature into competent, self-reliant adulthood!

Justice is the only 'deity' worthy of man's esteem. His acolytes are knowledge, and his disciples are those who seek after their own accumulation of wisdom. Let their mental baptism wash away "ignorance." That is the "original sin" of mankind. Thereafter, may we all pray not for sanctifying grace (a fraudulent, non-existing, commodity!), but for the ability and opportunity to learn unendingly. Every morsel of fact that replaces faith is a vitamin that aids our intellectual growth. Each fragment of learning is a sliver of a virtual Heaven. Metaphorically, every injustice is a further psychic injury to our forever-earthbound bodies. Absolute justice is the most desired beneficence that an all-knowing Deity could bestow upon His created creatures. The indisputable fact is that we humans are perpetually burdened with the exact opposite; that being: with ubiquitous "injustice." This convinces me that there positively isn't any all-wise, all-loving, and ever-acting Deity functioning anywhere in the Cosmos. Patently & irrevocably, Mankind has always been intellectually alone in the Universe!

DISCREPANCY IN THE ANOINTING AT BETHANY

All four Gospels tell of a woman who anointed Jesus with expensive oil (spikenard). This would seem to authenticate the incident. There are serious discrepancies however, when the four versions are compared. An inescapable conclusion intrudes itself because of this: The authorship of "Matthew" or the authorship of "John," or both, must be doubted. Furthermore, this forbids Divine inspiration of that story (stories?) by the two non-Apostle Evangelists.

For instance: John writes that the anointing took place in the home of Lazarus sometime after Jesus had restored him to life. John further informs that it was Mary, sister of Lazarus, who poured the perfumed oil. [Cf. Jn. 12:1-8]

Matthew and Mark report the event as taking place in the home of Simon the leper. The woman is not identified in their respective versions. [Cf. Mt. 26:6-13 & Mk. 14:3-9]

Luke records the event as having taken place in the home of Simon the Pharisee, and he records that an unnamed "sinful" (trollop?) woman performed the rite. [Cf. Lu. 7:36-50]

There is also disagreement as to what part of the body of Jesus was anointed. John tells us the woman anointed the feet of Jesus. Matthew and Mark write the woman anointed the head of Jesus. Curiously, Luke agrees with John that the woman anointed the feet of Jesus. However, Luke also mentions the lack of anointing of the head of Jesus. Recall Luke places the event in the home of Simon the Pharisee. Jesus censures Simon for his neglect of the formal courtesy offered to a respected guest. That is, the anointing of the head of one's house guest.

> *"Do you see this woman? I came into your home, and you gave me no water for my feet, but she has washed my feet with her tears and dried them with her hair. You did not welcome me with a kiss, but she has not stopped kissing my feet since I came. You provided no oil for my head, but she has covered my feet with perfume."* [Lu. 7:44-46]

Clearly, if the differences noted here don't prove that, far from being divinely inspired, these Gospel stories are the imperfect recollections of human beings unaided by any Deity, then no other evidence, however inarguable, will be able to prove my contention either.

The miraculous catch of fish is similarly reported in two (suspect) differing versions. Luke reports the incident as occurring early in the ministry of Jesus. John records the event as occurring after the Resurrection. Matthew and Mark are both ignorant of a miraculous catch of fish.

Luke reports the catch as occurring during the call of the first followers, Simon (Peter), James, and John. (Andrew isn't specifically named here.) [Cf. Lu. 5:4-11] John records the miraculous catch as one of the post-Resurrection appearances of Jesus. [Cf. Jn. 21:1-14] Matthew and Mark record a call of the first followers, but omit the catch of fish. [Cf. Mt. 4:18-20 & Mk. 1:16-20]

This is very confusing. Did the catch of fish take place at the beginning of Jesus' ministry; at the end of His ministry; or did it not take place at all as Matthew and Mark testify? How can anyone believe that God inspired every word in the Bible when there are so many internal proofs that the entire compilation is a premeditated deception? Divine inspiration is a pious delusion that has deceived Christianity for two thousand years, and it continues to do so.

Yes, anyone can make a mistake. But it is more than a mistake when religionists willfully close their eyes to all evidences that repudiate their assessment of divine guidance in the composition of the "Sacred Scriptures." In my judgment, studied religionists are guilty of flagrant deceit if they fail to inform their followers of discrepancies such as those exposed in this book. Have I exposed all the problematic segments there are? No, I have found far too many, and I suspect I have missed many more discrepancies that are contained within the Bible.

For twelve years of my sub-adult life I attended Mass almost every Sunday and never once, in all those years, did the preacher (priest) mention a single incongruity or potential inconsistency in the Bible. Since then, I have read hundreds of books and pamphlets written by Protestant authors, and not one of them admitted to anything questionable in the Gospels either. In frankness, the Protestants are more brazen in their proselytizing. They extract quotes wholly out of context, and use them to their own mercenary advantage. One might excuse a proponent of any persuasion for not divulging the weak points in his propositions. This may be acceptable in secular matters. But not with religious matters! Christian teachings are proffered as grounded on ethical standards. Because of this, truth must be held paramount, even if the truth engenders confusion by raising doubts. What proselytizers most fear are defections, if their sacrosanct deceptions are exposed!

My position is similar; though not identical. I recognize that I must be truthful to my readers. Wherever I have quoted the scriptures, I have quoted them accurately (within the constraints of my abilities). No claim of infallibility is made here, only honest endeavor. That which is only my opinion, or altogether my interpretation, has been clearly indicated as such. At no point in this book have I knowingly misled my readers. I am not a biblical scholar, and I have not presented nor intimated myself as one. I have studied the Bible often, and I have read many books dealing with religion. But, in essence, I remain just an average person searching alone to determine the reality of religion, i.e., belief in a personal creator god, or its falsity!

The impetus for this book was gradual. When I began writing, this was chiefly for my own purposes. I am not a persuasive public speaker. I wanted to inform my immediate family, and a few close friends, why I had lost my faith. Yet, I knew I could never do so convincingly if I had to rely on oral arguments alone. I decided to write down my reasons for not believing in Heaven or a life hereafter, for my family to read. It was not my first intention to un-convert anyone, but merely to vindicate my own conclusions.

From a modest beginning of approximately twenty pages, my research has grown to more than six hundred pages. At the moment these words are conceived, I am uncertain anyone other than me will ever read them. My notebooks are in general disarray. My sparse talents working with word-processing computer programs lay years in the future. I don't have the foggiest notion of how to get this composition published. Yet, despite this daunting uncertainty, I am self-compelled to deal honestly and forthrightly with my future readers, if such there ever will be?

Please don't misconstrue here. I experienced no imperative, then or now, to authenticate any portion of the Bible. We, the general non-clerical populace, have been swamped with pro-religion propaganda. Each day brings a fresh onslaught from religionists. It is well past time for some contrary arguments to be aired. Quite frankly, the number of books published that debunk religiosity surprised me. But many of them have been timorous, and have only attacked tangentially as if reluctant to initiate a full frontal assault. Or alternately, they had been written so intellectually that the average person is too intimidated to read through these scholarly compositions. Perhaps those authors were wiser than your author, who is quintessentially "the average man." Only time and circumstance will confirm if my literary efforts are worthy of scrutiny.

Enough self-analysis: Let us return to the Bible and renew our investigation. Begin by repeating an oft-raised question: Can the Bible contain provably false information and still be deemed inspired? Ultimately, you will decide this for yourself; I can only point to provable or suspect areas. For myself, I am convinced that none of the four Gospels, in their present form, was written by their reputed author. They are worded in second-hand fashion, and that is precisely how they were composed: second-hand.

I believe that the man Jesus (Yeshua) lived and performed many inspiring deeds. Several incidents in His life were spectacular, and soon after His death, they became glorified into miracles. But I do not believe Jesus was a God, nor any part of a God. There never has been a human God! Neither is there a spirit God. In melancholy fact, there is no God at all!

There are universal truths of which man is, as yet, unaware. Application: Man is unaware of the explanation of these realities; Man is not unaware that enigmatic truths exist. Early man invented gods (gods in the sense of super persons) to account for the inexplicable and the unknown. Today, we know our ancient explications were entirely without merit. We now know that every event that occurs in the natural world has a natural cause. God isn't merely dead; He is superfluous!

Why should we pray to God for rain for our crops when we can build a reservoir and irrigate our fields? If my wife is barren, I can have doctors create a test-tube baby to be implanted in my wife's womb. Alternately, I can hire a surrogate mother to carry my child. Evidently, 'God's Will' can now be modified and even thwarted. There isn't anything the ancients ever petitioned God for that can't be accomplished today by men of high intellect and technical training. Man's brain is his salvation. Man inaugurated eternal life when he invented speech and writing. Once the thoughts of man could be remembered indefinitely (recorded), mankind became immortal. Pictures & videos, as is writing, are communicative extensions of speech.

Excuse the minor detour: I was discussing the second-hand nature of the Gospels. What I think happened was that after Jesus died, and after a few of His disciples thought they had seen Him arisen, they began to publically proclaim Him as the promised Messiah. The stories of His life were told, and retold, and then repeated many times over. Each recounting added a touch of glorification until the stories attained a consensus. Finally, possibly fifty years after He died, the stories were collected, embellished, and composed in written form.

The ersatz 'Evangelists' gathered all the extant stories of His life and began to collate them. I suspect this was no simple task. From the beginning, I believe, two opposing objectives moderated their actions. Their first impulse must have been to render coherent what must have been a conflux of disparate stories. A secondary impulse would have been to present the stories as faithfully as they had been broadcast. The result is that now we have four versions of the life of Christ, none of which are historically factual; yet, none of which are wholly fictitious.

Yes, the Gospels have been emended from their very second rendering. But the tampering (editorial rewriting) never became wholesale fabrication. The ending of the story of the woman anointing Jesus in Bethany is representative. (As portrayed by Matthew and Mark at the beginning of this segment.)

The final verse of Matthew's and Mark's account of the anointing reads thus: *"Now remember this! Wherever the gospel is preached, all over the world, what she has done will be told in memory of her."* [Mk. 14:9 & Mt. 26:13] This is a direct quote of Jesus. Can you picture Jesus speaking of a 'gospel' to Simon the leper? Nowhere else does Jesus personally mention the word "gospel." No, this is a pious addendum to the story of the anointing that is found only in Matthew and Mark. However, not all accused additions are so straightforward to identify.

The above ends this segment that had as its purpose a now familiar theme: The proof of the falsity of the gospels is to be found within those very gospels. God didn't dictate to man. Religious man has tried to dictate to the rest of mankind as if he was an implicit spokesperson for the faux universal Deity!

HUMAN ANATOMY EVOLUTION
OR DIVINE DESIGN?

Religionists advise us all — to look around ourselves to discern the handiwork of the Creator. The vast oceans, the imposing mountains, the plains and the forests, every fragrant flower, every wondrous creature, are visible proof of the Omnipotence of the Almighty. Indeed, the substantiation of God's existence is seemingly everywhere. Still, is this what the above delineated evidences indicate?

I have already written on the diversity of life forms and what their variety proves to me. The properties of inert matter, I think, speak against a God whose sole purpose for creating was to design a morality testing ground for human beings. What about man himself? What does the existence of man prove? To treat this question fully and fairly would require a separate book at the very least. Consequently, in prudence, I will just touch on a few aspects of that topic in this work with the purpose of making my premiere point from yet another perspective.

Fundamentally, the human body can be separated into male and female. What, if anything, is learned by this distinction? Much and little at the same time! There is no natural imperative for dividing individuals within a species by gender. In fact, there are several species that change from male to female depending on natural or biological factors. Also, there are many life forms that are self-replicating without an opposite gender.

Why did God create this sexual division in humanity? He could have created elsewise. Is any theological purpose served by the anatomical differences between man and woman? If humankind was created in God's image, does this inform us that God is a hermaphrodite? Is God exclusively male? Or is God exclusively female? If God is neuter, why did He make His most beloved creatures anatomically dimorphic? Couldn't God, if He so desired, have crafted humans so that each individual would be complete within his, or her, self? Yes, He could have; many plants do possess this self-impregnating method of reproduction (parthenogenesis).

But He didn't! (Convention, or male bias, impels me to use the masculine pronoun.) Because He didn't, I must ask why this difference exists. Evolutionists tell us that sexual differentiation is one of nature's successful mutations. We who are evolved from sexually differentiated primates inherited this biological regeneration method from the ape family of creatures. This proposal isn't conclusive. But it is persuasive! A religionist would merely argue that this was 'the Will of God.' But this is no argument at all. I could set aside all arguments supporting the Personal Creator hypothesis by stating "That's just not the way things are," with the same want and lack of proof.

Neither of the above answers the germane question of why women differ physically from men. Women differ psychologically from men also. This raises questions that religionists can't answer with anything more substantial than the 'Will of God' inanity. The totality of differentiation between the sexes is an enigma theologically. But, for an atheist armed with scientific information and evolutionary theories, the mystery is progressively unraveling. The mystery threatens, in all practicality, to be fully resolved in the not-too-distant future.

There is an additional point, *apropos* human anatomy, that I wish to make now. It has to do with the act of procreation, but isn't included here salaciously, nor with a furtive intent to titillate. The observation, presently to be expounded, is just another indication of a natural genesis for mankind, and concomitantly, is a refutation of our imputed Divine design.

Several years ago, an instructional pamphlet for a feminine hygiene product came to my notice. On the pamphlet was pictured a side view of a woman's torso in cut-away illustration that depicted the female reproductive organs. In this illustration, the vaginal canal was seen to bend in the same convex curve as does a woman's lower abdomen, including her womb, when viewed from the side. This isn't anomalous; rather, this is the exact curvature one would expect. A man's reproductive organ, when erected, also has a natural curvature. Now whenever two curved surfaces come in contact, they can either be in agreement, or in opposition.

If one were to visualize the act of copulation in humans, keeping the above in mind, then the male mounting from the rear of the female would place the two curvatures in agreement. Whereas: a male penetrating a female from her front would place the curvatures in opposition. This would seem to indicate that the 'natural' method of human copulation is from the rear, not face to face! Yet, face to face is the common position the overwhelming mass of humans prefer. By observation, almost all animals copulate in the opposite, that is, the 'natural' position.

How can this incidental fact be explained best? If God fashioned our human bodies wouldn't He have known of our preference for frontal copulation. Logic informs He would have. Orthodox theology would insist that He did know this! But, if it is true that we have evolved from the animal kingdom, then it is understandable why our genital configurations would/could be akin to that of primates. This seems to be the exact case. Of course, none of the foregoing is incontrovertible proof of either evolution or creationism. But, if it can be read as a clue, then that clue points toward evolution and away from creationism.

Any and all serious investigators should gather their evidence as they find it; not as they wish it to be! Religionists look at mankind and state, "Only (a) God could have created a human being." Yet, if one looks scrupulously, rather than sanctimoniously, humans are physically very frail. Via compensated comparison, man is a veritable weakling. Only a superior brain grants us dominion over all other life forms. Be aware, our brain isn't different in kind. It differs by degree. This verifiable fact supports an evolved brain, not divinely infused intelligence.

Stated another way, Parakeets have small wings; consequently, their flight ability is limited. Eagles have large wings. They can fly much higher and cover much greater distances than smaller birds. Still, both are dependent upon wings for their ability to fly. If a bird existed that had no wings: yet still was able to fly; then this bird would provide proof that the Creator is all-powerful.

Similarly, if man had no brain at all, yet could still reason: this would be proof positive of an Omnipotent God! The evidence is otherwise. Man has a brain that is more evolved than a gorilla's, yet is little different in structure. Animals, especially the higher animals, aren't lacking in intelligence. They just aren't as broadly perceptive as are humans. But then too, all humans aren't equally endowed with intelligence. Sadly, but truly, some severely retarded humans have less practical intelligence than do the smartest primates. Is this because "God made them that way"? No! Genetic imperfection creates retardation, which has many diverse natural causes. Unwittingly, our science has generated several forms of mental retardation caused by the coincidental side effects of either chemical ingestion or environmental pollution.

Is my latest premise clearer now? If He had so desired, couldn't God have endowed humanity with superior intelligence without the need for a brain? Couldn't our intelligence have resided in our soul or our spirit, both of which are non-corporeal, thereby invisible? Why must God always work His wonders through biological (physical) instrumentalities?

Debatably, the most damaging query a person may ask is, 'Why is there always a "natural" explanation for every eventuality that religionists faithfully ascribe to the realm of the "supernatural"? God, that is! (Example: In biblical times mentally defective persons were "possessed by demons." Today, we know that mental illness is most often caused by a chemical imbalance in the body affecting the brain.)

The answer, of course, is that no God whatsoever is active in the affairs of planet Earth. In every instance, what occurs are the interactions and reactions of physical phenomena. There always has been, and always will be, a natural cause for every occurrence. The term 'God' is nothing but a shibboleth for 'Nature.' Humans are only one of many possibilities created by natural elements interacting with each other. Mankind evolved from a lower life form. Life isn't some mysterious infusion from the heavens. Biological life is every bit as natural as is the formation of a mountain range, or the discharge of a bolt of lightning. Nature is the ever inscrutable reality that we humans have perverted into a universal deity. Yes, we can know of Nature, but Nature can never know of us. Nature ("God" in religious vernacular) is a process, not a personality!

THINKING ABOUT ANGELS

What are angels? Angels are pure spirits that can never be detected without divine dispensation. Because they are non-corporeal, there is no way for mortals to verify their existence. There just isn't any found method to coax angels into a bodily appearance. Angels can only be seen when they are on a mission for the Deity. Apparently at these times, God turns angels into virtual human beings. At the Resurrection tomb angels appeared in the guise of men. At His birth they appeared to the shepherds as standard (?) angels. Whatever angels factually look like? In Genesis, Chapter 18, two Angles, in company with the Lord (Yahweh?), appear as three ordinary men to inform Abraham and Sarah that she will birth a son (Isaac).

Do angels have wings? What about demons who are, as revealed, only rebellious angels? What do they look like? Do the rebellious angels ever make earthly appearances? If they do, are their appearances bodily, or angelic, or demonic? Before 'The Fall,' I imagine that all angels looked alike. Did God change the appearance of the now-fallen angels to prevent them from posing as faithful angels? Paul writes that demons can change their appearance to imitate *"Angles of Light."* [2 Cor. 11:14] We literally know very little about angels, or devils, in most aspects of their existence. Yet, there are areas where our knowledge of spiritual beings is quite extensive.

These observations are inserted here only to prompt you to think about angels. Here are a few more questions: God created Angels, hence, there was a time when angels didn't exist. Will there come a period in the future when angels will no longer be necessary? Pointedly: 'beyond the end of the physical world? When all human beings have been assigned to their eternal destinies (Heaven or Hell), will God still need angels? 'Probably not!

Can we speculate that God will expunge all angels the moment they have fulfilled their divine purposes? 'Probably so! What would be the point of keeping them around? Of course, God might still need the demon angels. After Doomsday, who is going to keep an eye on those wicked souls in Hell? The Devil's usefulness will probably continue until Hell comes to an end. But Hell fire is an eternal damnation, you state. Thank you, that is correct. Hell is scheduled to last for all eternity! The bad angels will live forever as attendants of the fiery torment. I almost could have forgotten that. Is what I have written about Hell to this point essentially correct theologically? I believe it is. What is more, I believe you now will have discerned my point. The rebellious angels are eternally necessary. The steadfast angels will be rewarded for their fidelity by being willed out of existence. This is blatant ignominious treatment for entities that are entirely sinless.

Okay, we will grant that God won't destroy the good angels. What does this prove? What difference does it make if all angels live or die? We are told that the greatest reward in Heaven is the sight of God. The angels have never been without the sight of God. Why they merited Heaven without having first earned it, as humans must do, is beyond my comprehension. Nevertheless, the angels were created and placed directly into the ineffable bliss of Heaven. This didn't stop the Angel of Light, Lucifer, from fomenting a revolt. But we will overlook that here. We have conceded that the good angels will live for the remainder of eternity. Then what happens next? Nothing, you say! You are probably correct, for I know of no biblical prognostications that extend beyond the "End of the Age." The story of Christianity ends after the final judgment. '… And they lived happily ever after! 'Or unhappily in the case of the damned!'

Bravo! The play is ended. I trust 'The Saga of Mankind' has been a smashing success. The lone spectator to this monumental drama has been God. I can only hope that He has been gratifyingly entertained, for there will be no encore performance. Our story ends with God being gleefully embraced by an undetermined number of ecstatic saints and dimwitted angels. Yet, why angels merited Heaven continues to haunt my reasoning. Nonetheless, the angels were created and placed directly into the bliss of Heaven, and a minimal number of human beings have joined them there in wonder and joy. Or are they all simply mesmerized into automatons by God's manifestation? 'No matter! The Saga has ended with all the players mindlessly immersed in endless time and space.

Frankly, this silliness is just as difficult to write about as it is to believe. Angels are no more existent than is God. How can humans be so gullible as to believe in spirits? If I have a spirit, why can't I control it? Why can't I perform spiritual acts? Why can't my spirit fly around to observe what is happening elsewhere? If you state that my flesh imprisons my spirit, then I want to know how mortal flesh has the power to subdue spirit essence. Can spirit essence be restrained? I thought spirits could pass through solid walls? I thought spirits could fly unhindered, anywhere they pleased? You can't have it both ways. Either spirit essence is impervious to physical matter, or it is subservient to physical matter. The true explanation is that there is no such invisible substance as spirit essence. Angels were postulated as the soldier-slaves of the fictitious god king, Yahweh. Consequently, angels themselves are fictitious.

Angels are more than illogical; they are unnecessary! God doesn't need anything or anybody. If He created angels and gave Heaven to them, why did He create men and make them earn Heaven? If the angels revolted once, then they can do so again. Who knows? This time they may succeed! Would we learn of it if they did? God punished the angels who rebelled against Him. Did He reward those who remained loyal? How do you reward someone who is already in Heaven, the utopia of all places?

The story of the Fallen Angels is too nonsensical for serious evaluation. So, too, is the rationalization that humans were put on Earth as a trial to prove their deservedness to reside everlastingly in Heaven. If God knew beforehand that created man (Adam and his descendants) would be so wicked that shortly thereafter He would have to destroy every creature on Earth except Noah and his family: why didn't God just start with Noah and his family? Did God know of Lucifer's rebellion before He created angels? God is omniscient, He must have known. Therefore, God created the epitome of evilness (Lucifer-Satan) in a deliberative act. God Himself thereby fabricated the rebellion of the disloyal angels.

Did God foresee that the creation of man would inevitably result in the mortal crucifixion of His Son, who is imputed to be co-extensive with His divinity? If He did, then He abetted His own death. It should be obvious to all by now that the founding premise of Christianity is preposterous. Don't speculate why Christian religionists insist that you reflect on the mysteries of your faith exclusively with pious acceptance. If they had told you to examine those beliefs intelligently, you would have been scandalized by their absurdity and their ludicrousness.

Summarizing this segment: A question: Why are all angels male? Why aren't there female angels? However, angels are only minor players in the fiction of religiosity. God is the main character in the myth of man's creation. God is a literary devise composed by mankind. So, also, are His (male) angels. Finally and unalterably, all spirits are a fiction. Treat them as such, and I am persuaded you will have advanced your intellectual maturity toward full adulthood. Once enough of us have reached this state of self enlightenment, the demise of human supernaturalism (that is, 'religiosity') will have commenced. I could pray to see such a day, but alas, I shan't. Those enlightened persons who do persevere until that day dawns, will realize bliss far greater than any spiritual heaven could ever confer upon them.

EDEN'S LOCATION

While scanning books on Christian theology, I am somewhat unsettled when I read the almost standard comment that a "Senior Church Official" (theologian) hasn't yet ruled on this or that obscure theological point. The inference is always that although the debated or debatable point is a mystery to most, the mystery will be revealed by the Official at a time in the future. Of course, most congregants will readily espouse whatever doctrinal position that Official establishes. This is a politically safe stand, but intellectually, it frustrates factual analysis. The stated belief is that God (or Christ, or the Holy Ghost) inspires the Christian Organization; consequently, all their theological pronouncements are unalterable revealed 'truths.'

Once more though, I ask you to forgo the humble, unquestioning acceptance of this indoctrination. Examine instead, the evidence readily available to formulate your own conclusions. A detailed history of the

Ecumenical Councils of the Church would be appropriate here. But they would, likewise, be extremely lengthy; more so, if I added my thoughts and observations. So it is with sincere regret that I apologize for not commenting on each one of the twenty-one General Councils.

Yet, this work would be incomplete without some mention of the Councils; 'the reason for their convening; 'the events leading to; 'the events transpiring during, and the actions that shaped their conclusions. A reasonable application of intellectual honesty would reveal that the decrees of those Councils, by and large if not wholly, were arrived at by the same process as are our present-day laws. Specifically, most of those disputes were settled through political expediency, cronyism, compromise, coalition voting, or just plain power politics. No one postulates the Holy Ghost as the real author of our national laws, and neither should anyone credit Him with authorship of any one of the Christian Church's decrees. (Protestant, Catholic, or Non-Denominational)

The similarities between our Legislative Congresses and the Councils of the Church are most striking. The chief difference being that our Congress is composed of two generally antagonistic political parties, whereas the Church ostensibly had only one homogeneous Christian party. However, in practice, most Church Councils were called because of factional splits within the Church hierarchy. Disputes that were so deep, and that had champions on each side so powerful, that only the Church in Council could resolve their doctrinal disputes. In the earliest Councils the side that numbered the Emperor and his soldiery was invariably the faction whose doctrinal tenets prevailed.

All the participants of these gatherings professed to seek the guidance of the Holy Spirit. But few really desired His spiritual presence unless they could have been assured beforehand that He would be predisposed to their preferred theological advocacies. Reading of the chicanery that preceded and accompanied the Councils (usually on both sides of a controversy) I can sympathize with the absence of the Holy Spirit. Had He made an appearance, He could never have escaped 'guilt by association' denunciation *with* one of the disputing factions.

Notwithstanding the foregoing, what difference did (or does) it make if Jesus was true man at the same time that He was true God? 'If His human nature was superior to His divine nature? If He possessed one will or two wills? Here, indulge me to list several early Councils of the Church to settle internal controversies. [Cf. (1st ever Ecumenical Council) Council of Nicaea – AD 325; (4th E.C.) Council of Chalcedon – AD 451; and finally the (6th E.C.) Third Council in Constantinople – AD 680-81] These Council disputes were/are egotistical minutiae that only stimulate pedants, or their virtual kin: the theologians.

If God sent His Son down to live among humans, there must have been a cogent reason for so doing. We can disregard the particulars here of just how He accomplished this, and concentrate solely on His motive. What was God's purpose for sending Jesus to live as a man? Early Christian thinkers asked the same question: "Why?" It obviously wasn't for the reason the Old Testament taught. Viz., that the Messiah would come and establish God's earthly kingdom. Everyone who lived after the Resurrection could witness that no earthly kingdom had been established. They also could observe that Jesus no longer lived on Earth. Nor was there the slightest evidence that He provided any guidance or protection for His fledgling organization. But there was ample evidence for their opposites.

The persecution of the early faithful, along with the perfidy of the later powerful ruling Church leaders, arouses my suspicions. Then and now, all the evidence is arrayed against the existence of a personal God, and expansively so against more than one God, e.g., a Trinity of Gods. [Cf. (2nd) First Council of Constantinople – AD 381]

By now, we all know what God didn't intend. But we still aren't cognizant of what He did intend, assuming the divinity of Jesus is fact! The stock answer is that Jesus died for our sins. What sins? Those of us born after AD 33 hadn't committed any sins yet. 'True!' But Adam had. Adam had eaten of the Tree of Knowledge. For that unforgivable transgression, mankind has toiled and contended ever since. That is Divine Justice at work: 'One man sins and all mankind are punished.' [Cf. Num. 16:22 or Jos. 22:18] But fortunately, consistency is maintained because Divine Mercy is just as lopsided: 'One man is crucified, and all men are absolved of their sins thereby.' [Cf. 1 Jn. 2:2]

Are we dealing with fact here? Or is humanity being sold a literary elixir that is touted to cure all our ills without end? There is no reality in Genesis; it is a near total work of fiction. Adam's fall is the premise for the Incarnation of Jesus. Genesis 1 to 3 is a prosaic fable that ranks about midpoint in relation to other tribal creation myths throughout the world. Some are more imaginative and more interesting; others are more improbable and less entertaining to contemplate. However, the scantiness of our Christian creation story exposes its fabrication.

Take any folk tale! Examine the details of the story. Many inconsistencies and improbabilities that escape a cursory reading will become evident. Recall Snow White and the Seven Dwarfs. What did the dwarfs eat? Surely not meat; yet there was no vegetable garden seen in the movie. If the dwarfs mined diamonds, why weren't they rich? Why didn't they live in a castle?

Were they heterosexual? If they were, why hadn't some gold-digging Goldilocks moved in with them long before the arrival of Snow White? If homosexual, what attraction did Snow White possess that a local maiden hadn't already exhibited? If asexual, what allure did Snow White possess?

There are no wholly satisfactory answers to the above questions simply because the story is fiction. It never really happened, and couldn't ever really happen; therefore, the mundane but unavoidable necessities of workaday living aren't accounted. The Adam and Eve fable suffers from the same inherent defects. It didn't happen, and it couldn't happen. Consequently, verifying facts that authenticate the story are absent. My argument for this assertion follows.

Skip the first seven days of creation; they are too ridiculous to spend much time with. Begin with the Garden of Eden; did (does) it exist? The Bible states that it existed, and implies that it still does exist. *"Cherubim, and the flaming sword that turns every way, to guard the way to the tree of life."* [Gen. 3:24] I have read and re-read Genesis, yet nowhere do I read what became of the Garden of Eden; consequently, it must still exist exactly where God left it. The Cherubim ("im" pluralizes in Aramaic. Cherub is singular) must still be there guarding the wondrous tree. To advocate otherwise would be tantamount to revising the words of God. If Eden does still exist, why can't we locate it today?

Furthermore, if God was going to move Eden, or destroy it, why would He place Cherubim to guard the tree? Did He need time to do whatever He eventually decided to do? If He did, then He definitely wasn't all-powerful. Maybe He couldn't make up His mind, but this implies that perhaps He didn't have enough information to make the wisest decision.

Yet that too denies His omniscient power, and thereby is untenable. Finally, we are left with the inescapable testimony of the Bible. This being: That Eden still exists in the vicinity of the Euphrates River. 'It is yet accessible to mankind. As a consequence, the Tree of Life is still guarded by angels ("Cherubim") wielding a flaming sword(s). [Cf. Gen. 3:24] I wonder if a flaming sword would be effective against a modern tank. This is laughable today; but a flaming sword, in the days of the ancient writer of Genesis, would have been a formidable weapon indeed, and exceedingly so when brandished by angels.

Here is a question for all fundamentalist Christians: "If every word in the Bible is true, then where is Eden today?" For those who alibi the accuracy of the Bible by postulating some of the text as literal, and some of the text as figurative, I submit that all of the text is figurative. The entire book is a figure of many fertile imaginations. The Bible is either the entire word of God; or it is totally the word of man. If one tittle can be proved to have been added by man against God's will, then the theory of divine authorship must be forsaken. If He didn't inspire a true and complete (and unalterable) text, then His inspiration didn't fashion any part of the Bible. He is perfect; could He inspire an imperfect composition? Not if He wished it to be reverenced as the unassailable word of Infinite Wisdom!

ELIJAH REBORN

In Matthew's Gospel, Jesus declares that the Baptist is (the rebirth of) Elijah. *"John is Elijah."* [Mt. 11:14] In John's Gospel, the Baptist is asked by the messengers of the priests and Levites *"Are you Elijah?"* The Baptist answers categorically, *"No, I am not."* [Jn. 1:21]

Where is the unadulterated truth? Did Jesus lie, or did the Baptist lie? Why does the Bible contradict itself if God inspired its authors? Both of these authors (Evangelists) were Apostles. Which one of them wrote falsely?

O. T. PROPHECIES FULFILLED IN THE N.T.

In keeping with the title of this chapter, "Curious Questions," a pertinent question arises. It is this: Why are the Old Testament 'prophecies' pertaining to the arrival of the Messiah scattered so ubiquitously throughout the Old Testament? Take just the first three chapters of Matthew's Gospel as an example: Matthew records nine separate O. T. prophecies between verses 1:1 and 3:17. Each is declared a fulfillment of a prophecy. Yet, if I research these prophesies in the O.T., I find them significantly separated and completely immersed in texts that are not prophetic of N.T. events. Is this point clear? It's as if the author of the Greek Mythologies had decided to make a hundred or more Messianic predictions pre-AD that would not be fulfilled entirely until between the years AD 2000 and 2003. Yet instead of lumping them altogether in a cohesive unit, the myth makers (at the behest of a celestial editor?) scattered them willy-nilly throughout the various Greek Mythological tales without expressly identifying them in those unrelated, incongruent text locations as Messianic predictions.

Here follows a listing of nine Messianic predictions found in just the first three chapters of Matthew's Gospel. There are many more to be found throughout the N.T. books. My point can be made without researching all of those. My question is this, 'Why would God, the Heavenly Inspirer, want to conceal His Messianic notifications in a hundred or more places, obscured among O. T. Chapter and Verse that had nothing to do with predicting the 'Coming' of His Redeeming Son? At best, this is devious. At worse it is diabolic, in that few if any future exegetes would recognize the importance of these obscure verses beforehand. I can fathom no sensible reason for doing so. If those verses can only be discerned "after the fact" as are every one of Matthew's (and his contemporary N.T. authors), then what purpose did these verses serve in the first instance? Most were so effectively disguised within other O.T. biblical verses that no one ahead of time could accurately predict any future scenario that would describe the eventuating method for the Messianic Redemption of the Sin of Adam and Eve.

The verses referred to at the start of this segment from Mathew's first three chapters along with the [bracketed] O.T. predictive Messianic chapter & verse follows: 1:21 [Si. 46:1 apoch.]; 1:23 [Isa. 7:14]; 2:6 [Mic.

5:2]; 2:15 [Ho. 11:1]; 2:18 [Jr. 31:15]; 3:3 [Isa. 40:3]; 3:4 [2 Ki. 1:8]; 3:12 [Ws. 5:14-23 apoch.]; 3:17 [Gen. 22:2, Ps. 2:7, Isa. 42:1]. What any reasonable person should conclude from this mish-mash of past predictions is not 'inspiration from a divine being.' Rather, hindsight matching by a future exegete striving to find verses in the O.T. matching with his own messianic reportage, or the messianic composition of other written verses in the N.T. Almost any verse one might compose can find a matching or predictive verse in the O.T. simply because the O.T. is rather large, and because there are so many obscure, ambiguous, or enigmatic verses contained therein.

Yet, the one prediction that we find in the writings of three N.T. authors is that Jesus will return before everyone alive in AD 33 has died. [Cf. Mt. 16:28; Mk. 9:1 {8:39} & Lu. 9:27] That thrice repeated prediction has failed utterly. Two thousand (2,000) years later, we are still awaiting the swift 'Return of Jesus.' [Cf. Mt. 24:30] 'The Kingdom of God is at hand!' [Cf. Mk. 1:15 & Lu. 10:11]

WHY HASN'T JESUS RETURNED AS HE PROMISED?

Perhaps here, we should have a brief review of what we have accomplished heretofore, and how we have accomplished it. I write "we" because I believe that anyone who has ventured this far into my writings will have long since been reverse converted. If this isn't the case with the present reader, please make the necessary mental adjustments and proceed.

We (I) have scoured the Old Testament and found much to attack. The four Gospels provided a wellspring of additional ammunition. The Epistles fared no better. Only the Apocalypse (Revelations) has remained virtually unscathed. Here that will change. The Apocalypse is so overladen with oblique symbolism that frankly, I have never been able to sit down and read it through even one time. At different times I have encountered references to various sections, and at those times I have examined the cited material. In these disjointed efforts I probably have covered most of the germane material contained therein. 'Perhaps? But not precluding all possible doubt!

Now, after the previous disclaimer, I will continue. The most striking feature evident in the Apocalypse is its immediacy. All the predicted events will be realized (presumptively) during the lifetime of the first readers. The author of this last book of the New Testament believed that all of his visions were imminent! This is why "Revelations" (The Apocalypse) was addressed exclusively to seven churches and not to Christians in general. The thrust of this present segment will be to show that the author was wrong about the immediacy of his nightmare scenarios. When I prove this point, I also will have proved concurrently that no deity inspired the text. This accomplished, I will then ask if any portion of the Bible can be deemed inspired, if any other section can be proved uninspired, as is irrefutably obvious in John's Revelations.

Evolved Christian dogma must, and does, forbid the proposition of a partially inspired Bible. Therefore, the object of this segment will be in harmony with all others in this book. Namely: To defrock the persistent myth of a Personal God. I do this not as an attempt at deicide, but rather, after the manner of the outspoken boy in the tale of The Emperor's New Clothes. The naked truth is that there isn't a Personal God. If I look and fail to see God, and speak out to say so aloud, perhaps everyone else will stop pretending that they can see Him. Once we all clear our eyes, we may just discover that clothing made of straw (i.e., a disconcerting truth) may be preferable to no clothes (pretend truth). Here then is my argument:

Revelations (Apocalypse) specifically records that Jesus will return "shortly" in at least nine verses. Verily, I am aware of the insertion in the Second Epistle of Peter the phrase: *"One day can be as a thousand years."* [2 Peter 3:8] But that doesn't apply here. The passages under scrutiny refer directly to a brief time span, and not to days or to years. The next-to-the-last verse in the Bible reads thus: *"He {Jesus} who testifies to these things says, 'It is true, I come quickly!'"* [Rev. 22:20] [Cf. Rev. 1:1; 1:3; 1:7; 3:11; 22:6; 22:7; 22:10 & 22:12]

Notice that the author, speaking in prophecy from Jesus, doesn't say He will return in a few days. He says Jesus will return 'quickly.' If we distort the meaning of this adverb to anything other than 'rapidly,' or 'speedily,' we not only deceive ourselves, but we likewise admit that the author of the text was deceived by his inspirer. Assuming that John the Apostle was the author of Revelations, I ask: Did the Spirit of God purposely delude John into believing the return of Jesus would be prompt? If the words of John were inspired, then you must answer my query affirmatively. God inspired John falsely!

Here is a verse with time citation: *"And the angel said to me, 'These words are trustworthy and true; and the Lord, the God of the spirits of the prophets, sent his angel to show to his servants what must shortly come to pass.'"* [Rev. 22:6]

Even more indicative of the immediacy of the return of Jesus prophesied in Revelations is this quote: *"Behold, he cometh with clouds, and every eye shall see him, and they also which pierced him: and all kindreds of the earth shall wail because of him. Even so, Amen."* [Rev. 1:7] John, attested throughout the ages as 'inspired by the Holy Spirit,' predicted that those *"which pierced him"* would still be alive when Jesus returned 'shortly.'

Did John believe he was the object of divine inspiration? Answer: Yes! Did John think that Christ Jesus was returning soon? Answer: Yes! Was John correct in either instance? Answer: No! John was twice wrong! He wasn't the recipient of mystical foreknowledge. He deluded himself. If we believe his false prophecy, we delude ourselves. John wasn't even writing to Christians in totality. He specifically directed his revelations to these seven churches: Ephesus, Smyrna, Pergamum, Thyatira, Sardis, Philadelphia and Laodicea. [Cf. Rev. 1:11] Do any of these churches still exist? Who knows? Would it matter?

Don't agonize if you study the convoluted symbolisms contained in Revelations (Apocalypse) and find them utterly obscure. They were written to an audience two thousand years removed from you. To determine the veracity of John's predictions, let the words of Moses guide you.

"If you say to yourselves, 'How can we recognize an oracle which the Lord has spoken?' Know that, even though a prophet speaks in the name of the Lord, if his oracle is not fulfilled or verified, it is an oracle which the Lord did not speak. The prophet has spoken it presumptuously ...." [Deut. 18:21-22]

John presumed that Jesus (under the aspect of the Holy Ghost) inspired him, but the test of Moses exposes John as a false prophet. For those who rationalize that Jesus may still come, I rebut you: Too much time has already transpired to redeem the failed promise of John. If Jesus were to appear tomorrow, this would still be more than nineteen hundred years too late.

Essentially this concludes the segment. What more is there to write after this quote: *"But any prophet who falsely claims to speak in my name or who speaks in the name of another god, is to be put to death.*" [Deut. 18:20] Revelations is exposed as just so much obscure, paranormal, non-inspired phraseology.

Know this; it doesn't pleasure me to debunk religiosity. Frankly, I would prefer that there was 'Someone' up in the sky to importune. 'To pray to; or even just to commiserate with. There isn't; this is sad. But, this doesn't leave us without hope. What is it that we desire from a Personal God; "Love"? Yes, but it must be actual love, not conjured love; not conjectured love; nor postponed love. Do we desire God's respect? Of course! But respect granted without deservedness is perfunctory at best. Now consider Justice. Isn't the swift imposition of prescribed retribution against our adversaries, combined with the coincident mental respite, that we all determine ourselves to be entitled. Isn't this what each of us deems as our inherent 'just reward' in life?

Justice! Justice! Justice! This is what we all need, and this is all we need. We need it here! We need it now! For if there is no true justice, then there is no real Justifier! Eternal bliss is much more than I could ever earn. Eternal damnation far exceeds any just punishment I could warrant. My human limitations preclude either absolute joy or absolute pain as proper recompense for my human deeds or misdeeds; whichever may be decisive! The ancients were correct in their expectations from the deities. If I am good, then reward me now. If I am evil, then punish me with that same immediacy. That is just!

Someone much wiser than myself once stated: "Justice delayed, is justice denied!" {William E. Gladstone} To my mind, no aphorism ever spoke a more profound truth with such succinctness.

IMPLICATIONS OF THE SHROUD OF TURIN

No one knowledgeable in the sphere of the Christian religion could overlook the implications of the Shroud of Turin. This artifact is purported to be the very linen cloth that covered the deceased body of Jesus during the time lapse between Good Friday afternoon and Easter Sunday overnight, two thousand years ago. Truth insists that I admit, when I first learned of the Shroud, I decided instantly, and with scant knowledge, to declare this relic a fraud. Historically, how many other relics have been exposed as shameless hoaxes? The miracle-credited bones of Saint Rosalie of Palermo proved, upon examination, to have come from a goat. Slivers alleged to be from the original Cross, if gathered together, would supply enough wood to build another Ark! Had all the spearheads claimed by their owners to have come from the lance that pierced the side of Jesus been authenticated, Jesus would have been rent asunder by the soldier's thrust.

But, my early encounters with mentions of the Shroud were different. The official Church was reticent; it was cautious. That wasn't too surprising. What was remarkable was the matter-of-fact tone of the references I read. The spokespersons were as guarded in their affirmations, as was the official Catholic Church. Gradually it dawned on me that here was a phenomenon that might derive its merits on its own witness, without the artificial impetus of religious fervor.

At the bookstore, however, my enthusiasm was tempered. There was no lack of information about the Shroud. However, each book I glanced through started with the premise that the Shroud had already proved itself, and proceeded from that premise. I didn't purchase a book that day. A year later, quite fortuitously, a small pamphlet distributed by the Salesian Missions came into my wife's possession. To me, the pamphlet was a revelation. Unlike the works I had skimmed at the bookstore, this pamphlet was quite matter-of-fact. It omitted all but a few of those "Gloria's" and "Hosanna's" that permeate most religious works. Predictably, its brevity, coupled with its factual presentation, rekindled my desire for more knowledge of the enigmatic Shroud.

I shan't here list all of the books I subsequently read from the library. Two titles remained in my memory long after I had forgotten the others: The Shroud of Turin, by Ian Wilson, and Verdict on the Shroud, by Stevenson & Habemus. I recommend both books to my readers. The discussion point here will center on the consequences inherent if the Shroud is deemed authentic. Frankly, the evidence accumulated heretofore is compelling in favor of authenticity. Without personally attesting to its genuineness, I will proceed with this dissection conceding its authenticity. Accept for the moment that the Shroud is truly what it is purported to be; namely, it is the burial cloth of Jesus.

First, the image on the linen cloth that comprises the Shroud is said to "prove" that Jesus factually did resurrect after His crucifixion. This just isn't so! The image on the Shroud is in the likeness of a deceased adult male. How the image became imprinted onto the cloth remains a mystery, and to date, can't be replicated. This aspect of the Shroud is spectacular, perhaps even miraculous. Yet, I repeat: "The image on the Shroud is that of a dead man!" What is proved is that a corpse palpably formed an image on a covering burial cloth; not that a physical resurrection took place!

Second, the Shroud is credited with a protective power for the city of its residence. Why this is reputed cannot be fathomed, for the Shroud's conjectured history unambiguously contradicts the premise. The exact history of the Shroud isn't known. In this discussion I accept author Wilson's speculations concerning the Shroud's travels as accurate, and discourse accordingly. Edessa, its first home (AD 35?) outside Jerusalem, was alternately Christian, Pagan, then again Christian. The Byzantines later gained control of the City from the Parthians. Still later, the Persians ruled there. During much of this time the relic was hidden in a niche above a city gate for safety from both man and nature. (Edessa was a frequent site of floods, as well as of wars.)

As you can read, Edessa was anything but protected during the Shroud's residence there. The Shroud itself remained hidden above the gate for almost five hundred years. Finally, in the year AD 944, the attacking Byzantines obtained the Shroud in ransom for sparing Edessa, and transferred that relic to Constantinople There it remained until AD 1204, when, during the Fourth Crusade, the perfidious knights of Western Christendom detoured their attack against the infidel Muslim invaders of the Holy Lands. Instead, they directed their larcenous intentions to sack and loot the Christians in Constantinople. At this point in history, the Shroud disappeared again. (Perhaps to hide its total embarrassment at being unable to protect its then host city?)

The Shroud came to light almost a century later in, of all places, Acre. 'Not far from its starting point of Jerusalem. Alas, Acre soon fell to the Muslims, and the Shroud was hastily transported to Paris. Nor was the Shroud safe there, as the English and French were active combatants (against one another) during most of this period. Over the next several hundred years the Shroud had many homes, and was involved in much controversy.

Oddly, the notion persisted that the Shroud conferred divine protection on its owners and their environs. That the notion was unfounded is an imperative puzzler. Then, on December 4, 1532, a mortal blow was delivered to the Shroud's attributed protective faculties. A fire in the chapel housing the hallowed relic caused permanent damage to the Shroud, and narrowly missed destroying it altogether. Observably, the Shroud couldn't even protect itself; much less anything else!

None of the foregoing relates specifically to the authenticity of the Shroud. But it definitely adds nothing to its credibility either. The passiveness of the Shroud during all of its adventurous existence is mute testimony against any miraculous property emanating from the Shroud itself. The Shroud has appeared to be normal in every respect save one: it displays the image of a brutalized and crucified man whose replica bears evidences of most everything we know of the crucifixion of Jesus! The scourging; the beating; the cap of thorns; the pierced side; and (in a negative aspect) the absence of broken legs, are all visually apparent, and all visuals match with the known travails of Jesus.

Several factors do cast doubt on the continuity of the Shroud. One factor is this: During its sojourn in Constantinople, the Shroud (if factually it was the Shroud) was known as the Mandylion, per author Wilson. The Mandylion always was represented as a disembodied facial image on a cloth the size of a small towel; not the double imaged fourteen-foot linen that we know today as the Shroud. Author Ian Wilson (T. S. of T.), offers an astute deduction to account for this ostensible discrepancy. He posits the Shroud being folded and encased so that only the face was visible. Yet the possibility remains, the cloth we call the Shroud, and the cloth known to history as the Mandylion, may be two separate objects. In this circumstance, the history of the Shroud can only be traced back to the fourteenth century. One of the reasons that era was infamous was because so many counterfeit relics were manufactured during the period. This should be recognized as a caution flag for any prudent investigator.

The second factor is this: In the late 1980s, the Church permitted a small swatch of the Shroud to be carbon-14 dated. The test indicated that the Shroud was manufactured more than one thousand years after the crucifixion, between AD 1230 & 1360 (?). This would seem to doom the authenticity of the Shroud. It doesn't, because the sample may have come from a more recent replaced portion of the Shroud. (After its fire damage.)

Also, there are queries about the dating process itself. Later contamination of the Shroud is also a possibility. During testing, any sample provided is completely destroyed; thus the Church has so far refused to supply an original swatch large enough to guarantee an unquestioned result. My guess is that the dating question will remain unresolved until a less destructive test, or a test with less need for subjective interpretation, is devised.

Advocates for the authenticity of the Shroud point out that over the centuries, countless persons have handled, kissed, pressed religious objects against it (crucifixes, *et al.*), and have generally contaminated the linen cloth. Mere exposure to the atmosphere could have compromised the carbon-14 results through the settling of plant spores and other air-born contaminants upon the Shroud. With a larger sample of cloth, these impurities might be removed completely beforehand so as not to confound the testing. (Developments in 2002 have further rendered unreliable the carbon-14 dating test results of 1988.)

Another factor that must be weighed into the evaluation is the historic rumor that copies or imitations of the Shroud had been produced in the past. Because of the Shroud's tangled history and multiple ownership (and questionable continuity!), a serious researcher has to ponder what the imitations looked like. How authentic did they appear? How were the imitations prepared? None of the rumored copies is extant. In honesty, how can we be certain that our extant Shroud isn't a counterfeit of an original Shroud? Previously, ingenious testing of the Shroud by professionals in several fields of knowledge seemed to verify this Shroud as genuine. Yet, if we possessed a known forgery for comparison with the Turin Shroud, we could be more confident in our conclusions.

Lastly, still advocating that the Shroud is authentic, I ask: "What divine motive did the resurrected Jesus have for leaving His image behind?" No explanation suggests itself to me except that it exists so that this generation could prove that the crucifixion of Jesus was historical. No other previous generation has had the technical expertise to verify the Shroud's authenticity beyond all refutation. In this event, the present custodians of the Shroud are thwarting God's purposes. They have been overly reluctant to even display the Shroud. They have permitted some scientific testing of minute strands of the cloth, and have permitted limited examinations by scholars. But not enough to satisfy the prime germane question: "Is the Shroud of Turin a legitimate two-thousand-year-old relic?" Until a consensus of respected investigators attest to the Shroud's authenticity, nagging suspicions of forgery or delusion will detract from the perceived and conceded hallowedness of the Shroud of Turin.

SIGNS OF THE LAST TIMES

I reckon that if God sent us predictions so that we might recognize the advent of the Second Coming, then He shouldn't fool us with deceptive indications that recur, time and again, throughout the centuries. Every biblical prognosticator who ever scanned the last book of the Bible has envisioned himself as a uniquely endowed decipherer of God's secret code, namely, the final book of the Bible, Revelations (aka Apocalypse).

Even Charles Manson, the cultic guru of a mentally twisted band of murderous street urchins, perceived a hidden message within Revelations, intended (or so he imagined) for his personal enlightenment. To be sure, we can mock his self-delusion now. We view his folly in the clarified brightness of hindsight. But God must accept some share of Manson's error, if indeed He did inspire the words of Revelation. Charles Manson's interpretations prodded by Revelations were no more irrationally convoluted than anyone else's has been. There is an embarrassing lesson to be learned from Manson's misconceived (malevolent) deciphering of the Apocalypse. I doubt if any of our self-appointed, present-day disciples will be dissuaded from formulating their own apocalyptic predictions because of Manson's apocalyptic, perverted madness.

The entire book of Revelations is nothing more than symbolic swill, pious poppycock, and glorified gibberish. It is said that 'beauty resides in the eye of the beholder.' But, in the above instance, a more cogent adage should be coined: "The wisdom of the ages can be replicated from a can of alphabet soup. But eating a bowlful won't make you a wiser biblical decipherer: just full of soup!" The Apocalypse is so fantastically written that every age is able to extract counterfeit verification from its contemporary situation to fit the vagary 'signs of the last times' foretold by the author of the final book of the Bible. All with naught verification!

SAINT PAUL AND THE 'LAW'

We know from his letters that Paul was an ardent Pharisee before he adopted Christianity. [Cf. Rom. 7:5-6] Yet, in truth, his abandonment of Pharisaism came before his conversion. Paul had already forsaken the Law as a means to eternal life before traveling that fateful road to Damascus. [Cf. Rom. Chap. 7, e.g.] His persecution and pursuit of the original Christians (whom he considered heretical Jews, not apostates), was a renewed effort to win the mental salvation that had eluded him as a faithful practitioner of the Law. He deemed the Law as holy, good, and true. Yet, when he adhered to the strictures of Judaism, sin gained control of his life. Paul identified the Law as the occasion for his sins. [Cf. Rom. 7:8-9] His theology here is obscure to me. What he seemed to be conveying was this: When Paul lived according to the Law, sin became more potent in him. Accordingly, when he preached Christ, he dispensed his converts from the requirements of the Law. At the advent of the Messiah, 'The Old Testament Law,' by Paul's appraisal, had become an archaic anachronism. [Cf. Rom. 10:4]

Although Paul forsook Pharisee dictates, he never abandoned his hope for an eternal life; a key tenet of Pharisaism. To Paul, the Law was an impediment to his goal, whereas, Jesus became the vehicle to Paul's life-long quest. If Jesus truly was resurrected through God's power, surely God would likewise resurrect all who believed in Jesus. It couldn't be otherwise. Nowadays, we refer to these self-deluding notions as the 'Power of Positive Thinking.'

MULL OVER THESE PREDICTIONS!

"Woe to them that desire the day of the Lord: Why do you long for the day of the LORD? The day of the Lord is darkness, and not light."
[Amos 5-18]

"The House of (Virgin) Israel is fallen and it shall rise no more."
[Amos 5-2]

"And the Lord God said, 'The end is come upon my people Israel': I will not delay their punishment again." [Amos 8-2]

CURIOUS QUOTES

"Put not your trust in princes, nor in the son of man, in whom there is no salvation." [Ps. 146:3 KJV]

{Jesus called Himself the 'Son of Man' — Is this a Messianic passage?}

"He delighteth not in the strength of the horse: he taketh not pleasure in the legs of a man." [Ps.147:10]

{This KJV quote forbids both horseback riding and human foot racing.}

"Blessed be the Lord my strength, which teaches my hands to war, and my fingers to fight." {Psalm of David} [Ps. 144:1 KJV]

{This quote gives Divine instigation and approval for wars.}

"For I know that the Lord is great, and that our Lord is above all gods." [Ps. 135:5 KJV]

{From David we learn that there are other, 'lesser' gods.}

"Lord, who among the gods is like you?" {Per Moses} [Ex. 15:11 KJV]

{Moses believed in a multiplicity of deities.}

"But he said, Yea rather, Blessed are they who hear the word of god, and keep it!" [Lu. 11:28 KJV]

{What is the true meaning of God's "Word"? No one can say with certitude.}

"In those days the word of the LORD was rare; there were not many visions." [1 Sam, 3:1 NIV] There were few prophets having visions in Samuel's day.

(Just as in today's world!)

CHAPTER 22
Concluding Proofs

THE APOSTLES REFUTE THE TRINITY

The very last sentence in Luke's Gospel is convincing evidence that Jesus never intended to start a new religion. Also, it is coincident evidence that Jesus wasn't (a) God. The gist of the passage is this: having just witnessed the ascension of Jesus into heaven, the eleven Apostles were filled with joy and thereafter traveled to the Temple to give thanks to God. [Cf. Lu. 24:53]

Plainly, they considered themselves still members of the Jewish faith; not the first Bishops of a nascent religion. Likewise, they gave thanks to God (Yahweh), the God of their ancestors and figurative father of their race. "Thanks for what?" I ask. The only answer available from Luke's text is that they gave thanks to God for exalting Jesus above all mankind through His resurrection and ascension. Clearly, the Apostles attributed this power not to Jesus, but to His Father, Yahweh (the father of all righteous Jews).

Here, I want to urge all those who have reasonable, troubling doubts about the spirituality of the Bible to read it! Do so questioning everything that jars your sense of logic. Don't precondition your thoughts in a manner that represses your intellect. If God did create you, then the most wondrous attribute He endowed you with is your superior brain. Religionists would have you reject all that your intellect informs you. They ask you to believe the most absurd clap-trap that uninformed, devious man has dreamed up. Make no mistake about it; the Bible is not a record of God's inspiration. It is an inglorious testimony to man's unmitigated gullibility, and his willful misinterpretation of the interactions between humanity and nature.

Every facet of religiosity (and there are an indefinite number of facets) is liable to repudiation by man's intellect. The evidence against a supernatural force that can and does influence natural events is so over-whelming, that it does just that. It overwhelms mankind. Most religion-ists scoff at astrologers, and snicker into their palms when an adherent of astrology seeks to defend his beliefs. But how much difference is there between those two? 'Scant little! Religionists have merely substituted a personal God for the astrologers' planets and stars. The overall disparity betwixt those twin superstitious beliefs is too insignificant to embrace one over the other.

The one insurmountable query that thankfully I've never been asked by a religionist is this: "Prove to me that there isn't a personal God." Upon being confronted with that challenge, I would have thrown my hands up in despair. How can I disprove a concept that has no material manifestations, when all the evidence I can muster is the total absence of material mani-festations. One might arrogantly ask me to prove that I'm alive to a jury of dead men. How could I communicate my arguments to the corpses?

The chasm between the natural world and religionist's supernatural world is unbridgeable. The foregoing statement applies only in one direc-tion however. In the mind of a religionist, God bridges the chasm almost continuously. Only when a skeptic seeks acceptable proof of a paranormal 'Entity' do religionists take refuge at the edge of the chasm. God, angels, saints, demons and the Devil all cross the barrier in an endless profusion, but never predictably, and never in an open fashion that would silence virtually all doubt. Purportedly, certain favored individuals have made the crossing (died) and been returned (resuscitated). It seems that only those who most desire proof are denied it. By name, the skeptics, the doubters, and the unbelievers!

THE MESSIAH — DIVINE OR HUMAN?

There is a serious impediment to the belief that Jesus was both God and the Messiah. The Messiah was expected to be a man exalted by God to his lofty appointive (selected) position. The Old Testament never informs us that the Messiah was to be God Himself, or His Son. The thought of God having a true biological son would have been deemed shockingly blasphemous to every descendent of Abraham, especially a divine son born of a mortal woman! (There is no need to graphically elaborate this declaration.)

Still, Christians have insisted for centuries that God did, indeed, have a mortal Son. But how could Jesus be a mortal, if He was a God? Yes, for God nothing is impossible! So, accept temporarily, that God did make Himself into a mortal human being. Was He wholly human, or just perceptively human? No, you insist that He was one hundred percent human. Okay, I have granted your premise: Jesus was one hundred percent human! Now that I have guided you into an indefensible position, I will proceed to assail you.

If Jesus was entirely human, how did He come to be returned to His Godhead? Humans are not omnipotent. It isn't within the power of a man to turn himself into a God. It is also not within a man's power to work miracles, but I will forego that element for now. The vital question is: "How was Jesus able to become (a) God again?" If your reply is that God the Father wrought this miracle, then I will switch the topic to the question of how many Gods are extant in the Universe. You see, if three is one, and one is three, then all three of them ceased being God when Jesus became a man. Or should I have written, 'All One of Them?'

Athanasius (AD 293? – 373), the Bishop of Alexandria, purportedly answered that question with his "Athanasian Creed." His 'Creed' never replaced the Nicene Creed. It did attempt to elucidate an orthodox explication of 'The Trinity.' Later scholars discount Athanasius as the actual author of that Creed based upon the suspicion that the Creed wasn't formulated until after his death. However, for my purposes, Athanasius will be deemed the author of the Creed bearing his name. Incidentally, The Catholic Church has elevated Athanasius to sainthood, and several other Christian denominations likewise have decreed him 'sainted.' The five paragraphs below reprise the Creed of Athanasius.

ATHANASIAN CREED

Whosoever will be saved, before all things it is necessary that he hold the catholic faith; which faith except every one do keep whole and undefiled, without doubt he shall perish everlastingly. And the catholic faith is this: That we worship one God in Trinity, and Trinity in Unity; neither confounding the persons nor dividing the substance. For there is one person of the Father, another of the Son, and another of the Holy Spirit. But the Godhead of the Father, of the Son, and of the Holy Spirit is all one, the glory equal, the majesty coeternal. Such as the Father is, such is the Son, and such is the Holy Spirit. The Father uncreated, the Son uncreated, and the Holy Spirit uncreated. The Father incomprehensible, the Son incomprehensible, and the Holy Spirit incomprehensible. The Father eternal, the Son eternal, and the Holy Spirit eternal. And yet they are not three eternals but one eternal. As also there are not three uncreated nor three incomprehensible, but one uncreated and one incomprehensible.

So likewise the Father is almighty, the Son almighty, and the Holy Spirit almighty. And yet they are not three almighties, but one almighty. So the Father is God, the Son is God, and the Holy Spirit is God; and yet they are not three Gods, but one God. So likewise the Father is Lord, the Son Lord, and the Holy Spirit Lord; and yet they are not three Lords but one Lord. For like as we are compelled by the Christian verity to acknowledge every Person by himself to be God and Lord; so are we forbidden by the catholic religion to say; There are three Gods or three Lords.

The Father is made of none, neither created nor begotten. The Son is of the Father alone; not made nor created, but begotten. The Holy Spirit is of the Father and of the Son; neither made, nor created, nor begotten, but proceeding. So there is one Father, not three Fathers; one Son, not three Sons; one Holy Spirit, not three Holy Spirits. And in this Trinity none is afore or after another; none is greater or less than another. But the whole three persons are coeternal, and coequal. So that in all things, as aforesaid, the Unity in Trinity and the Trinity in Unity is to be worshipped. He therefore that will be saved must thus think of the Trinity.

Furthermore it is necessary to everlasting salvation that he also believe rightly the incarnation of our Lord Jesus Christ. For the right faith is that we believe and confess that our Lord Jesus Christ, the Son of God, is God and man. God of the substance of the Father, begotten before the worlds; and man of substance of His mother, born in the world. Perfect God and perfect man, of a reasonable soul and human flesh subsisting. Equal to the Father as touching His Godhead, and inferior to the Father as touching His manhood. Who, although He is God and man, yet He is not two, but one Christ. One, not by conversion of the Godhead into flesh, but by taking of that manhood into God. One altogether, not by confusion of substance, but by unity of person.

For as the reasonable soul and flesh is one man, so God and man is one Christ; who suffered for our salvation, descended into hell, rose again the third day from the dead; He ascended into heaven, He sits on the right hand of the Father, God, Almighty; from thence He shall come to judge the quick and the dead. At whose coming all men shall rise again with their bodies; and shall give account of their own works. And they that have done good shall go into life everlasting and they that have done evil into everlasting fire. This is the catholic faith, which except a man believe faithfully he cannot be saved. {End of Athanasian Creed}

Frankly, I cannot discern the tiniest shard of sensibility in Athanasius's definition of the Trinity. The Norse mythology, in its entirety, is more credible than is his edification as to how three separate, distinct Gods are arithmetically only one God. Additionally, anyone who questions this absolute contradiction in convoluted logic will be damned to hellfire everlastingly. St. Athanasius also dictates that we must believe, under threat of the same damnation, that Jesus was and is both God and man. There is no greater contradiction in all of philosophy, and in unalterable reality. If God and Jesus are "one," how can Jesus sit at the "right hand of God"?

Bogus premises are exceedingly difficult to defend intellectually. That is why religionists always resort to "faith" and "unquestioning belief" (backed up by threat of eternal penalty), to impose their impossible-to-comprehend doctrines upon all of us. I have a question for defenders of the Athanasius Creed. If God made us; if it was He who implanted us with a logical brain; why then are so many of the vital tenets of Christianity (or any other supra-natural belief) always contra-logical? Are the intelligent of this world being deceived via our logical minds so as to be doomed to unending torment in Hell? Theologically, this seems to be precisely their inevitable, inescapable, and <u>intended</u> fate.

ZECHARIAH'S MESSIANIC PROPHECY

Some exegetes find a prophecy of the death of the "shepherd" {Jesus?} in Zechariah (aka Zachariah). *"The Lord Almighty says, 'Wake up, sword, and attack the shepherd who works for me! Kill him, and the sheep will be scattered.'"* [Zec. 13:7] In his next chapter, Zechariah wrote, *"At that time he* {the Lord} *will stand on the Mount of Olives ... The Lord my God will come bringing all the angels with him. When that time comes, there will no longer be cold or frost, nor any darkness. There will always be daylight, even at nighttime. When this will happen is known only to the Lord."* [Zec. 14:4-7]

Note the words: 'shepherd', 'kill him', and 'Mount of Olives.' Superficially, they seem to intimate accurate foreknowledge of the death of Jesus. Yet, careful examination dispels the superficial accuracy of Zechariah's predictions. Zechariah foretold the death of the shepherd by sword. Also the shepherd is identified as (he) "who works for me", not as the Son of God! Jesus died on Golgotha. The prophecy says the Lord "will stand on the Mount of Olives." Jesus prayed in the garden of Gethsemane at the foot of Mount Olivet. Lastly, Zechariah foretold the coming of the Lord and His angels; *"Then the Lord will be king over all the earth; everyone will worship him as God and know him by the same name."* [Zec. 14:9]

Approximately two thousand and five hundred years have passed; where is the fulfillment of Zechariah's prophecy (circa 520 BC)? Especially, *"... the Lord my God shall come, and all the saints with him.* [Zec. 14:5] Here is yet another instance where the Bible's words predict near immediacy, but the historic actuality confirms the very opposite.

JUDGMENT DAY

Judgment Day will be God's day of reckoning. But how will He reckon? Christian theology teaches that God will judge every one of us at some point after we have died. Precisely when this judgment will take place has been the subject of much speculation. Some believe it will occur at the instant of death. Others believe the judgment will come at the end of the age. Still others have more bizarre ideas about the final judgment.

Also, if we are to have a 'final' judgment; are we first to have a 'preliminary' judgment, at some time previous to the 'final' one? If so, I wonder where we will pass the intervening days. (weeks; months; years; decades; centuries; millennia) Notwithstanding, I began this segment with a different thought, and it is this thought that I will focus upon here.

The question here is similar to questions posed in other portions of this work: Is God truly fair in His treatment toward His created creatures? Permit me to editorialize before you finalize your response to this question. If I were given the authority and responsibility of deciding who would enter Heaven and who would be sent to Hell, and my choice was between St. John the Beloved Apostle and Judas Iscariot, the decision would be uncomplicated. If between Joseph Stalin and Mother Theresa; again my choice would be simple. Total opposites are easily separated. But the world isn't comprised of only saints or sinners, felons or heroes. Yet, at the final judgment, there is going to be only Heaven or Hell for the adjudged. There is to be no intermediate destination after that last accounting.

To make my point applicable: Suppose there was a woman who spent alternate days, first in sin, then in repentance. On the final night of her life, as she lay asleep in her bed, a wind storm struck a tree beside her home causing the tree to topple over and crush the bedroom of the sleeping woman killing her. Would this woman go to Heaven or to Hell? What I am attempting to illustrate here is just how unfair the notion is that assigns an eternity of opposites when the determinant is intermediate. (Or, as in this hypothetical case, is vacillating.)

The criminal justice system will provide a clearer illustration without resolving the controversy. Grant that a law has been passed which stated that in all criminal cases only two verdicts are permissible: The death penalty, or complete exoneration. Later, you are on a jury deciding the fate of a man who confessed to willfully breaking a woman's leg that has caused her to be crippled the remainder of her life. How should you decide his just fate? Should this defendant be acquitted, or should he be executed? Either alternative would be a travesty. So, too, is it with Heaven or Hell for the identical reason. There is no reprieve from either one. Has there ever been a human being who was so bereft of redeeming qualities that he deserved to be punished all day, every entire day, for endless billions of years? Eternity is forever! His punishment will never end. If ever there was an example of arrant injustice, regardless of which decision is rendered, the Final Judgment is it!

{Two examples} Joe 'Goodness' was a decent fellow. He had never harmed anyone in his life. He gave to every charity that solicited his donation. Joe was exemplary in every respect, save one! His lone flaw was that he believed the Bible was nothing but a collection of Hebrew superstitions. Where was Joe consigned after he died? You and I both know. Joe went to Hell!

Fred 'Despicable' was a thoroughly evil person. He cheated, he stole, and he once raped a small child. If he were confident of avoiding detection, he would have murdered someone for a dollar. But, just before he died of extreme old age, a "born-again believer" converted him to Christianity. Fred truly repented his former life of evil. Where will we find Fred after the final judgment? According to *de rigueur* Christian theology: Fred will be resident in Heaven! Personally, I would rather share eternity with Joe Goodness.

Moreover, if I were Jesus, I would certainly keep Solomon away from my mother, Mary. Also, I would keep an eye on King David and Mary Magdalene in Heaven. {Absent sincerity} Most all of those Old Testament characters should be kept under constant surveillance, assuming they are resident in Heaven.

The last paragraph is typed with 'keyboard in fake mode.' But, there is enough potentiality in it that I won't apologize for composing it. The real key to an actual heaven is not piety; it is morality. Don't believe that you have to wait until you die to experience an everlasting reward. If we truly desire a Heaven, we are going to have to construct one on our own. Right here and right now is the right place and the right time. We should begin by selecting out the unrepentant sinners and punishing them forthwith.

The decisions that will save us are the judgments that we make today; those that we decide ourselves.

My point here isn't easily made. Our present criteria for entering Heaven are both simplistic and flawed. The only heaven we will ever attain is a heaven fabricated here on Earth by living, breathing, provident human beings. An eternal heaven far surpasses a prize any human being could ever rightly earn or deserve; an eternal hell far exceeds any punishment humanity should ever have applied against it. Both extremes are outrageous perversions of equitably administered justice. Man is incapable of deserving the one, or warranting the other. Candidly, there isn't any cosmic logic for the existence of a Heaven, or for a Hell. If an extant God is as intelligent as we postulate, then He should be cognizant that this is so!

WAS THE EARTH CREATED?

When Genesis states that God (Linguistically, "the gods") created the heavens and the Earth, does this mean that the contents of the heavens (scattered gaseous matter and accreted dust matter) plus the constituents of the Earth (rocks, minerals and various compounds) were created as unitary, complete entities? [Cf. Gen. 1:1] In other words, 'that the Earth didn't form from the congealing of cosmic debris that pre-existed in the cosmos.' God didn't merely create oxygen, carbon, silica, nickel, plus all the ingredients of life-supporting planetary matter, and then simply permit these elements to accrete to form our planet. Is my distinction clear?

The reason I raise this question is because it seems to me that it is reliably proved that the Earth itself has evolved. Pointedly: Was the Grand Canyon created *ab initio*, or did it evolve more than millennia after some previous act of creation? This question is crucial to determining whether God created, or if nature evolved. All the evidence posits that the Earth was never static. Had our world been created in an instantaneous act, some indications (if not all) should evidence this fact. This just isn't the observed case.

Geo-evolution isn't some hare-brained fable dreamed up by anti-Biblists. It is a logical deduction that was prompted by a dispassionate interpretation of the geological data. Sentient man gathered the strewn evidences of the Earth's topography together, and collated them into reasonable hypotheses that dependably explained the genesis of the Earth. To reject the evolution of the Earth is to demean and discredit a wide spectrum of sincere, intelligent, honorable persons. What is even more dishonoring of humanity as a whole is to reject geo-evolution on the discernibly ignorant witness of the Bible.

The creation scenario in Genesis, in actuality, is enormously indulged ignorance wrongfully elevated into sanctified enlightenment. Genesis has the stars and all the rest of the Cosmos formed in a single day. Yet, what does the stellar astronomical data indicate? There just isn't any indication at all of an instantaneous creation. Are the stars all the same composition, age, size, or even state of being? No, they are not, and neither are the galaxies. Everything we observe in the Universe is in a state of wildly random flux, i. e., instability. The theory of cosmic evolution is the only theory that shows any agreement with the gathered and continuously accumulating cosmological evidences.

The author(s) of Genesis was completely bereft of any factual knowledge about the Universe. To him (them), the entirety of the heavens was nothing but tiny lights affixed to a crystal globe that encircled the flat, unmoving Earth.

How does Genesis explain the hundreds of hominid remains (extinct humans, et al.) uncovered by archeologists? Adam positively was not the first human being! When we revere the Bible we aren't honoring God, we are only revealing our own species ignorance, credulity and superficiality. The Bible examined dispassionately and intellectually screams at you "MAN-MADE!"

WAS ANCIENT JUDAISM MONOTHEISTIC?

Did all the authors of the Old Testament subscribe to the theory of one, unique, solitary, unrivaled God? Today's Christians would insist that the response be "Yes." Yet, what does one find if he or she looks at the historical evidence? Need it be pointed out that the Bible contains many references that indicate a general belief in more than one spiritual Divinity? If this is so (and it irrefutably is), why didn't the earliest copyists remove these damaging statements? My reply is that we don't know what has been omitted. We only know what has been retained.

The references that indicate an inferred unambiguous belief in more than one god are few. I have read seven. But recall, I haven't read the entire Bible, nor have I noted the verse number each instance where I encountered a reference to belief in multiple Gods. Below are seven instances that I have recouped:

> *"Now I k*now that the Lord
> is greater than all the gods ...." [Ex.18:11]

> "There is none among the gods like unto thee,
> Oh Lord ...." [Ps. 85:8]

> "For the Lord is a mighty God,
> a mighty king over all the gods ...." [Ps. 94:3]

> "The Lord is great ... he is to be praised
> over all the gods ...." [Ps. 96:4]

> "I know that our Lord is great,
> greater than all the gods ...." [Ps. 135:5]

> "For the Lord is great ...
> he is to be feared above all gods ...." [1 Chr. 16:25]

> "The Lord your God is supreme
> over all gods and over all powers." [Deut. 10:17]

Harken to the words of Samuel: *"Samuel said to the people of Israel, 'if you are going to turn to the Lord with all your hearts, you must get rid of all the foreign gods and the images of the goddess Astarte.'"* [1 Sam. 7:3] The ancient Israelites believed in Monolatry,* not Monotheism.

(*Monolatry – **noun:** the worship of a single god, but without claiming that he or she is the only god)

WHAT NATIONALITY WAS JESUS?

The answer to this segment-heading question would seem to be obvious, and the question therefore pointless. Notwithstanding: the question remains. This is the reason I ask it: Jesus came from Galilee; the people from that area were a mixed population as a result of the Assyrian Captivity (740-722 BC). [Cf. 2 Ki. 15:29] The ten northern tribes (Israel) had split from the two southern tribes (Judah) shortly after the reign of Solomon (c. 930 BC). This division was not only political, but was religious as well. [Cf. 1 Ki. 12:25-33]

In Samaria, a branch of Judaism formed that denied the paramount status of the city of Jerusalem, and, indeed, of the preeminent position of the Temple. Their 'holy site' was Mount Gerizim. The people of Samaria and Galilee weren't only religiously separated within Judaism, they were ethnically different too. After the Assyrians defeated Israel in the eighth century BC, the Assyrians deliberately set about resettling populations that they controlled. Samaria and Galilee were repopulated with Mesopotamians, while the former inhabitants of those areas were removed to Mesopotamia. [Cf. 2 Ki. 17:24] Despite this biblical evidence, one might embrace the belief that the Galileans retained their Hebrew nationality. This is more wishful thinking than probable fact. If there is one item that an invading army always leaves behind, it is this: its seed! This has always been, and shall always be. World-wide, most women find 'different' men irresistible.

Ethnically, no one who belongs to a group that has prolonged contact with a different population group will be pure blooded. The most tempting individual nature has to offer is a strange and attractive member of the opposite sex. Visible ethnic difference seems only to enhance the appeal. Forbidden fruits are the most desirable fruits. This reality, as much as any other, is a prime cause for the inferior civic status of women throughout history. Men leave their sexual dalliances behind them. Women birth theirs. This is biology, not philosophy.

How did the question of Jesus' nationality enter my mind? A religionist would credit the Devil. It was a Catholic publication that started me thinking along those lines. The February edition featured an artist's rendering of what Jesus may have looked like based on the facial image on the Shroud of Turin.

As you will have no doubt anticipated, Jesus is quite handsome in this rendering. But, even more predictably, He is depicted as indisputably Caucasian! Today, we stereotype Jewish men as having large noses, generally hooked downward at the tip. In this representation, Jesus is anything but typically Jewish. We could excuse this artist's nationality bias rather effortlessly, except for the fact that the face does closely resemble the face on the Shroud. That person had a long, slender, straight nose. So, also, does the face on the pictorial re-creation.

This nationality identification imponderability won't be solved here. The Jewish religion forbade the imaging of human beings. Because of this prohibition, no one knows what facial characteristics the Jews of Jesus' day bore. Despite all the foregoing, I will concede that Jesus was a Jew. The question of His nationality was only inserted here to get you (my reader) to think; to question; to wonder. Only if one reads the Bible (and collateral sources) with an intelligent, quizzical mind can he or she discern any truth. The truth is that human hands wrote the Bible; the human mind conceived the Bible; only human longing for self-aggrandizement encourages the imputation of Divine Inspiration of the Bible.

BELIEF PROMPTED BY IGNORANCE

Arguments in support of a personal Supreme Being derived from the writings of several eminent scholars, as quoted from the book: <u>Rebuilding a Lost Faith</u>, by John Stoddard. Mr. Stoddard refers us to Sir Francis Bacon … "who had one of the keenest intellects ever given to man." {*sic*} Bacon is quoted from his essay on <u>Atheism</u>: "I had rather believe all the fables in the Legend, and the Talmud, and the Koran, than that this universal frame is without a mind."

If this quote truly is an argument for a Creator, then to my mind, it is a weak one. Bacon is merely informing us that he would rather believe. What is it that he would rather believe? He would rather believe that the Universe is guided by a "mind", instead of by mindless physics. Is this proof of a Cosmic Creator? I don't think it is. To me, Bacon is longing for a Creator; as do all who embrace religiosity! The observant reader will also note that Bacon refers to the Koran and the Talmud as "fables." (The Koran being the Sacred Scripture of Islam, and the Talmud being a "sacred" book of Jewish Commentaries) The Talmud sets civil and religious law as extrapolated from the first five books of the Torah. The Torah is virtually the first five books of the Christian Old Testament as well.

Bacon is not so much condemning Atheism, as he is promoting Christianity. He dismisses the religious "fables" of contrary believers unequivocally. Still he, presumably firm in the Christian faith, accepts the parting of the Red Sea, human resurrection, and multiple other biblical fabulosities without a glimmer of skepticism. This isn't scholarship; it is biased advocacy. In this instance, Bacon the Philosopher has unwisely co-opted Bacon the Scientist.

The Universe awes all of us. The vast Cosmos seems to go about its everyday imperatives completely oblivious to puny man. It doesn't need us, nor does it heed us. It ignores our presence. We don't matter to the Universe. The vanity of the religionist won't tolerate this situation. All life forms are subservient to mankind; consequently, so shall the Universe heel to man's command. Our species arrogance doesn't permit anyone, or anything, to pay no heed to the presence of Man.

Accept the foregoing as fact and then re-examine the Bible. What do you discern as the overriding theme of that book now that you have primed your objectivity? Do you perceive the real message of the religion-ist? I believe so. For the impetus behind its composition isn't man's salva-tion, nor is it his enlightenment; it is his self-elevation to supremacy in the Universe. Religiosity is vanity blatantly pandered! Quite literally, religious man's goal is the establishment of the Nobility of religious mankind and the Enthronement of its theological leaders.

God is nothing more grandiloquent than an instrumentality to achieve this goal, just as a mountain is only incidental to the mountain climber so that he may achieve his ends. The mountain climber's goal isn't exclusively just to scale the mountain. Rather, it is to bask in the accolades that attend the accomplishment of that feat. So, too, does God merely pro-vide the medium for religious man to exalt himself through ostentatious posturing, audible prayer, and especially through successful proselytizing!

What profit is there for God to provide mortal man with an eter-nal shelter (heaven)? What loss does He suffer when man comes up short of this self-appointed destiny (damnation to Hell)? One theory of the Godhood insists that God must be immutable. If God truly is immutable, what difference does it make if man achieves Heaven or not? The same difference it makes to a mountain when a climber fails. Or, for that matter, if its climber doesn't fail!

Bacon isn't the only famous person who was infected with pernicious religiosity. Read now, a few more quotes from Mr. Stoddard's book. Sir Isaac Newton: "The whole variety of created things could arise only from the design and will of a Being existing of Himself."

Charles Darwin (pondering the Universe): "I feel impelled to look to a First Cause, having an intelligent mind in some degree analogous to that of man."

(Johannes) Kepler: "My Supreme desire is to find in myself the God, whom I find everywhere outside."

There are other quotes contained in Mr. Stoddard's book, but those already presented will satisfy the purpose. All agree to a degree that some higher force or intelligence exists beyond their knowledge. No one, not even Atheists, can successfully argue against this ubiquitous postulation. But what specifically were these eminent scholars expounding?

Bacon was a philosopher and statesman of the Elizabethan era. Darwin was a nineteenth century naturalist who formulated the original Theory of Evolution. Kepler was an astronomer, and is best known for his Three Laws of Planetary Motion. Newton, arguably the most intellectually endowed of the quartet under discussion, was a mathematician and a scientist. He discovered the Principle of Gravity, and also invented Calculus.

All were great men of notable accomplishment. Dare I dispute them? "No," if I enter into their fields of expertise. "Yes," with religion, because thereby all humans are susceptible to error. Note this well: there is no science of religion! The theory of a personal God rests solely on indirect inference. Now, if you will recall what each man offered as the core of his belief, you will clearly see that each is an opinion, presented as an opinion, not as a law, or as a certainty!

No one has ever proved that a personal God exists, although countless numbers of the mystically minded have attempted the feat. This entire book is an attempt to disprove the many arguments offered in support of the 'Personal God' proposition. It is impossible to positively prove a negative, especially in the immaterial spiritual world. All I can do is to force a proponent of the Godhead theory to give me a single 'positive' proof of God's existence. Having forced this, I can then prove that his 'positive' proof is flawed, or outright false.

This is the only "evidence" an Atheist will ever be able to demonstrate. But that should suffice, because I have yet to encounter even one substantive proof for the existence of a personal God that couldn't be rebutted easily. Praying to God isn't a proof of His existence, but it is a logical corollary of the presumed, and sometimes fallaciously attested, actions of a Supreme Being. Concede an argument here, and I will develop my point. Grant that God exists, that He acts, and that He hears our prayers, and then ponder the following.

In the Fall of 1985, a long dormant volcano erupted in Columbia. The eruption itself was very destructive, but even more devastating were the many mudslides that followed. News stations around the world broadcast the tragic events within hours of the disaster. That very night a well-known television Evangelist reserved an individual moment to direct his audience in an elegant, beseeching prayer asking for God's mercy. He petitioned God's help for the injured and homeless victims of the tragedy. The next day a secondary shock hit the area and even more people were injured and killed, most by mudslides.

After the second day, a local television station aired the reaction from the Vatican in Rome. The Pope read aloud a prayerful petition asking for God's compassion and mercy on the maimed, and he entreated God to aid the tasked rescuers of those buried alive in the mudslides.

What was God's reaction to Pope John-Paul II's call for heavenly assistance? On the third day, another tremor struck and still more people died! Didn't God hear the prayers of these two Christian leaders and their congregations? If there is a God, then He must have heard. Why, then, did He flout their pleas? Instead, in response, God lashed out and caused more death and destruction? Were the prayers the impetus for the further destruction? It could seem so! If the disaster situation had reversed, and all the mudslide victims were rescued, religionists would joyously have announced God's respite responsibility.

The TV Evangelist had his audience lower their heads, close their eyes, and clasp their hands tightly against their breasts while praying. This was an emotionally moving experience, even for me. This world-famous minister couldn't have been more eloquent, or more humbly beseeching.

No compassionate person could have denied his plea. Yet, God did! The Pope's intersession was likewise ignored.

Here, then, is the conclusion I desire you to reach from this subchapter: The opinions of the noteworthy religionists carry no more weight in the field of importuning God than do ordinary people. Religiosity isn't a science. It cannot be experimented with in any manner that will prove or disprove any of its tenets. What it is, is an exercise of the imagination in which humans fantasize all sort and manner of pseudo-realities predicated on the actuality of an invisible sky divinity; in name, God the Father, in the belief of Christians.

So what if Bacon detests a mindless Universe? What is proved by Newton's creation confusion? For him, it was too fabulous to believe in a creator-less Universe, so he postulated a creator-less Creator. I fail to discern any logical preference between these two impossibilities. Both require a negation of our innate reasoning.

Lastly, we come to Darwin. He looked for the first intelligence. I do likewise! But shall we find intelligence anywhere except in living matter? No, we shan't. Only living matter possesses intelligence. Intelligence is a physical attribute. It requires a physical sensation center (a brain) even to exist.

Mental retardation is the profoundest proof on Earth of the absence of a 'Grand Design,' plus a Grand Designer! All the extant species, the extinct species, and the not-yet-existent species provide evidence beyond rebut that God isn't directing a life drama script. Instead, what we observe is a kind of Murphy's Law of existence; "If it can exist, it will exist! If it lives, eventually it will die!" This law applies equally to both individuals and collections of individuals, i.e., groups, that are in reality only linked, stereotyped individuals. Every bio-entity is, in verity, an individual. Every occurrence, no matter how wide its effect, nor how vast its reach, nor how long its duration, is composed entirely of individual events. Any patient, objective observer will recognize this. Random occurrence is the cosmological recurring eventuality throughout the Universe. (Always has been! – Always will be!)

So why are some individuals born retarded? Not because God so ordered it, but simply because it is possible. Why can't whales fly? The answer: Because they are encased in a ton (or more) of blubber to shield them against frigid waters. Also, for the reason that they have evolved dense bones to support their bulk. Additionally, their upper limbs have evolved into flippers instead of wings. It wasn't because God didn't want whales to fly.

Intelligence is only one of the arbitrary possibilities in the Universe. Lack of intelligence is another possibility. Ask a live clam if it believes in a God, and then be guided by the clam's response. Intelligent people invent gods for the same reason, and in the same manner, that children invent imaginary characters when they play with toy figures. That being: companionship that is totally predictable, and wholly controlled by the mind of the one who imagines the characters!

Accept this premise of your author, and then re-examine and re-evaluate the next "holy man" you encounter. I am confident that the honest evaluator will recognize that my characterization of all religious proselytizers is universally applicable. Evangelizers control the common perception of their espoused deity in order to manipulate their cultic adherents in a manner that bestows glorification upon the evangelizer himself or herself.

WHAT DO YOU BELIEVE?

One of the perplexing revelations that became manifest to me while I was writing this book was the fact that most people subscribe specifically only to their own personal beliefs. I wonder if anyone else has had that same revelation. What specifically do you believe? If you are Roman Catholic: do you accept as irreducible fact every single tenet the Catholic Church proclaims? If you are Lutheran: do you believe every Lutheran doctrine, and only Lutheran doctrine? If you are Muslim: do you accept the entirety of the Koran, the entirety of its teachings? If so, which division of Islam? Judaism has at least four sub-denominations; which one professes the totality of your Jewish beliefs? How many divergent doctrines exist in the totality of Christianity?

Every Religion, every Sect, every Denomination, every division within a denomination has one or more articles of faith that differ from that of their spiritual competitors. This is precisely why we have so many different religions. This is why we shall continue to create ever more factions, if not the outright creation of new faiths, from the existing milieu. One assumes (In error, it develops!) that all members of each individual faith adhere to the specific beliefs that separate it from another faith. Undeniably, this is generally true. Alas, on close examination, it devolves that specifically, this isn't the case in most instances. People join congregations for many divers reasons, but seldom is the deciding factor total belief in every tenet! I wonder if a professing majority ever embraces the totality of any religious theology.

The impetus for this segment was the declaration of a practicing Catholic woman of my acquaintance who admitted to me (without pretext) that she didn't believe everything the Catholic Church teaches. This admission to me was prompted by pointed inquiries aimed at Catholic doctrines that are difficult to accept. After speaking with her, subsequently, I purposely initiated conversations with women of other persuasions in my work situation. Some men were also quizzed, but they were more reluctant to discuss their religious beliefs in detail, so I concentrated my inquiry mostly on females.

It eventuated that women were more frank and were more cooperative, when I explained why I was questioning them so deeply. What I learned was this: Almost no one is one hundred percent converted! That is, no grouping can lay avowal to being totally free of their own plurality of 'Doubting Thomas' followers. No Christian denomination was completely exempt from undeclared/undetected heretics within their particular congregations.

Even to this day, it seems to me that everyone generally believes in his/her denomination's declarations. Yet, simultaneously, they reject (not always openly) any proposition that conflicts with their own personal mores, or with strictures that hinder their own preferred lifestyle. Provided that no one challenges them about their heretical beliefs, they remain ostensibly devoted adherents of their respective denomination.

The most obvious instance of this observation is the continuing standoff within the Catholic Church over birth control. The Bishops of the Roman Church continue to forbid it, while the laity of that Church continues to practice it. Protestant ecclesiastic authorities are openly disregarded in a related controversy. Protestant Church leaders denounce abortion as murder, while many Protestant congregants seek after, and have, abortions. Jewish Rabbis exhort their faithful to observe the Mosaic dietary laws, while Jews throughout this country continue to enjoy pork products. Few of the Muslims that I have known pray five times daily while facing Mecca. Still, no denomination has a monopoly on either sin or of piety. {The foregoing are examples, not <u>stereotypes</u>}

Adherence to behavioral strictures in all organized religions runs the gamut from burning zeal, through tepid acceptance, culminating in chilly minimal compliance. Yet, as this segment asks: What do you believe? Most people would rank themselves with the tepid. (They are incorrect!) Of the remainder, a few would rate themselves burning; while a lesser sliver would admit coolness. However, if an objective observer could deduce actuality; more people would be classified as well below the midpoint of required beliefs than ever would recognize themselves as truly low (frosty) in the rankings.

Most people practice their religion much the same as they would conduct themselves at a buffet luncheon. They pick and choose only those food items (beliefs) that entice their palates. They eschew the remaining food items (beliefs) without rationalizing their rejection. They will proudly announce their fidelity to this favored restaurant (religion) provided they aren't forced to consume and extol every food item (belief) displayed on the buffet table, (participate in every ritual, or affirm every tenet, extending the analogy)

But religious doctrines aren't voluntary choices on a sacred menu. If all doctrines come to us via inspiration from the Deity, then all beliefs and all restrictions are obligatory! There is no choice, no personal selection, no sampling, and no skipping over. Just as the Christian Church of the Middle Ages insisted: 'God decreed; therefore all must obey!' There can be no review of any of His dictates. And, more detrimentally, there can be no rewriting of sacred doctrine to accommodate future human fad or fancy. Here, my examples will undoubtedly enervate feminists. Read the words of Peter, Chief Apostle of the nascent Christian Church.

"In the same way you wives must submit yourselves to your husbands, so that if any of them do not believe God's word, your conduct will win them over to believe. It will not be necessary for you to say a word, because they will see how pure and reverent your conduct is. You should not use outward aids to make yourselves beautiful, such as the way you fix your hair, or the jewelry you put on, or the dresses you wear. Instead, your beauty

should consist of your true inner self, the ageless beauty of a gentle and quiet spirit, which is of the greatest value in God's sight. For the devout women of the past who placed their hope in God used to make themselves beautiful by submitting themselves to their husbands. Sarah was like that: she obeyed Abraham and called him her master [Lord]. *You are now her daughter if you do good and are not afraid of anything."* [1 Pet. 3:1-6]

For the past two decades, women have been petitioning for (and frequently attaining) ordination as ministers in the various Christian denominations. They insist that women must be permitted to perform every sacred function previously biblically reserved exclusively to men. This insistence seems reasonable and justifiable to almost all of today's liberal Christian hierarchy. Nonetheless, this policy, when adopted anywhere in Christendom, violates an 'inspired' dictum from God, via the Holy Spirit ... As in 1 Peter above and 1 Corinthians below:

"As in all the churches of God's people, the women should keep quiet in the meetings. They are not allowed to speak; as the Jewish Law says, they must not be in charge. If they want to find out about something, they should ask their husbands at home. It is a disgraceful thing for a woman to speak in a church meeting." [1 Cor. 14:34-35]

How does a Christian woman circumvent God's unalterable commands? Personally, I have never heard a refutation of these scriptural dictates from those demanding the ordination of females. Allow me to re-emphasize from the above quote: *"Women should keep quiet in the meetings ... It is a disgraceful thing for a woman to speak in a church meeting.... They must not be in charge."* Without an outright rejection of the divine inspiration for these verses (Thereupon rejection of the Holy Spirit), how does one in belief elude God's laws? Paul seemingly anticipated today's revisionists one verse later: *"If anyone supposes he* {not she!} *is God's messenger or has a spiritual gift* {the gift of tongues is one such}, *he* {not she!} *must realize that what I* {Paul} *am writing to you is the Lord's command. But if he* {not she!} *does not pay attention to this, pay no attention to him* {or to her!}." [1 Cor. 14:37-38]

Then there is also more in Timothy, where Paul expands upon the proper role of women in the Church of Jesus Christ. In this Epistle, Paul admonishes women to be modest and sensible in their dress when attending religious services. He especially instructs women not to adorn themselves with *"fancy hair styles"* or with *"gold, pearls, or expensive dress."* [1 Tim. 2:9] Is Easter Sunday included above? Paul further instructs women to *"learn in silence and all humility ...."* He then appends what I deem a virtual eleventh commandment. *"I do not allow them to teach or to have authority over men; they must keep quiet."* [1 Tim. 2:11-12]

Just prior to that Paul informs women that they should acquit themselves with *"good deeds, as is proper with women who claim to be religious."* [1 Tim. 2:10] Paul ends Chapter 2, with these words: *"For Adam was created first, and then Eve. It was not Adam who was deceived; it was the woman who was deceived and broke God's law. But a woman will be saved through having children, if she perseveres in faith and love and holiness, with modesty."* [1 Tim. 2:13-15] I can find no loophole in this divinely-inspired directive for women to have children. Yet, in cooperative defiance of the foregoing, the Christian women of Europe and North America are not birthing enough children to replace themselves. Western women have decided that a working career is preferred to the motherhood that facilitates the continuation of their European Racial heritage. Their men are all enabling accomplices in the modern women's defiant actions of purposely limiting the number of children born to their legacy. So to my future female readers I exclaim, 'If these texts express the Holy Writ of God, then obey them! If the words are not God's commands, then believe this book!'

AFTER GOD … WHAT?

What philosophy will get us to heaven after we have deposed King God? The ultimate philosophy that ends our quest for life philosophies may never be formulated. My guess is that the quest itself must sustain us. The most important factor in the quest however will be our leadership. How to keep our exploratory sloop on course presents a challenge that cannot be dispensed with. We shall be continually afloat in uncharted waters, seeking new worlds (knowledge) and encountering strange natives. (Unexpected facts that must be dealt with) Our fate, as always, rests in the hands of our captain. He must be chosen well. But who, pray tell, (just punning), will choose the Master of our vessel? The answer to that question is at once both disarmingly simple and fearfully complex. The "best" man for that job should be chosen with great care. One of the vital components of "best" is intelligence.

Although some may not agree, we do possess a means of determining human intelligence. I. Q. tests do just that. Demonstrably though, these tests fail to project another equally pertinent factor, viz., the degree of emotionality our leader candidate is afflicted with. Emotionality is a holdover from our pre-civilized past that counteracts our intelligence. Accordingly, our selectee should be as free from emotionality as is possible.

Decisions made wholly or primarily via sentimentality will always be regretted either presently or eventually. Religion is pampered "sentiment." All religious experiences can only be expressed by describing the emotions they aroused. St. Paul in one of his epistles relates how he was caught up to 'third heaven' in a religious reverie. [Cf. 2 Cor. 12:2] All sudden converts to religiosity credit some personal ecstasy, or another highly-charged emotional incident, as the impetus for their spiritual conversion. Persons predisposed to such commitment-reversing tendencies will make flawed leaders in an intelligently administered society. Excising religion from my proposed secular government would concurrently eradicate sentimentality from governance.

Full citizenship in this proposed society would await full mental maturity, and would not be granted automatically by age; much less would it be subject to conference upon demand. (As some of our 'privileges' now are demanded as 'rights') Everyone would be given the opportunity to prove himself or herself competent to citizenship. Proving one's self 'capable' would be a mandatory requisite. Obviously, intelligent women would participate in governing, but not on a quota or equity status, or any other non-competitive basis.

But now I am projecting much too far into the future. All of this is predicated on divesting ourselves of the shackles of superstition. The trouble with most people is that basically they are mentally languid. They would rather be told something, than to labor to discover it for themselves. (This author included)

There are scarce few persons willing to attack the unknown frontally if it entails much work, or uncertain results. Even some of the super-intelligent are halting in the face of possible/probable failure. Perhaps we have placed too high a premium on achievement, and neglected to bestow due deference to effort? That is one area where institutionalized religions' methods have succeeded. Christian Churches reward effort and downplay negative results; initiating the need for 'confession.' Any preacher worthy of his collections will tell you that you need not become pristine in the Christian faith to be saved; providing only that you make a pious attempt toward that end. Catholic theology is more stringent; vis-à-vis, an unforgiven "mortal sin" infraction.

All Christian Churches exhort you to admit that you are a sinner. If you do so, God will forgive you. Thereafter, you may go out and sin anew! (The last portion of that statement isn't explicit, but you will concede that it is implicit!) Just as Jesus admonished the woman caught in adultery, so too, the Church should counsel its adherents: "Go and sin no more!" [Jn. 8:11] Because all humans are indeed 'sinners' by Church definition, we must necessarily examine just why we are, one and all, 'sinful.' Is it because the strictures of the Church are too restrictive? Are we utterly undeserving of the love of the Supreme Worthiness? Which are we: creatures of Satan reaching out at times toward God; or are we God's creatures conceived imperfectly, thereby tainted by sin from birth? We are, in verity, neither! The force that created us isn't a benevolent spirit, nor is it a malevolent specter. It is Nature. Nature is what happens. Nature is impersonal. It is never judgmental.

Does the natural power process that destroys your home via an unexpected tornado care whether you are kneeling in prayer, or watching pornographic movies? Does the force that activates a bullet know whether it is propelled toward a holy man, or toward a murderer? Do earthquakes destroy only brothels, and leave churches standing? Does the Sun warm saint and sinner equally? Of course it does! But why is this so? It's because the Sun is totally oblivious that it is even shining; how, then, can it know whom it is shining upon? God isn't up in the heavens orchestrating the Universe, and neither is any other entity.

Ignorant or deceptive men have humanized God (the God concept) and endowed 'Him' with every mortal personality trait. Even we humans, His secondary creatures (presumably Angles are prime), are at times loathsome to Him, as when men have a nocturnal, involuntary emission. [Cf. Lev. 15:16] Or when a woman has her monthly menstruation, she is deemed unclean for seven days. Anything that she touches, or that touches her, during that seven day period is decreed "unclean." [Cf. Lev. 15:19-23] How perfectly unenlightened are God's Old Testament decrees when they are judged by today's enlightened (?) comprehension.

It is factual that neither of the above decrees are present-day tenets of the Christian Faith. Continue reading Chapter 15 of Leviticus from verse 24 through verse 33. Then ask yourself if there is any known Jewish or Christian religious sect that demands adherence to God's menstruation or semen flow strictures as recorded therein. But the relevant fact is that those Leviticus pronouncements were given by God to Moses as unremitting strictures to be perpetually enforced.

That the Christian Churches (and the Judaic Faith as well) have rescinded the 'Laws of Moses' repudiates the doctrine that these "laws" came directly from God (Yahweh). The relevant Church hierarchies have abrogated to themselves the authority to re-write the "words of God." The reality is that the Christian Churches, or any other religious body of whatever otherworldly persuasion, have as much legitimate authority to set universal (or global, or national, or even community) law as does the 'man in the moon!' Perhaps less so, for the Christian Churches are evermore earthbound; whereas the 'man in the moon' is ceaselessly to be found in God's domains, that is, "in the heavens."

I believe it is time for humanity to advance forward, not backward by expecting the Bible to provide the solution to every human problem. Put your Bibles away, but retain your morality. Begin investigating the entirety of the cosmos for the factual revelations of "Nature." Intelligent mankind has the ability to learn practically everything. All we lack is the will to attempt that goal minus all the superstitions that have always held us back from exploring for the absolute truth. You will not (you cannot) learn the absolute truth by worshipping a book replete with sanctimonious fictions. The Bible (& the Koran, et al.) is a book written by the most deluded, or the most deluding, individuals who have ever trod this "flat" earth. Truth is not a variable. The absolute truth perpetually remains: God isn't dead. He simply never existed!

CHAPTER 23
The Verdict

PRELUDE TO THE FINAL WORDS

Much ground has been covered in this book, but much more could have been uncovered. The main theme has been: there is no personal God; consequently, He cannot act! Everything else is secondary, and in verity, owes its conception and inclusion to this paramount proposition. Yet, if the God concept is expunged, as I believe it should be, what will mankind be left with? In the concluding pages of this book I will outline several items we stand to lose if we renounce religiosity.

Perchance, we will both be praying to God for expiation thereafter. For a start, we can alter our coins to read, "In Gold We Trust." Seriously! Formerly our coins had intrinsic value in addition to their assigned value. Today, the coins themselves are almost worthless.

The human denominational divisions of religion created by disparate beliefs and customs should disappear. Morality can be enforced on the basis of its inherent desideratum, not because some supernatural being commands it. Decency in all civic matters would be enforced for secular reasons on believers and on non-believers uniformly! Community standards could be set without consultation with ecclesiastic hierarchy. Senseless "Blue Laws," such as closing businesses on Sundays to honor God only induced scorn, mockery and disregard. No statute that solely pandered to mystical tenets would ever be enacted, obviating arbitrary enforcement. Any law, regulation or other forced behavior via religion should be abolished and forever anathematized.

When the President outlines a course of action for the country to follow, he can foreswear the ineffectual rejoinder, "with God's help." In the past this has led some to await divine intervention, and to postpone appropriate remedial human action. How many times have I heard this groundless shibboleth stated as an indisputable fact: "The Western Allies won the Second World War because God favored their side." That nonsense is venerable rubbish. Read the history of that war and you will soon discover that a plethora of debatable military decisions on Hitler's part were the prime causal factors in Germany's defeat. If we insist that God had input in those decisions, then Hitler didn't possess a free will. In which case, he can hardly be held accountable for the Holocaust!

Of course, we can always postulate that God only interferes in adventures that are resolved via the approval of that person responsible for the postulation. This type of rationale is always one hundred percent accurate. Whichever way events unfold, that is the way God caused them to happen! How can anyone argue with that proposition? Why should anyone bother? The absence of logic in that declaration is appalling. Yet this type of thinking does serve a purpose; it demonstrates typically the major fault of all religiosity. Namely, if you can convince a person to accept unquestioningly one unproven and improbable proposal, then you will surely have less difficulty inducing him to believe any other proposition, however absurd!

The personal God hypothesis is patently illogical. Therefore, once you espouse that hypothesis, from that day henceforth you will reject all reasonable arguments against the hypothesis. After you have tuned your mind in to the fantastic, coincidentally, you will have tuned out prudent skepticism that could result in intelligent analysis and verifiable reality.

CLOSING ARGUMENTS

The time has come, and may even be overdue, for the dissection of the monolith we call Christianity, along with every other hyperphysical delusion. {Meaning: Every last belief system invoking a supernatural person or any spiritually directed ideology.} My goal soon after the start of this book was simply to state a case debunking Heaven, and to let you, my prospective reading jury, return an affirmed or a rejected verdict. That was so initially. Then (predictably?), I waxed to the task.

Demonstrably, Heaven is nothing but a pious dreamer's fantasy. Yet, religiosity encompasses more than a hopeful rebirth of the human psyche. Faith permits the mental attainment of the physically impossible. Theology encourages the imagination to function irrationally. Ritual places magical powers into the hands of the powerless, thereby rendering them hypothetically potent. Sacraments make feigned winners out of perceptual losers. The weak are given fancied strength: religion teaches us to naively believe such!

So what is wrong with any of the above? Just this: Fancied conceptions exist only in fantasy worlds, not in the real world. The existence of the Christian Faith (a fancied conception) for two thousand years might seem to give lie to the last statement, but it doesn't. The unabated fragmentation of the Christian Religion that began in the days of the Apostles (And continues expansively into our own age) gives witness to the actual fact. The Bible doesn't encompass an 'eternal truth.' It causes 'eternal divisions.' Likewise does the Koran divide!

Absolute truth shouldn't need faith to sustain it. If God lives, it should be impossible to prove otherwise. Let someone today try to prove that the world isn't a globe. It can't be done because we have far too many proofs to the contrary; beside which, all the former 'proofs' of the flat earth have long since been disproved. Even St. Paul (Saul of Tarsus) broadcast his ignorance when he wrote in Philippians, *"That at the name of Jesus every knee should bow, of things in heaven, and things in earth, and in things under the earth."* [Phil 2:10] The Earth has no underside; what *'things'* {sic} could occur *'under the earth'*?

Further, the proposition of a Deity, and the even more preposterous notion of the divinity of Jesus, is a blemish tarnishing the brilliant collective intellect of mankind. In our racial adolescence it was acceptable for us to believe that the only way to reach God was through the rising smoke of a burnt offering. (Sacrificial holocaust) Three thousand years ago our species ignorance excused us. But now, despite the determined hostility of the Christian myth, mankind has matured to early racial adulthood. We now know that rain falls whenever warm, moist air masses come into contact with cool, dry air masses. We formerly thought rain fell because God knew we needed it, or to punish us, as with the Flood! We can be forgiven for our former naiveté only if we admit presently, how supernaturally ignorant we were formerly.

An adult who continues to believe in the Easter Bunny forfeits his niche in responsible society. He or she should be relegated back to a grammar school level of responsibility. Yet, we continue to heap accolades on religious proselytizers who are every bit as credulous as were the first religionists. Why? Is there any more proof of the reality of a Holy Spirit Dove than there is of a basket filling rabbit? There isn't! Well-intentioned adults lie to their children to foster the belief in a yearly return of the Easter Bunny.

Religionists lie also. They tell you God loves you; yet you learn you have incurable cancer. Then they tell you that God hears your prayers; so you pray earnestly and humbly to God for the miracle you are told He has performed for others. You beseech God with all the humility you can muster. And, beyond anticipation, several months later you are told you have experienced total remission of your cancer. Your joy is unbounded; your prayers have been heard and granted; 'God loves you!' The following week your spouse has an automobile accident, is killed, and now you wish you had died of that cancer.

Is this the Will of God? No, and don't allow anyone convince you that it is. The God whom religionists preach, and the God whose actions we observe, are unalterably incompatible. This isn't to affirm that either God exists. They don't. The first postulate is precluded by our verifiable observation. The difficulty in attributing to God the unpredictable happenstance of life emanates from its observationally arbitrary occurrence.

The individual authors of the Old Testament were dupes of their own delusions. They composed their stories around the preconceived notion that God was directly and immediately liable for every episode that befell the Israelite-Hebrew-Jewish peoples. If you read the Bible and find a contradiction, then you know that God had nothing to do with its composition. But don't reverse this logic in the fashion of religionists who employ that self-evident proposition as proof that the Bible doesn't contradict itself. 'God inspired the Bible; therefore the Bible cannot contain any contradictions.' This states the essence of a religionist's deceptive rationale to counter obvious contradictions found throughout the Bible.

There is a common proposal that states that God is Truth. It took many years before I grasped correctly what the proposition implied at its core. Now, however, I understand its meaning. I know that the proposition is reversed: Truth is God! A Truth can't be contradicted; if it can, then it never was an actual Truth. Religionists have turned truth inside out. They state that the real world, which we can see, and feel, and react with, isn't real! They offer in its stead an imaginary world of Paradise. To them the spirit world is the real world. Heaven can't be seen, nor felt, nor reacted with. Nonetheless, they insist the spirit world is the only universal reality.

Does man die? Of course he does! Is man reborn? Of course he isn't! These are incontrovertible facts that everyone can verify. Despite the absolute verity of death, and the positive falsity of rebirth, I ask: How would a religionist reply to the previous two questions? Their response would be the exact opposite! Essentially, both intellectuals and believing religionists seek an identical objective. This objective is Ultimate Truth. What is truth? A Truth is an Absolute that can't be amended or repealed. Until it is tested, a Truth is only a theory; then, should the evidence repudiate the theory, we didn't have a Truth, we had a false theory.

Long ago, religionists took a blundering turn in their quest for Eternal Truth. They have yet to recognize their error. The postulation of a dynamic Personal Deity preempted the search for natural knowledge, and led religionists into a vast quagmire of superstitious ignorance. Intellectuals, likewise, have made many an erring detour on their journey toward Perfect Understanding. Yet, my bet is wagered on the intellectuals as the only ones who will ever approach to finishing the quest of discerning 'total universal truth.' The religiously deprogrammed intelligent have the surest likelihood of propinquity to that desired objective: ultimate wisdom!

But first, our intelligentsia must abandon their private sanctuaries, and speak publicly against the perverse conception of an emotion-laden Creator. Some already have; more need to do so! A Creator who is saddled with human emotionality is, perforce, a less-than-perfect Deity. Likewise, let them reveal the juvenility of the dogma that states 'that man was created by God in the image and likeness of God.' The literal reverse is the actual and undeniable reality. God was crafted by mankind in the image and likeness of mankind.

The proof of the humanity of the anthropomorphic God concept is readily at hand, if we will only take it in our hands and read it. All the debunking evidence anyone could desire is contained within the Bible itself. Genesis informs us that God walked in the Garden of Eden. [Cf. Gen. 3:8] He also spoke face to face with Adam and Eve. After hearing of his exile to the land of Nod, Cain lamented to God: *"...from Thy face I shall be hidden."* [Gen. 4:14] Cain spoke face to face with the Divine Presence and didn't expire?

Today, we read those humanized passages about God figuratively. Yet, how did the author intend those passages to be read? Open your Bible this minute and read in Genesis: *"Let us make man in our image, after our likeness..."* [Gen. 1:26] This was God speaking.

Now read further into Genesis. *"When Adam had lived a hundred and thirty years, he became the father of a son in his own likeness, after his image, and named him Seth."* [Gen. 5:3] In these passages we find the same words, written by the same author, yet you know positively that we, today, interpret these two identical statements in two completely opposite contexts. Permit me to point out to those who corrupt the Bible thus, that the above quotes are identical because their author intended them to be understood identically. Namely, Seth had the same form and appearance as his father, Adam. Adam had the same form and appearance as his divine creator, Yahweh. Yahweh is the precursor Divinity to 'God the Father.'

We can pervert the sense of the texts in this age, but we can't disregard a known fact that exposes our misconstruction. The Hebrews, as is well known, forbade the depiction of any image of God. This alone tells us that they believed God's likeness could be imaged. More saliently, they also forbade the imaging of man. Why? I am convinced now, that everyone can appreciate the prohibition. The Hebrews forbade the imaging of man, because this was the same as replicating the image of God. God's image and man's image are counterparts.

So how should we visualize God? If we use the Old Testament as our guide, exactly as humans observed worldly rulers at the time the O.T. Bible texts were composed. They visualized God with a human head, with eyes, ears, nose and mouth; a torso with arms attached at the shoulders, and legs attached at the hips; and lastly, a gluteus maximus (buttocks) so that our presumptive king may sit upon his conjectured throne in regal comfort. Through cognition, we discover that God isn't a 'Supernatural Being at all.' In our perception, He is a perceptual "Human Being" with superhuman powers.

Each and every supernatural belief (aka "religion") is an irredeemable abomination against human intelligence. Only in mankind's imagination can the unreal become real. Mickey Mouse has more actuality than does every single imagined, thereafter preached, belief system. The concept of "GOD" has many diverse names throughout human history. Every last one of them should be defined as a defamatory indictment against the intelligence of mankind, and should be unspoken forevermore!

Proselytizing any religion is the most pernicious felony one human being can commit against another human being. The First Commandment of the entire universe should read: "Do not believe in any supernatural being whatsoever. They are all false. There is no God, consequently, there is no Son, there is no Prophet, there is no Supernatural anything, and never has been! All religion is an invented Deity Fairy Tale!

END OF CRITIQUE

I have already asked the question that this book must resolve if I am ever to end it. The question is this: Now that your faith in all religions has been eradicated, what will replace it in your life? My reply must be divided into two parts. The first concerns religiosity. What I deem as 'religiosity' is primarily 'reverent superstition. 'Only knowledge can dispel superstition! Whenever you are told something incredible in matters of faith or religion: get the facts. This could provoke a critical diagnosis of all sanctimonious delusions.

If someone claims to be miraculously revived from death, find out if the Medical Authorities accepts the claim. If not, try to learn why they rejected the claim. If you hear of someone being cured at a miraculous Shrine, ask your informant how many people have gone there, and haven't been cured. Ask him why. Don't accept the 'whimsy' of God as an answer. (Or a similar alibi)

If anyone vows that he or she has been aided through the intercession of a particular Saint, learn all you can about that Saint. After study, ask yourself why this Saint has any more influence with God than you do. Once you have read the lives of most of the Saints, you will find that, early on, they were every bit as humanly flawed as was any other mortal being that has traversed this Earth.

Restating an off-repeated declaration herewith: "All religiosity is a sham." What one needs to do is to study religion dispassionately to discover how utterly untrustworthy is the entirety of supernaturalism. Unbiased research is the key. Knowledge dispels superstition! Alas, science does have the answer to a religionist's insistent question of how we got here. However, while the scientific explanation may be accurate, for many persons it isn't flattering. The human ego would prefer to view itself as an adopted child of God, rather than as the bastard child of Nature.

The second part of the explanation encompasses morality. Morality is praiseworthy in and of itself. Morality doesn't need a Supreme Being to legitimize its value to humanity. Ethical behavior stands on its own merits. We need controlled, predictable, civilized behavior from our fellow human beings. That is how we became so enamored of religiosity. Until now, us Christians thought the two, "morality & religiosity" were one. Not only can they be separated; imperatively, they must be separated. Religiosity is to be chucked into the nearest trash receptacle, from there it should be taken to an incinerator, burned, and the ashes scattered to the (figurative) four winds. Moral, sensible, governed behavior must be elevated to the pinnacle of human homage. Emphasizing its morality component has shielded religiosity from an impersonal and unbiased scrutiny of its misbegotten paranormal (religious) tenets.

Morality is what has been so appealingly "right" with religiosity ever since Moses came down from Mount Sinai. Moses added an incontrovertible dimension of authority to his moral laws by attributing their authorship to God Almighty. (The identical is applicable to Mohammed and the Koran.) Morality, back then, shouldn't have needed a prop to render it incontestable. The witness of history proves that it did.

The persistence of Christianity is due almost exclusively to its conceded pseudo-legitimacy, *vis a vis*, its espoused morality. Without morality, Christianity is reduced to just another compilation of incredible deity tales.

Moses striking a rock and bringing forth water [Cf. Ex. 17:6] belongs in the same category as Cinderella's Fairy Godmother when she used her magic wand to transform a pumpkin into a beautiful carriage. The story of Adam and Eve in the Garden of Eden is in no way superior to other creation myths; it is only different. Instead of a gigantic plant stem rising up to the clouds, as in Jack and the Beanstalk, we have two trees with magical fruit; the Tree of the Knowledge of Good and Evil, and the Tree of Life. [Cf. Gen. 2:16-17 & 3:22] The Tree of Life would have conferred eternal life to both Adam and Eve, had they been sly enough to eat from it before being expelled from the Garden of Eden. How intriguing and even enchanting is this Holy Book folktale.

No one bothers to examine the tale of the fate of Lot's wife. She is the one, you will recall, who disobeyed God and looked back at the destruction of Sodom and Gomorrah. For this less-than-heinous indiscretion, God punished her by turning her into a pillar of salt. [Cf. Gen. 19:26] Why a pillar of salt? By Twentieth Century standards, this punishment would be condemned as both cruel and unusual. Religionists might argue persuasively against the charge of cruelty, but they surely couldn't quibble about the punishment being unusual.

Why would God turn someone into a pillar of salt? There are a myriad of other ways He could have chosen to kill a human being. Again I ask: Why a pillar of salt? The answer, not unexpectedly, is gleaned through knowledge. The towns of Sodom and Gomorrah were situated in the Dead Sea valley. This valley, which is the lowest point on the surface of the dry Earth, has abundant salt formations. Present day geologists know, and can explain the reason for the existence of these salt formations. Yet, the ancient people who lived there had no inkling of how those salt pillars were generated. The Dead Sea, which may be the saltiest body of water on earth, through evaporation, will leave behind variously-shaped salt formations. The downright unpredictability of crystallization ensures that various diverse shapes will form.

To the ignorant ancient observer, for unknown reasons God created those oddly shaped structures. Some of these natural formations superficially resembled the human form. It is no great wonder, then, that someone didn't put "Y" and "Z" together and come up with "X" (the unknown) for an answer. Their solution to the "X" puzzle of the salt formations was to propose that God had mystically transformed human beings into pillars of salt as a punishment for sin. Lot's wife chanced to be chosen by the ancient mythmaker who reported the destruction of Sodom and Gomorrah story, with Lot, his family, and two Angels appended.

We should dismiss all the biblical myths. What should be embraced is Judeo-Christian morality. The real problem is how? How can we exorcise the mysticism associated with religion without stripping away the moral ethos also? This is truly a case of "saying is easier than doing!" Yet it must be done. We daren't lose our ethics, when we discard our superstitions.

One possible scenario would be to form an advisory panel whose function would be to define moral issues for us. Note that I wrote 'define,' and not 'dictate.' The definitions of this panel would be a guide to the law-makers of the community, not inalterable dictates. As an instance: On the question of abortion, who should determine if the intentional termination of a pregnancy is legal or illegal? What rights does an unborn fetus possess? Is the community obligated to nurture and rear unwanted children? Or is this a matter for individual initiative and community charity? These questions, and thousands of others, are community matters. The answers aren't as uncomplicated as most religionists would insist.

In the case of abortion, most Protestants agree that life begins at conception. It is comforting that they agree. But they are absolutely wrong! A woman's ovum and a man's sperm are both very much alive before they unite. The Catholic position against the use of contraceptives is entirely valid, religiously considered! Every viable sperm cell or fertile ovum is a potential human embryo. Any action we perform that hinders the natural union of these two reproductive cells before, during, or after, sexual intercourse terminates a human being!

You can banter all you may about the technicalities. But the actuality of the matter is that a unique and irreplaceable human is lost every time a male sperm fails to impregnate an ovum. This is why male masturbation is defined as sin. Anticipating that you may not agree that the use of contraceptives is technical homicide, consider this: A freighter navigating in the middle of the ocean sights survivors in a lifeboat from some unknown ship sinking. For some unstated reason, the ship's Captain refuses to render assistance to the stranded shipwreck victims, thus damning them to death. The Captain was not responsible for the sinking of the other vessel; all he did was to refuse to render help to the survivors. What is the position of the law in this matter? We all know that he would be charged with criminal and willful manslaughter in permitting the death of other human beings that he should have saved. This Captain would be certain to be punished for his actions, or rather, for his lack of a specific action.

But no! Protestants draw the line at the moment of conception. Catholics draw the line at the moment of orgasm. I have just drawn a line at the moment of abnegation (of coitus). An arguable case could be formulated against married persons who follow the 'rhythm method' of avoiding pregnancy. Every individual reproductive cell frustrated because of this contrivance would be eligible to file an ideological malfeasance (nonfeasance?) grievance against its human conniver. Fertile males having intercourse with known infertile females (or vice versa) are sinning against their potential descendants. Sterilization, for whatever reason, should be an unpardonable offense for it dooms to oblivion every reproductive cell that would have been formed in the reproductive system of the sterilized individual.

Where should the line be drawn? If we can't agree among ourselves, how then, can we condemn pro-abortionists who don't draw the line until the fourteenth week of gestation; or even up to the last seconds of a pregnancy, as in 'partial birth' abortions? If it appears here that I have carried a reasonable proposition to unreasonable lengths? Perhaps I have! This may be the best way to illustrate the full spectrum of my contentions. The answer to the abortion question is beyond resolution under the auspices of today's morality. The problems of today are unsolvable precisely because everyone reckons that they are privy to some absolute power of 'beyond challenge' reasoning.

Religionists deem they know the Divine Will; rendering them infallible. Liberals read the Bill of Rights (selectively), and thereby, become undisputed authorities on the interpretation of laws pertaining to personal freedom. Social activists climb atop soapboxes and expound ebulliently on the cosmic correctness of their (pseudo) philanthropic philosophies that have no foundation in our Constitution at all.

How convincingly these various activists deliver their diatribes. Their arrogance is intimidating. Their sanctimonious statutes have been etched into the very weft of the Universe; or by their own declaration, they should be! Yet, should I wonder at the hubris of these persons? No,

I know the foundation of their spurious authority. It is the same source as a religionist's authority, 'Cosmic truth' extrapolated from the Bible! Or appropriated by persons who are self-appointed moral dictators, that is, 'secular clones' of Moses without input from a spiritual creator entity.

Some people just have the unwarranted arrogance to assume that only they can perceive the ultimate light of cosmological wisdom. To this I charge, "Pompous delusion" (or more explicit!). No single person knows every answer. The reality is that no individual knows any one unequivocal answer. There is no decree in all of creation that is indisputably unimpeachable. (Apart from this last axiom?)

No one person has either the right, or the authority, to define absolute certainty unless he has been delegated that prerogative by those over whom he exercises his authority. What is said here is this: "No one has any inalienable rights whatsoever." Rights can only be granted. No one has any birthrights simply by being born. What we are born with is a responsibility to ourselves —period! Excepting only the incumbent responsibility of parents to nurture and instruct their offspring until self-sufficiency has been taught to and attained by the child.

Each of us is accountable for the overall welfare of our own existence. This inherent surcharge doesn't force us into indulgent hedonism; it does the opposite! The overall well-being of mankind is best served by creating and maintaining a harmonious human community, starting with our very own family. Thereafter, ideologically extending ever-outward until the entirety of our nation can be included within the term "community."

This may appear to be egalitarian, and might seem to result in a totalitarianism that would be devastating for the human race. This isn't so, however, if we discharge our responsibilities with undaunted and complete fidelity. Our vacillations in the application of justice cause us more harm than any alternate action we could perform. We simply don't have the implacable boldness to be the final impartial arbiter in all things that affect mankind. The "Right of Governance" can only be granted to politicians by the consent of those they govern.

Reading the last several paragraphs you could conclude they present a paradox. They don't. Man, alone, possesses no rights. Men in elected assembly have the right to enact any ordinance they collectively choose. These ordinances needn't conform to anyone's sense of uniformity or consistency. The civilized future I envision for our nation won't need a Supreme Court. The laws of man aren't surrogates for the laws of nature, or of God. Properly, laws should be guiding propositions that state in a general way that which our society deems detrimental to the common weal. Secular strictures often (But not always!) make the mistake of trying to define precisely what is a crime (sin), detailing every conceivable nuance of violation.

Ironically (at least I thought it ironic), the Bible does contain the only immutable rule we need to guide us. The sense of the passage is found several places in the Bible, but is first recorded in Leviticus. *"Love Thy Neighbor as Thyself."* [Lev. 19:18, et al.] What more needs to be said? Respect thy worthy neighbor would be more exacting, thus preferable. But know this: only another Israelite (Hebrew/Jew) could become your neighbor. Foreigners or strangers were never to be considered a "neighbor." [Cf. Deut. 15:1-3]

Incidentally, I don't credit Yahweh, the fearsome God of Moses, as the originator of that 'neighborly love' maxim. That vengeful deity long since should have been arraigned before some Cosmic Court of Justice and been sternly condemned. Yahweh never existed. This is a fact that I hope you now can accept. But His self-appointed religious Regents did exist. It is they who should receive the punishments accruing to the ongoing saga and ubiquity of religious tyranny.

So here, then, is my proposal: Inasmuch as no single person is fit to decide the fate of another, then only those who are proven capable can discharge this function. We can learn who is best able to direct us through the agency of unbiased testing. Contrary to the pronouncements of societal rights activists, we do have an unbiased method of determining human abilities in fields requiring mental acuity. The method is known as I. Q. testing. If we link these tests with aptitude and emotional stability testing, we should be able to discover the best-qualified candidates in many essential areas. Jurisprudence and Civil Administration are just such fields.

All political Parties would be prohibited. In all of human history we have never made intelligence the prime factor in selecting those who should administer human affairs. Today, if we possessed the determination, we could do just that. We should demand intelligent leadership.

I am not stating that we have never had intelligent people leading us. What is said is that this hasn't been the overriding consideration in selecting them. But it should have been. We pick the strongest men to do the heaviest work. We seek out the fastest to represent us in a race. Traditionally we have chosen the bravest to lead us in battle. Yet, the wisest among us have always been somewhat suspect as leaders. This is largely the result of the incessant calumny of less-than-intelligent secular and clerical aspirants to leadership. We are urged to fear the sage man more than anyone else, and this has impeded our civilized evolution.

The formation of any 'group,' for whatever purpose, should be discouraged. Each time two or more people band together in a common cause, many others are certain to suffer. People form groups to obtain for themselves, as individuals, some benefit that they would not be entitled to singularly. Groups performing charitable works could be an exception. No political group should ever be permitted. Separation by States should only facilitate the goal of keeping the Federal Government from becoming a Washington, D.C. oligarchy. The Federal Government should be prevented from becoming dictatorial down to the level of legal individual deportment. Unequivocally, the Government should never legislate what we must think; regardless of the issue! Hate Crimes are undisputable hate-generated, ergo they break their own law.

Try to picture the United States if every law on the books was repealed immediately. In place of this hopeless welter of minutiae, we penned in this simple statement: "Any action any person performs, or fails to perform, which any other citizen considers detrimental to the communal welfare may be brought before the Bar for Judicial Review to determine: (1) Is there a crime? (2) Is he/she guilty?"

This concept provokes emotions of dread and uncertainty. But it needn't. Remember, all juridical positions would be parceled to the very best candidates we could identify. They would be our judges; the best and the brightest! An intelligent group specifically instructed in impartiality to discharge this function would perform jury duty. There would be a penalty meted out against the accuser in the case of frivolous charges. Worthy charges would be adjudicated without automatic penalty against either the accused or the accuser. Sustained charges would have punishment meted out without hope of appeal. The premise being that if we select the best possible jurists and jurors in the first instance, then no review would ever become necessary.

All Government functionaries could have accusations brought against them. The defense "Yes, I took the gratuity, but it didn't affect my decision" would be forever unacceptable by anyone in a position of authority. Any single instance of dissembling would bring immediate lifetime disbarment (Impeachment). "Oh, the business deal that greatly enriched me was completely forgotten; that is why I didn't report it as I should have," would be utterly unacceptable, thus criminal! All persons in positions of authority must comport themselves in a manner that renders them unambiguously 'beyond reproach' and 'above suspicion.' Under these conditions, (All?) most of today's politicians would fail to qualify for their present positions. (Ruefully!) Private practice of the law would be abolished. Lawyers would all be government employees paid by the week, by the state. They would earn their promotions through the proper (honest) application of absolute justice, or as near thereto as humans can achieve!

All laws would be specifically applied only in the smallest, viable political unit. Few laws would be enforced nationally. Every law passed by the national legislature (Congress?) would have to be ratified individually by every governing unit to which the law was intended to apply. All laws, excepting only those most necessary to the nation as a whole, would be enforced through or by the local community. Minor differences of law between communities would be acceptable, perhaps even desirable at times. Infractions of the law would always be adjudicated at the lowest possible level of governance. Every law would need to be confirmed and reestablished periodically. A national "Bill of Rights" would consist only of a set of guiding principles, not as inviolable writ from on high. If this scenario appears Utopian; it is! But is it also viable.

If we strive honestly to obtain the best possible administrators, and we come up short of our goal, then we will have done the very best we can. I think we can abide with less than undiminished perfection. But I don't think we are going to persist harmoniously with our present whimsical, vacillating illogic.

Today's liberal tenets proclaim that anyone can perform any task. All we need do is appoint them to the position according to some senseless "diversity" quota system. Talent and ability are never inherited proportionately or ubiquitously. Neither are they distributed by gender, race, nationality, sexual orientation, or any other grouped manner. We should not even attempt to apportion government positions by any other criterion than aptitude, capability and intellect. The only real separator between mankind and the remainder of animate life is intelligence. The absolute, unqualified, and unquestionable fact is that 'we are all a minority of one!' Let us, accordingly, cause this to remain so forevermore. Merely advocating the formation of virtually any group (i.e., organization), regardless of purpose, would bring the law down harshly upon its sponsor and its supporters.

Ladies and Gentlemen, the philosophy that group balance must be maintained in governance is going to prove fatal to our advanced civilization. The designation of a government entity to ensure that a public entity doesn't offend or harm a generally disparaged group: aids, abets, encourages, and even creates "prejudice." The postulate that only a member of an aggrieved (?) group can judge fairly another member of his group is tantamount to proclaiming an inherent difference between groups. If there is a difference, then this difference can be quantified; thereby, "superior" or "inferior" are injected into all group-versus-group relationships.

Religion has contributed greatly to our present predicament. Religious theology and doctrine are the most divisive of all the (fraudulent) philosophical divisions separating humanity. Religious beliefs are the nadir of intellectual reasoning. The basis for my accusation follows. First, God created us all equal. Second, He has said, *"the wisdom of the world is foolishness in the eyes of God."* [1 Cor. 3:19] Lastly, He has said that He is going to end this world and provide a heaven for us to enjoy. Consequently, we needn't strive for intellectual advancement ever. God, in His Infinite Wisdom, will provide us with a perfect angelic existence in this spiritual Heaven shortly after our death! [Cf. Mt. 5:12]

I don't accept any of this. I don't believe Jesus is returning, and neither do I believe that the end of the world is coming. Not at the hand of God, factually! I think the closest we will ever approach to Heaven is when we reform (hence, transform) our own Earth into a Paradise. As observed at the outset of this concluding chapter, the social morality of Christianity is impeccable. We have only to renounce the burlesque notion of an arbitrary puppeteer Deity from our minds. Our foolishness has us headed for disaster. We must wake up and engage our intellects soon. We don't have till Doomsday. We are going to be either the initiators of a beneficent world Shangri-la, or the sorrowing survivors of an unwelcome Armageddon.

The fate of mankind is in the hands of man himself. God is dead. Let us hold the funeral and lay Him to rest so we can advance to the ultimate determinant for/of our existence: to grow in knowledge! We have to unleash our collective intellects. Let those expand! Heaven is within our grasp. No supernatural being is going to fabricate a Paradise for us. If we are ever to have one, we are going to have to create that one by ourselves.

Solitary Man isn't great. But working cooperatively, we can accomplish great things. Cast off whatever has shackled us in the past. Religion, primarily! If the Old Testament has taught us anything, it is this: Not everyone is going to enter the Promised Land. Don't be misled by the Golden Calf of ignorance and superstition. The only God who has ever existed for man is the 'God of True Wisdom.' May this "God" (meaning 'tested, proven knowledge') survive for all Eternity! And "IT" will! But only if we forthwith continually strive to serve that deified principle intellectually, devotedly and exclusively!

Examined intellectually and honestly, the entirety of the Bible is found to be an ego-enhancing fiction story for mystery-immersed, religiously-inclined adults. Factually: All religions are nothing but adult Fairy Tales!

Finis

R.ON.